Penguin E

D0649156

Introducing Sociology

Peter Worsley

Roy Fitzhenry, J. Clyde Mitchell,
D. H. J. Morgan, Valdo Pons, Bryan Roberts,
W. W. Sharrock, Robin Ward

Introducing Sociology

Peter Worsley

Roy Fitzhenry, J. Clyde Mitchell,
D. H. J. Morgan, Valdo Pons, Bryan Roberts,
W. W. Sharrock, Robin Ward

Second Edition

Penguin Books

Penguin Books Ltd, Harmondsworth, Middlesex, England
Viking Penguin Inc., 40 West 23rd Street, New York, New York 10010, U.S.A.
Penguin Books Australia Ltd, Ringwood, Victoria, Australia
Penguin Books Canada Ltd, 2801 John Street, Markham, Ontario, Canada L3R 1B4
Penguin Books (N.Z.) Ltd, 182–190 Wairau Road, Auckland 10, New Zealand

First published 1970
Reprinted 1971 (twice), 1972, 1973 (twice), 1974,
1975, 1976 (twice)
Second edition 1977
Reprinted 1978 (twice), 1979, 1980, 1981, 1983, 1984, 1985

Made and printed in Great Britain by
Hazell Watson & Viney Limited,
Member of the BPCC Group,
Aylesbury, Bucks
Set in Monotype Times

To our students

Contents

Acknowledgements

Our thanks are due to various colleagues who have helped us in producing this second edition: to Christine Jackson, Julian Laite, Peter Martin, Teodor Shanin and Daphne Taylorsen who read and commented on parts of the manuscript, and to Marjorie Gray, Eileen Lee and Cilla Macmillan who typed the manuscript.

Acknowledgement is made to the following for permission to use copyright material: two maps from *Beyond Vietnam: The United States and Asia* by Professor Edwin O. Reischauer, to Alfred Knopf, Inc.; Population Trends table from Richard Leete's 'Marriage and Divorce', to H.M.S.O.; Development Gap map from the chapter 'Problems of the "Have-not" World', by Peter Worsley, in *The Times, History of Our Times 1945–71*, ed. Marcus Cunliffe, to Weidenfeld and Nicolson Ltd; *One view of the political economy of sex*, an advertisement in *Spare Rib*, August 1976, to Graphic Workshop, 232 Mare Street, London E.8; Charles Schultz, *Peanuts* cartoon, to United Features Syndicate; Brian Jackson and Dennis Marsden, *Education and the Working Class*, to Routledge and Kegan Paul and Monthly Review Press; Colin Lacey, *Hightown Grammar: The School as a Social System*, to Manchester University Press; Tom Lehrer, 'Wernher von Braun', *Tom Lehrer's Second Song Book*, to Crown Publishers and Elek Books; Conrad M. Arensberg and Solon T. Kimball, *Family and Community in Ireland*, to Harvard University Press.

Manchester, 1976   P. W.

Preface

As we explained in the Preface to the first edition of this book, we have tried to avoid a simplistic 'talking down' to the reader coming to sociology for the first time: we assume that he or she is a critical being, interested in society, and interested, too, in examining a variety of different perspectives each of which obliges us to look at the social world from different angles and at different things in that world, though always with the attempt to relate these approaches, and the things they address themselves to studying, to one another, rather than being content simply to lay them side by side.

We have also tried to take account of the likely knowledge and interests of our readers. Most of them, for instance, are probably engaged in some course of study within one or other of the institutions of higher education. Hence, we pay attention to the sociology of the educational process. We have also assumed that the majority of our readers will be from the Western world, though many are not. Since it is not possible to write a universal textbook, which will deal equally effectively with what is likely to concern the reader in Malaysia every bit as much as the reader in, say, Sweden, we have compromised by varying the material we use and the topics dealt with so as to cater for this variety of interests. In any case, we believe firmly that it is vital for the Western reader to develop a much richer understanding of life in the Third World than currently exists, and so ask much deeper questions about the nature of communist society than is usually the case. The anthropological perspective to be gained from studies of tribal and other pre-industrial societies is also of especially great importance.

Conversely, people in the underdeveloped countries need to examine the experience of those which have industrialized, as much because they may constitute negative models as because they may be models to be imitated. The developed countries can learn a great deal by studying societies in the Third World – and vice versa.

We have retained a division into three Parts. The first deals with questions on the scope of sociology, its relationships with other disciplines, the nature of social science as distinct from the natural sciences, and the special ethical and political problems of the social sciences. We then examine the consequent problems of method, of doing research, and of constructing theoretical explanations or ways of understanding that are peculiar to social science.

In Part 2 we examine the family, education, and work, industry and organizations, then community and urban life, because these divisions relate to the reader's own experience of life, the normal experience being to be brought up in families, then to go to school, and later to go out to work within the framework of some organization in an urban environment.

In Part 3, rather than mechanically ploughing through every specialist field of sociology, from religion to mass culture, we have examined the inequalities and divisions in society in Chapter 8, and the ways in which the achievement of social order is variously conceived of in Chapter 9.

Throughout, we have tried to communicate our own interest in what is going on in society, and not only in sociology, and have drawn upon what we have found to be some of the more stimulating current research which conveys this. But we have also sought out that kind of work which carries out inquiries within a coherent theoretical perspective. Indeed, we have made differences of theoretical orientation much more explicit and visible than we did in the first edition, without, we hope, losing sight of the structures and processes these theories are meant to illuminate.

Inevitably, the subject-matter of the various chapters has dictated changes of different kinds and in differing degrees. Those dealing with basic issues of subject-matter and method (Chapters 1 and 2) have not been radically altered, except to reflect more definitely the recent growth of interpretive sociology, a development which is treated systematically in the last chapter, alongside functionalist, conflict, symbolic interactionist and ethnomethodological perspectives. (Don't worry: the meaning of these polysyllabic terms will become quite clear before long.) New developments in theory, too, are reflected in the attention given to Marxist work in various chapters, notably in Chapter 3 on the sociology of development, an area where the influence of Marxist theorists has perhaps been greatest.

Changes in the real world, too, have caused us to recast the chapters on the family and on education quite fundamentally, and we examine the central processes of urbanization much more directly than before, in particular by comparing contemporary urbanization in the Third World with the urbanization of Britain and the U.S.A. in the nineteenth and early twentieth centuries.

The rise of the Women's Movement, besides stimulating us to rethink the framework of the chapter on the family, has made us aware of the inadequate attention previously paid to the place of women in society outside the family, particularly their status as a disprivileged category. We have also added to the chapter on stratification a badly-needed consideration of race, ethnicity, and nation, and rewritten much of the rest, particularly the discussions of communist society and of the underdeveloped world.

Finally, the concluding chapter has been totally remodelled, and succeeds, we believe, in making clear even those theories that their own progenitors, from Parsons to Garfinkel, seem to be incapable of expressing in an accessible manner. We think that this explicit and systematic treatment of rival theories, and of the ways in which they respond to each other, is superior to scattering bits and pieces of theory and disconnected concepts around the various chapters.

We have been gratified at the response to our first edition, which has been used in about half the universities in the U.K., in many colleges of various kinds, and even – to our surprise – in schools, so that our students have often read it before they arrive at university! It has also appeared in Portuguese and Swedish, and in a special Indian edition (and shortly in Icelandic). With all modesty, we think this second edition a distinct improvement on the first. It also contains more material, nearly all new, without expanding to inordinate length.

At the back of the book the reader will find a list of references containing all the titles of books and articles referred to in brackets in the text; the list contains the author's name, followed by a year of publication, and then page references where needed (thus: Weber, 1952, pp. 100–121). We have tried as far as possible to use only writings that we think interesting enough to be worth reading in the original version, at great length. In addition to these references, we have recommended other works for further reading, chapter by chapter.

Finally, we should explain that each chapter was written by different individuals: Chapter 1 was written by Peter Worsley; Chapter 2 by J. Clyde Mitchell; Chapter 3 by Peter Worsley; Chapter 4 by D. H. J. Morgan; Chapter 5 by Bryan Roberts; Chapter 6 by D. H. J. Morgan and Robin Ward; Chapter 7 by Valdo Pons; Chapter 8 by Peter Worsley and Roy Fitzhenry; Chapter 9 by W. W. Sharrock. The texts have been revised, often painfully, in the light of our own experience of using the book in teaching, and in the light, too, of explicit criticism by students and others. Despite a great measure of agreement about what constitutes interesting sociology, there remain considerable differences of approach and emphasis between us, and the different chapters inevitably reflect the particular interests and approaches of their respective authors. These we have not tried to eliminate because we believe this to be a much more faithful representation of the diversity of contemporary sociology than pretending that there is one common body of thinking subscribed to by all sociologists. Finally, though we have responded with interest to expressions of opinion about the book, negative and positive, we have been amazed at how little response of any kind has emerged from such a wide readership. This itself says something interesting and rather disturbing about the machinery and practice of communication in our society. But because we would prefer communication to be two-way, we would always welcome your views as to the defects and virtues of the book.

Manchester University   PETER WORSLEY

Part One

Chapter 1
Sociology as a Discipline

One of the most striking intellectual developments of recent years has been the growth in popularity of the social sciences. Sociology has perhaps been the fastest-growing, though not the largest, of these disciplines. Yet it is by no means popular in all quarters. Some, indeed, fear the dispassionate examination of society: they think that things might come to light which are better left hidden or unexplained. Sociology is thought to make people (especially students) 'radical' or 'critical'. Radical students, conversely, attack it as being too conservative a discipline. Criticism sometimes goes further: it questions not just the uses of sociology, but even its claim to be a science. Thus a leader in *The Times* (9 July 1968) remarked that sociology 'whatever [its] other merits . . . [is not] a rigorous intellectual discipline'.

Because of attacks like these, sociologists have often reacted to criticism of their new science with a touchiness that sometimes takes the form of 'imperialistic' aggressiveness – claiming that sociology is the queen of all the social sciences – and sometimes that of an over-sensitive defensiveness. Others exhibit a conservatism of their own, asserting that the discipline is so exacting that it cannot properly be taught in schools, but only to more mature students.

So in capitalist countries, many think of sociology as a kind of academic synonym for socialism, whilst in communist countries it was banned for decades as 'bourgeois' ideology. Though physicists scarcely feel it incumbent upon them to 'defend' physics as a discipline, sociologists still write articles 'in defence of sociology'.

Despite these tribulations, sociology has continued to grow rapidly. It is this very growth, indeed, which excites some of the attacks from those who fear its social consequences or its academic competition. It has grown because yet others find it useful. Indeed, the more serious problem for sociology today is not so much that people look down on it, but that they expect too much of it. Today, sociology departments exist in dozens of British universities and colleges. In the United States, the American Sociological Association had fewer than 700 members fifty years ago; today it numbers over 12,000. And in the Soviet Union sociology is now an established discipline.

A second paradox concerning the growth of sociology raises even more fundamental issues. Within the last few years only, human society and culture have entered a new era. For the first time, men stepped beyond the bounds of their own planet. To do so, they had to overcome all kinds of limitations set by Nature, including those upon the human body. They succeeded because they were able to bring technical devices into being which overcame these natural limitations. From one point of view, this achievement is quite new in kind. From another, it is merely the latest in a succession of technological breakthroughs which go back in time to the earliest successes of humankind in inventing such crucial tools as the knife and the spear.

Yet even when we remember this, it still seems paradoxical that such an outstanding set of cultural innovations as are implied by space technology should occur at the very time that very popular books are seeking to remind us that Man is an animal – a 'naked ape' – and, for the most part, dwelling on his less endearing characteristics.

This kind of thinking about Man does not come about simply because we have now accumulated lots of facts about Man's habits and history. For the facts always have to be placed within some context which gives them meaning. From this point of view, the moral fables so characteristic of our time which we call 'science fiction' share a great deal in common with quite non-fictional science. For the latter, in the end, has significance for us to the extent that it helps us answer such questions as 'Where have we come from?', 'How did we get to this point?', 'What are we doing?', and 'Where are we going?'

These questions are not simple 'questions of fact', though facts are certainly needed in order to answer them. Fundamentally, they are questions about our evaluation of the significance of life: *why* should we do one thing rather than another? what is the *best* way of doing things? how are we to decide what *is* best? is there any ultimate purpose to it all? will our patent capacity for viciousness and destruction prove more powerful than that other part of our heritage: our ability to co-operate and to create?

Hence, when we look at the sweep of human history, we ask ourselves ethical and philosophical questions, questions of *value* as well as of fact. For though looking at Man as a natural species might seem a purely 'scientific' operation, to do so raises philosophical and ethical questions in particularly sharp form, for men have always projected their values, beliefs, prejudices, hunches, hopes and fears upon 'Nature'. In the nineteenth century thinkers drew many different conclusions from their studies of biological evolution: for some, their studies showed that Nature was 'red in tooth and claw', that 'the fittest' survived; for others, like the anarchist Prince Peter Kropotkin, they revealed a story of a cosmic progression towards co-operation and autonomy and away from competitive individualism; from being controlled and determined by Nature, to the exercise of collective reason so as to maximize human independence and self-determination. In fact, you can always read into the history of the human species, as into Nature generally, almost anything you like.

In the nineteenth century, though they were aware of mass poverty, mass war and mass disease, upper-class thinkers were usually confident that human history was the history of progress, ever onwards and upwards – 'Whig' history, as it was parochially called in Britain. Both conservatives and revolutionaries were optimists who believed that change, by and large, meant improvement, and that the present was the best because it was the latest. Today, though we all accept the patent evidence of human technological advance, there is much less confidence that such advance is necessarily accompanied by a parallel improvement in morality or in our ability to devise better social arrangements that would enable more people to live richer lives than they do now.

The contrast between lunar triumph and the hunger of the majority of men on earth is too striking to permit unqualified optimism today. Growing worry about the apparently inevitable exhaustion of crucial natural resources and pollution of the environment are the latest expressions of a mood of deep pessimism, which the experience of two world wars, Hiroshima, brainwashing and concentration camps had already established. Reactions to man's entry into space were therefore ambiguous. People wondered whether the conquest of space would not in the end lead to disaster, whether unintentionally (e.g. through contamination) or because one of the key rationales is, in any case, military. For only those whom C. Wright Mills calls 'cheerful robots' (Mills, 1959) can forget that equal human ingenuity has been deliberately called into service in order to devise chemical, bacteriological and nuclear weapons which now give us power to kill off the entire human species. Within a single decade, we have found it necessary to coin a new word to replace genocide – biocide.

If we do end in disaster, it will not be because we are animals beneath a cultural veneer. It will be because we were not as good at social innovation as we were at natural-scientific. Men are, as we know, aggressive; they are also animals. But they are not solely aggressive, any more than other animals, and when they are, it is often because this is culturally expected of them and instilled in them. Even in attacking each other, they use their reason and their social skills. It may sound strange to describe warfare as 'culture', for this is a term we normally reserve for string quartets, poetry, or – nowadays – films or jazz. But from the sociologist's point of view, it is vital to distinguish what is 'given' in man's physical heritage as an animal – the ways of behaving that he is *naturally* born with – from those ways of behaving that he learns. And the really striking thing about the human child is its dependence on people around it, normally its parents and kin, for a very lengthy period of time, for much of which it is fairly helpless. Unlike the newborn foal, which gets up and runs about within hours of its birth, humans cannot even walk for a long time. They are, however, from their first moments, subjected to an incredibly complex and intensive process of 'socialization', during which they acquire what social scientists call 'culture'. They learn how to behave, starting with control over their bowel-motions and eating-habits. As well as being so constrained and trained from earliest infancy, they are simultaneously encouraged to internalize norms of conduct, to practise *self*-control, as well as – most important – to develop their own capacity to learn and to innovate (within limits set by their culture) without somebody having to stand over them the whole time.

Biology and Culture

We often assume that many of the things we learn are not learned: that it is 'natural' to dislike people who look different from ourselves; that pain in childbirth is entirely natural; that different degrees of success in life reflect the amount of intelligence we are endowed with at birth; that poor countries stay poor because their peoples lack qualities of enterprise, etc. Yet slave-owners were so attracted to Black women that whole 'Coloured' populations emerged; the physical experience of childbirth varies enormously between cultures even though every woman belongs to the same physical species, *homo sapiens*; our society condemns many talented people to humble stations in life and elevates those less talented but who have 'chosen their parents wisely'; the passive Indians of the Andes are the lineal descendants of their imperial Inca forebears, and industrialized Wales and Scotland contain descendants of those the Romans regarded as primitive barbarians. Even something as basic as sex does not necessarily carry with it a 'natural' set of masculine and feminine behaviours. Unlike sex, 'gender' is a social product: 'One is not born, but rather becomes, a woman. No biological, psychological or economic fate determines the figure that the human female presents in society; it is civilization as a whole that produces this creature, intermediate between male and eunuch, which is described as feminine' (de Beauvoir, 1953, p. 9).

Plainly, these variations cannot be attributed to physical changes or differences. What does change is society and its stock of culture. For human culture, though it constantly cumulates over-all, taking the world as a whole, can also be lost or decline: whole peoples can be de-cultured or stand still, so that those who now lead may be laggards at some other time. True, in isolated areas, the rate of innovation may be almost imperceptible, as with the Australian aborigines before Captain Cook. But the constant enlargement of human culture as a whole is plain enough, as is the growing-together of the human species. (The very last pockets of peoples still not involved in what is in effect a single world society are today being broken into in the Highlands of New Guinea and the jungles of the Amazon.) But if we can talk in this way about general human advance, we do so primarily with reference to the enlargement of human knowledge, particularly technical devices and skills. Whether these advances carry with them any enrichment of the *quality* of life, or whether the Australian aborigines did not have highly complex religious cultures, constantly changing and enriched despite the fixity and poverty of their technical equipment, are not just matters of debate, but of debate according to philosophical criteria. This we cannot embark on here, just as we leave aside such questions as whether there might be other dimensions of experience altogether (accessible perhaps only via religion, hallucinogenic drugs, etc.) outside what we take to be normal waking life.

All we need to appreciate, at this juncture, is that conventional definitions of human culture, which usually restrict this term to the creative 'fine arts', are, to the sociologist, arbitrary and restricted. He is most unlikely to take the view that all human creations are of the same order of value – that 'pushpin is as good as poetry' – and will recognize as well as the next man that Beethoven or Angkor Wat are cultural products of a very superior kind. But these are philosophical and aesthetic evaluations; for sociological purposes he will regard as 'culture' *everything* acquired by human beings that is not physically inherited. From this point of view, sewers are as much 'culture' as symphonies. 'Culture', as traditionally defined, consists of certain forms of the conventionally approved arts: painting, sculpture, creative literature, music: these are indeed 'culture' in the sociological sense too, but so are hybrid wheat, brake-linings and strontium 90.

Our physical inheritance, indeed, includes very little human culture. Neither machine-guns, breakfast-foods, brassieres, existentialism, or the Goon Show are outcomes of biological dispositions or inborn behaviour. They are 'artefacts' or 'ideofacts', produced, communicated, handed down, stored up (in books, on tape, on film, etc., and in men's brains), internalized and taught, transmitted from man to man, and from group to group.

Nor can we explain the great diversity of human cultures by reference to our common biological equipment. For there are many *different* cultures and many 'human natures' which vary from society to society, not one single, physically determined 'Human Nature'. Though as individuals we have to learn everything 'from the beginning', as it were – whether in school, the family, or elsewhere – collectively we do not, for culture is both a social product and a social property, passed on through teaching from generation to generation, so that, as individuals, we are able to start where the last and most advanced person left off. Hence culture cumulates, and the most creative, too, are always adding to it: they do not merely inherit and receive. At the same time, our biological equipment scarcely changes.

It is this that marks off human society as a qualitatively distinct phenomenon from even the most complex insect 'society', for the insects do not learn to behave; they do so instinctively. Their society has no *culture* at all. Even the higher apes are sadly limited in the extent to which they can learn, and when they do learn, do not pass their experience on to new generations: the result is that their culture does not grow. Indeed, scientists have brought up chimpanzees and gorillas with their own children. The rate of advance of the apes has, in some respects, been more rapid than that of the children in early years, but the apes soon get left behind. Their fundamental limitation, of course, is that they can learn, invent, and hand on very few word – socially standardized sounds which convey meanings – and it is t inability to produce language (apart from physical limitations) keeps the apes as they are. For culture is only transmissible thr coding, classifying and concentrating experience through som of language. A developed language, therefore, is a unique a tinctive human trait, and human society is a higher level of organiz tion of behaviour than merely instinctive or animal behaviour. Hence any attempt to explain human behaviour in terms of lower levels of behaviour is bound to be inadequate.

Man, in fact, is the least biologically determined species of all, because he possesses features absent in other natural species. Whilst ethologists emphasize our resemblances to animals, the sociologist looking at human conflict, for example, sees that men co-operate even in order to fight: they create complex social organizations that far exceed anything animal packs are capable of. Nothing, indeed, is more organized, tight-knit, less 'personal', spontaneous or 'instinctive' than an army. Moreover, whatever potentials for aggression there are within the individual's psyche, the culture or sub-culture he lives in is a crucial intervening variable between his biological predisposition and the overt acting-out of aggression towards others, for if he is a Quaker his aggressiveness will be discouraged, whereas Nazi and Fascist theory and practice reinforced, indeed evoked, aggressive action. In other words, violence may be learned as culturally-expected behaviour in different kinds of society or sub-society: it is not simply 'instinctive'.

Man, though a producer, is certainly not always a creator – one who produces positive values which are helpful to his fellow men, for he creates also the means of destruction. But *reductionist* theories, which simplify the elaborate complexity and diversity of human culture by trying to reduce it to 'underlying' innate animal instincts are, of course, hard put to it to explain why, given, say, what is assumed to be a fixed 'sex instinct', human beings have developed so many different ways of 'handling' sex: within marriage, where there are many forms from polyandry and polygyny to monogamy (and, in Hollywood, what has been called 'serial monogamy'), to commercial sex, religious sex and other forms of extra-marital sex which range from the casual encounter to the long-term liaison, or even the deliberate suppression of sex-drives in the form of required or even self-imposed celibacy. We also know that cultural practices, such as erotic advertising and other public stimuli, can create 'appetites' that are often assumed to be entirely 'natural', and that non-erotic environments, such as many prisons, can result in a diminished pre-occupation with sex. Again, anthropologists have shown how hunters-and-collectors constantly on the margins of hunger have dreams, fantasies and obsessions about food rather than sex.

Human beings by no means simply produce material objects; indeed, these could not be produced unless thoughts and ideas were produced too. A particularly crucial set of human products are the social arrangements men live under – their social organization. Cultural innovation includes more, indeed, than simply technological innovation, for older social forms and cultural behaviours become outmoded as well as machines. Religions and monarchical institutions have decayed in Western Europe and new kinds of social phenomena have emerged across the globe: the Chinese commune, the Ombudsman, the giant metropolis, new 'youth cultures' and so on.

The relationship between technological innovation and the growth of culture is thus more complex than is often thought; not just because progress in technology does not automatically mean social

progress, but also because the same technology is compatible with quite different social arrangements. The same tools can be used within the context of quite different 'relations of production', for the relations themselves are not built into the instruments. Yet we are still sometimes tempted to talk as if 'technology' was some kind of quite independent moving force. Thus Clark Kerr and his colleagues assert that, by and large, modern industrialism has a 'logic' of its own, which will ultimately lead to a convergence between capitalist and Soviet society because both are industrial societies (Kerr *et al.*, 1962). It is true that there are no capitalist lathes and no communist lathes, but only lathes. Yet though both societies may employ common technical systems – capstan lathes and nuclear energy – they use them in different ways and turn them to different ends. The upshot is quite different kinds of society. In fact, there is no serious evidence of over-all 'convergence' at all (Goldthorpe, J. H., 1964). For basically, technology does not determine the total pattern of social arrangements; it is groups of men, with certain values they wish to realize, who pursue policies that determine what technology and its products will be used for. The patterns of relationship entailed in industrial organization are only part of the social order; society is much more than its technology. Similarly, neither the cultural variety of humankind nor the general patterns of development it has exhibited can be explained by demographic factors, such as population pressure – another common type of reductionist thinking.

The notions that society is directly shaped by demographic pressures or by technology or by economic arrangements are thus too simple; they are 'reductionist' every bit as much as the ethological theories we have discussed. Besides being reductionist, such theories are *deterministic*: they assume that these forces give rise to the same outcome everywhere in an inevitable fashion. This is not to deny that there are limits set to what is possible, and inherent requirements, too, imposed, for example, by the economy and by the technology on which the economy depends. These issues will be discussed more closely in Chapter 6. Equally, though we reject the view that social man can be understood simply in terms of his animal characteristics, this is not to say that there are not very important social implications which derive from the facts of man's physical condition. Chronic hunger will certainly affect both our capacity to work, as well as our attitudes towards work and towards those who are more fortunate. Different distributions of certain physical characteristics in different populations also have profound repercussions for society: in Europe, the growing proportion of the aged in the population is creating new problems of the social isolation of old people, at the personal level and nationally, because of the need to provide new social services and other sources of support for those who are 'old and alone'. In developing countries, where half the population is commonly under fifteen, the difficulties of absorbing this growing population into productive employment, and the availability now of revolutionary alternatives, makes for very explosive social situations.

The variety of physical population-characteristics also has consequences at other levels. Race (or ethnicity, more usually) is one of the 'ready-made' physical attributes which, if reinforced by inequalities in living-standards, political power or in social interaction, gives rise to conflicts which are only too obvious (and only too widespread and full of tension) today, whether at the interpersonal or global level.

Finally, there are immense social problems created by the changes in Nature brought about by Man. We are polluting the atmosphere and the waters, poisoning sources of food, and creating the means of universal destruction far faster than we are inventing means of overcoming these dangers. It is the shortfall in these social skills that is Man's greatest weakness. It is for this reason that the scientific study of society, so late in beginning, becomes an urgent need, not as some specialist activity for a few, but as a central preoccupation of all intelligent human beings.

The Divisions of Social Science

Sociology is only one of several social sciences, some of which have been in existence a good deal longer than has sociology, which only seriously emerged towards the end of the nineteenth century. Perhaps the most sophisticated of the longer-established social sciences is economics, which has developed elaborate techniques and a complex body of theory over two centuries. Psychology, anthropology and political science (including 'public administration') are the other disciplines most closely related to sociology, together with law, history and aspects of other fields of study (social medicine, social administration, etc.). All these disciplines have their own bodies of theory, techniques of inquiry and specialized subject-matter, to one degree or another. They have also become specialized occupations (law, business, medicine, etc.). Because of this, the relationships between the social sciences that logically ought to exist, in fact, are often quite weak due to 'professional' divisions and jealousies that are far from scientific in character.

Despite their differences, these specialized subject-matters are in fact all parts of one general subject-matter: man's social behaviour. Certain of these disciplines can be readily marked off as being focused primarily on one particular kind or aspect of general human behaviour. Thus the rather mis-named 'social administration' has in practice been concerned with the consequences of various kinds of social disadvantage, ranging from illness to unmarried motherhood, for which some kind of social provision has to be made. Yet those concerned with these social problems find that they have to study the organizational contexts within which welfare or medical work, for example, take place. In order to carry out such studies, the social administrator often finds that he has to draw on the theories and the 'substantive' knowledge developed within other related disciplines, such as political science, public administration or sociology. There are thus no hard-and-fast lines between the social sciences, even in the case of those disciplines like social administration which might appear to have a neatly marked-off subject-matter.

The absence of hard-and-fast lines of division reflects the fact that they deal with something that is, in reality – 'out there' – *not* parcelled up into discrete areas. What social scientists actually observe is human beings walking, talking and performing other kinds of physical acts. They then proceed to abstract out of this welter of activity certain aspects to which they give particular attention and to which they also attach certain labels. Certain kinds of actions become dubbed as 'economic' – such as those relating to production. In the process, the analyst will deliberately and consciously fail to pay attention to other aspects of the behaviour in front of his eyes. If he does his study via the use of statistics or documents, the degree of abstraction, of selection out of the complexity of the real world, is even greater.

We will see later that though, in studying factories, an economist might tend to see the work-force primarily as a 'supply of labour', the sociologist would be interested in other dimensions of the workers' social make-up which indeed make them very different *kinds* of workers. He will note that social relationships on the shop-floor are greatly affected by relationships developed *outside* the firm, and that the attachments and antagonisms within the factory are not necessarily produced by the requirements of work alone. So factories manned by unskilled Irish immigrants, skilled female Lancashire cotton-operatives, or craft-conscious engineers, are very different kinds of factory, not just because the work is different, but because people bring their lives outside the factory into the work-situation. The sociologist, then, may study exactly the same scene, may watch the same people doing the same things that the economist or the psychologist observes. But whereas the economist normally restricts himself to looking at this reality through certain theoretical spectacles, and so restricts himself to the analysis of the interaction between the factors of capital and labour, or with the operation of the market in terms of price or demand, the sociologist will be further interested in the interconnections of all this with other dimensions of social relationships in the work-place or the market-place, and with the way work fits into non-work life.

The sociologist, then, does not question the expertise of the economist in dealing with those special aspects of human behaviour that he chooses to concentrate on. Rather, he attempts to relate 'economic' behaviour to other kinds of behaviour, or, more accurately, to see 'economic' behaviour as simply a partial abstraction from the total social behaviour of the individual.

Though the sociologist needs the economist's expertise, he himself is able to contribute this wider perspective. But a discipline which claims an even wider perspective than this, with much justice, is anthropology. 'Social' or 'cultural' anthropology is concerned with the variety of arrangements which men have created over millennia. Its perspective is highly comparative, or 'cross-cultural'. Anthropologists have been especially interested in studying cultures very remote from their own, sometimes by going back into history, but more normally by going to still-existing tribal, exotic and often (though not always) simple societies in the contemporary world. In arriving at an understanding of how such societies work, anthropologists have inevitably thrown a flood of light on general principles of social organization and have enabled us to see how, on the one hand, apparently exotic customs are simply ways of coping with common human problems that we handle in different ways, and that our ways are not necessarily the best or the only ones possible, or, in other cases, that some societies have altogether quite different preoccupations from those that dominate our thinking, so that by studying them we can see ourselves as only one particular kind of society with its own limited concerns.

In some ways, then, anthropology is much wider-ranging than sociology. On the other hand, precisely because of its search for what is culturally different, anthropology has paid little attention to developed societies which are particularly important to us. The great value of anthropology then lies in its comparative 'cross-cultural' vision. Conversely, though some sociologists talk about sociology as the 'widest' social science that includes all others, in fact sociologists have largely confined themselves to contemporary societies, principally industrialized ones, and only latterly to agrarian societies in the underdeveloped world.

The enormous field of the study of *past* societies has rarely attracted sociologists, who have left this field to the historian. There are many kinds of historians, some of whom see history simply as 'meaningless' or even 'patternless', unique sequences of events which can only be described quite separately rather than looked at in terms of common patterns or trends shared with other societies. Such writers are suspicious of 'theory' and claim to stick to the concrete facts of the particular situation. This 'empiricist' approach will be discussed later. Suffice it to say here that such approaches, common enough among historians, represent quite non-sociological ways of approaching the study of past societies, however great the value of such researches may be as industrious compilations bringing order into chaos and knowledge out of ignorance, or as implicit analysis. Nor would we claim that the sociologist who turns to past societies necessarily does better research than his historian-colleague (he is probably likely to be as long on theory and short on fact as the historian is the converse). But the best history is, in fact, sociological: the sociology of the past.

What we may claim for sociology, at its ideal best, is a distinctive *perspective* rather than, say, any specific substantive subject-matter or type of human behaviour: it is a way of looking at Man's behaviour as conditioned by his membership of social groups – a perspective which may seem self-evident to some, but is by no means accepted by those, for example, who see history as determined by the activities of great men, or those who see Man's social behaviour as simply the outcome of his animal nature. To make the contrast, a reductionist is likely to see warfare simply as an outcome of aggressive instincts which people, as individuals, are born with. Thus Anthony Storr remarks: 'We are the cruellest and most ruthless species that has ever walked the earth – each one of us harbors within himself those same savage impulses which lead to murder, to torture and to war' (Storr, 1968, p. 9). War, here, is the outcome at the social level of pre-social human characteristics inherited by the individual. The social scientist, on the other hand, is sceptical of this appeal to instincts, noting that 'three out of four die from causes other than violence', that 'most forms of human rivalry explicitly preclude the use of violence' and that 'Man is not just a wild animal whose ferocious instincts must be curbed by society or sublimated into other channels, [but] . . . a social animal who is taught by society to exhibit hostility in some situations and friendliness in others. The difference is fundamental' (Leach, 1968, pp. 26, 28).

Sociology is thus concerned with socio-cultural behaviour, a different – and higher – level of behaviour altogether than those kinds of behaviour that are the outcome of innate drives built into the individual. This is not to say that the latter do not exist, simply that they may be overlaid, elaborated, repressed, counteracted by complex sets of social forces which the individual is subjected to *because he lives in society* and because he is not an isolated entity who simply 'behaves' in response to internal or external physical stimuli or psychological drives. Perhaps the best-known attempt to interpret society in terms of innate instincts is Freud's psychoanalytical theory, which places such great emphasis upon inborn drives, particularly the sex-drive. Yet Freud himself constantly stressed the way such drives could be frustrated by cultural controls, and towards the end of his life placed more and more emphasis on culture as against simple instinct.

Psychology is a sister-science that contains both sub-social and social 'wings'. Physiological psychology is concerned with the physical processes through which thinking, feeling, etc., take place. But most of the rest of psychology is in fact to one degree or another *social*. What is commonly labelled 'social psychology' is in fact only a part of this wider 'social' part of psychology. Social psychology usually deals with a rather arbitrary collection of topics, not necessarily related, such as the study of small groups or of crowd behaviour. But *all* non-physiological psychology is in effect 'social' psychology, since it is concerned with the processes by which human behaviour becomes culturally standardized, expected and obligatory: in other words, the ways in which society enjoins certain patterns of behaviour upon the individual.

Are not both psychology and sociology, then, it might be asked, equally concerned with the way individual behaviour is socially conditioned? The answer is 'Yes', but the psychologist's point of attention is usually the individual, the sociologist's that of the groups and categories to which the individual belongs. But that is to put it too crudely, for psychologists do study groups and categories, too: the attitudes, say, of miners, disc-jockeys, sadists, or women. The real difference is that the unit or frame of reference for the psychologist is the behaviour of the individual, whether his inner 'psyche' or its external manifestations observable in his relationships with others. The sociologist approaches perhaps exactly the same piece of behaviour 'from the other end', as it were, and asks what the significant regularities and patterns in a person's behaviour are that enable us to see him as typical of others who have been similarly socialized, undergone parallel life-experiences, or belonged to similar groups. Social behaviour is thus not simply the putting together of all the separate 'natural' behaviours of many individuals – what is called 'aggregate psychology' – it is a qualitatively different *level* of behaviour, not 'given' in the *individual* psyche independently of its experience of society, as it were, but produced *in social groups* and internalized within the individual as a result of exposure to the pressures of these groups. Both the psychologist and the sociologist, then, may study the same behaviour and ask similar questions. It is not, crudely, that one studies the group and the other the individual, but that the focus or 'point of entry' will be the individual for the psychologist, and for the sociologist the society and culture of which the individual is a part. They will thus frequently converge in their studies, and at the borderlines it becomes rather arbitrary whether one labels a study 'psychology' or 'sociology'. Yet the psychologist, basically, is interested in the way the individual's behaviour is organized so as to constitute a 'personality', the sociologist in the way the individual as a person relates to others.

The differences between sociology and psychology, on the one hand then, are differences of *perspective*, in the same way as the differences between a sociologically minded historian and an 'empiricist' historian are differences of perspective. The differences between law, political science and economics, on the other hand, are differences of what one might term *domain*, in that each has a prime interest in certain substantive areas only within human behaviour in general, that is, the lawyer in the study of the way men resolve 'trouble issues', the economist in the study of production and consumption. Of course, at the widest, the lawyer who looks at the connection of law-making agencies to the rest of society, or who studies how different kinds of behaviour become defined as 'good' or 'bad' and how these definitions become embodied in law, is studying law in very sociological ways.

Researches within any one specific discipline may be vital to another: thus the sociologist may draw upon the economist's knowledge of the female labour-market as a part of his study of the family; conversely, the economist may use the sociologist's national surveys or local, intensive studies in order to enable him to estimate where and when likely supplies of labour, or demand for commodities, can be expected.

Thus the different divisions of the social sciences are only relative; they cut off what is in reality a 'seamless web' for convenience of analysis and in order to permit specialized study, so that where we see people behaving, we label their different actions variously 'economic' behaviour, 'religious' and so on.

Sociology itself has been subject to the same processes of specialization that characterize industrial production, the arts, or the natural sciences. Within 'sociology' as a general perspective, there are now specialized 'domains' also, of which medical sociology and the sociology of education, in Britain at least, loom large – for obvious reasons, since both deal with key social institutions which employ sociology and sociologists, finance research, etc., on a scale that is not the case, for instance, with the sociology of religion or law. These special areas or domains are, however, held together by a common body of theory and a common body of available methods. Other major divisions are urban sociology, political sociology, social stratification, race relations, the sociology of the family and so on. All these, of course, are only divisions of convenience. There can be, in principle, as many sociological domains, or sub-domains, as there are classes of social activity. Thus we have a 'sociology of jazz', of dying, of war, and even a sociology of sleep, since sleep is, in part, a socially conditioned activity (Aubert, 1965, pp. 168–200). And the sociology of deviance, that is, the study of those activities stigmatized and designated as 'improper' or 'nonconformist' behaviour – from prostitution to membership of marginal religious sects – is a well-developed field.

Sociology studies all these separate topics only as particular manifestations of its overall subject-matter: men's social relationships to one another. Although each domain does develop its own special body of theory, it always draws upon the *general* theory of sociology. In its turn, it contributes to general theory, so that industrial sociologists may learn a great deal from theoretically oriented (as against merely descriptive) studies of schools, and a sociologist studying religion may profit greatly from reading studies of child-rearing. Certainly, anyone who sticks too rigidly to his chosen specialism is likely to be both a poor specialist as well as a poor sociologist-in-general.

Sociology in Society

So far, we have defined sociology by discussing those special characteristics that mark it off as a discipline distinct from other, related disciplines. This definition is in fact an ideal statement of what sociology *ought* to be about. We now need to look at sociology, not so much in logical or ideal terms, but in terms of the actual organized forms in which it is found 'on the ground', and in terms, too, of the kinds of things sociologists actually do. For, like any other science, sociology exists not just in people's minds, but in the form of institutions within which sociological work is carried out. And though the field claimed for it is extremely wide – no less than the study of social relationships, of whatever historical period and in whatever culture – nevertheless, sociologists do, in practice, concentrate predominantly on certain kinds of problems within certain kinds of societies.

When sociology emerged as a new science at the end of the eighteenth century, it was very wide-ranging and comparative, covering the whole development of man. It attempted to classify the variety of forms of society throughout human history and throughout the world, and to locate these different species of society within a general theory of the development of society. Under the impact of the Darwinian revolution in biology, most major nineteenth-century sociologists continued this tradition. The great sociological theorists – Marx, Saint-Simon, Comte, Durkheim, Spencer to name no others – all developed evolutionary schemes that embraced all the main types of social organization then known.

Yet in the later nineteenth and early twentieth centuries, during the period when sociology was becoming an established academic discipline in universities, there was a turning away from such ambitious comparative and developmental study in the direction of an increasing preoccupation with contemporary industrial societies, usually the study of the society in which the sociologist was living. Underlying this shift of attention was the assumption that the industrial countries which dominated the world then were the 'wave of the future' and that the rest were outmoded 'traditional' societies, destined to follow in the wake of the advanced countries. Sociology thus became both less cross-cultural and less historical, concentrating mainly on contemporary society, and witnessed a revolt not only against evolutionist thinking but against large-scale generalization of any variety concerning the over-all direction of man's social development.

This loss of historical and comparative vision has persisted to the present day, though of late there has grown up a revival of interest in the larger problems of 'development' under the stimulus of the arrival on the world stage of the new revolutionary societies of the U.S.S.R. and China, and the transformation of many former colonies into newly independent states, all bent upon rapid modernization.

In this century, then, sociology has, until recently, primarily concentrated upon the analysis of the social systems of a very limited number of highly developed societies. It has mainly flourished in the

United States and in Britain, France and Germany. Within these countries, it has existed in institutionalized form in the shape of a discipline taught in universities and colleges, and in the form of research conducted in these places and in special research institutes. It has also been found in governmental research units; in market-research and consultancy bodies (usually commercial organizations); within pressure-groups and 'cause' organizations. There is plenty of perceptive writing about society by people who are not professional social scientists: journalists, novelists, etc. – people who have that special capacity to generalize intelligently from their own experience, to relate this experience to the lives of others, and to trace out the forces shaping the conditions under which people live out their relationships with one another. People who lack these gifts, however, and who are at the same time ignorant of the literature of the social sciences, nevertheless readily pronounce about society. They are likely simply to produce spurious 'conventional wisdom' at best, and positively dangerous nonsense at worst.

Often, laymen tackle issues, too, that are neglected by professional social scientists. The neglect of such key problems by sociologists may be in part, of course, simply a function of the small numbers of professional sociologists: until about fifteen years ago there were only 450 members of the British Sociological Association, and not all of these were working sociologists. But the causes of such neglect run deeper than this: it is also a failure of intellectual nerve and a narrowness of horizons that has been excoriated by C. Wright Mills in his book *The Sociological Imagination* (Mills, 1959).

We do lack sound scientific studies of many areas of social life, and sociologists commonly defend themselves for not having produced such studies on the grounds that they cannot produce scientific analyses where the basic research has not been done. Against this one can argue that we will probably never have all, even much, of the data we would ideally like. Yet we do have available data of various kinds, which we can use within a sociological framework of analysis. If we wait for perfect information, we will never be able to say anything.

Mills declares that the shortage of data is not accidental. Academics, he suggests, are usually people of middle-class (and nowadays often working-class) background. Their upbringing and work rarely involves them in any direct acquaintance with the lives led by the wealthy and the powerful; they mostly occupy lower and middle level positions in institutions such as universities which are separated off from the worlds of business and politics where the key decisions are taken. The academic, too, often interprets the scientific ideal of objectivity to mean 'non-involvement' in public issues, and refrains from researching such controversial areas as 'Who runs Britain?' and from expressing any views on such matters. He is in danger, Mills suggests, of becoming exactly what the Greeks – who thought men should be engaged in their society – defined the 'idiot' to be: the completely private man. The result is that many of the 'big', the controversial, and therefore the really important problems never get researched into at all. Conversely, the social scientist, all too often, confines himself not just to small-scale studies (which are perfectly justifiable), but to studies of the socially marginal and unimportant.

Since every one of us knows something about society, to many people the study of society does not seem to call for any special expertise. And as we noted, journalists, creative writers and others – not social scientists alone – write perceptively about society.

Yet increasingly people are coming to appreciate that to study society scientifically demands special skills, and produces, though it does not displace, a quite different kind of understanding from that provided, say, by the novelist. They hope, too, that this knowledge will be of use, just as sociology emerged in the nineteenth century in response to the needs of various kinds of groups – mainly governments and social reformers – interested in using social science. The contemporary 'customers' for social science are equally varied.

We will now consider the uses made of social science under three broad heads: the demand for information; the need for explanation; and the use of sociology in policy-formulation and execution.

The Assembling of Information

It would be naïve to assume that governments, any more than ordinary people, necessarily only want accurate information. They may want to mislead others with lies; they may be incapable of facing the truth, and may wish to have their favourite prejudices comfortably supported; or they may use 'inquiry' itself as a political device to avoid actually doing anything, whilst making it appear that something is being done. Thus the Morton Royal Commission on Marriage and Divorce in 1951 in Britain has been described as 'a device for obfuscating a socially urgent but politically inconvenient issue' (McGregor, 1957). Nor does the inclusion of a sprinkling of social scientists on a commission guarantee by any means that the inquiry as a whole will be scientific. Even less does it ensure that any conclusions will be translated into action. The Kerner Commission into the U.S. riots of 1967 concluded its report with these words from Dr Kenneth B. Clark, a distinguished Negro psychologist called as 'expert witness':

I read [the report] . . . of the 1919 riot in Chicago, and it was as if I were reading the report of the investigating committee on the Harlem riot of '35, the report of the investigating committee on the Harlem riots of '45, the report of the McCone Commission on the Watts riot.

I must again in candour say to you members of this Commission – it is a kind of Alice in Wonderland – with the same moving picture – reshown over and over again, the same analysis, the same recommendations, and the same inaction (Report of the National Advisory Commission on Civil Disorders, 1968).

But governments, like firms or individuals, do need a great deal of information, too, and many inquiries are mounted in order to get it. The coming of industrial society made it increasingly imperative for governments to assemble information about populations that were highly mobile and therefore highly unsettled, as hundreds of thousands of people were pushed or pulled off the land into the new, teeming cities. In the era which followed the French Revolution a terror of Jacobinism akin to the McCarthyite fear of Communism in this century gripped the comfortable classes. Simple repression was the main response: early trade unions were banned and more troops faced the Luddites in Britain in 1812 than Wellington had had under his command in Spain in the Peninsular War.

But, increasingly, governments found that the sword brought no solution to problems that were essentially rooted in social distress; they turned, in consequence, to analysis of these sources of popular discontent and began investigations of the lives of the new masses who now lived in cities and worked in factories, and who responded in new ways to these new conditions of life. Before action could be taken, the size and nature of the problem had to be estimated. How many people were there? How many were literate? What did they earn? How did they make a living? Did they make a living at all? The asking of such questions in Britain, the first industrial society, underlay the introduction of the Census (1801), the classic Reports of the Factory Inspectors and the Poor Law Commissioners. This was the beginning of what we now call the 'information explosion'; complex societies, from thence forwards, could no longer be run on the basis of ignorance.

Many of the great series of nineteenth-century governmental inquiries were also concerned with modernizing ancient institutions. The Civil Service, the Army and the Public Schools were all redesigned in this way. Disasters were a singularly important stimulus to such critical examination, as when the cholera epidemic of the 1830s, and the ignominious performance of the British Army in the Boer War, led to agonizing reappraisals of the health of the nation.

Studies of popular responses to these new conditions, however, were less common. The Religious Census of 1851 was an exception, and was not repeated. But public official inquiries are not the only way to assemble information. Popular moods and organizations were in fact watched, and less respectable ones were watched in less respectable ways: by police-informers and *agents-provocateurs*, just as the C.I.A. and F.B.I. do a great deal of un-public research in twentieth-century America and elsewhere. The records of these public private eyes, and the archives of court and prison, only become available to later generations, if at all. They are as valuable to the social historian as they once were to those who paid for them, and have enabled historians like George Rudé to add to the *dramatis personae* of traditional historical studies those who inhabited prisons rather than palaces (Rudé, 1959).

Though governments produced information for their own purposes, they could not prevent their opponents using Government publications for their own, quite different, purposes. Reforming radicals and revolutionaries made great use of official reports. Karl Marx used them to write *Capital*; social reformers used them as ammunition. But the radicals and reformers mounted their own independent inquiries as well. Liberal reformers like Francis Place, Ernest Chadwick and Lord Shaftesbury helped pioneer the modern extensive survey, and Marx's colleague, Frederick Engels, pioneered the sociology of the new industrial cities in his classic study of Manchester in 1844 (Engels, 1975). Later the Fabians, notably Beatrice and Sidney Webb, developed the factual social survey in a monumental series of studies that helped shape the entire cast of thought of the Labour Party.

The long tradition of fact-collecting surveys in Britain, and their use by the Establishment and its opponents alike, in part explains why so many people still see social science as simply the collection of facts, and why so many people make the further assumption that since facts are neutral, the collecting and ordering of the facts must be a neutral operation too. The facts, they believe, speak for themselves.

Now if there is one thing that facts never do it is to speak. What does happen is that *men* select certain facts, interpret them, and then take actions which may or may not be closely dependent upon the analysis they have made.

There is, obviously, some element of truth in this popular assumption that fact-collecting is 'scientific'. The scientific aspect of fact-collecting lies in its being *uninhibited*, in two senses; firstly in the sense that the scientist imposes as few barriers as possible on himself (even if others may do so) in collecting the evidence he needs, and in analysing and publishing it 'without fear or favour'; and uninhibited in a second sense, in that the scientist tries to free himself from fixed preconceptions, prejudices, *a priori* judgements, 'pet theories', etc. Ideally, he questions everything, even his own habits of thought. For him there are no tabooed topics, no areas where inquiry should be avoided for fear of breaking rules imposed by non-scientists – whether they be political rules ('security'), or just social conventions (e.g. taboos on discussing sexual experience) – and thereby offending authority or the general public or some particular interest-group. The slogan 'publish and be damned' reflects the spirit of this aspect of social science well.

In more academic form, the same spirit manifests itself as what is called *empiricism*. The empiricist model assumes an individual researcher who runs across or thinks up some intellectual problem, which stimulates him to collect facts in an open-minded way, which lead him in turn to certain conclusions which he publishes without any consideration for practical implications and without committing himself to any moral judgement or to recommending any course of action. Though this model contains elements of truth, *in toto* it is quite inadequate as a sociological model of the way science works. Firstly, it assumes that facts can be collected without the prior existence of a framework within which they can be put into some kind of order. Facts do not order themselves, and even in the simplest inquiry there are theoretical assumptions built into the researcher's mental equipment that suggest to him what sort of facts to look for, what kinds of facts are likely to be irrelevant and may therefore safely be ignored, what likely causes to search for, what connections might be worth following up, and so on. Moreover, as we shall see in Chapter 2, very little research actually follows the postulated sequence of operations.

Because of this constant endeavour to take nothing for granted, much of the time the scientist appears to be simply documenting the 'obvious'. In fact, much that is held to be 'obvious' is anything but, and 'received ideas', 'conventional wisdom', or popular stereotypes are often quite misleading. Not that popular assumptions are necessarily wrong: the real inadequacy of such ideas, from a scientific point of view, is simply that they are unexamined and untested.

The scientist does more than question particular interpretations of the facts; he questions the very claim that they are the relevant facts, and asks whether other relevant facts might not have been ignored. For all facts are a selection from a complex mass of phenomena which confronts us. Out of this welter of events, we select some for particular attention because we think them to be relevant to some problem we have in mind. Not all facts are relevant: it is the 'frame of reference' which determines which are likely to be. Even where facts seem to be self-evident, then, we are already reading significance into them by selecting them for attention.

Such problems arise even when we are engaged in such apparently 'factual' matters as estimating the distribution of income. First of all, what do we include under the term 'income'? In peasant economies, food produced for subsistence is often the biggest item in a peasant's total income, but it is not purchased for money: can we impute a value to it in money terms? Next, what is the income-unit: the individual, the family, or the household? Can we lump together the profits of small shopkeepers, the wages of skilled workers, the pensions of the retired, etc., as 'income', merely because they receive the same amount of money? Are they not different *kinds* of income?

When we start asking such questions, the simple notion that obvious facts are lying around waiting to be collected can be seen to be an illusion. The categories we use to select and order facts will depend upon our purposes: to follow our example, a taxation official will only classify as 'income' those kinds of income specified by legislation as liable to tax. A sociologist studying the family might regard as 'income' forms of wealth such as trusts and covenants which are not conventional individual income (Titmuss, 1962).

If the categories we use are affected by our purposes, so are even the things we perceive, for we are conditioned by our cultural training to perceive some facts and not others. We do not inevitably even see the same things when we do look. 'What a man sees', Kuhn points out, 'depends upon what he looks at, and also upon what his previous visual-conceptual experience has taught him to see' (Kuhn, 1962). Thus a farmer and a landscape artist both *look at* the same reality, but *see* (or 'perceive') quite different things: the one a valley good for wheat, the other a pattern of tonal values. We may be trained to see the world differently from the way other people see it, especially if we are intending to be a specialist. The police-recruit, for example, must not look at everyday reality as everyone else does, but instead is taught to look for clues which might indicate the existence of crime. Most of us do not see the world as being filled with potential miscreants. The policeman's role demands that he does exactly this:

As he walks through the beat with a mature officer, persons who to him appear legit are cast in the light of the illegal activities in which they are engaged . . . The lovely young lady alighting from a cab is now observable as a call-girl arriving for a session. The novice is shown how to see the streets as, so to speak, scenes from pornographic films (Sachs, 1972, p. 285).

It is not the case, then, that we 'see' identical things which automatically register themselves on our minds, like light on photographic paper producing identical images on each sheet of paper. Rather, we are all equipped with different pieces of sensitized paper, since we have all had different cultural experiences: our cultural conditioning sensitizes our minds to special kinds of things which we share only with those similarly sensitized.

But it is not only the observer who is socialized into interpreting the scenes he observes. The people he is observing, too, are themselves doing the same thing all the time. They may even be observing him. This, indeed, is the basic difference between most of the natural sciences and the social sciences: that the former do not have to cope with *consciousness*. For unlike rocks, amoebae or machines, men think, appraise and feel: they have aims, grievances, aspirations, hopes, fears, dreams, utopias, horrors. This consciousness is not simply *cognitive* knowledge, for men also *evaluate* their experiences as 'good' or 'bad' and react to them with feelings, whether of pleasure or fear. Because of these special features of human behaviour, Max Weber, the classical German sociologist (1864–1920), insisted on using the phrase 'social action' to distinguish such behaviour – behaviour characterized by *meaning* – from man's purely animal behaviour or from the behaviour of plants or insects.

Some of our behaviour is of the latter kind. Just as an insect reacts to a source of light by flying towards it, so we, because we are animals, respond to physical stimuli instinctively: a sudden shout makes us jump. But we control our natural tendency to jump out of our skins, because we don't want to seem 'seven-stone weaklings' in the eyes of our girl-friend (we evaluate the social effects of our own actions on others). Behaviour of this kind is not 'natural' at all: it is social. We also immediately interpret such behaviour. We try to find out who has shouted, what he was shouting about, whether he is hostile, or perhaps simply someone we know giving us an over-hearty greeting; whether he is addressing himself to us at all or perhaps to some other person; and we adapt our own response accordingly.

Even when we are physically quite alone, we carry our society around with us in our heads, just as Robinson Crusoe did on his island. So we refrain from stealing a handbag we find in an empty room because we have absorbed ideas about honesty from our society. Conversely, we may be socially quite isolated, though physically surrounded by people: we can be very lonely in the big city. David Riesman, indeed, has characterized our whole urban civilization as the life of *The Lonely Crowd* (Riesman *et al.*, 1950). Loneliness is a social, not just a physical, condition.

Social action, then, is action which takes into account, or is affected by, the existence of others. It involves understanding or interpreting the meaning of their behaviour – estimating what they are thinking, feeling, and trying to do. We project ourselves into other people's minds. And, of course, they are doing exactly the same *vis-à-vis* our behaviour. This two-sided process has been called 'double contingency'. More complex still, we calculate what others are thinking *about us*, and so on. This is no piece of abstract academic complication for its own sake. It is a perfectly normal part of everyday life, certainly familiar to Lucy and Charlie Brown (see next page).

Though social action takes place at one point or period in time, it is affected by events that have happened before – by 'history'. Thus our estimate of a person's likely behaviour will be affected by our past experience of him, or someone like him in similar situations we have lived through or heard about. Any act thus involves the past as well as the present. We carry history around with us, locked up in our heads, and are constantly referring to it all the time, as historians rightly emphasize. But in acting at any time, we are also making estimates about the future. We pre-figure the outcome in our 'mind's eye'. Even so-called traditional or habitual behaviour – where we 'do this because our forefathers always did it that way' – carries with it the implication '.... and it will therefore work equally well in the future'. Sociologists, who concentrate usually upon the study of contemporary situations, often underemphasize the extent to which contemporary behaviour is thus conditioned both by the past and by orientation towards the future. In order to understand why trade unionists are sensitive to technological innovation, one has to know what the experience of the Depression has built into their consciousness. In order to understand why the sons of comfortable upper-class families go off to live in jungles as guerrillas, one has to understand their ideas about the coming of a new kind of society. The simplest piece of behaviour thus involves past, present and future.

In so far as all behaviour contains an element of intention, all behaviour is 'future-oriented', even if the future turns out to be just a repetition of the present. Marx pointed out that this characteristic is peculiarly human: even the so-called 'social insects' do not possess it. 'A spider conducts operations that resemble those of the weaver, and a bee would put to shame many a human architect by the construction of her honeycomb cells. But what distinguishes the worst architect from the best of bees is that the architect builds his cell in his mind before he constructs it in wax' (Marx, 1976, p. 284).

'Double Contingency'

The capacity to imagine involves a further crucial human skill that the insect lacks: our capacity to 'dream up' future states that have never yet existed in reality, such as 'utopian' societies or 1984s and similar 'anti-utopias'.

It is this capacity to imagine that is the source of innovation and therefore of human development, for men try to bring these utopias into actual existence, and dreams of a heaven upon earth or a classless society have been powerful springs of action in human history. Karl Mannheim called them 'utopian' orientations (Mannheim, 1948), in contrast to those social ideals which merely justified and helped preserve the present social order. These he called 'ideologies'. Our orientation to the future, then, includes not only what we think will happen (our expectations), but also what we want to see happen (our aspirations).

To understand other people's behaviour we have to make complex calculations about such mental states that underlie their actions. We also have to look at our own actions 'from the outside' as it were; to 'see ourselves', as we say, 'as others see us'. One's own behaviour becomes an object of scrutiny to oneself. George Herbert Mead, the American philosopher (1863–1931) therefore tried to persuade us to stop thinking of the individual as a unitary thing called the 'person', a self which exists, as it were, quite independently of others, but to think of the self as a complex with several different dimensions, built up out of our relationships with what he called 'significant others': people whose behaviour has social importance or consequences for us (Strauss, 1964). The individual actor is a different person to different Others, both because he acts differently towards them, and they to him, and because each interprets the Other's behaviour differently. When the individual considers how his behaviour looks to Others, he becomes a Me (the Self as object of scrutiny) to his I (the self as subject, who is doing the scrutinizing).

The skills needed in interpreting the behaviour of others are thus quite different from those needed in analysing non-social, physical behaviour. They are acquired directly by practising them in everyday life, and indirectly from other people and from special stores of cultural experience – books, films and so forth. Since no two of us have been through quite the same set of identical social experiences – we have each had different parents, have been of different seniority in the family, have had different teachers in school, read different books and had different friends, etc. – each of us ends up (apart from being differently endowed by Nature) with a distinctive personal store of culture. It is this idiosyncratic culture that constitutes our individual personality. Conversely, millions of us occupy quite similar life-situations, have lived through the same events and have been raised in very similar ways, so we also share social characteristics with millions of others. If we did not, social science would be impossible, for society would be composed of a multitude of unique cases.

This rich variety of social contacts sets us a problem, then, for each role we play connects us with others who have expectations about what we are likely to do, and ideals to which they try to get us to conform. The attempt to pressurize other people to conform to our normative expectations is what we often call 'politics' or 'social control'. There is, indeed, a coercive element in all behaviour, not just the behaviour of governments and political parties.

But different Others have different norms. Each tries to get us to behave in the way he wants. We cannot satisfy everybody. Yet we must, in the end, act. Sometimes we can arrange things so that we meet these competing Others separately; we solve the problem by behaving 'situationally'. In so doing, we are not simply being hypocrites. Total inconsistency we call 'being all things to all men'; yet social life certainly requires what we more generously call 'flexibility'. Words like 'hypocrisy', 'inconsistency' and 'flexibility' are different *moral* evaluations of what, sociologically, is an inevitable consequence of social relationships. For every role we occupy brings us into contact with several different people, each with different expectations of us. And we enact many such roles, as we will see when we discuss roles and role-sets below (pp. 295–7). In some situations we cannot so easily compartmentalize our behaviour, however. We may have to decide to risk hurting A because, in the end, B is more important to us. Or we may try to strike a balance, by behaving in a way that will totally alienate nobody even if it totally satisfies nobody either. Often, then, we have to calculate 'How will people *in general* treat us or respond to our behaviour?' We produce a kind of lowest common multiple or highest common factor of behaviour in adapting it to the differing expectations of all those different Others. Mead called it adapting our behaviour to a *Generalized* Other.

The Construction of Explanations

Given this complexity of social meaning, even in 'simple' social acts, we can see how inadequate the notion of simply 'collecting the facts' is. Strictly, we cannot separate information-gathering from explanation, which involves interpreting the meanings social actors attach to their behaviour. Secondly, the theories we have in our heads will tend to influence not simply the explanation of the facts we assemble, but the very process of assembling them and the categories we use to classify them.

Much of sociological theory consists in the clarification and development of these categories, for without agreement upon them we cannot even speak the same language about society. Terms such as 'role', 'socialization', or 'pluralism' are necessary tools of the trade, just as natural scientists have their terms with agreed meanings. But we need to distinguish two types of terms. Firstly, there are those like 'hydrogen' or the 'matricentral family' which describe some particular arrangement of matter (in the first case), a particular structure of social relationships (in the second). They describe bits of reality which exist 'out there' in Nature and society. Let us call these, following mathematical practice, 'parameters'. Terms like 'role', on the other hand, are not particular kinds of social arrangement in certain societies, but can be applied to the analysis of any piece of human behaviour. The difference is such that people in a given society can recognize a 'clan' or a 'trade union' for themselves, and indeed have a word for such parameters as the 'clan' and names for particular clans, whereas they do not necessarily have any equivalent for such sociological concepts as 'social mobility' or 'interaction', 'deviance' or 'bureaucracy'. A lot of sociological work, especially in cultures less familiar to us, has consisted simply in creating a 'parametric terminology' by labelling the institutions of which the society is made up – what a 'clan' was, or how 'patronage' worked, the structure and functioning of families, trade unions, parties, etc., in a given society or type of society. 'Concepts', however, are tools we need to tackle the study of *any* society. Both kinds of category are needed in order to analyse social arrangements.

Similarly, in constructing explanations, two different kinds of operation are involved. One researcher may be interested primarily in the religious beliefs of the English. Another may only be interested in these beliefs as a particular example of 'ideology' in general, or as an instance of the wider problems of how human beings respond in a variety of ways to the universal situations of 'birth, copulation and death'. He may, that is, be interested in religion rather than the religion of the English.

Most researchers are interested in both, but the two approaches are distinguishable. Just as we have distinguished 'parameters' from 'concepts', so we can distinguish that kind of sociological theory whose prime focus is upon the culture of the specific society or societies under study as 'substantive' theory (because it is concerned with the content, the 'substance' of the society) from that kind of theorizing which concentrates upon establishing general propositions about the properties of human relationships – which we call 'formal' theory. Formal theory thus deals in concepts and propositions applicable to various kinds of behaviour that differ widely in terms of their 'subject-matter'. 'Substantive' theory on the other hand is theorizing about particular kinds of cultural phenomena: the Soviet power-apparatus, or the English medieval family, or, more widely, single-party states or family-systems in industrialized societies.

Formal theory often develops from and is applied to real social situations. Conversely, concepts developed in formal theory are useful in research which is quite practical in orientation. Thus 'small group' theory developed in quite artificial situations (by studying American students through one-way glass screens) has then been used to study real-life street-corner gangs.

The most abstract kind of formal theory focuses upon kinds or dimensions of social relationships that are universal. This extreme kind of theorizing is typified by the work of the German sociologist Georg Simmel (1858–1918) who was concerned with such matters as conflict, authority and interaction, whether they appeared in religious or economic contexts, in ephemeral interpersonal encounters or in permanent organizations (Simmel, 1950). Thus a formal sociologist concerned with the study of 'authority' could equally well study authority in strip-clubs, the Athenaeum, or old people's homes.

Most of the sociology the reader is likely to be familiar with is of a very different kind: sociological research into specific problem-areas such as crime, race relations, housing, or the family. It is usually research into areas where it is believed that things have 'gone wrong'. The concern of such researches is usually with quite substantive matters – documenting and explaining the patterns and causes of delinquency, illegitimacy, or overcrowding. Its primary aim is not the construction of theory or simply to arrive at an intellectual understanding of why things are as they are.

Men whose prime aim *is* simply to theorize in this way are not irresponsible people, unconcerned with human problems. As citizens, they are often quite as concerned about social problems as the next man. Indeed, they may choose to specialize in theorizing precisely because they believe it necessary to understand the workings of society clearly before one can act in ways likely to prove effective. Their main aim as scientists will thus be to help people think more clearly about society, for we cannot solve social problems until we have thought about social problems sociologically.

Social problems are not the same things as sociological problems. Sociology is a scientific mode of analysing social relationships, and a problem, for sociology, is any pattern of relationships that calls for explanation; the challenging problems are those where the relevant factors and causes are not obvious. A 'social problem' is some piece of social behaviour that causes public friction and/or private misery and calls for collective action to solve it.

Now if a sociological problem is constituted by any piece of behaviour of which we want to 'make sense', it will be obvious that it is not only with 'trouble' problems – problems of breakdown, welfare, or so-called 'social pathology' – that the sociologist is concerned. The explanation of why divorce happens, why it happens to some people with certain social characteristics and not others, or its rise and fall, constitutes problems of explanation for the sociologist. Divorce thus throws up sociological problems. It is, at the same time, a 'social problem'. But the sociologist confronts equally different problems of explanation when he looks at marriages which persist rather than break down, for any husband or wife knows that marriage is no bed of roses; it is a relationship suffused with tensions, even where – indeed, because – there is a specially close relationship. Again, Finer has argued that whilst the series of recent military take-overs in African states is a social phenomenon requiring explanation, equally interesting is the sociological problem of explaining why it is that the military, who have decisive control over the means of violence, do not take over in *every* society (Finer, 1962, p. 5).

So 'normalcy', persistence, continuity, order, the things we regard as 'natural' and 'normal', are all quite as much sociological problems as are those of breakdown, conflict or deviation from normalcy – homosexuality, marital discord, etc. – the phenomena we conventionally label 'social problems'. From the point of view of the State or the neighbours, that is, 'quiet' families are not 'problem families'. Sociologically speaking, they are.

Since sociology emerged largely in the context of movements of reform or modernization, we tend to retain nineteenth-century conceptions of social science as the study of 'social problems'. More than that, we retain nineteenth-century definitions of only certain *kinds* of issues as social problems; delinquency and crime, unemployment, disease, malnutrition, poverty, drug addiction, alcoholism, prostitution, bad housing, sexual deviance, divorce, etc. The major things that these quite diverse items have in common is that they are all things which the nineteenth century saw as *bad* things, and about which people used sociological inquiry in order to provide them with ammunition in an essentially political and moral debate. This debate centred on the issue of whether these things occurred because the individuals involved were personally inadequate, or whether social arrangements and not simply individual shortcomings led them into such straits.

Even today 'social problems' are still thought of in a way that reflects a nineteenth-century preoccupation with problems of poverty and with an individualistic approach to its solution. Thus the social services are largely focused upon a 'case-work' approach to solving the individual client's personal problems. Only very recently have 'community-action' approaches to problems of health, education, poverty and housing, or approaches to these questions in terms of the political economy of the entire society, begun to break away from the individualistic 'case-work' approach. Moreover, increasing leisure is seen as the source of new kinds of social problem; problems of 'affluence' as well as poverty. Further, researchers like Titmuss (1958) see such individual problems not merely as the product of inadequate interpersonal social relationships within the family or within the firm, but as outcomes of decisions and arrangements at national level and as part of national politics. For 'welfare' problems cannot be fully analysed without relating them to the wider structure of society which produces such problems for the individual as being out of work. Others are trying to transform 'social administration' by applying sociological theory developed in the study of steel plants or insurance offices to the analysis of welfare organizations, hospitals and case-work agencies.

Deviations from normal, respectable behaviour create social problems not just for the individuals who suffer, but also for their neighbours, their kin, the State, etc., who have to bear the consequences of their suffering. Such tragedies, that is, are rarely purely private, either in causation or in their consequences. Nor are the individual's problems usually peculiar to him alone. The sociological imagination, C. Wright Mills has argued, consists in the ability to appreciate that the 'troubles' that afflict the individual are the outcome of much wider arrangements within which his life is lived out, and that these arrangements affect the local family and work milieux within which most of his life is acted out. Most people never get beyond seeing their personal troubles as simply personal. Even some social scientists tell people that their problems are mainly caused by personal inadequacy, by inability to adjust, that they are the outward manifestation of innate anti-social drives, etc. The development of a sociological imagination, Mills suggests, enables the individual to see that his 'personal troubles of milieu' are connected with 'public issues of social structure'; that his personal history (biography) is shaped by what is happening to his society (history); that to 'understand what is happening in themselves', men have to see themselves as 'minute points of the intersections of biography and history within society' (Mills, 1959, p. 7).

The causes of constantly recurring mass and personal distress, moreover, are to be found in the functioning of what to those more fortunately placed appears to be a 'normal' and satisfying society. Thus, in an educational system like that in Britain, 'educational opportunity', which represents for some children the achievement of higher education, necessarily entails the 'de-selection' of the rest. Failure for the majority is a condition of the normal functioning of society. We know, too, that large numbers of the most talented children are excluded while many of the less-gifted go on to college and university. This, also, is part of the 'normal' functioning of society.

Those who suffer, therefore, often criticize the structures that produce these results as themselves constituting 'social problems'. Traditional 'social problems' research, they say – the study of what has been variously defined as the study of 'nuts and sluts' (or 'peers and queers') – merely deals with the end-products of this normal society: its 'welfare' problems. But this social machinery itself, as well as war, political corruption, the private ownership of newspapers, the starvation of millions at home and abroad, are every bit as much 'social problems'.

The 'sociological imagination', then, involves acquiring an understanding of how the day-to-day life of the individual is connected to the higher levels of social organization and to wider processes in society.

The sociologist thus sees society as exhibiting order: patterned regularities, not just a collection of random, disconnected events or facts. A society is a *system* insofar as it is made up of parts which mesh together. Changes in one part will have effects on other parts (though the effects may not necessarily be direct or powerful). To relate together these different parts of society and different areas of experience, to draw a coherent 'intellectual' map of the world and to locate ourselves on this map, we need to match together the different pieces of our mental furniture also. Some of it may need consigning to the rubbish-heap because it does not fit the over-all intellectual pattern or style, or is worn-out and needs replacing by more modern and better-fitting furniture.

In order to understand these interconnections in the world 'out there', then, we need a body of theory which itself is systematic. We cannot, in social science, operate effectively with bits and pieces of ideas unconnected to each other, as we so often tend to do in everyday life. Most people in Britain, for example, use bits of classical liberalism, bits of socialist ideas, and bits of Christianity, without necessarily subscribing to any one of these belief-systems as a whole, and without fitting the bits together very systematically in their minds. True, few people see no interconnections at all; their life would be very chaotic if this were so. But they are quite capable of refusing to believe, for instance, that Hell exists as well as Heaven (Gorer, 1955, p. 252) – or where they acknowledge the existence of Hell, refuse to admit that anyone they know and love is destined for Hell.

Scientists can be quite as inconsistent and unscientific in their private lives as anyone else. They are obliged, however, in their work to order their thinking more rigorously, if they are to make serious sense, and be able to demonstrate to their colleagues that they have made serious sense. Without some kind of intellectual scheme which is comprehensible and acceptable to their colleagues, they cannot do this.

Once we begin consciously to relate our ideas about society to each other to form a more coherent outlook, we are beginning to think systematically. The most unlikely and apparently remote phenomena may now be seen to be related: thus Max Weber argued that the rise of capitalism in Europe and the rise of Protestantism were by no means unconnected (Weber, 1952). There is, of course, a danger of artificially *over*-connecting things. There are sociologists who seem to think that if there are two football teams in a town, one must be Protestant and the other Catholic (an assumption which holds true probably only in Glasgow).

Systematic thought is essential for comprehending the world that itself is a system. We can, indeed, look at the whole world as one single social system (Worsley, 1967, ch. 1). Within this world system are sub-systems such as the nation-state. There are also sub-systems within the State: county and parish levels of government, for example, as well as other separate and parallel organizational sub-systems within the same society: national organizations of transport workers, national associations of motor-car owners, dahlia-growers, etc., each with its own internal divisions and levels. There are also non-organizational systematic regularities, as when all families – both by legal requirement and long-established custom – are systematically monogamous. There are thus regularities even though there is no formal organization to which all families belong. The concept of system allows for the existence of many kinds of system and sub-system, as well as *levels* of society, from the lowest level of direct face-to-face interactions in 'primary groups' to the level of nation-wide and even international groups and associations.

Though today what goes on in any one country is profoundly conditioned by world-wide developments – so that no nation-state is an island – most of the groups and categories that immediately affect our lives are still contained within the nation-state. Between the level of the nation and the level of the primary group, there are many types and levels of society: Parliament, a housing estate, or a school class in their form-room. Theory can be said to be high-level or low-level according to the different levels of society it deals with. Thus theories about the functioning of the national party system are often described as 'higher-level' theory than studies of local party branches. This implies that the level of a theory is a function of the range of phenomena it deals with, and some go on to argue that the study of national organizations or of such nation-wide units as the family (e.g. by carrying out national surveys) necessarily engenders theory which is 'higher level' than that which arises from studying twenty families intensively.

Now in one sense a theory which deals with a larger area of reality is, of course, more 'general' than one which handles smaller portions. But very good theory can be generated out of studies which are quite limited in size. Thus Elizabeth Bott studied only twenty families, but produced some of the most stimulating ideas about family life in general that have come out of recent sociology (Bott, 1957). Again, general theory can be applied to, rather than emerge from, small-scale or low-level situations, as when a psychiatrist applies all his knowledge to the cure of a single patient or when industrial sociologists intensively study a single shop in a factory. It is possible, if one is equipped with an adequate sociological vision, to study the Chinese Revolution through the examination of only one village (Hinton, 1966).

We can thus classify a theory not only according to the *level* of social organization to which it applies, but also according to the *range* of phenomena the theory covers. The kind of theory we have called 'substantive' is said to be 'high level' when it tackles things which are large in scale or widely distributed. But the degree of generality of *formal* theory is of a quite different kind and is measured by the extent to which concepts and propositions are fitted together to form a coherent body of *ideas*, rather than the degree to which the theory concerns a particular level of *society*.

Formal theory, then, is concerned with theoretical range rather than with social level. Extreme formalists aim at establishing propositions which will hold good for any social situation in any society in any epoch. Naturally such proportions are very abstract and limited in number. Thus, we may see certain resemblances in three-party relationships, whether these be the 'eternal triangle' or nations at war, but the differences between these are much more crucial than any such resemblances.

But in order to comprehend processes of development, and especially the emergence of quite new social forms to displace older ones, a more historically informed sociology is needed. The great sociological theorists, such as Max Weber and Kark Marx, were thus neither simply 'formal' or 'substantive' theorists. It seems best to label them 'general' theorists, for while they developed complex bodies of theory concerning the basic properties of human society, they used this to delineate the general patterns of human historical development within which studies of particular societies were located.

Many theorists have been attracted to formal theorizing because they have hoped to be able to establish general laws of human behaviour that would hold true irrespective of what particular society was being studied in what particular period. They hoped to emulate the natural sciences by working out the laws governing social behaviour. Once we knew these laws, we could become 'social engineers', able to control the future by taking the appropriate action.

This set of ideas about the role of science in society is known as *positivism*, a term coined by Auguste Comte (1798–1857), the man who also coined the term 'sociology'.

Positivism is based on a number of assumptions. First, it assumed a mistaken conception of the natural sciences, for natural scientists do not simply 'collect' facts any more than social scientists do. Different scientists develop different theoretical frameworks or 'paradigms', as Kuhn calls them, and these are often in rivalry, as when astronomers began to find that Ptolemaean conceptions of the cosmos could not explain certain observed movements of the heavenly bodies. Copernicus then devised an alternative 'paradigm'. Science proceeds by the resolution of such problems, not simply by the amassing of more and more facts.

Secondly, modern natural scientists no longer conceive of the operation of the laws of Nature in the way that their predecessors did in the eighteenth century. The conception of law with which the natural scientist operates today is based upon notions of probability in the statistical sense, rather than upon notions of an absolutely determined universe. In this conception of law, there is still order, but the behaviour of any particular item cannot be exactly foreseen – unless we can acquire exhaustive knowledge of everything that might possibly affect it (which we can never do, though we can get near enough to it for many practical purposes including some extremely sophisticated ones). The positivistic social scientist, then, is really modelling himself upon outmoded, not contemporary, natural science.

In any case, we cannot assume that there is only one way of doing science, a standard set of procedures which we can use to test whether a proposition is valid or not: as we will see in the next chapter, there is little agreement as to what 'the basic scientific method' is. Some argue that the test of a good theory is its logical consistency; others emphasize that this kind of 'internal' consistency is not enough (some forms of madness, like paranoia, being extraordinarily consistent – *too* consistent and thereby impervious to experience). Rather, they say, a good theory must make sense of the complexity of the world out there. Others consider the ultimate test to be not one of logic at all, but of capacity to predict what will happen. Opponents of all these kinds of positivism object that what happens in society does not simply happen, but is *made* to happen – by coordinated human action. Others emphasize that this man-made order is always mediated by the ideas that men carry round in their heads. By 'ideas', in this wide sense, they imply not only the intellectual (or 'cognitive') categories we use to make sense of the world, but also our emotional states, and dispositions (wants, fears, etc.), and, too, our ethical beliefs about right and wrong, what is desirable or disapproved of: in a word, our *values*.

These ideas do not emerge, or persist, or die away, simply in mysterious ways. Even the most scientific of knowledge is related to the structure and purposes of the society it is embedded in. It was, for instance, the demands of industry and commerce for better navigational instruments, mining machinery, and sources of power that led to the establishment of the Royal Society in Britain in the seventeenth century. Military needs similarly produced usable atomic power, electronics, and antibiotics in the Second World War. Conversely, a 'genius' like Leonardo da Vinci may produce notions and inventions that are 'ahead of their time', since the level of industrial development of his day did not permit many of his inventions – the jet-engine, for instance – to be put into production.

Perhaps the main theoretical school in social science which emphasizes these interrelations between science and society is Marxism, which we will discuss in several of the following chapters.

Marxists – and others – have argued that the intellectual categories we use, and the theoretical framework we operate within, are affected by our existence in particular situations in particular societies at particular points in time. Obviously, this includes those relationships that are governed by our being employed by others for their ends (e.g., the making of profit), but this is only one particular – though, in class society, crucial – instance of the much wider social determination of knowledge and of the process of 'doing science'. Whereas positivism conceives of the thinker or scientist as if he were disconnected from any social context, individualistically pursuing knowledge wheresoever his intellect leads him, and not allowing himself to be affected by considerations as to whether his discoveries might harm anyone – whether those who employ him, or his or their friends or enemies – or benefit anyone. Knowledge, in this model, is treated as an end in itself, subject to no particular direction.

Classical positivism, too, conceived of a separation between the theorist and the objects he studies – usually thought of as 'facts' to be looked at, 'objectively', from the outside, by the scientist. Parts of what scientists observe are then selected as having the status of *scientific* knowledge, that is, knowledge that has been acquired in a particular way; the rest may be knowledge, but not scientific knowledge. If it accords with scientific findings, it may be called 'folk-knowledge'; if not, it simply gets labelled 'error'.

Now sociologists do not generally suggest that all knowledge is of the same status, any more than they question that the world is real even though many of us see it quite differently. But they do point out that what ends up in textbooks is only a part of what scientists do, and that the ways this knowledge is arrived at is usually 'doctored' or 'written up' so as to conform with an ideal of scientific method (the hypothesis, the testing of that hypothesis by experiment – artificial and 'natural' – and consequent proof or disproof).

Such an account omits, in the first place, the role of 'hunches' or 'serendipity' – that which gets found or thought of *not* as a result of careful design. We usually call this 'accident', but it is no random happening when a scientist like Sir Alexander Fleming 'happens' to notice an unexpected culture growing on a plate – and so comes to 'discover' penicillin. He did so because he was looking for that sort of thing, knew what to look for, and observed things non-scientists might simply have written off as 'mould' and scraped into the dustbin.

Much of what scientists do is completely excised, too, from the accounts of their activities given in textbooks, which usually just give those things accepted, now, as their lasting contributions to science. Thus Sir Isaac Newton's deep preoccupation with modes of religious thought that were regarded as backward-looking and superstitious in enlightened circles of his day is not mentioned in conventional histories of physics. The connection between science and industrial or governmental patronage is also usually ignored, together with the existence of personal values other than the commitment to the pure search for knowledge; and the crucial nature of motivations such as personal ambitions, the search for status, power, and money – motivations which, of course, are not *purely* 'personal' since they are instilled in the individual who lives in a competitive, individualistic and hierarchical society.

Historians and sociologists of science, in recent years, have therefore questioned traditional presentations of how and why science gets done. The study of changing conceptions of madness, for instance, has been shown to be related to wider changes in ideology: the new eighteenth-century belief in Reason, for instance, gave rise to new methods of treating the insane. Such changes were not due solely to changes in ideas, however. In the rapidly growing, post-colonial U.S.A., with enormous social mobility, the sick, the destitute, the insane and the poor could no longer be provided for or dealt with as they had been hitherto, by being taken into care or custody within the community in other people's houses or in special houses little different from and modelled on the ordinary household, in which they spent only a short period. The asylum, the prison, the workhouse and the long-stay hospital had to be invented in their place.

The ideology of science, however, continues to emphasize the free and unfettered, pure pursuit of knowledge, and a radical difference in kind as between scientific and non-scientific thinking. Yet anthropologists have found that the operation of witchcraft is strikingly logical, and students of scientific thinking and practice have come to observe that though scientists certainly use 'scientific' techniques and modes of thought, they often deviate from those canons even in the pursuit of scientific work. Thus, certain frameworks of thought – 'paradigms' such as the Ptolemaic conception of the universe, or the medieval belief in the 'humours' – persist over centuries and virtually all scientific work takes place within these frameworks. As Kuhn points out, young people are socialized into these ways of thought and accept them as authoritative, not only because they are labelled 'scientific', but because science is socially organized, and those scientists who dominate academic and industrial scientific practice have both the prestige and power to impose the orthodox paradigm on others. To break away from it – as Copernicus, Galileo, Darwin or Einstein did – may entail challenging the dominant intellectual orthodoxy, the scientific Establishment, and secular and even religious authorities, too.

Innovation is most likely to be officially sponsored when society urgently needs to innovate, as in times of crisis, such as wartime. More rarely, persons less socialized into orthodoxy, such as the young, are lodged in marginal positions in society (perhaps even supported and licensed to innovate, as academic and research institutions develop new unorthodoxies).

A third major tradition, which stands in opposition both to positivism and to Marxism, is the set of related approaches we can roughly label 'interpretive' sociology. Whereas positivism emphasizes the fact that society exists outside the observer, interpretivism stresses that this 'external' world can only be known to us through the operation of our minds, and that our minds are not blank, but furnished with mental structures which affect our perception and understanding of that world. Hence, it is argued, social science cannot imitate the natural sciences. Most importantly, this special way of coming to terms with the world is not restricted to social scientists: the sociologists' 'subjects' are not inert substances, but conscious, active men themselves. These approaches will be discussed in Chapter 2 and especially in Chapter 9.

One of the major implications of this, we have seen, is that men can retain their experience, storing it up as 'culture'. They also increase it by innovation. Hence, social life is characterized not only by communication of culture, from one society to another and from one generation to another, but also by the emergence of new forms. Social development tends to show sharp discontinuities as well as more gradual change, since a society may be converted to Islam, or undergo a revolution, whereas no ant society is ever going to be affected by the ideas of other ants, because they do not have any.

The construction of a body of sociological theory capable of handling the variety of human society and culture over time is, plainly, enormously difficult. It encourages social scientists to give up the attempt, and to concentrate instead on becoming specialists in only some limited areas. Sociology becomes a series of compartments: there is now industrial sociology, 'small group' sociology, conflict sociology, and so on, rather than, simply, 'sociology'. The results are often disastrous: theorists spin elaborate structures which are ill-connected to researched knowledge, and field-researchers fail to demonstrate what the general theoretical implications of their work might be. And in what should be a dialectic between theory and society, theorists tend to become interested only in endless comparisons between the latest fashionable, and preferably obscure, theories. The work of looking at what is going on in the world they leave to others, who often, therefore, tend to lack as sound a theoretical background as they ought to have.

It is thus possible to divide the varieties of sociological theorizing into positivistic, interpretivist and Marxist schools. To do so is to assume that the important differences are those of theoretical orientation. But this is only one way of conceptualizing divisions within the discipline, and for other purposes other ways of dividing up the subject are both possible and useful. One obvious and simple way is according to divisions of subject-matter into 'substantive' fields, such as the sociology of education, or the sociology of health and illness, or other similar institutional areas of social life. Similarly, looking back at the nineteenth century, Nisbet has discerned a set of 'unit-ideas' which preoccupied both the precursors of modern sociology and the members of the societies they lived in: community, authority, status, the 'sacred', and alienation (Nisbet, 1970).

We can, alternatively, distinguish between *levels* of theorizing: broadly, as between 'micro-' sociology and the 'macro'- sociological study of whole societies and cultures – or even, at the level of formal theory, the attempt to generate propositions which would be universally valid.

Other suggestive ways of conceptualizing the main types of theorizing use quite different yardsticks. Thus Dawe has argued that there are basically two major modes of approach to the study of society: a sociology of action, on the one hand, and a sociology of social system, on the other (Dawe, 1971), the first emphasizing the actor's awareness of his world and his attempts to adopt that world to his own ends; the second, the way in which the requirements of social organization are imperatives governing the life of the individual.

Sociology and Political Action

One unfortunate, and all too common, consequence of this compartmentalization of subject-matter, and specialization of theory and of methodology, has been a loss of all-round intellectual vision: the capacity to see the relationship between the particular subject under study and the rest of both society and sociology. A loss of moral perspective, too, has often accompanied this loss of intellectual focus.

C. Wright Mills has pointed out that some areas are remarkably understudied, considering their social importance. This neglect he saw in part as the expression of a limited 'middle level' imagination which the social background and social role of most researchers engendered. But is also occurred because academics simply gave in too readily to social pressures not to delve too deeply into areas that the powerful might prefer to keep shielded from scrutiny. What gets studied clearly depends greatly upon whether support for research is forthcoming. What is done with the studies equally depends upon people other than the sociologist. But he does have some say himself, and at this point, science, politics and ethics are all involved, and create problems of choice and of social responsibility for the sociologist.

For social research to take place at all, research must normally be sponsored and paid for. Moreover, various groups in society are interested in using the results of the inquiry, either simply to clarify their understanding of social processes or in order to develop and carry out specific policies.

But even the act of publishing or reading a quite 'academic' book is a social act which has social consequences. The reader may have his beliefs undermined, his prejudices reinforced, or his 'eyes opened' by being exposed to new possible interpretations of the world. The specialized production and consumption of knowledge, indeed, has become a source of unique power in an age where mass communications become more influential.

The 'pure' scientist professes to be unconcerned or unaffected by such things. But the distinction between 'pure' and 'applied' science is quite misleading if it is taken to mean that the scientist, even if he is unconcerned about any possible applications of his work, bears no responsibility for its social consequences, or that there *are* no social consequences to 'pure' science. However 'pure' research is intended to be, the distinction between 'pure' and 'applied' science is not absolute. All that we can really say about 'pure' science is that it is either that knowledge which has not *yet* been used, or that which is 'fundamental' – basic to other scientific work. For we cannot know what the applications of even the most abstract theory may be. After the dropping of the atomic bombs on Japan, Einstein, on whose early 'pure' and utterly 'academic' mathematical work the development of nuclear weapons depended, remarked, 'Had I known, I would rather have been a watchmaker'. Conversely, theoretical findings of great importance have resulted from research undertaken for quite practical purposes, as the scientific breakthroughs of two world wars demonstrate.

In fact, the scientist faces moral dilemmas at every stage of his work. The classical liberal view of science does not prepare him for these problems, for it teaches him that science is neutral. It also contains within it ideals which most of us accept as highly desirable – the ideal of the untrammelled search for the truth, and the ideal of the unrestricted free interchange of knowledge between fellow-scientists and between human beings generally. Yet we know that in reality knowledge may be used for evil purposes: there are people whom each one of us, if we could, would debar from acquiring certain kinds of knowledge because we know they would use it for anti-human ends. Such decisions, in reality, are more often made *for* the scientist than *by* him: control of the flow of information is a matter of institutional rather than individual decision. But the individual still has to decide whether to conform to that decision.

Society, in fact, by no means always allows the pursuit of knowledge as an absolute. Much natural-science information is 'classified' for 'security' reasons; social science, too, is inhibited by refusal of research facilities, restrictions upon publication, or upon communication with foreigners.

Thus the liberal conception of science fails to provide an adequate sociological model of the practice of science. Nor does it even pose satisfactorily the ethical problems of science. It holds that science cannot flourish without the submission of knowledge to the critical inspection of the whole scientific community, because we need to co-operate with other minds. 'Secrets', therefore, are said to be a hindrance to science. Yet, clearly, the communication of knowledge is not what the patrons or controllers of science are necessarily interested in at all; they are as much, sometimes more, concerned, notably in the fields of atomic and bacteriological research, with preventing knowledge getting to other scientists, who work for their political rivals and enemies. Knowledge produced by social scientists, if important, is usually labelled 'intelligence'.

Scientists themselves also secrete their findings, perhaps less dramatically. They may do so for reasons quite unconnected with the 'reasons of State' we have so far mentioned. Scientists are no more or less ambitious, avaricious, idealistic or egoistic than other human beings, as Watson's account of his work on DNA vividly shows (Watson, 1968). The institutionalized pressure to 'publish or perish' in the race for personal advancement, or consideration of status, can induce researchers to treat their findings as private property, giving them an edge over their professional rivals, and preventing the latter from 'jumping the gun' by publishing first.

Not only is the liberal ideal of the free flow of knowledge a long way removed from the actual practice of science, but its strict necessity becomes dubious in an age when scientific organizations are now so large that they can live largely off their intellectual resources, just as big corporations finance their growth out of retained profits. Being big, these organizations automatically attract recruits, as big nations do via the 'brain drain'. By impoverishing scientific institutions elsewhere, they have less need to pay attention to the work of other, minor bodies. Moreover, such advanced scientific work can be carried out within quite unfree societies, for scientists can work and live in 'encapsulated' privileged worlds or be allowed freedom in their work only. The production of knowledge within massive organizations – however 'socialized' it may thus have become – is clearly by no means dependent on free communication and co-operation. Furthermore, the utilization of this knowledge can be used to the disadvantage of people, or in ways repugnant to the values of the researcher.

It is unscientific, then, simply to assert that science is intrinsically 'liberalizing' or beneficial. It can be used to destroy as well as construct. Social science, likewise, is increasingly being used as part of 'counter-insurgency' programmes, brain-washing and village-concentration campaigns, as well as for the activities with which it has been more commonly associated in the past: town planning, social welfare, etc. Though science has always been put to harmful uses, today it is being used for purposes which its least optimistic and liberal forebears might have found horrifying.

The classical liberal model of science further asserts that the scientist should not refrain from scrutinizing *any* area of human behaviour because he finds it abhorrent or sacred, because of fear of offending the mighty or of offending against social taboos against the frank examination of certain topics or institutions, or from some desire to protect his own pet beliefs from scrutiny or testing.

On the other hand, privacy is a major value, too, and people have the right to freedom from social science inquiry into their lives. And there are scientific studies we would not do. None of us would study the concentration-camps, even though Erving Goffman (1961) has shown how the literature of the camps usefully helps us understand behaviour under much less appalling conditions, in 'total institutions' such as the ship, the mental hospital, or the army unit (see pp. 313–14).

Peter Berger has called this capacity to alter one's perspective 'alternation'. Others call it 'relativism'. It is embodied, in more popular language, in such sayings as 'seeing the other man's point of view'. By looking at very unfamiliar social situations, we are undoubtedly enabled to escape from our conventional ways of thinking about society, even about our own society. This has moral as well as intellectual implications.

Such shifts of perspective may be destructive of dogmatic beliefs or habit. Social science, indeed, often does show that dogmas are unfounded, that 'the facts' can be interpreted differently, or that there are assumptions, acts of faith, beliefs or values lurking behind what people think to be 'self-evident' truths or 'natural' behaviour. If this left us in a position of absolute relativism – believing that nothing is true, or that everything is true, depending on how you look at it – it would be morally unnerving. But insofar as we avoid this and the opposite absolute – that there is one simple and self-evident truth – we are encouraged to think relatively and critically.

Comparative sociology thus leads us to challenge uncritical modes of thought. It is unlikely to eliminate them entirely, since men do not hold their views solely because they have arrived at them as a result of hard thinking. They are least likely to alter their thinking when there is one socially approved way of thinking and to think differently would invite social loss, as when to challenge racial stereotypes would be to invite ostracism, or raise fears of social competition for houses, jobs or sexual partners.

There are limits, then, upon the power of scientific knowledge alone to effectively change people's thoughts and actions, for they are adept at 'compartmentalizing' their thinking, and also at compartmentalizing their thinking, feeling and acting, so that to accept an idea intellectually does not necessarily mean that this will change one's whole behaviour. People live quite happily with contradictory beliefs. They believe in spermatozoa and ovulation in the biology class, and the 'divine spark of life' in the religious instruction period. We believe in democracy and equality – but often only for 'people like us'. We think, that is, *situationally*.

Most people are, in fact, hardly concerned with systemizing their world view at all, they are concerned with solving their particular problems: what to do about those coloured people who have come to live next door; how to avoid getting called up for the Army; why it was that my child, and no other, died of the 'flu.

Some intellectuals make such problems their work. Many, as we have seen, are as 'fragmented', even in their work, as the non-intellectual. But if intellectual systemization eludes him too, the scientist in the laboratory situation, on the other hand, does come near to the ideal of criticality. Yet even in the apparently purely technical activity of carrying out experiments, he is driven by a complex of personal and social motivations which have little to do with the pursuit of knowledge, and a lot to do with the pursuit of money, status and power, with religious or political beliefs, or even with sexual insecurity. The white coat is worn as much to emphasize rank, to tell the world that one is a professional, as for reasons of hygiene. And when he goes home and is talking to the children about sex, for example, the scientist may be as bigoted and inept as the next person.

To understand the causes of social problems does not, of course, necessarily enable the scientist, or anyone else, to solve these problems, any more than a knowledge of the causes of an illness necessarily enables us to cure it every time. However convincing analysis may be, however sensible proposals for reform, decisions as to what will be done, or even whether anything will be done at all, lie in other hands.

In one way, most of us will be heartened to realize that the power of the social scientist is limited, for besides having hopes of social science, we are also all haunted by the 'anti-utopian' nightmares of totally controlled societies master-minded by sinister social scientists who manipulate the people who inhabit these Brave New Worlds and 1984s. The social scientist is in fact never likely to be in this position, both because real power lies elsewhere – with the élites and with the masses he manipulates so easily in the nightmare – and because our scientific knowledge of society is never likely to be as perfect as the positivistic social engineer thinks it can be.

We need not be overly pessimistic or humble about what social science *can* do:

A sociologist worth his salt, if given two basic indices of class such as income and occupation, can make a long list of predictions about the individual in question . . . , about the part of the town in which the individual lives, as well as about the size and style of his house . . . , the interior decorating of the house and . . . the types of pictures . . . and books or magazines likely to be found . . . , what kind of music the individual . . . likes to listen to . . ., which voluntary associations [he] has joined and where he has his church membership . . . , [his] political affiliation and his views on a number of public issues. He can predict the number of children sired by his subject, and also whether [he] has sexual relations with his wife with the lights on or off . . . (Berger, P., 1963, pp. 96–7).

Yet, in the end, we cannot, however carefully we examine the present, accurately predict the future. Rather than predict what *will* happen, in some foredoomed sense, social science enables us to make up our minds in an informed way about what the problem is and how to go about solving it in the way that we would prefer. The social scientist may well provide people with improved information and explanation and with better intellectual tools which they can use for themselves. But decisions, in the end, will be made as the outcome of sets of complex pressures from many kinds of people: idea-mongers, power-wielders, organized citizens, etc., not social scientists alone, and not solely on the basis of knowledge or reason.

Some kinds of prediction can be made, both long-range predictions about large-scale processes, and short-term projections about small-scale matters. We can be fairly confident both about some of the bigger looks into the future – that there will be major famines by the 1980s, for instance – and about lesser extrapolations, such as the projection of divorce-rates for the next decade, or even smaller predictions such as the likelihood of a particular newly-married couple's marriage ending in divorce and when, or their chances of producing a child within a given time. The last example may seem so simple as to be merely commonsense or trivial. Since it is the kind of calculation we make every minute of the day, we do not usually think of it as 'prediction'. But it is, just as we go to a popular film-show early, because we *know*, in advance, that there will be a queue.

To be accurate, most of the explaining we do in social science is not 'forward' prediction at all. It demonstrates the interconnections between events at a given point of time, rather than explaining how they came to happen or what will happen in the *future*. Strictly, research is 'retrodiction', looking backwards at past events and making sense of them. From this point of view we may attempt to extrapolate forwards, to make what some contemptuously call 'prophecies' because our estimates about the future cannot, in the nature of things, be as definitive as retrospective analysis.

There are special reasons why there are limits upon successful forecasting in the social sciences. The social scientist's data is especially complex not just in volume – in that there are so *many* factors to be taken into account – but in quality, because consciousness is both part of his subject-matter and because he, too, is a conscious human being who can never completely insulate himself from involvement with his subject-matter.

People may be objects of study, but they are also subjects with their own consciousness and interests. People can change their minds, can think and act in one way in one situation, and differently in another, under different sets of pressures. They can even deliberately set out to mislead those who seek to govern, bamboozle, or even just study them.

They resist other people's pressures upon them, and may reject official orthodoxies and develop their own definition of the situation, creating their own group life embodying their own separate culture and independent interests. Even the most all-embracing, repressive, or complex organization can never establish total social control. There is always a degree of latitude, autonomy, conflict, looseness of 'fit', even if in exceptional situations, like that of prison, the room for manoeuvre may be very restricted indeed. The larger and more complex modern organizations become, moreover, the more they depend upon the harmonious working-together of all the parts, and the more vulnerable, in consequence, to the malfunctioning of even one part. Thus the withdrawal of labour by even a few hundred key workers can bring to a halt plants employing tens of thousands.

It would be foolish to underestimate the power of those who control large organizations. But it is also possible to underestimate the degree to which self-assertion and capacity to make changes are possible even in 'organization society'. To take the very different situation of agrarian societies, the passivity, even fatalism, of peasants was assumed to be a 'natural' characteristic of a population bound to the unchanging rhythms of the agricultural year, and, as often, bound by oppressive laws, by landlords and money-lenders. But in the twentieth century, peasants, far from being passive, have been a major revolutionary force. People can, then, respond to a given social situation in new ways, once their consciousness is changed or their capacity to act altered (e.g., when a revolutionary party gives them direction).

The subject-matter of the social sciences – the relationships of people to one another – is thus peculiar, owing to this special capacity of people to think about themselves and to modify their behaviour. It is a capacity which separates Man from the rest of Nature, and therefore the social from the natural sciences. It inevitably makes for special difficulties in making extrapolations about future behaviour on the basis of an examination of the past.

Nevertheless, sociologists often do make such prognostications. They even make recommendations, though here they are acting as citizens rather than scientists. A social scientist, *qua* scientist, cannot tell anyone what to do. He can make reasonable guesses as to what will happen if we choose to do A rather than B, but that does not tell us whether A is *better* than B. Whether it is or not depends on the values you hold. If you are shown that wealth is unequally distributed, you may react with disgust, indifference, or possibly pleasure (if you are wealthy yourself, say, or believe in the inevitability of inequality).

Whether he openly prescribes or not, a sociologist's assumptions, theories, values and attitudes always shine through. Any skilled reader can usually tell what they are, just like any intelligent reader of the daily Press when he observes the way different newspapers treat the same events. Sociologists, however, sometimes refrain from making explicit recommendations or forecasts (though there are always some possibilities they silently exclude) because they regard it as their job to analyse, not to prophesy. Even less do many of them consider it their duty to prescribe: to say what should be done. For to recommend involves taking up a position, the abandonment of a 'neutral' position. The search for knowledge is held to be an absolute; if the scientist takes sides, his open-mindedness is likely to be impaired. He may close his eyes, consciously or unconsciously, to things which he would prefer not to see because they might offend his deepest beliefs, his party or his religion. We may refuse to subject those beliefs which our values would lead us to like to believe were true to the test of rigorous scientific method. These procedures will be discussed in the next chapter.

There is a real danger that we may close our eyes precisely where they need to be kept open. It is for this reason that the scientist does not so much set out positively to *prove* a particular hypothesis, but deliberately to test its validity by subjecting it to precisely that kind of evidence that he thinks might *dis*prove it.

We should not confuse objectivity with neutrality. The social scientist, indeed, cannot escape from the social implications of his roles as scientist or his other social responsibilities either. He has inescapable moral obligations towards the people he studies and thus tries to avoid publishing anything which might damage people who have helped him. The moral choices he faces are not always so easily made. They are not even necessarily perceived as moral issues, nor, if perceived, can a single answer acceptable to everybody be given.

The ethical problems of social science, then, do not reduce themselves to such simple issues as whether direct recommendations are made or not. Even if there are no recommendations, there are social effects, no matter how few people read one's work. The more diffuse consequences are often forgotten, because the more direct consequences are the more obvious – as when people protest publicly about interpretations contained in a research document, or when a social scientist's work is used to somebody's disadvantage, say, to make money out of them or control them. The social scientist bears responsibility for the social implications of his work at every stage. He cannot shrug it off with the all-too-familiar response: 'the social scientist only reports: he does not recommend – that is the politician's choice', or 'the social scientist simply indicates what the likely outcome will be if alternative courses a, b, c are followed'.

There are ethical choices throughout. Who pays for research, who uses it, who ignores it or censors it, are some of the major issues. They involve the social scientist in taking decisions in the light of his values as a citizen, not simply according to some kind of 'purely scientific' criteria devoid of value-implications. For social science, like the social scientist, exists within a social context, which does not disappear however much the scientist wants to be uninvolved, thinks he can be, or tries to be. The position of being 'uninvolved' is, of course, itself a position. It tacitly entails letting things go on as they are. It is for this reason that the notion of total uninvolvement has elicited the sardonic remark that a man can be 'so open-minded that his brains fall out'. The ultimate immorality of total non-involvement has been expressed in the words Tom Lehrer credits to the nuclear technician:

> Once the rockets are up, who cares where they come down?
> 'That's not my department,' says Wernher von Braun.

Chapter 2
The Logic and Methods of Sociological Inquiry

Given that the sociologist has his own values, just like everyone else, he is likely to be influenced by them at every stage in his research, both consciously and unconsciously, unless he exercises particular care to take account of such biases when making observations about the character of social relationships and drawing conclusions from those observations. Problems of 'method' of this sort are an integral part of any scientific discipline, and sociology is no exception.

By 'methods' we do not simply mean 'techniques' – the use, say, of statistical tests of significance, or the case-study, the interview or the questionnaire. Such techniques themselves depend upon *prior* assumptions, often of a philosophical nature and often unexamined, about human relationships, about the legitimacy of making general statements about behaviour, and about the whole notion of 'science' as applied to society. That is why we entitle this chapter the 'logic and methods' of sociological inquiry, rather than, simply, 'methods' or 'techniques'.

There is in fact a very wide range of markedly different approaches to sociological investigation, for each of which certain techniques are appropriate, while others are not. This variety of approaches can be reduced to two polar extremes, each reposing upon different fundamental philosophical assumptions about the way we acquire knowledge about our environment. The first approach, deriving from the positivism of Auguste Comte, regards the procedures used in social science as fundamentally of the same kind as those used by natural scientists. It assumes that social phenomena constitute a reality which exists in its own right, quite independently of how the observer acquires information about it. Those who adopt this stance feel justified, therefore, in using the procedures of the natural sciences to collect data relating to social phenomena and to analyse these data. Their analyses are therefore phrased in terms of 'variables', and use statistical procedures to establish relationships among the variables and express their findings in terms of causal explanations. The 'survey' based on interviews or questionnaires, is the best-known instance of this kind of study.

Indeed, many people think that all sociological research uses this kind of method, and call all sociological studies 'surveys'. Sociologists who work in the other major tradition – the 'interpretive' approach, stemming ultimately from Kant – assume that all knowledge is acquired through the operation of the mind on the observer's sense-impressions. Sociologists who work within this framework therefore lay particular emphasis on the observer's direct understanding, often intuitive, of the phenomena being observed, and tend to see those phenomena as falling into particular patterns, as wholes, which the observer must interpret to bring out their wider and deeper significance. The observer is thus said to 'construct' social reality by the way in which he interprets what he learns about it.

The sorts of procedures sociologists within these opposed epistemological camps use to assemble the information they need to substantiate their interpretations of social phenomena naturally tend to be dissimilar. Those who adopt a *positivistic* or 'scientific' approach work with the method – more technically, the 'hypothetico-deductive' method – shown in Figure 1 on p. 75.

The process is cyclical: the researcher starts at any point in the process and then proceeds through the steps back to the same point; more accurately, the process is spiral: he arrives back at a slightly changed position. He may commence, for example, with the formulation of an hypothesis – a tentative explanation. He starts out, therefore, armed with the knowledge of existing theory about social relationships or social actions, and anticipates finding certain relationships. From his knowledge of existing theory, for example, he knows, without needing to do research on the matter, that delinquent gangs tend to operate with a set of values different from those of their parents and local representatives of authority. The researcher then *deduces* that in a community which is sharply alienated from the larger society – as in a Black district in the United States, for example – where this community's values are likely to be opposed to

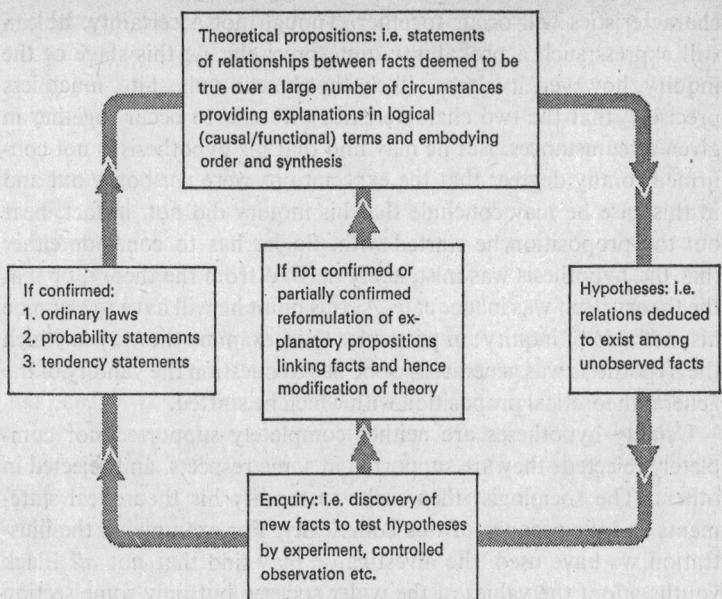

Figure 1 The paradigm of scientific method

those of the larger society, young Blacks who revolt against their parents are likely to do so by adopting the cultural characteristics of the very Whites to whom their parents are opposed. At this stage, he has merely generated an *hypothesis*. The next step is to see whether what he expected in fact turns out to be true. To do this, he looks for a situation that reproduces these conditions; that is, a Black community which, as a whole, rejects the values of the larger society. He then sets out to see whether the young people in this community do in fact adopt the values of the wider society.

The outcome of the inquiry may in fact confirm his hypothesis, in which case the research worker begins to have a little more confidence in the general theoretical framework out of which this particular hypothesis was developed. He may then go on to make a generalization about the relationship between dominant values and the values of delinquent youths, postulating either that the relationship always holds true and constitutes a 'law', or – more likely – that because it is true more often than not it reflects the 'probability' that the two characteristics will occur together. Though not a certainty, he can still express such a probability quite precisely. At this stage of the inquiry, however, it is more likely that he can only state, much less precisely, that the two characteristics will *tend* to occur together in given circumstances. But he may find that his hypothesis is not confirmed to any degree: that the expectations were *not* borne out and in this case he may conclude that his inquiry did not, in fact, bear out the proposition he started with. So he has to conclude either that the hypothesis was mistakenly derived from the theory, or that the theory itself was inadequate. At this point he will have to examine his methods of inquiry: in particular to re-examine the way in which the hypothesis was generated; or he has to question the validity of the general theoretical proposition with which he started.

Usually hypotheses are neither completely supported nor completely rejected: they are supported in some respects, and rejected in others. The sociologist then seeks to modify his theoretical statements to take account of this complexity. For example, in the illustration we have used, the investigator may find that not *all* Black youths adopt the values of the wider society, but only some section of them – as for example the children of *middle-class* Blacks. This then poses a new problem for the investigator and should make him refine and widen his theory.

This is to speak as if scientific inquiry always follows a rigid pattern. But the *logical* procedures by which hypotheses are developed and tested should not be confused with the way in which scientists, whether natural or social, actually carry out their inquiries. Scientific method, that is to say, is the *logic* of the procedure not the *practice*. The 'perfect' scientific method is more like a systematic set of rules which scientists use in order to organize their analysis in ways acceptable and understandable to their colleagues. But this is usually a very abstract reorganization of what they actually did, arranged so as to bring out the connection between the various aspects of the scientific procedure in a clear and logical way. If a scientist is to expect his colleagues to accept his arguments, he must be able to cast his procedure in the form of the model or paradigm in Figure 1.

In real-life scientific work, the actual carrying out of research – of theorizing, testing, hypothesizing and reformulating hypotheses so as to arrive at theoretical insights – takes place at one and the same time and in a much more haphazard way. Few scientists in fact actually sit down in cold blood and follow the sequence of working out an hypothesis from an existing theoretical notion, developing an appropriate experiment or inquiry, then systematically testing the hypothesis and finally spelling out the consequences of their finding for theory. Rather they may happen to be reading a research report on some quite specialized topic; see that it suggests certain general theoretical issues; half-remember some inquiry which was relevant (perhaps something *they* have done); develop an hypothesis from what they already know and then pursue inquiries (perhaps using strict experimental procedures) to demonstrate the relationship which they already know very likely exists. Scientists may thus in fact develop the 'theoretical background' only as the inquiry begins to yield preliminary results. In the process they modify their hypotheses or change the direction of the inquiry.

All this may seem very haphazard. In fact it is not: it is simply that sociological research, like any other intellectual pursuit, has to be organized in a systematic way when it comes to making a careful analysis, but the way in which ideas come to scientists does not take place according to neat procedural rules. When scientists come to write up their results they must, however, present their findings within a framework which allows their colleagues, whether friendly or hostile, to check the validity of the steps in their arguments. Here the model of the scientific method as set out in Figure 1 becomes important, for it is only through using an explicit model that their colleagues are able to examine the validity of the procedures they have adopted and to see whether the conclusions they have drawn are in fact justified.

Those who work within the 'interpretive' framework tend to go about their studies in a totally different way. Since they aim to start from their appreciation as ordinary human beings of the social phenomena they are studying, they tend to see prior hypotheses about the phenomena as more of an impediment than a help. They try, therefore, to become involved in the activity or situation they are seeking to interpret and pursue their understanding of it through learning what other people involved in the activity or situation understand about it. They deepen and expand their direct appreciation of the situation by whatever means they can. Language, in particular, is a fruitful route to their appreciation of social phenomena, but symbols of any type may provide the observer with insights into the way in which apparently unrelated aspects of social life are in reality connected. The end-result of the analysis is an interpretation of the social phenomena under study which, if successful, immediately makes sense to his colleagues and reveals subtleties and insights, and connections, which hitherto had remained obscure or even unobserved. The emphasis is on making apparent a pattern of relationships amongst what were formerly seen as unconnected elements.

Sources of Data

Whether the sociologist is working within a positivist or an interpretive perspective, however, there must be rules or procedures by means of which other sociologists are able to assess the plausibility of the analysis or interpretation being proffered to them.

The sociologist is primarily interested in seeking out generally valid interpretations of regularly recurring patterns of social phenomena. The framework of ideas and concepts which he uses in this process constitutes sociological theory. These concepts and notions are abstract mental constructions in the same way that 'gravity' is in physics, or 'valency' is in chemistry. The sociologist arrives at these concepts by making a very basic assumption: that there is a regularity or pattern in the things he observes. Equally, he may infer the existence of an underlying characteristic from the presence of certain signs or indicators. A sociologist may, for example, notice that the behaviour of workers in a large factory and that of children in slum areas of a large city have certain similarities which may be characterized as a lack of identification with their fellows and a lack of confidence in those who wield authority. He may identify this characteristic as a manifestation of the abstract condition of 'alienation'. He may be able to isolate certain actions or characteristics of people which he regards as indicative of this underlying condition. Later he may wish to relate the 'alienation' of a particular category of people to their class position, or possibly to the way in which they vote.

There is thus a two-way interaction between observation and conceptualization. The sociologist selects from the welter of social actions going on around him a limited number, which he then interprets in terms of an underlying concept (such as 'alienation'). As we have seen, there is no such thing as completely passive observation: the observer perceives social relationships or social actions, and the act of perception implies that he invests his sense-impression with some meaning. In so far as sociology is concerned, then, a fact is simply some element of perception which is related to the sociologist's conceptual scheme.

The observations of the sociologist are guided by certain abstract concepts which the sociologist himself brings into his observations. So the best materials for his purposes are those with these ideas specially in mind. Ideally, when the sociologist is collecting information, he ought to be doing so in order to advance some general interpretation of the material. Unfortunately, this is a counsel of perfection which is not or cannot always be followed. Often sociologists have to make do with information which has already been collected (even if *they* have collected it themselves) and carry out their analysis, or make their interpretations, after the event. Some of the most imaginative and stimulating sociological thinking has been based on re-interpretations of existing data. Nor does adherence to accepted procedures ensure that one's analysis will produce valuable results – it only makes it easier.

So we may classify the material which sociologists have available either as that which has been collected with specific concepts and purposes in mind – and upon which, therefore, *primary* analysis can be conducted – or material which has been collected for some other purpose, or with quite different purposes and concepts in mind, which the sociologist may, however, re-interpret and analyse in terms of his own constructs and concepts. In other words he may make a *secondary* analysis of the data.

Existing Material

The amount of material potentially available for secondary analysis is enormous, since it includes all the information about social relationships and social actions from any source whatsoever, whether it has been assembled for sociological purposes or otherwise. For convenience let us classify these as (i) statistical records, (ii) historical sources, (iii) contemporary records and personal documents.

Statistical sources

Government statistics – particularly censuses – or statistics produced by large industrial or commercial firms, trade unions or other organizations, provide one important kind of data which sociologists can use in their analyses, and which in fact they commonly do use. An outstanding example of the imaginative use of official statistics, in the positivist tradition, is the study of suicide made by the famous French sociologist Emile Durkheim (1858–1917) in the last decade of the nineteenth century (Durkheim, 1970). Durkheim set out to expose the social basis of this apparently most individual of all acts, and to do so he used official statistics, firstly to identify the sorts of people who were most likely to commit suicide, and secondly to identify the sorts of circumstances under which people were most likely to commit suicide. He found that the incidence of suicide varied between different social groups: that there were different *rates* of suicide. This suggested that proclivity to commit suicide was not just an individual matter. By carefully searching through the official suicide statistics of the Europe of his day he was able to show that some hypotheses about the causes of suicide did not hold water (e.g., that 'Latins' commit suicide more easily than 'Nordics'), whereas other features of suicide rates were very general and were to be found in country after country and from year to year. Durkheim then concentrated on these regularities, and in order to try to account for them erected several hypotheses about the way in which the individual is integrated into social groups to which he belongs.

This assiduity which Durkheim displayed in the use of these mountains of statistics are a model even today. But the difficulties he ran up against illustrate the difficulties we always encounter in using official statistics and other kinds of data not collected by sociologists themselves. The first is that the statistics are classified into categories drawn up by officials for their own purposes. These categories, however, may present difficulties to sociologists who try to use them. Suicide statistics are notoriously prone to difficulties of this kind. For example, for 'social' reasons the cause of death for a clear case of suicide may sometimes be entered as some other 'cause' on the death certificate from which the mortality statistics are compiled. Sometimes, indeed, it is very difficult to say whether the person who killed himself had in fact intended to do so. If such distortions of recorded cases of suicide occurred purely at random, they would not lead to much distortion in an analysis based on these figures. But the factors which lead to an under-registration of suicide are frequently social – because of the shame that surrounds suicide, for example, in small intimately organized social systems, or among Catholics or Moslems, and this distortion may not be apparent from the official statistics: a point taken up and developed extensively by an 'interpretive' sociologist (Douglas, 1967). For similar reasons, crime statistics are notoriously unreliable foundations on which to base sociological analysis.

A second difficulty is that characteristics which are important for sociological purposes are frequently simply not recorded. Durkheim found this when he wanted to relate suicide rates to religious persuasion, for the religious persuasion of the victims of suicide was not recorded in official statistics. Yet it was important for his hypothesis that he should be able to measure the effect of religious persuasion upon the propensity to commit suicide. He had therefore to rely upon a questionable statistical procedure, that is, to compare suicide rates in predominantly Roman Catholic parts of Germany with rates in predominantly Protestant parts.

What is relevant for official statistics, which are often collected for fiscal or electoral purposes, may not, then, be important for the sociologist's purposes, and what the sociologist wants to know about may not be of interest to governments. It would be of great value to sociologists if church membership, social class, ethnicity and personal income could be collected in population censuses and in health and mortality statistics. But sensitivity on these issues precludes this, and sociologists must accordingly make do without these categories of information in official statistics.

A third difficulty arises because statistics are sometimes not presented in a form which is most useful for the sociologist, even when the appropriate categories have been included. Distributions of characteristics, for example, may be presented independently of one another, whereas the sociologist is likely to be interested mainly in the way in which one characteristic varies in relation to other characteristics. Durkheim ran into this difficulty also, for although data on suicide by age, sex, conjugal status, presence or absence of children and province were available, these characteristics were not related to each other in official statistical publications. Accordingly he had to get one of his students, Marcel Mauss, to tabulate by hand the details of 26,000 suicides recorded in documents held by the Ministry of Justice in Paris. The table Mauss prepared enabled Durkheim to separate out the effects of marriage, childlessness and age respectively on the propensity to commit suicide, a finding he could not otherwise have established. This was of particular importance to Durkheim, but was clearly of no direct interest to the Ministry of Justice.

But the greatest difficulty that sociologists encounter in using official and other statistics is the extent to which the categories in terms of which the statistics are collected may be held to reflect significant sociological variables. Durkheim was particularly interested in the cohesion of social groups, and the extent to which this cohesion influenced the behaviour of its members. He found that members of élite regiments of the Army, for example, were more inclined to commit suicide than members of other regiments. This he attributed to the high emphasis on *esprit de corps* in these regiments, with a consequent sinking of the individual's personal identity in that of his regiment and therefore an under-emphasis on individual survival. Durkheim looks at the same issue in several different contexts – long-term soldiers as against short-term; soldiers who have re-enlisted as against those who have joined for the first time; non-commissioned officers as against 'other ranks'. But it would have suited his purposes much better if he could have used a direct measure of the subjugation of the individual's identity to the ethos of the regiment. This he could not do because he was in fact conducting a secondary analysis. Instead, he could only examine a whole series of instances which he took to illustrate indirectly the abstract notions he was trying to demonstrate.

These dangers are made clear in a much more recent study in which the author wished to show how the growth of towns stimulates and accompanies extensive changes in social systems (Reissman, 1964). He based his study on material drawn from the recent history of

Western Europe and then proceeded to test how four different characteristics of social organization vary according to the level of development of society. These variables are urbanization, industrialization, the growth of the middle classes and the development of nationalism. The only available method of examining the way these variables vary together is to look for such indicators of them as are available in official international statistics. The author does not have much difficulty in finding reasonable indicators of the degree of urbanization and industrialization of various nations, but the other two variables present him with difficulties. As an indicator of the prevalence of middle classes he takes *per capita* income. As an indicator of nationalism, he takes the percentage of people over the age of fifteen who are literate. The use of the latter indicator is based on the argument that if nationalism is to be an effective determinant of attitudes and behaviour, it is necessary for those responding to it to be able to imagine unity in the face of manifest diversity between the peoples of a nation. Such abstract ideas, he argues, do not come easily to illiterate persons, who tend to equate reality only with sensed experience. A minimal skill in reading and writing can therefore justifiably be used, he considers, as an index of the ability of populations to understand the concept of 'nationalism'.

Reissman is well aware of the weakness of this position and he warns readers that his approach is tentative. But even so, to try to represent such a complex phenomenon as nationalism by such a simple indicator as the proportion of adults who are literate is scarcely adequate, even if we were to accept the validity of Reissman's justification for it. A combination of *several* suitable indicators might get nearer the mark, if they could be found, but there is in fact no way of measuring nationalism by means of official statistics.

Much of what has been said about difficulties in the use of official statistics would apply to the 'secondary' analysis of social surveys conducted by other sociologists. It is true that such surveys are likely to include more variables which are potentially important to sociologists, and that many of them include such categories as social class, membership of social groupings, value-orientations, and so on. It is also likely that the results of social surveys conducted by other sociologists will contain more cross-tabulations of findings, so that the association between variables can be estimated. But even here a re-analysis is likely to involve asking questions which the original survey was not designed to answer.

Historical documents as sources of data

Records and accounts of a qualitative (i.e. non-statistical) kind – for example, relating to beliefs, values, social relationships or social behaviour – may also provide data for sociologists, especially those working within an 'interpretive' framework. Such records and accounts may be contemporary or may refer to earlier periods. But in using either kind of data, similar problems arise and there are specific advantages and disadvantages whichever kind of data we have available.

Consider first the use of documents and records relating to former times. The sociologist is interested in tracing regularities in social relationships and social action. Data from earlier times are therefore particularly valuable in providing information about the extent to which patterns of social relationships persist as contrasted with the extent to which they change.

But several difficulties immediately present themselves in the use of records from the past. The most important of these is that few chroniclers of the past have been interested in recording observations of social relationships and social actions in the systematic way in which sociologists are. There are often intriguing and sympathetic accounts, of, say, peasant life, but information which is vital to the sociologist is often missing, presumably because the chroniclers of those times did not think these points significant. Thus, from studies of African societies, we know that who accuses whom of witchcraft is a valuable indicator of wider social oppositions and tensions in small face-to-face communities. A systematic study of witchcraft accusations in a seventeenth-century English village, therefore, might equally throw light upon social conflicts within it. But records of witchcraft accusations are limited to those that were brought to court, and these were probably only a small proportion of all accusations made. Where records of accusations do exist, they frequently lack the detailed information which would enable us to see the framework of social relationships within which the witch and her accuser operated.

As with official statistics, a sociologist using historical records has to accept the fact that the records have been created for purposes other than for sociological analysis. If he wishes to use these materials for his own analysis he must try to assess these purposes and make allowance for them in order to make his own interpretations of the material.

One attempt to do this is J. A. Banks's study of *Prosperity and Parenthood* (Banks, 1954), in which the author sets out to examine the relationship between standards of living and family-limitation in England during the Victorian period. Methods of preventing the conception of children had been known for a long time before the late 1870s when evidence of a clear decline of fertility among middle-class people became apparent. The problem then is: 'Why was it that voluntary control of the size of the family became popular when it did, and what was the relationship of the decline in fertility to the economic circumstances of middle-class people at the time?' For although the number of children a couple may have decided to have may appear to be a highly personal matter, as with suicide, there is little doubt that general social circumstances influence these personal decisions, since, for example, middle-class couples began to limit the number of children they had earlier and more generally than did working-class couples.

This problem arose out of the population controversy at the end of the eighteenth century, when Thomas Malthus pointed out that population numbers inexorably pressed upon the means of subsistence available to that population. By the middle of the nineteenth century, it was becoming common for members of the middle classes to postpone marriage until they could afford both to have children and at the same time to maintain the standard of living to which they had become accustomed. The incomes of middle-class people were expected to rise in such a way as to allow them to support their children in a middle-class style of life as they grew up. But incomes did not continue to rise. Some twenty-five years after the expansion of standards of living in the 1850s, that is, in the middle 1870s, there was an economic recession which forced middle-class parents to limit the number of children they had, or, alternatively, to suffer a decline in their standards of living.

In order to examine the relationship between standards of living on the one hand and size of families on the other, Banks searched through contemporary records and reports of many different kinds. Some were papers written for learned societies; some were official government reports, others were books, both popular and learned, on a variety of topics. Banks also used pamphlets written for propaganda purposes, letters to the papers, and novels of the time (particularly those by Jane Austen and Anthony Trollope). He was able to show convincingly how the attitudes and opinions of representatives of the middle classes reflected their concern with the public demonstration of their social status, as shown by their standard of living, and how the expense of bringing up children – particularly of educating them and giving them a start in life – conflicted with this desire. Yet, as Banks points out himself, the final steps of his argument are not filled in. The need to keep family size under control to ensure a middle-class standard of living did not alone provide either necessary or sufficient conditions for voluntary limitation of the size of a man's family. To complete the causal connection between these two aspects of social life, we would have to document how the couple came to the conclusion that they could not afford another child, what choices they had before them, what factors induced them to make the choice they did, and finally, what action they took to prevent the conception of another child. Information bearing on these vital links in the argument was not available to Banks. If he were studying this problem in contemporary England, he could, of course, endeavour to find out about these matters and so complete the links in the argument. But since he had to use data assembled without these questions in mind, his argument could not be definitively demonstrated.

Contemporary records

Similar difficulties arise in connection with the use of contemporary records when used as a source of information in sociological studies. Contemporary records are seldom used as the sole source of information in sociological research; they are usually one source of a particular kind of information. We may, for example, use them to study ideologies. Thus, in the field of communications-research a great deal of attention has been paid to the way in which ideas or values are presented through various media.

Studies of newspaper readerships, for example, involve the

analysis of the way in which different newspapers, directing their sales towards different types of audience, present the same item of news in different ways. This method is also applied for commercial purposes by advertising and market research agencies, etc., to the study of political, religious or other doctrines as they are presented in such mass-communication media as newspapers, magazines, radio broadcasts or television programmes. Here the object is to identify and characterize the content of the communication and not to test sociological hypotheses. A sociologist, however, is more likely to use information derived from an examination of contemporary records to test some hypothesis which suggests links, say, between people's aspirations and the frustrations, material and otherwise, that they experience in everyday life.

Contemporary and historical records are sometimes analysed through systematic procedures known as 'content analysis'. This involves constructing categories for classifying information about certain themes in advance. The records are then perused and the incidence and use of the categories and themes noted. Sociologists also examine records less rigorously by creating a 'quantitative index' in which the frequency with which themes are mentioned is counted *without* first establishing a list of themes on the basis of some theoretical assumption. (In some questionnaires, again, the questions are laid down in advance in order to elicit a precise answer: other questions are designed to allow the subject to respond freely.) The sociologist is left with the problem of reducing the 'freer' responses to some systematic set of categories he can use for his analysis. It is here that a quantitative index is useful, for by means of such an index he can record the number of times the different themes are mentioned in response to a question. Coding the responses to these questions is usually a tedious task, but recently some steps have been taken towards using computers to recognize patterns of words and to count up the themes mentioned by enumerating the different word-patterns that emerge.

The distinction which is significant here, however, is not that of whether a record is analysed by 'content analysis' or a 'quantitative index', but that between records which come into being by reason of a sociologist's inquiry with a specific hypothesis and conceptual scheme in view, on the one hand, and records which have come into being originally for some other purpose, but which the sociologist nevertheless uses as a potential source of information, on the other.

Our emphasis so far has been on records produced for purposes which are not those of the sociologist. We must now turn to information which the sociologist gathers directly for his own specific purposes.

Data Collected with Analysis in View

When a sociologist sets about systematically gathering information about a problem that he wishes to find an answer to, he is faced with certain conflicting demands on his time. On the one hand he needs, ideally, to extend his inquiries over a large number of instances in order to take account of the full range of variation in the phenomenon he is interested in. On the other hand, he needs to become sufficiently well acquainted with each particular case to enable him to obtain enough understanding about it in order to be able to make trustworthy judgements. Clearly, the more he satisfies the one need, the more he frustrates the other. The techniques of information-gathering available to the sociologist therefore may be ranged along the two dimensions of 'numbers involved' and 'personal involvement'. Clearly those working within a 'positivist' orientation will tend to work towards the 'large numbers/low personal involvement' end of the continuum, whereas those working with an 'interpretive' orientation will tend to work towards the other end.

Social surveys

The basic procedure in surveys is that people are asked a number of questions focused on that aspect of behaviour the sociologist is interested in. A number of people, carefully selected so that they are representative of the population being studied, are asked to answer exactly the same questions, so that the replies of different categories of respondent may be examined for differences. Since one of the virtues of the survey lies in the large number of respondents that can be included, it follows that both the method of getting the questionnaires completed, and consequently the formulation of the questions to be asked, must be very carefully worked out.

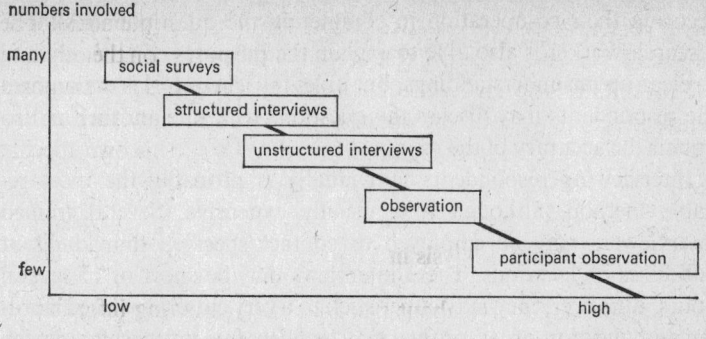

Figure 2 Relationship between number of respondents and degree of personal involvement of sociologist

One type of survey relies on contacting the respondents by letter and asking them to complete the questionnaire themselves before returning it. A variation of the procedure is that an assistant delivers the questionnaire to the respondent, asks him to complete it, and makes an arrangement to pick it up later. Sometimes questionnaires are not completed by individuals separately but by people in a group under the direct supervision of the research worker, as for example a class of students in a university or a group of workers at a trade union meeting. In other surveys a trained interviewer asks the questions and records the responses on a schedule for each respondent. These alternative procedures have different strengths and weaknesses.

Mail-questionnaires are relatively cheap and can be used to contact respondents who are scattered over a wide area. But at the same time the proportion of people who return questionnaires sent through the post is usually rather small. The questions asked in mail-questionnaires have also to be very carefully worded in order to avoid ambiguity, since the respondent cannot ask to have questions clarified for him. The questionnaire which is picked up by an assistant, similarly, must be very carefully designed. The personal attention of the assistant usually ensures a higher rate of completion, but it obviously costs more than a mail-questionnaire. Using *groups* to complete questionnaires means that the return rate is good and that the information is assembled quickly and fairly cheaply (though difficulties are encountered in selecting appropriate groups and in securing their co-operation in completing the questionnaires). The research-worker is also able to explain the purposes of his study and to clear up misunderstandings, but unless strict control is maintained the respondents may discuss the questions with one another and so impair the accuracy of the results.

Interviewing respondents individually is probably the most reliable method, although it is usually expensive. Several trained interviewers may be employed to contact specified individuals at addresses or locations. These interviews may be short or of several hours' duration; they may either stick to a very closely specified wording and question-order, or they may be fairly free interviews in which the interviewer is allowed to pursue the topic in an indirect and oblique way. Different topics may require different methods of interview.

Where 'attitude' questions are included, great care must be exercised to see that the wording, emphasis and intonation are standardized between different interviewers and from respondent to respondent. Respondents may react to slightly different intonations or difference in wording; this can make results obtained by one interviewer systematically different from those another interviewer obtains, and make the results useless for comparative purposes.

As a rule the questions will cover two somewhat different types of information. One part of the questionnaire will be concerned with the main (or 'substantive') part of the inquiry. If the inquiry were concerned with the factors influencing family planning, for example, a number of attitudinal questions might be asked about people's aspirations for their children; conceptions of the satisfactions and dissatisfactions which might come from having children; their attitudes to methods of contraception; their value-orientations in respect of marriage and the family; a number of factual questions on the number of children desired; their actual practice of contraception, and so on. The other part of the questionnaire (sometimes called 'face-sheet data') would consist of a set of factual questions about the couple's education, social background, religious persuasion, income, ages, date of marriage and so on. Much of the analysis which follows will involve seeing whether respondents with specific social and demographic characteristics answer the questions in the substantive part of the questionnaire in the same way or not.

An important aspect of the survey, as in other procedures of data-collecting, is the way in which the units of inquiry are chosen. The kind of unit selected depends on the frame of reference of the inquiry. It may be a group, or organization, or an individual. In an ideal world, the sociologist would be able to examine every unit he wanted to acquire information about. Sometimes this is possible – there are, after all, a limited number of trade unions or political parties in any one country. More commonly, however, there are more units than a research-worker can possibly contact in any practicable way. He must therefore employ other tactics. One of these is to limit the units to be examined to a number which he can handle given the time and resources he has available. The research-worker, then, must first of all decide how many units of inquiry he can examine, taking into account how long each investigation (or interview) will take, how long it will take him to get there, whether he will be able to analyse all the material he collects and so on. Having decided on the number of units he can handle, he must now choose which actual units he will examine.

Immediately a problem presents itself: how can he ensure that the units he selects really reflect the characteristics of the whole population about which he wishes to make generalizations? Several devices are used to achieve this. One of these, known as 'quota sampling', requires that certain specified characteristics of the units should be present in the sample in the same proportion as they are in the general population. For example, if the sample were of adult males, and we wanted to find out the extent to which they belonged to voluntary associations, the sample may be so designed that the proportions falling into different age-groups, incomes and occupations are the same as those in the general population. The interviewers then have to contact a given number of males in these specified age-groups, income-categories and occupations. This type of sampling is used widely in public opinion polls, and has the great advantage that it is relatively simple and cheap to administer. But there are certain difficulties with it. One of these is that the final selection of units is left to the interviewer, who may unconsciously introduce a bias. Another is that certain statistical tests based on probability theory cannot justifiably be applied to the results.

For scientific, as against commercial, work, some form of 'random' sampling is usually recommended. Random sampling does not mean *haphazard* selection. It is instead a method of selecting units for study in such a way that the probability of selecting each unit can be exactly specified. This means that formulae based on probability mathematics can be used to calculate within some range of accuracy, what the chances are that the sample so drawn is typical or not typical of the wider population from which it is taken. The commonest way of doing this is to allocate a number to each unit in the whole population (or 'universe'), and then to use a set of 'random numbers' to select the actual units to be included in the sample. The way in which the set of numbers is constructed ensures that no bias is introduced into the selection of the sample and that the probability basis of the sample is maintained. Note that the actual proportion of units drawn out of the total population does not play a very important part in the procedure. Rather the minimum number of cases that will allow adequate cross-tabulations of characteristics, and the maximum number that can be handled with the resources available, is decided upon. The actual size of the sample is determined by these considerations, and this in turn determines the ratio of the size of the sample to the population out of which it is drawn, that is, the 'sampling fraction'. If the sampling fraction turns out to be rather large (say, over 10 per cent) then adjustments will need to be made to some of the calculations. But this is done later – at the stage of *analysis* – by modifying some of the values in the computations, and does not affect the sample.

It is essential that before a sample is drawn, all the elements of the population being studied (it may be a 'population' of industrial concerns or schools) should be identifiable and open to selection by the method of sampling chosen. These requirements may present some difficulties. Let us suppose that we wish to obtain a representative sample of the young people of England and Wales. Let us further suppose that we are able to define those people of ages fifteen to twenty-four who have been in England for one year at the time of the survey, as constituting the universe of people about which we want to make generalizations. Ideally, our sampling requirement demands that we should have available a record of each person with these qualifications, so that he or she is exposed to the possibility of being selected. But how do we in fact give each person with the requisite characteristics a number which may be used to select a sample from our table of random numbers? There is no easy answer. In fact, the problem is usually solved by choosing first of all a number of geographical areas in a random way. Sub-areas are chosen within these, and sub-sub-areas within these, until we arrive at a unit of identifiable residences. These are then sampled in turn to find out whether there are in fact people with the appropriate qualifications in the households. Some of the elaborate procedures involved are discussed in books on methods of social investigation such as that by Moser and Kalton (1971).

Before the inquiry can begin it is usually necessary to conduct a 'pilot' study, in which preliminary ideas about the problem, the over-all research strategy, the design of the 'research instruments' – the questionnaires, interview-schedules, etc. – are tested. It is usual for the preliminary schedules, for example, to be tried out in the field to see whether they present any particular difficulties in use. Only when the schedule has been tested in the field will the stage be set for the full study. A workable set of research procedures should thus emerge from the pilot study.

There is usually a good deal of office organization needed to run a social survey. Schedules must be prepared with sample identifications (for example the addresses of houses or firms). If a mail questionnaire is to be used, the envelopes have to be addressed, stamped and posted. If the inquiry is based on interviews, the interviewers will have to be very carefully briefed. When the schedules are completed and returned, it is usually necessary for someone to read them through to see if all questions have in fact been completed so that omissions may be attended to. Then it is usually necessary for the individual responses to be translated into a code which can be punched on to a card, or on to paper tape or transferred to magnetic tape for computer analysis. The preparation of a code, and the actual coding, often takes longer than the actual interviewing: a fact which has led to the tendency to prepare a code in advance ('pre-coding') so that the way in which the interviewer records the reply (as, for example, by putting a ring around a number printed on the schedule) *automatically* codes the response to the question.

There has been a good deal of controversy about the reliability and validity of results obtained from social surveys. Many of the critics of social surveys have little idea of the care that goes into the design of such studies, the wording of the questions, the testing of schedules before they are used, and the precautions taken in training interviewers and in selecting the sample. Commonly, too, uninformed people criticize individual questions without taking into account their relationship to many other questions in the schedule, or without appreciating how the research-worker proposes to use the responses to this question. There are undoubtedly limits to what may be inferred from a particular kind of response to a question in a social survey, in the same way that indicators may only partially represent an underlying phenomenon. But within these limits, the results of social surveys can be useful and meaningful.

There are other objections to the use of the survey method in sociology, however, which are more difficult to counter. One of these concerns the extent to which *individual* characteristics may be assumed to relate to social properties – a point which will be discussed further below. Another concerns the validity of the replies to questions which are obtained in social surveys. This objection is based on the argument that the interview in a social survey is a special kind of social situation and that social interaction under these conditions may influence the way in which respondents react to some types of question. Some factual questions, such as age, occupation, or educational level reached, may be relatively straightforward (though this is not always so: it is difficult to get middle-aged women to say what their real age is, for example). But certain attitudinal and opinion questions may be sharply influenced by the nature of the interview-situation. Information about private aspects of behaviour such as the use of contraceptives or sexual habits may be difficult to collect, mainly because respondents tend to give 'safe', standardized and not necessarily accurate responses to these questions.

Clearly the means used to collect data must be suited to the sort of information that is required. While mail-questionnaires may be perfectly adequate for information on a number of straightforward and unambiguous topics, other topics may require the more subtle approach of a skilled interviewer. Social surveys, therefore, may or may not involve interviewing, depending on the topic being studied. Where interviews are involved, however, new problems are raised.

Social surveys, as we have seen, may depend either on questionnaires which are self-administered, or on schedules which are completed by trained interviewers or by the research-worker personally. Interviewing, then, is not a method of data-collection distinct from social surveying, but rather a technique which may vary from the brief formal contact – as when the interviewer is working for a firm of public opinion consultants or a market-research organization and simply asks a housewife a few highly specific questions on a limited range of topics – to a long and rather rambling interview in which the research-worker allows the respondent to develop points at leisure and take up others as he chooses. The brief formal interview, in which the wording of the questions and the order in which they are asked is fixed, is called a 'structured' interview, while the more free discursive interview is called an 'unstructured' interview.

The object of using structured interviews is to standardize the interview as much as possible, and thus to reduce the effect that the interviewer's personal approach or biases may have upon the results. And even when structured interviews are used, proper training can do a lot to ensure further the reliability and validity of results. Tests made with both untrained and trained interviewers showed that more accurate and fuller results were obtained from trained interviewers, and that there were also fewer refusals and 'non-contacts'. Not only the personality of the interviewers, but also the social characteristics which the respondents attribute to him, may influence the results. His accent, for example, may lead to different reactions from people of different class backgrounds from himself. Little can be done about problems of this kind apart from using, where practicable, what are known as 'interpenetrating samples'. Here each of several interviewers with different personal characteristics are allocated interviews at random in each of the areas to be surveyed. The effect of interviewer bias can then be estimated by comparing one interviewer's results with another's.

The problem of interviewer bias in *un*structured interviews is much greater. Here the interviewer is left largely to his own devices as far as the way he approaches the respondent is concerned. There is no fixed list of questions to work through; instead, the interviewer may work from a guide which will remind him of the topics he wishes to cover. But what topic he raises first, and how he leads on to the next is left entirely to him, as long as he eventually covers all the issues in the guide.

Clearly the training of the interviewer is crucial here: not simply training in the social skills of keeping a conversation going on a topic which the respondent may not be very interested in, but also in acquiring a sensitivity to those things his respondent tells him which are specially relevant to the theoretical topic he is pursuing. This means that unstructured interviews can only be carried out by people trained in sociological theory. They are then able to seize upon stray comments made by respondents which can be developed and lead on to important theoretical insights.

A good example of unstructured interviewing is provided by the study Elizabeth Bott made of twenty London families (Bott, 1957). She was interested in the way in which husbands and wives divided the domestic tasks between themselves, and wanted to relate this division of labour to the structure of friendships the couple had with others. It would have been difficult to use other methods of investigation. A structured interview was hardly appropriate on a topic as delicate as this and was in any case impracticable, since Bott had not yet worked out the details of her hypothesis. This was done only *during* her inquiry. If she had decided to work by observation alone, she would have had to confine herself to the few families she was able to live with.

Her best procedure was a series of unstructured interviews, covering the background of the families, the organization of family activities, the informal relationships of the family with outsiders, the formal relationships of the family with outsiders, and the set of value-orientations the different families worked with. On average, Bott conducted thirteen interviews with each family. These lasted, on average, for about one hour and twenty minutes, about ten minutes being spent in initial conversation, an hour covering the topics she wished to explore, and about ten minutes casual conversation at the end. Bott introduced the topic to the couple and the couple discussed it with her. If they wandered off the topic, she did not bring them back to it immediately, because part of the study was to see how the couple managed their interpersonal relationships. The interviews tended to be a friendly exchange of information rather than a matter of question and answer.

There is little doubt that interviewing of this kind can provide a sociologist with immensely useful insights. But there are difficulties. One of these is that an interviewer, whether conducting a structured or an unstructured interview, is in fact playing a role and the content of the communication between the respondent and the interviewer may be very heavily influenced by their individual conceptions of that role. Interviewing after all is a kind of formal social interaction in which the actors adopt behaviour which they consider appropriate to the situation. The fact that most sociologists would be thought of as members of the middle class, for example, in a working-class area is likely to colour the information sociologists collect by interview in such an area. Interviews on emotionally-charged topics such as race relations, religion and political attitudes are particularly prone to biases of this kind.

But it is not simply a matter of the stereotyped roles that a respondent may attribute to an interviewer. If the role is recognized the interviewer can make some allowance for it in recording his findings. But it may be very difficult for a respondent to understand what exactly an interviewer is trying to do. The notion of a scientific inquiry concerned with some apparently abstruse theoretical issue may be very difficult for the ordinary man in the street to grasp. He may therefore attribute to the interviewer a role quite different from the interviewer's own conception of what he is doing, and may quite unconsciously structure his comments in accordance with his conception. This may lead him to avoid the very issue in which the sociologist is really interested, and it will be very difficult for the interviewer to appreciate that this has happened.

Bott found that she acquired *three* (partly contradictory) roles in relation to the couples she was studying. First, she was, of course, a *scientific investigator* interested in obtaining certain information, the import of which was not always clear to her respondents. She also tried, initially at least, to present herself as a *friend of the family*, so that in the early interviews she 'submerged' the role of scientific investigator and did not take notes in front of the couple nor raise specific topics. Thirdly she was looked upon to some extent as someone who was interested in the 'problems' of the couple which she could 'put right'; that is, as a *therapist*. The contradictions between these different roles led Bott into difficulties, which were considerably reduced when she defined her role clearly as *scientist* and started making notes in front of the couple and 'directing' the interviews to specific topics.

One major danger, we have suggested, is that when people are asked to report on their own behaviour, or to consider in abstract terms the ideas and values that lie behind their actions – as they might be asked to do in an interview-situation – they may tend merely to state the formal rules of social behaviour, rather than recount accurately how they or other people actually behave. Bott found this in her study. She knew that one woman held strong views about the desirability of easy divorce. Yet in a meeting of a women's association, the same woman spoke out *against* easy divorce. In the formal public meeting, clearly, she felt it necessary to emphasize the 'respectable' norm of the sanctity of marriage, even though her private opinions were at variance with this. The same thing can happen in interviews. People may simply reiterate formal norms and values and behave quite differently in practice, or make a general statement about their behaviour, when in fact they behave differently in different situations.

Observation: participant and otherwise

Some of the difficulties arising out of the use of interviewing in sociological data-collection can be overcome by combining observation with interviewing, or perhaps by using observation alone. The rationale behind the use of observations in sociological research is that the sociologist should become party to a set of social actions sufficiently to be able to assess directly the social relationships involved. The degree of involvement may vary considerably from being merely a watcher on the side-lines to being deeply involved and part of what is going on.

Completely non-participant observation is as rare as full participant observation. In social psychology, one-way observation screens have been used to watch groups in action so that they are unaware that they are being watched, and the observer cannot affect their actions by his presence. But in sociological studies, which are usually studies of everyday situations, the observer is usually visibly present in a situation. Sometimes he may be relatively unobtrusive, as he might be when studying a football crowd, where he appears merely to be another spectator in the situation and does not influence the situation any more than any other member of the crowd. But more commonly, the sociologist is visibly present and part of the situation either as a sociologist or in some other guise. Simply entering into personal relationships with a number of people will involve a sociologist in a set of obligations towards them, so that he will have to explain to them what he is doing. Much will depend upon the sort of relationship the sociologist becomes involved in and the situation he finds himself in. As a member of the football crowd, where the interpersonal contact is slight, little explanation of his role seems called for, but in situations involving deeper personal involvement as in studying a gang, for example, the sociologist would need to justify his presence in order to be able to have access to the information he needs. In any case, professional ethics demand that the sociologist should not deceive his subjects: they should know he is a sociologist studying *them*.

Where the sociologist is merely an observer it is usually assumed that he knows enough about what the actors are doing to be able to understand their behaviour. It would be pointless, for example, for him to attempt to study the behaviour of some quite foreign people merely by observation, for he would know so little about the culture of the people that he would have difficulty in understanding why the people were doing what they were doing. Even the uninitiated Englishman watching American football is in this position. Any sociological observer has then, to some extent, to be a participant observer – he must at least share sufficient cultural background with the actors to be able to construe their behaviour meaningfully.

But the degree of participation and of sharing of meanings may vary considerably. The fact is that all people who join groups come to play some part in the activities of these groups. This means that, like the interviewer, the observer is allocated a role. The role that he is allocated will at least be defined by such basic characteristics as age, sex and possibly ethnic or racial status. Even if he participates only very little in the activities of the group, like some social anthropologists in the past, at least he will be given some minimal roles, and his ability to gather information will be affected accordingly. A man will find much of the behaviour of women beyond his observation, and vice versa: a young researcher may find it virtually impossible to associate with the old in order to see what they do and what they talk about, and vice versa. Coloured people and Whites may have associations from which people of the other colour-group are virtually excluded. The role that the observer assumes or is allocated, therefore, has a considerable influence on what he may see and hear.

To escape this dilemma, some observers have attempted to hide their observer role completely. They have adopted roles which were familiar in the groups they wanted to study, and carried out their observations clandestinely. Thus a group of American social scientists wanted to study a very exclusive cult which believed that the end of the world was to come on a certain specified day, and took part in its meetings by pretending to be believers (Festinger et al., 1966).

The ethical dubiousness of this sort of subterfuge is obvious. Here, however, we are concerned primarily with the procedural difficulties involved. One of the advantages of an overt as against a covert participant-observer status is that the observer is able to ask for certain obscure aspects of behaviour to be explained to him. The people who have accepted him into their midst acknowledge his observer role, as well as any other role that he may have taken. Though he may never be fully accepted into the group, therefore, he does have certain rights and a certain special degree of freedom at the same time.

The roles that participant observers assume – apart from the basic roles dictated by age, sex, etc. already mentioned – vary considerably. Ideally, it should be a role which will enable an observer to sink himself in the activities of the group but at the same time give him the maximum opportunity to see and hear what is going on, and, if necessary, to take notes about what is going on. Frankenberg, who studied a small Welsh village, found it convenient to take on the role of Secretary to the Football Club. This gave him a *raison d'être* for being at all the meetings, for knowing what was going on, and also for keeping extensive 'minutes' of the meetings which could double as field notes (Frankenberg, 1957). Lupton, who made a study of the social relationships of workers in an engineering workshop, took on the role of a sweeper, which enabled him to circulate freely amongst the workers and to talk to them all (Lupton, 1963).

But to remain an observer when one is becoming more and more involved in the activities of the group may prove difficult. One of the best accounts of the problem of participant observation is by William Foote Whyte, who made a study of an Italian slum 'street corner' gang in Boston just before the Second World War (Whyte, 1953). Whyte was introduced to the leader of the gang, Doc, who became his patron. Whyte learnt Italian and participated in all the activities of the gang – gambling, bowling and even participating in rather shady electioneering for a senator – while at the same time being known to the gang as someone who was 'writing a book' about the slum. But he eventually became aware that he was becoming so absorbed with his life as a gang member that he had stopped being an observer. He commented 'I began as a non-participating observer. As I became accepted into the community I found myself becoming almost a non-observing participator.'

Indeed, the peculiar strength of participant observation demands not complete detachment, but the involvement of the research-worker in the lives of the people he is studying. (He has, of course, to submit this experience to dispassionate analysis.) His general experience and knowledge are extended by his contact with the actors, and his sharing of their activities with them. He is then able to understand the meaning they attribute to the actions of others, and so better to appreciate the logic of their behaviour. This gives him a deeper insight into the behaviour of the people he is studying.

But to do this involves the investment of a good deal of time and energy in achieving this closeness to them, so that he can only become really accepted by a few groups. Clearly the problem of choosing which groups to study is a difficult one, since it does not depend entirely on *his* choice but also on whether a given group *allows* the sociologist to become 'one of them'. Whether the group is representative of a wider set of groups he is interested in is not always within his power to ensure. Thus intensive studies have their problems as well as 'extensive' (e.g., survey) ones.

In so far as the intensity of personal contact and numbers of persons involved are concerned, participant observation is at one polar extreme, then, and the large-scale social survey at the other. There is often much debate about the desirability of one method of collecting sociological data as against another, with the protagonists of survey methods commonly arrayed in hostile ranks against equally belligerent supporters of participant observation. The Solomonic judgement, of course, is that the method of data-collection must be related to the sort of problem on hand and to the social situation which presents itself to the sociologist (Bechhofer, 1974). If we were to undertake a sociological study of a small group – say the operation of a Board of Directors of an industrial concern (given that access to it is possible) – there would seem to be little point in trying to use social survey techniques. Participant observation can be turned to good account in practically any situation, but the findings which emerge from its use will be of a different kind and quality from those derived from a social survey. A study conducted by participant observation provides detailed examination of the actions of persons occupying specific social positions in particular social situations, together with their appreciation of the meanings those people attribute to the actions. But we would not be able to say how general this behaviour was, that is, whether it occurred in other situations or in other groups. For this, data derived from a *series* of observational studies or from some carefully designed social survey would seem to be necessary.

There is, then, no one 'best' way of collecting data. The sort of generalization that the sociologist wishes to make, and the nature of the subject-matter he is dealing with, will jointly determine whether he primarily uses existing material, a social survey, interviewing, or observation, participant or otherwise. The danger is that the ease of accessibility of information will determine the sort of data the sociologist collects and therefore indirectly determine the sort of problem he considers. It may be easier to conduct a social survey than to involve oneself in participant observation, even though the problem at hand demands participant observation techniques. If the sociologist is swayed by the ease of data collection then the quality of his analysis may be severely impaired.

The Analysis and Interpretation of Data

The purpose of assembling sociological data, of course, is to present some theoretical analysis or interpretation of it. But the processes of observation and analysis or interpretation are rarely independent of one another. Problems often become redefined as the research proceeds, and this means changing the kinds of observation made. In the social survey, for example, the pilot stage is vitally important, since the sociologist derives preliminary information from it which he then uses to test existing hypotheses in a crude way. He may then have to modify both the hypotheses and in consequence the techniques: for example, the schedule that he is using. Unstructured interview-techniques and observation are particularly suitable where the questions must be changed as the analysis begins to throw up new problems which demand new information, perhaps even new kinds of information, in order to answer them. But once the sociologist becomes immersed more in analysis than anything else, he must obviously stop collecting data – at least for a while. A successful analysis is one which explains much of what has already been observed, and directs the sociologist's attention to new areas of observation. Thus having related youth sub-culture to delinquent behaviour, he immediately has to ask why some kinds of youth behaviour involve sub-cultures and others do not.

The analysis of data, therefore, involves sifting through observations with the object of determining in what circumstances certain relationships manifest themselves and in what circumstances they do not, or to check that field notes support one interpretation rather than another.

At this stage it is necessary to raise two difficulties in the use of sociological information for analytical or interpretive purposes. The first of these is called the *reliability* of the data. This refers to the extent to which investigations are repeatable: that if the same procedures of data-collection, the same conceptual categories, and the same rules for establishing the veracity are used on the same subjects by different observers, or by the same observer on a different occasion, no relevant change having taken place in the meantime, results comparable with earlier studies should be obtained. Obviously if different answers emerge from inquiries which should yield the same responses, then the data may not be used to represent an assumed underlying regularity. If the analyst believes that the underlying regularity does in fact exist he will need to look to the way in which he has assembled his data to seek out reasons for this unreliability before he may use them. These reasons may, of course, be legion: the contexts in which the data were collected, the effect of the personality of the person who collected the information, subtle differences in expression or behaviour of the inquirer, unappreciated changes in the willingness of people to respond to inquiries or any other circumstance leading to differing responses. The measures which the sociologist can take to overcome unreliability in responses will depend upon what procedure he is using to collect the information and what types of analysis he wants to make.

The second difficulty, the problem of *validity*, is even more difficult to ensure. Validity refers to the extent to which the sociologist's interpretation of the underlying characteristics he wishes to reflect is in fact a faithful representation of that characteristic. The sociologist working within a positivistic framework may wish to represent some abstract notion such as 'alienation' by a set of relatively easily identified indicators. He may, as we shall see (p. 112) attempt to combine these indicators into a single index of the characteristic he wants to represent. Having done this, however, how can he be sure that his index reflects the characteristic of 'alienation' accurately? Sociological research-workers frequently rely purely upon the plausibility of the arguments they use in justifying their choice of particular indicators, and the further justifications they produce for using such indicators to construct indices in this way. But all indices should be tested empirically, and the usual way to do this is by using indicators on samples of subjects who are known from other evidence to be 'alienated' or 'not alienated'.

The problem of validity is equally difficult for those working within an interpretive framework, for they must be sure that the meanings they attribute to people's statements, actions or gestures are the same as those that the people themselves attribute to them. This is in fact extraordinarily difficult to establish, simply because people are not accustomed to putting their perceptions and feelings about meanings into words and may offer stereotyped responses to direct questions rather than accurate accounts of those meanings. The interpretive sociologist must therefore often rely on his sensitive appreciation – almost his intuitive understanding – of the unstated assumptions lying behind people's actions and behaviour. The observer, in the end, is driven to establishing his own assessment of the 'meaning', and this assessment carries with it as many difficulties about validity as the indices constructed by the positivists.

Given, however, that the sociologist is reasonably satisfied with both the reliability and the validity of his data, how does the analysis or interpretation proceed? This depends upon the framework within which the sociologist is working. Within a 'scientific' framework, the sociologist will be interested in testing some hypothesis which he has derived from theory by examining the connection in his data between some specified 'dependent variable' and some set of 'independent variables' which, he suspects, have some causal influence. This implies that the initial stages of the analysis, which may be going on while the data are being assembled, must be concerned with identifying the variables and in deciding what criteria may be reasonably used to represent these variables, a problem we have already raised with the inadequate way in which Reissman attempted to operationalize the concept of 'nationalism'.

Only after the 'scientific' sociologist has satisfactorily defined and operationalized the variables he wants to use to test the causal proposition he is postulating can he proceed to this test. The classical scientific way of doing this is by conducting controlled experiments. Experimental procedures, however, are seldom feasible in sociological analysis. Experiment involves selecting two sets of cases which, at a given point of time, are considered to be identical in all observable (or measurable) relevant characteristics. An experimental stimulus with observable (or measurable) effect is applied to one of the sets of instances (the 'experimental' group), while the other set (the 'control') is isolated from the effect of the stimulus. The observable characteristics of both experimental and control group are then examined to see whether any changes in them have taken place. Changes in the experimental group which have not taken place in the control group are attributed to the experimental stimulus.

It is not difficult to see why these classical experimental procedures are not common in sociology. To create a situation in which a designated group of people are isolated from some social stimulus, while another group identical in relevant characteristics is exposed to the 'same' stimulus, is hardly feasible. It is true that sometimes something approaching this state of affairs may occur by accident. For example, in several parts of Africa the arbitrary acts of statesmen have divided a single tribe so that one part has fallen under the colonial administration of one nation, while the other has fallen under another régime. It has been possible to study the differences between the two parts of the same people after a lapse of time and so to estimate the effect of differences in political culture upon them. But there are many difficulties in this procedure, the most important being that it is almost impossible to prevent people from moving to and fro across international boundaries, and so intermixing the two experimental populations; or at least communicating with each other, thus violating the rule that the experimental stimulus should apply to one group and not to the other.

Some sociologists have tried to achieve the advantages of the classical experiment by starting with a random sample of subjects and then carefully matching pairs of subjects in the sample so that each pair has the characteristics in common that the sociologist wants to hold constant and differs only in respect of some assumed causal influence. The extent of this causal influence may then be gauged by the difference between the effect in the sample which shows the causal variable and that in the sample which does not. It is, however, very difficult to isolate sufficient cases in which the variables are matched, especially if there are a number of such variables, to make the ensuing analysis feasible. In one of the most famous studies of this sort, in which the investigator wished to assess the effect of college education on occupational advancement, while holding six other possibly relevant influences constant, she found that only 46 subjects out of an initial 2,127 could be matched adequately enough to be included in the study. This was when only six relevant characteristics were being held constant (Chapin, 1947). Had the investigator tried to hold even more variables constant the final sample would have been reduced even further.

Not surprisingly, matching procedures are not common in sociology. Those sociologists who work within a 'scientific' framework, therefore, have perforce to adopt other procedures. At present the most promising line of inquiry seems to be a method of analysing material collected *at one time*, whether in a social survey or during participant observation, in which the research-worker tries to unravel the effects of a number of factors *all of which operate at the same time*. A procedure of this kind – there are several – is referred to as 'multivariate' analysis. The procedure usually aims at estimating the effect of any one of a number of 'independent' variables on a specified 'dependent' variable, on the assumption that all the other independent variables are held constant. Such multivariate analyses are essential if controlled experiment is not feasible – and it usually is not in sociological inquiry – because a relationship between two characteristics may arise simply because they derive from a common circumstance and have no sociological significance other than the 'spurious' relationship through the common factor.

An example is provided by the association between the imports of toilet requisites into Rhodesia, on the one hand, and the number of marriages contracted in the following year (over the period 1938 to 1949), on the other. The relationship is shown by the graph in Figure 3, in which the points, labelled by the date to which the information refers, are placed at the appropriate place in relation to the vertical axis (number of marriages in succeeding year) and to the horizontal axis (value of perfumery and toilet preparations in the stated year). The line is drawn through the points in such a way as to make the deviations from it as small as possible.

It is clear from these figures that as the value of perfumes and toilet waters imported varied, so did the number of marriages that took place in the following year. The degree of association may in fact be measured by a 'correlation coefficient' which takes the value of $+1 \cdot 0$ when two characteristics vary in the same way exactly; $-1 \cdot 0$ when the two characteristics vary together, but in exactly *opposite* directions; and a value of 0 where there is no association at all. In this case, the correlation coefficient is $+0 \cdot 82$, which is high. But commonsense leads us to distrust the implication of this correlation. We can scarcely believe what some advertisers would have us believe

	'38	'39	'40	'41	'42	'43	'44	'45	'46	'47	'48	'49
Value of perfumery and toilet preparations imported (Base, 1938)	100	100	129	140	128	91		192	233	349	376	314	472
Number of marriages registered in following year (Base, 1938)	100	83	76	75	60	69		70	101	107	122	117	119

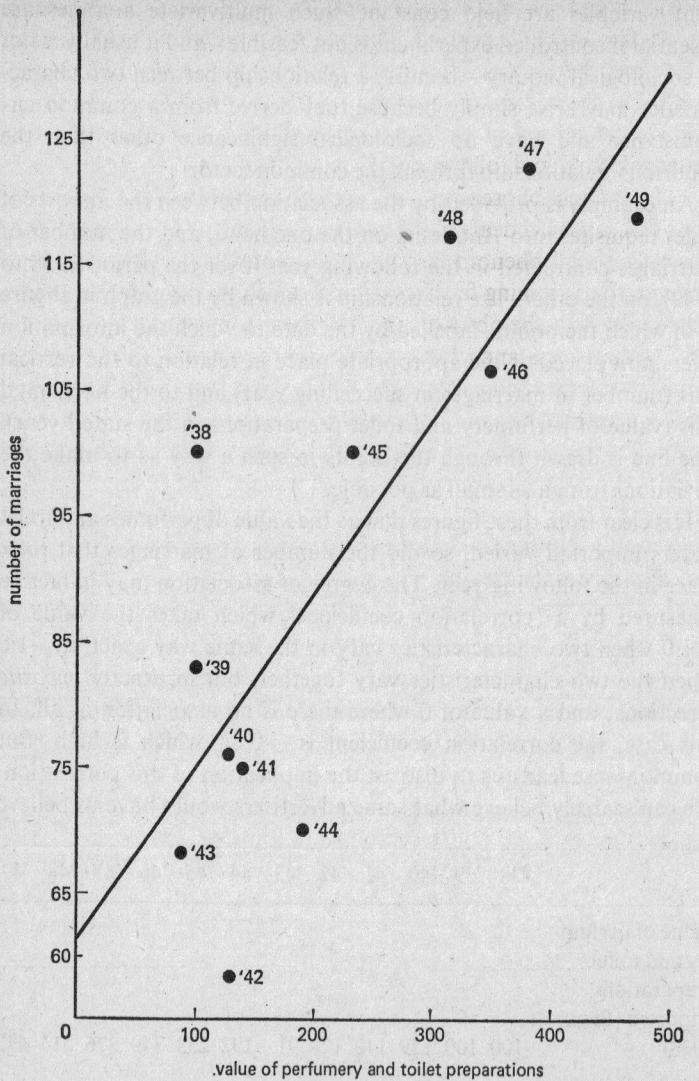

Figure 3 Relationship between value of perfumery and toilet preparations imported into Rhodesia and the number of marriages registered the next year : 1938–49

– that marriages are brought about primarily because men cannot resist the allure of perfume! Though a correlation can be found, therefore, there is no direct *causal* connection. Rather, both marriage rates and the volume of imports of perfumes were the consequences of a common set of circumstances – a period of marked over-all change during and following the war.

The example chosen was deliberately simple. In actual practice the position is a good deal more subtle and difficult to disentangle. This is because social phenomena are usually interconnected and affected by *many* determining factors, some of which may not be immediately appreciated by the observer. Let us return to the example of suicide. We know, for instance, that suicide is more common among divorcees than among married people of the same age and sex. But there may be *several* explanations of this. That suicide is caused by the distress and isolation experienced after divorce is one possible explanation. In other words a third factor, such as isolation, distress or perhaps financial strain, has intervened between the divorce and the suicide, explaining the causal connection between them. Diagrammatically we may represent the situation thus:

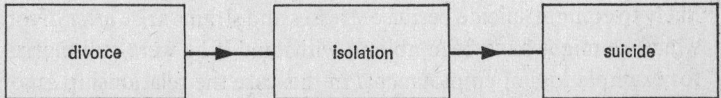

But there is also the possibility that it was the very personality characteristics which inclined the person to commit suicide which also put the marriage under strain and led eventually to its break-up, in which case the assumption that suicide was the consequence of divorce is spurious, so that the position is as follows:

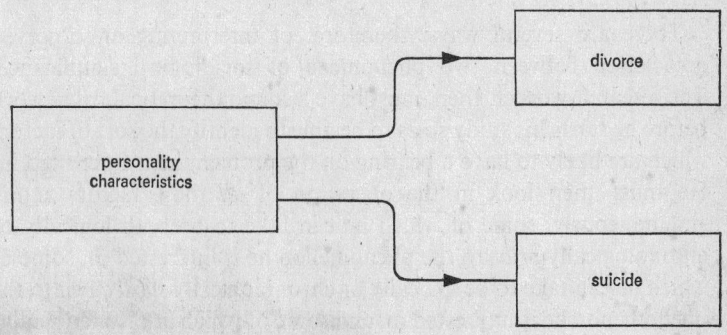

There is also the further possibility that the divorced person will commit suicide only if certain other factors are also present (say, for example, if he has no children – children normally being a 'protective' influence against suicide). Or perhaps there need to be *several* such 'conditions' before a divorcee is likely to kill himself, giving rise to the following situation:

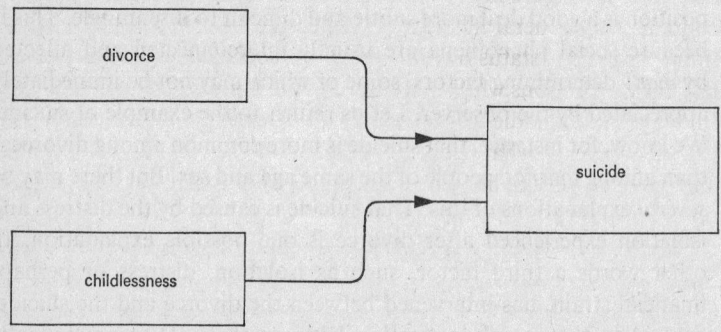

Finally, there is the possibility that a divorced person may only be likely to commit suicide because stresses and strains arise *after* divorce which he might have been able to withstand if he were still married, for example loss of employment. In this case the relationship among the events would be:

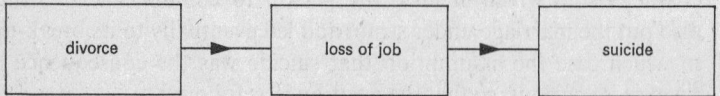

There are several ways, therefore, of interpreting an observed association between two phenomena of sociological significance. The research-worker, then, must have a sound theoretical framework before he starts his study so as to be able to identify the sort of factors which are likely to have a bearing on the problem he is interested in. He must then look at the operation of *all* these factors acting simultaneously, some of which he can take to be both logically or chronologically *prior* to the phenomenon he is interested in, some of which he can take to be logically or chronologically *subsequent* to the phenomenon he is interested in, and some of which are 'functionally'

related to the phenomenon he is interested in – that is, they may be taken as *either* cause *or* effect with equal validity.

Scientific analysis is mainly concerned with stating causal or functional relationships between variables in this way. But before this can begin, the positivistic sociologist must make sure that the abstract notions he is chasing are adequately contained in the events he has been able to capture in his observations. The language of sociologists contains very general abstract concepts like 'social status', 'alienation', 'anomie', 'status inconsistency' or 'social cohesion', as well as less abstract notions which refer to relationships like 'kinsmen of', or 'manager' or 'middle-class person', all of which, he assumes, manifest themselves in what people do and in how they *interpret* what they and other people do, but which are in fact not open to easy and direct observation.

Sociologists argue that even if they are not open to *direct* observation, they are nevertheless open to *indirect* observation. A label such as 'middle-class person', for example, is usually based on the examination of a large number of characteristics related to social class and cannot be determined from any single characteristic of an individual. The argument is that different attributes of individuals may reflect, in different degrees, the middle-class status of that individual. For example, each single attribute – where he lives, what school he has been to, his taste in music, the job he does – may not by itself be a trustworthy indicator of the 'class' of the individual, but a consistent response on all of them will be much more reliable. Some summary or adumbration of a number of these 'indicators', therefore, will enable the sociologist to gauge the dimensions of the intangible underlying disposition he wants to reveal.

The underlying disposition is sometimes referred to as a 'genotypic' phenomenon, that is, as the phenomenon which gives rise to the external and observable characteristics. The observable characteristics, on the other hand, sometimes called the 'phenotypic' phenomena, are directly observable and apparent. Many of the problems of devising indexes and scales in sociology arise from the difficulty of inferring underlying characteristics from their observable manifestations. The logic of most of the procedures turns on the notion that if we select a number of characteristics of individuals or groups which, our theory suggests to us, reflect some underlying disposition we are interested in, they ought, if they are all manifestations of the same underlying disposition, to vary in the same way when the underlying disposition varies. Therefore, if we examine a number of sets of indicators of, say, social status, we would expect them all to move in the same direction as we successively move from looking at the behaviour of 'upper-class' people to looking at 'middle-class' people and then 'working-class' people. We would anticipate, however, that some of the indicators would reflect social status differences more faithfully than others. Different indicators could then be weighted by their relationship to the underlying disposition and be combined into a single index of social status. Something like this was done by the American sociologist Lloyd Warner (Warner *et al.*, 1949). He devised a mathematical expression which allocated a person to a social 'class' on a scale made up out of a combination of indicators: occupation, amount of income, source of income, education, type of house and residential area. The statistical reasoning behind such procedures may be fairly complex and may depend upon certain mathematical assumptions, but with the widespread availability of computers to cope with the arithmetic involved, the use of these techniques should become commonplace before long. Sociologists will therefore have to know how to use these techniques, though they will not necessarily have to know how the answers are in fact worked out, in the same way that a psychologist may use a complex piece of equipment to study the operation of the brain without knowing much about the electronic circuit upon which it is based.

In computing such indexes and constructing such scales, however, there is one serious difficulty that the sociologist must take into account. The basic assumption behind these procedures is that the characteristics we observe are the characteristics of *individuals*. Our interest as sociologists, however, lies not in the individuals themselves but in the relationships the individual has with other individuals or the beliefs and values that he shares with others. The underlying sociological relationships must usually be adduced from these personal characteristics: they are usually not immediately observable. Often, when statistical tables are prepared in which the personal attributes of many individuals are cross-classified, the sociological phenomena that they are taken to represent are not made explicit. What passes for sociological analysis merely becomes what Coleman (1964) has called 'aggregate psychology', that is, the behaviour of the persons is seen to be the summation of a series of individual reactions, without any reference necessarily to their common beliefs and values, or the social relationships they have to one another.

If we correlate the incidence of suicide amongst men and women, young and old, married and single, town-dwellers and country-dwellers, for example, we are merely dealing with the joint occurrence of characteristics in a collection of atomized individuals. We are saying nothing about the social relationships between these individuals, including the meanings which people give to the actions of others. Much social survey analysis, indeed, does not go much beyond this.

Personal characteristics such as age and sex may be construed in several different ways. They may be related at one level to personality structure, so that the relationship of suicide to the characteristics can be understood in the framework of general personality structure. But age and sex, at a sociological level of analysis, may be taken to signify social relationships, so that being both old and a man may indicate the social isolation that characterizes men in industrial society when at the later phases of the life-cycles they have stopped working and lost their position in the family. In terms of Durkheim's analysis an isolated person of this kind is particularly prone to commit suicide. The personal characteristics in this sort of analysis, therefore, indicate abstract sociological notions: the propositions are about these sociological notions and not directly about the observed personal characteristics at all.

Models

An effective test of the validity of the necessary connections among abstract notions postulated by any theory is the extent to which these abstract notions may be linked together as elements in a set of inter-relationships in such a way that the repercussions of a known change in any one of the elements may be traced on all the others. A set of elements linked in this way is called a *model*.

In sociology model-building has not yet reached the pitch that it has in economics. It manifests itself mainly in what are known as 'simulation' studies. These are models which set out to show what will happen when some specified changes take place. One field in which simulation studies are widely used is in international relations and in conflict studies generally. In these studies, ordinary individuals are given roles to play representing people in important positions in the structures whose behaviour is to be simulated, for example, nations. The decisions they make, and the effects of these decisions upon one another, are correlated and co-ordinated and fed back to the actors. They are then in a position to make new decisions in the light of this information, and these decisions are, in turn, fed back into the situation. The social scientists who make these simulation studies are then able to examine the possible outcome of different decisions, and their effect on the pattern of social relationships in their models. Ideally, the extent to which the behaviour of the simulated structure resembles the behaviour of real structures should be assessed, but there are several difficulties in estimating this, due to the complexities of real social structure as compared with the necessarily simple models we have to use.

A simple example of this procedure is provided by a study in which a model of organizational behaviour, much respected by sociologists, was tested by linking the various components of the model in an appropriate way in a computer. By feeding arbitrary values into the model and testing to see how the interconnection in the model affected the various components it was easy to show that the model as set out by the author simply could not work: in this way the *logical* coherence of the model could actually be tested (Markley, 1967).

A more restricted use of model-building is by starting with some very simple assumptions, and then developing more complex arguments from these. In this technique, the consequences of people's actions are traced out on the basis of these elementary assumptions. These are then compared with an example of what happens in fact, and the initial assumption then modified. An example is provided by Coleman (1964) who predicted the pattern of migration among a number of towns on the assumption that movement between them was conditioned partly by the size of the towns and partly by the distance separating them. Next he compared his predictions with actual migration statistics and found several significant departures. He tried then to explain these differences in terms of the specific characteristics of the cities involved, for example the amount of travel to the Federal capital, Washington, travel to Washington being disproportionately large considering simply its size and location in relation to other cities. The attraction in these procedures lies in the fact that the basic assumptions and the logical relationships involved are explicit and clear. Models start from a number of postulates about the relationships linking parts of a structure: the extent to which the model predicts observed phenomena is a measure of the adequacy of its explanatory power.

The Methods of Interpretive Sociology

So far we have been discussing the procedures adopted by sociologists working with a positivistic approach to the understanding of social reality. But, as we have seen, by no means all sociologists subscribe to the assumptions underlying this orientation. Many sociologists see their subject, as we have said, as more akin to literature or history than to the natural sciences in the sense that they seek to reflect the pattern or 'meaning' in a set of observations they have made. Yet others – those identified as ethnomethodologists – consider that the basic problem of sociology goes back even further than this and is concerned with the processes by which people come to establish meanings in social phenomena. Sociologists of this conviction deny that 'variables' accurately reflecting the unique qualities of human life can be constructed at all, and that to try to establish regularities in terms of relationships among such 'variables' is a misplaced activity from the start.

The disagreement is a fundamental one: over the nature of the philosophical assumptions the proponents of the different approaches make concerning the way we come to know about what is taking place in the world outside ourselves. These assumptions, however abstruse they may appear to be, have dramatic consequences for the way in which the sociologists who operate with them go about their business.

Some interpretive sociologists – those identified as 'symbolic interactionists' for example – are content to operate with a relatively naïve set of assumptions about how we come to know about social phenomena. They are prepared to accept the meanings that the actors attribute to social phenomena at face value, and proceed to erect their systematic interpretations on these foundations. This implies that the sociological observer must exercise sufficient discipline on himself to ensure that it is indeed the *actors'* meanings that are recorded in his notebooks and not merely his own. It is obvious that if the sociologist is studying a people with a culture vastly different from his own then he is obliged deliberately to learn a foreign language, gestures, sets of values, customs and ways of looking at things quite different from his own. But if he is studying people from his own cultural group he may fall into the trap of assuming without question that the meanings that his subjects give to gestures, to verbal expressions, to symbols of all kinds, to the actions of other people, will be the same as his. They may well be, but the assumption must be checked before the meanings may be used in any interpretation of the sociology of the group that he is studying. It implies also that the observer would need to check the meaning of the same social phenomenon with several of the actors concerned to make sure that he has not inadvertently sought his information from an idiosyncratic member of the group he is studying.

If the study were left at this level of analysis we would have a description of the commonly accepted meanings that people attribute to social phenomena: we would have in short an *ethnography* of the people – an account of their *culture*. But this is only the first step in an interpretive analysis, for the sociologist is interested in understanding social phenomena in *general* terms. Accordingly he must move beyond the folk-meanings of the phenomena and try to discern patterns and regularities in these meanings, which he can represent as cultural 'themes'. Further patterns and regularities running through these themes may in turn be represented as 'configurations' of themes which, taken together, may be held to characterize the essential characteristics of whole cultures. In this way, the anthropologist Ruth Benedict characterized the cultures of some American Indian peoples as 'Dionysian', that is, given to extreme and frenzied states of being, and others as 'Appollonian' – always seeking moderation in behaviour and cultural expression. She achieved this by tracing these features through a wide range of their manifestations in the cultures of the people she examined (Benedict, 1934). These interpretations of meanings at different levels of abstraction are all informed and guided by the ultimate motive of establishing concepts which provide sociologists with a *general* way of understanding human activities and beliefs (cf. Bruyn, 1966).

Thus far we have been considering the data-collecting and analytical procedures adopted in sociological studies in which the meanings attributed to social phenomena are based on commonsense interpretation of behaviour by both the actors involved and the observer. Some sociologists say that this does not go far enough. The aim, they say, is not simply to identify and record the meanings that people have assigned to situations but to understand the ways in which they generated those meanings in the first place. The idea that it is important to understand 'how the world looks' to those who live in it is approved of by these critics, but they argue that this is not, in itself, the end purpose of inquiry, for the final emphasis should be on the ways in which they – the members of society – come to see their world in the ways they do.

Since most meaning is transmitted through language, sociologists who want to study the 'interpretive procedures' which members of the society use to attribute meaning typically focus their attention upon speech exchanges in which the participants are involved in 'making sense' of each other's talk. The emphasis is upon the study of the ways in which people in actual situations of interaction come to 'see' what the other person is meaning. An example of this kind of study is Cicourel's study of juvenile delinquency (Cicourel, 1968), in which he traces the way in which young people come to be categorized as 'juvenile delinquents' by the police, probation officers, the courts and so on.

In this study Cicourel tried to show how policemen and other officials, through talking to adolescents who are brought before them, arrive at decisions about those adolescents, come to 'see' that they are 'a lost cause', 'not a bad kid', 'someone who'll end up in jail', etc. Cicourel shows that the way the adolescent sits in a chair, his tone of voice, the look in his eyes, whether he pauses before answering questions, are all used by the officials dealing with them as signs of their 'attitude', as bases for the inference that the adolescent is 'defiant of authority', 'rude', 'hostile', and so on and that these inferences are used to make out that the adolescent is a potential delinquent.

The decisions as to whether someone is to be classified as a delinquent or not are made because the officials involved in making the classification attribute meanings to the adolescents' physical and verbal activities. The order of phenomena arises, then, from the ways in which actors attribute meaning to the events and activities with which they have to deal, rather than from the inherent order of some social structure or some 'objective variables' (such as, in the case of delinquency, 'broken homes' or 'low social class') which positivist sociologists assume characterize the materials they are dealing with.

The kind of information a sociologist of this sort requires to substantiate his analysis is quite different from the information needed, say, by interpretive sociologists operating with commonsense meanings, and certainly from that needed by sociologists who try to express abstract variables in terms of 'indicators' and to establish postulated relationships between the *variables* by using the numerical relationships among the *indicators*. Direct observation is undoubtedly the most fruitful procedure, accompanied by extensive verbatim recording of conversational exchanges among the actors involved. More recently, tape-recorders have increasingly been used, and in some instances video-tape recordings have been made so that the sociologists may have the opportunity of analysing not only the detail of the wordings of exchanges and the intonations of the voices but also gestures and facial expressions which may provide important clues to the way in which meanings are communicated. More formal laboratory techniques may well be used, as in one well-known experiment when thirty students were asked to take part in an experiment with 'psychotherapeutic procedures' (McHugh, 1968, Garfinkel, 1967, pp. 79–88). This experiment is discussed in detail below (pp. 559–63). The experimental subjects were told that they were to consult a therapist who would be concealed from them by a screen and who would answer their questions only by 'yes' or 'no'. The subjects were to seek help from the therapist by asking him questions through an intercom. In fact, the 'therapist' was just an experimenter answering the subject's questions in a quite arbitrary way (through following a table of random numbers), and the aim of the experiment was not so much to see if a certain kind of therapeutic technique would work but simply to see how the experimental subjects would understand what they believed was a therapist's advice.

The experiment was aimed at understanding how people 'make sense' of other people's talk, and a quite 'artificial' situation was used to explore practices which the experimenter assumed are used in real life.

Case-Studies and Life Histories

So far we have referred to analyses and interpretations of quite different kinds and at different levels of abstraction. Normally these different kinds of analysis are kept separate from one another. They may, however, be brought together if they are related to one particular set of events. This is what happens when a case-study is made.

The case-study starts from observation and proceeds to show how general abstract explanatory principles manifest themselves in one piece of observed reality. The approach here is similar to that of a medical scientist who has before him a diseased person and a history of the course of the disease up to that point. He also has a number of symptoms and clinical signs, and possibly a number of other diagnostic aids such as blood-counts, microscopic examinations of tissues, serum-reactions and so on. The medical scientist weighs up these various indicators and fits them together into a meaningful whole, guided by what he knows about the patterns of disease in general. Given this interpretation, he is able to check his assumptions by carrying out further tests.

In the same way, a sociologist making a study of a 'wildcat' strike may have before him a history of events leading up to the strike, an analysis of the structure of the factory, and a knowledge of the relationship of the various actors in the situation to one another. From his general knowledge of industrial sociology, he will be aware of a number of generalizations about the role of informal relationships among workers in industrial organizations, the differing effects of authoritarian and permissive managements, and so on. By examining the course of events he may be able to make a number of propositions about the way in which social relationships operate in industrial situations, and the courses of action workers may adopt in such situations.

The time duration of the case-study may vary from a single isolable instance – a social situation – through to a series of situations which develop one from another in a connected series of events, possibly over several years. Both types of analysis, however, share one basic characteristic: the situation, or set of situations, provides a 'natural' occasion on which the sociologist is able to point to the operation of certain basic principles of social organization. Turner (1957), who calls his extended case-studies of one African people 'social dramas', uses situations of crisis to examine the latent conflicts in social life. 'Through the social drama,' he says, 'we are able to observe the crucial principles of the social structure in operation and their relative dominance at successive points in time.' The sociologist using this technique, therefore, may select a 'typical' set of events – or a very special event – a demonstration or a dispute – and use his general knowledge of the social situation in which these events are taking place, and his detailed knowledge of the actors, to show how the actions of the *dramatis personae* reflect the various positions in the social structure.

In arriving at his interpretation, the sociologist makes use of as much knowledge and information about the actors and their social relationships as he can assemble. He draws on historical data, official records, social surveys, interviews with people in strategic positions, and insights and understandings he may have acquired through participating in the activities of the people concerned. He also uses his knowledge of the social system as a whole as a backdrop against which he interprets the behaviour of the individual actors. All this is fitted together so that the whole forms an intellectual synthesis in which the connections between the actions of people occupying positions in a social structure and the meanings informing those actions are made understandable.

The general validity of the analysis does not depend on whether the case being analysed is representative of other cases of this kind, but rather upon the plausibility of the logic of the analysis. The generality is of the same kind that enabled Sir Ronald Ross to announce the 'cause' of malaria when he found the malaria parasite in the salivary gland of a single female Anopheles mosquito in 1897.

The demonstration of the logical connection between events gives the researcher the means of asking further questions about the phenomenon he is examining. To answer these questions he has to start once more systematically collecting and analysing data. The subject thus grows by constant interaction of the painstaking and systematic checking of observations and the inferences that may be made from them, on the one hand, and insightful, imaginative synthesis – as in model-building or case-studies – on the other. Together they allow order to be seen where formerly none was discernible.

Chapter 3
Development and Underdevelopment

So far, we have talked of 'societies' or 'the society' implicitly in terms of the modern nation-state, without discussing other kinds of society or the often highly varied patterns of structure and culture within nation-states, the major types of society that we can distinguish, or the relationships between societies. The first of these issues will be central to every chapter of this book. Here we examine, more explicitly, the major classifications of contemporary societies used in sociology and, more widely, in the world at large, and the differing conceptions of the world within which these types of society are encompassed.

The world as we know it today is a novel formation. Before the nineteenth century, however extensive the empires or religions of earlier epochs, there was no 'world order' in the sense of a global system of trade, an international system of political relationships, or world-wide communications networks which makes it possible for people from one culture to know about the culture of the rest of the world (Worsley, 1967, ch. 1). The nation-state itself only began to emerge a few centuries ago (and may well, ultimately, disappear). The classifications we find useful today, then, differ fundamentally from those we might need to construct in order to study the past.

Today, it is the 'development gap' between the 'mechanized rich' and the 'rural poor' that is most immediately striking: British expenditure on deodorants and slimming foods, for instance, exceeds the entire gross national product of Botswana.

We can extend this distinction by re-drawing the map of the world in terms of this great disparity between wealth and population, instead of according to land area, as in conventional use. The relative importance of the various countries will then look very different,

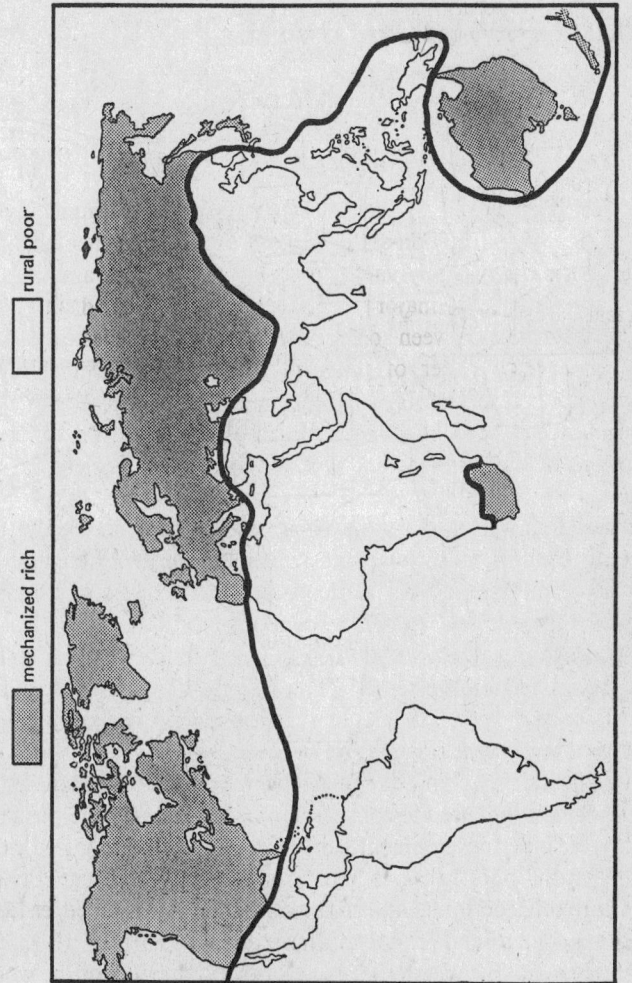

Figure 4 The development gap
(Source: *Times History of Our Times, 1945–71*, p. 44.)

mechanized rich

rural poor

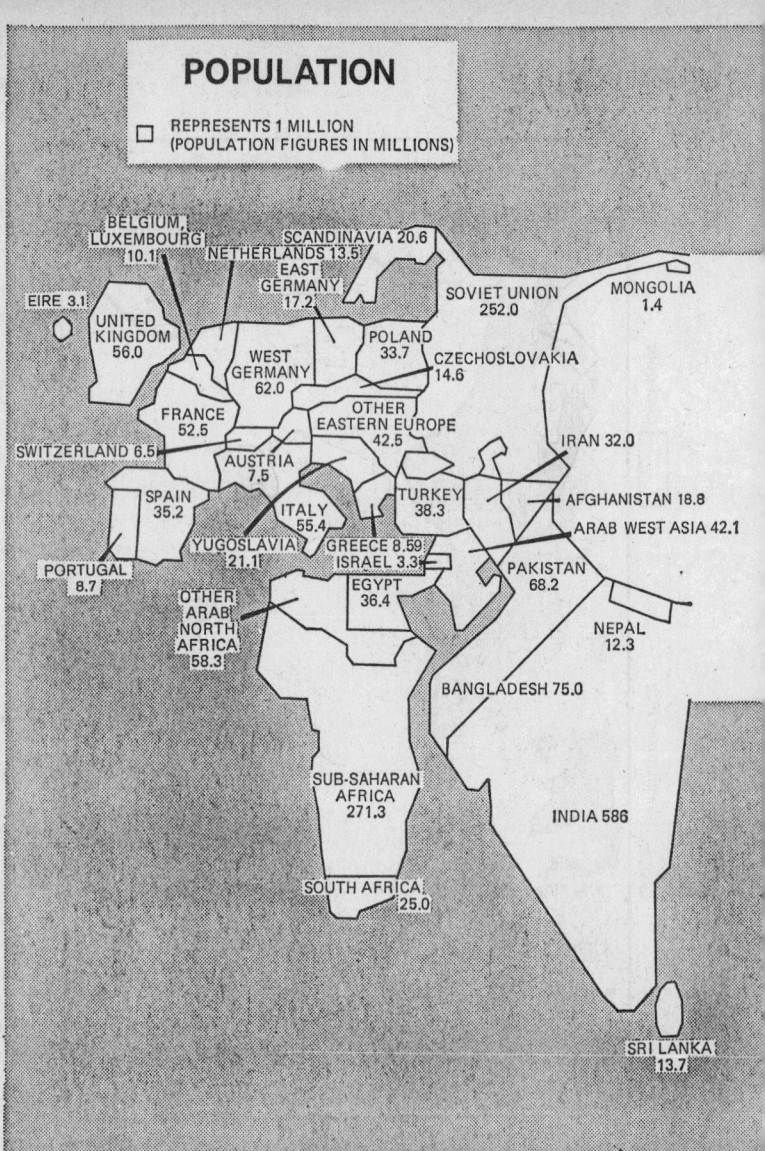

Figure 5 Population
(Source: Edwin O. Reischauer, *Beyond Vietnam: The United States and Asia,* Knopf, 1968.)

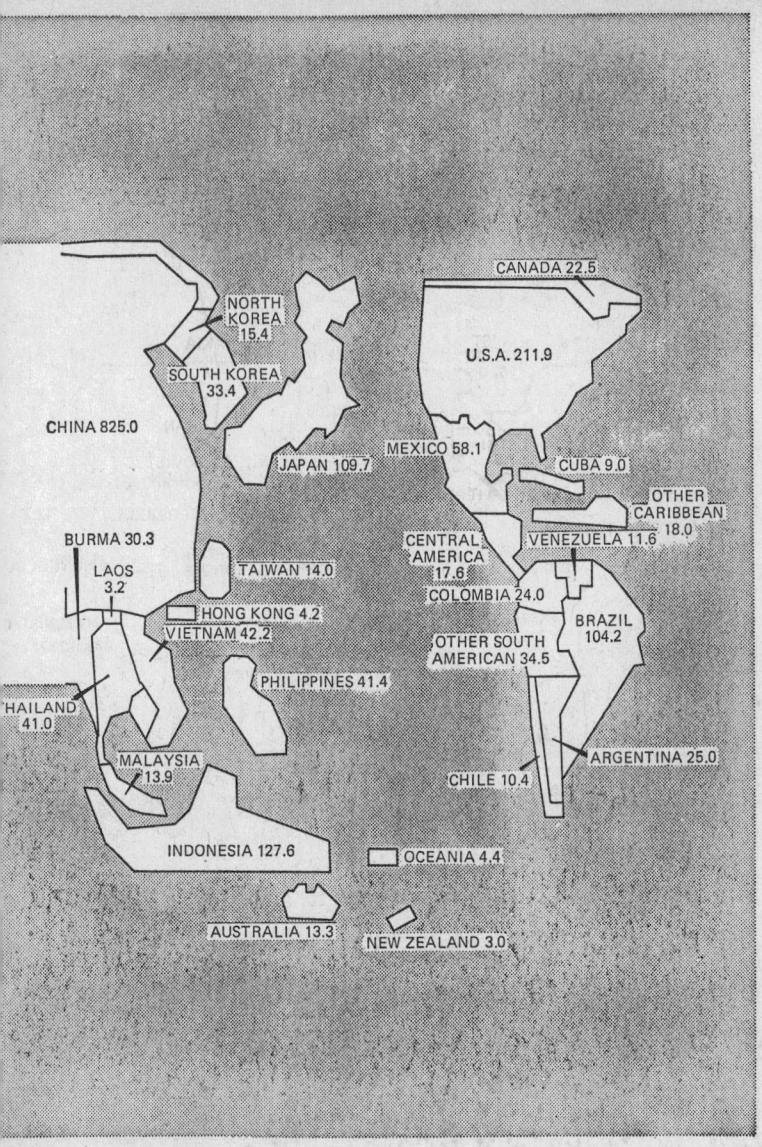

CANADA 22.5

U.S.A. 211.9

NORTH KOREA 15.4

SOUTH KOREA 33.4

CHINA 825.0

JAPAN 109.7

MEXICO 58.1

CUBA 9.0

OTHER CARIBBEAN 18.0

BURMA 30.3

LAOS 3.2

TAIWAN 14.0

CENTRAL AMERICA 17.6

VENEZUELA 11.6

HONG KONG 4.2

COLOMBIA 24.0

BRAZIL 104.2

VIETNAM 42.2

PHILIPPINES 41.4

OTHER SOUTH AMERICAN 34.5

THAILAND 41.0

MALAYSIA 13.9

ARGENTINA 25.0

CHILE 10.4

INDONESIA 127.6

OCEANIA 4.4

AUSTRALIA 13.3

NEW ZEALAND 3.0

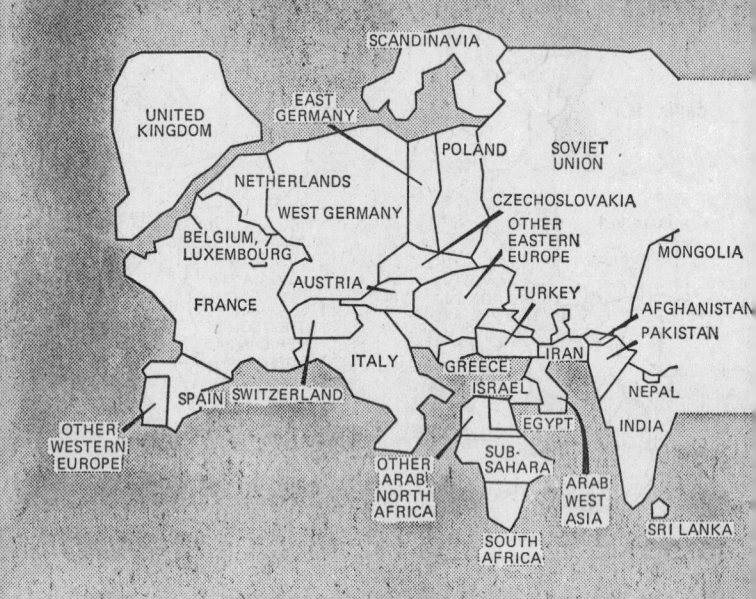

Figure 6 Gross National Product
(Source: Edwin O. Reischauer, *Beyond Vietnam: The United States and Asia*, Knopf, 1968.)

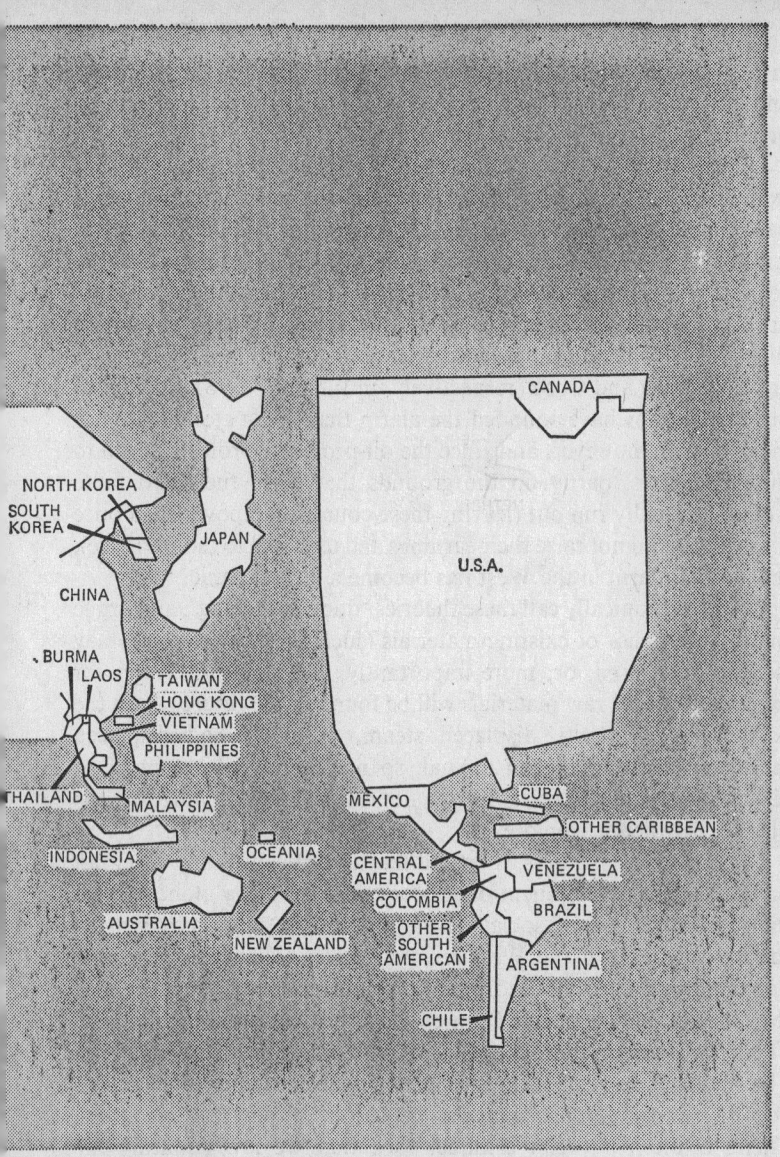

according to the criterion emphasized. In terms of population, for instance, China and India easily outstrip the U.S.A. and the U.S.S.R., and countries like Indonesia are of major importance; in terms of production, the picture looks very different.

Other ways of classifying the world's population are called for in examining other kinds of issues. In the last decade, for instance, it has become generally recognized that we need to think not simply in terms of population, or the relationship between population and the economy, but in terms of an 'ecosystem', involving the separating out of 'human resources' (in qualitative terms of skills as well as sheer size) from natural resources (raw materials) (see Readings 1 and 2, Ogburn and Cook, respectively, in Worsley, 1978). Ecological pressure-groups have sounded the alarm that raw materials are not inexhaustible, however, and since the oil-producing Powers began to raise oil prices, partly on the grounds that fossil fuels and finite would eventually run out (leaving these countries impoverished once more if they did not raise their earnings and use them to industrialize), the note of alarm in the West has become a virtual panic.

Others sardonically call these theories 'doom-watching', and argue that new supplies of existing materials (such as North Sea oil) may well be discovered, or, more importantly, that new substitutes for existing fuels and raw materials will be found in the future. As in the past, when electricity displaced steam, as steam had displaced muscle-power, human and animal, so nuclear or solar energy, or technologies and materials as yet not contemplated, will take the place of petroleum, iron ore, etc.

These problems, others assert, ultimately depend, in any case, not on the level of development of science and technology alone, but on the level and kind of social development. The preoccupations of 'doom-watchers' in the West are thus seen in China as reflecting not the limitations imposed by Nature on humanity generally, but the crisis of one particular form of social organization – capitalism. Their own social system, they believe, will overcome these problems. The ecology movement in the West, again, extends its analysis beyond simply emphasizing the depletion of physical resources. Theirs is often a social critique, too: that we are polluting the natural environment and producing inhuman man-made environments, for the sake of 'planned obsolescence', 'consumerism' and profit.

Man's relationship to Nature is thus itself the subject of theoretical reflection and controversy. But thinking about Man's use of Nature, or the constraints Nature imposes on us, inevitably involves considering the ways in which we co-operate and conflict with others in the process, the equipment we use, and the relationships we are involved in outside the sphere of production.

Thought and debate about these matters, are, of course, by no means modern phenomena.

Though sociology only emerged as the new 'science of society' in the last century, from the beginning of humanity people – both ordinary people and specialist 'thinkers' – have always striven to understand the world around them, and their place in that world. Philosophers in ancient Greece debated the merits and demerits of the rival systems of tyranny, democracy and oligarchy; medieval Arab scholars like Ibn Khaldun saw history as a dialectical interaction between the way of life of the pastoral nomadic desert-dwellers and that of the settled cultivators and city-dwellers.

These contrasts reflected the social formations and the social changes of their day. Rapid changes – military, economic, political, technological – did, of course, occur; a Hun invasion, or the doubling of China's population in less than a century, due to the introduction of new varieties of rice.

Great empires, such as those of the Mongols, the Aztecs, or the Zulu, rose and fell in Asia, America and Africa, sometimes on a scale dwarfing anything Europe had known. The regular army in tenth-century China contained one-and-a-quarter million men, and the Bow and Crossbow Department's central workshops alone were turning out 3·24 million weapons a year by 1160 (Elvin, 1973, p. 84).

The history of the world, then, is by no means the history of Europe. But the developments that did decisively link up the entire globe for the first time happened in Europe, and favoured those states which had succeeded in developing social institutions which assisted the vigorous development of capitalist industrial enterprise, from the joint-stock company and the independent town, to State patronage of science, technology, invention and discovery. The *avant-garde* capitalist countries were ultimately to dominate not only Europe, but the whole world. What those 'favourable' conditions were exactly, however, is, as we shall see, a question that has continued to exercise scientists and practical men alike.

In the early centuries of their contact, the gap between Europe and the rest of the world was small. Initially it had not even been a difference between industrialized and non-industrialized countries, for agriculture only slowly transformed itself into capitalist agriculture, and industry remained quite subsidiary, despite the growing home and foreign markets for manufactured goods. But in the late eighteenth century the whole process was stepped up: in British agriculture, by the application of rationalized management, based on production for the market, economies in labour and new capital inputs which were only possible on large farms using science-derived technical innovations, from new strains of seed to machinery. Other countries, which modernized much later, inherited a large peasantry which had been swept away long before in Britain. The effects – as the struggle over collectivization in the U.S.S.R. as late as the 1920s shows – were to influence profoundly the different paths of development taken by these countries (Moore, 1973).

These technical and organizational changes in British agriculture could not have happened without two crucial societal transformations: the production of a labour-force and the accumulation of capital.

By enclosing large tracts of land formerly worked in small parcels, or taking over common land into private ownership through enclosure, a sizable segment of the former tenant-farmer and small independent farmer population could be eliminated, or at least greatly reduced in numbers. Some became agricultural workers, working for a wage. Most had to leave for the city. A 'proletariat', rural and urban, had been created.

The capital needed to finance both the new capitalist agriculture and machine-based industry was accumulated out of the profits generated by rising output and increased productivity of labour (both via intensive exploitation of human labour power and by increased use of machinery), channelled through new mechanisms for raising money on the market. But most, initially, came from 'primitive' accumulation – the application of military and political, as distinct from economic, power to ruin and despoil those unable to resist, whether at home or in the parallel growth of what Weber called 'booty capitalism' abroad – the destruction of the Inca and Aztec empires in the case of Spain, or the preying upon Spanish treasure-fleets by the English. The latter, however, were to translate this capital into means of production, while the Spaniards did not.

France and Britain emerged as the great rival empires, with the Netherlands a minor third. They clashed in every part of the globe. Each consolidated its possessions by imposing a rigid system of political control on their colonies, and by eliminating competition for home manufactures: thus the Indian textile industry was destroyed to make way for Lancashire textiles made from Indian cotton. The process of 'underdevelopment' had begun. Such countries now became producers of raw materials for the industries of the West. Capital, too, flowed back to Europe in the form of profits, to finance modernization of European industry and the conspicuous consumption of a small ruling class.

Such gigantic social transformations finally brought to maturity a set of interrelated conflicts of interest over political, economic and even religious questions between the new capitalist bourgeoisies and the established land-owning aristocracies who had traditionally monopolized government. These struggles lasted over centuries, and occurred at quite different points in time as well as having their own distinct rhythms and character from country to country. The creation of a centralized State, for instance, was a necessary condition for capitalist modernization (though not a sufficient one, for ancient Egypt and Rome were centralized polities). In England, it had begun as early as Henry VIII's reign. In Germany it was not accomplished until Bismarck. Sometimes the final transfer of power came about as a result of political breakdown and the application of violence and counter-violence, as in France's Revolution. In Britain, the Civil War, the Restoration and the 'glorious Revolution' of 1688 produced a less clear-cut outcome, in which old landed aristocracy and new bourgeoisie intermingled.

But whatever the particular differences or compromises, the new owners of industry were now predominant within their societies, and the new capitalist States they dominated also came rapidly to control the rest of the world.

In Western Europe the coincidence of the Industrial and French Revolutions (Hobsbawm, 1964) brought to an end the key institutions of the traditional land-owning classes, and the division of society into the 'estates' one was born into. Now one was a 'citizen', no longer a serf or a nobleman. Yet the legacy of the feudal epoch did not disappear entirely, and although feudalism was inevitably condemned by those who destroyed it, it was by no means a totally negative inheritance. The 'parcellization' of sovereignty, for instance, involving the claim of interest-groups in society to representation in government, rather than the concentration of power into the hands of a monarch, or his servants, became an important right which continued into the era of capitalism. And the claims of quite new interest-groups, particularly the working class, to some say in government – even for a transformation of the whole system – had now to be met if their potentially overwhelming power was not to be directed against the existing social order and the State. By 1885, the extension of the vote in Britain to a wider electorate (which still excluded the poor and women), and the creation of new mass Conservative and Liberal parties, ensured that the political weight of the masses was channelled into institutions which were supportive of the political system. The extent to which this 'incorporation' of the working class was made possible either because the living standards of a superior stratum of the working class – an 'aristocracy of labour' – or, as others argue, of the *majority* of the working population, improved over the nineteenth century, is a subject of intense debate among historians. Some theorists, among them revolutionaries from Third World countries, from Lenin to Fanon (Lenin, 1975; Fanon, 1967), have argued that this 'incorporation' was possible because of the possession of an empire. Others accept the more dominant view that the dynamic of growth *within* the metropolitan country – as in Germany or the U.S.A. – was the principal source of wealth, wealth so great that a skilful ruling class could use a portion of it to 'buy off' the working class, or enough of them, or, later theorists argued, turn them into consumer-robots (Marcuse, 1968).

It is, of course, impossible to treat the flow of capital from abroad, subsequently used in the further development of the already developed industry of the 'West', as if it were separate from and external to the 'home' economy. Similarly, the very fact of colonial political power, as distinct from purely economic dominance of the world market, has meant that in the twentieth century the growth of the new states outside Europe and the Americas has been deeply affected by the ideas and institutions introduced by colonial Powers, from constitutions to school curricula. They were never carbon-copies of metropolitan ideas or institutions. They were adapted to and often specially produced for colonial conditions. Firstly, there were separate systems of rights for the rulers and the ruled, usually reinforced by social 'closure' in the form of the colour-bar. Democracy was not exported to the colonies, and colonial subjects were taught to regard their own history and culture as either nonexistent or barbarous. The road to civilization lay in an infinitely slow process of becoming French or British: thus African children in French colonies read history books about 'our ancestors, the Gauls'.

The interaction between the colonizer and the colonized thus affected both, in a complex, and by no means solely economic, dialectic. Hence the phases of development typical of Europe were not reproduced east of Suez. Socialism, for example, of the 'social democratic', 'reformist' variety which grew up in the wake of liberalism in nineteenth-century Europe, never got off the ground in the colonies, nor did it appear in the same sequence. There, radicals soon became revolutionaries, and revolutionaries, like Mao Tse-tung and his young friends, sought for and quickly found a doctrine much more relevant to their needs, Marxism. Others experimented with 'populist' ideologies, or with institutions which they thought would bring about development faster than Western liberal democracy: whether 'modernizing autocracy' or military government or one-party rule.

These differences constitute a general process, generally labelled 'uneven development', rooted in, but not confined to, the basic economic inequality. Perfectly 'balanced' development has probably never occurred anywhere, and gulfs between rich and poor, and town and country, are not restricted to the colonial situation. But the gross inequalities between the deliberately underdeveloped colonies and the imperialist metropoles were structural differences generated by imperialism and giving rise to new and spectacular extremes of wealth and poverty, and massive gaps between town and country. Attempts to restrict the economic development of colonies, and resistance to such attempts, are not wholly recent, however: settlers in the New World, both in South and North America, were the first to revolt against Spanish and British control. Haiti achieved her independence from France via even bloodier revolution.

The extension of colonialization, however, inevitably meant that the traffic was predominantly one-way, in which the imperialist Powers exported both institutions and ideas.

The revolt of the 'first new nation', however, as Lipset has called the U.S.A., had been of a different kind from revolt in the contemporary underdeveloped world. Far from being underdeveloped, the American colonies had been able to develop an agriculture and industry as vigorous as that in England. Unlike today's poor countries, the world's market was not dominated by entrenched rich countries. The society that grew in North America had inevitably developed its own distinctive pattern, whatever the attempts of Britain to impose either colonial institutions or duplicates of English institutions. The feudal legacy of England, in particular, had scarcely taken root in a country where a vigorous capitalism had emerged, both in the plantations of the South, based on slave labour, and in the northern cities, where a growing home market, based on ever-increasing immigration and the availability of abundant natural resources, led to a rapid growth of the economy. The 'open frontier' to the West, too, permitted tens of thousands of families to establish small independent farms, occupying land which the State helped clear of Indians and sold at nominal prices. Railroads completed the process to the Pacific, and took cattle and crops to the market. Later, millions, mainly from Europe, were to follow these pioneers.

Revolution in the New World might be 'as American as cherry pie', in Stokely Carmichael's words, but it was no monopoly of the United States or of the colonies. The transition to capitalist mass democracy was to prove equally traumatic in France; from there it was transmitted by Napoleon's armies to the rest of Europe. But the successful reaction to this export of revolution by Russia and Austria-Hungary, and the delay in achieving unification and industrial modernization in Germany and Italy, resulted in the existence of a set of latecomers who found the world market already carved up. Those who industrialized late not only did so under 'forced-draught' and authoritarian auspices, but came into conflict with the established world Powers. The struggle to redivide the world was to take two world wars, and was to result in fascism in Germany and Italy. This latecoming was, in Germany's case, advantageous, since that country modernized its industries on the basis of centralized financial institutions and advanced technology, while Britain was working with a legacy of comparatively small-scale industrial enterprises (Hobsbawm, 1969).

In Russia rapid capitalist economic growth, late in the nineteenth century, in a country still ruled under ancient autocratic institutions, was broken by a communist revolution. Given such conditions of backwardness, modernization became a State-imposed process, profoundly modifying socialist ideals in a way that had great consequences for the rest of the world, firstly because this vast country exported its revolutionary ideas and practices, and secondly because it eventually succeeded in becoming the world's second most powerful nation, and thereby a model for others seeking rapid industrialization.

In Asia the only country which successfully accomplished a purely capitalist modernization was Japan. The reason lay in the conditions of Japanese society before the Meiji Restoration of 1868, for until then Japan was the only major society outside Europe where the word 'feudal' can be accurately used to describe its institutions (Anderson, 1974b). Furthermore, Japan was never brought under Western colonial control, and therefore never 'underdeveloped' by the West.

The modernization of the other great East Asian Power – China – on the other hand was impeded by her lengthy subjection to several European colonialisms. Her pre-capitalist heritage of a strongly centralized society is again reflected in the contemporary structure of China, now unified once more under a strong Communist Party, which historians tend to view as the modern equivalent of the imperial Civil Service or 'mandarinate', with Marxism as a State ideology analagous to Confucianism. But contemporary China is more the product of Marxist ideas about 'democratic centralism' and the unifying effect of decades of highly-organized military struggle. The history of China, then, includes the colonial and Marxist legacy as well as the Confucian, and the Great Proletarian Revolution of 1965–7 cannot be understood without reference to the profound influence of the U.S.S.R. on Chinese communism, and the eventual reaction against the Soviet model.

Any modern society, then, has to be located within a world system of political and economic relations, and its historical legacy, both of external and internal relations, continues to influence the pattern of its development.

Theories of Development

All these transformations altered not just institutions and economies, but also conceptions of the world, even of the human personality. It was no longer possible so easily to accept the belief that society was the outcome of an unchanging 'human nature'. Too much had changed for that. The notion that human institutions were somehow ordained by God also took a severe blow as kingdoms and established religious orthodoxies crumbled and new kinds of polity and ideology emerged. Looking backward into history, to the Greeks, Romans and Persians, and also at the newly discovered variety of humankind reported by explorers, the European thinkers of the eighteenth-century Enlightenment had concluded that change, even radical change, was not only normal, but followed definite laws – a concept they took from the sciences of Nature, where Newton's exposition of the laws of mechanics and optics provided the model for the scientific study, now, of human society. With Darwin's later demonstration that even Nature had a history, that older forms (species) had died out and new ones had emerged, the triumph of science seemed complete. We had only similarly to apply our minds to social arrangements and Reason would show us not only how to make sense of the social world, but also to predict what would happen in the future. And that knowledge would further give us the power to intervene in and direct events – to create new and better social institutions. Man could control his own destiny.

This optimism was reflected in the widely influential 'positivism' of Auguste Comte, and, in Britain, in Herbert Spencer's equally popular social evolutionism. Things were not only changing, they thought, but changing for the better: in a word, progress. Though social theorists constructed different evolutionary schemes, all agreed that human society, like natural species, had evolved through a number of stages, and that we were now on the edge of something like perfectibility. As to what this new society would look like, however, or the causes of social development, there was no agreement at all. For the conservative Comte, a corps of intellectual priest-like rulers were to guide us into a new era of 'rational' capitalism. For Marx, age-old class society was about to experience revolutionary demolition and the transition to an era of classless communist society.

This variety of interpretations has been characteristic of sociology from its earliest days. The French Revolution produced the counter-reaction of the post-Revolution. To German thinkers, the British Industrial Revolution seemed the acme of heartless reduction of humanity to Economic Man (they called it 'Manchestertum'). Socialism emerged as a new dread for some and a hope for many more. Confidence in human capacity to develop and innovate was often qualified by the belief that such capacity was only given to a few. Hence sociology emerged profoundly concerned with the problem of order, in one form or another; how to preserve the existing social system, how to scientifically improve it, or how to replace it with new forms of organization and relationships. By breaking up 'political economy', until then a unitary 'science of society', into separate disciplines – economics, political science, sociology, psychology – economic and political structures could be 'left out' of sociological analysis, and taken simply as 'given'. Hence, where Comte's mentor, Saint-Simon, had been attracted to socialism, Comte took the capitalist economy as a 'given', and sought only its rationalization. In the same line of intellectual descent, Durkheim was to call for 'vertical' joint organizations of both employers and workers in each industry, to counteract the 'pathological' separation of interests which otherwise gave rise to 'horizontal' conflicts of classes.

European thinkers, impressed by the evidence of the conquest of the entire world by the advanced capitalist industrial States, often assumed that not only their society, but the 'archaic' cultures and societies of the rest of the world would inexorably disappear and be replaced by rational European institutions and ways of thinking – not only incorporation into a global capitalism, but also the eclipse of non-Western culture in all its aspects. Macaulay asserted that 'a single shelf of a good European library was worth the whole native literature of India and Africa'.

Revolutionaries, too, saw that the capitalist world economy and its technology was transforming the East:

England has to fulfil a double mission in India: one destructive, the other regenerating – the annihilation of old Asiatic society, and the laying of the material foundations of Western society in Asia (Marx and Engels, 1975, p. 386).

This was no 'purely economic' impact, then. Political institutions, attitudes towards authority, forms of the family, religious practices and beliefs – all of these would inevitably be affected by changes in the mode of production.

But the transformation capitalism wrought in the colonies and ex-colonies did not turn India or Peru into new capitalist industrial countries. Instead, their development occurred in a special way, as appendages of the metropolitan countries.

Moreover, the cultures of these societies simply failed to disappear. Marx and Engels had noted that the sequence of development, and the kinds of societies known in the East, had not been the same as in European history. Feudalism, notably, had not existed. Hence, future paths of development and forms of society might differ, too.

In Europe's own history, economic transformation had not occurred by itself, but involved changes in the whole social system. In particular, the rise of capitalism had been accompanied by the rise of Protestantism.

They suggested one aspect of that link: that the rising bourgeoisie, in its struggle against the entrenched feudal land-owning classes, necessarily developed an outlook on life which expressed quite different values from those enshrined in Catholicism, the dominant ideology of the medieval European world. Beyond suggestions, however, they did not proceed very far towards analysing what the essential differences were in the content of Protestant and Catholic belief respectively, or how these differences fed into worldly behaviour.

Max Weber, always influenced in his thinking by a usually unspoken 'debate with the ghost of Marx', noted that recent empirical research in Germany had demonstrated the striking continuity of this relationship between Protestantism and capitalism right through into his own day.

There must, then, he believed, be some special 'affinity' between Protestantism as a body of ideas and the requirements of modern capitalism. There was nothing, however, in much of the content of Protestant theology – about beliefs in consubstantiation as against transubstantiation, about saints, miracles, or conceptions of the beginning and the end of the world, or the nature of the afterlife – that made it all that fundamentally different from Catholicism, or either more or less relevant as a source of behaviour which might make for success in capitalist enterprises: little connection between these ideas and the world of looms, steam power and stocks and shares. But capitalism did call for particular kinds of attitudes and related behaviour – notably, orientations towards saving and accumulation on the one hand, and orientations towards work on the other. The 'spirit of capitalism' fitted well with certain key *ethical* values in Protestant *religious* doctrine, which – although they did derive from quite religious preoccupations with Man's relationship to God – were nevertheless particularly compatible with values needed for success as a capitalist.

Certain varieties of Protestantism contained this 'ethic' in its purest form; they also required of the believer not only that he believe, but that he act in accordance with that belief. Calvinism, in particular, insisted that people were individually accountable to God for what they did on earth, and could not shrug that responsibility off onto others. Hence, they were preoccupied not solely with the afterlife, but with right living in this life as a basic duty and condition of salvation in the next world. This produced attitudes towards work favourable to the effective running of capitalist enterprise. Calvinists were also accountable to their congregations, which made sure they led proper lives.

Deviation from this austere code was inhibited because of the hold the beliefs themselves had over men's minds, and by virtue of the social control that was exercised by others to ensure that they did not backslide. The 'Protestant Ethic' also converged with the 'spirit of capitalism' in that the less fortunately placed were also induced to accept their predestined lot – and to work hard at their 'calling'.

The rapid growth of capitalism, then, could not be attributed solely to scientific discoveries or to new machines. These, in any case, were the outcome of new modes of thought. So though Weber accepted fully Marx's emphasis upon the importance of the division of labour, and particularly the appropriation of the product, not by the producer, but by the owner of the means of production, as well as Marx's belief that these relationships gave rise to social institutions and to quite abstract ideas – e.g., concepts such as the notion of the individual person or notions of natural law – Weber insisted that such ideas had their own roots, independently of economic developments, even if they were connected to the latter. Ideas, for him, were more autonomous than Marx had allowed, and were not simply caused by economic forces. Indeed, they could profoundly affect practical social behaviour, including the economy.

Since Protestantism is scarcely important as a modernizing ideology in the modern world, this debate might seem archaic. Yet, in modified form, it still lies at the heart of contemporary arguments about development. How far, for instance, is development simply or primarily a matter of technology or of economic organization? Can it be stimulated by changing people's attitudes or ideologies? Are Marxist theory and communist parties latter-day equivalents of Protestantism and the Protestant sects? Do certain kinds of technology have built into them consequences for the way people come to think and behave both at work and outside it? Or does the existence of different development ideologies lead to different ways of organizing the economy and distributing its products?

In the twentieth century capitalist development is no longer the sole mode of development. Capitalist development has certainly occurred in formerly backward agrarian and dependent countries: Brazil, for instance, produces $6\frac{1}{2}$ million tons of steel a year. But with the major exception of Japan, which was never incorporated into any Western colonial empire, the countries which have most dramatically made the leap from agrarian backwardness to industrial society – notably the U.S.S.R. – have done so under the theoretical and practical aegis of Marxism. Those remaining least developed are predominantly part of the capitalist world.

Hence Marxism has become the major alternative development ideology of the twentieth century, especially attractive to backward countries like Russia, China, Cuba, North Korea and now Viet Nam. And even though the U.S.A. still produces about a third of the capitalist world's production and consumes a very large part of the raw materials produced in the whole world, the new economic crisis in the West, the experience of two world wars and of defeat in Viet Nam, plus the continuing poverty of the capitalist Third World, have eroded confidence in the inevitability of capitalist progress.

Development, moreover, is not to be measured solely in terms of how much steel is produced or how many TV sets per head, for much depends on how that production is achieved, how the product is distributed, and what it is used for – what kinds of relations are fostered between people and the kind of society and culture generated. Infinite consumption is not the only value. Moreover, as under-developed countries begin to industrialize, and to cater for an internal consumer market, inequalities of income increase, and the incomes of the bottom 25 per cent of the population are many times smaller than those of the top 25 per cent.

Increased production is one way of meeting unsatisfied demand; redistribution of wealth another. A further alternative is to limit wants. In a world where, even in 'wealthy' countries, few own more than a house and a car, and most not even that, and where, outside those countries, most people go to bed hungry, the reduction of wants is a philosophy that has appealed more to the privileged, as in the communes of the U.S.A., than to the poor, for whom both increased production and increased income are seen as preconditions for a better life, and the redistribution of existing wealth, too. A return to pre-industrial simplicity, a rejection of worldly consumer materialism and of the consumption of natural resources and destruction of the environment which ever-expanding growth entails, together with hostility towards the centralized corporate institutions of the modern industrial State, and in particular its machinery of force, are typical of the contemporary mood. By contrast, the optimism of Marxism could lead Mao Tse-tung to contemplate even the 'unthinkable' – nuclear war or the less catastrophic evolutionary end of humankind – positively:

There is nothing in the world that does not arise, develop, and disappear. Monkeys turned into men, mankind arose; in the end, the whole human race will disappear, it may turn into something else [and] the earth itself will also cease to exist . . .

When the theologians talk about doomsday they are pessimistic and terrify people. We say the end of mankind is something which will produce something far more advanced than mankind (Schram, 1974, pp. 110, 127).

Despite this kind of confidence in progress, and in communism as the visible future for the whole of humanity, communism has yet to come to power in a single advanced industrial country. The twentieth-century revolutions have not occurred in the most advanced capitalist countries, which Marx predicted. They have occurred in poor, agrarian countries like China, usually as a reaction to Western imperialism.

Communism, like seventeenth-century Protestantism, thus supplies an 'ethic' of modernization which is equally highly 'achievement-oriented'. But it departs from the older belief-system in three crucial respects: (a) it has no 'other-worldly' content; it is a theory based on 'historical materialism'; (b) it is based on a collective and corporated ethic of 'serving the people', rather than on individualism and acquisitiveness; (c) it is strongly egalitarian; (d) institutionally it has developed the 'democratic-centralist' party as the agency of social mobilization: modernization is not left to the individual or the market. Since both in its theory and its practice communist modernization not only differs in kind from capitalist, its very existence puts into question any idea of a unitary process of development, such as the theories of the nineteenth century which, in extreme form, postulated that all societies *had* to go through the same sequence of stages as those the advanced countries had gone through. Since these beliefs have been severely discounted by subsequent history, theorists have been led to query the notion of 'inevitability'. In the inter-war period anthropologists, indeed, turned their backs on the whole question of evolution, emphasizing the functioning of social systems, abstracted from any wider social context, such as colonialism (Asad, 1975), and conceived of as being in 'equilibrium'. The revival of interest in social change, including revolutionary as well as evolutionary changes, naturally accompanied the sometimes smooth, sometimes violent ending of colonial rule. It also led to a new emphasis on co-operation, emancipation and revolution, and the role of the under-privileged (Wertheim, 1974, especially chapters 1 and 2).

Unilineal theory was faced by a crisis, too, because of the increasing evidence of effective alternatives to capitalist development, and also the increasing evidence of *failure* to develop in the colonial world. One response to this crisis was simply to emphasize the peculiarity of each country's pattern of development or non-development, and – following Weber – that political institutions, legal codes, religions, etc., were not simply functions of the economy or technology, but each had its independent existence and contribution to development (Bendix, 1969).

More simplistic schemes of a refurbished evolutionist kind, however, proved more popular. Perhaps the most influential development theorist of the 1950s was W. W. Rostow, who postulated a unitary series of 'stages of economic growth' which all countries, communist or capitalist, would go through: firstly, a 'traditional' stage; then a stage in which the 'preconditions' of modernization were established (from financial and educational institutions to infra-structures of communications, etc.). In stage three, the 'take-off' to modernization begins; in stage four, the 'drive to maturity'; and in stage five, the epoch of 'high mass consumption' (Rostow, 1960).

Debates about how to achieve this take-off sometimes assume that what is needed is some purely technical input. Engineers believe in improved roads and railways as stimuli to the production of cash crops, or the provision of power supplies, or the importing of machinery. Biologists advocate new strains of seeds.

But they usually recognize that social changes are needed, too. Economists usually emphasize capital accumulation, or a free labour market, while psychologists insist on the necessity of inculcating a 'modernizing attitude', some contemporary equivalent of the 'Protestant Ethic' – notably David McClelland's advocacy of 'achievement-orientation' (McClelland, 1961). Educationalists insist that a vast expansion of schools is necessary to bring this about and to provide the necessary cognitive knowledge of the modern world.

Despite the variety of these specialist pleadings, certain common assumptions run through all of them.

(a) That no fundamental structural changes in the social distribution of power and resources need be involved.

(b) That those in power will endorse the changes envisaged.

(c) That they can primarily be planned and carried through by wise and benevolent experts acting from above.

(d) That the changes will benefit the mass of the population.

(e) That the models for growth are those of the advanced capitalist world (usually the U.S.A.).

(f) That the means of 'modernizing', from tractors to ideas, also have to come – as 'aid' or via 'diffusion' – from the advanced countries.

For Rostow communism was a 'disease of transition'. Specifically *communist* institutions, policies and ideas would disappear as the U.S.S.R. moved into the era of high mass consumption. But these aspects of communism obstinately refused to disappear. A more sophisticated idea was the notion – in what came to be known as 'convergence theory' – that capitalism and communism were *both* 'transitional' phenomena, which, with full development, would disappear. In a truly developed society the State would play a key role (as it already does, even in capitalist societies). The new society would be shaped by the requirements of modern industrialism, and would develop a class system based, not on private property, but on the recruitment of the most competent, via 'meritocratic' open competition for entry into mass higher education, and thence to membership of a new managerial élite controlling both the economy and the State. By this stage, the older justifications of class and sectional interest (the ideologies of Business and Labour) would have become irrelevant in a world of abundance for all, and would therefore lose their appeal. Much as Comte conceived of the beginning of 'the positive' era in his day, some sociologists thought that in our time we would witness what Daniel Bell called 'the end of ideology'. For most of them, the pattern of the future was the U.S.A. There, Lipset claimed, the conditions for the disappearance of 'ideology' already existed:

democracy is not only or even primarily a means through which different groups can attain their ends or seek the good society; it is the good society itself in operation (Lipset, 1960, p. 403).

The backward countries, however, were not developing as unilineal theory envisaged. Not only were they not catching up with the developed world, even where they followed American recipes for growth, but the gap between the advanced and underdeveloped worlds was *increasing*: the underdeveloped countries, it was said, were actually 'underdeveloping'.

In popular consciousness, such failure has often been attributed to 'natural' factors (poor natural resources, too little or too much population) or to inferiority of mental or biological endowment, either racial or individual. Such theories, long discounted in more academic circles since they had been discredited during the period when racism was identified with fascism, began to reappear, e.g., in the psychological writings of Eysenck and Jensen in the sixties (Richardson and Spears, 1972).

The major challenge to the assumption of the necessity of a specifically capitalist mode of development, not surprisingly, came from Marxist writers. In 1957, Baran and Sweezy, in the U.S.A., argued that the reasons for continuing underdevelopment lay not within the underdeveloped countries themselves, but in their weak position within a capitalist world system in which they were dominated by the industrialized Powers who kept them underdeveloped. They would remain so until they broke away from extreme imperialist control and internal capitalism (Baran, 1957). Other sociologists, however, continued looking for causes of underdevelopment *internal* to such countries. Many of them identified the enemy as 'traditionalism'. On the institutional side, this could mean 'feudal' ruling classes, solely interested in maintaining the agrarian social order they dominated, or the Indian caste-system which kept people in the station in which they were born – and thus discouraged mobility and innovation, particularly entrepreneurial innovation. Ideologically, it meant 'other-worldly' religions, which devalued life and activity on this earth as unimportant; or 'irrational' particularisms, old and new: attachment to tribal, ethnic, even nationalistic values instead of an open 'universalism'.

Such growth-models generally retained the nineteenth-century emphasis upon the need for innovation and entrepreneurship. Its critics, however, castigated precisely these aspects as 'possessive individualism' (Macpherson, 1970), competitiveness and aggressiveness, arguing that they undervalued the possibilities of co-operative endeavour and the possibility, too, of mobilizing the latent energies of the mass of ordinary people.

This view questions the assumption that the interests and outlooks of ruling classes and élites, however successfully imposed on or disseminated in society generally, necessarily also promote the interest of those they rule. The latter, too, may not accept the ideas presented to them, not simply because of failures of communication, but because they do not agree with them. They may also produce counter-ideologies, cultures, organizations or movements.

More orthodox sociologies, however, largely derived from the work of Talcott Parsons (see below, pp. 495–502), who took the view that what holds a society together, ultimately, is the extent to which people share in a common set of basic cultural beliefs, a 'value-system'. It was further assumed that the governing élite were the guardians of these 'sacred' values (Shils, 1972; Shils and Young, 1953). The crucial source of social disharmony – and of failure to develop effectively – was the failure to successfully disseminate and keep alive these values. Alternatively, the messages might be misunderstood or misinterpreted by those to whom they were addressed. Basically, that is, the failures were failures of communication, rather than of social control.

Plural Value-Systems or Counter-Cultures?

Critics of this position argued that we cannot assume the existence of a 'common' value-system; that the 'sub-systems' of society are not as tidily interdependent as 'systems theorists' would have us believe (Gouldner, 1970, pp. 210–16); that power is unequally distributed, anyhow; and that society can be seen, instead, as a 'balance' between contending forces, always shifting, in which groups (especially classes) excluded from power and wealth endeavour to alter the balance of forces in their interest. Each contending interest-group has its own set of values which it protects and extends by mobilizing its basic sectional support and its allies.

The ruling class or élite, however, tries to represent and 'sell' its own ideology as the ideology of the whole society. Thus, nationalism is often promulgated in this way by conservative elements: as an 'organic' community of interests shared by everybody, rich and poor alike.

'Plural' value-systems are not the only kinds of ideologies held by separate classes, or corporate groups, however. People may be loosely linked by common beliefs and shared cultures, as in Islam or Hinduism, but without any 'church' structure or hierarchical priesthood to link separate communities together. Members of different classes may also belong to the same church, for instance (even if they interpret doctrine somewhat differently). As Max Weber showed, several ideological systems can coexist, too, as in Imperial China, where Taoism and Buddhism were drawn upon by all classes, in addition to the official orthodoxy, Confucianism. These religions were not mutually exclusive, with different memberships and congregations, but *resources* upon which people drew, in different situations, according to their needs: on Taoist magical practices when they were ill, for example; on Buddhist conceptions when – as in the life-crises of birth, marriage or death – they were faced with handling, intellectually and socially, 'ultimate' problems of the meaning of life and of their place in the world; and on Confucianism as a practical guide to the conduct of everyday social relationships (Weber, 1963). The 'practical' religion used in everyday village life – the 'Little Tradition' – anthropologists have shown, is not the same as the religions of the 'Great Tradition' – Hinduism, Buddhism, Christianity, Islam, etc. The custodians of the Great Tradition are theoretical specialists, usually priests and monks living separately in churches, monasteries, etc., who expound, preach and proselytize, and, above all, intellectually systematize those doctrines. Ordinary believers are less systematic, even quite ignorant, sometimes, of just what the orthodox doctrine is. They also commonly interpret doctrines in their own way, and infuse them with their own social interests, selecting certain features of religious belief and practice for attention (e.g., those relating to the life-stages) and ignoring others. Thus unorthodox, even heretical and illegal, 'secret societies' in China drew upon Buddhist notions of a heavenly after-world and of a Messiah (Maitreya Buddha) as ideas which could even justify peasant rebellions (Chesneaux, 1971), as did their counterparts in Europe and Oceania (Cohn, 1957; Worsley, 1970).

If orthodox beliefs can be interpreted and used in ways those who govern or who formulate and transmit official ideologies never intended – the Italian Marxist, Gramsci, called them 'hegemonic' ideologies – the notion of a 'common' value-system, even in pre-capitalist societies, is thus hard to sustain, or at least (rather than assuming that 'everybody' shares the same outlook) must be taken as an open question, calling for empirical examination of the actual extent to which those who are politically or economically dominant succeed in spreading their ideas and beliefs, or the extent to which their *claim* to represent or to be custodians of 'the' value-system all share can be demonstrated. They may, that is, be more or less successful in these respects. Thus, in Britain, it has been shown that many Christians believe in heaven, but not in hell; in the U.S.S.R. 'dialectical materialism' is a compulsory subject in schools and colleges, like 'Religious Instruction' in Britain, endured as a chore rather than believed in. Deviance and dissent, or what Wertheim terms 'counterpoint' values (Wertheim, 1974, pp. 105–17), often have to be disguised or expressed lightheartedly – from graffiti to jokes about the high and the mighty.

The maintenance of ideological conformity is thus not solely a question of the inherent plausibility of the ideas alone, but of power: the capacity to control resources, including not just jobs and prisons, but also communications. In the case of Imperial China, for instance, the civil servants ('mandarins') strictly controlled the land-owning gentry, even though they themselves came predominantly from their ranks via open examinations, much as our own Civil Service recruits by examination, again disproportionately, from the upper and middle classes. They equally prevented owners of industrial enterprises from becoming too powerful as a class. The State therefore ran many key workshops itself. Hence, a vigorous independent bourgeoisie did not develop, and Confucian orthodoxy was never challenged by any equivalent of the 'Protestant Ethic'.

But when millions of Chinese emigrated to South East Asia, and were removed from the controls both of the State and the family, they threw up capitalist entrepreneurs *par excellence*, as contemporary Hong Kong and Singapore bear witness (Goldthorpe, J. E., 1975, pp. 228–37). Thus the failure of capitalism to develop in China was not due to something inherent in an unsuitable value-system alone, important as that was, but to the power of a dominant class to *im-*

pose its ideology of obedience and conformity upon others, in large part via the family, in the interest of preserving the existing social order, and to repress other ways of thought and behaviour. In analysing why some societies change and others do not, then (and why if they do they do so in particular directions), we have to take into account the political power to control ideas, and the material *interests* at stake, not just intellectual 'values' (which are often simply rationalizations or justifications of vested interests).

Both unilineal and convergence theories generated a growing volume of criticism, which culminated in A. Gunder Frank's attack on the 'functionalist' theories which underlay them (Frank, 1969). Firstly, he criticized the whole notion of 'stages of growth' on empirical grounds: had, for example, the 'traditional' stage ever existed in the form Rostow assumed? The label 'traditional', he argued, 'denies all history to the underdeveloped countries', or any significant differences in their history. Some, like India, had possessed flourishing industries (which the European colonizers destroyed): other areas (North and South America, the Caribbean) were unpopulated or underpopulated, or had had their populations exterminated. Hence failure to modernize could scarcely be blamed upon some common 'traditionalism'. Rather, it was colonialism that had been the common causal factor holding back the development of the rest of the world in the interests of the advanced capitalist Powers.

At a more theoretical level, he argued, 'achievement-orientation' was as prevalent in tribal societies as in the U.S.A.; conversely, values assumed in functionalist theory to be typical only of pre-capitalist societies (such as 'particularism', e.g., favouring kin in economic transactions, say, rather than non-kin, even though the latter may possibly be more efficient or offer better terms) were just as typical of the practices of directors of giant corporations. In any case, he argued, it is not 'roles-in-general' that are crucial in society, but the roles of those who govern.

Most fundamentally, Frank argued, we could no longer talk of 'societies' as discrete entities, anyhow. Modern imperialism had unified the entire world, in the interests of capitalism, and today still dominated the colonial and ex-colonial countries. International capitalism was the cause of underdevelopment, not traditionalism. It caused underdevelopment to develop: underdevelopment did not just happen, but was made to happen and kept that way.

Marxist writers like Frank took their point of departure from Lenin's *Imperialism*, written in 1916. There, Lenin had noted that the early capitalist countries had had no particular 'lead' over the rest of the world, in the mercantilist era, until 'machinofacture' had revolutionized production in the capitalist metropoles. Then, capital had become more and more concentrated and centralized in fewer and fewer firms, as the weaker ones were swallowed up or went to the wall. By the late nineteenth century, finance-capital (the banks) had come to merge with, then dominate, the capitalism of industrial entrepreneurs and factory owners. As the 'organic composition' of the capital invested in industry had shifted from capital primarily needed to pay the wages of labour to capital invested in machinery, the rate of profit had diminished. Less labour was needed, and unemployment, even starvation, ensued.

Capitalism, he argued, following Marx, always sought to push the workers' wages down to the minimum. The impoverished masses could not absorb the ever-growing output of industry, as consumers, so that periodic crises of over-production resulted. Hence the opening-up of new outlets for investment abroad became vital because there, not just profits, but 'super-profits' could be made, since colonial political controls kept down the cost of labour, and therefore of raw materials, by force; new markets for Western goods could also be developed. Imperialism was thus a product of 'late' capitalism, the expression of its inability to resolve its problems at home, and the source of new conflicts abroad.

Capital invested in colonial countries was thus not a 'market' capitalism, in which commodities found their own price, including labour. In the colonies, settlers, feudal lords and chiefs, mine-owners, banks and investors were specially assisted by the State. Prices were fixed to help them, and labour-costs kept very low. This, then, was a politically-induced and enforced capitalist growth, different in kind from the earlier 'classical', *laissez-faire* capitalism of the British Industrial Revolution (Hobsbawm, 1969).

From the beginning, too, colonial capitalism differed from that of the metropoles in that it was developed in the interests of the latter. It was not an independent growth. Finally, Lenin argues, so great were the super-profits that a skilful bourgeoisie could use a part of them to 'buy off' a section of the working class in the metropolitan countries – the skilled craft workers, foremen, etc. – who now became a new 'aristocracy of labour'.

Here, then, was a theory of *world* development, but of *unequal* development. Lenin also acknowledged the possibility that the specially-oppressed peoples of the colonial world might revolt in a way which might decide the future of capitalism everywhere – rather than the earlier Marxist assumption that the proletariat of the advanced capitalist countries would be the bringers of revolution to the world. The view that capitalism would bring about the industrialization of the colonies, just as it had done in Europe, was soon falsified by events. Rather, capitalism was seen as holding back their growth. Other Marxists, however, continued to expect an indigenous capitalism to develop which would come into conflict with imperialist capitalism. Indigenous capitalism was, they believed, 'progressive': it would bring about the expansion of the productive forces of society; it would bring into existence a new class – the proletariat – which would eventually overthrow capitalism; and it would create also an indigenous capitalist class which would come into conflict with foreign capital. This class would be also 'progressive' (and should be supported, therefore, by the working class) because it would likewise oppose 'feudalism' (i.e., the land-owning classes).

But indigenous capitalism failed to grow, since it was essentially a 'comprador' bourgeoisie, dependent upon importing manufactured goods from Europe and exporting raw materials. By the 1960s Frantz Fanon could scornfully dismiss the new bourgeoisies of the independent African countries as 'good for nothing'. They might have total *political* power, but the economy remained in foreign (capitalist) hands; they would never transform the economy therefore, as European bourgeoisies had done (Fanon, 1967).

These 'dependent' capitalists were at the mercy of those in the metropoles who set low prices for raw materials and high prices for manufactured goods. These inequalities for exchange, however, reflected the more basic underdevelopment of *production* in the ex-colonies, particularly modern industry. So powerful was foreign capital that it had also completely transformed colonial and ex-colonial agriculture by establishing large-scale capitalist production-units (plantations) and turning peasants into producers of cash crops for the world market. 'Feudalism' (usually loosely used as virtually interchangeable with 'pre-capitalist', or even 'agrarian' – like the term 'traditional') no longer existed. It had become penetrated by and incorporated into a single global system of production for a world market. The nation-states of the West and their empires, the kingdoms, tribes and empires of the rest of the world, had begun to merge together to form a new global political economy as early as the sixteenth century. Hence the 'society' was no longer the widest unit of analysis – the 'whole' – but the world (Frank, 1967). A more extreme version of the notion of the world as a 'total' world-system was developed later by Wallerstein, who argues that countries are simply either 'core', 'peripheral', or 'semi-peripheral' components of this system (Wallerstein, 1974).

Such theorists have been accused, however, of exaggerating the degree of integration achieved by capitalism, since by concentrating on the world *market* (a system of *exchange* rather than of production) they arbitrarily dismiss the fact that the commodities which arrive on the world market for sale are not necessarily produced by capitalist enterprises (plantations, factories, mines, etc.), using wage labour (Laclau, 1971). Peasant small-holders selling a part of their crop; surpluses extracted as tribute, in kind or in the form of labour; taxes paid to the State rather than to a lord or chief; all these and other pre-capitalist ways of extracting a surplus from the producer do become sources of commodities and of profit on the capitalist market. The worker-and-employer relationship is by no means the only one within the capitalist world system. Such persisting pre-capitalist production-systems, too, have been sources of resistance to the domination of capital, whether on the part of independent peasants or of village communities sharing land or practising mutual aid, to 'feudal' *hacienda*-owners running virtually independent private empires based on serf labour and in rivalry both with urban capitalists for control of the State (and especially control over export policy) as well as with foreign capital.

Against this view, capitalism was said to have penetrated into every village and family, or that if it had not yet, the process would soon, and inexorably, be completed; that 'feudalism' no longer existed; and that indigenous capitalism was incapable of independent growth. The only forces which would fight imperialism, then, were the working class, the exploited small peasants and their dispossessed landless cousins. Others argued that the urban working class was too small or too well-off, to become militant.

Such models have been criticized as being 'over-integrated' in a second sense. Societies are neither permanent, nor internally homogeneous or unitary. Rather, they are made up of assemblages of different modes of production, articulated together via the market or the State, or both. Thus, in inter-war Peru, one found small-holder peasant agriculture, village communities holding land in common but worked by separate families, capitalist plantations, 'feudal' *haciendas*, and capitalist industry, all within the same economy. To emphasize this historical process and variety, Marxists began talking about 'social formations' rather than 'societies'.

Orthodox historiography had usually assumed the nation-state to be the key modern unit of analysis. Now Marxist writers were, on the one hand, 'decomposing' societies into constituent modes of production, and on the other treating societies simply as components of a world 'totality'.

A very different kind of Marxist analysis is represented by Anderson's study of the emergence of European capitalism. For him, this was not simply a story of the universal triumph of a single economic system, but of a complex growth, out of feudalism, of institutions which had accompanied these economic changes. The linking-together of the constituent modes of production within any given 'social formation' was never achieved by the market alone. The growth of the Absolutist state, as in Henry VIII's England, had thus been vital to this process.

Furthermore, though capitalism eventually triumphed throughout Europe, the process was never identical for any two countries and occurred at different points in time, because each inherited different institutions from the past, and hence capitalist *society* developed in significantly different ways, at different rates. (Thus Russian absolutism lasted until the twentieth century.)

Feudalism in England, too, had been much more centralized than in other countries, due to the Norman Conquest. More usually, sovereignty, under feudalism, was 'parcelled' out amongst a variety of feudal lords, with no very strong or simple hierarchy of authority, and therefore with a weak kingship.

Finally, other institutions, notably the Roman law and the Catholic Church, which cut *across* societal boundaries, were crucial in the growth of modern capitalism (Anderson, 1974a and 1974b).

Another Marxist writer, Samir Amin, rejects the idea of a 'mode of production' as some kind of building-block used in the formation of particular societies, and continuing, unchanged, alongside other, quite separate, modes of production. Rather, he sees the main modes of production – primitive, tribute-paying (including feudal); slave; simple commodity-production; and capitalist – as each, in turn, dominating other, subsidiary modes and whole epochs. In the modern era, capitalism has dominated all others, and hence capital accumulated from the entire globe has been concentrated in the advanced metropoles. The peripheral countries, locked into the economy of the advanced world, only do 20 per cent of their trade with each other. Conversely, the advanced countries do 80 per cent of their trade between themselves. The exports of the periphery, moreover, mainly come from capitalist enterprises in those countries, particularly multinational corporations: 40 per cent are oil and crude minerals; another 40 per cent agricultural products, half of which come from plantations. The rest of the economy – the subsidiary modes of production which employ most people – is stunted in its growth. Hence underemployment, poverty, static levels of production and productivity, and flight to the towns ensue. Underdeveloped countries, then, though formally independent, and no matter how authoritarian their governments, are at the mercy of those who control world markets and prices, and cannot effectively control their own destinies (Amin, 1974).

Frank's model had little to say about the persistence of pre-capitalist modes of production, so preoccupied was it in demonstrating that we have had 'one world economic and social system for half a millennium'. It equally had no clear place for the emergence of new *non*-capitalist countries, notably the Second communist world, or for the relationship between that world and the First world. Wallerstein did take the socialist countries into account, treating them, however, simply as part of a still-dominantly capitalist world market. For him, 'socialism in one country' was, as for Trotsky, simply a contradiction in terms. Socialism could only flourish when it dominated the world-totality.

In similar vein, Amin sees the socialism of the communist countries, though different from and superior to capitalism, as essentially transitional and therefore inevitably distorted, both because it has arisen in backward countries which have had to mobilize to develop, and because their survival, economically, politically and militarily, is always threatened by the still-dominant capitalist world. Socialism could only begin to flourish without 'deformations', such Marxists argue, when an international system of co-operating socialist states has become world-wide, or at least predominant.

How Many Worlds?

The model of the three 'worlds': the world of advanced capitalism; the communist* 'Second' World of the U.S.S.R., Eastern Europe, China, North Korea, Cuba and North Viet Nam (and later all Viet Nam), and the 'Third' World of the underdeveloped capitalist countries, became commonly accepted after the Second World War. It was used, for instance, by the United Nations, which grouped countries into 'economically-developed private enterprise economies', 'centrally-planned economies', and 'primary-producing countries'. Similar models became widely used by agencies as different as the C.I.A., on the one hand, and 'aid' lobbies or groups working for the elimination of world poverty, on the other. They might appear, therefore, to be 'neutral', unproblematic categories devoid of ideological assumptions. In fact, they are none of these things, nor are the three worlds conceived of in an identical fashion.

In what we may call the 'ideological' version, communism is assumed to be a unitary phenomenon: Communism with a capital C. This assumption is scarcely tenable, however, in a world where the two principal communisms, those of the U.S.S.R. and of China, are in bitter conflict, or when the once undisputed leadership of the U.S.S.R. has given way to 'polycentric' tendencies, even in Eastern

---

*The countries we label 'communist', of course, call themselves 'socialist', since communism is seen by them as an advanced stage of abundance and freedom – involving the ending of class society – which they have not yet reached.

Europe, and in Western Europe has led to the abandonment of such sacred Marxist principles as the 'dictatorship of the proletariat'. This model, it should be noted, is not strictly a *development* model at all; it is an ideological/political one which *ignores* differences in levels of development as between the backward agrarian communisms (Cuba, Viet Nam) and the industrialized/industrializing ones (and the success of formerly backward agrarian communist countries in industrializing). On the other hand, the model does revert to *developmental* differences when it treats the Third World as different in kind from the First – even though both are capitalist – because of the low levels of development obtaining in the Third World.

In the 1950s and 1960s Third World governments, from 'modernizing autocracies' to 'populist' régimes (Ionescu and Gellner, 1969) rejected the categorization of themselves as simply peripheral capitalist countries, and either saw or presented themselves as economically different from either communism or capitalism, even as a third 'way of life' (usually some kind of 'national' socialism). Such a claim has been rejected, e.g., in Jenkins's sarcastic description of the Third World as 'owned, run and underdeveloped by the imperialistic nations' (Jenkins, 1970, p. 18), and has also been heard much less often since the 1960s, as most Third World countries have become more explicitly and visibly capitalist, particularly with the spread of military and other forms of authoritarian rule in the face of rising radicalism and revolution.

The second major version of the notion of three worlds takes levels of development of the productive system as the crucial differentiating criterion, and relegates ideology/social system differences to subsidiary status. In this version, the advanced industrial countries – *whether capitalist or communist* – (the U.S.A., U.S.S.R., Japan, E.E.C. countries, Australia, South Africa) become the First World. The Third World is the *poor* world (both capitalist and communist poor (Goldthorpe, J. E., 1975, p. 1) and the Second World, those countries *en route* to industrialization (e.g., Hungary, Brazil). The *very* poorest countries were sometimes called the 'Fourth' World, or the 'Third World of the Third World'.

The Chinese model of the world pushes this version to its logical conclusion: the two Superpowers alone make up the First World. All other capitalist countries and Eastern Europe fall into the Second-world level of development (Jen, 1974). The model is not simply a technical one, however: it assumes common interests, as against imperialism (U.S. or Soviet version), shared by all underdeveloped countries. This is the 'principal contradiction', and it considers the differences between the 'revisionist' communism and Western-style capitalism to be of secondary importance. Rather, they are 'convergent', because revisionist communism leads to the revival of class society – the 'capitalist road', as the Chinese call it. Other theories than the Chinese also treat communist societies – *including* China in their model – as neither truly socialist or communist at all, but as some kind of intermediate or 'late' form of capitalism (e.g., 'state capitalism'), or as 'deformed' communism ruled by a 'New Class' (Djilas, 1957; Trotsky, 1974). Finally China, as a poor country, locates herself firmly within the Third World; with her primary commitment, therefore, to other poor countries, nations and peoples.

In the 1950s the direct economic legacy of colonialism was so recent that the capitalist world was seen as unquestionably divided into advanced and backward segments, at least in terms of levels of economic development. Communism, too, was identified then with backward, agrarian societies, the major exception, the U.S.S.R., having suffered severely from the war.

Yet the newly independent countries did not develop along Western lines. Instead, they remained economically backward, to such an extent that many believed the gap between them and the advanced countries to be increasing. Politically, one-party states, military régimes and the like displaced Western-style parliamentary constitutions, a process interpreted by those who took the presence of these institutions to be the touchstone of advanced culture as evidence of societal immaturity – in Finer's phrase, 'low political culture' (Finer, 1962). This immaturity was conceived of either as a legacy of traditionalism, or the consequence of colonialism which had prevented the free expression of interests, and the development of experience in governing, by concentrating power in the hands of all-powerful foreign élites.

Radicals, on the other hand, saw these developments as evidence of the irrelevance, for the underdeveloped countries, of bourgeois parliamentarianism. The pattern followed in the West could not be imitated, they argued, since these Powers had conquered the globe and now prevented similar growth in new States. Since poor countries could never accumulate capital, the mobilization of the masses politically and economically was the only alternative social resource. Right-wing theorists, however, resisted any intrusion of these masses into decision-making.

All these models can be subsumed within one 'meta-model' based on two criteria; level of development, and type of social ideology. It allows for the existence, therefore, of poor agrarian communisms as well as rich, industrialized/industrializing ones, and also of developed and underdeveloped capitalist societies.

	Developed	Underdeveloped
Communist	U.S.S.R. .... Eastern Europe	China, Viet Nam, Cuba, N. Korea
Capitalist	U.S.A. .... E.E.C., Japan, Australia, S. Africa	capitalist 'Third World'

'Ideological' models read *across* these rows, treating all communisms and capitalist societies as falling into two great, opposed 'camps'. 'Technical' models read *downwards*. The Chinese model requires the separating of the Superpowers – above the dotted lines – from the 'intermediate' developed countries below the lines.

This reflects real shifts in the world balance of forces, politically, and the emergence of a 'semi-developed' group of countries, which, some suggest, has now grown so large, with so many countries scattered along a *continuum* of development rather than grouped into quite sharply marked-off polar categories, that perhaps the majority of countries will soon become 'intermediate'. In other words, development is taking place, they claim, even in the Third World.

The rise of multinational corporations, on the other hand, has been seen as further consolidation of the domination of the world by the advanced capitalisms. The burden of debt accumulated by those countries which have borrowed finance under 'aid' programmes, too, has been taken as a new imperialist device to keep poor countries poor. Yet the multinationals have increasingly retained a rising proportion of their profits within the underdeveloped countries, sometimes willy-nilly, as when nationalistic governments, notably oil-producing countries, have either taken a greater share in direct ownership or have wholly nationalized the corporations' subsidiaries operating on their territory, or raised oil prices, or the level of taxes. By so doing, they have diverted a huge flow of capital away from the West, and created a critical situation for the economy of the First World, both economically and politically.

One consequence has been the stepping-up of growth in manufacturing. The proportion of gross domestic product contributed by manufacturing in the underdeveloped world was already over one half of that in the developed world (Warren, 1973). In countries like Mexico, South Korea or Thailand, 16·7 per cent, 9·5 per cent and 13·2 per cent respectively of the total active population were working in manufacturing industries by the 1970s, in industries producing mainly for the home market, not for export, and including chemicals and basic metals as well as light consumer goods. In almost every Latin American country, manufacturing now makes a greater contribution to gross domestic product than does agriculture.

Some growth, then, is taking place in a few Third World countries. The gap, for most, remains enormous: most of Africa, for instance, has a GNP of less than $100(U.S.) per head per year, and the three most populous countries of the Third World – India, Indonesia and Pakistan – had $89, $129 and $104 respectively, in 1969 compared to $3,694 in Sweden and $4,664 in the U.S.A. 80 per cent of the exports of the Third World are still raw materials, foodstuffs and fuels; half the 'manufacturing' is craft production on the part of a man and his family. Nor is the growth of manufacturing the only index of development. U.S. agriculture is the most productive in the world, and the major U.S. export is not steel, electronics or even armaments, but food. The majority of the world's people, conversely, are underproductive, poor, peasants. Finally, it is only a privileged élite which benefits from what growth there is: 5 per cent of the Brazilian population receive nearly 40 per cent of personal income (Emmanuel, 1974, McMichael, Petras and Rhodes, 1974).

Much of this growth takes place under the aegis of the State, usually in agreements with foreign corporations. Profits still flow out, often, now, in the form of payments for patent rights, management expertise, etc., or in payment (at high prices) to parent companies back home for goods and materials used by their local subsidiaries ('transfer pricing').

The State, then, plays a key role in this kind of development, despite the absence of a capitalist class of the kind that had constructed capitalism in the West (Alavi, 1972). Those who control the State constitute a new kind of bourgeoisie, with high living standards patterned on those of the expatriate officials they had replaced, made possible because of the opportunities for investment offered them by the State and by foreign corporations (Leys, 1975).

These new models, then, recognize the existence of growth, however limited or distorted, as a few at least of the formerly underdeveloped countries move from 'Third' to 'Second' levels in the capitalist world, and as development proceeds apace in both agriculture and industry in the communist countries.

Models of growth can never, of course, be purely intellectual classifications (taxonomies), for although some seek 'growth-in-itself' and eschew any kind of ideology, the kind of social arrangements that accompany economic growth – patterns of class, political institutions, educational and family systems – and, most basically, who gets what, depend upon the development strategies chosen by those who control the levers of power, and by those who try to influence them.

Growth models are therefore usually also 'models' in the sense that they have values built into them; ideals and anti-ideals: recipes, formulas, and strategies for building the kind of society which one sees as good, and not just any kind of development. Striking examples of each are held up to be imitated or shunned.

The U.S.A., in this sense, was the dominant value-model in the development sociology of the West in the 1950s and 1960s, and remains very influential. But the influence of Marxist theory has increased as communist countries have successfully demonstrated the possibility of alternative growth-models (Foster-Carter, 1974). Yet most Marxist theorists have examined the history of Soviet development critically, trying to analyse what went wrong in a strategy for industrial growth that cost so many millions of lives, particularly during the forced collectivization of the peasantry. In the process, too, many believe, the ideals of socialism withered. The Soviet model has its appeal, however, to non-Marxists who consider that capitalist development is impossible in countries without capital accumulation, without a modernizing entrepreneurial bourgeoisie, and given the domination of foreign corporations.

Those fearful of either major 'ism' have often looked to populist régimes, of which Tanzania, with her communitarian *Ujamaa* villages, her 'intermediate' (or 'appropriate') technology policies, and her emphasis upon low-level participation rather than centralized planning, remains the most popular example in the capitalist Third World. Among the communist countries, China's attempt to maintain an egalitarian impetus, in the shape of the Cultural Revolution of 1965–7 – by combating bureaucracy and élitism, by decentralizing participation in decision-making to the level of the commune and the factory; and by closing the gap between town and country, mental and manual labour, and industry and agriculture (the 'Three Great Differences') – constitutes a major departure from previous communist strategies, which have been highly centralized, highly hierarchical, and have based industrial development on the exploitation of the peasantry (Worsley, 1975).

Part Two

Chapter 4
The Family

Introduction

The family, with its strengths and its weaknesses and its possibilities for the future, is today at the centre of a lively and concerned debate. Legislators consider the role of the family in shaping social policy, and social workers, academics and churchmen organize conferences and symposia around such themes as 'The Future of the Family' or 'The Family Today'. Some see in an apparent decline of the family and the erosion of familial values a threat to the future of civilization itself, while others see the institution of the family as the main barrier to the full liberation of women – indeed of humanity – in our society. Some see in the apparent 'weakness' of the contemporary family and parental authority the source of many contemporary evils such as juvenile crime, vandalism and drug abuse. To some it is an institution vital to the health of the individual and of society as a whole, while to others it is an oppressive and outmoded survival from an earlier period of human history. Accounts of alternatives to the conventional model of the conjugally-based family range from evolving patterns of 'living together' and 'open families' to a wide variety of communal experiments, and frequently attract the attention of the mass media and social scientists.

Yet, at the same time, it would appear that for a large section of the population 'normal' family life goes on, apparently untouched by these deliberations. The overwhelming majority of those who are of appropriate age will marry, and a large proportion of these will have their marriage solemnized in a religious setting (see Table 1 and Figure 7). The birth of a child, too, is still a social event, so much so that it is likely to be recognized by some form of religious service in a society not otherwise deeply 'religious'. Married couples still main-

Table 1

Percentage of Males and Females Ever Married at Selected Ages (England and Wales)

| Year | Per cent – ever married | | | |
| | Males Aged | | Females Aged | |
	20–24	45–49	20–24	45–49
1931	14	89	26	83
1939	17	90	34	84
1951	24	90	48	85
1961	31	91	59	90
1971	37	90	59	92
1974	35	90	58	93

(Source: Richard Leete, 'Marriage and Divorce', *Population Trends*, 3, Spring 1976, H.M.S.O., p. 3.)

tain effective and meaningful ties with their parents and in-laws and recognize these ties on major ritual occasions such as Christmas, birthdays, weddings, baptisms and funerals. And while the divorce rate has been rising, a large proportion of divorced people will find other partners and remarry.

In 1965, 11% of the 370,000 marriages involved a divorced bride or groom; this increased to 22% of the 426,000 marriages in 1972, and increased further to one in four marriages in 1974 (Leete, 1976, pp. 6–7).

The varieties of family themes, tragic and painful as well as happy and rewarding, often form a central part of conversations between neighbours, friends or strangers, and provide an almost inexhaustible fund of material for comedians, popular songs, novels, poetry, films and television series. The family, so close to the universal concerns of sex, birth and death, is so much part of what is 'given' for any one individual, that it seems deeply rooted in the natural order of things.

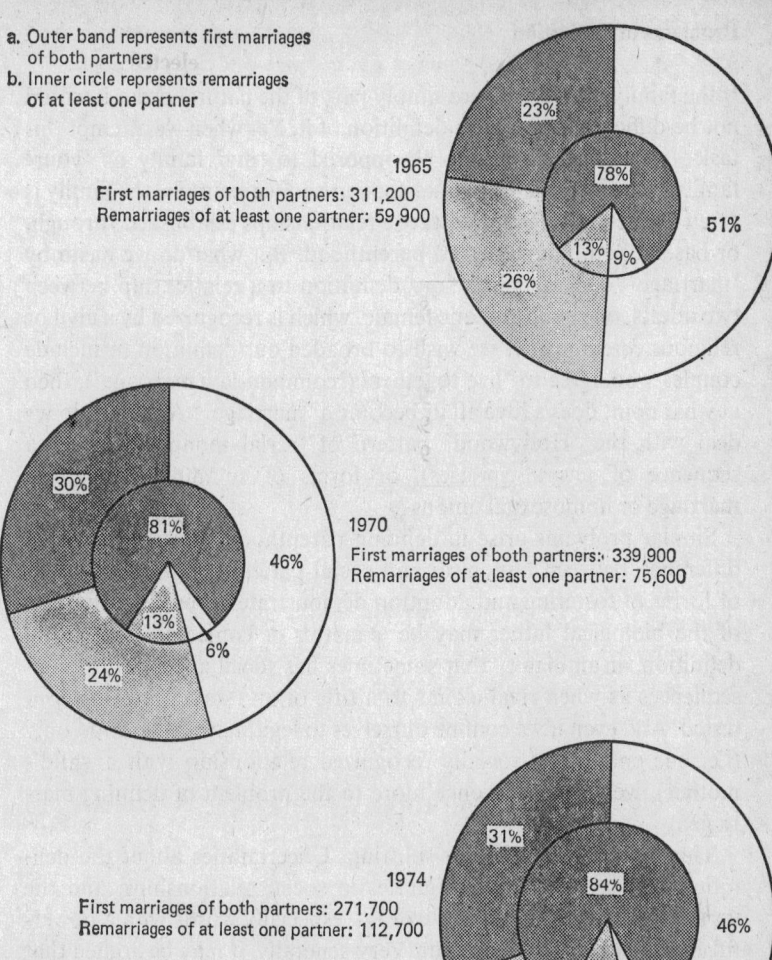

a. Outer band represents first marriages of both partners
b. Inner circle represents remarriages of at least one partner

1965
First marriages of both partners: 311,200
Remarriages of at least one partner: 59,900

23% · 78% · 51% · 13% · 9% · 26%

1970
First marriages of both partners: 339,900
Remarriages of at least one partner: 75,600

30% · 81% · 46% · 13% · 6% · 24%

1974
First marriages of both partners: 271,700
Remarriages of at least one partner: 112,700

31% · 84% · 46% · 12% · 4% · 23%

■ Civil ▨ Other religions ☐ Church of England

Figure 7 Marriages : manner of solemnization, England and Wales
(Source : Richard Leete, 'Marriage and Divorce', *Population Trends*, 3, Spring 1976, H.M.S.O., p. 8.)

Problems of Definition

If the family, however, were simply part of the natural order it would not be difficult to provide a definition of it. Yet when we attempt this task – to define *the* family as opposed to 'my' family or 'your' family – considerable difficulties soon arise. For example, the family is often defined as referring to those relationships established through, or based upon, marriage and parenthood. But what do we mean by 'marriage'? Do we confine our definition to a relationship between two adults, one male and one female, which is recognized by a civil or religious ceremony? If we wish to broaden our definition to include couples who agree to 'live together' ('common-law marriage'), then at what point does a love affair become a 'marriage'? And how do we deal with the 'Hollywood' pattern of 'serial monogamy' (i.e. a sequence of several spouses), or forms of communal or group marriage or homosexual unions?

Similar problems arise in defining parenthood. Clearly there is a difference between biological and social parenthood, as the variety of forms of fostering and adoption demonstrate. Even the definition of the biological father may be a matter of conjecture and social definition, an ambiguity that sometimes has social and political consequences as when rival claims to a title or an estate are being contested. And even if we confine ourselves to legitimate fatherhood only (i.e. one entailing a socially recognized relationship with a child's mother), we come back once more to the problem of defining marriage.

This is not academic hair-splitting. Uncertainties about the definition of words reflect ambiguities in social relationships, and the variety of uses to which these words – especially words with a powerful emotional content – are put. Very generally, it may be argued that when familistic words such as 'father', 'mother', 'daughter' and 'son' are used, they are used not only to indicate and distinguish a particular kind of relationship in an analytical or logical sense but also to make an evaluation about the quality of that relationship. For example, the use of the term 'brother' may be a simple factual statement that the two males (or a male and a female) recognize the same parents; it may also indicate something of the quality of the relationship that, it is felt, ought to exist between those who may behave like brothers even when they are not. Thus, the largely unemployed black males described in Liebow's study of street-corner life in Washington D.C. may describe a relationship of friendship between two men as one of 'going for brothers' (Liebow, 1967, p. 167). By using this term they seek to indicate a quality of relationship that is felt to have more strands of obligation and meaning than simple friendship or mere acquaintance. In most cases, these two elements involved in the use of family terms – the simple statement of fact and the more complex statement of moral expectations – coexist in uneasy partnership, but they may easily become separated or even come into conflict, as we see in 'tug-of-love' disputes over children between adoptive and biological parents.

In our culture, these ambiguities increase when we move to kinship relationships and terms outside the immediate family. For example, the term 'uncle' might refer to:

(a) A brother of an individual's father or mother. (In contrast to many societies studied by anthropologists, we do not have separate words to distinguish uncles on the mother's side from those on the father's side.)

(b) A term of respect adopted towards an adult male friend of a child's parents or, possibly, towards a male who shows appropriately 'avuncular' qualities.

(c) A term used to describe a mother's lover.

Thus, when we use the word 'uncle' we are making a complex statement which may be compounded of any of the following elements: genealogical position in relation to oneself; relative status in terms of age; and some more general and less well-defined notion of 'avuncular qualities'.

If, therefore, we assume that in talking about the family we are dealing with connections established by marriage and parenthood, we are merely indicating a broad area of social relationships in which many questions still remain open. We should beware of giving the idea of 'the' family some fixed 'thing-like' quality, thereby perhaps smuggling in some notion of a universal or unchanging family. To put the matter another way, all of us, in society, are engaged in the business of defining 'the family' by the ways in which we think and act in relation to those whom we label as family or non-family. Furthermore, these definitions change over time. Raymond Williams has pointed out how, prior to the mid-seventeenth century, *none* of the meanings attached to the word 'family' had the connotations, so common today, of a small group of immediate kin sharing a dwelling (Williams, 1976, pp. 108–11). In studying the family, then, we need to investigate the different ways in which people in a particular culture understand, use and evaluate the term 'family', together with the whole set of terms available for family and kinship relationships.

So far we have considered marriage and parenthood as the key elements in a possible definition of our field of inquiry. There is, however, one further element that we should include and that is *residence*. This element poses further problems for investigation rather than supplying some definitive static notion of the family. A couple may 'live together' and not be married; a couple may be married and yet not live together. Lodgers and servants may live under the same roof and be treated as 'one of the family', while a son or daughter may live far away, out of sight and out of mind. A useful distinction is often made between 'family' and 'household'; part of the definition of the latter term provided by the 1961 Census is as follows:

A household comprises one person living alone or a group of persons living together, partaking of meals prepared together and benefiting from a common housekeeping (quoted in Stacey, 1969, p. 35).

Certainly the element of residence is an important one at arriving at an understanding of the family in society. The house is often also the home, and to 'return home' (still a poignant theme in drama and literature) is to return to one's family of origin, the family in which one was brought up.

This discussion of the definition of the family may be summarized in the form of a chart and a diagram (Figure 8). The chart shows possible combinations of the elements; marriage, parenthood and residence. The diagram, based upon this chart, consists of three overlapping circles. Clearly the degree of overlap will vary between and within societies, as will norms as to which particular set of combinations are the most desirable or 'natural'. The representation of possible definitions of the family in this manner does not, of course, resolve all the problems; there is still, for example, plenty of room for debate about the constituent elements of this definition, such as 'marriage'

Figure 8 *Possible Combinations of Marriage, Parenthood and Residence*

	Marriage	Parenthood	Residence	Examples
1.	Yes	Yes	Yes	'Complete' nuclear family, with or without additional kin.
2.	Yes	Yes	No	Family dispersed through separation of spouses or through children leaving home.
3.	Yes	No	Yes	Childless couple.
4.	No	Yes	Yes	Couple 'living together' with child ; unmarried parent with child.
5.	Yes	No	No	Separated childless couple. (Form of 'marriage in name only'.)
6.	No	Yes	No	Illegitimate child adopted or otherwise removed from its biological parents.
7.	No	No	Yes	'Living together'.

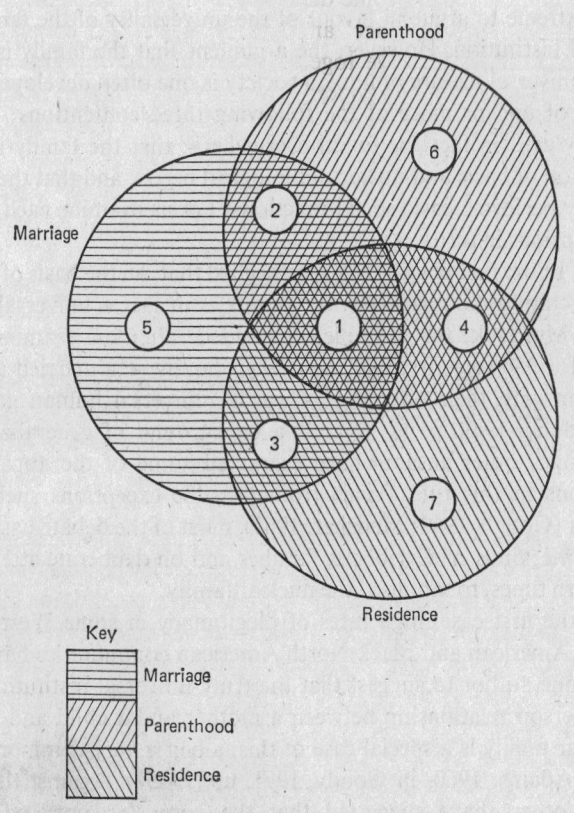

Key

Marriage

Parenthood

Residence

and 'parenthood'. Yet the diagram can serve as a point of departure, and even those who argue that the family only 'really' exists at the point of intersection of all three circles will also probably agree that other kinds of relationships, outside this central area and yet located somewhere within the area covered by the three circles, will also possess some 'family-like' qualities.

The Family: A Universal Institution?

In the light of this brief discussion of the difficulties involved in defining the family it would appear to be even more hazardous to attempt cross-cultural or international comparisons, and dubious in the extreme to argue in favour of the universality of the family as a social institution. However, the argument that the family is a basic and universal feature of human society is one often developed on the basis of one or more of the following three contentions: that the family can 'in fact' be found everywhere; that the family is an expression of basic and universal biological needs; and that the nuclear family performs basic social functions. Let us examine each of these contentions in turn:

(a) In the first place it has been argued that, on the basis of detailed cross-cultural comparisons, the family is in fact a universal institution. Murdock, for example, concluded, after an examination of data for 250 societies, that the *nuclear* family – 'a married man and woman with their offspring' – was a 'universal human grouping' (Murdock, 1949, p. 1). Against a background of generalization of this kind, other authors have examined some of the apparent exceptions to this rule. Apart from possible exceptions such as the Nayar (Gough, 1960; Mencher, 1965), most of the debate has focused on some kinds of Caribbean families and on deliberate attempts, in modern times, to 'abolish' the nuclear family.

In the first case, high rates of illegitimacy in some West Indian, Latin American and Black North American communities have led at least one author to suggest that the truly universal institution is the two-person relationship between a mother and a child and that the nuclear family is a special case of this, albeit a very common special case (Adams, 1960, in Goody, 1971, pp. 19–37). Against this argument others have suggested that the *norm* (as opposed to the *practice*) in these societies is still the nuclear family based upon marriage, and that the fatherless families found chiefly in the poorer sections of these communities are ultimately a product of past historical experience of slavery and of continuing, contemporary discrimination and low employment opportunities (Goode, 1960, in Coser, 1974, pp. 64–77; Staples, 1971, in Skolnick and Skolnick, 1974, pp. 536–64).

In the second set of cases it has been argued that attempts to abolish the family in modern times have apparently always failed. Thus, in spite of early revolutionary anti-family legislation, the nuclear family has remained a strong institution in the Soviet Union. In contemporary China, while the traditional patriarchal relationships (of men over women and fathers over children) have declined in significance, the family is still an important and valued institution (Davin, 1976). Again, the return of familism, over a few generations, in the Israeli kibbutzim would also apparently support the view that the nuclear family is a basic and universal institution. Radical communal experiments in North America which sought to abolish 'selfish' and exclusive sexual ties, such as the Oneida community (Carden, 1969), tended to last for less than a generation, while communities where the family was always a definable entity (such as the Hutterite brethren) remain a flourishing and going concern. All these 'deviant cases' are instructive, but they need to be studied in their historical context. Thus the Soviet case cannot be understood properly without taking into account the effects of two world wars and internal political struggles, and the short-lived character of some North American communal experiments cannot be considered without examining the wider, and often hostile, community within which they were placed.

Clearly there is much to argue about in these examples and counter-examples. But the difficulties experienced in attempting a definition of the family in the context of our own society and the realization that several different kinds of relationships could be viewed as having 'family-like' qualities should make us especially cautious about attempting cross-cultural comparisons in terms of our own conceptions of, say, 'marriage' or 'legitimacy'. Such generalizations that we are able to make may be at the expense of ignoring the different meanings that these arrangements have in different cultures to their members. Furthermore, concentrating on the conjugal tie between spouses or the nuclear familial relationships of mother, father and children leaves out of the picture the very diverse ways in which these ties relate to other networks of social relationships, such as kin, neighbours or friends and to other social groupings or categories such as generations, lineages, social classes and ethnic groups.

(b) Another argument for the universal necessity of the nuclear family is that the nuclear family is the natural outcome of certain basic biological needs. This kind of argument stresses certain basic facts about human existence, such as:

i. The need for the human species to reproduce itself. The individual expression of this is via the sexual drive.

ii. The basic human needs for nutrition and protection from natural and social dangers.

iii. The fact that the human infant is not in a position to seek its own food or to protect itself, and requires others to do this on its behalf. Furthermore, the human infant remains in a state of dependence for a much longer period than other animals.

It is possible to accept such premises about certain basic human needs without accepting the conclusion that the nuclear family is necessarily or logically the *social* institution that must always fulfil these *biological* needs. It does not follow, for example, that *all* persons need take part in the process of reproduction; for example, in all periods of history, celibacy has not merely been practised by some groups and individuals but has, indeed, often been regarded as a highly moral or religious state. More generally, it is misleading to think of sexuality as some abstracted animal drive, separated from the particular social institutions and cultural symbols in which and through which it is expressed. Sexuality can be stimulated (as in advertising or erotic films) or repressed. Further, it is not necessary for the biological parents to remain with their joint child. Similarly, it does not appear to be essential for the biological functions of reproduction, on the one hand, and the basic requirements of care and protection of immature infants, on the other, to be met by the same set of persons. Finally, we should stress the dramatic impact brought about in our own times by the fact that it is possible, through increasingly effective and available means of contraception, to separate the sexual act from reproduction. In short, the range of possible cultural arrangements that might be made in response to a set of basic biological needs is very wide.

(c) A third kind of argument for the universal necessity of the nuclear family, somewhat similar to the previous set of arguments, is to maintain that the nuclear family performs fundamental *societal* functions. The argument stresses not so much basic biological needs of individuals as the basic needs of society as a whole. Thus, in one formulation, Murdock argues that the nuclear family fulfils four basic functions – the sexual, the economic, the reproductive and the educational (Murdock, 1949, p. 3). Functionalist theories of this kind raise many complex issues which we will not take up at this point, but we should note that they generate difficulties similar to those we encountered when considering the relationship between biological and social parenthood. We may agree that certain basic prerequisites have to be met if society is to survive as a collectivity. Human beings reproduce themselves biologically, but they must also reproduce themselves culturally, i.e., the accumulated and constantly enlarged and revised skills and knowledge of previous and existing generations embodied in spoken and written language, must be passed on to subsequent generations. But it does not follow from this that the nuclear family is the only institution capable of fulfilling all these societal functions theoretically assigned to it. The nuclear family *may*, in a given culture, fulfil all the functions attributed to it by Murdock and others, but this is not the same as saying that this particular social institution is *necessary* for the performance of these or any other particular set of social functions. Thus it is important to see how far these functions are shared with or performed by other institutions such as schools or nurseries, or sets of people other than kin, such as neighbours, godparents or friends.

But we are not saying either that the nuclear family is a totally arbitrary institution. Throughout the world and throughout history, relationships between adult men and women have, at some point in their lives, been formalized and recognized in a way which might reasonably be described as 'marriage'. Similarly, children are not arbitrarily brought into the world but are given some kind of social identity, usually in relation to their socially defined parent or parents. Indeed, so important is this theme of the provision of social identity through parenthood that one anthropologist, Malinowski, outlined a universal principle of legitimacy which stated 'that no child should be brought into the world without a man – and one man at that – assuming the role of sociological father' (Malinowski, 1930, in Coser, 1974, p. 59). The basic biological individual needs which we have outlined, together with the needs of society for economic co-operation and continuity over generations, have set distinct limits on the range of variability to be found in the family or its surrogates. Nevertheless, the differences between human societies in these respects are – perhaps increasingly – at least as impressive as the similarities.

So far our attention has been largely focused on two entities, the family and society. These terms are too general for our purposes. We need to examine whether the nuclear family exists as part of a wider network of kin extending over two or more generations or whether it exists in relative isolation. We must ask ourselves whether, within the family, there is a sharp differentiation between the roles of the spouses, or whether these roles are weakly differentiated. We need to discover whether the family is responsible for a whole cluster of interrelated functions, or whether it shares these functions with other institutions outside the family. These, and other questions, require us to look, comparatively and historically, at how the family is linked to and located in wider social networks and structures, and how it ultimately forms part, often a discordant or contradictory part, of society as a whole. In these and in many other respects, the family is a changing institution, and it is this process of change, particularly in modern industrial society, that we must examine in some detail.

The Family in Industrial Society

To write the words 'the family in industrial society' is to make a lot of assumptions and to open up a complex range of questions. It assumes, firstly, that there is something unique or special about the family in such a society, and, secondly, that this uniqueness is in some way associated with an easily recognizable phenomenon called 'industrialization'. Further it assumes that the differences between the forms and functioning of the family in 'industrial' and 'pre-industrial' societies are greater than any differences that might exist within these two categories such as, in the former, between capitalist and socialist societies. Even if we agree that these kinds of assumptions have some general validity, the questions that then stem from them are equally complex. If we can associate certain patterns of family living with the process of industrialization then what were these particular patterns, and were they *caused* by industrialization or a necessary *pre*-condition for it? Finally, as industrial societies do not remain static – indeed some sociologists are already talking of a 'post-industrial' society – what further changes, if any, are we likely to see in patterns of family living or in the development of alternatives to what we usually understand as 'the family'?

The nature of the changes

Whether or not particular authors take industrialization to be the main engine of change, or whether they include other factors, such as urbanization and bureaucratization, three generally agreed themes seem to emerge from the writings of many sociologists of the family. From reading these accounts it would appear that three main changes have taken place in family structure and functioning over the past one or two centuries:

(a) The family has become a more isolated unit, relatively separate from wider sets of kin, and functioning chiefly as a conjugal or nuclear unit.

(b) The family has either lost many of its functions or has become more specialized in these functions. In particular, the family has lost its central functions as a *productive unit* in the wider economy.

(c) Internally, relationships within the family have become more egalitarian, both between husband and wife and between parents and children.

It should be noted also that many sociologists would argue – particularly Goode, for example (Goode, 1970) – that these changes are not simply confined to Britain and the United States but are taking place throughout the world, although at different paces and starting from different points.

Sociologists differ as to the amount of weight they place on each of these changes and the way in which these changes are evaluated. Thus the more pessimistically inclined will write of a 'loss' of functions of the family, while the more optimistic sociologists will talk of the 'change' in and 'specialization' of these functions. The final alleged change – that of growing equality within the family – is perhaps the most controversial and the one which is most challenged by contemporary feminist writers who argue that the family is, and continues to be, the major unit sustaining the exploitation and subordination of women. Thus despite the apparent consensus among many sociologists about these changes in family form and functioning, there is still considerable debate and controversy. Let us consider each of these debates in turn.

(a) *The isolation of the nuclear family*. Those who argue that the modern nuclear or conjugal based family is a 'relatively isolated' unit do not deny that individual family members may maintain strong relationships with members of the families in which they were brought up (their families of origin) even after they have married and formed their own families (their families of procreation). The overwhelming body of evidence for Britain and the United States is that such ties are maintained after marriage and that this is not simply a matter of recognizing connections at Christmas and birthdays plus occasional visits or telephone conversations. Married couples may live close to one or other set of parents or their own children and their spouses. Each may provide assistance in times of infirmity or sickness or in the provision of baby-sitting or other services. Kin may still be of importance when it comes to seeking work or accommodation. Furthermore, these kinds of effective ties are maintained not only among traditional working-class or immigrant communities, where factors such as economic need and outside hostility may cause them to depend more upon each other, but also among the more mobile members of the middle class. Here, parents may provide valuable financial assistance to their married children in the early stages of their family life-cycle, when the head of the household is beginning a career, and when the young couples are faced with the initial expenses of setting up a home and providing for young children (Bell, 1968).

Early exaggerated statements by sociologists about the tendency, in modern society, for the nuclear family to become 'isolated' had the effect of masking the existence and strength of these intergenerational ties, which persist in spite of geographical distance or social mobility. But taking a wider historical and comparative perspective, there is some truth in these statements. Marriage today is seen as a matter for the couples themselves and not something to be decided upon by members of some wider kinship grouping. The couple is expected to set up a separate residence for themselves on or shortly after marriage (that is, and has long been, a general European pattern), and the chief obligations of the spouses are to each other and to their children, and only after that to their own families of origin. The emphasis is, therefore, on the *conjugal* bond, to such an extent that marriage has become an index of 'normality' or 'settling down' and is now a status formally open to almost everyone of the appropriate age (see Table 1, p. 166). This 'democratization' is, as Bernard reminds us, a relatively new trend of the last hundred or two hundred years, and one which contrasts with an earlier situation where marriage was '. . . a kind of privilege, a prerogative, a gift bestowed by the community' (Bernard, 1976, p. 123). Furthermore, there is no clearly bounded or defined kinship unit – such as a clan or a tribe – outside this nuclear or conjugal family. Rather, the conjugally-based family exists in the context of a fluctuating network of kin, neighbours, friends and workmates. In many cases, kin may be 'chosen' (and other kin ignored) just as friends may be chosen, and individuals may choose to go to non-kin instead for particular kinds of help or services. To some extent, then, kin can take on the status of friends, perhaps involving special kinds of obligations and pressures, but also subject to the influence of factors such as distance and the preference of the couples themselves, rather than determined by blood relationship. This network of kin and non-kin has no clear boundaries; at the far edges are individuals who are simply 'known' or 'recognized' as kin, while towards the centre there are more effective ties, perhaps involving frequent visits and exchanges of goods and services. Rules within this network about how couples should relate to particular categories of kin are often unclear and subject to considerable variation between families, and this ambiguity itself provides a clue about the nature of the modern nuclear family. A good illustration of this is the lack of certainty that many young people have over the question of how to address their parents and parents-in-law after marriage. Some will use the first name or parental terms (such as 'mother', 'father', 'Mum', 'Dad', etc.), others will adopt more formal modes of address ('Mr Smith', 'Mrs

Jones'), while many find this awkward situation eased somewhat when they themselves have children and they are able to use the term 'Gran' or some equivalent (Firth *et al.*, 1969, pp. 418–22).

(b) *The loss of functions*. It would appear to be an easy task to show that the nuclear family has progressively lost many of its functions over the past two hundred years. Its economic functions, for example, have become severely limited; once a unit where the members produced jointly (on a farm or in some form of domestic industry) as well as consumed jointly, the nuclear family has now simply become a unit of consumption only. The link between the family and the economy have become more indirect, mediated through the wage-packet. Similarly, it can be maintained, the educational functions of the family have been taken over by more specialized agencies, as have the functions of leisure and protection. Even the so-called 'sexual function' of the family – that is the function of regulating and channelling sexual activity – would appear to be of more limited significance today, although supporters and opponents of the 'permissive society' alike may both be guilty of confusing talk about and representations of sexual activity with actual practice. (For some of the evidence see Schofield, 1968, and Reiss, 1967.) In many respects, therefore, it would appear that the family is a much less important institution in modern society than it was in the past.

Yet, while this account of loss of functions and dwindling significance might appear to be almost self-evident, many sociologists – most notably Talcott Parsons (in Parsons and Bales, 1956, pp. 16–17) – have argued that this picture is much too simple. The family, he maintains, has not so much *lost* its functions as it has become more *specialized* in its functions. The family is doing fewer things, but it is doing these things rather well. Parsons argues that the specialized functions of the nuclear family today are twofold: the socialization of immature children (often called 'primary socialization'), and the stabilization of adult personalities. Taking the first function, while it is true that the education (and hence, also, as we shall see in a later chapter, socialization – since the two cannot be readily separated) of children and young adults has increasingly been taken over by agencies outside the home such as schools, play-groups and youth organizations, the basic primary socialization of the child is still very much a responsibility of the nuclear family. It is in this family that the child is taught to make basic distinctions between self and others, or between male and female, to acquire and to use language, and to develop a framework through which to understand, interpret and evaluate the world outside. Through what is sometimes called 'role-playing' within the family, the child is taught to anticipate certain adult roles and identities, particularly those identities associated with being a man or a woman. Children's toys, for example (dolls or 'Action Man'), clothes (pink for a girl, blue for a boy) and names help to establish and define stereotypical patterns of behaviour associated with being male or female. Here, Parsons points out, the task of socialization may be much simpler in our culture for girls, because the role-model – the mother – is usually close at hand around the home and the daughter can imitate her behaviour much more readily. For sons, on the other hand, socialization may be more in terms of broader, more stereotypical notions of masculinity such as may be manifested in horseplay at weekends or evenings, rather than in terms of the more specific features of the father's role at work, which may often be hidden from the male child.

Perhaps the most important feature about all these, and other, aspects of the primary socialization process is that *a large part of it is unplanned and non-deliberate*. (In a later chapter, we shall see that this is also true of education in schools.) Socialization within the family is manifested in subtle cues of things said and things not said, of facial expressions and gestures which arise in the course of day-to-day living within the same dwelling. The daily ritual of meal-times, for example, may often contain a wealth of deliberately and non-deliberately imparted information for the child, in part confirming his status *as* a child (children should be seen and not heard, children should finish their cabbage because it is good for them), in part defining the stages of growing up (older children sit on 'proper' chairs, drink out of 'proper' cups, and use knives and forks), and in part defining and reinforcing certain adult identities (father carves the joint, mother brings food from the stove). When some sociologists talk of the 'socialization function of the family', therefore, they are not talking of a family deliberately and consciously performing a function assigned to it from outside by 'society', but rather of a more subtle process that arises out of the facts of being married, of sharing a residence over a long period of time, and of parenthood. In so far as any one institution is responsible for this basic stage of child socialization – literally, making *social* – then that institution is more often than not in our society the nuclear family. Furthermore, if outside agencies – such as courts or social workers – decide that socialization has in some way been inadequate, it is to the family that they are most likely to turn in the allocation of blame or responsibility.

The modern nuclear or conjugal family, however, does not simply fulfil the function of socializing children; according to Parsons, it also fulfils functions for adults. In a society which is increasingly bureaucratized, and characterized by impersonal relationships in the work-place or the streets of the city, the home forms a major setting where adults may enjoy primary social relationships. So many popular expressions maintain that the family is the place where one can 'be oneself', where one can 'let one's hair down' and so on. The values of privacy and the values of home are closely interwoven, especially in contemporary middle-class culture. The family home, for example, is the one place where adults may indulge in 'childish' behaviour (perhaps with and through their own children) without incurring moral disapproval. A further aspect of the family, linking these ideas of privacy, home and self-expression, has received considerable attention in the last few decades with the growth of popular psychology manuals on how to enjoy or improve married sex and, more recently, encounter groups and sexual therapy. Even mate-swapping or 'swinging' may sometimes be seen as an adjunct to a stable, adult family life.

These two features of the family in industrial society – its relative isolation and the specialization of its functions – may together suggest that the family enjoys a relatively *autonomous* status in contemporary society. If the family can be said to perform functions for the society of which it is a part, it performs these functions indirectly (that is, through the individuals who, as adults, move out of their own families of origin and form families of procreation), and possesses a certain degree of latitude as to the performance of these functions. Modern society, it may be argued, is not like a set of neatly intermeshing and well-oiled cogs, but rather a game in which groups of players have considerable discretion so long as they keep within a set of rules which are often themselves rather loosely defined or at least open to negotiation and change. Hence families in this kind of modern society are not all alike, although there are limits to the range of variation.

This account of the functioning of the family in modern industrial society may be considered to be defective in a variety of respects. Ignoring for the present some of the difficulties inherent in functional analysis, we may note, for example, that the account of socialization ignores the variety of other agencies that play an important part in socializing the child. Schools and play-groups have already been mentioned, but there are many other less formal agencies: direct, such as other children, other kin or neighbours; and indirect, such as television. To some extent, of course, these other agencies are often filtered through the family and evaluated by the parents on behalf of the children: the mother may 'censor' the amount and kind of television that enters the home, or parents may discourage, with varying degrees of subtlety, their children's choice of certain 'undesirable' friends. Yet in this respect as in many others, few families are a complete law unto themselves, and many children are able to participate in the culture of the playground or the street in happy ignorance or gleeful defiance of adult wishes. The reader is recommended to consult the work of the Opies as an example of a vivid reconstruction of the semi-autonomous world of children's songs, games and folk-lore, a culture often carried on and elaborated over generations (Opie and Opie, 1959).

More important, perhaps, is the fact that this account of the family may be considered defective in that it ignores the *varieties* of patterns of family living that are to be found in a modern industrial society. Specifically, we are presented with a rather bland, urban or suburban, middle-class model of family living as if this were a model of or for society as a whole. Of course it may, and indeed has, been argued that the middle-class model *is* the model for the future – this argument will be considered later in this chapter – but for the present we may simply note the variety of modes of family living that continue to exist and flourish. We have already mentioned that kin continue to play an important part in family life and that families vary considerably in the density and complexity of their kinship networks. Rural communities in Wales or the North of England,

Italian immigrant communities in London, or Pakistani communities in Rochdale, working-class communities in Bethnal Green or Liverpool, French Canadians in Quebec; all these patterns and many others can be said to exist within industrial societies and yet do not clearly conform to the model presented earlier. Relevant factors underlying these variations are linguistic, ethnic or cultural identity, discrimination on the part of the host community, mobility or lack of mobility and economic differentiation. This last factor is of particular importance. Long working hours, shift-work, large families and overcrowded dwellings may limit the possibility of privacy and of personal growth through the shared marital culture which Parsons's model postulates.

Finally, it may be noted – as this previous point suggests – that the account presented by Parsons and others has tended to dwell on the *eu*functions (positive functions) at the expense of the negative or *dys*functions of this pattern of family living. The private dwelling which may be the course of personal fulfilment and growth may also be the centre and source of child- or wife-beating. Here the value of privacy may act against the interests of family members; neighbours may consider that it is not their business to interfere and the beaten wife – at least before the growth of women's self-help centres – may find that she has nowhere to go (Pizzey, 1974). The family has probably always been a major source of violence – consider the wealth of folk stories and songs that deal with cruel sisters, feuding brothers, and infanticide – but now the violence may be more hidden, less open to immediate social control from the wider community, at least until it is too late. The violence, of course, may not be physical; in some of the families that Laing and his associates have described, privacy becomes isolation, togetherness becomes a mutual and corrosive manipulation, and love becomes a commodity or weapon (Laing *et al.*, 1970). It may also be asked – and it is being asked with increasing urgency – whether this family that has been described is not the one remaining institution that prevents women from fully developing as individual personalities? This theme will be taken up in the next section.

(c) *Towards a more egalitarian family structure?* In outlining the main changes that have taken place in the family in industrial society it has sometimes been maintained that one of the most important changes has been the evolution of a more egalitarian or more democratic family structure. In the first place it is argued that this growing equality has been a 'relational' equality between men and women in the home. Women are free to choose their spouse, and have moved towards the development of equal rights in such matters as divorce and control over property. The spread of readily available and simple means of contraception has meant that the wife is less likely to spend much of her life in the bearing and rearing of children and is more likely to seek employment outside the home, thereby developing a source of income and interests outside her traditionally defined role:

... in Britain the proportion of all wives in paid work went up from 10% in 1911 (as it remained in 1931) to 26% in 1951 and 42% in 1971 (Young and Willmott, 1975, p. 101).

She has become a more equal partner in decision-making, in the enjoyment of sex, and in control over domestic resources. Similarly, the husband is playing a greater part in domestic tasks associated with the house and children.

In the second place, it can be argued that similar changes have taken place in the relationships between parents and children. The traditional patriarchal structure has been eroded, partly because the formal head of the house has moved out of the home into the completely separate sphere of work, and partly because the authority he derives from control over economic resources and property is eroded in an urban, money economy. Child-rearing is more 'permissive', and while children may not be granted the status of equal partners in the family decision-making process, they are no longer simply expected to be seen and not heard. The relationships between husbands and wives, and between parents and children, have, it is argued, become permeated with a democratic ideology.

The evidence, however, reveals a much more complex pattern. There are, in the first instance, many resistances to these processes within our society. In the case of child-rearing, commentators may confuse the development of 'permissive' child-rearing *theories* with a growth of permissiveness in *practice*, and assume that the former also entailed the latter. Certainly, there is little strong evidence of an unambiguous growth in permissive child-rearing practice, at least in the United Kingdom. At the very least, we need to consider variations according to social class as Table 2 (taken from the Newsoms' study of child-rearing practice published in 1963) demonstrates. This suggests, too, that the very notion of 'permissiveness', and its converse, is a slippery one; in many cases it would seem to mean little more than an exchange of more overt physical controls for more subtle emotional controls. In both cases, the actual *structure* of authority between parent and child remains unchanged. Similarly, in the case of relationships between spouses, it can be shown that clear divisions between the woman's sphere and the man's sphere persist, and the illustrations of this do not come exclusively from rural or traditional working-class communities. In professional or managerial families, for example, the husband's career is the dominant consideration, maintaining the traditional division of labour between the husband as breadwinner and wife as housewife (Pahl and Pahl, 1971). Studies which show apparent equality in decision-making between husbands and wives often omit or do not give due weight to many of the more important decisions such as where to live, when to move or when to buy a new car (Gillespie, 1972). In most cases, the role of the husband as chief income-earner is still likely to be the deciding factor in any marital power struggle.

More significantly, it is possible to point to certain paradoxical elements in the apparent development of a democratic family structure. In the first place it must be asked why, if this growing equality between spouses has been achieved over the past hundred or so years, has the militant feminist movement grown throughout the world during the 1960s and 1970s? In part the answer might lie in a 'revolution of rising expectations', a growing, perceived contradiction between the overt ideologies of equality and the apparent growth in opportunities for women opened out through the educational and employment systems, on the one hand, and the actual experience of being a woman on the other. A woman may not be bound by her role as a housewife but it is still the case that in so far as any one person is left with the main responsibility for the housework, that person is the woman. Even in cases where the husband and wife contribute equally to the family budget, there is no guarantee that both will contribute equally to the day-to-day running of the home and caring for the children. In short, the growing participation

Table 2
Class Differences in Infant Socialization

Registrar-General's class	I and II	III White Collar	III Manual	IV	V
	%	%	%	%	%
Aged 21 or less at first birth	24	25	40	46	53
Breast feeding: at 1 month	60	50	50	51	34
at 3 months	39	34	24	22	12
at 6 months	20	12	11	11	7
No bottle after: 6 months	10	9	4	1	1
12 months	50	47	29	21	15
Dummy: at some time	39	53	71	75	74
still at 12 months	26	38	55	57	46
Bottle or dummy to go to sleep	23	36	47	52	51
if wakes	24	36	40	47	42
Bedtime: 6.30 p.m. minus	47	31	29	24	31
8.0 p.m. plus	7	12	20	23	26
Sleeps in room alone	54	42	20	18	3
Diet inadequate	5	10	13	13	32
Potty training not started (12 months)	12	16	17	13	32
Of those started, never successful	36	38	46	42	79
Genital play checked	25	50	57	69	93
No smacking	56	38	32	42	35
General smacking	39	53	60	54	58
Frequent tantrums	9	8	14	15	23
Father's participation: high	57	61	51	55	36
little or none	19	6	16	18	36
Baby-sitting: once or less p.a.	25	36	42	42	59

(Source: J. and E. Newsom, *Patterns of Infant Care in an Urban Community,* Penguin, 1963, p. 229.)

One View of the Political Economy of Sex.

of women in the labour-force has not been matched by an equal growth of male participation in the home. Furthermore, this very development of the family as a relatively private and semi-autonomous sphere has, at one and the same time, left the wife free to develop interests outside the home but also, through the increasing stress on the importance of the home in childhood socialization and the growth of adult personalities, laid much of this new domestic responsibility on women. The woman, therefore, is placed under a severe set of conflicting pressures: on the one hand to develop her identity outside the home and, on the other, to develop and improve new and subtle human 'skills' as a housewife and as a mother. At the same time, in contrast to earlier eras, the housework is more likely to be carried out in isolation, without reference to others or without any external standard of comparison from which she might derive status or recognition for her particular skills as a cook or a housewife. Furthermore, the long hours of housework are, as many feminists have stressed, unpaid and do not receive any recognition as productive labour in national income statistics.

Another paradox may be noted in the case of children. On the one hand it would appear that they are less likely to be clearly subordinated to traditional patriarchal authority. At a time of rapid social change, for example, and through the educational system, the child may acquire a degree of independence as a result of the new knowledge and experiences that he comes to possess. In some respects, also, the parents may be more inclined to treat the child as a person with views of his or her own. At the same time, however, the child's status *as a child* is perhaps more tightly defined through employment legislation, the raising of the school-leaving age (thus depriving the child of an independent source of income as well as retaining him or her within an institutionalized system of control), and the growth of a market geared to particular and distinctive images of childhood and adolescence. Writing of modern, mass-produced toys, Barthes argues:

... faced with this world of faithful and complicated objects, the child can only identify himself as owner, as user, never as creator; he does not invent the world, he uses it: there are, prepared for him, actions without adventures, without wonder, without joy (Barthes, 1973, p. 54).

This perhaps overstates the case but at least reminds us that the modern child is provided with images of himself as a member of a distinctive category just as, a few years later, teenagers are presented with a variety of images defining what it is to be a teenager, each stressing a collective autonomy and independence. The child is in some respects freer than his predecessors while, at the same time, less able than might have been the case in the past to participate in adult culture.

It is possible to summarize this account of the family in industrial society? Certainly, by now, we should have learned to be cautious about simplified statements which attempt to outline the central features of 'the family in modern society'. In the first place it is clear that 'modern', 'Western', 'industrial' or 'capitalist' society is not some homogeneous whole but one which contains many varieties of patterns of living, many different communities and sub-cultures with differing degrees of openness to the wider society, differing historical experiences, differing ways of relating as families and as individuals to the major changes in the economy and in ways of earning a living. The task of sociology is to develop tools and modes of understanding these different patterns and responses and to relate them to the broad strands of historical change. In the second place, the account that has been provided has been shown to be open to differing interpretations of *value*; in other words, while we may agree what the main changes in the family have been, we may disagree over whether or not we approve of these changes. To some, they are signs of an overall decline in the family and in familistic values, to an extent which threatens the fabric of society itself; to others, they indicate a successful adaptation on the part of the family to economic and social change; to yet others, the changes have meant deeper and new contradictions in the role of women and more subtle patterns of sexual exploitation. Another part of the sociologist's task is to investigate these diverse and conflicting values, to examine the social forces shaping them, and to explore the effect they have in actually shaping the institution of the family which was the original subject of inquiry.

One final warning is necessary. The attempt to talk about 'the family in industrial society' implies some contrast with the family in 'pre-industrial society', thereby apparently lumping together feudal Europe, the major empires and kingdoms of the Middle and Far East and the Americas, and the many forms of tribal, hunting, nomadic and peasant societies that have been found throughout different parts of the globe. Such an approach is not only unscientific; it is also arrogantly ethnocentric. Finnigan has demonstrated how misleading it is to describe 'primitive societies' as if they were all in some way 'dominated by kinship' (Finnigan, 1970, pp. 171–94), and Laslett and his associates at Cambridge have shown how, in many ways, the composition of the family in pre-industrial England was similar to that of the family of today (Laslett, 1965). Then, as now, the norm was that young married couples should live in a residence separate from those of their families of origin, and the three-generational household was as rare then as it is now. These qualifications and cautions become particularly appropriate when we come to consider the historical and social sources of these broad changes that we have attempted to outline.

Perhaps the least contentious way of describing the family in contemporary society is to characterize it as a 'relatively autonomous' institution. At a more theoretical level this characterization has some affinities with Gouldner's concept of 'functional autonomy':

In conceiving of systems as made up of more or less functionally autonomous elements . . . the elements are not merely 'parts' but are seen to exist in and for 'themselves'. They are seen to have an existence apart from any given system in which they are involved; their reality does not depend solely upon their involvement in the system under examination (Gouldner, 1970, pp. 215–16).

More concretely, and with particular reference to the institution of the family, we have seen:

(a) That there is no generally recognized familistic unit other than the nuclear family.

(b) That this unit is relatively 'shallow' genealogically speaking, i.e., that it tends to consist of two generations only and that for many couples the main tie of commitment and responsibility is the conjugal one.

(c) That the relationships outside this conjugally-based family are, to varying degrees, reflections and expressions of choice, rather than of firm and unambiguous duty.

(d) That this relatively autonomous conjugal unit is supported by a familistic ideology, which stresses the importance of relationships between the spouses, and between parents and children, and which tends to equate the values of independence and privacy with this kind of family unit.

Finally, and following from these previous points:

(e) That the relationship between this family unit and other sectors of society, notably the economy, are indirect and subject to considerable variation.

To describe the family of today as a relatively autonomous, conjugally-based unit is probably the best way to do justice to the variety of patterns that not only still persist but which continue to evolve and develop, and to recognize some of the sources of contradiction and tension within the family as well as some of the sources of strength. Finally, to describe the family in these terms is not necessarily to argue that societies other than those so-called 'industrial societies' may not possess some of these familial features as well.

To talk of 'the family in industrial society' implies, as we have noted, that in some way the family has changed with the process of industrialization. But what does this mean? Does this mean that industrialization *caused* certain changes in the family; or that certain changes in the family were a necessary (if not sufficient) precondition for industrialization to take place; or that, more vaguely, there is some degree of 'fit' between a certain type of family and a certain type of economy?

The historical and comparative evidence, as well as the evidence drawn from our own society, presents many difficulties in the way of reaching any clear decisions on these matters. Thus we have seen that there is considerable evidence of a living and functioning *network* of kin (some sociologists write of a 'modified extended family') in modern industrial society and how some historians have shown how many similarities exist between the family in pre-industrial Europe and the family of our own times.

Some further evidence of the complexities involved in handling the problems of the relationship between social and economic change and change in the family comes from accounts of the way in which families handle problems of migration in societies undergoing processes of urbanization and industrialization. Rapid urbanization and industrialization takes place with the growth of a new, mobile labour force recruited from rural areas or from other, more rural, countries. Such movements, however, do not necessarily and simply entail the substitution of a smaller conjugally-based family for a traditional extended family; rather it would appear that at these times kin may take on a new significance, and that we may need to look at a network of relationships much wider than the conjugal family. Thus:

(a) Families in the rural areas or in the countries of emigration may provide financial assistance for some of their unmarried males to travel many hundreds of miles to seek employment. Reciprocally, such families may receive financial remittances from their migrating members once they have established themselves, and those left behind may derive prestige in their local community from the successes of their sons in the cities or the new countries.

(b) Kin already established in the countries of immigration or in the city may provide all kinds of assistance to related newcomers, whether in terms of accommodation, short-term financial loans or in finding work. Less tangibly, but almost of equal importance, the newer migrants may obtain advice on how to adapt to the urban way of life with its newer and more 'sophisticated' ways. A wide-ranging network of advice, information and assistance may develop, linking the families left behind and those who have migrated on a seasonal, short-term or longer-term basis. Such patterns have been noted, with considerable variation, in Latin America, Africa, India, rural North America and Britain at the time of the Industrial Revolution.

This brief examination of the inter-relationships between family, migration and urbanization should serve to illustrate the point that it is often difficult to establish any clear pattern of causation. Changes have certainly taken place, often dramatic and painful changes, involving exploitations and deprivations. Yet, at the same time, there has not, in most cases, been a sharp break between one way of life and another but rather a process involving subtle shifts in emphasis, whereby one set of relationships – kin, friends and neighbours – take on new significances in place of or in addition to older or earlier established relationships.

This brief discussion should also illustrate the point that we have, implicitly, adopted a very broad definition of industrialization, taking the term to include not simply the adoption of new techniques of production (factories and corporations) but also wider and related changes such as the development of industrially-based cities, migrations to these cities, the growth of bureaucracies and, perhaps, less tangible changes in values. In a more detailed analysis it would be necessary to separate out these different factors and to attempt to assess how each has contributed or is related to changes in the family. Thus, talking of industrialization in this sense would entail an interest in such topics as a growing separation between home and work, and the growing transformation of the family into a unit of consumption linked to the sphere of production through the separate and specialized earnings of its constituent members. When we are considering the impact of urbanization, we focus upon the way in which changes in the family and economy are affected by physical distance and spatial separation, the increasing need to travel to work, and perhaps the substitution of primary social relationships in a relatively stable territorially-based community such as a village by more secondary, more impersonal and fluctuating social relationships – which may, under certain circumstances, cause the members of the nuclear family to become more dependent upon each other. When we talk of capitalism, we are concerned with a system which is based upon the need for what Weber calls 'forever renewed profit' through the selling of the worker's labour power to the property-owning employer, and the consequences these socio-economic relationships have for the family. When we talk of mobility, we are talking about movement that is both geographical and social, and about the way in which these movements separate family members as well as, perhaps, creating new ties between other family members. Clearly the task of separating out these different strands of historical change is an enormous one but the mere outlining of these problems reminds us that the sociologist must always be sensitive to the differential cultural and historical experiences often hidden under such general and abstract labels as 'industrialization', 'migration', 'urbanization', 'capitalism' and so on.

If, therefore, it is difficult at this stage for us to establish with any certainty general patterns of cause and effect between 'industrialization' and the relatively autonomous conjugal family, it may be possible for us to argue that there is at least a degree of fit, a congruence, between these two elements. This involves a recognition that societies have some kind of pattern and that certain features of a society appear to 'hang together'.

An example:

Love and Marriage in Western Society

As an example of this kind of argument we may look at one part of the analysis of the family in modern society, that is the process by which mates are selected. The 'rules' according to which marital partners may be selected in modern Britain or the United States may be stated very simply:

(a) There are very few *pro*scriptions as to whom one may *not* marry (apart from those governed by laws dealing with incest, bigamy, age of consent, etc.) and no *pre*scriptions as to whom one *should* marry or, indeed, as to whether one should marry at all. However, we should note that the prescriptions and proscriptions of particular religious or ethnic groups may almost have the force of law, in that an individual must either adhere to them or face exclusion from that particular community. Thus some religious sects demand of their members that they should not be 'yoked to unbelievers'.

(b) More positively, mates should be selected by the prospective partners themselves. The ideal expectation is that marriage should be based upon love, a strong emotional and physical attraction between two unmarried persons which stresses the personal qualities of the one in the eyes of the other, rather than the expectations of the parents as to the ideal mate for their child.

Of course, in practice we know that this is a very over-simplified picture. The law may appear to be very permissive in this respect but we know that in actual practice homogamy – the tendency of like to marry like – is as much part of our actual marriage-patterns as formal freedom of choice. Marital partners tend to come from the same area, to be of the same social class and educational level, and to be of similar ages. Even within the broad categories of age and social class it may well be that parents are exercising subtle pressures in the background as to who is to be considered a desirable match for their offspring. Furthermore, it is likely that love and marriage are not so inextricably linked as the popular song would have it and that many couples take a more pragmatic view in choosing a mate, or indeed recognize the possibility of falling in love outside marriage. However, in spite of these qualifications, it still remains the case that marriage is a matter of choice by the partners concerned (except in cases such as royal marriages) and that love is viewed as being an important, if not the sole, element in this choice.

Sociologists have noted that this process whereby prospective mates choose each other, a process apparently so 'natural' to people within our culture, is, on a wider historical and comparative basis, a very unusual one indeed. Many other societies have or have had much more specific rules about whom one should or should not marry and about who should decide on prospective marriage partners. A well-known example is the traditional Islamic Arab pattern whereby the groom often did not even see his bride until the actual wedding day, and where selection of partners was firmly in the hands of the elders (Goode, 1970, pp. 88–101). In these cultures, love, if it played a part at all, was viewed as something that should develop after a marriage had been arranged, celebrated and consummated, rather than before. What used to be called the 'Hollywood' notion of love might often appear to be laughable or grotesque to people in other cultures. Gluckman, writing of traditional African society, notes:

One observer has said that a man seeks companionship with other men, loves his sister and sleeps with his wife. This is an exaggeration, but it stresses the need to examine family relations in the light of these wider social relationships (Gluckman, 1956, p. 78).

The 'romantic love complex', it is argued, is a feature peculiar in the first instance to Western industrial society, and one which grew out of the earlier pattern of courtly love and was slowly adapted by the more puritan members of the new middle classes for the needs of that society.

Thus it is argued that the presence of this romantic love complex is not an accidental matter, but is something that 'fits in' with other features of Western society, particularly the economy. Thus the particular pattern of marriage based upon love and free choice might be linked to the wider economic system in a variety of ways:

(a) The labour market 'requires' that individuals should be prepared to move to the most appropriate jobs, either socially through the educational system or geographically (or both), and such a system presupposes a relative weakening of kinship ties. With social and geographical mobility as the central requirements of such a society, parental controls – in marital and other matters – are thereby weakened, since unmarried individuals have greater opportunities to meet each other in situations far removed from the parental home. Negatively, a system based upon strong and wide-ranging kinship ties and controls would act as a severe brake upon an economic system requiring this degree of mobility.

(b) This weakening of kinship and other primary based ties and controls as a result of the requirements of the economic system means that married couples are thrown more upon each other and that they may feel a need or an obligation to develop a deep personal relationship within this conjugally-based unit. The stress, therefore, is upon compatibility based upon prior exercise of choice and selective dating and experimentation. (The use of computers in this process is a logical extension of this tendency.) One corollary of this process may be increased divorce rates, a reflection of the perhaps over-high yet under-precise expectations generated in respect of the marital relationship.

(c) The economic system, together with the democratic ideology, places a high premium on individual achievement and self-fulfilment. The freely-chosen marriage and the independent household 'fits in' with this ideology.

The relationship between mate-selection based upon romantic love and free choice and the capitalist economic system is buttressed by the historical legacy of Protestantism (itself related to capitalism and individualism), including Protestant attitudes towards sexuality. Furthermore, we are dealing with an evolving system. On the one hand, Protestantism as a dominant religious force has declined, and with it the idea of the strict connection between love, sex and freely-chosen marriage. In a more secular and commercial society, love and sex have been given a separate, commodity-like status through the institutions of advertising and the mass media. Yet if love and sex are no longer seen as being necessarily identified with the institution of marriage, the dominance of the idea that marriage should be based on free choice and characterized by free sexual expression remains, and reinforces the individualistic view of love.

This analysis implies, therefore, a fair degree of 'fit' between a particular aspect of family living and the economic system, between the part and the whole, and between family values and wider ideological themes. There are, however, certain difficulties with this analysis, reflecting some of the problems we experienced above in trying to place a particular kind of family system within a particular kind of economic system. In the first place, it is clear that attitudes to love and marriage are much more complex than this account allows for. Popular attitudes towards love and marriage would often seem to suggest the possibility of a tension between the two rather than an automatic affinity. Also, as has already been suggested, contemporary attitudes to sex – marital, pre-marital or extra-marital, heterosexual or homosexual – would also suggest a range of possibilities rather than the simple bracketing together of sex, love and marriage and that all these possibilities could exist within the same or similar economic systems. Secondly, it is easy to slide from a theory of the historical *origins* of the romantic love complex (whether true or not) and of how this cult became incorporated into capitalist culture, to some notion of the historical inevitability or functional necessity of this process. Thus, although the United States, Japan, Italy, Britain and the Scandinavian countries may all, to some extent, be described as 'capitalist' countries, it is clear that they all reflect varying attitudes and practices in relation to love, sex and marriage. At the very least such comparisons should remind us that we are dealing with a broad *range* of patterns or tendencies rather than a fixed set of relationships between family and economy. This range of variation is an example of the concepts of relative or functional autonomy that we outlined earlier in this chapter.

Finally, it is important to note that this assumption of the fit between romantic love and capitalism or industrialism smoothes over and obscures tensions and contradictions within the system, especially in relation to the position and exploitation of women. To a large extent love and marriage, while they necessarily involve men, appear to form a central life-interest for women in the same way that work, in our society, is often a central life-interest for men. Women, for example, are much more involved in the business of organizing and preparing for weddings and are much more likely than men to demand that their wedding be a 'correct' one (Barker, 1972). Women, more home-bound and less involved in the economic and political spheres than men, invest a much greater part of their selves in love and marriage and thereby stand to lose more, emotionally as well as financially, in the event of a breakdown of these relationships. Love, therefore, may also be seen as part of an ideology which masks the sexual and economic exploitation of women. It is important to remember, therefore, that there are different ways of evaluating the inter-connections between love, marriage and industrial society or capitalism.

Functionalist and Marxian Perspectives

This extended analysis of the place of love and mate-selection based upon free choice was included in order to illustrate wider problems in the analysis and evaluation of the degree of 'fit' between the particular kind of family system that has been outlined and the economic system in which it is placed. The wider theoretical implications become clearer if we go on to contrast and compare two approaches to this problem, the functionalist and the Marxian (see also Middleton, 1974).

Version 1: the functionalist

The main themes in this theoretical approach have already been outlined at different points in this chapter. It is argued that the conjugally-based, relatively autonomous nuclear family system, with its emphasis on free mate-selection and relative weakness of kinship ties and obligations outside the immediate family, is the family system best suited to the needs of a mature industrial economy. In particular, this version holds that this family system is the one most likely to facilitate free mobility of labour and to provide the maximum opportunities for advancement based upon individual strivings and skills, unhindered by kinship obligations (Parsons, 1964, pp. 191–2). Furthermore, the conjugal family unit – with the stress on privacy and individual growth and development – is the one best suited to provide an emotional counterpart to the tensions generated in the economic system, in the large factories and impersonal offices. Finally, in this version, the nuclear family, relatively autonomous and therefore indirectly linked to the social system, is probably the most appropriate unit for the socialization of young children into the central values of individualism and independence.

Version 2: The Marxian

In this version, the nuclear family is the main unit through which the capitalist *system* reproduces itself. This is not simply a matter of physical reproduction, the process of providing new members to work in the system. The operation of the sexual division of labour, whereby the woman's main sphere is defined as that of the household and housework, is the cheapest and most effective means of sustaining the male worker on a day-to-day basis, providing him with the basic physical, emotional and sexual needs. Furthermore, the fact that the worker has to provide not merely for himself but also for his wife and children serves as a powerful inducement to him to remain at work and to conform to its disciplines on a regular basis. Finally, via the family, the labour-force and the capitalist system as a whole reproduces itself over generations, since new members are born into it and are socialized, in later years in association with the educational system, into accepting the values of hierarchy and obedience (combined, paradoxically, with the values of individualism) so essential for the maintenance of capitalism. One Marxist writer likens the position of women in the household under capitalism to the backstage workers in the production of a play, essential yet invisible (Secombe, 1974). In this version it should be remembered that we are dealing not simply with a functioning system but with a system that is stratified into antagonistic classes and that we would therefore expect the family to function in slightly different ways for the different classes. Amongst the property-owning classes, for example, the family serves to maintain the system of private property through the institution of inheritance. At all levels, the family is the major institution through which the class system reproduces itself.

These two versions have been necessarily over-simplified but it is already possible to see some points of comparison as well as of contrast. In the first place, the two accounts are surprisingly similar in stressing the close degree of 'fit' between the family and the economic system. For the Parsonian functions of 'socialization of children and the provision of emotional stabilization for adults' we may substitute the Marxian version of 'reproducing the capitalist system'. Both, therefore, seem to be open to the similar criticism that they fail to do justice to the variety of family patterns that can coexist within one economic system. We have already noted some of the difficulties in this respect with the functionalist model. Some of the objections against the Marxian model may now be noted. This account, like the functionalist, seems to presuppose a traditional model of the nuclear family where there is a married couple with children, where the husband is the breadwinner and where the wife stays at home to deal with the housework. This is, in fact, the pattern which is adopted by many couples in our society, and it is becoming clear that even the increasing participation of married women in the labour-force has only meant a slight shift in emphasis in the traditional sexual division of labour within the home. Yet, theoretically at least, there seems to be no logical reason why the 'dual career' pattern (Rapoport and Rapoport, 1971) of husband and wife making equal contributions to the family income and to the running of the home should not extend beyond the more privileged sections of the professional middle classes. At the very least it may be that this Marxian version, like the functionalist version, does less than full justice to the opportunities for experimentation and change *within* the existing framework: crude versions of historical inevitability (like crude versions of functional necessity) present a particular and specific historical pattern as if it were some kind of more general law. It is likely, for example, that capitalism would continue to function if the major activities of the nuclear family (care of children, feeding, etc.) were socialized – that is carried on outside the home – to a much larger extent. Factories under private ownership could provide crèches for the children of their women workers, just as such facilities were provided during wartime or as they are provided in socialist countries. The experiences of migrant workers in Europe and Southern Africa, for example, where the male workers live together in barrack-like accommodation, provides a disturbing illustration of the way in which capitalism might be able to continue without a direct and immediate dependence on the nuclear family. (Of course, it is recognized that these migrant workers are often supporting nuclear families in their countries or areas of origin and that their growth in numbers reflects the growth of capitalism as a world system; the point again is to suggest the wide range of variation in family experience that is possible within any one economic system.) Or again, is the introduction of payment for housework inconceivable under a capitalist system? Would it liberate the housewife or merely transform her into a new kind of wage-worker, with her husband as employer? The extent to which the liberation of women and/or the abolition of the family is possible within a capitalist system is an important subject of debate within the contemporary feminist movement.

There are, of course, significant differences between the two versions. In the first place, the functionalist version tends to speak of 'industrial society' (or some similar variation), whereas the Marxian version talks more specifically of capitalism. If the former is too broad, the latter is probably too specific, tending to ignore some of the similarities in family systems between capitalist and socialist (e.g. East European) countries. In the second place, the functionalist version tends to see family and economy in some kind of reciprocal partnership, whereas the Marxian version posits the economy as the 'dominant partner'. Finally, the Marxian version directs our attention towards some of the sources of contradiction and change within the system, a feature often more muted in many functionalist accounts. To put this contrast another way, the functionalist version tends to suggest that family and economy exist together in a relationship of relatively stable equilibrium, while the Marxian version, working within a framework that deals with conflict and class antagonisms, views the system as containing within it a variety of contradictions which are inherently unstable.

It is certainly true that the functionalist theory does allow for change, largely through the process of 'structural differentiation', whereby the economic functions initially performed by the family are taken over by factories outside the home, hence splitting the functions of consumption and production. It does also point to some sources of tension within the system. These sources of tension are, however, seen as deviations from the norm or *mal*functions of the system and not as possible sources of change, or the positive development of alternative and possibly better patterns of living. Marxist theorists, on the other hand, point to contradictions within the system which can, they argue, be resolved only through some fundamental change. This is most clearly illustrated in the case of the examination of the position of women in capitalist society. One social contradiction for women lies in the affirmation of the values of independence and individualism in the economic system and the political system, and the denial of these same values in the context of the family. Again, as we have seen in the discussion of love and mate-selection, the marital relationship is formally based upon the idea of a contract between equal partners, while in practice, in terms of power, decision-making and total life-experience, it often appears as a denial of this very idea of equality. Furthermore, the growing participation of women in almost all spheres of the labour-force, and the development of universal education, introduces further contradictions between opportunities formally open to women and the actualities of their day-to-day experiences. Such discrepancies and contradictions, when realized and perceived, may give rise to organized movements on the part of women which seek to overcome them. The feminist movements of the latter part of the nineteenth and the second half of the twentieth centuries may in part be understood in these terms.

Perhaps both the functionalist version and the more overly-schematic versions of Marxism do not fully recognize the ways in which people, individually and collectively, experience defects in the domestic or economic situations in which they find themselves, and seek both to understand and to change them. Sociological accounts of 'social change', too, often appear to present social change as an external 'thing' or 'process', something which happens *to* people rather than something to which they may respond and play an active and conscious part. Capitalism has never been short of its critics from within the system, and the same applies to the associated patterns of family living. Protests against the subordination of women and the institution of the family – which was seen as the main source of this subordination – came from both men and women (Mary Wollstonecraft, John Stuart Mill, Virginia Woolf) throughout the nineteenth and twentieth centuries. Such protests sometimes led to organized movements or pressure groups designed to overcome particular aspects of this exploitation (such as the suffragette movement or pressure groups for equal pay and against discrimination in employment) or to confront the system as a whole (as is the case in many of the contemporary feminist movements). Alternatively, a growing sense of dissatisfaction with the existing domestic system sometimes led to more individualistic or partial attempts to develop and evolve alternative patterns of family living. Some of these alternatives and possibilities will be considered in more detail in the next section.

The Future of the Family

In one sense, to talk of the 'future of the family' is to take us back to our starting-point, the question of the definition of the family. To ask the question 'What is the future of the family?' is to presuppose some existing and agreed definition of *the* family. If we include a couple not formally married yet living together, perhaps with children, within our definition of the family, what of two or more couples living together in some form of group or complex marriage? What kinds of changes, for example, could be counted as indicating the 'abolition of the family'? Does this mean abolition of all existing forms of family living, or does it mean the abolition of one particular form of family life? Again, it should be stressed that this debate is not simply 'about words', but about lived experiences – and the words and rhetoric that people use to describe and shape these experiences.

Clearly, also, how we view the family of the future will depend to a large extent on the way in which we view the family of today. If we view the family as a biological necessity, then it would seem to follow that the family must last as long as human society lasts. If we regard the family as an institution performing vital functions which cannot readily be performed by any other institution, then the family should continue or society must face the consequences. Alternatively, it might be possible to regard the whole of human history as being, in a sense, the overcoming of biological necessity, and perhaps the ultimate recognition of this may be in the transcendence of the family as a basic institution. The development of 'biological engineering' to the extent that motherhood is rendered obsolete, and the development of more collective forms of socialization (communes, kibbutzim, etc.) may to some represent the possibilities of a humanist utopia and to others a science-fiction nightmare, a dystopia. But the possibilities – perhaps first set in motion with effective control over conception – cannot be discounted from our model of the future.

In the light of these observations, let us consider a variety of possible alternatives and futures that have been developed or proposed:

(a) *Communes*. Much attention has been paid to the development of varying patterns of communal experiment, chiefly in North America, over the past few years. Of course, the creation of such 'intentional communities' is not new in the history of North America;

economically self-sufficient communities, often with a strong religious ideology, flourished throughout the nineteenth century. What is perhaps new is the range of variation, the sheer volume of communal experiments, and the amount of publicity and research that is being given to these communities. The range is certainly very wide, from austere and disciplined communities of Zen Buddhists to apparently anarchic 'hippie' communes; from economically self-sufficient rural communes to looser networks of relationships in an urban environment; from communities founded on 'rational' or 'scientific' principles by followers of Marx or Skinner to mystical communes with close connections with the drug culture. The types of family relationships represented within these communes are equally various. There may be complete celibacy, clearly defined nuclear families within a wider communal setting, loose alliances of couples with varying and permissive degrees of permanence, or more elaborate forms of complex or group marriage. Turning our attention to children, these may be socialized by the community as a whole – and may even be regarded as children *of* the community – or by couples. There may be complete or near-complete equality between the sexes, or there may be a reassertion of more traditional 'frontier' styles of division of labour. Just as it is difficult to talk with any confidence about *the* family in modern society so it is also difficult to talk about *the* commune, and it is possible to see the looser types of urban commune merging imperceptibly into more open family networks.

Communal living, whatever form it may take, is still very much a minority activity, chiefly, although not exclusively, among the young and particularly among the White middle-class young. The difficulties that such communities have experienced – for example the need to reconcile a 'do your own thing' and anti-materialistic ethic with the need for some degree of co-operation and economic planning – are enormous, and few of them appear to last for more than a year or two. But importance is not necessarily simply measured by life-span, and the interest shown in these experiments spreads far beyond those who participate in them. It is possible that increasing numbers of people will come to spend at least a period of their lives in a commune or community of some description and that the ideas that these communes represent may have a much wider influence.

(b) *Variations in Marriage Pattern.* At a more modest level, perhaps, some sociologists have examined changes that may be taking place within the institution of marriage itself. In other words, a kind of commitment between partners may continue to exist, but the relationship may differ in many respects from traditional models of marriage. The chief dimension along which change can be expected concerns the degree of equality in decision-making and the division of domestic responsibilities between the sexes. Thus, Young and Willmott point to the growth of a 'symmetrical family', a growing pattern of egalitarianism between spouses which is already with us among sections of the middle class and is likely to be followed in the future by a much wider section of the population (Young and Willmott, 1975). Other writers have stressed the central importance of employment. In the increasing number of cases where husband and wife are both working and contributing equally to the joint income, it is likely that equality of participation in decision-making within the home will follow. The Rapoports have described the 'dual careers' followed by some professional married couples (Rapoport and Rapoport, 1971), and Bernard looks to a future where husband and wife each have a part-time job only and where each contributes equally to the running of the home (Bernard, 1976, pp. 260–77). The notion of 'open marriage' includes this shared-work pattern as one of its elements, but would also extend the idea of openness to include friends and leisure-interests and also the possibility of sexual relationships with other partners that are not necessarily labelled as adulterous and providing grounds for divorce.

Theoretically, all these patterns are possible, and in practice they are all being lived by a few couples, chiefly in the professional middle classes. But data for these professional middle classes (including that of Young and Willmott) also suggest that the traditional sexual division of labour is still very much with us, that the husband's career is the strongest influence, and that the husband simply 'helps' his wife in domestic chores (particularly the more pleasant ones such as taking the children for a walk) rather than participating equally in the running of the home. The possibility of egalitarian marriage may have been demonstrated, but the barriers to its realization and the limits to the extent to which this pattern can extend throughout society are considerable.

(c) *Feminist Variations.* Some of the strongest criticisms of the contemporary nuclear family have come from members of the women's movement. The nuclear family, and particularly the institution of housework, has been seen as the main obstacle to the full liberation of women, severely limiting whatever advances may have been made in the fields of employment or politics. Generally, discussion on possible alternatives to the nuclear family has focused on the ways in which it might be possible to separate the various present 'functions' of the family. Thus, socialization of children, largely the exclusive responsibility of the nuclear family (in practice, the mother), should be made more of a responsibility of the community as a whole, both formally in nurseries and play-groups, and informally in a wider network of relationships between individuals and families. It is not so much, therefore, a question of the formal 'abolition' of the family as of the development of viable alternative ways of meeting its present-day functions. Juliet Mitchell, for example, sees hope in the development of a range of alternatives which will include experiments in communal living (Mitchell, J. J., 1971, pp. 144–51), while Firestone lays more stress on the possibilities of biological engineering, particularly more effective controls over conception and artificial reproduction, and linking the feminist movement with radical ecology (Firestone, 1972, pp. 183–224).

We could extend this discussion of alternatives for several pages. It is difficult to opt for one version of the future as against another (for one thing, the concept of 'the future' itself, which can refer to next week or the next century, is inherently ambiguous), but it is possible to pick out some of the key features in our present society which may shape, while not rigidly determining, the future of the family. The first consideration is that attachment to the central ideas of family and marriage is still very strong. Some of the evidence for this – the continued popularity of marriage and remarriage, for example – has been cited earlier in this chapter. The second consideration, in opposition to the first, is that there is a growing degree of concern about and awareness of the weaknesses and possible defects of the nuclear family as it exists today. This concern is reflected not simply in the feminist movement but also in the concern aroused by publicity given to battered children and battered wives, the aspirations of women who may not be formally attached to any overtly feminist group, and the popularity of writers like Laing and Cooper.

Proposed solutions to these problems, however, may vary considerably, from a strengthening of the family through a more deliberate channelling of social assistance through family ties (for example, in the care of the aged, the sick and the handicapped) and the growth of family counselling, to the developments of the alternatives that have been outlined above. It is difficult to see any clear consensus emerging out of these claims and counter-claims. It is likely that patterns of experimentation will continue, perhaps growing at a modest rate, alongside the slower changes taking place within more orthodox family patterns. It is possible that the institution of the family will, in some respects, become demystified, that people will be more willing to face its ugly side and to criticize its more obvious defects. It is likely that new ties and commitments will emerge and that individuals will be less willing to use the language of family relationships – the rhetoric of the family – to describe these new relationships. Couples living together, for example, may be more willing to use the labels of 'man and wife' as labels on behalf of others. The task of sociology in this debate is not to stifle hopes or discourage innovation in the name of biological inevitability or functional necessity, but to subject all arrangements and experiments to critical scrutiny and to assist in a process of mutual understanding and communication through the lucid presentation of variations of family living and the relationships that are evolving or being worked out.

Conclusion

The reader may feel that this chapter has not 'said anything' about the family of today or of its future. The aim, however, has been not so much to present a set of facts about the family but to remind the reader that there are various ways of understanding and interpreting these facts. The family, although a very small unit, is also a very complex unit. Its complexity derives partly from the fact that it includes people of different ages and generations whose relationships to each other are constantly changing through processes of aging, the establishment of new relationships and the breaking off of old ties. Its complexity also derives from the fact that most of us have been or are deeply involved in and shaped by these family experiences, experiences which seem unique and personal to each individual. Neither happy nor unhappy families are all alike, yet the fact that we can understand something of the family experiences of others reflects a sharing of a similar culture and history. In the sociology of the family we attempt to come to terms with these similarities and differences in ways which do not do violence to the uniqueness of individual family life and yet in ways that are aware of the extent to which the family is a product of factors outside it. The family, facing both ways – towards the individual and towards society – plays a vital role in mediating between what C. Wright Mills has called 'personal troubles' and 'public issues' (Mills, 1970, pp. 14–15), and for this reason alone should continue to excite our attention and concern.

Chapter 5
Education

Formal education in schools and colleges has assumed a massive importance in modern society. In the United States, for example, education has become a full-time activity for a substantial section of the population: a third of the population aged 18–24 were enrolled in higher education in 1974, and in the same year over three million people were employed as teachers in educational institutions (Bureau of Commerce, 1975). As a consequence of its importance, education is the centre of attention of powerful and, at times, competing interests. Governments are interested in the 'output' of education as trained labour power; employers are worried about the 'quality' of contemporary education and whether it provides suitable recruits for their enterprises. Many parents are concerned that their children get a 'good' education, one that will allow them to obtain higher qualifications and well-paid jobs. Educational systems are also blamed for contributing to social and economic inequalities because, for example, they segregate children of one race and one religion from another or because children of poorer families are not as successful in obtaining educational qualifications as children from richer families. Indeed, changing the educational system is often identified as a major instrument of social reform aimed at remedying social and economic inequalities.

In the heat of these debates, certain characteristics of formal education and of educational systems are often forgotten. First, a system of education is an integral part of society, and the content and organization of education are likely to reflect the prejudices, inequalities and social and economic priorities of that society. Education is not an autonomous agent which can be used in a socially neutral way, to change or 'improve' society; in other words, education is not a malleable tool of social engineering. One of our arguments in this chapter is that the strength of the external pressures to which educational systems are subject limits educational innovation and makes education a less-than-rewarding experience for school children and college students.

Second, what is learnt in school is not simply a fixed body of knowledge which is necessary to the performance of subsequent occupational and social roles. Learning in schools and colleges is itself a social process. When sociologists study the learning process they are not simply concerned with the acquisition of subject-matter knowledge and how that acquisition is influenced by variations in school organization. Values and social skills are also communicated through the system of formal education. This is often done deliberately as when, for example, a school seeks to impress upon its pupils values of achievement and loyalty to the flag. Skills and values will also be communicated to pupils informally, by their teachers and fellow pupils. Not only are civic ideals communicated in the school, but also basic ethical notions of honesty and solidarity and social norms encouraging say, individual competitiveness, group loyalty or even 'anti-school' attitudes. The communication is often not overt; it occurs via the playing of games, in informal classroom interaction among pupils and between them and teachers, in the life of school societies and in the rituals of school prayers and assemblies. This form of learning has been described as a 'hidden curriculum'. The learning of social skills and values also takes place outside the school and, indeed, occurs throughout life. The social skills and values learned outside and within the school may, at times, conflict and will certainly influence each other, thus contributing to blurring the boundaries between formal education and the rest of society.

The main contributions that sociologists have made to the study of education are, then, (a) the analysis of education as part of the system of social stratification and (b) the examination of the learning process within schools and colleges. We begin our discussion by considering the various ways in which the social environment affects education, and to do so we will consider the extent to which even so apparently fixed an attribute as intelligence is influenced by environmental factors. We will see that, to sociologists, 'environment' includes a considerable range of factors, such as the home and family, neighbourhood, social class and the overall system of social stratification. All these factors affect, and are affected by, the educational system. In the second half of the chapter, we consider the organization of education within schools and colleges and examine the social processes internal to educational organizations. Finally, we close the chapter by comparing educational systems in various countries to see how societal differences in social stratification affect educational systems.

Heredity and Environment

One possible objection to the sociologist's emphasis on the importance of the social environment is that learning is a mental process which is affected, primarily, by the innate capacities – the intelligence – of the child. Those who hold this perspective would not deny that environmental factors influence education and that, for example, the learning of all children could be improved by a better teaching environment, or, in the case of poor families, by improved material conditions. Yet the thrust of their argument is that innate differences in intelligence will determine the educational achievements of the children: some children will learn quickly and proceed to high educational levels, while others will be slow learners and will be incapable of grasping complex bodies of knowledge. From this perspective, intelligence is an objectively identifiable and relatively fixed human capacity.

Those who hold to the notion of innate intelligence argue that differences in intelligence can be determined at an early stage and the results of the tests can be used to provide the kinds of education 'suited' to children of different intelligence levels. Intelligence tests and IQ (intelligence quotient) were devised as scientifically-based and impartial measures of intelligence, allowing a child's true potential to be determined without the 'biases' introduced into educational performance by such factors as extra coaching or temporary lack of interest (Burt, 1961, pp. 447–50). As Sir Cyril Burt expressed the matter in discussing the advantages of IQ testing: 'Capacity must obviously limit content. It is impossible for a pint jug to hold more than a pint of milk; and it is equally impossible for a child's educational attainments to rise higher than his educable capacity permits' (ibid., p. 448). Testing, it is claimed, is highly efficient for educational organizations, permitting them to make the best use of scarce resources: children with little chance of reaching higher educational levels can then concentrate on the types of skills appropriate to their intelligence level and teachers and schools can specialize in educating children of different innate capacities. Such arguments have exerted a profound influence on educational thinking: the IQ test and the division of schooling to cater for children of different innate capacities have been two of the mainstays of education in Britain and elsewhere.

The emphasis on innate intelligence has, from the beginning, been associated with the idea that intelligence is mainly inherited. Eysenck, for example, argues that some 80 per cent of the variation in IQs within a given population is the result of heredity (Eysenck, 1971, pp. 61–5). Eysenck does not claim that there is a total fit between the intelligence level of a child and that of his parents, but shows that there is a high probability that children will have similar intelligence levels to those of their parents. He points out that in any society open to the talents, there will always be a degree of social mobility occasioned by the downward movement of the less intelligent children of the élite and the upward movement of the more intelligent children of the less privileged classes. In the United States, Jensen has claimed that it is hereditary factors that explain the persistence among Blacks of low levels of educational attainment and of inferior IQ scores when compared to Whites.

The arguments of Eysenck and Jensen are cast in scientific terms. They claim that intelligence is determined genetically, that is by the pool of genes (the basic particles of heredity located in the chromosomes of each cell) which individuals derive from their parents. Genes are known to determine a range of human characteristics, such as the blood-group, eye and hair colour, and reflexes to stimuli. Not enough is known about genes for it to be possible to test directly the relationship between an individual's genetic make-up and his intelligence, and consequently the proponents of heredity have relied on indirect tests of the association. Their arguments have been based on comparing the IQs of parents and children from different social classes, on the persistence of class or racial differences in measured intelligence (despite improvements in the material conditions of the less privileged) or, in the case of the Black–White comparison, on comparing racial groups (Black, Whites, Mexican-Americans) who have similar incomes and occupations. Those favouring the heredity explanation have also drawn support from studies of relatives and twins, such as those, for example, which show that twins with similar genetic origins (identical twins) are closer in IQ than are non-identical twins (a critical survey of these studies is found in Bodmer, 1972, pp. 83–113).

These attempts to separate hereditary and environmental factors are not as straightforward as at first they might seem. Biologists see little value in distinguishing genetic and environmental effects, since, though both types of effect can be identified, they are inextricably intertwined. The biologist Steven Rose points out, in discussing the brain, that the genetic programme of the individual can never be expressed without an environment and that the nature of the stimulation provided by that environment determines which capacities are brought into play and which are allowed to wither and die (Rose, 1972, pp. 134–41). Another biologist, John Hambley, shows that it is wrong to think that single genes can be identified which determine specific capacities, such as intelligence; the action of genes depends on the presence of a large number of other genes and on the environmental circumstances which provide stimuli and switch genes on and off (Hambley, 1972, pp. 116–20).

Hambley goes on to question the utility of searching for any one quality as the measure of the talents needed either in education or in the wider society. Genetic variability is, he claims, one of the most important qualities of human biological make-up; the plasticity of an individual's genetic composition enables him to learn from and adapt to an environment. Differences between individuals in their genetic composition allow for a variety of adaptive modes and of talents to develop in society. Hambley sees the use of measures such as IQ as dangerous because they 'fix' one type of capacity as the most important quality needed for human survival. Education, he says, should encourage the development of diverse talents and, as he puts it, 'IQ is not a particularly inspired measure of what our future needs might be whether in this regard [to face uncertainty] or in regard to aesthetic and creative talents needed to sustain such a [future] society' (Hambley, 1972, p. 124).

Some would go further in their condemnation of the IQ test and argue that it is primarily an ideological device which is used to justify the different treatment and rewards that children receive in school and, later, in the occupational world. Thus, relatively small differences in IQ are identified as 'significant' by school authorities or employers and, with little supporting evidence, are assumed to determine occupational potential and provide a justification for paying low wages for one kind of work and high wages for another, more 'skilled', kind. As Bowles and Gintis put it: '. . . the emphasis on IQ as the basis for economic success serves to legitimate an authoritarian, hierarchical, stratified, and unequal economic system, and to reconcile individuals to their objective position within this system' (Bowles and Gintis, 1976, p. 116).

Sociologists and sociolinguists have also questioned the usefulness of intelligence tests by arguing that such tests cannot adequately detect the various ways in which the ability to reason or express intelligence are developed in society. Intelligence tests, as Eysenck himself admits, are always culturally biased in that they use words or refer to concepts which will be more familiar to one group of children than to another (Eysenck, 1971, pp. 54–5). The important point, for Eysenck, is that tests must be relatively culture-fair, using a vocabulary and set of concepts which do not require much schooling or much academic knowledge. Eysenck, however, misinterprets the significance of culture for the sociologist by emphasizing the biases introduced by differences in access to high culture rather than those arising from different uses of everyday language.

In a study of Black youths in inner-city areas of America, Labov showed that the non-standard vernacular these Blacks use, which could cause difficulty in answering most IQ tests, does not inhibit learning and is often associated with considerable reasoning powers and imagination (Labov, 1972). Swift argues that there is sufficient difference in vocabulary and concepts between, say, children from Liverpool dockland, South Wales mining townships and North London suburbs, for it to be impossible for tests to avoid language biases (Swift, 1972). Swift claims that IQ tests 'can mislead us into a culture-bound theory of intellect that is only a reflection of the dominant behaviour patterns in society. If we accept that the language of culturally deprived children is not a basically non-logical mode of expressive behaviour we will find great difficulty in justifying the rules of language which we impose upon children in schools and tests designed to predict school behaviour' (ibid., p. 158).

The quotation indicates that the argument against explanations in terms of heredity is that the latter misunderstand the nature and importance of the cultural diversity of society. By culture, the sociologist refers to the values, norms and particular styles of verbal and non-verbal communication that are shared by a group of people; this group could be a nation, a region or simply people who have interacted enough with each other on the job or in a neighbourhood sufficiently to need to develop their own means of communication.

Distinctive cultures, sometimes called sub-cultures, develop within a society, when a group lives or works in relative isolation, when a group perceives external threats to its welfare, or when a group has a common interest to defend against outsiders. Such cultures include the 'deviant' sub-cultures of teenagers in inner city slums, the working-class cultures of mining villages or upper-class cultures based on the suburbs and the golf club. People belonging to the same culture may develop preferences for the same types of material object, such as a certain type of motorbike or a preference for tea as against coffee; they are also likely to develop a special set of norms and values about the 'right' kinds of behaviour for people like themselves, and this 'right' behaviour will differ widely between the teenage motorcycle gang and the surburban business executive. People in the same culture will also be likely to have a special language – whether through idiomatic phrases, or fashionable and unfashionable slang.

When the sociologist talks about the effect of environmental factors on education, he does not simply refer to differences in material wealth or in the physical standards of housing or schools; the environment to the sociologist is nothing less than the social and cultural organization of society (Swift, 1965). It includes the system of social inequality in society and the views that people develop about the world as a consequence of this system of inequality. The environment, then, affects people's self-conceptions, their self-confidence and their readiness to stereotype others as unworthy, unintelligent and so on. Thus, comparing the IQs of Blacks and Whites who have similar incomes and occupations does not 'compensate' scientifically for the effects of two hundred years of accumulated racial prejudice (Bodmer, 1972). From this perspective, the environment is neither external to the individual nor a concrete object which can, somehow, be tested for. Swift contrasts the sociologist's approach with that of the psychologist:

... the sociologist complains that a psychologists' treatment of the environment tends to be a simple extension of his approach to the rat in the laboratory maze. That is the environment is treated principally as if it consisted of physical artifacts. It is something against which the individual barks his shins. On the other hand, the sociologist wishes to suggest that the vital aspect of the environment is its presence in the mind of the individual who imposes meaning upon the world around him through a process of symbolizing (Swift, 1965, p. 341).

Indeed the whole exercise of testing is itself a product of environmental influence and, as we shall see later, of those social and economic processes which led people to want to test for intelligence.

Let us now look at the various major facets of the 'environment'.

Home Environment and Education

In considering environmental effects on education, many observers have focused their attention on the home as the major environmental influence. *The Home and the School* was the title of J. W. B. Douglas's first book reporting the early results of a study of 5,362 children born in Great Britain in the first week of March, 1946 (Douglas, 1964). Douglas followed the educational careers of these children through primary and secondary school and, for some, to university, until 1962. His findings revealed a range of factors which influenced how long a child stayed on at school and how well he did at school. One of the most important factors was the impact of the social class of the family. Douglas measured social class mainly by the occupation of the father, though he also considered the educational levels of the parents and their own social class origins (Douglas *et al.*, 1968, p. 199). Douglas found that nearly 50 per cent of children of high ability from lower-manual working-class homes had left school by the time they were sixteen-and-a-half; in contrast, only 10 per cent and 22 per cent respectively of the upper- and lower-middle-class pupils of the same ability-levels had left school. In addition to these social class differences, Douglas found that other factors in the home environment also influenced educational careers. These factors included the extent of the parents' interest in education, their own educational histories, their occupational aspirations for their children, the degree of insecurity in the family (whether deriving from poverty, illness or the absence of a parent), size of family, and the child's position in the birth-order (Douglas *et al.*, 1968, pp. 186–91). Many of these variables can be seen as aspects of a more general phenomenon, however: the degree and quality of attention which a child receives in the home.

The advantages which first children have over later siblings, in Douglas's study, are best understood in terms of the greater degree of attention and responsibility which *most* first children are likely to receive from their parents, as well as the greater responsibilities they have to shoulder. Likewise, children from smaller families generally have higher educational attainment, since they are also likely to receive more parental attention than children in large families.

Focusing on parental attention in this way helps us understand why apparently unconnected factors all tend to work in the same direction. They also affect the child's behaviour at school as well as within the home. The amount and quality of child–adult interactions influence the development of the child's linguistic capacity, e.g., the range of his vocabulary. Likewise, the child's own interest in schooling, as distinct from that of his parents, and his sense of being at ease when at school, are affected both directly and indirectly by his awareness of the importance and value his parents explicitly and implicitly place on schooling.

The family itself thus constitutes a learning situation for the child. Nor is the child simply 'moulded' by the family environment. He or she is an active agent who has to learn to interpret that environment, as we will see when we look at the educational process within the school later. Consequently, when considering the effects of the home on educational attainment, it is not enough to see this simply as the result of the occupation and education of the parents. Family insecurity, for example, is not only produced by poverty, but also results when professional parents with busy lives spend little time with their children. Resentments built up through such family interactions may undermine the good intentions of parents to help their children perform well in school.

We can extend our understanding of how the home environment influences education by considering more carefully the ways in which the home influences the speech-patterns of children. A starting-point is the work of Basil Bernstein (Bernstein, 1962; 1965; 1971; 1975). We will discuss some of Bernstein's later work on curriculum and on the within-school learning process later. Here we examine his earlier work on the relationship between home environment and the speech-patterns of children.

Bernstein distinguishes two patterns of speech which he labels 'elaborated' and 'restricted' codes. These speech-codes are a set of rules or preferences for organizing speech which people learn as members of a group. Thus Jenny Cook-Gumperz sees the code arising in this way: 'The child, through learning how to talk and negotiate verbally his position in a group, acquires an ability to act as a member of the group, from which he can develop "rules" about how to act as a member of the group' (Cook-Gumperz, 1973, p. 8). The way a person organizes his speech – the words he uses and his grammar or lack of it – 'signals' to others his or her membership.

The restricted code expresses and relies on the shared meanings and assumptions of a group. When this code is used, speakers do not elaborate their meaning but use simple referents, as in, for example, 'I went to the pub'. This speaker presupposes that his listeners are familiar enough with local institutions and with his own behaviour patterns not to require a detailed explanation of what a pub is or why he should want to go there. In contrast, the elaborated code is more explicit and the speaker leaves his meaning less open to interpretation or dependent on shared assumptions, thus filling in the detail of his behaviour, providing explanations for that behaviour and so on.

The elaborated code leads, then, to longer, more complex and more long-winded speech. This code allows its user to communicate with others who do not have a detailed knowledge of the speaker, his assumptions or his environment. The elaborated code is also a code in Cook-Gumperz's sense since people learn how to use it through interacting with others who habitually use this code. Thus, in a home in which parents expect children to elaborate their meaning, we might find this exchange: 'I want to go to the shop, Mum.' Mother: 'Why do you want to go to the shop and what shop are you talking about, anyway?' In this example, the mother may know perfectly well why the child wants to go to the shop (to buy sweets) and also which shop is being referred to, but chooses to continue the dialogue instead of cutting it off with an abrupt 'No!' or a 'Shut up!' as a device to control the child by forcing him or her to recognize the 'impropriety' of such a request. The child will, of course, in turn learn the code and with practice may learn to phrase his requests to go to the sweet-shop in such elaborate ways that the mother will be caught at her own game and may even have to revert to the peremptory, 'Shut up!'

Bernstein attempts to connect the development of these codes to differences in the ways members of a family relate to each other, such as whether children are expected to participate in decision-making or whether children are simply assigned roles (oldest child, girl, the 'wild one' of the family) and are expected to behave in accordance with them (Bernstein, 1971). Both ways of relating to children are means of control, but in the participation case, control will be verbally oriented, while in the other case it is more likely to be imperative: 'Do this, because I told you so.'

The relevance of speech-codes to education is that Bernstein claims that formal education is itself based on the predominant use of one type of code – the elaborated code. Teachers use it in the classroom to elicit 'satisfactory' answers from pupils and most essay-writing involves an elaboration of meaning. Naturally, the elaborated code is, in some senses, a necessary part of education, but its use is also based on membership of a particular type of community – the educational community. For teachers, this use is reinforced by their own experiences in school and college.

Children from homes in which the elaborated code is often used are thus more likely to be familiar with what is expected of them in school. They will 'cue on' more quickly to teachers' expectations and know how to respond to them. Conversely, children whose main experience has been with the restricted code will be less familiar with what goes on at school and will be 'slower' to respond.

Bernstein suggested that the restricted code is more likely to predominate in working-class speech and the elaborated code in middle-class speech, though both classes make use of, and understand, both codes. He claimed that the working-class home environment is one in which control of children is more likely to be based on the imperative. Working-class parents are not likely to have high levels of education, and Bernstein saw their language as making extensive use of unelaborated, but commonly shared references to familiar places and people. The speech of the working-class home environment will include local 'slang' and non-standard grammatical forms. Conversely, Bernstein claimed that most middle-class homes use the elaborated code, as well as the restricted code. Middle-class parents are likely to have higher levels of education than working-class parents. They are also likely to have jobs (clerical and professional jobs) in which writing and the elaboration of meaning, the providing of justifications, is part of their stock-in-trade.

Bernstein's intent was to show how language intervenes in the educational process, making it difficult for the potential of children to be adequately recognized when they are 'judged' by *one* particular linguistic standard. However, he has been subjected to considerable criticism concerning the class bias of his analysis and his reification of differences in language use (Rosen, 1972; Holly, 1973; Labov, 1972). Bernstein has been accused of implicitly, and, at times, explicitly, saying that the speech-codes he identified function not only to differentiate the style of communication among children from different home environments, but also affect the very *capacity* to communicate effectively.

The point of this criticism can be illustrated by returning to William Labov's study of Black youth to which we referred in the last section. Labov launches a strong attack on those who view the educational failure of Black children as an instance of cultural deprivation (Labov, 1972, pp. 201–37). Thus, he criticizes the notion that it is the lack of adequate verbal interaction with adults that results in the inability of children to reason effectively or to express themselves adequately.

He points out that research into linguistic forms of cultural deprivation has not looked at verbal interaction within the natural setting of the home and local community. Instead, children have been placed in an *interview* situation, in which children are faced by an unfamiliar adult interviewer who imposes upon them a series of questions which they are expected to answer. The interview is thus like the teacher–pupil relationship in the classroom, in that it is a situation of unequal power over which the child has little control. The child has little familiarity with what is expected of him in the interview, and bewilderment and defensiveness show in the 'non-verbal' type of response. Labov contrasts the formal interviewing situation with other situations in which a child does feel at ease. In such a situation, an eight-year-old who had been previously classed as 'non-verbal' became highly verbal, using a range of vivid imagery, displaying detailed knowledge of local politics and commanding a rich array of grammatical devices.

Labov sees the ghetto as bathing children in verbal stimulation from morning to night. He shows that ghetto inhabitants make concise and ingenious logical arguments, despite the apparent irregularities of their grammar. For example, one of Labov's colleagues detects a flaw in an argument of a fifteen-year-old local gang leader over the existence of God:

Interviewer: Well, if there's no heaven, how could there be a hell?

Gang leader: I mean - - ye-eah. Well, let me tell you, it ain't no hell, 'cause this hell right here, y'know! (Interviewer: This is hell?) Yeah, this is hell right here! (Labov, 1972, p. 216).

In contrast, Labov points out that much of Bernstein's elaborated code is, in actual speech, mere verbosity, full of qualifiers and with the argument often lost in a mass of irrelevant detail.

Consider the reply of the normally forthright Mr Anthony Benn, Secretary for Energy in the British Government, to a parliamentary question as to whether a conference had helped him to decide if the steam-generated heavy reactor programme was to be scrapped or not:

The energy conference contributed to the education of all those who were present, including ministers, and civil servants, but people who had special interests in a particular form of energy may, by listening to others, have appreciated the wide range of interests there are in this matter (*The Times*, 20 July 1976).

Holly makes a similar point, arguing that middle-class speech often contains a high degree of ambiguity of meaning, and is repetitious and formalistic (Holly, 1973, p. 104). He criticizes Bernstein's examples of the verbal performance of working-class children because they are derived from formal interviewing situations. The first set of examples were obtained from interviews with day-release students conducted by Bernstein or by one of his co-workers. Holly contrasts this interview-situation with Bernstein's interviews with boys from private schools: 'For these boys [day-release students], Bernstein, like any other lecturer, must have represented the power structure which had willed their attendance and their curriculum. Similarly, for the public school boys, Bernstein must have been identified with "research", University College, the system which represented *them*' (Holly, 1973, p. 103).

The point of agreement between Bernstein and his critics is that language is an important variable in how children are treated by, and respond to, education. Language is a means of social as well as intellectual communication, reflecting the home environment of the child, its practices and its assumptions. The problem for education is, at times, that differences in children's ways of communicating socially are identified as differences in intellectual capacity. The success of the elaborated code in schooling may indicate an educational structure which rewards ambiguity, verbosity and formalism in speech, as often as lucidity and organization. For further discussion of these issues, readers should consult the work of Ginsburg and Cicourel on language use and school performance (Ginsburg, 1972; Cicourel *et al.*, 1974).

Neighbourhood, Social Class and Class Culture

In the last section, we restricted our attention to the home environment, though throughout we needed to refer also to the importance for their education of the neighbourhood in which children live and of the social class to which they belong. In this section, we focus on neighbourhood and social class and their relationship to the class culture we discussed briefly earlier.

In the first part of his study, *Home and the School*, Douglas stressed the importance of the neighbourhood for primary school education. Primary schools in certain neighbourhoods achieved a much higher proportion of successes at the 11-plus examination than did schools in other neighbourhoods. The explanation for such differences is partly that schools differ in the age of their buildings and in the quality of their teaching. Such differences are often associated with differences in the social class composition of the neighbourhoods. Thus, in a study of educational inequalities in Detroit, Patricia Sexton showed that low-income families tended to be concentrated in inner-city areas of old and decaying housing, where the schools were also old and ill-equipped; in contrast, the middle-class suburbs on the outskirts of the city had new, well-equipped schools (Sexton, 1961). Processes such as urban renewal and explicit attempts to counter the material educational disadvantages of children from low-income families have, in many countries, 'equalized' the physical content of educational facilities by building new, well-equipped schools in low-income areas.

Poor facilities are not, however, the only or even the main way through which the social characteristics of a neighbourhood affect education. Families with similar levels of income and similar types of occupation (i.e., 'white-collar' employment as opposed to manual work) tend to live in the same neighbourhoods of a town or city; thus schools that recruit their pupils on a neighbourhood basis tend to have pupils who are homogeneous in terms of their social class. Such homogeneity reinforces the effects of the home environment.

Schools which cater mainly for middle-class children are likely to receive considerable financial help from parents to provide extra facilities. The general 'climate' of the school is likely to be one in which educational success is highly valued and in which children are expected to carry on as far as possible with education. In such schools a high percentage of the children may be receiving help at home with their reading, writing and vocabulary. Though teachers may dislike and distrust such 'help', it will save time in class and allow more individual attention to be given to children.

Contrast the situation in a homogeneously low-income neighbour-hood: there, many children will come to school with few school skills and there *may* well be less parental support for the school. This lack of support is not a question of lack of interest but results from lack of money to spend on school events, unfamiliarity with school routines and, often, an uneasiness in dealing with teachers. Consider this excerpt from Jackson and Marsden's study of education and the working class in which they compare the attitudes to school of middle-class parents and working-class parents:

When [*middle-class parents*] chose a primary school they chose with care. They chose one which not only promised well for a grammar school place, but pointed firmly in the direction of college or university.

[*Working-class parents'*] reasons for preferring one [school] rather than the other were warm and child-centered, but extraordinarily short-term. Mrs Black chose in this way for her little girl: 'Yes, there *were* two schools in Broadbank but we didn't know much about them. Well, there were some children passing on the road and I said, "Which school do you go to?" and they told me to the Church School. So I told our Doreen, "Those children go to the Church School. Would you like to go to that school?" ' (Jackson and Marsden, 1962, pp. 28, 84).

Indeed, many middle-class parents often choose the neighbourhood in which they wish to live by finding out first where the 'good' schools are located. These considerations help us understand why such educational innovations as comprehensive schooling in England may do little to change the influence of social class on education. The residences of the different social classes are segregated in most cities of the world and even schools which recruit from wide areas, such as large secondary schools, often recruit children whose homes represent a narrow range of occupational and income differences. Comprehensive schools can, for example, be predominantly 'middle class' or 'working class' depending on the area of the city. This 'ecological' pattern of recruitment is one major reason why the desegregation of schools in the United States involved bussing children from one area to another; previous to bussing, schools in a city like Chicago were predominantly either all-White or all-Black because of the racial composition of different areas of the city.

As we will see in the chapter on social stratification, the relative homogeneity of neighbourhoods is itself a direct product of the system of social and economic inequalities in society. In capitalist societies, a minority have large 'unearned' incomes from shares, rents, etc., but most people gain their income from working for wages or a salary. Level of income, in its turn, determines the type of housing that can be afforded and the degree of choice which a family can exercise over housing; the differential cost of building and land leads to the development of housing either for sale or for rent, each in its own area, with a similar level of relatively uniform rents or purchase prices. Those with similar incomes tend to concentrate in similar areas, higher income areas having better amenities in terms of space and public and private services.

These inequalities are found in Britain, in Europe and in the United States, and often in even more exaggerated forms in under-developed countries. The shanty-towns which surround many cities in the underdeveloped world, for example, contrast sharply in over-crowding, insanitary conditions and lack of educational or other service facilities with the spacious suburbs of the middle classes. In the countries of the Eastern European communist bloc, differences in job status result not only in income differences but also in dif-ferential access to different types of housing in different localities. Though social class differences are generally less sharply pronounced in these countries than in many of the capitalist countries, relatively homogeneous class environments of this kind in part explain the inequalities of educational opportunity that are also found in these countries, despite government attempts to ensure equality of access to education (Boudon, 1974, Tables 3–4).

The residential segregation of different social classes and ethnic groups is one factor producing class and ethnic cultures. People with similar levels of income and education tend to live near each other, work close to each other, see each other socially or while shopping and so on. And though we have up to now spoken of the family as if it existed in isolation, the members of the family, of course, always have relationships with others about them – kin, neighbours, friends, work-mates. These relationships can be described as the social networks of family members and they provide social and often material resources for the family. Thus, the family's social network gives supportive help such as visiting when sick and retails infor-mation about where to buy goods cheaply or about sources of work. The social network also provides a means of obtaining favours in business or helps with access to government, local administration or school authorities.

A person's social class position is then not simply a matter of income or occupation, but includes his or her social relationships and a particular style of life. For the middle classes, their social relation-ships and style of life are as important as their incomes in ensuring that their children succeed educationally. These advantages are not necessarily secured intentionally, but often result from the 'natural' consequences of middle-class status, such as living in certain types of neighbourhood and having certain influential friends.

We can extend this argument by placing it within the context of our earlier discussion of language and education. It is possible to interpret Bernstein as saying that class situations generate typical speech patterns and that as a consequence of social inequality and the uneven distribution of power in society, certain speech-patterns are rewarded more than others. Particular speech-patterns and accents become effective means of circumscribing decision-making to particular groups of people. Such patterns serve to identify others who, by their background and experience, are likely to share the same interests as oneself. Language, in short, becomes a means of knowing whom to trust or with whom it will be relatively easy to co-operate, and becomes an integral element in any system of domination, facilitating the communication of the powerful.

In contrast, the Black vernacular of American inner cities provides an alternative source of identity and organization for Blacks. Thus an eight-year-old in Labov's study replies to the interviewer's question, 'Who can make magic?' with, 'I'm sayin' the po'k chop God! He only a po'k chop God! [other child chuckles]' (Labov, 1972, p. 210). A pork chop, Labov explains to the reader, is a Black who still has the traditional subservient ideology of the South, who has no knowledge of himself in Muslim terms, and the *pork chop God* is thus the traditional God of Southern Baptists. Labov points out that though this God and his followers might be 'pork chops', they still held the power in the world of his child informants. Hannerz, in his study of a Black ghetto in Washington, D.C., claimed in similar fashion that such concepts as 'soul', and the street language which developed among Blacks in the ghetto situation, were one of the bases of a common race culture which helped to override differences in income or job and facilitated their political organization at the time of the inner city race riots (Hannerz, 1966).

This perspective has been developed and applied to educational systems by the French Marxist philosopher, Louis Althusser (Althusser, 1971, pp. 123–73). To him, the school is the dominant State ideological apparatus, contributing to the reproduction of the relations of production necessary to contemporary capitalism. In the

Middle Ages, in contrast, the Church had a similar function. By means of compulsory schooling, the State secures a captive audience of all its future citizens. In school, according to Althusser, children learn not only the basic skills necessary for the economy, but also the attitudes required for the successful functioning of the capitalist system. They learn respect for private property and come to recognize the merits of individual competition. Children are also taught to accept as 'natural' and 'inevitable' the fact that people are rewarded differently according to their presumed abilities. Children learn, above all, to accept the rules of the established order by which, if they become workers, they 'submit' to directions from those with superior power or knowledge, and, if they become managers, they manipulate the ruling ideology correctly.

The ruling ideology thus determines the dominant culture of society, influencing what is taught in schools and universities and determining through education and the mass media what types of thought and language are seen as normal and are 'rewarded' by society. 'Counter-cultures' develop among those who find themselves excluded from the material benefits of society. One way in which sectors of the working class express their alienation from capitalist society is through rejecting the dominant culture and its values; this can take the form of anti-school attitudes or the 'aggressive' Black vernacular that Labov reports. We can see the same happening in Alan Sillitoe's *The Loneliness of the Long-Distance Runner*, a sensitive account of the way in which a correctional educational institution – a Borstal – attempts to use sport to impart values that the authorities want the boys to accept. The long-distance runner of the story sees running as a means of escaping the pressures imposed upon him by society. To the Borstal authorities the whole purpose of the running is to defeat a team from a neighbouring public school and thus uphold the 'honour' of the Borstal. The runner resolves the value conflict to his own satisfaction by 'winning' the race, but refusing to step across the finish line.

In Bernstein's later writings, he has come increasingly to relate speech-codes to the material as well as to the social culture of the different social classes, under the influence of a group of French Marxist educational sociologists represented by Pierre Bourdieu (Bernstein, 1975). Bernstein's recent work complements this Marxist approach by attempting to demonstrate the links between the kinds of material objects present in the homes of families from different social classes and the social interactions and the concepts and patterns of speech which develop within these families.

Whereas traditional conceptions of education commonly emphasized the way in which people acquire objective knowledge of the natural world, in this Marxist view such knowledge is always mediated by society, and it is knowledge of ways of behaving appropriate to the different classes in society that is learned at school. This group emphasizes the concept of *cultural reproduction*: the means whereby the system of class relationships in a society is maintained over time through the production and diffusion of ways of thinking and expressing oneself that come to be seen as natural and acceptable ways of behaving. The desire to accumulate consumer goods, for instance, is not an ingrained trait of human nature, but is generated by the cultural framework of a capitalist society. From this perspective, culture, and in particular, education, is an important means of reproducing the class relationships obtaining in society as a whole.

The fit, however, is never a complete one. The educational system not only acts to assign people to class positions and provides them with the skills and aspirations appropriate to those positions; it also provides the means by which people learn to function with some independence of mind – a necessary attribute of efficient work in any class position. This independence can become the basis for awareness of the exploitations inherent in a class system and a basis for organizing to change it.

Educational Inequality and Social Stratification

The patterns we have discussed in the last section make up a system of generalized social inequality and stratification in which several different class cultures coexist. It is now time to examine the specific ways in which, during formal education, social stratification generates increasing inequality of educational opportunity. Most evidence, for instance, indicates that the advantage of being of middle- or upper-middle-class background increases with length of schooling; it is at university and college level that these classes are most over-represented given their proportions in the population as a whole. Boudon brings together a set of data from Europe and the United States to calculate the relative educational advantages of children from upper-class families (Boudon, 1974, Table 3.2). He calculates that in Portugal, in 1963–4, the chances of an upper-class child attending college were nearly 130 times greater than those of a lower-class child; in Spain, 57 times greater; about 33 times greater in the Netherlands; between 20 and 30 times greater in France and about 14 times greater in Sweden. In the United States, he calculates that the chances of upper-class children attending college are about three-and-a-half times greater than those of lower-class children, and in Britain he estimates that the relative upper-class advantage is about seven times greater than that of lower-class children.

Social class is not the only source of inequality in education; consider the following table on the relative 'drop-out' rates of women in the American educational system. Whereas women are a higher percentage of high school graduates than men, they are not as likely to proceed to higher levels of education.

Table 3

Women as Percentages of Graduates in Different Stages of Education: United States, 1969–1972

	Men	Women
Graduate from high school	49·6	50·4
Graduate from college	58	42
Obtain a master's degree	59	41
Obtain a doctorate	84	16

(Source: Bureau of the Census, *Statistical Abstract of the United States*, 1975, pp. 135–61.)

The combined effects of being a woman and being Black on one's likelihood of staying on at college can be graphically illustrated in the relative drop-out rates of White students from their entering year (freshman) to their final year (senior). Only 35 per cent of Black females entering college as freshwomen are likely to continue until their final year; in contrast over 60 per cent of White males continue into the senior year (Figure 9).

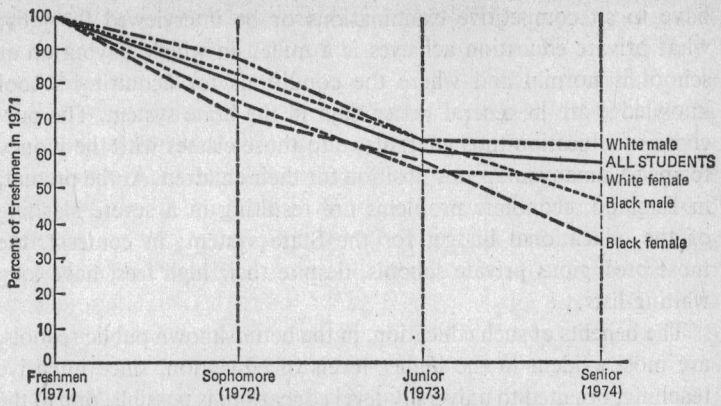

Figure 9 College enrolment in the United States of the 1971 freshman class: October 1971 to October 1974

(Source: Bureau of the Census, School Enrolment – Social and Economic Characteristics of Students: October 1974, *Current Population Reports* Series, p. 20, No. 286, November 1975.)

The increase in educational inequality is significant because it is not the result of the inherent incapacity of children to benefit from education. We have provided material in the previous sections to suggest why such a conclusion is unlikely: working-class or Black children may reject school but they are quite capable of learning the ropes should they wish to do so and should the school encourage them. Also, available evidence suggests that cultural factors, such as any inherent incapacity to learn, are not the reason why working-class children are *increasingly* disadvantaged in school. Raymond Boudon analyses a large variety of data from Western Europe and the United States, to make this point (Boudon, 1974). J. W. B. Douglas's conclusions from the study we reviewed earlier are similar and he points out that there is no evidence from his sample that working-class children become increasingly incapable (as measured by his intelligence tests) of schooling as they proceed to higher levels.

One important reason for the increase of educational inequality is the obvious, but often overlooked one, that money can buy higher levels of education. The existence of a large private sector of education guarantees to those who can afford the fees that their children will receive a relatively high-quality education which provides an easier access than does the State educational system to 'good' jobs or to higher education. Naturally, children in the private sector still have to sit competitive examinations or be interviewed for jobs; what private education achieves is a milieu in which staying on at school is normal and where the conditions for acquiring school knowledge are in general better than in the State system. The purchase of education thus guarantees, to those classes with the money to spend, an advantageous position for their children. At the present, in England, economic problems are resulting in a severe slashing of the educational budget for the State system; in contrast, the most prestigious private schools, despite their high fees, have long waiting-lists.

The benefits of such education, in the better-known public schools, are most evident in the higher levels of education, since intensive teaching, oriented to university-level education, is possible, due to the availability of skilled teachers working with small classes which high fees permit. Such schools also instil in their pupils modes of behaviour and of language which facilitate entry into élite positions (Wakeford, 1969; Weinberg, 1967). Since they are usually residential, these schools take on some of the attributes of Goffman's 'total institutions', as the child is removed from the influence of the parents, and lives with fellow-pupils, outside as well as inside the classroom, under the control of the teachers (Goffman, 1961, pp. 3–12).

Children from such backgrounds therefore succeed disproportionately in gaining entrance to the most prestigious universities, Oxford and Cambridge. In the United States, Mills shows, a similar career-route exists between private 'prep' schools and the 'Ivy League' universities (Mills, 1956, pp. 67–70). Those who do not succeed often opt for Edinburgh or Trinity College, Dublin, or join the grammar-school boys at other universities. Thus, a hierarchy of universities parallels the hierarchy of types of schools. Both hierarchies are interconnected, and set the student on paths which lead to different kinds of occupation (McPherson, A., 1973).

Raymond Boudon explains the increase in inequality of educational opportunity by considering the over-all structural effect of the system of social stratification rather than particular features of society such as the class differences in motivation, language and the like which we have discussed hitherto (Boudon, 1974). Boudon's explanation is basically simple: the higher the social-class background of a child the more likely he or she is to stay on at school; consequently, the more stages and choices there are in schooling, the more likely are children from higher social-class backgrounds to predominate in the later stages of education. Children from upper- and middle-class homes are not under the same pressures to leave school to earn money. For them, the 'cost of persistence' with education is less, both the economic cost of persisting with education, and the social cost of deviating from the normal practice of one's peers. Children from upper-middle-class backgrounds normally stay as long as possible in school, and staying on leads to occupations that are normal for their class. For them, it is difficult to leave schooling both because they will be abandoned by their friends, who will increasingly diverge from them in interests and activities, and because of pressure from their parents to stay on. The working-class child, by contrast, is under pressure from his parents and his peers to leave earlier.

Boudon also claims that children and parents from working-class backgrounds need to expend relatively more effort just to keep pace with what is normal for children of middle- and upper-middle-class background. For example, even obtaining the information required to make the 'right' choices of school or curriculum will be easier for those of upper- and upper-middle-class background because awareness of the range of courses, and what those courses entail, both in terms of their content and what they lead to, once finished, is more likely to form part of the normal background of these classes. Jackson and Marsden provide an example of this form of disadvantage in the encounter of one of their informants with his child's primary school headmaster:

> That's right, I saw the headmaster, and I said: 'We've got this form with these schools down, and we don't know anything about any of them.'
> 'Well,' said the headmaster, 'What's his father's job?'
> 'He's a lorry driver.'
> 'Well then you'd better be sending him to Mill Cross.'
> 'Mill Cross? Why, is that the best school?'
> 'No, it's not, but it's the best school for you.'
> 'How do you mean, it's the best school for me? Where would you send your lad?'
> 'Oh, I'd send *my* lad to Marburton College...'

So what do you think of that story? Fair cheek, isn't it? (Jackson and Marsden, 1962, pp. 90–91).

Since educational attainment requires special effort from those of working-class background – even where they have similar intelligence and potential to middle-class children – it is the middle-class children who will be more likely to persist with education.

Boudon's analysis of the relationship between social structure and education emphasizes the existence of several crucial 'branching points' within schooling, each leading to different classes of occupation. With economic development, there has been an increasing division of labour in society and an increasing degree of occupational differentiation. This process has been accompanied by an increasing sophistication not only in technology, but in economic and political organization, too. These changes have been similar throughout the developed world. Entry into occupations has become more specialized in the types of training demanded, and this specialization has usually meant that schools have had to provide different curricula, or even that there are quite different types of schools which prepare children for different kinds of occupations.

One implication of Boudon's argument is that a reduction in the number of branching-points in schooling is likely to reduce inequality of educational opportunity. He suggests that the lower level of educational inequality in the United States as compared with France or Great Britain is to be attributed in part to the lower number of branching-points in schooling. In the United States, that is, everybody normally goes right through primary and secondary education; from 'grade school' through 'high school'. Those completing high school, in most parts of the United States, are entitled to proceed to higher education. Students successfully completing a two-year junior college course after high school can proceed to the third year of a state college or state university. Though higher education is highly differentiated by type of institution and by prestige of institution, there is, at least formally, an equivalence of standard between institutions. In Europe, until recently, education was highly differentiated with a large number of branching-points, such as the choice between vocational, technical and academic grammar schools (*gymnasia*, *lycées*). Children entering certain branches, such as secondary modern schools in contrast to grammar schools, had little opportunity to proceed to higher education. The 'openness' of the American system is to talk in terms of formal qualifications and eligibility alone, of course, for in practice, children who drop out at any stage are not likely to drop in again, and the chances of a graduate of a state college obtaining as good a job as a graduate of Harvard are slim. Yet the power of Boudon's argument must be recognized: the later the educational system allows people to make those choices which affect their futures, the more chance there is for the socially disadvantaged to pursue one of the better careers.

We can see the implications of this argument by considering the proportions of children from different social classes who enter higher education in the United States and Britain (Table 4). The data from

Table 4

Social Class Origins of Entrants into Higher Education in Britain and the United States

Britain			United States			
Social Origin	Per cent of children obtaining *university* education. Those born in:		Social Origin	Per cent of children obtaining *college* education in:		
	Late 1930s	Approx. 1953/4		1960	1970 Male	Female
Professional and technical	10	35	Upper-and upper-middle	80	90	86
Administrative and managerial		18 · 21	Lower-middle	45	70	57
Other non-manual		10½	Upper-working	25	48	32
			Lower-working	6	20	10
Manual, all levels	1½	4				
Per cent of total age group	4	9	Per cent of total age group	33	53	41

(Sources: The British data are excerpted from John Westergaard and Henrietta Resler, *Class in a Capitalist Society*, Table 33. The American data are taken from R. J. Havighurst and B. L. Neugarten, *Society and Education*, Table 5.2.)

the United States include types of higher education not represented in the British data (Teachers' College, Polytechnics, etc.). Yet even if these were included in the British data, the proportions attending higher educational institutions would still not be as high as in the United States. Though *access* to education has increased in the United States, this increase has done little to reduce inequality of educational opportunity. In both Britain and the United States, social class remains an important determinant of higher education. There are more working-class children in higher education in the 1970s than in the late 1950s, but the proportions of children of middle-class origin have also increased considerably. The data on social class in the table are not strictly comparable, since the British and American data do not use the same categories for classifying students' social origins, but the middle- and working-class distinctions in the American data are broadly similar to the non-manual and manual distinctions in the British data.

The choices that affect one's career are not only a question of what types of school or college one goes to, but of the different curricula within those institutions. Eliminating the eleven-plus examination and introducing the comprehensive school system in the United Kingdom, for example, are unlikely to affect inequality of educational opportunity, when specialized curricula then develop within the comprehensive school, when these schools are internally 'streamed', and when a series of public examinations remain which filter entry to the higher education system in Britain.

There seems, however, to be a trend in developed capitalist countries for the most overt forms of education differentiation to decrease. In France and Germany, as well as in England, specialized secondary schools leading to different types of careers have been increasingly replaced by a common secondary school system. Increasingly, pupils attending all kinds of schools in these systems can go on to higher education by taking the requisite qualifications and examinations. Likewise, in recent years, there has been a convergence in many European countries in the direction of the American pattern of higher education, by allowing greater flexibility in choice of courses, and in the possibility of changing courses during the undergraduate career.

These trends derive from two interrelated factors. Firstly, the demand for higher levels of education has been rising consistently throughout the world in recent decades and, in many countries, the length of compulsory schooling has had to be extended. These rising levels have meant that secondary education has expanded rapidly. Such an expansion has itself created a pressure towards a less differentiated system which can accommodate, flexibly, the larger numbers of students staying on in school until graduation from secondary school, and this expansion of 'volume', irrespective of other pressures, has led to some decrease of educational inequality.

Secondly, in many countries, developed and underdeveloped, public debate, generated by the kind of research we have discussed, and by changes in political ideas, has led to recognition that rigid distinctions between types of schools and curriculum work against equality of opportunity, and criticism, especially on the part of the disprivileged, has to be taken notice of. More cynically, perhaps, as Burton Clark has suggested, reforms of this kind mean that social inequalities may still remain, but the way they operate becomes more difficult to observe in a more 'open' educational system (Clark, 1960).

Boudon justifies his argument with a range of empirical data and with statistical models of the consequences of the greater drop-out rate of working-class children. His main contentions, however, have also been documented, more descriptively, in British studies of the sociology of education. Jackson and Marsden's study of *Education and the Working Class* (1962) illustrates the dilemmas of working-class parents if they were to make the 'right' choices for their children's educational future.

Many a time you'd be out and the neighbours would say, 'Eeh, is your lad still at school? What's he going to be then?'

And I'd have to say, 'I don't know what he's going to be yet.' And they'd say, 'Doesn't he know yet?' and then I'd come home and I'd sit opposite our lad in the chair, and I'd say, 'What do you think you'll be when you leave school?' 'I don't know, I don't know at all, don't bother me,' he'd say and that was it. When the neighbours bothered me, I hadn't got an answer and I felt soft. They'd look at you as much as to say, 'Staying on at school all that time, and don't know what he's going to be, well!' (Jackson and Marsden, 1962, p. 116).

For this father and his neighbours the value of education was understood in terms of the job it would bring. The grammar school the son attended stressed more 'ivory tower' values, in which learning was seen as good for its own sake. The son was caught between these conflicting emphases and felt uneasy with both. The above excerpt also indicates the kinds of pressures that help explain why children from non-élite families concentrate on vocational courses, and children from élite families can 'afford' to take the less vocational subjects.

The social costs, for working-class children, in taking education 'above their station' are various. Not only does such an education create difficulties for the family when faced with their neighbours, but working-class parents are likely to find encounters with teachers a difficult and exasperating experience:

Well, we can't tell you much about bloody schooling because they didn't tell *us* so bloody much about the job! Once a year you went to that bloody college, a great big bloody queue, two or three minutes each . . . You'd see this bloody Glen-Smith fellow and he'd look at you and hum and bloody haw and he'd give you no encouragement . . . We never thought the lad had a chance, and there in the end he gets a scholarship to university (Jackson and Marsden, 1962, pp. 118–19).

Such instances are inevitably generated when schooling prepares people to move into occupations different from those of their parents, and when those parents are unfamiliar with the types and levels of education needed. Children coming from homes where the parents have themselves experienced extended education will be more attuned to the expectations of teachers and behave in ways acceptable to them; in their turn, the teachers will expect such children to succeed in their studies. Such children will often be automatically enrolled in advanced courses, be reminded how important certain school examinations are if they want to go on to post-secondary education; if these children fail to measure up to these expectations, teachers are likely to treat their behaviour as abnormal, and to see the children as having 'problems' and to take these up with the parents! Those children whose social class is such as to lead teachers to have no such expectations that they will 'naturally' go on to higher education, may, on the other hand, be automatically enrolled in courses or curricula which do not lead beyond secondary level education. The primary school headmaster whom we quoted earlier would certainly not have enrolled a lorry-driver's son in Latin or language courses which used to be essential prerequisites to entry into Oxford or Cambridge. Of course, children who are perceived to have high academic potential are likely to be encouraged by teachers, irrespective of social background.

The Impact of Education on Society

In the preceding section we considered how the system of social stratification affects education; in this section, we reverse our perspective and examine the impact of education on society, considering how education affects social stratification and what contribution education makes to the economy.

We can begin by using Ralph Turner's distinction between 'sponsored' and 'contest' mobility systems in education (Turner, 1962). Turner used the distinction to contrast what he saw as the dominant tendencies in the British and American educational systems. The British system, when Turner wrote, was what he called a sponsored mobility system in that the élite sets social as well as educational criteria for occupational recruitment, requiring the segregation of children into different types of schools which 'train' them in the values appropriate for different levels of occupation. Upward mobility is 'sponsored' under this system, because it occurs only through acceptance of the values and norms of behaviour established by the élites. The private schools trained pupils in élite norms and values; the grammar schools imbued children with the appropriate sense of responsibility for 'second-level' occupations such as clerks or managers; and the mass of the population was left to secondary-modern schools.

In contrast, Turner claimed, the American educational system creates a sense of open mobility in which children 'contest' to reach the highest levels. There is no educational segregation from an early age, and the possibility of reaching the highest levels of education are not foreclosed; in practice, only a few will ever succeed, and these, as we have seen, will come predominantly from the upper classes. Yet, Turner claims, the American system creates a sense of opportunity, and represents a device to 'integrate' Americans into the dominant achievement-values of the society.

His claim, then, is that education contributes to the *type* of the stratification in society – the particular ways in which class-differences are manifested and maintained. In the United States, accent or style of life are less important markers of class-differences than they are in England.

This form of stratification is related to differences in the ways in which the economies of Britain and the United States developed. This does not mean, as Mills has shown, that America is any more 'democratic' than Britain or that power is any less concentrated (Mills, 1956). Nor does it mean that the chances for upward social mobility are any greater in the United States than in Britain (though on this point there is continuing disagreement among sociologists).

The massive expansion of the U.S. economy, from the third quarter of the nineteenth century onwards, both in agriculture on the frontier and in industry, was made possible only by recruiting huge supplies of labour from abroad and from the rural areas. Tens of millions of immigrants flocked into the United States, bringing with them their indigenous cultures. Most of them, initially, found their way into the ethnic 'ghettos' of the cities. The American educational system made a massive effort to 'integrate' this labour by teaching literacy and the values of American society. Even during the massive immigrations of people from the non-English-speaking countries of Europe from 1870 to 1920, illiteracy among the *foreign-born* population of America was never higher than 13 per cent (Folger and Nam, 1967). This was achieved by the rapid proliferation of schools and the training of large numbers of teachers; it also led to the creation of a common school system throughout America.

In the same period, illiteracy among the American Black population ranged from 79·9 per cent in 1870 to 23·0 per cent in 1920. One of the major factors in the drop in the illiteracy of Blacks was their own migration to the Northern and Southern cities and their incorporation into the urban labour force. Education, then, was a major instrument in the early economic development of America, enabling the economy to make effective use of immigrant labour. The vitality of the American economy has, in part, continued to depend on labour mobility and on an integrative educational system. The different classes in America may consume different amounts, but they are different amounts of the same domestic goods and services. This 'mass' market, cutting across classes, is the motor of American economic development.

In contrast, in Britain, after the large-scale migrations from the countryside to the city in the early nineteenth century, the population of most British cities became relatively stabilized in comparison to the movements taking place within and between American cities. One of the major reasons for this relative stability was the concentration of employment in England in large-scale manufacturing and the slow rate of technological change in British industry. Work, for most working-class children, meant a job in the local mill or factory, often where their father or mother was employed.

Eric Hobsbawm points to the relationship between the British educational system and this type of economy: education did not promote scientific knowledge, nor did it serve to integrate the working-class into a national culture (Hobsbawm, 1969). Also 'a rigid educational system, a shaking economy, confined workers and their children to their own world. The able young proletarian still found the best opportunities for his talents within the labour movement – like Aneurin Bevan – or in schoolteaching. A secondary education for his son was not out of the question, though the Fisher Education Act of 1918 did not seriously widen the educational ladder' (ibid., p. 241).

It would be unwise, however, to assume that formal education makes a direct and necessary contribution either to occupational performance or to economic development. Despite the emphasis that governments place on finding the 'right' type of education for the needs of the economy, there is little evidence that education or any specific type of education (vocational, technical, social, scientific, etc.) promotes economic development. Indeed, 'success' in school has little relationship to 'success' in the occupational world, as is shown by analyses of the educational records of those with high incomes (Bowles and Gintis, 1976, pp. 102–24). Some occupations, of course, do require specific kinds and levels of education. Literacy, for example, is necessary to almost all occupations in modern society, whether underdeveloped or developed. Highly specialized technical occupations such as engineering, electronics or medicine require considerable training in technique before entry into that occupation. But *most* occupations and most jobs lie in between the extremes of requiring only simple literacy or advanced technical knowledge: the advantages of specific courses of education for occupational performance are by no means self-evident.

It is the assumptions of government and business, mediated by various professional organizations, which determine the kind and level of education appropriate to different occupations. The type of curriculum which these professions expect their members to have followed will also influence the academic choices of secondary school students, either explicitly or when children and their parents assume that certain subjects or certain combinations of subjects best prepare a child for a given occupation, whether this be in a factory, in business or in the Civil Service. Schooling thus prepares children for different occupational roles and is the first step towards entry into well-paid employment, on the one hand, or being 'shunted' to lower-paid jobs on the other. Inequality of educational opportunity is thus one of the major means whereby those holding privileged positions transfer those positions to their children.

In any case, occupations which have the highest average levels of education (school and university teachers) are not able to translate this 'intellectual capital' into obtaining access for their children to the best jobs and the best incomes. In France, for instance, these children do indeed succeed in education, but this success simply channels them into the moderately-rewarded jobs their parents have. In contrast, the sons of businessmen – whose capital is material rather than intellectual – 'succeed' less well in education, but end up with the best jobs and incomes.

The significance of education as a 'sorting' process, facilitating the differentiation of jobs by status and monetary rewards, has increased with the dramatic changes in the occupational structure of most countries. Thus the proportion of 'white-collar' jobs to manual jobs has risen consistently in all countries of the world, and in the developed countries, white-collar employment now provides almost half the jobs available. Thus, in 1970, 47 per cent of jobs in the United States were 'white-collar' jobs (professional, clerical, sales) out of a total of nearly 80 million jobs; in 1900, only 18 per cent of jobs were white-collar and the total number of jobs was 29 million (Bureau of Commerce, 1975). Even in underdeveloped countries there is also a change in occupational structure as the proportion of agricultural jobs decrease and the proportion of urban jobs increase. These occupational opportunities, however, are largely only available to those who do not go straight into work from school, but who stay on for further education.

We have already seen that schooling has become an important means of allocating people to occupational positions. Education has therefore become an intervening variable in the process of social mobility and stratification, for though social background is still the major influence on the job which a child will obtain, the effects of social background are mediated through the educational system. A father in a powerful position can ensure a well-paid occupation for his son irrespective of his school or college record; but it is usually necessary for that son to obtain first a certain level of education. Since high levels of education have become necessary credentials for entry into most well-rewarded occupations, educational qualifications are assets in social mobility. Competition for access to educational qualifications becomes an 'instrumental' means whereby the different social classes compete for social and occupational rewards rather than a search for knowledge in some pure or abstract sense.

This process is by no means novel. The public school system in Britain only emerged in the mid-nineteenth century, when the expansion of both the economy and of employment by the State (the Civil Service, the Army, etc.) led to new jobs. Up to that time, such positions had been monopolized by the landed classes, and usually filled via personal networks or by purchase. The new emphasis on the part of the rising middle classes upon efficiency and competition, and their new demand for a share in public office, led to public competition for office, usually by examination (notably into the Civil Service), and therefore stimulated demand for schooling which would prepare the young for these examinations. The strong cultural influence of the landed classes continued to manifest itself, in Britain, in the important place still given to 'classics' (Latin and Greek) in the curriculum, especially in schools and universities preparing people for entry into élite positions.

The expansion of jobs in public administration and in large-scale business corporations in the contemporary developing world has equally led to expansion of educational systems and intensified competition for entry into schools and universities, particularly by middle-class children. In Latin America, for example, the expansion of secondary and even higher education has occurred fastest in the middle-class-dominated, private sector of education. In contrast, the public sector of education in Latin America has inadequate facilities and there is often severe overcrowding in schools. This occurs at *all* levels of education. The National University of Mexico has, for example, some 150,000 students enrolled on a single campus that is hardly bigger than that of one of Britain's larger provincial universities. In contrast, private universities in Mexico have much smaller enrolments, have better facilities and better staff/student ratios. Because education becomes more crucial for one's future occupation in this way, the educational system inevitably becomes a focus of the class struggle. Most of the controversy over education, indeed, expresses the divergent interests of particular social classes. One reflection of this process is the defence of established school systems by the already-privileged in face of demands for greater access to education by social groups which have hitherto been excluded. The defence of the grammar school system in the U.K., or the violent clashes in the U.S.A. between White ethnic groups such as the Irish and the disadvantaged Blacks over the bussing of schoolchildren are other instances.

Yet as levels of education rise in a country, education necessarily becomes a less discriminating qualification for occupation. In the extreme case, for example, if everyone were to graduate from higher education, educational qualifications would be of little help in getting a job and a person's position in life would depend, as it did in the past, on his family, his personality and luck. Boudon stresses the social paradox which this situation creates: people strive to raise the educational levels of their children so that they can secure good jobs; but their success in getting their children educated means that these levels of education are no longer sufficient to obtain good jobs (Boudon, 1974, pp. 165–201). He shows that, in Europe, this process has meant that for children from middle-class families higher levels of education than those of their parents are not enough to secure jobs equivalent in status to those their parents held. In such cases, children will move downwards, despite the superiority of their educational qualifications, a situation producing social tensions, personal frustration, and anxiety over schooling. As more children finish secondary education, competition, whether for jobs or for entry into higher education, increases and gives rise to parental anxiety about the 'quality' of the secondary schools.

This growing demand for and reliance on formal educational qualifications – degrees, diplomas and certificates – has been labelled 'credentialism'. Job-seekers wishing to give themselves competitive advantages over others now have to acquire even higher qualifications; and employers wishing to differentiate among job applicants come to demand such advanced qualifications as a matter of course. It is this social process which may account for the rapid expansion of formal and especially higher education. For example, students in the United States who graduate from college with a bachelor's (first) degree and wish to enter business have increasingly found it necessary to stay on for a master's (postgraduate) degree in business administration. Such advanced courses were first established to meet a quite specialized and limited need for a particular kind of personnel in certain sectors of business, but they have now become 'further' qualifications that *all* intending business entrants take, whether or not the course is strictly helpful to the particular business career. Ultimately, of course, credentialism is likely to reinforce the effects of social background, since once these qualifications become general, and, for example, all applicants to a particular job are college graduates with the appropriate skills, employers fall back on such criteria as the 'quality' of the school attended, personal presentation, social contacts, and so on, in making their selections.

The interconnection of educational attainment, social background, occupational and income levels creates, consequently, a vicious circle. This is the argument that underlies Christopher Jencks's findings in his study, *Inequality: A Reassessment of the Effect of Family and Schooling in America*. Jencks brings together a range of survey data from American education to show that there has been little decline in inequality of educational opportunity in recent years. He shows that educational attainment has little influence on income that is independent of the effect of social class of origin: to earn a high income in the United States, it is necessary to go to college, but it is also necessary to be born into a middle- or upper-class family. He also summarizes data indicating that IQ has little 'independent' effect on earnings.

Jencks's conclusions were based in part on the series of studies sponsored by the United States Office of Education in 1965; these studies used a survey of some 650,000 students and their teachers in approximately 4,000 state schools. The major finding in all the studies was that the social background of students (mainly the occupational and educational levels of their parents) was the chief determinant of success in school, and that the influence of other factors on achievement such as differences between schools in facilities, curriculum and staffing, were negligible (Mayeske and Beaton, 1975). These conclusions are similar in many respects to those of Raymond Boudon who is also sceptical about the possibilities of education reducing inequality in educational opportunity by 'reform' of the educational system.

Jencks's findings for the United States are particularly striking, since it has often been assumed that American society is a 'meritocratic' one in which occupational position depends mainly on the objective merit of the individual as measured by his educational attainment. Michael Young's satire upon tendencies in British education – *The Rise of the Meritocracy* – shows how this kind of emphasis upon meritocratic achievement in education gave rise to a new kind of élitism (Young, 1961). In Young's account it leads, by the year 2033, to a highly rigid stratification-system, based on eugenics, in which only the intellectually deserving get any of the cake; fortunately by 2033 there are signs of increasing revolt against the system and hopes of return to a more 'primitive' age. The fundamental problem, as Jencks and Boudon point out, is *social stratification*: the jobs in society have different prestige and are rewarded with widely different levels of income. It is this fundamental inequality that generates inequality in educational opportunity.

So far, we have discussed social mobility as a personal phenomenon and as a class phenomenon. *Occupational groups* also seek to raise the status of their members, collectively, by raising the educational levels for entry and thus keeping down the numbers in the occupation, and by bargaining on their behalf for superior rewards and status.

Many occupations seeking to elevate their status begin to 'professionalize' themselves, modelling themselves on established professions such as medicine (which itself did not become a high-status occupation until the nineteenth century). Such occupations lay great stress on the existence of a body of specialized knowledge, theoretical and practical, and often esoteric, which has to be acquired via protracted training. Without this, it is claimed, people trying to do the job would be incompetent and liable to do harm to others. The classic case is usually taken to be the practice of medicine, where wrong treatment could lead, in the extreme, to death. Hence strict examination of a would-be entrant to the profession is required to see if he or she has in fact successfully acquired this knowledge. Once certified as knowledgeable and competent, the new professional is then licensed to practise that profession. Advancement in the profession also depends greatly on acquiring further professional qualifications. Such occupations demand the power for the professional body as such to control entry to the profession, not the State or the schools, colleges or even universities. This degree of control over access to jobs in such professions is a monopoly recognized by the State, and only paralleled by 'closed shop' trade unionism (or effectively hereditary occupations).

Yet the claim to the existence of a kind of knowledge which cannot possibly be acquired in any other way is usually dubious. The allocation of power to control membership is therefore difficult to justify on intellectual grounds alone. It is, of course, convenient for government and industry as a 'manpower planning' device, in that output of trained people in certain fields of education can be controlled without the necessity for governments to risk unpopularity by themselves directly controlling who gets or does not get access to certain kinds of jobs.

A more disquieting aspect of professionalism is the extent to which educational 'change' of this kind can impede the provision of adequate services to the public. Medicine is a good example of this. Thus, in countries as diverse as China and Mexico, effective mass medical services are provided by using, in addition to highly trained medical specialists, a large number of far less well-trained medical workers whose jobs are to minister to basic illnesses and to refer more complex cases to specialists. Thus in China, tens of thousands of 'barefoot doctors' deal with minor injuries, colds, and the like, supervise public hygiene, and immunize children against disease. Patients are treated in clinics on the communes and in urban neighbourhood medical centres, using medications most of which are only available on doctors' prescriptions in the West. Prevention of disease and early treatment of illness reduce the need for vast numbers of expensively trained doctors. Similarly, in one clinic in a poor area of Mexico City, students with nine months' medical training were able to handle 95 per cent of the cases which came to them. Checks by qualified medical personnel have shown that they had correctly distinguished between those cases they could handle and those they needed to refer – the other 5 per cent of the cases. In Tanzania, assistants using simple guides to symptoms have proved as accurate as, and quicker in their diagnoses than fully trained doctors. In countries like Britain or the United States, on the other hand, there is considerable pressure to diminish the role of paramedical help. In Texas, for example, the development of courses for such 'intermediate' services by nurses and medical students was recently stopped by pressures from the medical profession.

Considerations such as these have led some commentators to charge that education has become part of the system of economic and social exploitation in society. Ivan Illich's books – notably his *Deschooling Society* (1971) and *Medical Nemesis* (1975) – have the common theme that the economic and political dependence of the many on the few is created by the increasing professionalization and bureaucratization of society – a process in which formal education plays an important part. According to Illich, people are taught to rely upon the expert; government and the professions create and buttress the image of expertise by making their procedures much more arcane than they need be. We have seen how the professions elaborate a special language for their members, establish rules to circumscribe the numbers of those who can practice, and require extensive educational qualifications for entry. A similar 'mystification' of knowledge pervades the entire educational system. In most schools, knowledge is controlled by the teacher. As children move through the school, more and more of that knowledge is revealed; only those who have been educated to the highest extent are supposed, in this hierarchical system, to be competent to undertake specialized roles in society. Yet alternative approaches to learning, as we will see, are quite possible.

Though schooling and the educational system are often thought of as independent of pressures from society and State, they do, then, in complex and varied ways, reflect or reproduce the basic patterns of social and economic inequality. Moreover, education is subject to considerable direct external pressures – from government, business and the organized pressure groups of different social classes – who each want the education system to serve their interests. Illich and others argue, in contrast, that education should not be oriented to such extraneous ends; the purpose of education should be to develop a child's general potential for living, not training him or her for a predetermined job. Education should therefore, he argues, be freed from the pressures these various external expectations place upon it: we should find ways of making schooling as rewarding an experience as possible for the various kinds of children within it, rather than trying to use education as a means of maintaining and repairing the social and economic structure.

This perspective is a 'utopian' one, for educational systems can scarcely be insulated from the interests of the society of which they are a part. Such utopias, since they suggest new ways of approaching education, do, however, serve to counteract the pessimism or fatalism often engendered by the patent evidence of the association between social class and educational opportunity.

Schooling and Socialization

We have seen how particular forms of educational organization, their maintenance and their change over time, can be understood in terms of the social and economic structure of society. Educational organization, therefore, varies between schools and colleges in the same society. Formal curricula and examination requirements and standards are established and monitored by the State through systems of inspection and licensing, and through financial controls, exercised by a division of authority between central and local government, in most countries. A certain amount of latitude is, however, possible in the way in which the broad strategic policies of the educational system are put into practice. Thus the curriculum, the organization of school classes into streams or sets, the existence of subject 'departments' – or their replacement by 'area' and 'problem-oriented' studies – are matters of variation and areas of potential innovation in any school or college system. The size of an educational unit and the number of educational levels and specialities it contains are also factors which sociologists have found to contribute to on what students learn and how they learn it. In larger and more complex schools, it has been argued, students may feel isolated and frustrated. Institutions internal to the school have been developed partly in order to counteract such tendencies, such as 'houses' which cut across the age- and classroom-groups and provide an alternative focus of identity. (They are also used to bolster competitiveness and to encourage notions of loyalty and commitment.) Clubs based upon hobbies and other common interests, which often meet after formal school hours, constitute a further, more personalized, and, usually, intimate source of social support for the individual.

Size and complexity often lead students to rely heavily on this kind of grouping, and on personal friendships and cliques, for identity and support. Such groups are not necessarily committed to the formal academic or other goals of their school; indeed, they may reject them. Thus, in his study, *The Adolescent Society*, James Coleman found that in certain kinds of large American high schools, the importance of the esteem of their peers was sufficiently strong to make even academically successful youngsters downplay the value of their achievements (Coleman, 1967). Girls, too – even women at universities – often 'play down' their intellectual interests and knowledge when on dates, deferring to their boyfriends, and conforming to the stereotype of females as sex objects rather than people with minds and personalities of their own.

Many studies have attempted to determine what factors in college organization itself might affect the values and attitudes of the students in them (Feldman and Newcomb, 1969). Thus, in recent years, research in the field of higher education has often been concerned with the effect of college life on occupational choice or political attitudes. A frequent question posed in the 1960s was the extent to which the wave of student sit-ins and demonstrations reflected the increasing size and impersonality of colleges and universities. In these impersonal settings, it was hypothesized, the political issues of the day were likely to engage the attention of students more than they had done their predecessors, since students themselves were now experiencing the tensions of life in a 'mass society'.

These studies examined a range of factors, including the area of academic specialization, or the course of the student; whether the college was residential or not; whether the orientation of the college was vocational, religious, or general education; variations within student culture, such as the presence of fraternities and other groupings, were also taken into account, and even the influence of the teachers.

The conclusions of such studies have often been contradictory and the implications of their findings are unclear, since we do not know how lasting the effects reported were, as the researchers were rarely able to follow students beyond college. The major conclusion that emerged, however, was that the impact of higher education on student orientations is relatively weak Feldman and Newcomb concluded, for example, that the principal effect of college life and of college organization was to reinforce tendencies already present in students. Students selected their college and their subject in accordance with orientations developed in their family and at school; going to a particular college, or taking a particular subject, strengthens these dispositions, but there is little evidence that it fundamentally changes them.

We introduce these findings on the impact of school and college because they raise the fundamental issue of how lasting are the effects of schooling. The *assumption* that schooling is significant for a child's personal and intellectual development underlies such theorizing as that of Althusser or Bernstein when they characterize the school as imposing ideologies on children. The effects of schooling on a child's behaviour are usually discussed as part of the process of 'socialization': the ways in which people come to learn the norms and patterns of behaviour, and the values underlying these, which are current in their society. But formal education is not the only place where people are socialized. Children first learn about the practices of society within their families, and the home environment continues to be an important influence on children. Socialization, indeed, never really ceases, since we are constantly confronting novel situations in life and must learn how to handle them. Sudnow, for example, shows how, in a hospital, patients are 'taught' how to be good patients and, in the extreme case, are persuaded to die in a manner that will not unduly disrupt hospital routines (Sudnow, 1967).

Formal education, however, has often been regarded as the most important agency of socialization in modern society. For Emile Durkheim, the formal education system was a crucial component in the social and moral integration of a complex socitey. Schooling was essential in introducing children to the values and practices of other social groups in the same nation, and in providing them with an understanding of the variety of specialized roles required by the division of labour (Durkheim, 1973). In Durkheim's view, the school socialized children to be effective and tolerant citizens in societies whose increasing economic complexity made people more dependent upon each other, but which had also destroyed the basis of prior solidarities – e.g. those of the village where people collaborated to achieve common ends.

This argument was extended by Talcott Parsons, who analysed the ways in which the process of schooling introduced children to the behaviour patterns required for effective functioning in the economy and polity of modern society (Parsons, 1962). It is in the school, Parsons suggests, that children learn, among other things, to distinguish those situations in which they and others can expect to be treated primarily in terms of their achievement, as against those situations, such as the family, in which they receive affection and consideration by the fact of their personal relationships. This school learning process is not always an explicit one, but emerges from the pattern of interaction at school between teachers and children, and among children themselves. From this perspective, primary school children and also high school and college students learn not just facts and figures, but also enduring orientations towards action: orientations which are seen to be a functional part of complex society. In such a society, being able to treat people in terms of their objective needs or merits, rather than in terms of personal loyalties or prejudices, is often an important aspect of economic organization, administrative decision-making or even of personal services, such as the doctor–patient relationship.

These approaches to socialization indicate that it is not only the formal goals of a school or the particular content of a curriculum that must be considered in estimating the kind of impact which schooling has; the interaction process within the school is also a significant element in what is learned. Much of this interaction is not intended to have a specific effect, but occurs spontaneously in the school setting as children play games or exchange stories, or as teachers seek to impose order in a classroom or playground. Some sociologists have emphasized the incongruences which can arise between these different interaction processes. Whereas Parsons emphasized the way in which the patterns of schoolroom interaction developed orientations required by modern society, others have shown that the interaction situation in education can frustrate the explicit goal of the school. The most radical perspective is that the formal organization of learning makes it impossible for children to be 'truly' educated (Holt, 1971; Goodman, 1962). From this viewpoint, examinations and school bureaucracies 'teach' children to see education as a coercive and boring experience which gives them no opportunity to discover things for themselves, to use their imaginations or to collaborate with others.

In his study of innovations in medical education, Robert Merton emphasized a variety of features in educational organization which could produce consequences unintended by those who designed the training programme (Merton *et al.*, 1957). He noted that the sequence of courses, and the prestige of the person giving them, influenced students in their choice of specializations; students exchanged ideas with one another in an attempt to interpret the implicit as well as explicit aims of their training programme. In the course of these interactions, they developed orientations to medicine which often ran counter to the intentions of the school. In other medical studies, Anselm Strauss and Howard Becker have stressed the many unintended ways in which interactional situations within educational organizations influence student orientations. Becker and his colleagues described the processes whereby medical students prepare each other for the sight of their first corpse, and stressed that it is this kind of group situation which develops professional orientations rather than the formal teaching situation (Becker *et al.*, 1963). In another study, Becker emphasized the way in which the importance of the 'grade-point' average (the average mark given for each college course) becomes, in certain university settings, a major criterion by which students organize their lives. Though fraternities and sororities in the American system pressure their members to obtain a high grade-point average, the organization of the student body subverts the academic intention which lies behind the grading process: instead of being an incentive to learning, grades become viewed instrumentally. Students learn how to get decent grades by a variety of straight and crooked means, and it is skill at doing this, rather than the 'learning' contained in the courses, which gains most prestige on campus (Becker *et al*, 1968).

The conception of the school or college as the major agency of socialization also tends to over-emphasize the receptiveness of children or college students to orientations conveyed to them through the formal organization of learning. In practice, interaction situations in education are not coherent; a teacher may show favour to some children and treat others more impersonally. Moreover, children are likely to interpret the situation in a variety of ways; they may see what is happening as prejudice against children from their type of social background, or, if it suits them, as evidence of their intellectual superiority, or, alternatively, of the wisdom of not getting involved in an educational competition which is not for the likes of them.

Aaron Cicourel points to a more fundamental difficulty in using theories of socialization to understand what goes on within schooling. He argues that it is more convincing to view children as learning not only values or normative behaviour but how to interpret the varied situations in which they habitually find themselves (Cicourel *et al.*, 1974). In their family and everyday life, as well as in school, he argues, children are not confronted with a single consistent environment but with a range of often conflicting expectations and patterns of behaviour. Even in the home it is extremely unlikely that parents' behaviour is consistent towards their children. Middle-class parents, for example, may know the 'right' thing to say when answering questionnaires on the most desirable way to bring up children, but under the pressure of life in the home, their behaviour may deviate considerably, and inconsistently, from these expressed norms. In such a situation, what children learn is how to find out just what is expected of them in any given situation and to behave accordingly. But there is also a certain 'freedom of action' in any given situation, since children are, to varying degrees, able to act upon their own interpretations. They may choose to co-operate with teachers or not; they may choose to go along with their parents or to throw a temper tantrum. Children neither unthinkingly conform to organizational pressures, nor develop an entirely coherent set of values and norms of behaviour of their own.

Knowledge, Control and Classroom Interaction

Modern research in educational sociology has increasingly looked at the possession of knowledge and the power to communicate or withhold it as a major resource in the maintenance both of control in the classroom and of general control in society. Thus, Illich has argued that learning in schools is often organized as an hierarchical process in that a set of facts or concepts provided at one level are required before the student is allowed to progress to facts or concepts at a subsequent level. This form of presenting knowledge contains the implicit assumption that learning in school is a process of acquiring ever greater *amounts* of knowledge and ever greater understanding of the complexities of knowledge. At any given stage, the knowledge available to the child is only partial, and a full comprehension of the problem must await subsequent stages of education. The teacher in a hierarchically organized knowledge-system will claim to have access to that fuller comprehension and to be able to correct the partial understanding of students and lead them to greater understanding.

Such assertions about the nature of knowledge may, at first sight, appear to be self-evident and the hierarchical organization to be a necessity, given the structure of knowledge. Some of the most stimulating recent work in the sociology of education has, however, questioned such assumptions. Thus Basil Bernstein, Michael Young and their associates (Bernstein, 1975; Young, M.F.D., 1971), assert that knowledge and its attainment need not have a hierarchical structure. It is possible, rather, to acquire knowledge through learning how to solve problems; indeed, they claim, learning how to do something rather than accumulating information is the basis for all types of learning. Such a perspective is not a novel one, and has long been advocated by such educational sociologists as Jean Piaget. Bernstein and his associates point out that learning how to solve problems has implications for the organization of education very different from those deriving from a hierarchical concept of knowledge. In problem-solving, for example, it is much more difficult for a teacher to adopt a 'wait-and-you-will-find-out-later' attitude to his pupils; unless the 'solution' to the problem is convincing on the spot, teacher and pupils are unlikely to maintain interest and progress in the learning situation. Problem-solving is likely to introduce a more collaborative note into classroom interaction. Likewise, Paulo Freire has urged the need for dialogue in education: 'Authentic education is not carried on by A *for* B or by A *about* B, but rather by A *with* B, mediated by the world – a world which impresses and challenges both parties, giving rise to views or opinions about it' (Freire, 1972, p. 66). To achieve this dialogue, Freire advocates a teaching based on the use and discussion of terms and objects which are a crucial part of people's everyday reality: 'slum', 'work', 'wealth' replace, in Freire's teaching, the 'Peter', 'Jane', 'cat', 'garden', 'rug' of the 'Key Words' scheme of the British Ladybird reading books.

This approach challenges the basis of the hierarchical view of knowledge. It questions the value-judgements underlying that view which treats one body of data and concepts as inherently superior to another. Bernstein points out that the orthodox process of learning is usually a process of ever-increasing specialization. We 'progress' in education by knowing more and more about ever smaller bodies of knowledge. This may enable us to function efficiently in specialized occupational roles, though highly specialized knowledge can rapidly become obsolete. But specialization does not necessarily enhance our capacity to solve the more general problems we may meet in our everyday life, or in society as a whole. In this sense, to attribute superiority to the specialist in knowledge is simply to accept the claim of those specialists that that kind of specialized knowledge really is the highest kind.

These attitudes also create a sense of inferiority and dependence in those exposed to them. Children 'cooled out' by the educational process tend to see specialized knowledge as not for them, and are ready to delegate decision-making to those who claim to have specialized knowledge of politics or of the economy. Such attitudes do not arise from the cultural incapacity of any social group; they are the outcome of learning to think of certain kinds of knowledge as outside one's own sphere of interest or ability.

Research in this area of educational sociology has become increasingly concerned with the ways in which different methods of organizing the curriculum determine what is defined as knowledge. Bernstein, for example, has examined the implications of different ways of what he calls the 'classifying' and 'framing' of educational knowledge for social control, both inside and outside the school (Bernstein, 1971, pp. 205–7; 1975, pp. 85–113). By the 'classification' of knowledge he means the degree to which data and concepts are defined as being of the same sort and belonging together, and only secondarily related to other sets of knowledge. Where classification is strong, 'contents are well insulated from each other by strong boundaries' (Bernstein, 1971, p. 205). Rigid distinctions between academic 'subjects' such as history, economics or sociology are an example of classification: what is learned within one subject is defined as being quite separate from what is learned in another subject. Classification provides a frame of reference which helps subject-specialists to build upon previous work and to develop, systematically, knowledge of that subject; but classification also 'protects' them from having their assumptions questioned by information drawn from other areas of knowledge. Unwelcome data or forms of analysis can be dismissed, on the grounds that they 'belong' to another subject and, in this way, pupils are taught that knowledge is compartmentalized, divided into separate little boxes.

'Framing' refers to the degree of control which teacher and pupils possess over the selection, organization and pacing of knowledge – the extent to which they can decide what is taught, how it is taught and over what period of time. Framing also refers to the sharpness of the distinction between educational knowledge and everyday knowledge, so that 'strong' framing means that external experiences are ruled out as irrelevant to what is learned in the classroom. Nell Keddie describes how even in a particular social science project, children's everyday knowledge was treated by teachers as different from and even irrelevant to what was learned in the classroom (Keddie, 1971). In one of Keddie's examples, a teacher was so concerned to communicate sociological concepts that he ignored pupils' understanding of family relationships in order to get across a definition of 'the British family'. Strongly framed learning situations are authoritarian ones in which pupils are meant to learn a given body of material and to obtain credit for learning that and that alone. When strong framing occurs, a willingness to accept a teacher's definition of knowledge and to put aside everyday meanings may be essential to 'success' in school. Keddie coments wryly: 'It would seem to be the *failure* of high-ability pupils to question what they are taught in schools that contributes in large measure to their educational achievement' (ibid., p. 156).

The way that educational knowledge is organized in school via the curricula has important consequences, therefore, for both the types of relationships that are possible between teachers and students and the attitudes children develop towards the whole purpose of acquiring knowledge. They may view knowledge as a kind of private property, which gives a certain identity to its owner, as well as access to certain market opportunities, or, alternatively, may view the acquisition of knowledge as a collaborative venture, offering no such security. Bernstein also suggests that the organization of the curriculum affects the internal school hierarchy; in more 'pupil-oriented' situations, in which there is both relatively weak framing and classification of knowledge, subject hierarchies are weakened, as is the oligarchical control of departmental heads and headmasters or principals (Bernstein, 1975).

We should not, then, take the ways in which knowledge is organized in schools and colleges as unimportant. Knowledge is presented in socially stereotyped ways governed by the assumptions administrators, employers and education authorities have about the relevance of different kinds of knowledge. Their assumptions, in turn, normally reflect the economic or political interests of the dominant groups in society.

There is an implicit contradiction between this stress on the ways in which children are manipulated in a uniform manner by educational systems, on the one hand, and the emphasis of Cicourel, Labov and others upon children's capacity, despite apparent inadequacies in vocabulary or knowledge, to interpret the complexities of their environment and not to be 'fooled' by the speech and assumptions of their elders. Hammersley shows how both perspectives help us make sense of the classroom situation (Hammersley, 1974). He describes how teachers organize the participation of pupils in lessons through a question-and-answer form of teaching. The teacher has greater power than the pupils and is backed by the whole apparatus of the State. Outside the classroom, a teacher's opinion of a child will be accepted, while that of the pupil will be judged irrelevant or incompetent. Yet the teacher, as Hammersley shows, must keep the class under control and give lessons without having constantly to have recourse to the backing of higher authorities. To achieve this, he needs the co-operation of the pupils. His success in obtaining co-operation depends on his capacity to get the pupils to accept his authority, and on his ability, by the use of devices such as sarcasm, to persuade the pupils that he really does know better than they do.

The teacher's power consists in his right to determine the topic of discussion, to put questions to his pupils, to select certain pupils for participation and to accept or reject the answers given. The question-and-answer sequences which Hammersley reports show that many of the answers which the teacher gets are appropriate ones, but it is the teacher who decides whether to accept these as the 'right' answers, to reject them, or to declare that they are only partially correct. Question-and-answer sequences thus become a means of rewarding or negatively sanctioning pupils, and a strategy for getting students to cover the points which the teacher wants included: '. . . It is *his* talk which officially constitutes the lesson. Pupils are officially limited to making or trying to make contributions to his talk; their partici-pation is not on their own terms but on his; they are expected to listen to what he says and follow his development of the topic in order to "learn" ' (ibid., p. 365).

But the control is only partial. Children who provide answers which might be reasonable, but which get rejected, are aware of the ambiguities and inadequacies of question-and-answer procedures, and may decide not to bother any more. They may disrupt the lesson by creating disturbances, or by 'taking the mickey' out of the teacher by exploiting unintentionally humorous comments. Pupils may also turn the question-and-answer session into a competition among them-selves, seeking acclaim from other students as much as praise from the teacher. The enthusiastic choruses of 'Sir! Sir! Sir!' which domi-nate many of Hammersley's tape-recordings of classroom inter-action show that pupils find their own ways of getting enjoyment out of formal learning-situations, despite a teacher's attempts to 'control' their participation.

The effects of interaction in the classroom on educational perform-ance, and on attitudes to formal education, have also been studied by examining the process of stereotyping which takes place in the classroom. In his study of 'Hightown Grammar', Lacey argues that the ways in which schools are organized encourage stereotyping processes. By the fact of admission to the grammar school, all pupils represent an academically highly selected group of children. Yet within a grammar school, where pupils are allocated to 'streams' based on estimates of different levels of ability, the position of the stream at the bottom of the school hierarchy encourages the rise of 'anti-school' pupil groupings and leads teachers to type such pupils, who did well in their primary school, as unintelligent and as having little motivation.

Lacey provides a detailed account of how friendship groupings formed among the pupils he studied. Contributing factors to the way these relations develop are: the division of the school into classes, extra-curricular activities in the school, the grading of pupils between classes and within classes, the attitudes of teachers, the values emphasized by headmaster and teachers, and the social background of pupils. These factors interact and place every pupil in a set of social relations that gives him a particular position in the school. This position may also contribute to a child's failure. Consider, for example, Lacey's description of the case of Priestley, a boy from a middle-class home:

On another occasion, Priestley was asked to read and the whole class groaned and laughed. He grinned apprehensively, wiped his face with a huge white handkerchief and started to read very nervously. For a few moments, the class was absolutely quiet, then one boy tittered. Priestley made a silly mistake, partly because he was looking up to smile at the boy who was giggling, and the whole class burst into laughter . . . Finally, the master with obvious annoyance snapped, 'All right, Priestley, that's enough!'

This short incident, one of several during the day, served to remind Priestley of his structural position within the class and to confirm the opinions and expectations of the class and teacher towards him . . .

During this period of observation, I also noticed the significance of the behavior of another boy, Cready. Cready . . . although his form position was similar to Priestley's (twenty-sixth) habitually associated with a strikingly different group . . . Cready was a member of the school choir . . . members of the school choir sat in the row next to the piano and [the English master's desk] . . .

During the first three lessons I observed, Cready answered four of the questions put to the class. If Cready got an answer wrong he was never laughed at . . .

[Priestley] compensated for his failure in class and lack of academic success by learning the stocks and shares table of the *Financial Times* every week. This enabled him to develop a reputation in a field outside the sphere in which the school was competent to judge . . . Even this did not improve his standing in the school, especially with the staff . . .

Cready and Priestley do not . . . conform with the established correlation between academic achievement and social class. Cready, a working-class boy from a large family on a council estate, is making good, while Priestley, an upper-middle-class boy from a smaller family, is failing academically. However, this negative case highlights the point I want to make; there was a measure of autonomy in the system of social relations of the classroom. The positions of Cready and Priestley are only explicable in the light of an analysis of the system of social relations *inside* the classroom . . . Cready who had all the major external factors stacked against him, was able to use the system of social relations to sustain and buoy himself up, while Priestley, despite all the advantages that he brought to the situation, had fallen foul of the system and was not only failing but also speedily losing any motivation to succeed in the sphere in which the school was competent to judge him (Lacey, 1970, pp. 245–62).

Membership of friendship groups was thus used by teachers as a way of estimating the academic potential and ability of their pupils. Teachers labelled the individual members of the 'pro' and 'anti' school groups which formed in Hightown Grammar in terms of the 'typical' behaviour they expected from people in such groups ('good' pupils, 'lazy', 'Bolshies', etc.). When teachers talked with each other in the common-room about their pupils, they used such labels as an easy means of communicating their classroom experiences, and teachers who did not know the pupil being discussed soon learned what behaviour to expect from him. The process becomes a self-fulfilling one: teachers 'typecast' their pupils; these typifications become reinforced by interaction among staff and by the pupils' reactions to these stereotypes.

In his study of interaction processes in grade schools (primary schools) in the United States, Rist shows how even in a school in a Black ghetto teachers use class or ethnic stereotypes to sort out their pupils (Rist, 1970). The teachers he studied had particular expectations of the 'ideal' behaviour of their pupils, based on a Black-White, educated middle-class reference group. The teachers used these expectations in selecting children for special attention or to perform responsible jobs and these children sat together in the classroom. Other children were typecast, on the basis of their pattern of speech or personal characteristics, as not likely to succeed educationally; in the interaction of the classroom, they were made to feel by the teachers and other pupils both educationally and socially inferior.

The rhetoric used in the training of teachers, however, does not normally endorse stereotypes about children from different class and ethnic backgrounds. Rather, they are told that all children are indeed educable, and, in line with the dominant liberal ideology of the society, that each should have 'equality of opportunity'. More specifically, trainee teachers are told that the notion that intelligence or aptitude are inherited is scientifically dubious, if not wrong; they are taught that the assumptions upon which IQ tests are based (even the very notion of 'intelligence' as some relatively fixed and measurable entity) is also scientifically suspect; and that, because of these uncertainties, the practice of separating children into 'streams' of ability ought to be resisted, since it brings about the very differentiation it prophesies: children, they are told, are *made* into 'bright' or 'slower learners' by being treated and taught in different ways and by being segregated into classes composed of others stigmatized in the same way.

There are, however, limits on the effectiveness of such training. What is learnt in teacher training is often perceived by trainees as 'academic' knowledge, divorced from the realities of the 'real-life' teaching situation (Esland, 1971). In a country like Britain, with a strong empiricist tradition, in which 'abstract' thought is devalued and 'factual', practical experience is popularly regarded as superior to 'theory', lectures given at training college can be readily assimilated to this general category of 'theory', and contrasted with the 'real' experience of 'teaching practice', when trainee teachers actually act as teachers in classrooms for a few weeks at a time. Research in Britain shows the limited impact of teacher training programmes whose courses and teaching practice are designed to encourage teachers to be innovative in the classroom and to value the educational potential of diverse types of children. Yet the attitudes of trainees in such programmes towards teaching, within a year or two of finishing the training, were quite similar to graduates of more conventional training programmes. Likewise, in Chicago a Teachers' College founded in 1961 to encourage trainees to teach in the inner city, had little permanent effect on the generally negative attitudes of its predominantly middle-class students to such teaching. By the time students had extensive teaching practice and were preparing to take their first job, they were more likely than at the beginning of their training to say in response to a questionnaire that it was more important to give individual teaching attention to fast learners than to slum children. It was the other Teachers' College in the city – whose curriculum was more traditional – that had the most trainees prepared to teach in the inner city. These trainees were mainly of working-class family background and they had often been born and educated in the ethnic ghettos of the inner city.

On beginning teaching, educational theory learned in college is quickly modified in the light of the requirements of the teaching situation: those of keeping order in the classroom and of learning to work with other, established, teachers. These teachers are learning-models for the trainees. Older teachers also have the power to influence, by critical comment, formal and informal, the career-prospects of the new, junior teachers. In the hierarchical structure of most schools, maximum power lies in the hands of the head teacher and his or her assistants, supported by local educational authorities and official inspectors. In Britain and in many other countries, teachers are also rewarded for their 'success' in selecting a *minority* of students who enter higher education. The chief indicator most commonly used both of a school's 'success' and that of individual teachers is the number of children who have been 'got through' O- or A-level examinations. Such figures are cited by the teachers themselves, by the children, by parents, and announced on ritual occasions such as Prize Days. They are also used in appraising the performance of schools and teachers by local government authorities in making promotions, investing resources of staff and money and the like. The criteria of a teacher's success with the majority of the students is often his or her ability to keep a classroom quiet and trouble-free: lessons that interest children but result in noisy participation may lead to a teacher being seen as ineffective.

The obstacles to innovation in education are, however, more

fundamental than those deriving from the conservative orientations of educational hierarchies and of established teachers, as is shown in Nell Keddie's study of an experimental curriculum in a comprehensive school in Britain. In this school the humanities department introduced an examination course based on history, geography and social science, designed to be an undifferentiated programme suitable for teaching children of a wide range of abilities (Keddie, 1971). The teachers in the programme held 'progressive' educational views, favouring teaching mixed-ability groups and ascribing differences in educational performance to differences in motivation rather than to differences in intelligence. Keddie shows that these teachers accepted, uncritically, established concepts of what constitutes 'ability' and, while recognizing the influence of environment on ability, still operated with an idea of the 'ideal' pupil – i.e., a fast learner, probably coming from a middle-class family. She quotes this exchange between two teachers talking about the A-stream class:

TEACHER J: Some of the class have written to Oldham Town Council for material for the New Town project.
TEACHER C: They're really bright, are they?
TEACHER J: Mostly from middle-class families, well motivated (ibid., p. 137).

Teachers in the programme put a great deal of effort into thinking of ways of getting their material across to children from the 'less able' C-stream. Yet, viewing such teaching as a 'challenge', they accepted, with little question, that children in that stream were incapable of absorbing the kind of material that could be used with A-streamers. C-streamers were often not given the chance to use more complex material. They were also expected to be less academically sophisticated, and their, at times, critical attitudes to the material they were given were taken by teachers as further evidence of their lack of academic suitability. As we saw when discussing framing, the attempts of C-streamers to introduce their everyday knowledge tended to be seen by teachers as irrelevant to academic purposes.

Nevertheless, many teachers not only accept new ideas about education but are successful in putting them into practice, despite institutional constraints. Others deliberately seek employment teaching underprivileged children. Critiques of 'élitist' educational theory and practice have been a source of major change in the educational system and have led to significant institutional changes in the United Kingdom, notably the comprehensive school and experiments with 'educational priority areas'.

The learning process, then, requires teacher and taught to come to terms with each other's concepts and mode of communication; but it is convenient for teachers in organizing the classroom to look for simplifying criteria which they can use to judge and communicate progress. These criteria are readily available to them in the form of established stereotypes about the abilities of different classes and ethnic groups and in fixed views about the 'best' ways of organizing and communicating knowledge. Such rigid views make it difficult to recognize the diversity of potential present in a school class.

The Comparative Analysis of Education

The comparative study of education is not restricted to describing differences in the structure and content of education in different countries at any one time. It is also concerned with examining the way educational systems change at different stages in a country's development, the way in which the goals of society affect the education system, the role of education as a force in social and economic development, and the patterns, parallels and differences that may be discerned in the development of different countries at different times.

Within the advanced capitalist world – mainly North America and the countries of Western Europe – we have noted tendencies towards convergence between their educational systems; the types of school and college and the organization of learning within them have become more alike, gradually eliminating differences between the system of specialized secondary education in Europe and non-specialized secondary education in the United States. Likewise in higher education there has been an increasing movement, in Western Europe, towards shortening the length of the first degree. Both on the Continent and in Britain, courses in higher education at undergraduate levels have become more general and less specialized. The proportion of the age-group attending college in Western Europe has also increased and has begun to approach the levels of enrolment in North America. Other important convergences include the tendency for large, mainly non-residential, universities, such as the University of Paris, to be complemented by smaller, more residential units. Higher education in Europe has also become somewhat less differentiated. In Britain, for instance, the separate sectors of higher education – teacher education, technical education, vocational training and academic education in the arts and sciences – have become similar in structure in that it is no longer only universities which offer degree courses but also institutions of higher education such as polytechnics and colleges of education.

Such convergences can be related to common processes of economic development. We remarked earlier that the American pattern was based upon an economic expansion which required not only more highly trained people, but also considerable mobility and transferability of skills. This expansion was based, in the first place, upon the development of a large internal market for capitalist production which, over time, raised the level of consumption of the mass of the population.

The rapid development of a relatively undifferentiated educational system in the United States, we suggested, was a function of these developments: in the early twentieth century undifferentiated high schools, taking all the pupils from the locality, and mass entry into higher education first took root in those regions of the United States in which population increase and economic change was most rapid, especially in areas of rapid increase of population such as California.

The economic development of most European countries, in this period, was based on a different dynamic – on industrial economies whose markets were, to a large extent, external. In this context, the mass of the population did not have such crucial significance as consumers, nor did the type of industrialization require significant mobility of labour or transferability of skills, once high levels of population concentration had been established. The educational system was geared to providing different types of education suited to those occupying relatively stable positions in manual work, trade, clerical occupations, and management and administrative positions respectively. In this situation, most education was attuned to local circumstances, to the expectation that most children would continue in the same locality and even in the same kind of work as their parents. Specialized academic education (e.g., grammar schools in the United Kingdom, *lycées* and *gymnasia* on the Continent) creamed off a small proportion of the working class and prepared them to occupy the slowly-expanding number of jobs in clerical and other middle-class occupations. Once the more rapid growth of the 'tertiary' sector of the economy began, the middle classes also came increasingly to stress the importance of the academic grammar schools and to prepare their children for entry into them. Lacey suggests, for instance, that in the northern industrial town he studied, this interest of the middle classes in grammar-school education reflected the change in the local economy from a situation in which small businesses and small industries provided secure employment for middle-class children to one in which the major sources of middle-class employment consisted in clerical-type work in the factories and offices of large firms controlled from outside the town. Higher education in Britain became similarly differentiated between Oxford and Cambridge, the provincial universities, and the teacher-training, vocational, and technical educational insitutions. Oxford and Cambridge only emerged as educational institutions, rather than as places for socialization into the culture of an élite, when employment in the higher Civil Service and in business and industry offered the best prospects for upper- and upper-middle-class children. The provincial universities provided the relatively small numbers of 'second-level' managers and technicians required by a slowly developing economy.

It would be unwise to take this analysis too far; developments in continental European higher education certainly differed from those in Britain, and these differences were based on differences in political and economic structures. The American pattern of education has also been influenced by the nature of political institutions in the United States, particularly the federal structure of American government, the powers of the component states, and greater emphasis on local-level determination of educational policy. The general contrast remains, however, since higher education in Western Europe, as in Britain, caters for a relatively small élite which shares a homogeneous general culture as well as mastery of the economic and technological expertise in those societies.

The British and European educational systems, it has been suggested, began to converge with the American system when their economies began to emphasize the internal market and technological change. For Britain, at least, this has been a relatively recent phenomenon, beginning in the 1950s. It would require a great deal more evidence than we have at hand, however, to establish these relationships definitively. Again, the dynamic of the British and, to a certain extent, of the European economies, remains different from that of the American economy. It is quite possible that in Britain we will never develop our internal market to a similar extent to that of the United States; the rate of technological change and economic development is also likely to remain substantially lower than in the United States. These considerations, along with the continuing differences in the political structure of the two countries, are sufficient to indicate why it is unlikely that our educational systems will converge any further. Indeed, there are signs of divergence in, for example, attitudes towards higher education as educational expansion is discounted in Britain as the key factor in economic growth.

In the communist world the U.S.S.R. and the Eastern European countries have rapidly developed a mass system of education, with substantial proportions of the age-group which has completed secondary-level education (usually 18+) going on to higher education. These educational systems appear to have remained much more internally differentiated than is the case in the United States, in so far as different kinds of specialized secondary school channel students to different occupational destinations. The institutions of higher education are also sharply differentiated, making it difficult to transfer from one sector to another or to change courses after entry. This differentiation has been accompanied by policies aimed at ensuring an equitable social distribution of opportunities; children of manual workers or peasants, for example, are preferred for entry into higher education. Despite this, inequality of educational opportunity still persists in these countries, with children whose parents are non-manual workers being more likely to stay on in secondary school and to attend university than children whose parents are manual workers (Lane, 1976, pp. 185–91). In the case of Eastern

Europe, these educational inequalities are often marked and children from peasant families have much less chance of entering higher education than children whose parents are industrial workers; these latter children are, in turn, less likely to enter higher education than children of the intelligentsia (a category which includes most white-collar workers) (Boudon, 1974, Table 3.3).

We can understand these characteristics of the Russian and Eastern European educational systems in terms of the history of their different kinds of economic development. The U.S.S.R., for instance, achieved rapid industrialization in a country which at the time of the Revolution was still predominantly peasant in composition. Educational resources were channelled into training specialists for science and industry, while providing basic education for industrial workers. The extension of education to the peasantry was slower, and only expanded once agriculture became more technologically developed. The pressures of rapid industrialization created a highly centralized and stratified political and economic system in which differences of status increasingly came to correspond with differences in level of education. Industrial managers and party officials were largely recruited from the highly educated, while workers with low educational qualifications had few opportunities to rise into management positions.

Chinese economic development has had different consequences for education. There, rapid industrial concentration as the overriding priority is de-emphasized in order to bring the different sectors of the economy more and more into balance. Though industrialization is being strongly promoted in China, and is still mainly concentrated in certain cities and regions, 'micro'-industrial development is taking place even in the rural areas, and considerable use is made of underutilized labour-power and inventiveness to avoid, where possible, the purchase of machinery. Regional imbalances and differences in the standards of life in city and countryside are partially offset by ensuring the circulation of people and scarce commodities between areas, so that, for example, prices of most consumer goods are stable, and industrial workers help with the harvest in the village. Educated young people from the cities are encouraged to go and live in the countryside permanently.

These political and economic policies are reflected in the evolution of the educational structure in China and have been major factors in changing educational organization and curriculum. In the early years of the communist régime, until the Great Leap Forward of 1958, the Chinese educational system was a highly differentiated one. After twelve years of study in schools of different types, competitive examinations led to a range of higher educational institutions. Under Soviet influence, the emphasis on specialization and excellence in education increased until, by the 1960s there were signs of the formation of an educational élite who appropriated the best and most comfortable positions for themselves. As higher education expanded, its class composition became more unequal: students from worker or peasant background declined from 67 per cent of enrolment in Peking University in 1958 to 38 per cent in 1962 (Gardner, 1971, pp. 235–86). Courses of ever-growing length resulted in a small élite class of very highly educated people, and limited the scale and speed of economic development. To overcome these constraints, a new policy of both economic and educational decentralization was embarked upon following the Cultural Revolution of 1965–7.

Education is also strongly oriented to the practical needs of society and of production. The traditional deference paid to the learned and to established knowledge has been replaced by encouragement to question the intellectual authority of teachers and of received learning. Universities and colleges also provide courses for workers and use experienced workers as teachers in their courses. Part-time and work-study programmes at advanced level involve millions of people, many of whom go on to take up more responsible jobs in society. Courses have also been reduced in length.

In these ways, both hierarchies of knowledge and hierarchies of personal authority in school and classroom are challenged, as élite education for a few becomes replaced by mass higher education, even for those working in the factories. In the rural areas, local members of communes receive basic training which they then put into effect when they return home – as teachers, radio operators, mechanics, or 'barefoot' doctors. In Tanzania, Nyerere has attempted to direct educational policy in similar ways to avoid the creation of an educationally-based élite.

These developments have been made possible by destroying

hierarchies within education which might have become the basis for strong professional monopolies. China's policy of greater economic decentralization, then, as compared to Russia, is reflected in the more flexible and less differentiated organization of its educational system.

The educational systems found in the rest of the underdeveloped world also reflect their patterns of economic development. Levels of education in underdeveloped countries have risen rapidly in recent years, so that in continents such as Latin America there are few countries where the majority of the population of school age and above is not literate. In some countries the majority of the population will have completed at least primary education. This rise in educational levels is closely related to the pace of urban industrialization in the region (Roberts, B.R., 1973a); levels of education have risen fastest where the population has concentrated in urban places. This relationship has, in most countries, been a direct one: as the dynamic of the economy shifts to the urban industrial sector, this sector provides the best and often the majority of jobs. Education becomes more generally available so as to provide at least basic literacy for the mass of the population, and primary, secondary and tertiary education on an increasing scale. The type of education provided, however, even in the rural areas, is generally designed by city-based educationalists, and contains an urban bias. Examples in textbooks are often drawn from urban cultures, stressing the advantages of city life, for example. Hence, often unintentionally, the education given stimulates people to migrate to the city.

The contribution that rising levels of education can make to economic or political development in the underdeveloped world can easily be exaggerated. It has often been assumed, for example, that the extension of education will promote democracy in under-developed countries. The pattern has, in fact, been otherwise. Indeed, those countries in Latin America which have the highest levels of education are also those with the most dictatorial régimes – Argentina, Chile, Uruguay and Brazil. Nor does the relationship between levels of education and the distribution of occupations show that education encourages the development of economic enterprise.

The low level of development of the economy in such societies, then, sets distinct limits upon the development of education systems, and upon what can be achieved by the society, or by the individual, through education. The structure of the education system thus reflects the condition of underdevelopment. Differentiation in the type and quality of education provided at both primary and secondary levels is very marked. Rural schools in most of Latin America are considerably inferior to their urban counterparts; even in the cities, the quality of schooling varies widely between the poor and rich areas of the city. The differences in facilities, student–teacher ratios, and in the general condition of the schools, as between such areas, lead to substantial differences in the educational attainment of children before the end of primary school and to high rates of dropout. Most children never get beyond primary school. Conversely, expansion of private education in these countries, also rapid in recent years, has increased the educational advantages of the wealthier classes.

This situation is not simply one of economic underdevelopment; some countries, such as Mexico, Brazil, Hong Kong or Singapore, have become urbanized and industrialized, in different degrees. They remain, however, economically dependent on the advanced capitalist world. Hence in Latin American higher education there has been an increasing development of North-American-style education, providing a relatively intensive training for the children of the élite, and in textbooks, theoretical approaches, course-structures and general organizational structure based upon North American models. This education prepares students for work in large corporations which are often subsidiaries of, or linked to, foreign companies. In the case of some occupations, such as medicine or engineering, they also prepare students for migration to the advanced capitalist world. Thus, it is estimated that the United States would have to build and operate twelve new medical schools to produce the manpower being derived through immigration (Adams, W., 1968). The 'brain drain' to the United States alone absorbed no less than 58,000 trained professionals and technical workers from the Third World during the period 1962–6 (Godfrey, 1970). Nearly half the junior medical staff in the British National Health Service comes from overseas, mainly from India and Pakistan.

Educational systems in the Third World are differentiated and stratified not only by level and type of schooling, but by an emphasis on foreign or national cultures. Just as rural schools introduce children to 'foreign' urban cultures, so, too, specialized secondary schools (such as the foreign-language schools in many Latin American countries, usually attended by expatriate children also) and specialized higher education prepare students to work for foreign-dominated sectors of the economy. Attempts in recent years to 'nationalize' educational systems, by eliminating foreign-language schools and colleges, reflect the political and social tensions produced by such educational developments. However, it has been difficult for even the most nationalist of régimes to reduce the amount of foreign-oriented curriculum; such curriculum reflects the economic structure of underdevelopment.

Chapter 6
Work, Industry and Organization

Definitions of Work

In our own society the term 'work' would seem to have a perfectly unambiguous meaning. It refers to a special kind of activity, clearly marked off from other activities in space and time. Work takes place in an office, a market-place or a factory – somewhere separate from the home. Secondly, it occurs during periods of time – 'nine to five', the 'evening shift' and so on – which are likewise segregated from other periods of time.

Yet, while the meaning of this word would appear at first glance to be perfectly clear, there are, in fact, problems and contradictions in the way we use it. Thus a person expending considerable physical energy in his garden, or redecorating the front room, is not normally considered to be working. In our society, too, an artist or an athlete may think of themselves as 'working' while carrying out activities which to others would be 'leisure-time' activities. (The problem of defining an 'amateur' or a 'professional' in sport is an indication of this kind of ambiguity.) And schoolchildren will talk of 'school work' or 'homework', although these activities carry no financial remuneration at all.

One striking, and very much debated, example of this ambiguity is in the case of 'housework'. Housework, still very largely defined as the work of women (even if they are also in full- or part-time employment), is often physically demanding, and certainly accounts for many hours in the lives of women:

It has been calculated in Sweden that 2,340 million hours a year are spent by women in housework compared with 1,290 million hours in industry. The Chase Manhattan Bank estimated a woman's overall working week averaged 99.6 hours (Mitchell, J. J., 1971, p. 102).

Such work is clearly economically significant, and where this work is not performed by unpaid housewives the gap is filled by paid employees, such as housekeepers or servants, restaurant staff and nursery workers. Furthermore, the women who perform these unpaid activities generally regard what they do as constituting 'work', with all the connotations of monotony and excessive pace that this word often implies (Oakley, 1975). Yet these activities do not enter into national income statistics, are not carried out in return for a wage, and therefore, in that usage, do not count as 'work'.

Work, then, is not the same thing as physical effort although our use of the word may sometimes reflect these older, more general meanings. What is and what is not work is *socially* defined; it is not a quality inherent in any particular act. In modern industrial society work is socially defined as *paid employment*, work carried out for others in exchange for a wage or a salary. An unemployed person, a person 'out of work', is one who is deprived of a regular source of income, yet who needs or desires such an income.

Just as we do not equate work simply with toil or physical effort, we also think about work as more than just an activity which brings us an income or contributes to the national economy. The concept of work is invested with varying degrees and kinds of *moral* evaluation. Thus attitudes to work emphasized by Calvinism see it as a moral as well as an economic necessity. 'Idleness', and its many synonyms, are not neutral terms simply describing the state of non-working, but are redolent with moral disapproval. Such disapproval is not confined to capitalist countries; loafing and idleness are at least as much subject to disapproval and sanction in Cuba or China as they are in the United States or Western Europe. This is because these societies are endeavouring to develop quickly, and hence need to mobilize the energies of their people. By contrast, highly industrialized, wealthy societies have shown signs, in recent years, of developing an 'anti-work' ethic, as people fortunate enough to live in comfort come to value the creative use of 'free' time and self-fulfilment.

Marxist evaluations of work, more generally, stress its fundamental necessity for society and its positive value carried out within a communist society. They contrast this with life in capitalist societies, where men not only work *with*, but also *for* other human beings. In this framework, work comes to imply exploitation, as the distortion of 'creative' labour deprives it of some of its human significance. This critique of work merges with Romantic indictments of industrial society (reflected in the work of writers as different as Blake, Ruskin and Lawrence) which laid particular stress, not simply on the ugliness of industrial cities, but also on the stunting effects of an increasingly high specialized division of labour (Williams, R., 1958). The working life of most people appears to be controlled by impersonal forces because they rarely encounter the people who make the crucial decisions that govern and structure their lives. Thus, it is argued, they feel themselves to be cogs in a complicated machine, like Charlie Chaplin's assembly-belt worker in *Modern Times*, which satisfy their need for income but do not satisfy or even involve the 'whole man'. Hence we find many different, and sometimes contradictory, evaluations of work in contemporary society: work is both human and anti-human, work is necessary but unpleasant and yet idleness is a sin or a crime. Even the artist – often the idealized image of the fulfilled worker – may find that his work is no longer his, but becomes the possession of buyers or commerical advertisers, or the object of uncomprehending critics, or subject to the capricious tastes of a small intellectual élite.

Thus, there are not only different evaluations of work within our society but different evaluations of different kinds of work. Within a single society there is no general agreement as to what constitutes 'real' work and who are the 'real' workers, although there is a tendency among members of most occupational groups to reserve these labels for themselves and to apply more derogatory labels to members of other occupational groups. Some kinds of work are regarded as more 'fulfilling' or more dignified. Thus the terms 'vocation', 'career' or 'profession' are attempts to put a more elevated and positive label upon work than the monosyllabic word 'job', and a distaste for 'mere physical toil' is implied when such distinctions are made. This particular distinction partly reflects a long-established, largely upper-class bias. But it probably derives, equally, from a plebeian resentment of obligatory back-breaking labour. Such a low regard for physical labour is not found universally throughout society, even amongst those who have to perform it; those who have been called the 'upside-downers' regard *manual* work or work which is valuable to society as 'real' or 'true' work (Young and Willmott, 1957b). People highly evaluated in this way might include labourers or nurses. Something of this sentiment is conveyed in this popular image of clerical workers: 'those chaps who sit on their you-know-whats in offices and push pens' (Lockwood, 1958, p. 12).

Social Consumption

It would appear to be a straightforward matter to argue that work must be a central focus in society, since there are certain basic human needs – our needs as consumers – which have to be met, and which can only be met through work. While straightforward, such a statement in fact tells us very little. It does not explain how there has arisen such an extraordinary variety of patterns of production, distribution and consumption throughout history and throughout the contemporary world. In other words, society is not merely the *result* of economic or biological 'needs'; it is also, in a sense, the *cause* of these 'needs'. In fact, apart from the minimum level of calories needed to sustain life, the rest of what we strive to produce and consume is not required to meet *biological* 'needs' at all; we work in order to satisfy culturally-determined and acquired 'wants'. Economists go further and distinguish both wants and needs from 'demands', which are wants backed up by the ability to pay in cash or in kind for the things we desire. Thus I need food, I want salmon, and I demand kippers. Salmon here is wanted not simply because of its nutritional content but also because it symbolizes a particular status and style of life.

Even in the simplest societies, men prize material goods because of these wider social connotations. The Bushmen or the Australian aborigines, often on the edge of hunger, nevertheless produce and consume in order to satisfy their religious wants as well as their stomachs, and exchange food – even go hungry – in order to meet religious or kinship obligations. Yet because their customary level of wants is not very flexible – whereas our appetites appear to expand indefinitely – once they have satisfied basic levels of wants, the rest of their time may be devoted either to 'leisure-time' pursuits or acquiring luxuries. Thus Marshall Sahlins has described hunting and collecting societies – to the surprise of many – as the 'original affluent society' (Sahlins, 1972). The nomadic Hadza of Tanzania, for instance, spend six months of the year gambling! Richer preindustrial societies work hard overproducing food they do not eat at all, but destroy or simply display so as to enhance their social reputations. The Indians of British Columbia, for instance, in their 'potlatch', *destroyed* the food, canoes and other forms of valuable property they had accumulated through hard work, as rival tried to outdo rival in competitive display so as to enhance his prestige (Codere, 1966). Similarly, Malinowski has described how the Trobriand Islanders of Melanesia produced more, on their garden plots, than they actually required and might indeed even harvest twice as much as they could eat. Furthermore, they put more work into their gardens than was technically necessary, spending much time in making the gardens look neat and clean 'for the sake of ornamentation, in connection with magical ceremonies and in obedience to tribal usage' (Malinowski, 1922, pp. 58–9).

Many of these patterns of behaviour can be found in our own society. The display of wealth, rather than its consumption, is not an unfamiliar notion in a society where 'status symbols' and 'keeping up with the Joneses' are household phrases. To attend a dinner may serve to satisfy a person's hunger, but it may also have implications for his professional or business interests. Furthermore, to be invited to a meal places the guests under certain obligations because they are expected to reciprocate this hospitality just as obligations are generated through the giving of gifts at Christmas and birthdays. In short, we must see the economist's conception of 'utility' as something which involves much wider social, psychological, religious and political as well as material or strictly economic expectations. The economy, that is, involves the management of resources, their production and consumption, so as to maintain groups and individuals in relationships, not merely to produce enough calories to keep the body adequately fuelled.

Social Production

The process of producing materially-necessary and culturally-valued items so as to satisfy wants is a collective undertaking, involving organized co-operation between individuals and groups and interaction between individuals and nature. Relations of co-operation, involving specialization of complementary tasks, strongly excited the imagination of classical economists when they looked at the new industrial division of labour. Here is Adam Smith, writing in 1776, describing the quite ordinary process of pin manufacture:

In the way in which this business is now carried on, not only is the whole work a peculiar trade, but it is divided into a number of branches, of which the greater part are likewise peculiar trades. One man draws out the wire; another straights it; a third cuts it; a fourth points it; a fifth grinds it at the top for receiving the head: to make the head requires two or three distinct operations; to put it on is a peculiar business; to whiten the pins is another; it is even a trade in itself to put them into the paper; . . . the important business of making a pin is, in this manner, divided into about eighteen distinct operations . . . (Smith, 1950, p. 3).

Adam Smith goes on to describe the way in which this division of labour enhances efficiency. He omits here, however, some other divisions that might have been of more interest to the modern sociologist: for example, the division between the owner of the pin-making enterprise and those who work for him, in short, class divisions. Also omitted is the fact that the worker in the pin factory would usually be working to support a family at home and a wife who, in her turn, might be labouring at her housework to sustain him: in other words, the domestic division of labour.

Adam Smith's description, although written two hundred years ago, seems very familiar to modern ears. Indeed, it is so familiar that it might appear to be banal and obvious until we come to compare it with descriptions from other societies. To throw these features into relief, let us consider another work-situation, far removed from eighteenth-century English pin manufacture. Among the agricultural Ndembu of Zambia there is another form of the division of labour, that between the sexes. Planting is regarded as women's work, while tree-felling and clearing are regarded as men's work. Hunting is also seen as essentially a masculine activity, so that there is a clear association between hunting and concepts of social status and masculinity (Turner, 1957, pp. 21–3, 25–8). Such associations between prowess at work and notions of virility and masculinity are not, of course, unknown in Western culture, as illustrated in the legendary exploits of John Henry.

Yet although we talk of the 'division of labour' in both the English pin-making and in the Ndembu situations, the meanings and consequences of this division of labour are very different in each case. In the first place, Adam Smith was describing just a segment of the workers' lives. He omits as irrelevant any consideration of their relationship with their kin, with their neighbours or with their wives. He does so because he works within a particular theoretical framework, that of *laissez-faire* capitalism, which treats the relationship between worker and employer purely in market terms: the worker sells his labour(-power) on the market and the employer hires him. Each tries to secure the best economic bargain he can get. The employer, in particular, is not responsible in any way for the employee's fate outside the factory. Their relationship is governed by a *contract*: so many hours of labour for so much wages. Whether he has one or ten children is entirely the worker's private choice; whether he lives in a slum or in a decent house is no responsibility of the employer. Their relationship, in sum, is solely an economic matter, ultimately expressed, legally, in the contract, and economically, in terms of cash. 'Moral' or 'social' considerations are irrelevant. The Ndembu economy and pattern of social and moral relationships could not be more different. There, the people one associates with in the process of production are not just fellow-workers: they are also kin and others with and between whom there are often many ties and obligations.

Secondly, in the pin-making process it is formally irrelevant who actually performs the tasks; male or female, black or white, old or young. What does matter is whether the individual fills an occupational 'slot'. These kinds of distinctions are, however, of much greater importance in the Ndembu case. While a woman might, if given the chance, prove to be just as skilled at hunting as her husband, this fact will not permit her to take part in the hunt.

Sociologists have elaborated this distinction between these two kinds of 'work' situation by distinguishing between *ascribed* and *achieved* statuses. In the case of the Ndembu we are emphasizing ascribed statuses, that is positions one is born into, or which one occupies by virtue of the fact of possessing certain characteristics, such as being of a certain age, sex or colour. It must be stressed that this is not a biological determinism; we are talking about certain characteristics, which might be biological, but which are given special significance in a particular culture. (Other biological characteristics might be ignored.) In the case of Smith's pin-workers, however, we are emphasizing achieved statuses, which were acquired through one's own efforts, technical skill, ability or cunning. We are not, of course, arguing that ascribed characteristics are unimportant in the occupational structure of modern society; the kind of work a person may do or be permitted to do is often in practice influenced by considerations such as age, sex or ethnicity. What is important is that in formal job-descriptions or organizational charts, these ascribed characteristics play little part and the jobs can be performed by a wide variety of people.

Whatever kind of society we are talking about, the necessity to work – the application of human labour to physical resources in the production of goods – involves a variety of social relationships. Moreover, these relationships are not determined merely by what is technically more efficient or appropriate for the particular task concerned. People are not merely co-ordinated – or 'orchestrated' – at work. They are also controlled: power is exercised over them. That people must co-operate in order to produce does not necessarily mean, therefore, that such co-operation will be harmonious or conflict-free. Within the industrial enterprise employers exercise control over their employees in a variety of ways: through direct disciplinary procedures, through the system of payment, and through the total set of administrative and technological controls that confront the worker when he enters the work-place and which shape his experiences there. Conflict over the use of these controls has been referred to as conflict over the 'effort bargain', the negotiation of the relationship between rewards and efforts (Baldamus, 1967, especially pp. 34–7). As we shall see, these conflicting relationships within the productive process have been sharpened in modern society with the growth of capitalism, the development of an urban industrial society and the growth of bureaucracy.

Work Today

In the previous section we implied that there is a difference between the nature of work in industrial society and the nature of work in what might be called pre-industrial society. In Chapter 4, on the other hand, we suggested that these broad historical distinctions have their limitations, since they tend to ignore considerable areas of overlap between the two kinds of society and because they tend to ignore important differences within them. It is with these kinds of qualification in mind that we go on to examine some of the features of work in modern industrial society. The picture we present will undoubtedly be crude and incomplete but illustrates some of the major concerns of classical and contemporary sociologists alike, seeking to understand the changing society in which they live.

In the first place let us consider the question of the extent to which work really is a central concern in modern life. We have hitherto argued that it is and, by implication, will remain so even in the most advanced industrial societies. Yet the way in which work is central varies between societies. It can thus be argued that work is central today in that wage-labour is the main source of most people's incomes, and hence physical survival. Yet even this statement should be subject to closer examination. Less than half the population of the United Kingdom is classified as being 'gainfully employed'. Thus for every person at work there is slightly more than one further person dependent upon him or her. Looking at the proportion of time spent at work by men in the year 1972, Young and Willmott estimated that this varied between 40 per cent at the highest and 34 per cent at the lowest. Furthermore it is likely that this proportion has been falling steadily from the mid-nineteenth century (Young and Willmott, 1975, p. 132). So that while we talk of work as a basic activity, in fact it involves less than half the population for less than half of their working day. The worker spends much of his time not in working but in eating, resting and sleeping at home and a further amount of time in domestic and leisure activities. Yet, before rushing to the conclusion that we are entering an 'age of leisure', we should remember that more time may be spent in travelling to and from work (a rather indeterminate space of time, neither properly 'work' nor 'non-work') and that, once again, the activities of housewives do not enter our calculations.

However, it is important to see work not merely in terms of time spent but also in terms of its meaning for the workers, and in terms of the effect that this work has on other areas of life. While work may be an activity that is physically and perhaps socially segregated from home and leisure activities, it is not necessarily a completely separate undertaking in the individual worker's mind. In the first place, as we have seen, he will most likely go to work to support his family. Work may also affect his leisure activities, either directly – in that he spends most of his leisure time with his fellow-workers – or indirectly and negatively, in that he seeks to escape from his work in his leisure.

Work is certainly crucial in that it is a source of income. But the work a person does is also important in other ways, notably in that it gives that person identity and status within society as a whole. Thus, when we ask the question 'What is he?', the kind of answer that we normally expect is a statement about the work that person does – 'He's an engineer' or 'He's a dentist'. Such words are not merely labels which inform us about the kind of technical function a person fulfils in society, but a major key to placing and evaluating that person socially. It is not only sociologists who use occupation as a means of classifying or ranking people in the wider society; individuals in everyday life use these as a means of classification. Lockwood, for example, argues that the difference between 'white-collared' (or 'black-coated') workers and manual workers can be especially attributed to the fact that these two different kinds of worker are treated differently *at work*, even within the same firm. Clerical workers may come to work at different times, eat in separate canteens and use separate toilets, and are often physically and socially closer to management (Lockwood, 1958, ch. 3). Gouldner has shown how status differences between mine-workers and surface-workers in an American gypsum mine carried over into the community in which both groups lived (Gouldner, 1955, ch. 7). In this way, a person's work may affect his social standing in the wider community.

Yet, here again, the situation is not without its ambiguities. Many of the differentials of skill and occupation which are understood by one's fellow-workers often have little meaning in the wider society.

Even two academics within the same university may find that they have little further to talk about once they discover that one is 'in Ancient History' while the other is 'in Mechanics of Fluids', and, in the wider society, an attempt to answer accurately the question 'What do you do?' may give rise to a polite but uncomprehending 'How interesting!' In a more clearly defined community such as a mining community, by contrast, where everybody understands what the miners' work involves in terms of skill and danger, miners derive prestige and satisfaction from talking about their work with their mates and neighbours in a pub or working-men's club (Dennis *et al.*, 1956, p. 144). Such a close overlap of work and community does not often obtain, however, and a 'big man' at work may be somewhat smaller in his suburban house and garden.

There is a final sense in which work might be said to be 'central': the way in which it gives the worker a sense of identity, not just in the eyes of others but also in his own eyes. A sense of occupational pride is well illustrated in this quotation from a railwayman:

A real railwayman doesn't finish at the end of his shift, he finishes when he's finished the job (quoted in Salaman and Thompson, 1973, p. 90).

Yet this sense of identity is affected by changes in technology and the wider society, and hence in the way in which the job is viewed by others:

When I joined the railways, a railwayman was king of the working class; now he's a laughing-stock. From top to bottom in a lifetime! (ibid., p. 76).

Where a job has a low, or perhaps even a negative, status, its members may seek to redefine their tasks and hence their image in the eyes of themselves and others. Thus American apartment janitors, conscious of their negative image as drunken layabouts, seek to redefine their job as all-purpose handymen, electricians or plumbers rather than as simply passive guardians of a building (Gold, in Berger, 1964). Similarly, traffic wardens may seek to emphasize some of the more positive by-products of their job by utilizing their intimate knowledge of the streets to advise inquirers about directions or parking facilities, thereby, perhaps, reducing their purely punitive image (Richman, 1972).

The study of 'work satisfaction' is therefore a complex one, involving the image and status that a particular occupational identity has in the wider society, the actual physical and technological conditions of work, and the expectations that the worker brings to the work-place. Berger, for example, has suggested a three-fold classification of work. Firstly, there are those jobs which still provide some kind of self-identification and satisfaction: for example, professional, craft or artistic occupations. Secondly, there are tasks which are almost the exact opposite – they are seen as a direct threat to a person's identity, reducing him to the status of an 'appendage to a machine'. Berger argues that these two extremes have declined in modern society, the first because working for large bureaucratic organizations results in a loss of personal freedom; the second because many unpleasant and routine tasks have been eliminated in modern industry. Instead, a third kind of work, perceived as a 'grey neutral' region, has grown up which is neither a direct threat to one's personal identity nor a major source of identity. Such jobs are neither very hateful nor very pleasurable (Berger, 1964, pp. 218–19).

This is almost certainly too simple. In the first place, we have seen how individuals performing low-status tasks may try to redefine their work in relation to members of the public. In the second place, some jobs which to the outside observer may appear to be boring, routine tasks can be a source of satisfaction to the person performing them. Baldamus, in this connection, has developed the notion of 'traction' which may be roughly defined as the opposite of 'tedium'. He describes traction as '. . . a feeling of being pulled along by the inertia inherent in a particular activity. The experience is pleasant and may therefore function as a relief from tedium' (Baldamus, 1967, p. 59). Traction, he argues, is akin to a sense of 'rhythm', which a person develops even in performing routine tasks.

We have been assuming, implicitly, that workers expect to get some satisfaction out of the work that they perform. But work may simply be seen by the worker as a means to an end. In a sample of industrial workers in the United States, for example, Dubin found that three out of four workers did *not* regard their work and the place of work as a central life-interest. Only 10 per cent of them thought of their work as a source of their most important relationships. Their friends were not normally fellow-workers (Dubin, 1956). Similarly, English car-workers, while disliking many aspects of their job on the assembly-line – particularly the fact that the pace of the work is dictated by the speed of the assembly-belt – do not necessarily expect to find the work rewarding in any sense other than a financial one (Goldthorpe, J. H., *et al.*, 1969). The workers, it might be said, implicitly strike a bargain with the firm and say, in effect: 'We are prepared to accept these deprivations *in* and *at* work in exchange for high rewards *for* work.' Many of the workers in this particular sample had given up more skilled, but lower-paid, jobs in order to come to work for the car firm. One of the conclusions of this Luton study is that the sociologist cannot allow his investigations to stop at the factory gates, but must also consider the attitudes and expectations that the worker brings to his work-situation and the ways in which these are influenced by the family and the wider society.

Simply having a job is, then, for most adult males, and for many adult females, a major source of identity in itself, and being denied that job, through redundancy or retirement, commonly brings with it considerable problems in terms of redefining identity or self-image. But whether a particular job is satisfying or unsatisfying, of high status or low status, a major source of identity or simply a means to an end, are much more variable matters. The sources of some of these ambiguities may be examined further by considering other features of work in modern society.

One of the sources of the ambiguous status of work in modern society is the tendency for work and home to become two separate worlds, a theme that has already been considered in relation to the family. A person *goes* to work and *returns* home. This is dramatically illustrated in that decidedly modern figure, the commuter, who is involved in twice-daily migrations to and from work, across our major cities. This separation of home and work has shaped and is shaped by the development of the cities with their constantly changing patterns of residential life and modes of urban transportation.

This is a quite different state of affairs from that in which people used to work with members of their families or their kin, as in 'cottage industry'. There, status within the family was closely related to the kinds of tasks performed; co-operation was typically a division of labour between members of the same kinship group; consequently, there was not the same sharp dividing-line between work and non-work, between work and family, and between work and leisure. (There was also the intermediate situation of 'out-work', where there was often a separation between work (for cash) and non-work, but not a separation between home and work.)

Yet this distinction is too sharp. Even in contemporary Britain a worker may be influenced, and perhaps even assisted, by his kin in selecting a particular place of employment. Ties of kinship are still important at the highest levels of business, finance and government, and the term 'family firm' still has some meaning in contemporary society (see Lupton and Wilson, 1959). Furthermore, there are still plenty of jobs and occupations which may either be carried out from the home or which are characterized by a blurring of the boundaries between home and work. We include here a diverse range of activities from typing and sewing done (often by married women) at home (the modern version of the 'putting-out' system), to the work of clergymen, doctors and policemen. In the last three examples, the work-situation spills over into the home, confusing time-schedules and affecting relationships with friends and neighbours.

The separation of home and work is not simply a physical separation; it is also a separation between two different kinds of relationships. Outside one's work, relationships are often supposed to be based upon personal considerations, to involve strong emotions and tend to embrace many aspects of life. Work-relationships, on the other hand, are based upon *rationality*. We do not use this word in its popular sense, as meaning 'sensible' behaviour. Rather, rationality, as used here, involves the calculated use of resources for the achievement of a particular goal or set of goals in the most economical way possible. In the light of this definition of rationality we may speak of individuals behaving rationally when they pursue their goals with maximum efficiency and minimum cost. We may also speak of business firms, universities, government departments and hospitals behaving in this same rational, calculative way, and the general term for this kind of social institution is the *organization*, the subject of the latter half of this chapter.

Clearly, then, behaviour that would be considered desirable or required at home might seem totally inappropriate at work, and vice versa. Where personal or 'family-type' relationships enter into business decisions we often talk – pejoratively – of 'nepotism' or 'corruption', and the father who attempts to run his household like a corporation is likely to be regarded as a figure of fun. Sociologists from the nineteenth century onwards have attempted to generalize this kind of distinction in terms of a contrast between industrial and pre-industrial society. In the one, *rationality* prevails, and the typical institution is the *organization*. In the other kind of society, *traditional* action is said to prevail: action which lays the emphasis on what is handed down from the past, on what, it is believed, 'has always been'. Here the appropriate kind of institution is the *community* (see Chapter 7) or the *primary group*.

This is not to deny that there will be strong elements of 'rationality' in traditional societies, and of 'traditional' behaviour in industrial societies. As we have seen previously, this is a very crude and preliminary classification. Moreover, there is no one single pattern of rationality, even in developed industrial societies. Some economists may speak of the capitalist entrepreneur who works out his best responses to the swings of the market as behaving rationally; others regard the question of the rationality of the individual or firm as subsidiary. They point out that the market-system as a whole is unplanned and therefore 'irrational', whatever the behaviour of individual firms in that market. Thus communists regard capitalism as 'anarchy', and capitalists denounce Soviet-type planning as leading to bureaucratic rigidity and therefore 'non-rational' inefficiency.

A final feature of work in modern society, and one which has been a central theme in the sociological tradition, is the *alienation* of labour. Without going into all the implications and controversies surrounding this particular term (see Williams, 1976, pp. 29–32), we can say that 'alienation' literally means 'separated from' and refers, in the first place, to the position of the worker in the work-place and his relationship to his work. He is alienated from the means of production; typically the worker does not own the tools with which he works, or the capital which is employed in the production process. He is also separated from the product of his work. He produces not for himself or for a specific purchaser, but for an abstract market. Furthermore, in many cases, he produces not a complete item but a small part of a finished product and probably only carries out a simple routine operation. These may be described as the objective features of alienation. Much discussion, however, extends to considering how far the objective features result in subjective feelings of deprivation or estrangement; a sense of a lack of wholeness, a sense of frustration or of a loss of humanity. Thus many people come to feel that their lives and work are controlled by *things* – by money, by abstract 'market forces' or by technology – and not by processes which are ultimately of human origin. Alienation implies much more than just a sense of boredom at work; it also refers to a lack of power or control on the part of the worker. Thus alienation is not the same as a lack of 'job-satisfaction' and, indeed, in one sense the worker who states that he is happy in his work may be more alienated than the worker who does not.

The separation of home and work, and the increase both of rationality and of alienation, are closely connected and can be considered as different aspects of a general process. Thus rationality demands the increasing separation of home and work, a separation which manifests itself in the use of migrant labour in industrial countries and the development of multinational corporations. The rationalization of the market, that is, calls for cheap labour and economies of scale, and sweeps aside considerations of nationality. The separation of home and work is one aspect of this process involving the separation of various areas of life which are only linked by the wage-packet (in the case of home and work) or the cash transaction in the sphere of consumption. Finally the institutional realization of rationality in the forms of the organization of the bureaucratic machine represent further aspects of alienation. While a worker in a moderately sized local firm or a worker in a multinational car firm may both be, formally, in the same position in relation to their employers – in that they both sell their labour-power in exchange for wages – in the latter case the sense of remoteness and powerlessness is likely to be much greater. Multinational corporations, a logical development of rational capitalistic principles in the mid-twentieth century, have come to play an increasing part in the world economy and, therefore, in the lives of individual workers and consumers. In 1970, for example, the sales of giants like General Motors and Standard Oil exceeded the gross national products of several European countries, including Denmark, Austria and Norway (Tugendhat, 1973, pp. 19–20). The similar dominance of principles of rationality in the communist countries of Eastern

Europe suggests that the sense of alienation for the worker in Belgrade or Prague may be not all that dissimilar from the sense of alienation felt by a worker in Birmingham or the Ruhr.

These three interlinked features of work in modern society – separation of home and work, rationality, and alienation – help us to understand the ambiguities of work in modern society. Work is central in that it is necessary for the individual, for the family and for society as a whole. Yet it often appears to be marginal in that it is seen in strictly *instrumental* terms, as being simply a means to an end. On the other hand workers, it would seem, do not see work as an end in itself – as having any *expressive* qualities – nor do they expect to see work in this way. In the words of a Ford worker:

It's the most boring job in the world. It's the same thing over and over again. There's no change in it, it wears you out. It makes you awful tired. It slows your thinking right down. There's no need to think. It's just a formality. You just carry on. You just endure it for the money. That's what we're paid for – to endure the boredom of it (quoted in Beynon, 1973, p. 118).

Yet perhaps this is too pessimistic. At the very least, there may be a sense that there 'must be more to life than this'. To quote someone commenting on his experiences on the line in a tractor factory:

A man isn't just born to be a worker, like the bees, and nothing else. I'm sure every man can do something good for his life, apart from just slave all the time. You might not think so though if you listen to people who have never put their heads inside a factory gate (in Fraser (ed.), 1968, pp. 103–4).

We have seen how some workers or employees attempt to give their work meaning, in an individual way, often with what might seem to the outsider very unpromising material. Workers may also, collectively, seek to overcome the sense of powerlessness and lack of control. It is to this we now turn.

Work and Conflict

There are two images of relationships at work in modern industrial society, reflected in what has become a standard question in investigating work situations:

Here are two opposed views about industry generally: I'd like you to tell me which you agree with more. Some people say that a firm is like a football side – because good team-work means success and is to everyone's advantage. Others say that team-work in industry is impossible – because employers and men are really on opposite sides. Which view do you agree with most? (Goldthorpe, J. H., *et al.*, 1969, pp. 73–4).

The team-work view is one which is widely expressed, either as a statement of what ought to be the case or as a belief that this really is the case. And this view is not simply one held by managers or politicians: 67 per cent of the manual workers in the sample of Luton car workers held this view as well. Such a view, it is important to note, does not preclude the possibility of industrial conflict – indeed a strike took place at Vauxhall shortly after Goldthorpe and his associates had conducted their survey – but it suggests that being prepared to go on strike for better pay and conditions does not necessarily imply political militancy or the holding of an 'oppositional' view of industrial relations.

The 'team-work' and 'oppositional' perspectives both have their difficulties when it comes to understanding industrial conflict. Those who hold the 'team-work' view have the problem of explaining such manifestations of industrial conflict as strikes, go-slows and workings-to-rule. In this view, strikes tend to be explained as a manifestation of irrational behaviour on the part of the workers, as a result of the efforts of trouble-makers or agitators or of breakdown or failure in communications. (The assumption in all these cases is that, at base, the real interests of workers and employers are the same.) One influential school of thought and practice based upon these assumptions was the 'Human-Relations School' which developed in the United States during the inter-war period and which stressed the need to develop 'social skills' that kept pace with the development of technological skills and which could be applied to the problem of conflict and tension in industry (Mayo, 1949).

Those who hold the oppositional view have the problem of explaining not the presence but the relative absence of conflict. Given the assumptions that strikes are manifestations of a fundamental class conflict which generates a work-situation characterized by alienation, it becomes difficult to explain why workers resort to strikes or other forms of industrial action so infrequently. For, contrary to some popular images, strikes are relatively infrequent events and industrial accidents and certified sickness cost far more in terms of working-days lost than industrial disputes (Hyman, 1972, p. 34). The solution to the difficulty usually offered by the proponents of the 'oppositional' perspective lies in analysing the sources of the workers' 'false consciousness', the assumption here being that the real interests of the workers are obscured, masked or distorted by the ruling class or by their agents who work, ultimately, in the interests of the employers.

There are problems in explaining some aspects of industrial conflict with both approaches. For one thing, strikes are only one form of the manifestation of industrial conflict. Workers may respond to the work-situations in which they find themselves in a variety of ways: collectively and individually, openly or covertly. Collectively or openly, workers may decide to go on strike or agree on a programme of 'working-to-rule'. Collectively but less openly, workers may establish informal controls over their output and earnings (so-called 'restriction of output') or may perform certain acts of 'industrial sabotage' such as illustrated in the following quotation:

They had to throw away half a mile of Blackpool rock last year, for, instead of the customary motif running through its length, it carried the terse injunction 'Fuck Off'. A worker dismissed by a sweet factory had effectively demonstrated his annoyance by sabotaging the product of his labour (Taylor and Walton, in Cohen, 1971, p. 219).

Individuals or groups of workers may sing or evolve patterns of boisterous horseplay, or may engineer frequent visits to the stores or the toilets – or if all else fails, simply day-dream while automatically tending the machine. Other forms of more individual response include absenteeism, lateness or extended tea-breaks, or, perhaps, at a more subconscious level, sickness or industrial accidents. All these responses may be seen as attempts on the part of the worker or workers to gain some control over their work-situations, to make work in some small way reflect their needs, to gain some small victory over the management, the foreman or the owners. The problem for the sociologist is to explain why one form of action occurs rather than another in a particular situation.

A further problem in the analysis of industrial conflict is that of explaining conflict which is not simply between managers and workers (in the 'team-work' version) or between employers and employed (in the 'oppositional' version). If the cruder versions of the 'team-work' approach are too naïve, the cruder versions of the 'oppositional' approach are too simple. Conflicts take place within and between groups of workers (as we see in the case of demarcation disputes) and within and between groups of managers. In the latter case, for example, we may have conflicts between the sales and personnel staff on the one hand, and the more professionally-oriented industrial scientists on the other. The former, as part of the official established hierarchy, may regard the latter as 'boffins' with no respect for the realities of the hard business world, while the latter, in their turn, may regard the former as unimaginative and narrow bureaucrats (Burns and Stalker, 1961). Similarly, there may be conflicts in terms of characteristics which are formally irrelevant to the industrial setting, such as age, sex, colour or religion. A modified 'conflict' version of industrial relations would regard the work-place as not simply being either a team or a battlefield, but as an arena in which there exists a potentiality for all kinds of conflict, including the classic Marxian cl s₃ conflict.

Yet it is undoubtedly the case that when people talk of 'industrial conflict' they almost invariably mean strikes, and it is the strike which attracts most attention in the media, an attention which is often out of all proportion to the incidence or real 'cost' of such disputes (Hyman, 1972). There seem to be two main reasons why strikes often attract such disproportionate attention. In the first place, they are conscious and deliberate (and even wildcat or unofficial strikes may be made 'official' retrospectively by the union), unlike other possible responses such as sickness or absence from work. In the second place, they are collective actions and, therefore, to some extent, represent a form of action different from and apparently more threatening to more established and legitimate ways of 'getting things done', such as through the ballot-box, letters to the press or backstairs influence.

It should be clear from this line of argument that we do not regard strikes as a form of collective 'irrationality'. Even the occasionally well-publicized examples of industrial disputes of apparently 'trivial' matters (such as the length of a tea-break or a swearing supervisor) may be seen as possessing their own 'rationality' (itself a slippery term) when the whole context is more fully understood. They may be seen by the workers as one event in a whole sequence of events – 'the last straw' – or as one manifestation of a wider pattern of struggle for small advantages or recognitions. A strike may be a simple expression of solidarity on the part of the workers in a particular workshop or department. Hyman argues that strikes or the threat of strikes are, among other things, 'the means by which labour refuses to behave merely as a commodity' and that in this respect, all strikes may be seen as a challenge to managerial control (ibid., p. 151). Industrial disputes, like any other form of collective or individual behaviour, may have features which could be widely regarded as 'irrational' but 'irrationality' can never count as either an adequate description of or an adequate explanation for such disputes.

Yet in spite of the sense of 'moral panic' about industrial disputes, and in spite of the fact that public opinion polls often reveal considerable suspicion of unions and opposition to the use of the strike weapon (even on the part of union members and even of strikers), to a large extent unions and industrial conflict have become an institutionalized feature of capitalist society. Trade unions, and the strike weapon itself, have become legitimized as a result of successive pieces of governmental legislation, and the relationships of co-operation between union leaders and government (of whatever party) have grown, especially since the Second World War. Furthermore, in concentrating on issues of pay as the main overt reason for industrial dispute, unions have to a large extent accepted the 'rules of the game' under capitalism. Even if a strike may be in fact about some issue of managerial control or prerogatives, it is more legitimate to redefine the issue as being one of pay or differentials (Gouldner, 1954). Unions, therefore, in so far as they concentrate on issues of pay and working conditions rather than striving to achieve a coherent alternative to capitalist society, can be seen as being part of that instrumental orientation to work which we argued was one feature of work in our society.

Roles

If we focus our attention on any one work-place – an office, an assembly-line or a hospital – we find that we are faced with situations of considerable complexity. We find all kinds of patterns of conflict and co-operation and potentialities for conflict or co-operation. We have relationships which appear to be primarily shaped by factors 'internal' to the work-place – such as the way in which the work-flow is structured by the imperatives of machinery or of managerial planning or hierarchical systems of authority, and we have relationships which appear to be more responsive to factors 'external' to the workplace, such as sex, ethnicity and social status in the wider community. Thus relationships at work can be influenced by factors outside the walls of the factory or office. Similarly, we have seen how, taking a perspective wider than the work-place alone, relationships at home, in leisure-activities and in the wider community can be affected by the nature of work. These factors would include the physical demands of work (obvious examples would be shift-work, or work which takes the individual away for long stretches of time, such as deep-sea fishing), and the status (negative or positive) of the work, and the extent to which that prestige is recognized by the wider community and expected to influence relationships there. Thus senior professionals or management may be expected to play a part in local politics or charitable work (especially, perhaps, in North America), and, in the extreme, highly 'visible' workers such as policemen or clergymen are said to be 'never off duty'.

One set of tools that sociologists have developed to handle complex relationships such as these has been the set of inter-related terms surrounding the concept '*role*'. Some sociologists have elaborated these terms and concepts into models of considerable complexity, but the basic ideas are simple enough. In the first place it can be seen that a theatrical metaphor is being employed. We may therefore focus our attention on the actor, on the different performances he gives in different contexts, and on the different ways in which he is called upon to present himself (Goffman, 1969). Some modern occupations seem to demand more in terms of the performance of a role, especially such occupations as those of waiter or salesman which demand constant interaction with an ever-changing public. Yet in all areas of occupational life there is some role-playing and some recognition of the different expectations of different audiences; school-teachers may drop their pedagogic masks when safely behind the common-room door, and doctors, outside the consulting-room, may talk frankly about the prescribing of placebos for patients who expect a bottle of pills after a visit to their G.P. (Comaroff, 1976).

This emphasis on the actual performance of a role in relation to different audiences, and the way in which these various performances relate to an actor's sense of his *self* – his sense of who he *really* is – has represented an important strand in sociological and social-psychological investigation. Perhaps more relevant to our present concerns is the emphasis on the roles themselves, the ways in which roles, and the expectations surrounding them, are structured in relation to each other and persist over time independent of any one particular actor. To continue our theatrical metaphor, the emphasis is upon the part itself – the script – rather than upon any particular performance, on Hamlet rather than on Olivier's or Gielgud's particular interpretation of Hamlet. In focusing on the role's themselves, and the way in which they are linked into relatively stable and institutionalized patterns, we have to make one important distinction. In the first place we must note that any one individual has several roles to play. Thus a machine-operator in a factory will be playing one role in relation to his foreman and his work-mates, but may also be a member of his union, of the Labour Party and of the Methodist Church. He will also be a husband, a father, a brother, a cousin, an uncle, a ratepayer, a taxpayer, a neighbour and a voter. At certain times of his life he will be a patient, a guest, a customer and a passenger. All his life he will be a male. Some roles are played together; some are clearly separated. Some are played in a sequence; some played once and for all; some fleetingly and some over a period of years. Clearly there is scope for conflict within this multiplicity of roles. At a time of a strike, for example, the role of the family-man may conflict with the role of the unionist. When asked to go drinking in a working-men's club, a person's role as a Methodist may conflict with his role as a fellow-worker.

This is the case of *multiple roles*: the fact that one man plays many parts, a situation which must be distinguished from the situation which Merton describes as '*the role set*' (Merton, 1968, pp. 368–84). In playing any one particular role, the actor is related to several different 'role-others'. There role-others may be individuals or collections of individuals. Thus, our machine-operator will enact that particular role in relation to spec.fic role-others such as the machine-fitters, the foreman, the rate-fixer, his fellow machine-operators, and the shop-steward. There is thus potential for conflict within the role-set just as there is potential for conflict between the different roles. Thus the foreman may make demands which are incompatible with those made by fellow workers. Certain roles, particularly 'men-in-the-middle' roles such as those of foreman or shop-steward, may be particularly prone to this sort of conflict.

The distinctions between multiple roles and the role-set are summarized in Figure 10 on p. 298. One danger of role-analysis, however, is that it may tend to give too static or passive a picture of social life, a picture of humans conforming to rather passive and abstracted 'roles' or 'role-expectations'. Yet this need not be the case. Individuals may often have considerable leeway or autonomy in performing any one particular role (so that theatre critics do distinguish between different interpretations of Hamlet or Hedda Gabler). Collectively, over time, the image and expectations surrounding a particular work-role may be changed through union action or the formation of professional groups; to quote one striking example of the long-term up-grading of an occupational role:

In the past seventy-five years funeral directors have emerged from a semi-pariah sub-caste of gloomy-demeanoured 'dealers in death' to a quasi-professional, socially respected (with some latent antipathy) occupation capable of conferring middle-class status on its members (Habenstein, in Rose (ed.), 1962, p. 246).

Role-theory can, therefore, take account of social change, and can be particularly useful in directing our attention to the complex links between different institutions, between the individual and those institutions, and to the problems the individual may face in relation to other role-incumbents.

An Example: Women at Work

It may have been noted that for most of this chapter the male pronoun has been used; it has been assumed that the worker is, in fact, a man. While this could be cited as an example of unconscious 'sexism', it also reflects reality, in that the majority of workers are men and that men are expected to undertake full-time paid employment

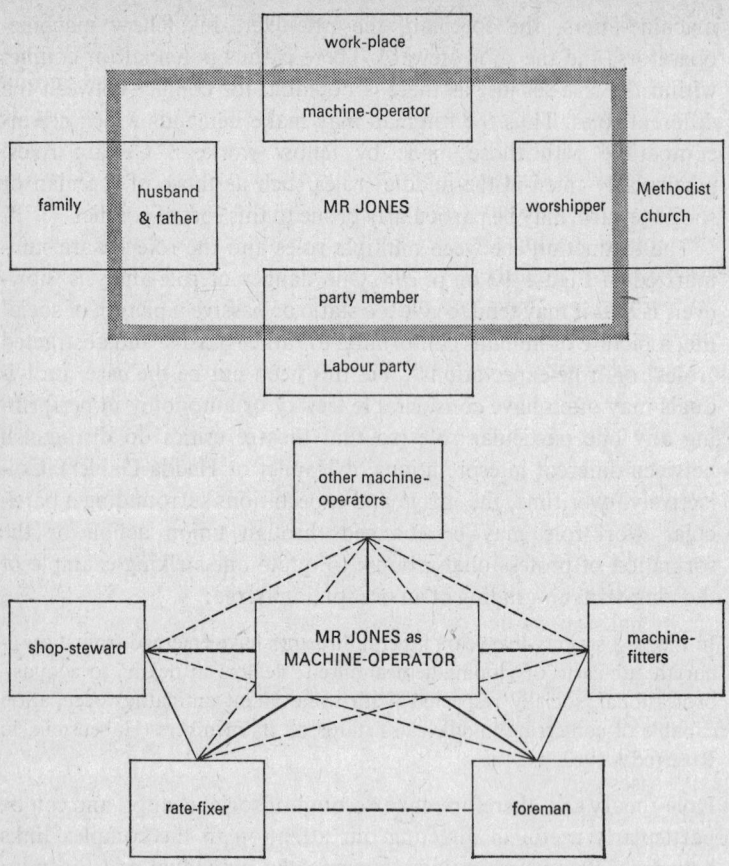

Figure 10 The role-set

for their adult lives (and are stigmatized as 'feckless' or 'work-shy' if they do not), whereas 'to work or not to work' is still presented as a choice for women. Yet increasing numbers of women (see Chapter 4) are coming to spend more of their lives working outside the home.

Sex-roles are one example of what, following Linton, we have already termed 'ascribed' roles (Linton, 1963, pp. 113–31), or what Banton has described as 'basic' roles (Banton, 1965, pp. 33–6). These very basic roles need to be distinguished from other, more specific roles, such as those associated with particular occupations. Gender-roles, based on biology although elaborated and given meaning by culture, are basic, in that they tend not to be confined to one particular area of life but pervade all aspects of life. This factor alone, in our society, can shape the original decision as to whether to go to work at all. It is true that many women *must* go out to work (mothers of one-parent families, for example), but it is also true that the dilemma – constantly reiterated in the media – of having to choose between being a mother or having a career hardly appears with anything like the same intensity for fathers.

Sex-roles are 'basic' in more ways than in simply determining whether a woman should work or not. They also play a large part in shaping what form of employment a women should enter and how far she may go in that field of employment. While there are few positions *formally* closed to women in an era of legal 'equal opportunity', it is also the case that women are more likely to be found in certain occupations than in others. These positions may be those which recognize her multiple roles and domestic obligations (for example, shifts in factories, or school teaching with holidays which correspond to the holidays of her own children), or which in some way reflect traditional notions about 'feminine' tasks. These may be jobs associated with skills traditionally defined as 'feminine', such as the nimble fingers of textile workers or workers in light engineering or the 'caring' skills of nurses, social workers or school teachers, usually connected to the 'personalistic' world of the home and the family. In some cases they may be jobs associated with a particular sexual image, such as air stewardesses or nightclub hostesses. In other cases, the jobs may be repetitive, without any obvious career prospects, and defined as 'feminine' because of their low status or low expectations, reflecting both prevailing attitudes to girls' education and employers' notions of women as a semi-casual labour force. Finally, women in employment are more likely to be judged women in a way which would seem very strange in the case of men. Newspaper reporters scarcely ever provide lengthy descriptions of President Carter's or Prime Minister Callaghan's clothes, or how they combine domestic responsibilities with high office. At a less elevated level, women in offices or factories are often likely to be at the receiving end of sexual banter and innuendo in a way which would not be necessarily taken as 'funny' were the roles reversed.

Thus while sex-roles may be basic roles, it would appear that they are more basic for women than for men. One consequence of this is that the dilemma of multiple roles may appear in a much sharper form for women than for men; to put it another way, there is a greater congruency between a man's role and his occupational role than between that of a woman and her occupational role, if she has one. Yet again, this should not be taken as a fixed situation. In recent years women have sought to redefine the situation, bringing pressure to bear on governments and exercising influence through the Women's Movement, and through particular occupational groupings. Roles, even 'basic' or 'ascribed' ones, can be subject to long-term negotiation and change.

We have pointed to certain paradoxes, perhaps even contradictions. In modern industrial society work is central; but it is also marginal. Work is undertaken as an isolated activity; yet it is closely related to other areas of life. How can these seeming contradictions be resolved?

In the first place we may note that there is no single pattern of attachment to the work-place. To say that work is central, in that it provides the worker with a wage to support himself (to return to the conventional sex-role model) and his family, is not necessarily to say that the work is *expressively* central for that worker or that the occupation is necessarily a source of status or identity in the wider society. Indeed, it is precisely this contrast between the material necessity for work and the low degree of personal involvement in it, for most people, which has led to the concern about alienation in modern industrial society.

We may similarly examine the second contradiction. On the one hand, modern economic organization demands that work be separated from the home and carried out without interference from domestic or outside considerations, and thought of and rewarded basically in terms of a given number of hours in exchange for a given rate of remuneration. At the same time, the work-place does not embrace the totality of the workers' lives. Role-theory reminds us that the worker is also a father, a man, an Irishman and many other things, and that there are inevitably links, and sometimes conflicts, between expectations arising out of work and expectations arising out of non-work involvements.

Within industrial society there are many ways in which work is related to non-work. In a mining village we may find a close overlap between home and work and leisure (Dennis *et al.*, 1956). In the newer estates of Luton, on the other hand, we may find that workers argue that 'mates are not friends' and that the major link – perhaps the only link – between work and non-work is the pay-packet (Goldthorpe, J. H., *et al.*, 1969, pp. 31–9). The fact that these differences exist *within* industrial society should at least persuade us to treat with caution crude contrasts between industrial and pre-industrial societies in terms of characteristics such as rationality or the separation of home and work. There are many similarities as well as many differences between both types of society.

We have examined work in terms of its position in society as a whole, its relationship to the fundamental economic problems that face any society, the values involved in various kinds of labour, and the patterns of co-operation and conflict which arise out of the social division of labour. The analysis of society in terms of roles is both an indication of the way in which sociologists handle the complexity of relationships arising from work in modern society and a reflection of the kind of society which generates this mode of thinking about human relationships. In other words, the *sociological* problems that role-theory sets out to solve – problems of the articulation between different sectors of society and the relationships between the individual and that society – are also *social* and personal problems faced by individuals within this kind of industrial society. One thing, however, that we have not specifically dealt with is the fact that many of these work encounters and problems occur within organizations and that much of our life is lived out within that kind of context.

ORGANIZATIONS

We have seen that work in small-scale, tribal societies is performed by groups of people who are not usually brought together solely for that purpose. Frequently, the family acts as a unit in the productive process; at other times, wider social groups, even a whole village, may co-operate to bring in the harvest or to move cattle from winter to summer pastures.

In industrial societies, however, work tends to be based on social units specially organized for that purpose. This process has been accelerated by the growth of modern technology, which has led to a rapid increase in the variety and content of work-roles and consequently has brought increasing problems of co-ordination. Work in industrial societies thus takes place in organizations: in factories, mines, offices, warehouses and similar units.

These changes are not entirely new, however. Factory production is at least four thousand years old. Other, non-economic kinds of organization are equally ancient. For centuries, as well as being employed in mines and factories, men have fought in armies, languished in prisons, sent their children to schools, prayed in churches, and played in gymnasia. Organizations have thus existed not only to facilitate production, but also, for example, to make and enforce legal decisions and to decide upon and administer government policy.

But such organizations were rudimentary in comparison with their modern counterparts. Let us first look at three quite different spheres of life in which organizations have come to the fore in modern industrial society: warfare, the law and mental health. Though wars have been fought for as long as history has been recorded, the warriors were not normally professional soldiers. They were usually peasants, who had to bring in their harvests before they could turn themselves into soldiers and fight battles. And when battle was joined, combat was largely an individual affair. Men brought their own weapons and used them as best they could. In industrial societies, by contrast, the military machine is much more sophisticated. Work-roles are more complex and diverse; recruits must be professionally trained; and the command structure is more intricately co-ordinated. It may still be 'a man's life in the Army', but what is demanded of the modern soldier is more often a technical skill, rather than an exhibition of a 'noble art'. The means of advanced warfare (tanks, guns, etc.), too, are owned by the organization – the Army. War is a social activity requiring complex and centralized organization and lengthy specialized training.

Again, legal systems, according to which certain behaviour is defined as wrong and the offender punished, have become increasingly organized. Only in fairly 'developed' societies is the definition of crime and the punishment of the criminal the duty of specially-constituted organizations – courts, police forces, prisons. Tribal societies often operate without judges, sheriffs and gaols, and rely more on the controls exercised over the wrongdoer by his kin or his fellow villagers. So societies have only gradually developed specialized organizations of social control, with legislative, judicial and penal functions. The blood-feud, for example, based on customary law, requires no official adjudication, and organized punishment is not carried out by specialist officials. Moreover, the solidarity on which the stability of society is based today no longer necessarily rests on a deeply-held agreement about moral values. Such agreement can be extremely powerful, and render prisons and policemen unnecessary. Malinowski quotes the case of a South Sea islander who was known to have had sexual relations with a woman with whom this was not permitted, and felt his shame so keenly that he climbed a coconut palm and threw himself off in full public view. And because such societies have not until recently been subject to rapid social change, ideas about what constitutes 'punishable behaviour' have not had to be regularly reviewed by any formal body. In *The Division of Labour in Society* Durkheim suggested that this kind of consensus has been replaced by what he called 'organic' integration, where society holds together not because of fundamental common agreement about ideas of right and wrong, but because its constituent parts depend on each other. Thus, though they have different functions and interests workers and management have to co-operate if production is to continue. Rapid change in society generally produces continual organizational change in specific institutions. Thus the pace of social change has involved constant alterations in the criminal law, and new ideas about the treatment of offenders have led to the development of a complex system in which prisoners are not simply kept in custody, but fed, clothed, educated, trained, employed and given access to specialized religious, educational, medical and other welfare services.

Finally, to take a quite different sphere of social life, the revolution in medicine has meant that the treatment of mental illness has also become highly organized. Mental hospitals, in fact, are a modern development. In the past, mental disturbances have often been put down to possession by demons, and offenders were put to death. The Mosaic law required that 'a man also or a woman that hath a familiar spirit or that is a wizard shall surely be put to death' (Leviticus, xx, 27). Similarly, the seventeenth-century treatise *Malleus Maleficarum* went into great detail in prescribing appropriate torture and burning for the medieval insane. As recently as the 1850s trippers went on outings to Bedlam to poke and prod at the chained lunatics. Modern concepts of the diagnosis and treatment of mentally sick persons, on the other hand, have led to the development of complex organizations through which these new ideas can be put into practice (Stafford-Clark, 1952, chs. 1 and 2).

These and other kinds of specialized organizations have not grown up by chance. Before they could develop, a series of changes in society had to occur; in particular, there had to be a sufficient level of scientific and economic development to produce a surplus of resources great enough to release personnel to perform specialized technical roles.

In industrial society these organizations have come to be widely accepted as the most rational way of solving the varied problems confronting such societies. Thus, the increasing specialization of work-roles and the complexity of the division of economic activities in production is paralleled by an even greater growth of complex organizational machinery of distribution, which channels the product to the market and, ultimately, to the consumer – market research, advertising, consultancy, and other specialized organizations. The ratio of administrative to productive employees constantly increases, and while this is partly due to the mechanization of production, it also reflects the increase in scale of corporations and the need for machinery to co-ordinate their diverse activities.

Hence our society has come to be called an 'organization society', peopled by 'organization men'. Indeed, some sociologists have emphasized the extent to which organizations have come to control men, rather than the reverse (Presthus, 1962). In the rest of this chapter we shall examine two principal aspects of this process:

1. We shall look at the basic structural resemblances between organizations which, at first glance, are of quite different kinds, noting the main 'types' of organizations, and observing how such structures mould the behaviour of the members.

2. We shall look at the way in which organizational behaviour reflects what participants bring to the organization rather than being

merely a consequence of the structural pressures exerted upon them in the organization. For whether people choose appropriate organizations for themselves – factories, churches, clubs, etc. – or whether *they* are chosen because of their 'suitability', and placed under various degrees of pressure to become members, as in prisons and hospitals, in either case they come with a variety of previous experiences, expectations and orientations towards the organization; they find their way into organizations through social networks in which they are embedded, that is, through their range of social contacts, and such networks may continue to influence behaviour inside the organization; finally they come bearing social characteristics such as Pakistani, professional, Catholic, pensioner, etc. and being categorized in such ways may be either an asset or a liability inside the organization.

The Structure of Organizations

Let us now tackle a question we have so far avoided: 'What do we mean by an organization?' Sociologists have often given examples rather than satisfactory definitions of what constitutes an organization. But usually they emphasize that organizations are bodies, persisting over time, which are specially set up to achieve specific aims (cf. Blau and Scott, 1963, ch. 1; Etzioni, 1964, ch. 3; Presthus, 1962, ch. 4).

Of course, those who control organizations may not be very effective in achieving their stated aims. In the first place, there may be varying degrees of *internal opposition* to these aims. For example, the interests of prisoners are largely in *conflict* with those of the staff. In industry, on the other hand, despite conflicts of interest, workers and management do, nevertheless, also have *complementary* interests in keeping the factory going. Finally, in churches, pastor and flock share *common* beliefs and have a common interest in the success of the church, though there may still be disagreements (cf. Thompson, 1975).

Secondly, there is likely to be *external opposition* which may inhibit the success of organizations. A religious sect, for example, such as the Jehovah's Witnesses or the Doukhobors, may be proscribed by Government; a business may be hit by new tax laws or by technological advance in other companies sharing the same market; a prison may find its task of rehabilitating inmates made more difficult by a public outcry for maximum security at all costs.

Thirdly, in all organizations members will have *personal interests* which conflict with official aims, and social relations will develop among members which have the effect of reducing organizational efficiency. This does not mean that they are trying to sabotage the organization. The fact is that most of the personnel in an organization may not be held or feel responsible for its success. But the way they express their sectional interests, and the social relations which develop, are limited by their attachment to the organization, the way they are controlled by it, and the need for it to remain a viable unit. Employees are aware that if a strike persists for too long, the factory may close down. If sufficient members of a religious sect develop heretical ideas, they may split the church in two. Even in prisons, inmates realize the advantages of acquiescing in the smooth running of the organization.

Thus there is some value in talking of organizations having goals. But we need to be careful how these goals are defined and how they are used to explain organizational performance. For instance, much organizational analysis has been based on the distinction between *formal organization* (which can be deduced from a consideration of organizational goals) and *informal organization* (which consists of aspects of organizational structure which appear to deviate from what could be expected according to the formally-defined basis of the organization's existence). However, Bittner (1973) argues forcefully that the use of terms which serve to define the formal structure of the institution, such as 'organizational goal', should be based on the study of how participants use them as common-sense concepts in the course of their everyday behaviour.

A further warning against the assumption that organizational goals have an existence apart from the objectives of all those individuals and groups involved in the life of the organization comes from Perrow (1970, p. 134), who argues that, strictly speaking, it is individuals, not organizations, who have goals. We may add, too, that many members may have individual goals which make it difficult for them to subscribe to what they take to be the institutional objectives: after all, prisons, factories and churches continue to function without their personnel regarding themselves as model prisoners or parishioners or having a zeal for productivity.

However, even those who stress the importance of analysing organizations from the perspective of their personnel, rather than by considering organizational performance against the yardstick of formally defined objectives, have used organizational goals or objectives as central features of their analysis. An excellent example of this is the work of Strauss and his colleagues on the sociology of the hospital. The rules of the hospital, they argue, like those of any other large-scale organization, 'tend to be written down, codified, and socially sanctioned':

[But] no-one knows what the hospital 'is' . . . unless he has a comprehensive grasp of the combination of rules, policies, agreements, understandings, pacts, contracts, and other working arrangements that currently obtain. In a pragmatic sense, that combination 'is' the hospital at the moment, its social order (Strauss *et al.,* 1964, pp. 312).

Rules, then, are not 'disembodied standards', but 'negotiable products'. The ways in which forces external to the organization impinge upon its life are considered later in the chapter (pp. 318–31 below). In the meantime we shall continue to examine structural features of organizations that obtain regardless of the environment in which they are set.

Organizations differ from communities and societies not only in having explicit goals, but in the means used to achieve them. Etzioni states that organizations are characterized by:

1. Divisions of labour, of power, and of communication responsibilities, such divisions being deliberately planned to achieve certain goals.

2. The presence of power-centres which control the concerted efforts of the organization and continuously review its performance, and re-pattern its structure, where necessary, so as to increase its efficiency.

3. The substitution of personnel, i.e., unsatisfactory persons can be removed and others assigned their tasks, and people can be transferred and promoted (Etzioni, 1964, ch. 3).

This definition is based upon the classic model of bureaucracy developed by Max Weber. We must appreciate that Weber looked at bureaucracy only as part of a much broader subject: the whole basis of authority in society. To him, one of the most striking features of industrial society was that when organizations were administered in a strictly 'bureaucratic' way, they were capable of achieving the highest degree of efficiency. Bureaucratic administration, he wrote, was 'superior to any other form in precision, in stability, in the stringency of its discipline, and in its reliability. It thus makes possible a particularly high degree of calculability of results . . . and is formally capable of application to all kinds of administrative tasks' (Weber, 1964, p. 337). Thus, bureaucratic administration was in principle equally applicable to businesses, charitable organizations, hospitals, churches and political parties, in so far as they were required to develop administrative systems. Let us turn, then, to a summary of Weber's conception of bureaucracy:

There is a series of officials, each of whose roles is circumscribed by a written definition of his power. These offices are arranged in a hierarchy, each successive step embracing all those beneath it. There is a set of rules and procedures within which every possible contingency is theoretically provided for. There is a 'bureau' for the safe-keeping of all written records and files, it being an important part of the rationality of the system that information is written down. A clear separation is made between personal and business affairs, bolstered by a contractual method of appointment in terms of technical qualifications for office. In such an organization authority is based on the office. Commands are obeyed because the rules state that it is within the competence of a particular office to issue such commands (Pugh *et al.*, 1964, pp. 6–7).

Under these conditions, far from being synonymous with irrelevant form-filling, red tape and inefficiency in general, bureaucracy, Weber says, can be the most efficient and rational means known of coordinating human resources to obtain desired ends. Yet the term has not come to have pejorative overtones without reason, and Weber's view needs some qualification.

It is precisely because men in bureaucratic structures perform specialized, 'segmental' roles, over which they may have no control, and in which they have little or no opportunity of using their rational judgement – the very features Weber praises – that they so often feel a sense of 'alienation' in industrial society. Instead of a man being responsible for his own behaviour at work, he feels that he is controlled by it and separated from the product of his labour. Bureaucratic relations are not conducive solely to efficiency: they may have unfortunate, even if unintended, consequences.

Merton, in his article 'Bureaucratic structure and personality' (Merton *et al.*, 1952, pp. 361–71), examines further possible 'dysfunctions' of bureaucracy. He shows how, to be effective, bureaucrats must behave consistently, and follow regulations strictly. This limits the capacity of bureaucrats to adapt to changing circumstances which were not envisaged by those who drew up the rules. The officials still think in terms of rules which are not to be questioned, and overlook the fact that absolute rules which make for efficiency in general produce inefficiency – even injustice – in specific cases. A different view is taken by Blau, who argues that such 'ritualistic' behaviour arises not from over-identification with rules so much as insecurity in established social relationships within the organization (Blau, 1963, p. 236). We shall look briefly at two examples.

Bureaucracy, as conceived by Weber, stresses that the official should be detached and not become closely involved in personal relations with his colleagues. But Merton stresses that this pressure for formal, impersonal treatment may be harmful when *clients* come to the bureaucracy, as in a maternity clinic or employment exchange, because they desire and need more individual attention (Merton *et al.*, 1952, p. 366).

Again, Blau, in the study of a state employment agency mentioned above, shows that the bureaucrats themselves who had to deal with clients disliked such an emphasis on formality, and that in a department in which impersonal treatment was stressed relations with clients were unsatisfactory. Impersonality produced a loss of efficiency. In another department officials tended to ignore the recommendation to treat all clients in a 'clinical' fashion, but instead dealt with them all as individual cases. This made the officials more satisfied with their work, and was also to the advantage of those clients that they enjoyed helping. But clients who were less 'rewarding' received worse treatment, so supervisors had to go back to bureaucratic regulations. Blau shows that in this and other ways bureaucratic practices instituted to increase efficiency have corresponding limitations. The task of management consists in continually adjusting bureaucratic and non-bureaucratic elements to secure the most effective combination at any time.

A key limitation upon the efficiency of bureaucratic administration lies in its difficulty in coping with uncertainty and change. Bureaucracy relies on tasks being convertible into *routine*. The more unforeseen contingencies arise, the less comprehensive and effective are the rules and regulations. Blau argues that in the agencies he observed bureaucratic conditions did generate favourable attitudes towards change. Officials welcomed innovations, for example, which would remove irritations in their present work-roles. They were identified with policies that required the expansion of the organization, etc. But it was not the bureaucratic elements in the administration which brought this pressure for change. Further, the fact that some of the officials favoured changes of a specific kind does not mean that the agency was organized in a way which would allow change in general to be easily instituted (Blau, 1963, pp. 246–7).

Again, Gouldner (1955), in a study of a gypsum mine and plant, shows how work-processes in the plant on the surface were largely predictable, and could be organized in a bureaucratic fashion. But the miners had to cope with much more uncertainty, and when a new manager tried to raise production by increasing bureaucratic control over the organization, this was successful in the plant, but the miners underground were able to resist it. The uncertainties of the physical environment made bureaucratic organization of the work-processes unsuitable, and the greater solidarity of the miners, partly a consequence of the uncertain conditions, enabled them to resist the imposition of bureaucratic controls.

Another major contribution to the study of bureaucracy uses a similar line of argument. In the course of their study of a number of firms in the electronics industry, Burns and Stalker (1961) found it necessary to use two models of work-organization. One, which they called 'mechanistic', was suitable where conditions were stable; the other they labelled 'organic', and used to describe situations where changing conditions constantly gave rise to unforeseen problems which could not be suitably resolved with a 'mechanistic' type of organization. The interest of this 'mechanistic' type is that it corresponds very closely to Weber's notion of bureaucracy, while the 'organic' system is notably different. Some of the bureaucratic principles of the 'mechanistic' model and their counterparts in the 'organic' system are contrasted below:

Mechanistic management system	*Organic management system*
Specialized differentiation of functional tasks into which the problems facing the concern as a whole are broken down.	Organization on the basis of contributions from various specialists to common tasks, across the boundaries of clearly-demarcated jobs.
The specification of what shall be done by whom, and the co-ordination of the separate tasks by those who are formally the immediate superiors for each level in the hierarchy.	Adjustment and continual redefinition of individual tasks through interaction with others.
Precise definition of 'responsibility' as a set of rights and obligations and of technical methods of work which are attached to each functional role.	The shedding of 'responsibility' as a limited field of rights, obligations and methods. (Problems may not be 'posted' upwards, downwards or sideways as being someone else's responsibility.)
Emphasis upon the rights, obligations and work-methods attached to a particular position at work.	The spread of commitment beyond the limits of immediate work-roles to wider levels of the organization.
Hierarchical structure of control, authority and communication.	A 'network' structure of control, authority and communication.
Insistence on loyalty to the concern and obedience to superiors as a condition of membership.	Commitment to the concern's tasks, and to the 'technological' ethos of material progress and expansion, is valued more highly than loyalty and obedience.

(Burns and Stalker, 1961, pp. 120–21.)

Burns and Stalker and Gouldner both point out a crucial ambiguity in Weber's original discussion of the bureaucratic model. Weber spoke of a man's authority being based upon his tenure of an office to which he had been elected on the basis of his technical qualifications. But Burns and Stalker show that, with the rapid growth in technical knowledge, not only does the hierarchy of offices become less distinct, but it is less obviously based on 'grades' of technical qualifications. That is, there comes to be a conflict between authority based on position and authority based on skill. In modern industry authority simply based on official position is no longer adequate. Rather, people contribute their special knowledge to whatever task is before them, and their standing is affected by the value of the contribution they make. Nor is this process confined to business organizations: similar changes have occurred in other types of organization, for example in the technical wing of modern military forces (Janowitz, 1964).

A further point which Burns and Stalker emphasize is the increased 'commitment to the organization' in the organic system. If a man's participation is not simply confined to a clearly-specified set of activities, involving only a limited part of his personality, then a great deal more of his human capacities must be harnessed by the organization. In the extreme, W. H. Whyte has suggested, not only must the modern technocrat be a 'company man', but his wife, too, must be sociable and adaptable to the requirements of the company (1957).

There are bureaucratic elements, then, in most formal organizations. Wherever routine administration is necessary, it is likely that it will be bureaucratic in character. So far, we have dealt mainly with economic organizations, in which much of the work performed can readily be converted into routine. The work of a Civil Service is even easier to reduce to routine. But we find bureaucratic elements even in organizations which work under much more difficult conditions: in prisons and hospitals, for example, where much of the work is performed not only *with* other people, but *on* these people, and there is a continuous change of prisoners and patients.

Yet sociologists too readily assume that the bureaucratic model can be used to study any kind of organization. From what we have already seen we should expect to find much less bureaucracy in organizations in which people participate as 'whole persons'. We shall examine next an extreme type of organization of this kind – that in which the members sleep, work and take their recreation on the same premises.

Total Institutions

Prisons, hospitals, monasteries, military camps, whaling ships, holiday camps and boarding schools all look vastly different – and are – but all do share one important common feature: they are all institutions in which participants *live* in the organization. They are, as Goffman calls them, 'total' institutions, in part formal organizations, in part residential communities (Goffman, 1961). All these organizations, he claims, have a basically similar social structure, regardless of the personal characteristics of the members. The basic arrangement of 'normal' society is that home, work and leisure are separate areas of life. People play, sleep and work in different places, in the company of different people, and under different controls. This is not so in 'total institutions'; here the members – whether they be patients, inmates, prisoners, monks or residents in a holiday camp – lead an enclosed, formally-administered round of life, and undergo similar experiences.

In each of these 'total' organizations, there is a prescribed 'career' for members (or 'inmates', as Goffman generally calls them), and a privilege system which is devised so as to reward them for conforming to this career and for their co-operation in causing as little inconvenience as possible to those who run the organization. Though inmates tend to react to this kind of régime in quite individualistic ways, they nevertheless see themselves as united in one respect: in their common opposition to the staff, who form a quite separate, superior category. They long for release, Goffman claims (thinking presumably of prisons and mental hospitals, which provide much of the illustration for his essay); but soon after graduation they are talking of the happy times they had.

Goffman shows that in such circumstances people become to a large extent the 'raw materials' of the routine work of the staff and that similar institutional arrangements are devised to administer them efficiently despite the different purposes the institutions serve (monasteries as against prisons, for example). Of course, there are also important differences *between* these various sub-varieties of total institution. In some, such as the holiday camp, entry is voluntary, in others, such as the armed forces, it is not necessarily so. There are also basic differences between those total organizations which exist to perform a work-task, such as ships and military camps, and those which exist to 'treat' people, especially without their ready consent, as in the case of some prisons and mental hospitals.

Treatment organizations, for example, often exist so that specialist staff can change the way the patients see themselves. A good deal of coercion is often necessary, and a natural rift develops between staff and patients. Patients (or inmates) in treatment organizations tend to be stigmatized, and frequently react by dissociating themselves from other patients, regarding themselves as different (i.e., 'normal'). Because they feel a need to preserve a set image of themselves, they are reluctant to form intimate primary groups with those from whom they wish to dissociate themselves.

In contrast, some work organizations have to be located in places which by definition make them 'total'. Thus, seamen live in a total community while at sea. The fact that a ship is a total organization does not imply that the crew need 'treatment' of any kind. This is simply a condition of their work. In such organizations the same division of labour is found as in factories on land, authority is not normally based on coercion, and close friendship groups are characteristic of such total communities. Thus, not only are there different types of total organizations; in some respects these different species are just as much like other non-total organizations as they are like each other. Schools, after all, have some similar features, whether they are day schools or for boarders.

| | | Organizational scope | |
		total	non-total
	work	merchant ship	factory
		military camp	department store
Organizational aims			
	treatment	mental hospital	clinic
		boarding school	day school

Goffman's essay on total institutions is important not because all total organizations are alike in every way – this is manifestly untrue – but because when people spend periods of their life within an enclosed space with the same companions, certain patterns of social relations tend to develop, whether it happens to be a prison, a monastery or a military camp.

The Classification of Organizations

We can divide organizations, as above, into work organizations and those which exist to act on people in a specified way. We now add a third type, those which provide a setting for people to share common interests, frequently referred to as 'voluntary associations'. These include religious, political and leisure associations. This rough classification thus divides organizations into three types on the basis of the kind of aims or goals they have.

A similar division of organizations is achieved by Blau and Scott (1963, pp. 42 ff.), who classify organizations according to the four different kinds of 'prime beneficiary' that organizations may serve. The main group to benefit may be the rank-and-file participants, in others the owners or managers, in yet others it is the clients, or 'public-in-contact' (people outside the organization who yet have contact with it), and in the last group it is the 'public-at-large', that is, members of society in general. These four types are correspondingly labelled 'mutual benefit', 'business', 'service' and 'commonweal' organizations.

Finally, let us consider one other useful classification which is based upon a different criterion for distinguishing types of organizations. Etzioni (1961) divides organizations according to the kind of power relations that exist between those administering the organization and its lower-level participants. Members may comply with the demands placed upon them by their superiors because they are coerced (they are made to conform), because of utilitarian considerations (they get material rewards, e.g. money or goods), or because they accept or share the assumptions, norms, ideas, values and so on, of those who take the decisions. Many of the significant differences to be found between one organization and another derive from the different kinds of power that are most commonly used and the corresponding variations in the way the members are involved.

Though this typology is based on a different criterion, in fact it produces much the same clusters of organizations. This correspondence does not occur by chance. For the utility of each scheme is not that it enables tidy-minded sociologists neatly to pigeon-hole organizations; rather each mode of classification concentrates upon one aspect of a whole set of interrelated structural features: power, compliance, aims, beneficiaries. Each scheme isolates one significant variable and systematically shows how it will have different values in different social contexts.

Though these typologies take quite different dimensions of organizations as their starting-point, then, there is an underlying pattern which links together their aims, their prime beneficiaries, the types of power used by the leaders and the involvement of the lower participants:

	Treatment organizations	Work organizations	Voluntary organizations
Prime beneficiaries (Blau & Scott)	Public	Management	Members
Power exercised by leaders (Etzioni)	Coercive	Remunerative	Normative
Involvement of lower participants (Etzioni)	Alienative	Calculative	Moral
Examples	Prisons	Factories Commercial enterprises	Clubs Churches Political parties

Etzioni's classification is based on the element of 'compliance', itself the product of these two elements: the kind of power wielded by those who take the decisions, and the kind of involvement in the organization of the lower participants. There are three types of power – coercive, remunerative and normative – and three types of involvement – alienative, calculative and moral. Etzioni argues that there is a tendency for certain types of power and certain types of involvement to occur together. Thus, in organizations where the staff have coercive power, the involvement of the members is alienative; where they have remunerative power, the involvement is calculative; and where they have normative power, it is moral. Etzioni admits that more than one type of power and involvement may be present in an organization at any one time. But these 'congruent' types of compliance patterns are particularly effective because they enable organizations with special kinds of goals to achieve them most easily.

Thus, in organizations which have what Etzioni calls 'order' goals, such as prisons, we can expect to find that the staff use coercive power and the inmates are alienated from the organization. We should expect friendships between staff and inmates to be rather brittle; and the problems of making prison industries efficient are partly due to the inadequacy of economic incentives for people whose involvement in the organization is alienative.

Secondly, we should expect organizations with 'economic' goals to have a utilitarian compliance structure. For example, a study of car assembly workers at Luton showed that they had a strongly marked instrumental orientation to their work (Goldthorpe, J. H., *et al.*, 1969). On the other hand, one school of industrial sociologists has emphasized the advantages of the 'human relations' approach in industry, and the benefits of permissive management. But these can only operate within the framework of a contract in which management and men agree on a suitable balance of labour and earnings. A utilitarian compliance structure is thus more appropriate in an economic organization than, say, coercion. Indeed, the collapse of slavery in some places has been put down to the sheer inefficiency of continually having to coerce workers to perform their tasks.

Thirdly, organizations with 'culture' goals are generally run on a basis of agreement. Churchgoers are not expected to get any economic benefits from their presence in the pews, nor do they expect to be pressured into church attendance; they attend because they hold certain beliefs, or respect social pressure to be seen at church – both are kinds of normative compliance.

Etzioni's 'congruent' types clearly apply to many organizations, such as prisons, factories and churches: his 'incongruent' types also help us to understand, for example, military organizations. He describes the peacetime military camp as an organization which is predominantly utilitarian, but has a secondary coercive pattern. The combat unit, however, is a dual normative-coercive organization. This contrast is reflected in the different recruitment methods used in peace and war. During peacetime, advertisements emphasize what recruits will get out of a period in the Army, for example, a degree, technical training, a chance to see the world. In wartime, however, 'your country needs you': the appeal is to one's duty, to sentiments which are shared with those in the fighting forces. But at any time recruits can be conscripted – coercion can also be used. In fact, many modern armies consist of both a core of economically-motivated regulars and a large body of conscripts. Strains may be set up within the organization where these two compliance-patterns occur together. Social background, career prospects, payment levels, indeed basic orientations to the military in general will tend to differ between these two groups.

External Influences on Organizational Behaviour

We noted earlier that people do not usually pick the organizations they want to join at random. They may follow their friends into a club, answer an advertisement for a job for which they are trained, or attend evening classes to develop a leisure interest. On the other hand, they were probably sent to school whether they liked it or not, and they may also have been obliged to go to hospital or to do military service. Whatever the circumstances, it is certain that either *they* thought they were suitable for the organizations they joined, or *someone else* – the State, the doctor, parents – thought they were suitable and had the power to get them to enter the organization.

The fact that people who belong to organizations are normally in some way 'suitable' for them is vital to the success of the organization. Schools admit children who are at a particular stage of physical and mental development; monasteries must select their recruits with the greatest possible care. People joining associations are often found to share similar political and religious backgrounds (cf. Stacey, 1960). And although prisons have to take all-comers, even here there are special prisons, or wings of prisons, in which men are separated from women, long-termers from short-termers, the younger from the more mature prisoners, etc.

That is, because of the selection procedures adopted, in most organizations new members will have characteristics that allow them to fit in without seriously disturbing the normal running of the organization: we may describe the ball-playing ability of recruits to a football club, the war service of members of a veterans' organization, the occupational training of people taking a job where they can use that skill as *manifest* characteristics. However, new members are also the bearers of *latent* status characteristics that have no direct relationship to the purposes of the organization, but which may significantly affect their attitude to the institution or the way they are treated by other participants; again the life of an organization is often affected by the networks of social relationships between members that developed outside. Thus, the character of an organization may depend to a great extent on the people who happen to belong to it, and these characteristics, part of the world outside will affect its internal organization.

We shall look at three aspects of this interplay between the organization and its environment:

1. How does the *orientation* of members to the organization affect its functioning?
2. How is organizational life affected by *latent status characteristics* which the members represent?
3. How do the *personal networks* in which members are involved affect life inside the organization?

Orientation to the organization

Let us take a few key examples of the quite different ways in which the orientations of members towards the organization affect the pattern of organization:

(a) Prisons are organizations in which the authorities almost always are obliged to administer people against their will. They therefore have to make arrangements to ensure that work continues despite opposition from the inmates. Thus, there are walls to keep them in, and constant checks to ensure they have not escaped or acquired the means by which they might escape. Such arrangements are not an inevitable consequence of organization. They are 'built in' to a particular *kind* of organization only – those in which the inmates have an 'alienative' involvement in, or orientation to, the prison. (It is a negative 'involvement', for they are alienated *from* the organization.) In one unusual prison in Scandinavia, however, which contains Jehovah's Witnesses who refuse to be conscripted for military service, no such 'alienation' exists, since the prisoners accept their sentence because of their religious beliefs. The internal organization of the prison therefore differs markedly because of these different attitudes: the only guards on the perimeter are there to keep sightseers out, rather than the prisoners in.

(b) A very different kind of organization is the monastery, where attitudes to the institution not only affect the monks' experience inside, but are crucial in determining even whether they are accepted as members at all, for applicants are only admitted after rigorous selection procedures. Yet though membership is voluntary, unlike the Jehovah's Witnesses' prison, the attitudes of the members are so positive that their *will* to play their part in the efficient running of the system makes utilitarian and coercive modes of control quite insignificant.

(c) Indeed, we can generalize further from monasteries to all 'voluntary' or 'mutual benefit' associations, in Blau and Scott's terminology, for, in this kind of organization, the prime beneficiaries are the members; hence we should expect their orientation to be of the greatest significance in determining the character of the organization.

Attitudes towards the organization will obviously vary according to the degree to which a club or church or political party branch is controlled from outside. If it is part of a centralized body, members may have less scope in moulding the organization according to their inclinations. This is, in fact, a frequent source of tension in voluntary associations: the headquarters staff are engaged in bureaucratic administration, and are relatively free from the pressures and attitudes that influence behaviour in local groups (see Rex and Moore, 1967, ch. 8). Union leaders will have different attitudes towards employers from branch members. A headquarters official of a religious sect will speak in a church meeting of 'our friends, the Roman Catholics' while local members are uttering veiled threats about 'popish devilry'.

But attitudes towards the organization are affected by what goes on within the local organization, as well as between the branch and the district or national centre, for instance over decisions about what kinds of activities a voluntary association is to undertake and how they should be organized. Should the R.S.P.C.A. campaign against blood sports? Should a village football (or county cricket) team be representative of the village (or county), whatever the results, or strengthen its side by bringing in outsiders? Personal relations as well as club organization in a 'social' tennis club will differ from one in which all the members are dedicated to becoming star players.

(d) One striking sociological account of the effect of members' attitudes towards an industrial organization is the study of car assembly workers already mentioned (Goldthorpe, J. H., *et al.*, 1969). Previous research in a variety of industries tended to emphasize the importance of 'internal' factors, such as management styles (cf. Roethlisberger and Dickson, 1964), or the technological environment (cf. Woodward, 1965), in determining how men reacted to their working conditions. But Goldthorpe and his colleagues showed that these car assemblers had a prior orientation to their work, which was not an 'internal' product of life on the job, but something they brought with them from outside, and which crucially affected the way the workers saw their situation. Their past experience of social and geographical mobility, their position in the life-cycle, their present patterns of family and community living, all helped to give them a distinctively 'instrumental' approach to their work. They were not unduly worried by the pressures of assembly-line jobs and the relative lack of 'social' satisfaction at work – 'belongingness'. The lack of such satisfactions *in* and *at* work was less important to them than a good, long-term 'money-for-effort' bargain (though, clearly, they did not enjoy repetitive ,'unsocial' assembly-line work).

Latent status characteristics

Having looked at the way in which the attitudes (or the 'orientation') of members affect the kind of organizational pattern adopted, let us now look at the way the running of the organization is affected by the categories that they belong to, that they put themselves in, or that other people put them in. People who enter organizations, whether they are schools, prisons, factories, clubs or other types, acquire a 'formal' role upon entry. They are expected to behave in a way that will enable the organization to function smoothly; they are given specific tasks, and are expected to conform to yet other rules and regulations which guide their behaviour more generally. Interpersonal relations between members, as we have seen, will naturally reflect their particular formal roles within the organization: their position gives them a certain amount of authority; it makes them dependent on others in order to carry out their work, etc. But every organization also has its 'under-life', its set of 'informal' relations, which is to varying degrees independent of the institution and is not 'laid down' by any formal rules.

Naturally, people do not enter organizations as blanks, waiting to be impressed with the organizational stamp. They have attitudes, feelings, beliefs. As we saw above, they have orientations to the organizations they join. Such orientations help to determine not only the formal life of the organization, but also the kind of underlife that develops. That is, their status within the organization and the way people behave towards them will depend not only on their formal work-role, but also on their latent status characteristics: age, sex, skin colour, social background, religion, etc.

Some categories may be of minimal social significance. For example, the fact that some of the members may have red hair will probably not affect their social relationships within the organization. The fact that all of them have addresses, again, will often not *mean* anything to their fellow members. Occasionally, however, a particular address, in a high or low status area, will be of social significance to other people in an organization – a junior manager who is already living in the stockbroker belt may find that this makes him more acceptable to his colleagues.

Other characteristics may be far more important. For example, members of racial minorities may find this status very significant in determining their life-chances. They may be equally qualified for and competent at a job, but because they represent a particular category of people, who are considered by racially-prejudiced people to be incompetent, they may be denied promotion. There are circumstances in which skin colour could be related to one's capacity to do a job. If an Englishman applied for a job as a waiter at a Chinese restaurant, for example, he would be turned down because of a category he represented – in this case a relevant one. But in most situations in which race is taken into account, it is quite irrelevant as far as the performance of formal roles within the organization is concerned. Instead colour categories are used to 'pigeon-hole' or 'stereotype' people, and provide a guide to others as to how to relate to them, by treating them in a standardized way irrespective of their other characteristics – their religion, their ability, their age, etc. These racial categories are a way of simplifying or codifying behaviour in situations where there is some ambiguity about what is appropriate, though, in fact, they *over*simplify (Mitchell, J. C., 1966, p. 53).

In principle, skin colour could be ignored in social relations in the same way that hair colour is. But, in reality, it is rarely ignored and so takes on a social meaning. This affects the lives of coloured members in two principal ways:

(a) People are treated in categorical terms on occasions when there is an element of doubt or ambiguity as to how they should be treated. That is, the more 'structured' the situation is (the more the relationship is clearly defined for the actors), the less scope there is for categorical relationships. Thus observers have been struck by the fact that when men are jointly engaged in combat, Black–White differences cease to be relevant. But under more normal conditions and especially in leisure activities racial status is likely to be important in military organizations. Again, there is some evidence that Black children in England in youth organizations with multi-racial membership have felt more at home where uniforms are worn, and where many of the activities are organized for members, than in those youth clubs where it is left to them to guide their own behaviour and establish their own activities according to their personal feelings and preferences.

(b) Categories such as racial or ethnic status may still be built up as an organizational requirement, no matter how irrelevant they may be in terms of a person's ability to do a job or to co-operate with others in doing it. In fact, other employees may simply not accept him. An employer may thus get into serious difficulty if he sticks to a purely 'technical' policy of recruiting men with the requisite skills, for he may thereby violate expectations that certain jobs should only be given to people of a particular ethnic group – a consideration that has nothing to do with individual skill at all, since it is only concerned with people as categories.

Such status characteristics as race or sex (and many of the points which have been made with regard to racial minorities apply equally to the position of women) may be of no social significance for much of the time. In other circumstances such characteristics may be an asset where they can be used to good effect. Frequently, however, such forms of categorization are a liability, since they are used to exclude people from organizations or restrict their opportunities within them.

There is no easy way of defining those situations in which attributes such as racial or sexual status will affect behaviour in organizations. For example, Reitzes (1960) described an American town where in the work-situation skin colour was entirely irrelevant: White and Black people performed the same jobs, belonged to the same trade unions, ate at the same tables in the canteen and had the same friends. Yet the same White people did their utmost to ensure that no Black family was able to buy a house in the select all-White quarter of town.

On the other hand many Black people in Britain may find their racial status in no way relevant to the process of getting housing (particularly in the public sector) but experience racial discrimination in getting a job.

Whether such characteristics are used to people's disadvantage depends on how those in a position to discriminate define their interests. A white work-force may fear a decline in their earnings and their occupational status if Black people infiltrate into the jobs they have traditionally held or, as in Reitzes' study, they may see potential racial divisions as something which employers could exploit to keep down wage-levels and conditions for the whole work-force, and therefore not sanction any discrimination on this basis (at least at work). The study of those aspects of a social situation which lead people to define their interests and act in such varying ways takes us into the area of social stratification, which is considered in Chapter 8 below.

Personal networks

We have shown the importance of the orientations of members towards the organizations in which they are involved, and of the categories they represent. These two factors are not of course entirely independent: orientations are partly a product of being Negro, or old or coming from a particular social background. All of these will influence the social networks of members. First, then, let us define what we mean by 'networks', and then suggest why they are important.

Although the term network is a comparatively recent addition to the language of sociology, it has already acquired numerous meanings. For our present purposes, however, we shall take a network to refer to the cluster of personal links which a person has around him, together with the links between these other persons. The importance of having the right 'connections' was appreciated long before sociology became a discipline. We use terms such as 'contacts', 'cliques' and 'nepotism' to refer to aspects of people's networks which are used for furthering their interests, often in a way that is not entirely approved of. In the same way, when sociologists and social anthropologists use the term, they stress that networks do not just 'exist': people are selected and incorporated into a network who can be relied on for support; they are a means of mobilizing resources.

Even before a man becomes a member of an organization, his network may be important in gaining entry for him. This has frequently been true of traditional industries such as the docks. It also occurs when applicants for membership carry some characteristic which is likely to impede their entry, such as nationality or skin colour. This leads to the rise of intermediaries whose networks include both management and men seeking entry, and who are rewarded by management for providing them with reliable recruits and by the men for securing them entry.

Once a man becomes a member of an organization, his network will gradually be built up, on the basis of all three of the factors we have already described. Thus, in the first place his structural position within the organization (the way his official role is defined) will largely determine those with whom he will have contacts: at one extreme is the prisoner who is specifically cut off from many social contacts and as a result acquires an intimate knowledge of a very small number of people who can be manipulated for various purposes; at the other extreme is the shop assistant who spends most of her time within the organization interacting with a large number of people in such a superficial way that it is difficult to 'use' any of these contacts.

However, whether in prisons or shops, a man's relations do not remain confined to those with whom he has formal dealings. Here his status-characteristics, or categories, become relevant: he will prefer to spend his off-duty time (tea-breaks, meal-times) with people whom he finds acceptable, possibly those from the same suburb, others with small children, fellow-Pakistanis. These have their uses: confidential information may circulate among them; he enjoys a game of cards with them; conversation with them helps the time to pass quickly.

Finally, he may go out and look for other contacts, not because they are people of the same sort, but because, having a certain orientation towards the organization, he is hoping to achieve some specific end, or at least build up contacts which will be useful in the future when occasion arises. Burns shows well two of the many ways in which networks are built up with such aims in view in his discussion of 'cliques' and 'cabals' in occupational settings (1955). These are both types of primary groups that are entered for the sake of building up support in specific social situations: 'cliques', in this usage, are groups of people in a precarious position whose mutual support reassures them that they have not in fact 'failed'; 'cabals' consist of aspiring people who use their influence to obtain illegitimate control and thereby success. In each case, groups are formed with a particular aim in view and cease to exist when that aim disappears.

An excellent study which shows the way in which networks can be used to explain social behaviour in an organization is Kapferer's analysis of a dispute between two operatives in an electrozinc plant in Broken Hill, Zambia (Kapferer, 1969). One of the older workers, Abraham, complained to Donald, a young man, about his fast working pace. Donald retorted angrily suggesting that Abraham was using witchcraft on him. Abraham admitted this, saying that those who did not respect their elders deserved to be bewitched. Each of them appealed to others for support, and in the end Donald had to back down and signalled his defeat by applying for a transfer to another department.

Kapferer analyses the networks of the two protagonists to show why Abraham was able to mobilize more support, although in some ways he was in a weaker position; why it was Abraham who made the accusation and not one of the other older workers; why Donald was accused and not his partner, who was working at the same pace; why in the course of the dispute more stress was laid on subordinate issues, such as whether Donald was showing disrespect to an older man, than the basic question of rate-busting and the accusation of witchcraft. All these questions are answered by identifying each man's sources of support in the department, and the support which the supporters themselves could call upon.

Sociology thrives on the resolution of contradictions, not simply on the cumulation of uncontroversial findings. The scientific method is based on continuously refining hypotheses as a result of comparing conflicting findings which have to be explained. Such conflicting interpretations are prominent in the sociological study of organizations. An important area of controversy derives from the fact that while one study emphasizes the significance of internal factors in understanding organizational behaviour, another stresses factors influencing members from the outside. Thus some studies have explained why it is that mental hospital patients do not easily form friendship groups by examining their social position and their place in the communications network inside the hospital; they may be desperately keen to present themselves as 'normal' people, in contrast to all the other unfortunates, with whom they prefer not to associate (Salisbury, 1962). They find it difficult to maintain friendships because, in the hospital communications system, things spoken 'in confidence' are, in fact, often taken into account in evaluating patients' medical progress and used as evidence against them. On the other hand, the reason for patients being in the hospital at all may be that they have found it difficult communicating in the outside world.

There is some evidence that particular types of explanation in this area have been fashionable at different periods during the development of sociology. For example, in reviewing studies of social organization in the prison, Schwartz (1971) shows that an emphasis on the *characteristics of members* in understanding life in the prison was followed by a stress on the way in which the carrying out of the *objectives of the organization* heavily sanctions the behaviour of members. Thus a landmark in the study of prisons was the work of Sykes (1958) which stressed that, in contrast to earlier studies, the inmate community is organized largely as a response to the 'pains of imprisonment' which affect all inmates, whatever their previous background, by depriving them of self-determination, sexual opportunities, goods and services, freedom, etc. (see also Sykes and Messinger, 1960). This structural pressure, he argued, was responsible for the development of the inmate code, which stressed a collective opposition to the staff and provided a set of statuses which could be met by members.

More recent studies, however, have stressed that Sykes's results were based on the examination of a single maximum-security prison where all the inmates were serving long sentences and where the range of social backgrounds, previous criminal careers and attitudes towards prison of the inmates was fairly narrow (see Irwin, 1970; Heffernan, 1972).

In contrast Irwin, in studying the parole-behaviour of inmates, found it necessary to go back to their varying lives before coming into prison to understand how they were likely to react to parole. Whereas other writers had stressed the strength of the 'indigenous' prison-culture which arose in response to the shared deprivations of prison, he divided inmates in the California State prisons into eight different categories based on pre-prison career. Some of these categories are, for example: *thieves*, who made a profession of stealing, particularly from large corporations, and believed that it was the world that was corrupt and saw nothing wrong in what they were doing; *disorganized criminals*, who came from the same background as the more professional thieves but had not found their way into the criminal sub-culture and existed in a state of confusion drifting between the conventional and the criminal worlds; *dope fiends*, whose reliance on hard drugs brought them into contact with the law; '*state-raised*' *youth*, who had grown up from childhood in state institutions and had become thoroughly 'institutionalized', so that for them the reality was the world inside the prison; and '*square johns*', members of conventional society upholding normal values who through some 'mistake' got themselves into prison where they found themselves surrounded by real criminals.

A crucial distinction between these categories is the way those in them react to the pains of imprisonment. One adaptation is what Irwin calls '*doing time*', that is, serving one's sentence as comfortably as possible, keeping out of trouble and waiting to resume one's criminal career outside. A second response to imprisonment is '*jailing*', that is, adapting to life inside, so that it is what goes on in the prison that is important rather than the world outside. The third main type of response he calls '*gleaning*', that is, using the time profitably by taking advantage of the educational and other resources provided by the prison. Significantly, Irwin found these three types of response clearly associated with his eight categories of inmates, defined according to *pre*-prison career. For example, predictably it was the 'square johns', who did not come from a criminal background, who spent their time in prison taking advantage of the facilities, whereas the 'thieves' he observed to be 'doing time' until they could resume their criminal career. The 'disorganized criminals' tended to drift in prison, as they did outside, displaying the reactions of whatever groups they happened to be placed among.

In another study Heffernan (1972) came to very similar conclusions. After a detailed analysis of a women's prison in Virginia, she argued that there were three different means of adapting to life in prison which varied according to the background and type of offence committed by the women. One category, who had no previous criminal career, reacted to life in prison in a way that led her to describe them as 'the square'; they took the same opportunities for 'gleaning' as Irwin's 'square johns'. A second category adapted in a way that justified the description 'the cool'; their previous criminal careers indicated that they saw crime as an occupation, and the 'cool' reaction was similar to that of Irwin's thieves who were 'doing time'. The third category were habitual criminals for whom alcoholism and other forms of drug addiction were a regular part of their pre-prison career. Their reactions to time spent in prison led Heffernan to call them 'the life', a concept similar to Irwin's notion of 'jailing'.

Thus, two studies of different prisons carried out at the same time showed the same variety of reactions to life in prison, and the same close relationship between types of pre-prison career and types of adjustment to imprisonment. However, these findings do not mean that people coming into prison are not significantly affected by the fact of incarceration or the nature of the prison régime.

Schwartz attempted to put these two approaches together by measuring how much of the adaptation to life in a penal institution for delinquent boys in Pennsylvania was due to 'cultural drift' (i.e.

the pre-institutional factors stressed by Irwin and Heffernan), and how much was due to 'indigenous influence' (i.e. the effect of situational factors inside the prison such as those emphasized by Sykes). In general, he concluded that factors internal to the prison were more responsible for determining the pattern of *behaviour* inside, and pre-institutional factors were more responsible for the *values and identifications* the boys held (which are less open to view and therefore less easily sanctioned either by other boys or the staff). This conflicts with Goffman's view that the personal identity of inmates, as well as their behaviour, is radically reconstructed in total institutions.

The analysis of the prison as a formal organization is a good example of how sociology can systematize and develop our common-sense understanding of how organizations work. For example, common-sense might lead us to take the view supported above that when people enter organizations, their behaviour is likely to be determined by what the organization is trying to achieve and by the system it uses for achieving those ends. However, the values and attitudes people bring to the organization are less likely to be affected, even in organizations where entry is involuntary, as in the prison, for prison staff are likely to be more concerned with securing the compliance of inmates than with totally resocializing them.

The systematic approach of sociology to such questions, however, allows us both to test how far such common-sense notions are true, on the basis of research, and to discover the reasons for these variations. This does not mean treating every case as unique – that would spell the end of sociology – but it does mean that the infinite complexity of social behaviour cannot be adequately *explained* by a few gross principles. Rather, we can be guided by our awareness of such processes in examining what actually happens in a given institution.

In conclusion, we should stress that the social experiences that members undergo within organizations feed back into their life outside, into primary groups such as the family, and into their general relationships in the community and elsewhere. We have suggested that – whatever their official philosophies – organizations, despite their structural constraints, never operate without taking account of what their members bring to the organization. Equally, however, social behaviour in the 'outside world' is affected by people's experience within organizations. As we go on to look at community life and patterns of stratification, we shall do well to remember that 'No organization is an island': that while we all belong to families, most people in developed societies spend most of their time within the framework of one organization or another.

Chapter 7
Communities and Cities

We have so far discussed a number of specialized institutions, groups and organizations which can to some degree be analysed as if they were independent systems of social relations. We now turn to the nature of communities, and the perplexing variety of settings for social life which the villages, towns, cities and metropolitan regions of the modern world provide for man. Our progression from specialized social units to the community may at first seem simple and unproblematic. In fact, however, the study of communities involves us in numerous problems.

We often still think of a 'village community' in much the same way as Mary Russell Mitford did, writing in the 1820s, as 'our village' – 'a little world of our own ... where we know everyone and are known to everyone, interested in everyone, and authorized to hope that everyone feels an interest in us' (Mitford, 1951, p. 3). But the term can also carry quite different connotations, as when we speak of a 'metropolitan community'. In this case our minds may turn not to cosiness but to the discomfort of commuting to work, or the dullness and uniformity of supermarkets, or the bewildering effects of advertising and television, or the tedious routines of mass-production. In short, the metropolitan community is often seen not as a setting for friendly mutual relationships but as a place of 'anomie', of 'alienation' and of 'mass culture', of individual impotence in the face of industrialism and capitalism, and of personal struggles against impersonal bureaucrats and technocrats. The 'village community' and the 'metropolitan community', so conceived, are but two extreme kinds of settings for life. Others that readily come to mind are the 'local town' which may be the service centre for a surrounding rural area, or the 'urban village' which, unlike the isolated rural village, may be embedded in a modern metropolis yet inhabited by people who share a distinctive way of life.

As the term community can evoke such varied images, we must question whether it has any value in sociology. One response might simply be that we need to define the term more closely. But sociologists have already expended much effort in trying to define community without reaching any appreciable degree of consensus. Thus, after reviewing ninety-four definitions, Hillery (1955) claims that 'beyond the recognition that "people are involved in community" there is little agreement on the use of the term'. A second closely related obstacle to clear thinking is that the term is commonly used for different purposes in the description and analysis of society. Thus it may be used to refer to particular spatial or geographical units (e.g., a village or a city) or to denote sets of units (e.g., villages and small towns, as against, perhaps, cities and metropolitan centres), but at other times is used in an evaluative way, as when we say that this village is a 'real' community but that one is not. A 'community of scholars', again, has no geographical focus at all. Nor, to take an example from world history, does 'the Jewish community'.

These difficulties stem, in part, from the fact that the term comes from everyday life. So we need to distinguish between the layman's uses ('folk models') and the sociologist's uses ('sociological models'). In common parlance, the term community generally refers to people inhabiting a certain locality, having some degree of political autonomy, a sense of fellowship, a uniform set of religious beliefs, perhaps ethnic homogeneity, and often a particular dominant occupational function. Numerous small-scale preliterate societies display all or most of these features, as do many groupings in the modern world. One example from Western society is the French-Canadian parish of St Denis studied by Miner in the 1930s. In his introduction to Miner's account, Redfield sums up the salient features of St Denis as follows:

The *habitants* [small farmers] live in terms of common understandings . . . rooted in tradition . . . The fundamental views of life are shared by almost everyone; and . . . find consistent expression in the beliefs, the institutions, the rituals and the manners of the people. In a word, they have a culture. Furthermore, the sanctions which support conduct are strongly sacred: the faith which all share provides endorsement of certain behaviour and con demnation for other behaviour. The priest tells them this is right and that is wrong; but the point here is that the people feel the right and the wrong and act from such a feeling, not from expediency. Furthermore, this society, like many others more primitive and outside of the European world, is strongly familial . . . the family system is strong, pervasive, and certain in its effects . . . There is little disorganization and little crime (Miner, 1963, pp. 13–14).

St Denis clearly constitutes a community in a common-sense way, and some sociologists use the term primarily to denote groups of this kind. But which of the criteria used are *essential* to the conception – 'the fundamental views of life . . . shared by almost everyone', or the 'familial' fabric of society, or the low crime rate? Are some features more central to its existence as a community than are others? Clearly the notion of community applied to St Denis is very different in meaning from the notions of a 'metropolitan community', an 'urban village' or a 'local town'. In urban areas people do not normally share the same views, nor are ties of kinship and marriage so prominent. Yet we still use the notion of community in relation to them. The principles governing life in St Denis are thus not the only ones which çan produce 'order' and 'stability'.

When we move to towns and cities we often encounter quite different systems of social control. As Norton Long (1961) stresses, most urban communities lack any inclusive, over-all organization. In a middle-class suburb, for example, a plethora of seemingly 'private' voluntary organizations all contribute to the maintenance of a social order which, however, also depends on the controls and constraints of various 'public' bodies and official municipal and national bureaucracies. Such a combination of agencies may at first sight not appear to make up any indentifiable community. Yet closer observation invariably reveals a multiplicity of interconnections. The middle-class suburb of Toronto, analysed by Seeley, Sim and Loosley in *Crestwood Heights* (1963), differs greatly from St Denis, but these authors clearly see it as a community. A wide variety of organizations intermesh in such a way as to co-ordinate everyday activities into distinct patterns, however unplanned or unwilled by any one of them. Again, in slum communities like those analysed in *Street Corner Society* (Whyte, 1955), or in *The Social Order of the Slum* (Suttles, 1968), gangs, rackets, and other similarly 'disreputable' institutions are important agencies of social control. Yet these institutions might be regarded by many middle-class people as symptoms of 'disorganization' rather than of 'organization'. St Denis, then, is only one kind of community; and it is itself part of a wider 'community' – that of all the *habitants* of French Canada.

The Community as a Unit

Many sociologists, however, have continued to treat the community primarily as a unit, despite the many different forms it may take and the different contexts in which it may occur. König (1968), for example, sees community as 'a basic form', which does not in his view disappear or dissolve in the wake of industrial and urban revolutions, as has often been argued. Similarly, Schnore (1967) categorically asserts that the 'community is a basic unit of social structure'. But such authors invariably leave it unclear as to whether they are using terms like 'basic form' and 'basic unit' to imply that the community actually exists as an objective *thing*, a reality, 'out there', or whether it is an analytical category used to describe aspects of social organization abstracted from the 'real' world.

The view of the small community as a basic entity in society was most explicitly developed by Robert Redfield, who, in his book *The Little Community*, made the unambiguous claim that 'humanity presents itself to the view of common-sense in just a few kinds of integral entities'. The 'little community' is one of these; others are a person, a people (*ein Volk*), a nation-state, and a civilization; each of which can be studied as separate units (Redfield, 1955, p. 1). For Redfield the 'little community' had four defining qualities: distinctiveness, small size, self-sufficiency and homogeneity of inhabitants. This conception, like many others similar to it, has been criticized on a variety of grounds. Firstly, the defining qualities listed by Redfield are not distinguishing criteria of the 'little community' in any strict sense of the word 'little'. Small communities seldom, if ever, have boundaries as clear-cut as Redfield implies. Secondly, homogeneity and self-sufficiency are relative and arbitrary characteristics. Most villages of the modern world contain people of different occupations and different social ranks; their religious and political affiliations often vary, and so on. Again villages are usually tied into a market-system, whether on a small or a large scale. In the twentieth century, villages in all continents, and in both developed and underdeveloped countries, have become progressively more involved in economic and market systems which pervade the entire world and are truly international in range.

Redfield was, of course, aware that the autonomy of the 'little community' had diminished over the course of modern history and that there were few self-sufficient communities left. Indeed, he argued that 'we must reckon with parts that have their centres and principal being elsewhere than in the village'. But even where 'little communities' still have their own distinctive cultures – perhaps specializing economically in agriculture, or possibly possessing their own 'little traditions' in religion, which in many cases focus upon the seasons, the crops, and individual and family life-crises – they are now no more than 'part-societies': parts of the 'rural sector' of the total economy in which cities are dominant, whether in terms of the market for peasant products or through the city-based governments, banks, armies, and other large-scale institutions which lie outside villages, yet exercise ultimate power over them. Again, most 'little traditions' in religion are influenced or even engulfed by the 'Great Traditions' of one or other of the world's main religions of Christianity, Confucianism, Buddhism, Hinduism, Islam and Taoism; there are very few corners of the globe where these have not penetrated. Thus Redfield's 'little community' cannot be taken as a description of reality. It is, rather, an 'ideal-typical' construction.

By 'ideal type', a term first brought into sociology in 1904 by Max Weber, we do not mean a type that is ideal in the sense of being *desirable*, but in the sense that it is an imaginary perfect representation of the essence of any particular phenomenon. Redfield himself expressly dwelt on the nature of ideal-typical constructions in his discussion not of the 'little community', but of 'folk society', a notion closely related to the 'little community' (Redfield, 1947). Here he makes the assumption that 'folk society' had certain features which enable us to think of it as a type in contrast to 'urban society'. Thus, 'the people who make up a folk society are much alike . . . having lived in long intimacy with one another', and so on. But, he explains, this *type* of 'folk society' is an 'imagined entity, created only because through it we may hope to understand reality'. Similarly, we might perfectly well set out to construct an ideal type of, say, totalitarianism – taking those features of totalitarianism which we consider to be *essential* aspects of that phenomenon in its 'pure' or 'ideal' form though it may never occur in reality, since it will always be mixed up with the other kinds of political arrangements which constitute departures from the 'pure' or 'ideal' type. Thus a given society may be predominantly totalitarian, but allow, say, a degree of self-expression to trade unions as long as they confine themselves to matters concerning work. Again, an ideal type of democracy might well include, say, popular participation in government and representation on the basis of universal suffrage, even though we know well that free decision-making 'by the people' is always subject to the constraints imposed by political party machines, by a powerful Press, and the like. But though no pure democracy exists in the real world and active social reality confronts us with many different kinds of democracy, it is a useful category for organizing our thoughts. Redfield's ideal type of the 'little community' must therefore not be judged according to whether it adequately represents reality, but in terms of its *heuristic* use in trying to understand reality.

But we still have to ask, as Redfield did, whether it is useful to 'describe as a whole a community whose life is modified by bits of other communities'. This leads us to consider two notions of community that differ slightly from the self-contained village model: communities within communities, and overlapping and interpenetrating communities. Instead of thinking of a village as discrete, we can conceive of it as akin to a magnet exercising its pull over a magnetic field. Social relationships take place within fields of force at the centre of which there may lie, not a magnet, but, say, a village, a farm settlement, or a town, each exercising attractive power over a certain area. Strong magnets (such as towns) exercise their attraction over larger areas within which weaker magnets (say, villages) also exercise some more limited pull. There are thus a whole range of overlapping social fields for every unit (person, village, etc.) and one may be subjected to the often contrary and unique pulls of a number of magnets. The town exercises a wider attractive pull because it provides more specialized or better-quality services than the village, even though the latter may be nearer. But, for everyday shopping, the village is good enough.

These 'fields' differ from geographical areas since they are relative, not fixed. Moreover, the metaphor breaks down because there are different kinds of 'pulls' – economic, familial, religious, etc. We may illustrate this with an extract from a rural study which follows Redfield's general mode of thought, while stressing that community life is not restricted simply to the physical boundaries of a village. In their study *Family and Community in Ireland*, based on field work conducted in the 1930s, Arensberg and Kimball observe:

In rural Ireland what we have called the 'rural community' is no simply defined geographical area. Any one of the recognized divisions of the countryside in Ireland, a townland, a group of townlands, a parish, an old barony, a mountain upland, a portion of a valley floor or plain, except perhaps the newer administrative divisions, is in a sense a community. The lines of relationship among the smaller farmers are continuous from one of these to any other across the land. Geographic barriers serve only to deflect the lines of this continuum, not to divide it.

We observe of a farmer of Luogh, for example, that he *coors* [co-operates with neighbouring farmers] largely in Luogh townland. But he has kinsmen scattered around about as far as Mount Elva, four miles to the north and Liscannor, three miles to the south. He attends the parish church of Killilagh, a two-mile walk from his house, but he sends his children to school at Ballycotton, only a mile off. He does most of his shopping in Roadford, a crossroad settlement two miles away. Yet he takes his larger produce for sale and his larger needs of purchase to the market town of Ennistymon, some eight miles off, or the smaller one of Lisdoonvaran, some five miles off. He votes and pays his taxes as a member of a certain electoral district which overlaps exactly with none of these regions. He associates himself in tradition with Clare and Munster as a North Clare man, rather than with Galway and Connaught, though he may have seen very little of either beyond his market towns. The smaller farmer of Luogh has allegiances to all these communities. He is quite ready to find his emotion stirred in any one of them. He is ready to back the men of Luogh against the men of the neighbourhood townland; to back those of the mountain regions against those of the valley lands; those of the parish against the rest; those of the countryside against the towns of Lisdoonvaran and Ennistymon; those of North Clare against other sections of the country; of his class against all others; of his religion against all others; of his nation against all others (Arensberg and Kimball, 1940, pp. 282–3).

From this, it is clear that any conception of a single unitary community would be grossly misleading: there are various interests or sets of interests which people pursue within a series of communities which do not necessarily add up to a clearly demarcated whole. (See also Frankenberg, 1957, on a village in Wales, and Littlejohn, 1963, on a rural parish in Scotland.)

In communities like these, the inhabitants interact with differing sets of people for different purposes, within differing administrative and institutional boundaries. Communities of this kind are not, then, basic *units*, but overlapping and multiple sets of social relations within a variety of geographical localities. The abandonment of the simple view of the community as a unitary whole thus leads us to consider overlapping and interpenetrating social ties. More widely, it suggests that we should not dwell exclusively on unity and harmony, but that we should equally look at division, specialization, conflict and competition. One major criticism of Redfield's ideal type is that it assumes that the 'little community' is an integrated homogeneous whole, free of tensions, and somehow more harmonious and unified than a large community. This assumption is highly suspect, for it may well be that internal conflicts, under certain circumstances, are much greater in a small community precisely because the members are closer to each other. Another telling criticism is that the whole notion rests on the assumption of an unchanging social order; in brief, that it is a-historical.

The force of such criticisms is well illustrated by the differing analyses produced by later researchers working with different perspectives on communities first studied under the influence of Redfield's assumptions. The first example we take is one of Redfield's own field reports – of Tepoztlán, a Mexican village, which he studied in the 1920s – and Oscar Lewis's re-study of the very same community in the 1940s (Redfield, 1930; Lewis, 1951). In his re-study, Lewis emphasized the lack of co-operation between villagers, the tensions between villages in the wider *municipio* of which Tepoztlán was a part, the political and other schisms within Tepoztlán, and the pervading quality of fear, envy and distrust in the interpersonal relations of the inhabitants. All this stands in sharp contrast to Redfield's account, in which he emphasized the co-operative and unifying factors in Tepoztecan society. And it is perfectly clear from Lewis's analysis that the differences between the two accounts cannot be explained away simply by the passage of time between the 1920s and the 1940s.

Our second example is of the difference between Arensberg and Kimball's study in Western rural Ireland in the 1930s (op. cit., 1940), and Hugh Brody's recent study conducted in the same area (Brody, 1974). Brody's analysis again differs from that of Arensberg and Kimball in a fundamental way. Whereas Arensberg and Kimball analysed Irish rural community and culture as functioning and self-maintaining social entities, Brody focuses on the process of change over time; and he directly challenges the earlier study of Irish rural culture as a balanced and self-sealing system, impervious to influences from the outside world. In particular he points to elements in 'the traditional situation' of rural Ireland which, he shows, have for long confounded and confronted each other. His study is thus centrally focused on processes of change and decline, rather than on an enduring culture.

Similar shifts of emphasis are evident in recent studies of formerly rather remote parts of most Western European countries, so much so that Boissevain notes how sociologists and anthropologists have largely ceased using such 'folk' terms as community, village and culture. Instead they have for some time employed more sophisticated concepts like the 'folk-urban continuum', 'absorption' and 'acculturation' – all adapted from earlier perspectives. But even these are no longer adequate to grasp the nature of change 'beyond the community'; if we want to understand modern rural Europe, Boissevain insists, we must now concentrate on the no less familiar, but very different, large-scale processes of industrialization, geographical mobility, the growing centralization of State power, co-operative arrangements in agriculture, and the like (Boissevain and Friedl, 1975, pp. 9–10).

'Contrast' Conceptions and Theories of Social Change

The arguments about community are not, however, new. As an analytical concept, 'community' has a long history, embedded in theories of the sociology of change developed in the nineteenth century and even earlier. These theories have commonly taken the form of elaborating contrasting pairs of categories, of which the most important are those between rural and urban communities, and between 'community' and what we may call 'non-community'. At this point in the discussion we therefore shift from a predominant concern with the local community (which the German language distinguishes as *Gemeinde*) to the community in general (*Gemeinschaft*).

Despite their differences, various theories of social change have tended to converge on one basic theme. All of them see social change as a movement from an 'old' to a 'new' emerging social order: a movement from the 'pre-industrial' order to the 'industrial' order, or from the 'traditional' to the 'rational', from 'folk society' to 'modern society', from the 'rural' to the 'urban' way of life, from small-scale 'personal' society to large-scale 'impersonal' society, from the believed simplicity of illiterate 'primitive' societies to the known complexity of 'modern' technologically sophisticated society, and so on. Implicitly or explicitly, all these theories of the general direction of evolutionary and historical development are based on some underlying notion of the changing basis of human relationships, such as the change from 'blood ties' to the 'cash nexus'. They also contain, within them, conceptions of the community and of its place in the changing social order.

Tönnies's book, *Gemeinschaft und Gesellschaft*, first published in 1887, makes quite explicit his assumption about these changes in social relations. The central categories he used in analysing the nature of human society, and its general direction of development, were the twin concepts of *Gemeinschaft* and *Gesellschaft*, usually roughly translated as 'community' and 'association'.

In Tönnies's view, the society of his time in Europe was in the throes of a relentless progression from *Gemeinschaft* to *Gesellschaft*. Urbanization was only one aspect of an interlinked set of social changes which affected the whole of society as it became ever less dependent on agriculture and ever more commercial and industrial. He conceived of *Gemeinschaft* as characterized by social order based on intimate personal living together. *Gemeinschaft*-like experiences satisfied fundamental wants and sentiments, and were built into deep-rooted and rich personal relationships. *Gesellschaft*, on the other hand, was characterized by impersonal and limited contractual relations established as a result of calculation and reflection. Tönnies developed and used these twin concepts in an elaborate way, as this brief passage shows:

All intimate, private and exclusive living together . . . is . . . life in *Gemeinschaft. Gesellschaft* is public life – it is the world itself. In *Gemeinschaft* with one's family, one lives from birth on, bound to it in weal and woe. One goes into *Gesellschaft* as one goes into a strange country . . . *Gemeinschaft* is old; *Gesellschaft* is new . . . all praise of rural life has pointed out that *Gemeinschaft* among people is stronger there and more alive; it is the lasting and genuine form of living together. In contrast to *Gemeinschaft*, *Gesellschaft* is transitory and superficial (Tönnies, 1955, pp. 37–9).

While Tönnies saw *Gemeinschaft* and *Gesellschaft* as two *opposed* ways in which men can be bound together, he considered that there were elements of both *Gemeinschaft* and *Gesellschaft* in all social relationships and all societies. They were not rigidly exclusive categories but aspects or dimensions of social relationships found in varying degrees in different societies. Nevertheless, over-all there was a definite trend of change, in the course of human history, towards an increase in the influence of *Gesellschaft* and a corresponding decrease in the influence of *Gemeinschaft*.

In a similarly seminal study, *The Division of Labour in Society*, first published in 1893, Emile Durkheim sought to show that undifferentiated societies – in which the social division of labour was not very marked, as there were few specialized roles – exhibited a particular kind of social solidarity which he referred to as 'mechanical', whereas societies with a marked division of labour and a high degree of occupational specialization were characterized by another type of solidarity which he called 'organic'. The major features of mechanical solidarity were the relative homogeneity of the population, uniformity of beliefs, opinions, and conduct, and the dominance of repressive criminal law. By contrast, organic solidarity obtained when a population was 'mentally and morally' heterogeneous, when there was diversity of beliefs, opinions and conduct, and when the principles of law become restitutive rather than repressive. Durkheim suggested that mechanical solidarity derived from the conformity of individuals to a common standard. He thus saw mechanical solidarity as based on the *similarity* of individuals, whereas he considered organic solidarity to be based on *interdependence*, arising out of complementarity between different categories of people. Like Tönnies,

Durkhiem saw change as progressive and irreversible: '... it is an historical law that mechanical solidarity, which first stands alone, or nearly so, progressively loses ground, and organic solidarity becomes, little by little, preponderant' (Durkheim, 1964, p. 174). There are important differences between the formulations of Tönnies and Durkheim. Thus, for example, Tönnies considered that the contrast he described arose from differences of individual attitudes and personality, whereas Durkheim rejected 'psychologistic' explanations of social behaviour in terms of the attributes of the individual. Our present interest, however, is in the similarities in their thinking.

Theories of this kind did not originate in the nineteenth century: they are variations on an eternal theme which can be traced back to the very beginnings of systematic social thought (Sorokin, 1955, p. 6). Nor did the appeal of such theories disappear with the passing of the nineteenth century. They have remained very influential in twentieth-century thought.

Thus, in 1909, Cooley coined the phrase 'primary group', now a basic concept in sociology:

By primary groups I mean those characterized by intimate face-to-face association and co-operation. They are primary in several senses, but chiefly in that they are fundamental in forming the social nature and ideals of the individual. The result of intimate association, psychologically, is a certain fusion of individualities in a common whole, so that one's very self, for many purposes at least, is the common life and purpose of the group. Perhaps the simplest way of describing this wholeness is by saying that it is a 'we', it involves the sort of sympathy and mutual identification for which 'we' is the natural expression. One lives in the feeling of the whole, and finds the chief aims of his will in that feeling (Cooley, 1964, p. 311).

Following Cooley's original enunciation of 'primary groups', various authors came to write of 'secondary groups' as, simply, all those which are not primary. Thus another pair of 'contrast' concepts was added to the discussion.

A further influential pair come from MacIver's variation on the theme of 'community' and 'association'. We can define a community, he suggested, as any group of individuals living together in such a way that they share 'not this or that particular interest' but 'the basic institutions of a common life'. 'The mark of community,' he wrote, 'is that one's life may be lived wholly within it, that all one's social relationships may be found within it' (MacIver, 1937, pp. 8–9). On the other hand, in contrast to a community, an *association* was a group specifically organized for the pursuit of an interest or set of interests. 'The difference is obvious,' he wrote: 'we contrast the business or the church or the club with the village or city or nation' (p. 11).

These formulations – and others of a similar kind – have passed into the intellectual equipment of present-day sociologists, both as particular concepts and as general characterizations of the processes of change. Just as Tönnies and Durkheim expressed these changes in the general formulae 'from *Gemeinschaft* to *Gesellschaft*' and 'from mechanical to organic', so Cooley's followers pointed to the gradual displacement of 'primary groups' by 'secondary groups', and MacIver's followers saw 'associational life' growing at the cost of 'community life'.

In the writings of Tönnies and Durkheim these 'contrast'-concepts formed part of wider sociological theories, characteristic of the nineteenth century. The pairs of concepts used by Cooley and MacIver, however, were not used so much in the analysis of changes in entire patterns of society and culture as in analysing fairly specific and limited aspects of particular societies. This difference reflects an important change from the 'old' to the 'new' in sociology itself. Tönnies and Durkheim were writing in a tradition of the creation of *general* theories of historical and evolutionary development; Cooley and MacIver were contributing to the formation of a later tradition with great emphasis on fieldstudies and the consequent demand for more specific *operational* – as distinct from *analytical* – concepts. Tönnies's and Durkheim's concepts are essentially ideal-types, whereas Cooley's and MacIver's were formulated more as operational definitions for use in the analysis of field materials.

We can now see that Redfield's ideal-type constructions were not original, but simply further variants of the general motion of the rural-urban contrast: he treated 'folk society' and 'urban society' as polar opposites in much the same style of contrast as *Gemeinschaft* and *Gesellschaft* or 'mechanical' and 'organic' solidarity. Urban society constituted a 'disorganized' social milieu, whereas 'folk society' was, like the 'little community', more orderly and harmonious. Because Redfield tended to see the essential qualities of community as those expressed in his notion of the '*little* community', he naturally inclined to the view that 'urban community' is virtually a contradiction in terms. Such views were initially influential in urban studies, but were to come under increasing criticism.

The Community in Urban Studies

The growth of towns and cities and the urbanization of the modern world constitute a major challenge to the sociologist. Large-scale urbanization is a recent historical development of which laymen are of course aware, though few perhaps realize the scale and speed of the process. The world's first cities were probably developed over 5,000 years ago, but were small and surrounded by an overwhelming majority of rural people. The growth of more fully urbanized *societies* began only about 100 to 150 years ago. Before 1850 no society could be described as predominantly urbanized, and in 1900 there was only one, namely Britain. Today, however, most industrial nations of the world are in effect urbanized societies, and there is also remarkable urban growth in countries with little industrialization. The timing and speed of urbanization in Western industrial nations is well illustrated by the U.S.A., where in 1790 only about 5 per cent of the population was classified as urban; it rose to 40 per cent by 1900 and to 74 per cent by 1970; and projections suggest that it will be about 85 per cent in the year 2000 (Advisory Commission on Intergovernmental Relations, 1971, p. 25). In less industrial nations, especially in the Third World, the timing and rate have been different but just as relentless. In India, for example, the percentage of the population classified as urban was about 11 per cent in 1901, and had risen to only about 14 per cent in 1941; but between 1941 and 1971 it rose to 20 per cent, thus doubling the rate of the earlier decades of this century. Moreover, there has been a rapid increase *in the population of large cities*. In 1901, only 23 per cent of Indian urban-dwellers lived in cities of 100,000+ whereas in 1971 the corresponding figure was 52·4 per cent (Bose, 1973, pp. 114 and 133). The general contrast between industrial and non-industrial nations is seen in extreme form in the difference between, say, England and Wales or the U.S.A., and Kenya or India, as shown in Figure 11, adapted from Davis (1965) and updated. In the more industrial nations the rate has been closely related to the

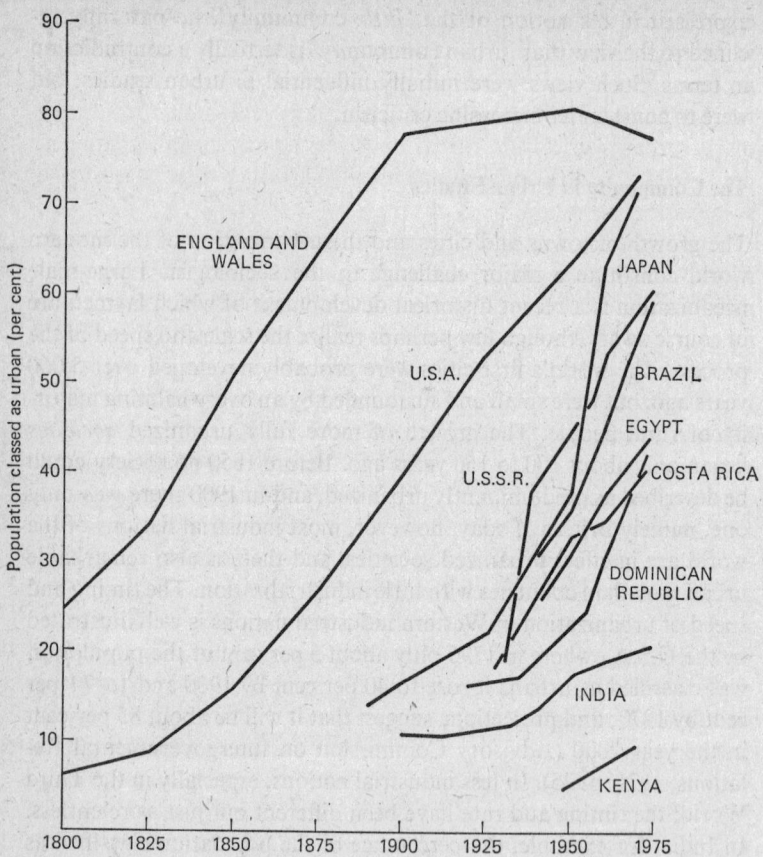

Figure 11 Rates of urbanization in ten selected countries
(Source: adapted from K. Davis 1965.)

pace of economic development; whereas in the less industrial nations the increase is largely attributable to the rapid rise of the *total* population. Despite the lower level of urbanization in non-industrial countries, however, Davis estimates that in the year 2000 well over a half of all humans will be residents of cities with populations of 100,000 or more.

Writers like Tönnies and Durkheim were clearly aware of the increasing pace of urbanization in the Europe of their day, but they could scarcely have envisaged the rapidity and extent of large-scale world-wide urbanization as it was to develop. This perhaps helps account for the fact that their points of departure were invariably the rural rather than the urban world. Their observations and experience of the urban world were often much less solidly based, being impressionistic, and to some extent imagined, rather than based upon systematic observation.

From the early decades of the present century, however, American sociologists in particular have increasingly focused on the urban community and it is initially to their work that we now turn. As our starting point we take the concept of 'urbanism' as formulated by Louis Wirth, who was a key figure in a whole programme of studies in Chicago in the 1920s and 1930s. Despite Wirth's awareness, through these field studies, of the vast metropolis of Chicago, his approach to the problem of community remained in many respects very similar to that of Redfield. In his well-known essay, 'Urbanism as a Way of Life', written in 1938 (Wirth, 1963), he claimed that our starting point for the analysis of city life should be the contrast between 'rural-folk' and 'urban-industrial' societies: these are what he calls the 'basic models of human association in contemporary civilization', the opposite ends of a continuum of social organization. But Wirth was less concerned with producing a comprehensive theory of community than with exploring patterns of life *in* the city. His essay was written as a tentative statement intended to guide empirical research; yet he also thought that some principal features of urban life had already been well established as enduring and invariable.

Thus Wirth believed that among the salient features of urbanism were the *substitution* of secondary for primary contacts, the *declining* social significance of the family, and the *disappearance* of the neighbourhood. 'All these phenomena,' he wrote, 'can be substantially verified through objective indices.' He also claimed that the city was not conducive 'to the maintenance of the home as the focus of a whole round of vital activities', and he thought the low and declining urban reproduction rates of the 1930s were an unchangeable feature of city life. Again, he considered that the city reduced man to 'virtual impotence as an individual', and that this was the reason for the urbanite exerting himself to join with others in organized groups; hence 'the enormous multiplication of voluntary organizations directed toward as great a variety of objectives as there are human needs and interests' (Wirth, 1963, pp. 60–61).

Forty years later we can see that history itself has proved Wirth wrong in certain particulars, while better and more comprehensive analyses than were available in 1938 have proved him wrong in others. To illustrate the former, we take his view that the failure of the urban population to reproduce itself was 'a biological consequence of a combination of factors in the complex of urban life', which led him to see cities as 'consumers rather than producers of men'. He was equally led to assume that large-scale rural–urban migration was, and would remain, universal and permanent. Some of his assertions about urban life had long been current in Europe. For example, in the nineteenth century, it was widely believed that London's population could not reproduce itself. The country immigrant was considered by many employers to be innately superior to the London-born, and some writers, influenced by Darwinism, later formulated what amounted to a theory of urban degeneration (Stedman Jones, 1971, pp. 127–32). In fact, however, by and large, such propositions now have little validity. For example, in the Western world cities are clearly producers, just as much as they are consumers, of men; and it is no longer essentially true that marriage tends to be postponed in cities as compared to villages.

Findings from more recent investigations have also proved Wirth wrong on a matter more basic to his general formulation of 'urbanism'. These concern the supposed 'substitution of secondary for primary contacts' in the city, and the supposed 'disappearance of the neighbourhood'. Since the 1930s many studies have shown that both primary contacts and neighbourhoods remain important in the daily life of many city people. Nor is the joining of voluntary associations a *general* feature of town life. Wirth was certainly correct in pointing to the multiplication of voluntary organizations in urban communities, but investigations in Britain, such as Bottomore's (1954) of 'Squirebridge', and Stacey's (1960) of Banbury, show that membership of formally organized groups is widespread only in certain specific sections of the population, namely in the middle class and then principally among the middle-aged. Again, numerous studies have shown that the home still remains, within limits, 'the focus of a whole round of vital activities'. Young and Willmott's study of Bethnal Green

(1957a) is one of the best-known examples. The basic weakness of Wirth's formulation is that it had one central (and defective) assumption in common with Redfield's thinking. As long as we retain the models of rural society and the rural community as our reference-points, we are likely to think of city life as being threatened by 'disorganization'. And as long as we are influenced by this view, we are less likely to develop better perceptions of just how city life *is* organized.

But does this mean that the concept of community as applied to urban studies is invalid? Arguments for and against its use in urban sociology still persist. One particularly forceful view is expressed in Norman Dennis's essay on 'The Popularity of the Neighbourhood Community Idea' (Dennis, 1958). The concept of community, Dennis points out, continues to exercise a great hold on people's minds, despite the fact that it means many different things to different people. In an urban context, it may refer simply to the houses and people located in a given area, even though living near others does not necessarily generate social relationships with them. Normally, though, a community is said to exist only when there is a great deal of interaction between people living near one another. Others think that the community is a *microcosm* of the entire social system, containing all the main elements of the wider society – political, economic, religious, educational, scientific, artistic, ideological, and the like – on a smaller scale, and that because of these multiple ties there is a rich, common life. Again, even though enemies 'interact', community is often taken to imply the existence of agreement over *shared* values – common views, and policies expressing those views – whereby the inhabitants of a community exercise 'autonomous social control' over each other.

These differences in the way people conceptualize community are not just matters of definition: they are part of wider ideologies, and contain important implications for social policy. Thus, at one end, some regard the analysis of local interactions as trivial: it is, they say, the nation-wide (even international) common ideas and social groupings (classes, trade unions, churches, etc.) that are decisive. Enthusiasts for the local community, however, point out that such places do still exist – not only in rural or suburban communities, but in towns like 'Ashton', where in the mid fifties 70 per cent of the work-force were miners (Dennis, Henriques and Slaughter, 1956).

And where community of this kind is absent, they argue, it must somehow be revived. They often believe that crime, delinquency, 'deviance' of all kinds, from premarital pregnancy to vandalism, could be eliminated if only people had a greater loyalty to the community. Hence planners and social administrators have tried to foster the neighbourhood spirit, modelled, usually, on the rural village, and, sometimes, the urban one.

Yet, as Dennis observes, the city today is geographically specialized; the urban locality is not a complete social system. The housing-estate, for instance, is the locus of only a few shared activities. Apart from being a place of residence, and of family life, it may provide schooling, shopping and some leisure facilities. But most people have to leave the local estate or suburb to go to work, to secondary school, to the pictures, and so on. Most key functions, that is, occur at the level of the city, where people interact with quite different others, such as officials and fellow-workers. Many important relationships do not even involve face-to-face contact at all: they occur via forms and documents, as when we communicate with invisible officials, or with 'pseudo-personal' faces on TV. The crucial centres of power also lie at an even higher level of society: outside the framework even of the city. Historically, Dennis argues, the deliberate fostering of local community life has been motivated by fear of class conflict, and a consequent attempt to divert working-class energies into controllable local channels of expression. Underlying such notions is the more fundamental assumption that 'differences, conflict, and the desire for change, are essentially unrealistic and pathological phenomena' (Dennis, 1958, p. 203).

Dennis's views tend to converge with those of numerous other twentieth-century commentators. Robert Nisbet, for instance, argues that the 'quest for community' in the modern world is part of a pervasive and fundamentally conservative ideology, running through a great deal of academic thinking.

Somewhat similarly, Nisbet claims that modern social thought is overly preoccupied with 'personal alienation' and 'cultural disintegration', a tendency which, already very marked in the nineteenth century, has become dominant in the twentieth century. In his view, this tendency now runs through all literature, including sociology in which even apparently quite empirical studies are suffused with a profound regard for established values (Nisbet, 1962). The concern about community, then, reflects much more than an interest in the actual details of the pattern of daily life in village or city: it is part of a moral and intellectual evaulation of the past and of the place we ourselves occupy both in history and in the contemporary social order.

In dwelling on rural studies, we noted how differing underlying assumptions about community have produced quite different analyses. To what extent, we now ask, has the same taken place in urban studies?

The Eclipse of Community?

We have seen that Wirth was acutely aware of the relative newness of the modern city and of large-scale and widespread urbanization in the Western world generally. In part, his continued preoccupation with the rural–urban contrast conception seems strange, until we remember that Chicago in the 1920s and 1930s had received millions of immigrants from predominantly rural backgrounds in Europe – from Bohemia, Poland, Russia, Italy, Ireland, and elsewhere. The rural–urban contrast was, therefore, a first natural mould for much of the work of the Chicago sociologists. Inevitably, also, they were confronted with the process of the assimilation of European immigrants into 'the American way of life'. These immigrants faced a host of problems on account of their foreign and ethnically hetero-geneous origins – problems in many ways similar to those en-countered in some of the major cities of the Third World today. Explorations into the life of the poor and the underprivileged thus led the Chicago sociologists to use the concept of the 'ghetto', not only in relation to areas occupied by Jews, but by all stigmatized ethnic groups. It also led them to develop other urban perspectives: one of these was the 'ecology' of the city, to which we return later; another dwelt on the integration not merely of first-generation immigrants, but also of second- and third-generation foreigners. They saw Chicago as a 'melting-pot', in which immigrants of different generations faced different problems. This interest in turn led them on to examine the processes of social mobility – of 'trickling upwards' – and of occupational specialization and increasing involvement in occupational cultures or sub-cultures, which progressively differentiated some erstwhile immigrants from others. They explored all these themes in great detail; yet, in a general way, they never fully abandoned their underlying rural–urban contrast conceptions. Nor did they pay much attention to the work of other American urban sociologists who had begun to develop new kinds of urban 'community studies' with quite different underlying assumptions about the problems of 'order' and 'organization'. Indeed, Wirth wrote somewhat disparagingly of 'the miscellaneous assortment of disconnected information which has hitherto found its way into sociological treatises of the city' (Wirth, 1963, p. 62).

The 'looseness' of many 'community studies' does, however, have a certain virtue, for it means that they are not shackled by hard-and-fast preconceptions such as those of Redfield and Wirth. They often suggest new ideas, which can then be fed back into further field studies. Concepts and perspectives developed through this kind of checking back and forth between field observations and their interpretations have been referred to by Glaser and Strauss (1968) as 'grounded theory'. Stein puts it well in his book, *The Eclipse of Community*:

On first reading . . . any good community study, the ordinary reader is likely to be overwhelmed by the mass of detailed facts included. Observations pile upon observations so that the guiding themes are not introduced until the final chapters, if they are made explicit at all . . . Community studies cannot be read like geometry text-books in which the argument proceeds from postulates to inferences in exact sequence. Instead, the reader has to allow his impressions of the social structure to grow gradually – *quite as does the field worker in the original situation*. Details have to be mulled over as their meaning changes with shifts in context, and general comparisons must be treated by renewed inspection of the reported data [italics in original] (Stein, 1960, p. 8).

The field sociologist, one might add, learns how the community functions, and what its norms and values are, by following many of the procedures which anyone entering that community is likely to follow, from relying on expert authoritative figures for factual knowledge to acquiring, or being told of, the 'proper' ways of behaviour in that community.

Stein sees the purpose of his book as being to develop 'a framework for relating disparate community studies to each other' and 'to devise an approach to community studies in which each investigation becomes a case study illustrating the working of generalized processes in specific settings'. In order to accomplish this task, he examines a series of well-known American community studies including some from the Chicago school, the Lynds' two studies of *Middletown* and *Middletown in Transition* (published in 1929 and 1937, respectively), and the 'Yankee City' studies by Lloyd Warner and his associates (published from 1941 onwards). In the course of this review, he comments on the seemingly disparate materials before him:

The range of variation found among the many community studies in the literature is great, making the task of reconciling them difficult. Each research report is a synthesis by the author of several orders of data about a particular community, arranged according to his *sense of significant social structures and processes*. This synthesis rarely takes into account the relation of the material to other related studies nor do most research reports contain chapters which satisfactorily present generalized conclusions. *The community sociologist has been a better ethnographer than a theorist and this is probably as it should be.* Weaving the scattered strands of a single community into a coherent picture is in itself a difficult task [our italics] (p. 4).

Despite the lack of any direct connection between most of the studies, Stein is able to show some continuities and resemblances. Starting with the Chicago studies of the 1920s and 1930s, he recalls the nature and rate of growth of the city, at that period, and dwells on some of its consequences for the Chicago sociologists. In his re-analysis of the two studies of *Middletown* and *Middletown in Transition*, he draws our attention to the important differences in the theoretical problems they dealt with as compared to the Chicago studies. Middletown was a town of only 35,000 inhabitants when first studied in 1924, with an almost all-White population largely made up of persons born locally or in the immediate rural hinterland. It had received its initial urban stimulus from a gas boom in 1890, when it was little more than a large village. *Middletown*, then, was essentially *a study of industrialization*, while *Middletown in Transition* dealt with the effects of the economic depression in the 1930s on the pattern of life created by the industrialization reported in the first study. Stein shows how the two studies add up to an intriguing analysis of change in community patterns stemming from quite different sources. He also compares Middletown and Chicago. The foreign origins, the relative lack of skills, and the ethnic heterogeneity of much of the population of Chicago contributed to the emergence of a slum- and ghetto-population which was far more vulnerable to the Depression than any class of Middletowners. The large mass of new Chicagoans simply lacked the educational and cultural equipment to cope with their difficulties, and usually possessed only very localized and incipient forms of 'community' organization.

From the Lynds' work, Stein turns to the 'Yankee City' studies conducted between 1930 and 1935. He dwells in particular on *The Social System of the Modern Factory*, in which Warner and Low (1947) analyse a strike in the local shoe industry which paralysed the entire community. Yet to understand why this strike occurred, the authors had to analyse the local firm's new involvement in the operations of a now larger national company, the state of the national economy, and the increasing bureaucratization of the trade union concerned. Their study of the strike thus led them to study social events and developments outside the community that they never intended to study. This in turn caused them to observe certain features of the community that might well not have emerged at all, or not so centrally, in a more orthodox 'community study' rather than in the study of a *strike*.

Warner and his associates had in fact specifically chosen Yankee City in the first place because they wanted a city where the ordinary daily relations of the inhabitants were not in a state of confusion or rapid change. They wanted to study a 'stable' community. As it turned out, however, they found themselves in Yankee City at a time of severe industrial unrest and were thus unable to study 'stability' as against 'instability'. Instead, they turned their investigation into an attempt to explain why a community with a previous record of weak small-scale union organization, and of 'good' industrial relations, had rapidly transformed itself into a community with strong union organization and antagonistic industrial relations. Stein shows us how events within Yankee City had to be seen as the outcome of an interplay between the growth of bureaucracy in industry and an increase in the control exercised over the local community by external forces in the national economy. In brief, the analysis of Yankee City inevitably became not only a study of urbanism, but also of industrialism and of bureaucracy.

The analyses reviewed by Stein, then, concentrate on *social change* at one particular historical period in the U.S.A. But Stein uses them to compare various communities in differing situations and at various stages of development; and, instead of viewing them as discrete studies, each with its own peculiar historical and cultural features, he compares them, and relates them to each other, in an attempt to produce a model of social process *in* and *of* the urban community more general and more flexible than the rural-urban contrast model. His work is a good example of 'grounded theory' to which we referred earlier, using field reports to illustrate three major general processes in contemporary society: *urbanization, industrialization* and *bureaucratization*. These processes do not necessarily operate together, or in the same way, in other political and economic settings, but in one combination or another they are distinct dimensions of what has come to be called 'modernization' in the economically underdeveloped regions of the world – *in rural as well as urban areas*. Urbanization inevitably affects the hinterland of the towns and cities, as rural peoples are absorbed into the factories and neighbourhoods of the city, and have to adapt to an unfamiliar culture.

It is partly because these processes can be seen to operate at national or even international levels that many sociologists have abandoned the notion of community in their work, whether as a unitary or an evaluative concept. Yet, we may ask, do the processes of urbanization, industrialization and bureaucratization necessarily spell the '*eclipse* of community'? Stein's own view is quite explicit. Writing of *Middletown in Transition*, he notes 'the final breakdown of any sense of character or working of the whole community among its residents' (Stein, 1960, p. 65). Similarly, he remarks that in Yankee City 'relations between [workers and managers] . . . were henceforth to be mediated by impersonal contacts arrived at through negotiation between representatives of the top echelons of the two bureaucracies – management and labour . . .' (p. 90). But this conception of the passing of community does not seem to us to be well founded. As we see the problem, Stein is in his book as a whole drawing attention to two different aspects of community. On the one hand he points to certain specific interlocking structural consequences of urbanization, industrialization and bureaucratization: notably the increased interdependence and decreased local autonomy of previously well-defined territorial communities, and the growing determination of the life-chances of local inhabitants by national and international forces outside local communities. On the other hand, he also points to criteria of a different kind involving subjective notions of personal relationships and identity: the feeling of change experienced by the inhabitants, the feeling of some that they were becoming strangers in their own towns, and the uncertain identity of newcomers. But such sentiments cannot by themselves be taken as marking the eclipse of community. If we do use such criteria on their own, we are in effect again working with a one-sided model of largely undifferentiated and harmonious communities which, as we have seen, is fraught with misleading connotations.

Slums and Suburbs

Patterned and stable relationships exist in conurbations and metropolitan areas, in slums as well as in the middle-class suburbs of major industrial cities, and even among the teeming millions in the cities of the Third World. Indeed, social organization in the kind of slums which were once thought of by the Chicago sociologists as the quintessential zones of '*dis*organization' is impressive. To illustrate this we refer, first, to several studies of poor and underprivileged areas, both in the West and in the Third World. We shall then turn to studies of areas inhabited by the more privileged.

In *The Urban Villagers*, a study conducted in the 1950s, Herbert Gans examined the life of the 'West End', one of the three slum areas which then surrounded the central business district of Boston in the U.S.A. The average Bostonian rarely entered the West End and usually glimpsed it only from highways or elevated trains. From there, he could see only a series of narrow winding streets flanked on both sides by rows of tenements, many poorly maintained, some unoccupied, and opening onto rubbish-strewn alleys: the classic image of a slum area. Here European immigrants – and more recently Blacks and Puerto Ricans – have tried 'to adapt their non-urban institutions and cultures to the urban milieu', in areas Gans describes as 'urban villages'. Often they are described in ethnic terms such as Little Italy, The Ghetto or The Black Belt (Gans, 1962, pp. 3–4).

The population included various ethnic and other identifiable groups: first- and second-generation Italians, Jews, Poles, Albanians, Ukrainians and Greeks; a residue of Irish families which had once been numerous there, but now consisted mainly of old people; some 'pathological households' of people in extreme poverty or suffering from physical or psychological disabilities; post-war newcomers attracted to the area because of its low rents (including Gypsies, 'squatters', artists, 'bohemians' and students); and finally a few middle-class professionals, mainly working in the local hospital.

The area was earmarked for redevelopment, but in the meanwhile the inhabitants organized their lives in a variety of ways: partly along the lines of 'class' divisions as expressed in differences in income, occupation and education; partly on the lines of ethnic affiliation; and partly in terms of *relationships developed through the very necessities of living in the neighbourhood*. The area thus offered a variety of opportunities:

The average West End resident had a choice between anonymity and total immersion in sociability. A few people had moved into the area to hide from the [outside] world, and, while visible to their neighbors, could discourage contact, and thus feel anonymous. Generally speaking, however, neighbors were friendly and quick to say hello to each other ... Deviant behavior, as displayed by the area 'characters', the bohemians, or the middle-class residents was, of course, highly visible. As long as the West Enders were not affected personally, however, they were tolerant. Yet this tolerance was ambivalent: people objected to deviants grudgingly but explained that such kinds of people must be expected in a low-rent neighborhood. At the same time, they found deviant behavior a lively and readily available topic of conversation, which not only provided spice and variety for gossip, but also an opportunity to restate and reaffirm their own values ...
Many West Enders had known each other for years, if only as acquaintances who greeted each other on the street. *Everyone might not know everyone else; but ... they did know something about everyone ... especially within each ethnic group*. Between groups, common residence and sharing of facilities – as well as the constant struggle against absentee landlords – created

enough solidarity to maintain a friendly spirit . . . Alcoholism, mental illness, desertion, the death of a loved one, serious financial difficulties, and even violence were familiar to everyone . . . [and when such] emergencies occurred, neighbors helped each other readily; other problems were solved within each ethnic group. For most West Enders, then, life in the area resembled that found in the village or small town, and even in the suburb [our italics] (Gans, 1962, pp. 14 and 15).

The West Enders themselves did not see their area as a single or discrete neighbourhood. It had long been known as the 'West End' by outsiders, but the residents divided it up for the purposes of everyday life into many inter-related sub-areas, depending in part on the ethnic group which predominated, and in part on the extent to which the tenants in one street had reason or opportunity to visit other streets. But they had little interest in privacy of the kind demanded by middle-class families in suburbia. While they wanted 'to be left alone' on occasions, they were 'not averse to the aural or visual closeness of their neighbors'. As everyone 'knew everyone else's activities' anyway, it was impossible to 'hide anything by physical privacy'. Moreover, 'hearing and seeing their neighbours' activities gave the West Enders a share in the life that went on around them, which, in turn, made them feel part of the group' (pp. 20–21).

At about the same time as Gans was studying the West End of Boston, Valdo Pons was studying a poor and remote corner of a White-dominated African town, Stanleyville (now Kisangani) in the then Belgian Congo (now Zaire). In a detailed study of one avenue – 'Avenue 21' – Pons (1961 and 1969) analysed the nature of neighbourhood relations in an area of the town inhabited mainly by illiterate and semi-literate Africans. Most of the residents were unskilled first-generation migrants from the countryside with little or no previous experience of urban life, though a few were urban born. Obviously, the town of these urban-dwellers was vastly different from Boston, yet certain patterns of social relationships were strikingly similar to those described by Gans. Both in the West End and in Avenue 21, ethnic affiliation and socio-economic status were important in ordering day-to-day life. And in both cases, the experience of *sharing a common local life situation* engendered additional bases of alignment and division.

Stanleyville in the mid 1950s had a population approaching 50,000, of whom some 4,000 were Europeans. The Europeans lived in the central part of the town and the Africans in outlying 'townships', where they were completely segregated from their colonial masters. Over eighty different African 'tribes' were represented in Stanleyville, which was by far the largest single town in the vast northeastern sector of the country. The town was a colonial creation with a short history. In the early decades of this century it was little more than an administrative outpost, but it had developed rapidly after the Second World War. The European inhabitants were employers and 'teachers', the Africans employees and 'pupils' under a strongly paternalist colonial régime. The African 'townships', rigidly administered, allowed and promoted the development of certain kinds of social relationships while inhibiting – and in some cases prohibiting – others. Thus Africans in the 'townships' were often landlords and tenants to each other, but very seldom employers and employees; they were frequently suppliers and consumers of a limited range of petty goods and services, but very seldom on a large scale. They lived in a situation which was, as a result of deliberate Belgian policies, highly conducive to the stabilization of urban families and to their permanent involvement in town life – unlike some other colonial 'towns' where migrant labourers lived in barrack-like 'compounds' without their wives and families. The inhabitants were, however, strictly prohibited from associating for political purposes, and even voluntary associations with social and cultural aims were supervised and controlled by the colonial administration (Pons, 1969, p. 41).

Avenue 21 was a quiet area on the periphery of Stanleyville. It consisted of twenty-three plots of land allocated to individual title-holders who had built small houses of sticks, mud and leaves for their own use and for letting to tenants. Its appearance was fresh and village-like, with palm-trees along the avenue and lush vegetation around the houses. A few of the house owners were residents of long standing, but there was a high turnover of population, as many temporary residents, accommodated either as rent-paying tenants or free of charge as kinsmen, were constantly on the look-out for opportunities to build their own houses or to move into better temporary accommodation. Most inhabitants used Swahili as their *lingua franca* and various vernacular tongues with members of their own 'tribes'. The constant turnover of the population combined with its ethnic heterogeneity to give Avenue 21 an atmosphere of diversity and flux which was further heightened by the intensity of social interaction. A large part of the daily routines of preparing food, cooking, eating and washing was conducted out of doors. People could see what their neighbours were doing, watch comings and goings, and could talk to each other from house to house. There was a great deal of ready contact and co-operation involved in drawing water, in selling and buying petty goods, in the exchange of services, and the like. Privacy and anonymity were thus virtually impossible.

In both the West End of Boston and in Avenue 21, ethnicity and 'class' or status were important principles of cleavage and alignment, but many groupings arose out of other kinds of face-to-face relations. In both communities, people associated and co-operated *across* the barriers of ethnicity and class; equally, they became estranged from each other within these same barriers. The two studies illustrate how, even in very different settings, the routines of local daily life can lead to certain basic underlying similarities in the conduct of members of urban populations characterized by cultural heterogeneity, poverty and a strong element of personal insecurity for many, and a small hard core of well-established residents with clear 'social investments' in the area.

On the other hand, there are equally cities in which ethnic, religious or political cleavages do divide people so categorically that everyday neighbourliness virtually disappears. This is well illustrated by F. W. Boal's study of 'Territoriality in Belfast' (1969). Focusing on a small inner-city area which was in the late 1960s inhabited by both Protestants and Roman Catholics, Boal shows how, *despite their sharing of a common locality*, social segregation between the members of different religious affinities was almost total. Here, then, is a case where loyalties and affiliations to 'outside' groupings and traditions largely override the factors making for social differentiation on the basis of local day-to-day life.

We also have to consider yet other types of inner-city areas. 'Urban villages' like those described by Gans and Pons are not the only kinds of slums. Some can more appropriately be described by Gans's label of 'urban jungles': areas where many inhabitants are 'hiding from society or themselves', and which often provide 'the more disreputable of illegal-but-demanded services for the rest of the community' (Gans, 1962, p. 4). The red light districts or Skid Rows of our cities are characterized by vice and crime, prostitution, gambling, illicit liquor trading and the like; and their populations are often even more transient, more depressed and more brutal than in 'urban villages'. The inhabitants are commonly in constant states either of fear of, or of collusion with, the police.

In his classic pre-war study of 'Cornerville' in 'Eastern City' in the U.S.A., for example, Whyte (1955) shows that the primary function of the police there was not so much 'the enforcement of the law, but the regulation of illegal activities', and that police officers were often subject to 'sharply conflicting social pressures ... [for] the "good people" of Eastern City ... demand that the law be enforced ... [while the inhabitants of Cornerville] have different standards and have built up *an organization which depends upon freedom to violate the law*' (our italics) (p. 138). The trouble with Cornerville, Whyte concludes, was not 'lack of organization but failure of its own social organization to mesh with the structure of the society around it' (p. 273). This conclusion is broadly similar to that drawn by Ellen Hellman (1948) in *Rooiyard*, one of the pioneering studies of African urban life, conducted in a 'Skokiaan' (illicit liquor) yard in Johannesburg in 1933. There, however, because of a very different political and racial situation, the inhabitants lived in fear of the police, rather than in collusion with them.

The squalor of Rooiyard, as described by Hellman, is strongly reminiscent of the notorious slum of 'Little Ireland' in Manchester of the 1830s and 1840s as described by Kay-Shuttleworth (1832, pp. 34–5) and Engels (1845, pp. 93–4). Rooiyard was typical of many 'yards' in those areas of Johannesburg where non-Whites were at that period still allowed to reside. It consisted of 107 rooms which were badly built, poorly ventilated, scarcely maintained by their White owner, unbearably hot in the summer, extremely cold and draughty in the winter, and altogether shocking by any slum standards. The population consisted of 376 men, women and children who between them shared six latrines and two water-taps. There was also a shop in the yard – the property of the same owner – which served as a kind of concession store, for the inhabitants were in effect compelled to use it. If they did not do so, the tenancy of their rooms was jeopardized.

The *leitmotiv* of the life of Rooiyard was the economic struggle. Most of the men held menial poorly-paid jobs. A small proportion of the women also had 'legitimate' occupations, but their main incomes came from the illicit beer-trade:

In every discussion with Rooiyard women their anxiety regarding their 'business' – and by 'business', beer-selling is understood – and their dependence on it were revealed. In the statements that 'beer is Kafir-tea' and that they 'eat from beer', two . . . women expressed concisely and tersely the two motives which make the illicit beer-industry such an integral portion of their lives . . . The one is to satisfy the demands of the male head of the family and to add to his comfort and well-being, and the other is to supplement his earnings which do not cover the necessary expenditure of family living . . . Beer-making, arduous in the extreme, demands the expenditure of considerable energy. The chief labour is involved in cleaning the tin, which is buried several feet below the level of the ground, in digging up the opening every time beer is put in or taken out, and in firmly plastering down the earth again so that the police may not notice any unevenness in the ground. The work demands rapidity and alertness, having to be performed in the intervals between police inspections (Hellman, 1948, pp. 39–40).

Beer-brewing and beer-selling, combined with some casual prostitution, were at the very centre of life in Rooiyard. Without beer-brewing for male customers at night, the residents could not have survived. Their survival was, however, precarious and dangerous, especially for the women. The need to escape detection had, Hellman writes, become 'part of the very fabric of Rooiyard life'; and arrests and convictions – with fines or imprisonment – were regarded as 'normal'. The illegality of the main activity in the yard also made the inhabitants wary of each other, for jealous neighbours could well become police informants against a too-successful brewer. Yet beer-brewing had also given rise to distinct forms of co-operation, as is well illustrated by the institution of 'stockfairs'.

The Rooiyard 'stockfairs' served two purposes: to dispose of any surplus beer unsold over the week-end as the beer could not be preserved for later use, and to act as a kind of savings society. A number of women – members of one 'stockfair' – would meet every

Monday morning, each bringing a stipulated sum of money to that week's 'owner' of the 'stockfair'. The 'ownership' rotated weekly between the members. In return for their weekly contributions to the 'owner', the members drank as much as they wished, and the 'owner' cut her losses over unsold beer from the week-end (ibid., pp. 33–4). Life was difficult and insecure in Rooiyard, yet it was clearly 'organized' and highly sociable.

This conclusion is stressed by most of the studies we have of the poor sections of large urban populations. Similar conditions obtain today in the *favelas* (hillside slums) of Rio de Janeiro as described by Frank Bonilla (1970). In appearance, the *favelas* are rather like the 'shanty-towns' or *bidonvilles* of Africa; unlike Avenue 21, they *look* depressed, consisting largely of shacks made out of odd scraps of wood, tin sheeting, canvas and the like. They are by no means the only poor and depressed areas of Rio de Janeiro; in fact they are to some extent a paradox, for they are partly a result of efforts to eliminate the city's more conventional slum areas. As Bonilla describes them, they 'crawl in cancerous disorder up the steep *morros* (hills), divided by labyrinthine paths and gullies that serve as precarious avenues of movement and [also as] natural sewers', and they appear as 'an incongruous anomaly ... perched above the gleaming glass and concrete of modern Rio' (p. 74). The population, unlike that in the African cases above, is racially mixed: 38 per cent are Blacks; 29 per cent mixed bloods; and 33 per cent Whites. Some Brazilians point to this composition with pride as evidence of the country's 'racial democracy'!

The *favela*-dwellers are 'plagued by all the ills that beset their kind everywhere': illiteracy, malnutrition, alcoholism, criminal violence and so on. But, once again, we find 'some working forms of human co-existence and social cohesion' forged through forced intimacy which breeds both conflict and a variety of forms of organization to deal with common problems (p. 75). Indeed, Bonilla sees the *favela* as an important agency of socialization into city life for migrants from the countryside. But this does not mean that the *favelados* feel closely integrated in the city, or that they participate in the wider society in any regular manner. Their main urban identification is, rather, with the immediate locality of their existence. This is revealed in a curious way by an inquiry reported by Bonilla into the attitudes of a sample of *favelados* towards various institutional agents outside *their* 'social world'. Surprisingly to some, labour unions and university students – two groups that have stood as champions of the poor in Latin America – were viewed as among the *least* helpful, and *least* interested, in the life and welfare of the *favelados*; priests and school teachers were regarded as somewhat more sincere in their efforts to help; but most appreciated of all were police officers. Policemen, we are led to conclude, are in closer touch with, more accessible to, and better understood by, the people living in the harsh reality of the *favelas* than other representatives of the wider society.

Further examples of broadly similar findings could be drawn from all corners of the world. But the above must suffice to illustrate some of the basic principles on both cohesion and division in the varied settings of the urban poor – in 'urban villages' or in 'urban jungles', in 'shanty-towns' or *bidonvilles*, in neatly administered 'townships' or in slum yards, in *favelas* and *villas miserias* or in Indian *bustees*. Accounts such as those we have reviewed reveal that the poor in the cities of the world do not lack a sense of *urban* identity. Nor do they lack social organization. Their life is miserable and wretched, usually far beyond the knowledge or comprehension of the middle classes, and equally beyond their concern. Referring to Manchester in the 1830s and 1840s, Cooke Taylor (1842) wrote that 'in our wisdom we have improved on the proverb "one half of the world does not know how the other half lives", changing it into "one half of the world *does not care* [his italics] how the other half lives"' (p. 164).

Yet, despite the wretchedness of material conditions for the urban poor, there is clearly a degree of *communality* in their lives; a communality which is generally lacking among the more well-to-do. Hence the latter often have recourse to more formal voluntary associations as a means of regulating their activities and staving off objective 'loneliness'. This was clearly in Wirth's mind when he wrote of 'the substitution of secondary for primary contacts' in the process of urbanization. He was partially correct on this point; many urban-dwellers are 'joiners' of formal associations, but 'joining' is a more prominent feature among the relatively well-off than among the poor. We have already noted the selectivity in membership of voluntary associations in two British studies by

Bottomore and Stacey, and evidence from many others points in the same direction. For instance, the abundance of voluntary associations among the educated élite of Stanleyville in the 1950s contrasted sharply with the absence of formal associational life in Avenue 21. A. L. Epstein (1967) similarly noted that on the Zambian Copperbelt the lower one's position on the scale, the fewer were the associations to which one belonged; and, for Latin America, Bryan Roberts's study of two poor areas in Guatemala City (1973) also shows that the poor participate less than the better-off. Again, studies in the U.S.A. show that although Blacks belong to a far greater number of voluntary associations than do Whites, *within* both the Black and White populations affiliation is more frequent in higher than in lower socio-economic strata (Babchuk and Thompson, 1970).

Another common feature reported in several of the above studies – and made particularly clear in Stacey's account of Banbury – is that voluntary associations of the middle classes and the élites tend to have links *between* them, and so constitute bases of influence, if not of direct power, in the community. Once again, we find similarities between towns and cities otherwise as different as, say, Banbury and the new urban areas of the Zambian Copperbelt. So *one* difference between 'slums' and 'suburbs' is, certainly, that social organization in the slums is less regulated by voluntary associations or other relatively 'formal' agencies of social control; and, conversely, casual face-to-face interaction and spontaneous sociability are more prominent as a feature of the overall texture of social life. But there are of course other differences which we now examine by turning to studies of residential areas inhabited by people who are wealthy, either in absolute terms, or by comparison with the inhabitants of the studies we have dwelt upon so far. We will first consider Crestwood Heights in Toronto, and then Churchill Gardens, a council housing estate of tall flats in Pimlico, London.

Crestwood Heights is a prosperous, upper-middle-class suburb where most adult males are independent businessmen, professionals and senior executives who leave their suburban homes daily for nearby Toronto. Thus one major life activity – work – scarcely enters into the analysis. Yet the authors still explicitly refer to the suburb as a community:

Crestwood Heights is officially a separate municipality within a greater metropolitan area, [but] it is also something else. It exists as a community because of the relationships that exist between people – relationships revealed in the functioning of the institutions which they have created: family, school, church, community center, club, association, summer camp, and other more peripheral institutions and services (Seeley *et al.*, 1963, p. 3).

The authors explain how one central feature of social life in Crestwood Heights gives it coherence as a community. Unlike many urban communities – for example, where the factory providing most people with jobs adjoins a housing estate or where there are other strong links between a particular industry and the community (as in 'Ashton') – work is not, in Crestwood Heights, a factor making for local identification. Nor does Crestwood Heights offer the kind of opportunities for social mixing or the necessity to mix, which we noted in the West End of Boston, or in the slums of the Third World. Yet Crestwood Heights is much more than a residential area or mere 'dormitory' of Toronto; people do reside there, but they do more than simply reside. Crestwood Heights is, the authors stress, the locus of a common life and a shared set of activities and concerns. 'Its major institutional focus is upon child-rearing' (p. 4).

Its adults are united in their concern to pass on certain ideals about manhood and womanhood to their children; and all the suburb's institutions are geared, directly or indirectly, to turning out young people to certain specifications that are well accepted in the community.

Educational facilities are always a prime concern in such middle-class areas, where parents are sensitive to the implications of formal education for their children's adult life-chances, even as early as kindergarten. In many Western countries – as in Britain today – education on the national scene is a 'political football', and the solidarity of the middle classes on this issue is most clearly crystallized in suburbia. Similarly, American studies show that substantial middle-class suburban communities usually gain control over the school system in ways which are not open to inner-city residents (Fine, 1958).

Another crucial agent of socialization is the mother: 'Mummy' in middle-class areas, and 'Mum' in working-class areas (Young and Willmott, 1957a). Particularly for women, there is a close identification with one's mother, since children and homes are common interests cutting across the generations; it is from her mother that a young wife acquires traditional (often, therefore, conservative) lore about how to run the home and bring up the children. And this lore is fostered and sustained through networks of gossip in the community – whether these networks are informal and 'on the street' or partially formalized within voluntary associations. Hence researchers speak of the 'matri-central' family, and of the close rapport between the three generations of grandmother, mother and daughter. Fathers may wield more or less 'patriarchal' influence over the family's life, but it is commonly the mother who is there in the home as a regular influence over the children's behaviour. Fathers do of course identify with their sons, but not so much across the generations; nor are they necessarily engaged in the same daily work-routine. These traditional family patterns of town and city dwellers' lives are, however, changing. With some half of married women in Britain at work, substitutes for the traditional mutual services provided by mothers and grandmothers have been developed. 'Convenience foods' and late-opening supermarkets are one response. Poorer women going out to work have to resort to baby-minders, often illegal and nearly always untrained, since public provision of such services is very restricted, while the middle classes achieve their leisure-time away from the children by paying for baby-sitters or arranging 'pools' of families who baby-sit for each other in turn.

Suburban areas are obviously not communities according to the criteria of, say, Redfield or MacIver. Nor are they neighbourhoods of intensive interaction in the streets, or in small restaurants or bars, or in the many opportunities for casual social intercourse as in the localities of the poor. But, as shown in the case of Crestwood Heights, they may be held together by complex networks of social relations organized within local areas and taking place within limited sets of converging institutional structures, especially schools, and sports clubs. They are, thus, 'interest communities'.

The differences between the urban experience of the residents of areas like Crestwood Heights and those in the slums and depressed areas of major cities are extreme, but both are in turn rather different from other types of urban experience, such as living on a council housing estate. The suburb is often thought of in Western society as the dominant type of dwelling-area for people who work in the central city; we often equate suburbia with 'dormitory towns', 'bedroom cities', and essentially middle-class life styles. But it is very misleading to think of all suburbs in this way (Schnore, 1958, p. 29). Vast numbers of people continue to live in inner-city areas, many of which are no longer run-down slums but redeveloped municipal or 'private' estates.

As a striking example of inner-city redevelopment, we take Churchill Gardens, a group of 'high rise' council flats in London, studied by a research team from the Centre for Urban Studies (1964). Their analysis focuses mainly on a lively Tenants' Association which arose among the inhabitants there and contributed to giving them an identity of their own.

The tall flats of Churchill Gardens were built along the Thames Embankment in the late 1940s on the site of a pre-war slum:

Glittering by night, assertive by day, . . . [they] . . . represent an attempt to create a new kind of urban environment . . . There are shops on the ground floors of the long seven-storey blocks which line the main street on the northern boundary of the estate. There are pubs on the site – two old ones, and a new pub with a terrace overlooking part of the estate . . . Both the layout and architecture . . . contribute to the diversity of the scene. The skyline and the ground level views change as one walks from one part to another. Blocks of different heights and facing materials are intermixed. Between them are green open spaces, across which one catches glimpses of the river. There are some playgrounds – including two 'adventure playgrounds' with unusual equipment (pp. 256–7).

Churchill Gardens cannot be taken as typical of 'high rise' developments since the war. On the contrary, apart from its unusually imaginative design, the authors stress that they chose to study it partly because from the beginning it 'had an exceptionally vigorous Tenants' Association' (p. 258). But studies of a-typical cases often do shed light on the nature of more typical ones. Over four in ten of male earners in Churchill Gardens were non-manual workers, mostly in relatively low-status occupations such as clerks and salesmen, and a slender majority were manual workers. The social class composition of the population was thus rather different from that of most municipal housing estates in Britain, and its relative heterogeneity – resulting in a strong awareness of what was seen by some as the injustice of means-testing – was an important factor giving rise to the Tenants' Association which first developed as a 'protest' movement against differential rents. But the Association did not remain a purely protest organization; at the time of the study, eight years after its formation, some 80 to 90 per cent of the households belonged to the Association, which was by then publishing a monthly bulletin and running whist, chess and other games clubs, a tennis club and a badminton club, a drama society, an Old People's Club, groups of Cubs, Brownies and Girl Guides, and a Boys' Club. No attempt had been made to cut off the estate by organizing activities only for residents and some of the clubs drew their members from a much wider area. Situated in the centre of London, it is not surprising that Churchill Gardens was not a closed community or a self-contained world of its own. What is of particular interest is that, despite the manifest involvement of its residents in the life and work of the metropolis, it still achieved its own identity and developed its own set of voluntary organizations.

It would, however, be quite misleading to suggest that local communities are always vigorous and strong. Not all city-dwellers live in 'urban villages' or 'urban jungles', in pleasant suburbs like Crestwood Heights; or in 'high rise' flats with successful neighbourhood organizations. Many attempts to establish tenants' associations or community councils have been dismal failures, as Dennis emphasizes (1958, pp. 77 ff.); and there are in our towns and cities wide expanses of residential areas which appear featureless, and whose inhabitants seem to lack identity and have no grass-roots institutions.

We know, too, that life in urban areas often creates tragic problems for the 'unattached' and members of the 'lonely crowd' – to use the term coined by Riesman, Glazer and Denney (1950) in a study of 'the changing American character'. The simple fact is that most towns and cities have areas of drabness *as well as* arresting townscapes, and that 'anomie' and personal loneliness are as prominent features of urban life as are rich and fulfilling interpersonal experiences and intensive small-group participation. This may seem paradoxical at first sight, but it is easy to understand once the complexity of urban life is appreciated. L. S. Lowry's paintings of industrial Lancashire, and of Salford in particular, are often assumed to be faithful depictions of 'loneliness in the crowd', but Robert Roberts in *The Classic Slum* (1971), also based on Salford, conveys a very different picture: one of poverty and material deprivation, but certainly not of loneliness. Yet it would be difficult to claim that Lowry was 'right' and Roberts 'wrong', or vice versa.

This conflict of perspectives upon city life is a particular instance of the general sociological 'dialectic' we discussed at the beginning of the book: the interplay between objective structure and our ideas and feelings about them. One attempt to cover both aspects of urban social reality is Hunter's *Symbolic Communities* (1974), a study which attempts to analyse the whole metropolitan area of Chicago in terms of three distinct 'dimensions' of its over-all social structure: its 'ecological structure', its 'organizational structure', and its 'symbolic structure'. The ecological dimension refers, of course, to the distribution of population and the relation of differing types of spatial or geographical areas to each other within the metropolitan area. The 'organizational structure' refers to the total complex of institutions and organizations – churches, voluntary associations, recreational facilities, service agencies, local newspapers and the like – which exist in the local areas of all large cities. Finally, the 'symbolic structure' refers to the collective representations and moral sentiments shared by the residents of different areas. We shall dwell on Hunter's discussion of the third of his three 'dimensions' in particular.

Taking the seventy-five local areas of Chicago first delineated by members of the Chicago School in the 1920s, Hunter attempts to determine the extent to which residents' definitions and perceptions of these 'local communities' have changed or persisted over time. He also tries to assess their evaluations of, and attachments to, these areas. In essence he poses three questions: (a) how do residents delineate 'local communities' in the sprawling conurbation of Chicago? (i.e., what are their *cognitive* definitions?); (b) on what bases do they *evaluate* them, as 'good' or 'bad', 'desirable' or 'undesirable'? (c) to what extent do they express *sentiments* of attachment to, and identify with, these localities?

In all three respects, Hunter found appreciable variations in outlook as between different sections of the population when divided, for example, into categories of age and sex, of Blacks and foreign-born Whites, of high and low economic status, and of length of residence.

He then attempts to relate this 'symbolic structure' of Chicago to the social positions of the residents *both in their respective local communities and in the city as a whole*; and shows that cognitive definitions, evaluations of areas, and sentiments of attachment to, and identity with, localities are all related to *both* the local and the non-local social positions of the inhabitants. Thus, for example, the evaluation of various localities as 'good' or 'bad' is more marked on the part of people with positions of high social standing in the city as a whole, whereas attachment to particular localities – 'good' or 'bad' – is, not surprisingly, highest among those who belong to local associations and have the most local links of friendship and kinship there (p. 183).

More generally, Hunter claims that there are in the 'symbolic structure' of Chicago various '*levels* of community'. The highest level includes large 'regions' within the city, such as 'the Roseland area' or 'the West Side', or 'the South Side'. Then there is a level which is approximately the size of the seventy-five 'community areas' delimited by his predecessors of the Chicago School in the 1920s, and he calls these 'local communities'. Below these are yet two lower levels: smaller residential units which he refers to as 'neighbourhoods' and even smaller distinguishable areas he calls 'social blocks'. Far from accepting the view that mass society leads to the dissolution of community, Hunter claims, on the basis of this study, that life in a complex modern society provides the city-dweller with the possibility of a great variety of identities:

Although we may have 'lost' the unique natural urban community of the past, with its strong local culture containing a common name rich in connotations and a distinct set of shared 'natural boundaries', we have 'found' in its place a dynamic system of 'symbolic communities' that meaningfully organizes the complex and rapidly changing social and spatial milieu of today's urban resident (p. 186).

In another study also based on Chicago and carried out with Suttles, Hunter discusses some of the principles according to which local identities are established and maintained (Hunter and Suttles, 1972). They argue that residential areas do not usually gain their identities simply because of certain gross features that mark them off from other areas. Such clearly-distinctive local communities and neighbourhoods do exist, but many which recognize themselves as clearly distinct in fact differ from each other only in slight degree – for example, in the proportion of wealthy residents or of Blacks living there. Nevertheless, these slight differences are seized upon as indicating a separate identity. Thus community or neighbourhood identity is not something which necessarily arises 'within itself': it arises by virtue of comparing one's own area with others. To some extent then, neighbourhoods and local communities acquire their identities by virtue of contrasts people draw, exaggerate, and even construct, as between their own and other areas; and they do so through what Suttles and Hunter call an 'on-going commentary between insiders and outsiders, between residents and non-residents' (pp. 50–51). Not *all* residents, however, define and evaluate local areas in the same way, or identify with them to the same degree: many are indifferent about their localities, perhaps more so than in the past.

Urban Imagery

While the exploration of the subjective aspects of urban life has received less attention from sociologists than have the objective structures of towns and cities, a major stimulus was given to this field of study by Anselm Strauss's *Images of the American City* (1961), and *The American City* (1968), a follow-up 'source-book' of urban imagery. Unlike Hunter, Strauss is more interested in the historically-rooted 'images' of towns and cities as wholes than in the symbolic structure of neighbourhoods and local communities. Indeed, his interests are even broader, and extend to the ways in which Americans, throughout their history, have developed their *conceptions about city life in general*.

Strauss points out that urban dwellers do not simply 'exist' in their towns and cities; they *use* their urban environment, and they do so for a perplexing variety of purposes. The different interests they have govern what they take notice of, and they select some aspects of their surroundings for attention while suppressing others. In doing so, they inevitably interpret and evaluate their environment and embody these ideas into 'mental maps', 'mental directories', and the like. Some of these they construct for themselves; others are part of the cultural heritage of the city concerned; and yet others are only shared by certain categories of people or by members of sub-cultural communities and classes within a city. 'Imagery' consists of sets of constructions in our minds or within our imaginations, but these seldom resemble the static pictures of a still photographer. These constructions are, to be sure, reductions and simplifications: as Strauss puts it, 'expressive declarations of [a city's] literal incomprehensibility', for cities as wholes are 'inaccessible to the imagination unless reduced and simplified' (Strauss, 1961, p. 8). But the images are often unclear and ambiguous, and in some ways this renders them more valuable for us, for it allows us to manipulate and define them as we wish for various differing purposes. We have to note, too, that they may be of several different kinds: temporal, economic, cultural, spatial, and so on.

Taking Chicago as his main example, Strauss illustrates how multifaceted the imagery of a city can be: Chicago is a great midwestern industrial and commercial centre, but it is also a cosmopolitan and world city both in aspiration and in attainment; it is the home of so many, and such diverse, ethnic groups as to make it the world's 'second largest Polish city', its 'sixth largest German city', and its 'second largest Swedish city'. At the same time, it is also a prairie city, an old city for some, but a new and unfinished city for others. One of the crucial implications of such a complex set of images is explicitly drawn out by Strauss:

When Chicago's residents lay stress upon one or more of those images, they also systematically *understress* certain other images; ... To say that certain urban populations within Chicago link, stress, and avoid certain public images is already tantamount to saying that these images have functions and histories not immediately apparent [our italics] (p. 34).

Another reason for diversity in the imagery surrounding a city is that the vantage-points of the 'image makers' – as of the residents themselves – are liable to vary, and of course to change over time. In making this point, Strauss traces the manner in which novelists have delineated various perspectives on New York – as a place of diversity, as a place of fun and adventure, as a place contrasting with the countryside, and so on. Dwelling in particular on John Steinbeck's experiences of New York, he explains how each time Steinbeck came there he was, in some sense, a different man, and that on each occasion 'he perceived and therefore used the city quite differently'.

But, Strauss writes, 'perceived the city is not quite the right term; conceived would be better' (1968, p. 5). And this particular correction – his preference, on second thoughts, for the notion of 'conception' rather than 'perception' – is significant, for it repeats an important point we have already made: that people are not passive observers of their environment, but active pragmatic users of it, and therefore have to bring order into the ways they think about it.

A city, therefore, is not the same physical fact, seen in the same way by everybody, or even by the same person at different times. Our conceptions of any particular city are mediated by our social positions inside or outside that city, by our knowledge and use of that city, and by our conceptions of other particular cities as well as of cities in general. Sets of views tend to crystallize, sometimes in quite contradictory constellations. In Stanleyville, for example, some residents saw the town both as positively attractive in itself and as a refuge from the difficulties and hardships of village life; others were overawed by it, even frightened, shocked, perplexed, and aggrieved by the demands that living there made on them and by the relative disregard in daily life for the time-honoured morals of tribal life. Yet others, who had visited or lived in very much larger and more vital cities, tended to regard Stanleyville as a rather quaint and backward town (Pons, 1956, pp. 667–9; and 1969, pp. 192–4).

In some towns and cities, the dominant imagery may strongly emphasize the notion of community; in other cases not. What these variations are, is, of course, something that can only be discovered by empirical investigation. In one form or another, however, towns and cities carry sets of images – whether positive or negative – which are often very complex and which affect the daily responses of the inhabitants. But variations in these responses, and the fact that towns and cities in the modern world are not unitary entities, do not necessarily mean that certain general images may not be widely shared, whatever the positions occupied by various people in the urban social structure and in any variety of communal sub-cultures. Moreover, while images may change rapidly they may also endure, with greater or lesser strength, for considerable periods of historical time.

A striking example of a city which developed a coherent image of itself that endured over a considerable period is Manchester in the nineteenth century. The dominant image was embodied in phrases which identified Manchester as the 'workshop of the world', and the 'symbol of a new age', expressed in maxims such as 'What Manchester does today, England does tomorrow'. Abroad there was the American saying that 'Manchester flogs England, and England flogs creation', and the German term '*das Manchestertum*', which reflected the character attributed to the city – one of industriousness, ruthless single-mindedness, and dedication to work and profit.

The social significance of such subjective expressions of the nature of particular towns and cities has received little systematic study from sociologists; in Britain, virtually none. Yet the frequency with which terms like 'community identity', 'civic pride', and 'local consciousness' are used in fiction, journalism and television documentaries must lead us to query whether they refer to real and important phenomena which call for study in conjunction with urban social structures, institutions and relationships. Certainly, *city* identities persist; and the fierce partisan support given to football and other local sports teams throughout the world suggests that the city is as much a ready-made focus for identity as either the village or the small town on the one hand, or the nation-state on the other. Cities are certainly not characterless, 'lonely' wastelands.

But it is not enough, for sociological purposes, merely to record the images that exist. We are also interested in how they are socially produced and communicated, and how they are *used* for various social purposes, which include their use as *instruments of power and control*. Again, this is an area of inquiry which has attracted relatively little attention from urban sociologists. But there are exceptions. One of the most striking and interesting is Lloyd Warner's *The Living and the Dead* (1959), the last volume of the 'Yankee City' studies, to which we have already referred. Here, Warner attempts a general analysis of the symbolic life of Americans as portrayed in that city. He ranges over a wide area of symbolism associated with life and death, with politics, with Protestantism, with sexuality and, indeed, with the totality of community life.

In analysing the construction and maintenance of the town's symbolic representations and cultural heritage, Warner dwells on Yankee City's Tercentenary, which took place during the period of his research, as a key occasion on which important social values were dramatically expressed over five days of parades, games, religious ceremonies, sermons and speeches, and which culminated in a grand historical procession watched by two or three times as many people as the entire population of the town. To grasp the significance of the procession, Warner studied the way in which each presentation was selected and produced. This involved him in investigating several distinct phases of the Tercentenary. The first was its early planning and organization, and the assignment of authority for its execution; the second was the period of preparation; and the third and final phase was the celebration itself. Through detailed analyses of all three phases, Warner is able to show how the conceptions put forward by the people of Yankee City were literally *created by social processes operating among them* at the time, for the nature and form of celebrations were planned and executed only after lengthy discussions on innumerable committees. The main interest of the leaders of Yankee City was manifestly not in the 'true' history of their town, but in what Warner refers to as its 'past made present and perfect' (Warner, 1959, p. 156).

In drawing on American studies, however, we are using literature which comes from a 'pro-urban' rather than an 'anti-urban' culture, with underlying value-judgements which are themselves only part of a wider conception of the nation's values. In contrast to the U.S.A., there is in Britain, and there has always been, a strong 'anti-urban' sentiment in the national culture. As Ruth Glass (1955) points out, the 'new urban colonization of the nineteenth century . . . [failed] to accept the concept of urban civilization', a failure which continues to this day, and which, she considers, may account for the overriding concern of British urban sociologists with the small-scale phenomena of urban life. 'Sociologists certainly share the nostalgia for the intimate, apparently discrete groups – the family, kinship and neighbourhood' (p. 19). This concern with the small-scale and personal levels of life may also account for the absence of British studies on the imagery of cities as wholes.

In this section we have considered lines of urban research which are poorly developed. The great bulk of urban research continues to concentrate on simply describing the various zones or 'social areas' of cities – residential or industrial, middle-class or working-class, ethnic ghettos or higher educational campus areas, slums or 'downtown' entertainment districts – very often without explaining the meaning of these areas either to those who use them or to those who do not. Yet modern research into deviance has shown that quite different 'images' may be held by different sets of people, and that however widely held, they can be quite false stereotypes rather than accurate pictures of reality. Thus the 'moral panics' which break out from time to time – about football hooliganism or battles between mods and rockers – are often wildly inflated by the mass media (Cohen, 1972), and some areas of our cities similarly acquire reputations which may be at variance with the actual quality of life there. Television documentaries and popular writings about our cities, and the 'social worlds' within them, are more numerous and influential than sociological studies. The discrepant accounts they offer also leave people confused as to how valid and reliable they may be as assessments of what actually 'goes on'. Studies of social work practice, for example, have revealed a vicious circle which begins by 'labelling' those who fail to conform to the often arbitrary definitions of respectability as 'problem personalities' and 'problem families', with the consequence that they are then 'dumped' in certain housing estates or slum areas, depriving them further of material and cultural facilities. Their passivity or 'anti-social' behaviour, in such milieux, is then blamed on their inability 'to cope', and on individual shortcomings rather than on cultural deprivation (Damer, 1974). 'Processing' individuals and families in this way has been seen, in many sociological studies, as a 'self-fulfilling' procedure which may well produce 'anti-social' behaviour, much as teachers' expectations about children from middle-class homes stimulates higher-than-average educational performance from such pupils. Images – 'true' or 'false' – thus affect the behaviour of people and are therefore important and worth studying: 'myths' and 'realities' constantly interact. Sociology, then, must also be constantly concerned with the dialectic between the two.

Ecological Studies

We have moved, so far, from detailed studies of small localities within large urban agglomerations to studies of images of cities as wholes. We now turn to a quite different approach to the study of urban organization, namely 'urban ecology', which was central to the work of the Chicago School in the 1920s and 1930s, and which has been widely influential since then. Ecological studies concentrate on classifying the different areas of a city in terms of their dominant patterns of use, and on the relationship *between* these areas – whether industrial, residential, commercial or recreational.

The early empirical studies of the Chicago School are so well known (and now so dated) that we have preferred to examine more contemporary studies in this tradition, of very different kinds of cities: of Paris, as studied by Chombart de Lauwe and his colleagues (1952), and of Cairo as analysed by Janet Abu-Lughod (1971).

In *Paris et l'agglomération Parisienne*, Chombart de Lauwe *et al.* delineate the populations and sub-populations of Paris in terms of social rather than administrative areas. For them, the population of Paris consists of *all the people for whom Paris is a centre of attraction*, and they thus include in their conception of Paris not only those who live there, but all who commute there daily, or who ever visit it for whatever reason. Once we accept that we must include all those who *use* Paris – or parts of Paris – in our analysis, we realize that there are innumerable interest-groups which pursue enormously diverse interests within any modern city. Some of these groups are concentrated in particular local areas, but other interests bring together people from all over the city, and beyond: supporters of football teams, members of political parties, or whatever. A community in this sense thus refers to those people who are linked together in any particular sets of activity or institutions, or those who share cultural characteristics which shape their behaviour or lead others to act in special ways – whether positively as, say, in the adulation of popular heroes or negatively as with stigmatized ethnic groups. There are as many communities, then, as there are interests and activities binding sets of people together (Webber *et al.*, 1964, pp. 108–20).

But in so far as boundaries remain significant, transportation routes play a large part in determining them. In the case of Paris, Chombart de Lauwe and his associates are led to liken the city to a roughly circular area with tentacles which protrude along railway lines and main roads. They also point out that Paris does not have one centre, but several. There is a business centre, a university centre, an industrial centre, an arts centre and so on. Further, Paris plays a number of different roles both in relation to France as a whole, and in relation to the entire modern world. Paris is, the authors point out, a part of the process of centralization of French society that the Napoleonic era consolidated.

The authors then divide the city into seven roughly concentric zones. In establishing these zones, they use differing criteria: the density of population, the time taken to travel to work, the relationship between areas in which people live and those in which they work, and so on. Thus, Zone 1 covers the *noyau* (the heart), the business core of the city (limits about 1 to $2\frac{1}{2}$ km. from the centre), and Zone 7 covers the extreme outskirts of Paris (in some places 30 or more kilometres from the centre), an area which they describe as being 'influenced by the proximity of Paris but not yet really integrated into it'. Between Zones 1 and 7 are other zones, roughly concentric, of a kind familiar to all who know any large metropolitan city.

In passing, we may point out that the relationship between any town or city and its hinterland always generates special problems. Thus, for example, in Britain, attempts have been made to maintain 'green belts' around London and other major cities as playgrounds for the urban dweller. In China, on the other hand, the relationship between city and country has been deliberately fostered in such a way as to bring the workers of the city and the peasants in the communes into closer relationship. No less than 190 communes are included within the municipal territory of Shanghai, and Tientsin covers an administrative area two-thirds the size of the Netherlands (Worsley, 1975, pp. 169–92).

Most ecological studies have, however, stopped short of examining the relationship between town and country. Nor are the historical, as against the contemporary, reasons for spatial arrangements always adequately analysed. The re-building of Paris in the nineteenth century under Baron Hausmann, for instance, took into account the revolutionary record of the city: the broad boulevards were constructed with an eye to counter-insurgency as well as aesthetics! (Chapman and Chapman, 1957.) But Chombart de Lauwe and his associates concentrate instead on the contemporary ecological structure of the city, distinguishing, also, between different sets of social areas which cut *across* the concentric zones, or are embedded *within* one or more of them. They equally point to various irregularities in the dominantly concentric pattern of spatial organization in Paris, caused either by the absorption of formerly independent towns or by the spontaneous growth within them of *quartiers* (neighbourhoods) with distinctive populations or distinctive physical features. Thus there are *quartiers* that are *bourgeois* as against those of the *ouvriers*; there are numerous ethnic *quartiers*, as well as *quartiers* which derive their distinctive characteristics from the fact that they are centred on a factory, or a park, or a square. This study of Paris, like many ecological studies in various parts of the world, is not a study of community in any of the senses previously discussed in this chapter; obviously, as we have noted, there are numerous overlapping and interpenetrating 'interest communities' in Paris, but the authors do not dwell on these.

The ecological analysis of cities is a vital but only a preliminary 'mapping' exercise in analysing city life sociologically. It does not *explain* how the pattern of social relations within different zones and social areas is sustained in everyday life or how the life of the city as a whole is co-ordinated and integrated. Nor do standard ecological exercises even begin to analyse the historical processes which created the cities concerned. This is not surprising, for any attempt to comprehend the full development of a city as complex as Paris over centuries would require a totally different conceptual framework or series of frameworks. As Chombart de Lauwe and his colleagues themselves stress, Paris exists as a product of the totality of European and even world history, but their own study had more limited aims and objectives.

A similar fascinating use of the ecological approach, this time to a non-Western city, is Abu-Lughod's *Cairo: 1001 Years of the City Victorious* (1971), a study which draws special attention to legacies from the past, even though it, too, does not extend its scope to a full historical analysis:

Cairo, far more than any Western City of comparable size, is a city of contrasts and contradictions, of extremes and anachronisms. Egypt is a society deeply committed to a basic reorganization of its economy, its social structure, and its political community. Is it any wonder, then, that both the old and new orders (and their intermediaries) should exist side by side in its capital city? Cairo combines the passing traditionalism and agrarianism of an Egypt that has existed for centuries with the industrial modernism of an Egypt yet-to-be. Reflecting this, her population consists of diverse groups, some barely emerged from village life, some still immersed in the small worlds of traditional neighbourhoods, some cut off from both village and neighbourhood and adrift in the demi-monde, some striving for mastery over the mechanical paraphernalia of the modern world, others seeking the harder mastery over its ideas and ideals, and a few, the most sophisticated, engaged in the challenging task of synthesizing the old and the new, the indigenous and the 'imported' (p. 182).

In Cairo the successive incorporation of the city into the empires of a succession of conquering powers, its cosmopolitan character as a trading city at the crossroads of the Mediterranean, its character as a centre of religious learning, and its dominant role in industrial and political life, have produced an ecological pattern very different from that of either Paris or Chicago. Different ethnic communities, often non-Muslim, tended to live in their own districts of the city, with their own representatives who dealt on their behalf with the central city authorities right into the nineteenth century. As in the case of all great Muslim cities, too, Cairo, unlike the cities of the West, was surrounded by a hinterland which included an important nomadic pastoral population, as well as a peasantry. Hence defence against nomad attack was a primary concern, reflected in the presence, at the heart of the city, of the huge Citadel; and the religious importance of the city is reflected not only in its mosques and universities but in its cemeteries, which are immense and elaborate. Today, these cemetery areas are populated and are the rough equivalent of the *bidonvilles* of many other African cities or of the *favelas* of South America.

Abu-Lughod depicts Cairo as consisting of thirteen major 'sub-cities', each of which has a distinctive 'life-style', different from that in adjacent areas. These differences are paralleled by differences in the physical appearance of the areas, in the kinds of housing and shopping facilities, and even in the dominant dress that their inhabitants wear and which often symbolizes different religious beliefs (p. 188). The thirteen 'cities within the city' follow a geographic pattern which has grown out of the past history of urban development of Cairo and which, for all its flux, shows a remarkable degree of persistence and reinforcement. Despite this variation from one 'sub-city' to another, Abu-Lughod also attempts to generalize about types of inhabitants and their origins. In particular, she distinguishes between three main types of inhabitants represented in different proportions in the thirteen 'sub-cities'. These main types are the people of 'rural' origin, the 'traditional urban', and the 'modern or industrial urban'.

The particular interest of Abu-Lughod's study, compared with those of Western cities, is that it shows how ecological processes are at work there, and have been for centuries, but that other principles of distribution and organization, pre-dating modern history, also have to be taken into account in order to find any coherence in the city of today. Any city, then, whether as ancient as Cairo or not, calls for analysis in terms of historical as well as contemporary processes.

Urbanization and Industrialization

As soon as we begin to think of cities as creations of history, we encounter a new range of fundamental problems, for cities, as we have seen, are not all of a piece: they have to be located within a cultural, economic, and historical context. This we illustrate by examining two cities – Calcutta of the mid 1950s and Manchester of the 1840s – which are extremely different from each other. Yet both are in fact 'modern', not ancient cities. We have already seen that *industrialization* and *urbanization* have often developed hand-in-hand. But they do not necessarily or inevitably go together. S. N. Sen's *The City of Calcutta* (1960) describes a vast city – the second largest in India and eleventh in size in the world – which has developed quite independently of industrialization: so much so that it has been labelled 'a premature metropolis' (Bose, 1965, p. 90). Sen's study is based on a series of socio-economic surveys conducted in the mid 1950s. These did not concentrate on the separate social areas of the city, as in ecological studies, but focused on *city-wide* processes. In the Manchester of the nineteenth century, on the other hand, we have a city which was the world's first industrial metropolis, and we are fortunate that Engels has left us a very thorough contemporary study of it in *The Condition of the Working-class in England* (1845).

The origins of Calcutta were colonial, dating from about 1700, when the British East India Company set up a Presidency in Bengal with Calcutta (up till then little more than a cluster of villages) as its headquarters. Later it became the seat of the British government for the whole of India, and remained so until 1912 when the government moved to New Delhi. The population grew from about 10,000 in 1701 to 140,000 in 1801, to about 949,000 in 1901, and to about a million in 1931. During the 1930s there was rather more rapid growth, associated with unemployment and underemployment *in the hinterland*. Migration to the city then increased greatly, firstly as a result of the Bengal famine during the years of the Second World War, and again in 1949–50 during and after the troubles following independence and the partition of India and Pakistan (Goldthorpe, J. E., 1975, p. 122). Then, for a period, migration to Calcutta did not rise as fast as to other Indian cities. In the decade preceding 1965, Calcutta's population grew by only 8 per cent as against Bombay's rate of about 39 per cent. Nonetheless, in the 1950s, by the time of Sen's studies, Calcutta had a population of over $2\frac{1}{2}$ millions spread over an area of about 32 square miles, and a new 'explosion' in the late 60s and early 70s has brought today's population of the whole of the Calcutta agglomeration to over 7 millions.

Our normal image of the 'exploding' cities of the Third World is, of course, a very general one – usually of large centres 'draining' their countryside hinterlands. This is, however, scarcely true of Calcutta; in the decade preceding 1965 when the city grew by only 8 per cent, the population of Bengal surrounding it jumped by approximately 40 per cent. Some consequences and concomitants of its peculiar pattern of growth – even as compared to India's other major cities – are reflected in Sen's statistics of the 1950s, which show that many of the demographic features of Calcutta's early history persisted: a large sex-disparity (65 per cent men and 35 per cent women), a small proportion of children (hence a large proportion of earners in its *total* population); and a very low proportion of workers in industry. In fact, *only 2·8 per cent of earners in Sen's samples were factory workers*, and only 16 per cent were engaged in any kind of manufacturing (even though the definition of manufacturing included such operations as the preparation of sweetmeats in small establishments and the making of food-products like fried rice and gramflour). By far the largest single category of workers consisted of those engaged in 'distribution of consumer goods' (25·5 per cent). Hence the biggest single male occupational group was *owners of retail shops* (9 per cent), closely followed by *domestic servants* (8·8 per cent). All families with incomes of more than 200 rupees per month (the average per capita income was 560 rupees) kept servants. The corresponding figures for all women *earners* were as follows: domestic servants and cooks 35·4 per cent; prostitutes 10·4 per cent; teachers 8 per cent; followed by nurses and midwives and sweepers with percentages of 4 or less, and a large variety of other smaller categories.

About a quarter of the population of Calcutta lived a single life without their families, and these single persons (mostly men) made up more than a half of the households in the city; 40 to 45 per cent of the population were first-generation migrants. As to residence, only about 7·5 per cent of all households 'lived in separate flats or complete houses with . . . amenities like a bathroom, water tap, kitchen and separate toilet'; about a quarter of the population lived in *bustees* (groups of huts), not only in slum areas but also cheek-by-jowl with modern apartment blocks or houses of the well-to-do; in some *bustees* the density of population was as high as 690 persons per acre, a figure three or four times as high as in the slums of most modern Western cities (Sen, 1960, pp. 1, 60 ff., 88 and 256 ff.; and Goldthorpe, J. E., 1975, pp. 121 ff.).

What these figures reflect is that Calcutta is essentially a commercial, mercantile, administrative and transport centre. It handles more than 40 per cent of India's total export tonnage, and is the nerve centre of the coal-mines and the tea-plantations of Bengal, which, though situated far away, are managed and financed by the business houses of the city.

Somewhat paradoxically, at first sight, Sen found that migrants had a lower unemployment rate than inhabitants born in Calcutta. The answer, however, is simply that migrants who cannot find a job go home, while many of the Calcutta-born residents have some education and thus can aspire to more than unskilled work. Being a commercial and administrative centre, Calcutta is a special, perhaps extreme, case, but some of its features are found to a lesser degree in many cities of the Third World. It has some resemblance, too, to conditions in London in the nineteenth century, where, as Stedman Jones (1976) has shown, factory employment was less important than in the northern industrial cities, such as Manchester, or the smaller mill and coal-mining towns like Oldham (Foster, 1968 and 1974).

A further seeming paradox is that Calcutta's average *per capita* income is 560 rupees, double the national average. The great increase in poverty in India in recent decades has been in the rural areas, and urban studies help us to understand why *peasant* discontent has been so significant. Yet the employment situation and living conditions of the urban population are scarcely privileged, even for those with regular wage-employment who have sometimes been called the 'labour aristocracy' of the Third World. Their wages are often so low that they supplement them by secondary jobs ('moonlighting') or by other kinds of 'informal' income-opportunities. These include illicit or socially-disapproved activities such as crime and prostitution, which are important 'industries'. To raise living standards in Calcutta would require not only massive job-creation, but also the provision of urban services on an immense scale. Thus Sen calculated that India would have had to spend some six to seven per cent of the funds available for the entire nation under the Second Five-Year Plan to give a decent job and housing to the population of Calcutta *alone*. And modern, capital-intensive technology, as in Calcutta's docks, has grown too slowly to absorb more than very small proportions of job-seekers. Such, then, are some of the problems, viewed broadly, of urbanization *without* industrialization.

By contrast, our final case-study is of Manchester in the 1840s, then an extreme case of a rapidly-industrializing city. Engel's outstanding pioneer work does not treat the city as if it existed in isolation, but locates its growth firmly within the context of the development of capitalist society at large. At the same time, it clearly delineates the different areas within the city in a way that foreshadowed modern ecological studies.

Though it is impossible to give the beginnings of Manchester as an industrial city any precise date, it had begun to develop as such by the 1770s. Before then it had been little more than a thriving market town. Its leading citizens lived in the town centre, while its more modest habitations were mainly located on its outer periphery. But with the development of industrial capitalism in the late eighteenth and early nineteenth centuries, this position was completely reversed, and the 'new' Manchester rapidly developed a dense concentration of slums in central areas of the city, adjoining the new mills. The middle and upper classes moved out into the countryside, initiating a pattern of divorce between place of work and place of residence still typical of the more favoured classes in Manchester, as in all industrial cities. This 'flight' of the wealthier population has contributed to the decay of the inner-city areas, exacerbated by the flow of local taxation (rates) to the suburban municipalities. Such change was already well advanced when Engels first set foot in Manchester in the early 1840s. By that time the population had risen to over 400,000 from a mere 30,000 or 40,000 in the 1770s and 1780s – an urban explosion typical of the contemporary Third World, though, as we have seen, not usually accompanied there by industrialization.

The changes that had taken place in Manchester in a few short decades are vividly recorded by Engels:

Manchester contains at its heart a rather extended commercial district, perhaps half a mile long and about as broad, and consisting almost wholly of offices and warehouses. Nearly the whole district is abandoned by dwellers, and is lonely and deserted at night; only watchmen and policemen traverse its narrow lanes with their dark lanterns. This district is cut through by certain main thoroughfares upon which the vast traffic concentrates, and in which the ground level is lined with brilliant shops. In these streets the upper floors are occupied, here and there, and there is a good deal of light upon them until late at night (Engels, 1969, p. 79).

Around this commercial area, Engels recounts, there were 'unmixed working people's quarters, stretching like a girdle, averaging a mile and a half in breadth . . . ' Beyond these were the areas inhabited by the middle and upper classes which, over the course of a few decades, had leap-frogged over the areas of working-class houses. He then describes the changing nature of the main arterial roads, noting how their character changed as they led out from the city centre and traversed the ring of poorer areas:

. . . the thoroughfares leading . . . out of the city are lined, on both sides, with an almost unbroken series of shops ... True, these shops bear some relation to the districts which lie behind them, and are more elegant in the commercial and residential quarters than when they hide grimy workingmen's dwellings; but they suffice to conceal from the eyes of the wealthy men and women of strong stomachs and weak nerves the misery and grime which form the complement of their wealth. So, for instance, Deansgate, which leads from the Old Church directly southward, is lined first with mills and warehouses, then with second-rate shops and ale-houses; farther south, when it leaves the commercial district, with less inviting shops, which grow dirtier and more interrupted by beer-houses and gin palaces the farther one goes, until at the southern end the appearance of the shops leaves no doubt that workers only are their customers (pp. 79–80).

This pattern of social segregation and insulation between the residential areas of the middle classes and the workers, and the differential pattern of use, whether for work or for recreation, were built into the spatial and physical structure of Manchester, its zones and its buildings:

The town . . . is peculiarly built, so that a person may live in it for years, and go in and out daily without coming into contact with a working-people's quarter or even with workers, that is, so long as he confines himself to his business or to pleasure walks. This arises chiefly from the fact that, by unconscious tacit agreement, as well as with out-spoken conscious determination, the working people's quarters are sharply separated from the sections of the city reserved for the middle class; or, if this does not succeed, they are concealed with the cloak of charity . . . This hypocritical plan is more or less common to all great cities. I know . . . that the value of land is greater near [the centre] than in remote districts; but at the same time I have never seen so systematic a shutting out of the working class from the thoroughfares, so tender a concealment of everything which might affront the eye and the nerves of the bourgeoisie, as in Manchester. [Yet] Manchester is less built according to a plan . . . [and is] more an out-growth of accident, than any other city . . . (pp. 78–81).

Even the climate differed for the different classes:

The east and north-east sides of Manchester are the only ones on which the bourgeoisie has not built, because ten or eleven months of the year the west and south-west wind drives the smoke of all the factories hither, and that the working-people alone may breathe (p. 92).

Manchester, then, was not planned in any formal or bureaucratic way, but its structure was nevertheless systematic, having developed – according to Engels – through both the 'tacit agreement' and the 'conscious determination' of the middle and upper classes. Engels's overall description contains in essence many of the key ideas informing ecological studies in the twentieth century. His attempt to set the analysis of Manchester in its wider social and economic context, however, gives his work a range and depth far superior to later ecological analyses. The essence of this framework is, of course, that the industrial revolution had wrought a transformation of society which he conceived as a series of interlocking processes, which were triggered by developments in science, in machine technology, and sources of energy, and then led to changes in the social organization of production. 'These inventions,' Engels wrote, 'gave rise . . . to an industrial revolution, a revolution which altered the whole civil society . . .' (p. 37). The factories in which the machines were concentrated, owing to technological imperatives, necessitated large and increasing investments of capital; and the larger the factories, the more profitable were they. From this, all else followed. 'Small employers who could not compete with great establishments were forced down into the proletariat . . .'; as capital became concentrated, so did the scale of the enterprise (with ever-larger factories) and the market as a whole. 'The rapid extension of manufacture demanded hands, wages rose, and troops of workmen migrated from the agricultural districts to the towns' (p. 51).

Concentration, polarization, and urbanization were thus natural consequences of the industrial revolution – as we saw in Stein's analysis of the interrelated processes of industrialization, bureaucratization and urbanization. Great industrial cities became the stage on which these major processes were brought into co-ordination. Even after outlining his analysis, however, Engels was himself amazed as to how 'the whole crazy fabric still hangs together' (p. 58). But hang together it did, and the value of his analysis lies precisely in his demonstration of how the city had to be studied within the overall context of a changing social and economic world.

Today, after a century of urban studies, and particularly of 'community studies', we have had to be reminded, once more, of the need, in studying even rural society in Europe, to go 'beyond the community', in Boissevain's words. In the final analysis, then, urban sociology – and *a fortiori*, community sociology – cannot be a subject with a distinct identity and a quite separate subject all of its own: it can only be a dimension or aspect of a general sociology of life in the wider society.

Engels's analysis has been taken up in recent years by Harvey (1973), who considers that it is far more consistent with 'hard economic and social realities' than that of the ecologists of the Chicago School. 'With certain obvious modifications,' Harvey writes, 'Engels' description [of Manchester] could easily be made to fit the contemporary American city: concentric zoning with good transport facilities for the affluent who live on the outskirts, sheltering of commuters into the city from seeing the grime and misery which is the complement of their wealth, etc.' (p. 133). Indeed, it is this stress on the social and economic processes that create the industrial city which distinguishes the work of Engels from that of twentieth-century ecologists who were more interested in the internal structure of the city as it affected the inhabitants than in the historical development of the political economy of the country. The study of the urban process involves not only the internal structures of urban areas, but also the city, the suburb and rural areas *in their relationship to each other*.

In some areas of the world, as in Britain for instance, the urbanization of the countryside is virtually complete and the old antagonisms between town and country now play a much reduced role, while new antagonisms have emerged in the heart of the city. In many regions of the Third World, on the other hand, as in the case of Calcutta in relation to the rest of Bengal, contrasts and antagonisms between town and country remain acute. Here the nature of the city was, and is, determined by a different set of processes, deriving from its colonial character.

A Marxist approach to the city, seen as a product of modern industrial capitalism, has also informed some recent research in Europe. Manuel Castells, notably, has argued that in the highly urbanized societies of the capitalist world the spatial and cultural distinctions between 'urban' and 'rural' are incorrectly founded (original 1968; English translation in Pickvance, 1976). The persistence of the contrast between 'urban' and 'rural' in much 'urban sociology', he believes, is due to a confusion of Western 'urban' experience with forms of urban-industrial development which are not invariant, and to a conception of 'urbanism' as a persistent *culture* rather than as a natural historical development. The term 'urban', that is, has become 'ideological', and implies that we can seek to explain life in towns and cities in terms of cultural patterns.

These theoretical ideas have been used in several recent case-studies, e.g. of urban 'developers' and their interaction with town planners, and of 'urban protest' movements. Thus Jose Olives, in a study of protest against the redevelopment of a particular area of Paris, argues that we cannot understand such a movement unless we take into account the activities of local authorities, the nature of central government pressures, and other powerful interests such as those of the property-developers and financial institutions (original 1972, English translation in Pickvance, 1976).

Studies like that of Olives's depart from orthodox sociology in that they repose upon a theoretical basis of historical materialism and operate with a structural framework of political economy. Do these developments spell the end of 'community' and 'urban' sociology? We would argue that they do not. The broad historical approach of Engels, and the more recent historical-materialist emphases, are immensely valuable in exploring the general setting for contemporary urban life; but the detailed study of how social life is actually 'lived out' on the ground by actual people in communities, towns and cities continues to call for modes of analysis better suited to that task than a macroscopic historical-theoretical framework. Clearly, however, intensive small-scale studies need to be far more consciously and explicitly articulated within broader theories of social structure, of the urban process, of the distribution and exercise of power in society and of social development and change, than they usually are.

In the past the main theories used by urban field-workers were ecological or functionalist or interactionist: sometimes explicitly so, at other times only implicitly. It is crucially important that social relations in towns and cities should now be viewed anew within a general framework which allows for change and conflict in economic and political institutions and processes, as well as in the social institutions of the family, the professions and the like. Though we can readily study internal aspects of a city through well-established sociological perspectives, a fuller understanding of *the urban process* requires more emphasis on the wider forces which *create, produce and maintain towns and cities*: the 'societal' and 'system' dimensions of urban sociology, of which, for example, the housing industry and related institutions such as building societies and governmental agencies are a central part.

We have in this chapter concentrated on certain theories and concepts at the expense of covering a wider comparative range of themes and of *types* of cities. In particular, we have not dwelt on pre-industrial studies as discussed by Weber (1960) and Sjöberg (1960) for Europe, or by Krapf-Askari for Yoruba towns in Nigeria (1969), or Stambouli and Zghal for North African pre-colonial cities (1976) (which, they show, resemble neither the towns and cities of feudal

Europe nor those of the great bureaucratic States of the East). Nor have we discussed the nature of cities in the Eastern European socialist states where urban growth is related to advanced industrialism, yet affected, as Musil (1968) shows in his study of Prague, by processes of centralized planning and State ownership unknown in Western Europe. Nor, again, have we discussed the contentious questions of power in the city, or for whose benefit modern cities are organized in their present ways (Pahl, 1975), or the manner in which modern cities are dominant bases of power in the society at large (Mellor, 1975). All of these topics merit close attention in any review of the study of communities and cities beyond the outlines of this chapter.

Part Three

Chapter 8
Social Stratification: Class, Status and Power

In using the term 'stratification' to refer to society, we are using an analogy. In geology, stratification refers to the way in which layers of rock are arranged one on top of another. Social stratification, similarly, refers to the division of a population into strata, one on top of another. But there are several most important differences between social stratification and stratification in nature:

(a) Between *social* strata there are relationships, whereas there is no kind of ongoing interconnection between successive layers of rock. Each class, that is, is part of a *system* of stratification.

(b) This interconnection involves the different strata in relationships of inferiority and superiority, usually of many kinds: political, economic, 'social', even religious. They therefore have conflicts of interest.

(c) Social strata are collectivities of people who themselves perceive these inequalities, and have their own conceptions of the stratification system which affect their behaviour. Their class-position, too, affects their behaviour even though they may not realize it.

(d) Social strata are not therefore inert: they tend to give rise to groups which recruit from the given stratum and which claim to express the interests of the stratum as a whole, and thus affect the rest of the system.

(e) Stratification systems change over time; they may do so suddenly or gradually (whereas rock strata have remained set, throughout human history at least).

Complex arrangements for classifying and stratifying people do not arise simply as an intellectual pastime. Stratification is in fact a means of regulating access to what the economist calls 'scarce goods', by which he means not just material objects of consumption like groceries or even material instruments of production like blast-furnaces, but rather all things *valued* (seen as 'good') in society and consequently sought after. So among 'goods' we include 'psychic' and 'immaterial' satisfaction, such as the distribution and receipt of prestige, as well as the distribution and receipt of material objects. As we saw in Chapter 6, people will commonly work hard and spend hard, in order to acquire not just the biological 'necessities of life', but also 'social' necessities (more accurately 'wants') which include using wealth to get power over others and respect from them. This often involves using one's resources not just for straightforward individual consumption, but using them to build up a political following or to maximize one's status.

We have used a very wide term, 'stratification', so far, because, although *class* stratification is the dominant kind of stratification found in the modern world – in capitalist societies deriving from differential access to private property, and in communist societies primarily from differential access to political power – there have been many other kinds of stratification in past history. 'Age-set' societies, feudal 'estate' societies and caste societies, for example, are quite different systems of stratification from those more familiar to people living in class societies.

Estate and caste societies, for example, distribute their members at birth into different strata according to one principal criterion – age, descent, rank, etc., and there is little or no possibility of moving out of that stratum. They also develop explicit theories explaining and justifying why such arrangements exist. In industrial societies on the other hand – whether capitalist or communist – however class-ridden or élitist they may be, there are no formal criteria of this kind which condemn a person to one particular class for his whole life. Class is thus much more informally institutionalized than, say, caste, but is nonetheless important. It will therefore help us to see the distinctive features of social class in advanced capitalist and in communist societies more clearly if we look first at two types of stratified 'pre-industrial' society more closely.

Let us look first at those tribal societies of the 'stateless' type described by Fortes and Evans-Pritchard (1940). These societies lack centralized administration and judicial institutions. The office of chief may not exist at all, or, if it does, often carries more ritual than secular power. Nor is succession to office necessarily hereditary. But though a society may be 'stateless', and lack chiefs (and thus be called an 'acephalous' (headless) society), it may still be stratified. Australian aboriginal tribes, for example, are stratified on the basis of age (and sex). Men move from one age-grade to another as they grow older, making successive transitions from boy to young man, from unmarried young man to married adult, and eventually to 'elderhood'. Membership of the age-grades is so important that it is socially marked by successive rituals, physically marked, too, on a man's body, in the form of cicatrices cut into his chest. In other societies, a whole age-group is initiated so as to form an 'age-set' together; it often takes a name derived from some contemporary event (Panyako: 'Pioneer Corps' was chosen in one African society because many young men were conscripted in 1940), or takes over a traditional name. These age-sets are the major basis of social organization – thus the age-set of warrior age was responsible for defence, and the older age-sets for various other tasks in the running of the society. Membership of these groups thus controls all aspects of life: it affects whom a man may marry, his right to own land, his ability to participate in certain rituals and so forth; hence membership of such a stratum has an extra dimension of religious significance that secular ideologies of class lack.

All aborigines, too, move through the age-grade system: a man becomes successively a hunter and a warrior and eventually reaches the heights of elderhood. His social development is identical with that of his age-mates, and is determined by the physical fact of ageing. So although a society like this is highly stratified and constitutes a 'gerontocracy', in which the older men hold the decisive authority, every man in his time becomes an elder. He is not fixed for life in a lowly position. Secondly, he performs exactly the same production-roles as his fellows: all are hunter-producers. Consumption-standards hardly differ either. Finally, there is room for any enterprising person of reasonably appropriate age to win himself a leading part in the economy, in settling disputes, or in ritual, if he wants to. To this degree, this kind of society is an 'opportunity' or 'open' society where ours is not, contrary to much popular assumption and even much sophisticated social theory about the 'open society'. Yet though there is change of personnel within the system, the pattern of stratification itself does not change – the basic determinants remain fixed: those of age and sex.

This kind of fixity is even more evident where a man is allocated to his place in the stratification-system by birth. In the caste-system of India, relationships in all dimensions of life were affected by a man's caste-membership. The caste-system exists at two distinct levels. One is an India-wide classification into priests, warriors (land-holders), merchants, and the broad mass of people on the land. The whole Hindu population, and a number of other groups, are fitted into these four *varna*. But these are not the basic units of caste at village level. Here, instead of the *varna*, we find a division of the local community called the *jati* (also translated as 'caste'). The *jati* is a group of individuals who live in a group of villages, who often (but not always) have the same occupation and who maintain their group-identity by marrying exclusively within the caste. It is this *jati* which constitutes the social reality of caste for individuals in rural Indian society and there are many thousands of such groups; all of them, however, can fit themselves into the four *varna*. A complex structure of norms and taboos derived from religious ideas concerning pollution also prevent members of one caste from eating with members of another or even touching them. The effect is to maintain social distance between the various *jatis* and to preserve the hierarchical system of ritual superiority and inferiority intact as a whole. On the margin of society altogether are the 'outcaste' Untouchables (now called 'Scheduled Castes') with whom caste-members could have only the most minimal contact for fear of pollution. Formally, the caste-system was absolutely closed, both to individual and group mobility. Nevertheless, whole groups have successfully improved their caste-position through the process known as 'Sanskritization', in which a group imitates the customs of a superior *jati*, via exaggerated observance of the ritual practices of that group, by taking up 'purer' occupations, by treating *jatis* of previously equal or superior status as ritually polluting, and by making demands for precedence over them in ceremony.

A caste is thus much more than an occupational group. It is an extreme example of what is usually called a status-group, because the term 'status' involves not just a position in a division of labour, but membership of a group marked off from other inferior and superior groups and accorded different amounts of prestige. Since all occupations are themselves evaluated as higher or lower in status, status is an intrinsic dimension even of a person's economic role. A caste is a very *closed* status-group, but status-groups can be much more open.

Sex and Gender: Are Women a Class?

So far, the systems of stratification we have discussed have really been systems of *male* stratification, though they purport to be about society as a whole. A woman's place in society is assumed to be simply dependent upon that of her husband or father. Yet many women, in our society, lead independent lives or contribute significantly to the household. Nor are even 'upper-class' women free from the dis-privileges involved in being a woman as against being even a lower-class male. Sociologists, it is true, usually do note that women are under-represented, *societally*, in the crucial decision-making centres of power and that their *social* contribution is also undervalued: both their place in the economy, and their place in the main area of society where they clearly predominate: the home. Their participation in both spheres is discounted as marginal, inferior or ancillary.

To understand how these evaluations – and the realities they express and sustain – work in society, involves us, at one level, in examining the social organization of sex and the family; at another, the polity and the economy.

How does it come about, for instance, that women are only allocated certain kinds of jobs? Why are those jobs, often vital to society – mother, housewife, educator – so undervalued and under-rewarded? Is it because there are too few women in positions of power to bring about an 'up-grading' of predominantly female occupations? If so, how did they come to be so under-represented at 'the top', and men to initially monopolize both the key jobs and the skilled jobs?

Male domination of society goes back for most of recorded history: far beyond the comparatively recent emergence of modern industrial society. By contrast, the class structure typical of modern capitalism is very recent, and class society of any kind, let alone capitalism, covers a much shorter span of historical time compared to the existence, over millennia, of 'primordial' inequalities between men and women. Some 'radical feminist' writers have consequently argued that oppression by males is a deeper, wider and more fundamental exploitation than domination based on control over the means of production or control over the apparatus of force. To examine this issue, therefore, we cannot restrict ourselves to the evidence derived from a handful of Western industrial societies in the last century or so. We need a much wider comparative sweep and a longer historical perspective. Sociology, that is, has to draw upon the related disciplines of anthropology and history.

Nineteenth-century evolutionary theorists believed, as do some contemporary writers of the Women's Movement, in the historical existence of a bygone 'matriarchal' age when women, not men, ruled society, or, alternatively, in a former state of equality between men and women. The existence of such a matriarchal epoch has been discounted by modern anthropology (which is not to say that women did not have a much more socially respected and central role in many cultures). But even in those societies where descent is traced through the female line (matriliny), it is nevertheless men who are the key leaders in most public affairs. Thus, it is the eldest male of the lineage who manages the affairs of the group of sisters who constitute the key kinship unit among the matrilineal Yao of Malawi (Mitchell, 1956). Again, the important part played by the king's mother, sisters and mother's brothers in many African kingdoms does not reflect some vestigial 'survival' from an earlier epoch when such women actually ruled themselves, but the value, to a king, of having advisors who were closely dependent on (and therefore loyal to) him for their high position in government, and at the same time (by virtue of their being female) ineligible for the kingship themselves and therefore unlikely to seek to overthrow him in a bid for power. The use of close female relatives in key offices was thus a guarantee of the monarch's security. Brothers and other males of royal birth, who might be Pretenders to the throne, were often eliminated at the accession of a new king, by murder or in succession-battles (Gluckman, 1963).

In the economic sphere, even where women's contribution, in the division of labour between the sexes, has been important – e.g., in hunting-and-collecting societies, where they contribute the bulk of the food supply (wild vegetables and fruit) – their role in political and religious life was inferior to that of men.

Just as we have to discount the idea that earlier matriarchal societies were overthrown by patriarchalism, we must also reject the common assumption that differences of role and status, as between men and women, are 'natural' in society, since they derive from innate differences of a biological kind which are truly natural, i.e., built into our physiques and minds through genetic inheritance.

History and anthropology show, rather, that the emphases placed upon sexuality, for instance – a singularly physical, non-social matter, one might think – have varied from epoch to epoch. Sexual behaviour itself is not some eternal, immanent characteristic, given in our biological constitution, which – like murder – will 'out', whatever the culture or kind of social organization. Rather, the kinds and occasions of sexual activity held to be appropriate for each sex are culturally defined, structurally institutionalized, codified in law and custom and entrenched in ideologies, and handed down by agencies of socialization, from mothers and priests to schools and T.V. commercials. Thus, respectable women were once thought by Victorian middle-class males to be incapable of, indeed 'above', such lowly, animal behaviour as sexual passion. Yet these same husbands freely explored and exploited the sexual services of a whole army of prostitutes, the 'fallen' women from the lower classes (Marcus, 1967).

Sex, like age or skin colour, is a natural attribute, and usually readily visible. But it has been culturally elaborated far beyond anything 'given' in our biological constitution, for biological differences of sex have been converted into social differences of *gender* (though we loosely continue using the word 'sex') (Barker and Allen, 1976). Gender is an artificial social product in the same way as linguistic gender, for instance, in which certain languages group all nouns into masculine, feminine and neuter (though there is nothing inherently feminine about a ship or a table, even if French treats them as 'feminine' nouns). Similarly, most 'sexual' differences in behaviour turn out to be cultural projections onto biological endowments, and then taken to be either 'natural' or deriving from Divine Providence.

Yet the social inferiority of women as a collectivity over wide periods of historical time is still often 'explained' in terms of genetic inferiority. Women, it is asserted, bear children and are therefore periodically immobilized; menstruation also hinders their continuous participation in social life; and their physique is less powerful than that of most men. These physical attributes are held to explain social inferiority in societies as different from each other as hunting-and-collecting societies, on the one hand, and industrial countries on the other.

It is true that one finds the biological process of menstruation everywhere treated as a condition of 'pollution', in both primitive and in advanced cultures. But menstruation is not dangerous to men: this is a social construction placed upon that physical state (reflecting the great importance placed upon birth, and the fear of anything abnormal). Neither menstruation, or even childbirth, necessarily restricts women in their physical activities. In fact, the immobility of women occasioned by childbirth, in nomadic societies, is usually limited to days, even hours (at whatever cost to the woman's constitution).

And wherever female labour has been needed in industrial societies, women have been removed from the home, and from child-rearing, as in Britain's Industrial Revolution, to drag heavy coal-carts, semi-naked, in underground mines, or to work long hours in cotton mills. In the First World War, they were used in millions in the munition factories, and in war work again in the Second World War, when provision was made for young children by the establishment of crèches (subsequently nearly all closed down).

The intellectual propensities of women have similarly been taken as 'natural', though the 'childishness' reported of Victorian women, assumed to be a natural deficiency, would now be explained by sociologists in terms of their restricted lives, spent mainly in the company of children and under patriarchal authority, and in terms of their limited formal education. (Slaves also developed parallel 'submissive' personalities (Elkins, 1963).)

Explanations of social differences in terms of some universal genetic endowment are thus abundantly contradicted by the evidence of the great variety of female behaviours. In the kingdom of Dahomey, women made formidable fighting troops; in Victorian England they were expected to recoil in terror at the sight of a mouse. The pressures of society, however, were so powerful that, over time, women themselves came to internalize whatever stereotypes were dominant, and to act in accordance with them. In Victorian England, women became what they were expected to become: timid, uncompetitive, submissive, 'personalistic' in their dependence upon men and their children both for meaning in their lives and for social identity limited to that of wife and mother. Stereotypes of the feminine character became 'self-fulfilling' prophecies (Merton, 1968). The behaviour predicted occurred; therefore the theory underlying the prediction – their natural timidity and incompetence – was taken as confirmed.

There is, however, it should now be apparent, no condition of 'womanhood' in general. Even at the same period of time, within the same culture, different kinds of women have been treated differently. Such differences between sub-sets of women cannot be logically explained in terms of innate common physical characteristics any more than similar disparities between the roles of the sexes from one society to another. Nor are cultures fixed. The position of women in society has thus changed greatly over time, and clearly changes in accordance with changes in the structure and economy of society as a whole. Women do not live on some isolated 'island' within society. A sociological explanation, therefore, has to examine both the institutional arrangements which determine what women can and cannot do, within a given society, the changes that take place in them over time, and the ideological notions of the 'proper' place of women that inform these arrangements.

Pre-sociological or sub-sociological explanations, like pseudo-history, could only flourish in an intellectual climate where historiography – the writing of history – has usually been history with the women left out. Usually women only appear in history books as royal wives or mistresses – usually, that is, as appendages of men, valued, instrumentally, as marriage-partners and breeding-stock, as means of obtaining access to property, because they or their sons might inherit land and kingdoms. Ordinary women have been even more invisible: a kind of 'silent half' of the population, even in an age when ordinary men have begun to be rescued from obscurity, for today historians no longer concern themselves solely with kings and queens, battles and Cabinets, but also study the activities – from domestic life to political involvements – of the ordinary mass of the population.

Until the Women's Movement of the last decade (Mitchell, J. J. 1971), however, the place of women in history remained severely neglected. The 'woman question' seemed to have been put on one side after the major (often violent) suffragette struggles around the turn of the century, when the solidarity generated in the common struggle for the vote gave way to an era when women were divided by differing ideas, along lines of social class, as to how to use that vote. Whereas the working class, which at first simply strove to elect working men to Parliament (usually as Liberals), ultimately developed a separate and 'sectional' party representing the distinctive and separate *class* interests of Labour, women, fully enfranchised by 1928, developed no such collective political identity. Women, however, continued to suffer important disadvantages, and it was to these issues that some turned, as women, in the inter-War era. One important area was that of sexual liberation – even, for the avantgarde, 'free love' – and the 'family planning' movement, much of it under the stimulus of Freudian psychoanalysis, which was now reaching a newly-literate and educated generation of women.

Since the latter kinds of issues affected women of all classes, offended the sensibilities of the orthodox, and affected all women in their relations with men, they tended to attract a great deal of attention. Innovation in these fields, too, was largely pioneered by educated and vocal middle-class women. While they were beginning, slowly, to break into male middle-class preserves (schools, offices, universities), working-class women were entering new areas of industrial, especially tertiary, employment, in vast numbers, and some even joining trade unions.

The problems of women, then, were problems of underprivilege and limited rights, affecting all of them in some respects. But women did not occupy identical positions in society. According to their class, they differed in the place they occupied within the domestic economy and in the extent to which unpaid housework was combined with wage-labour outside the home. (Many middle-class women also engaged in voluntary work with charity organizations, pressuregroups, etc.) Those involved in both sectors of the dual social division of labour – domestic labour and wage-labour – were obviously subject to strains unknown to those who remained in the home. But the latter became increasingly conscious, and resentful, of compulsory domesticity. Such differences reflected themselves within the women's movements themselves, e.g., within the suffragette movement, one wing of which was led by women from high society, concerned primarily with the vote, while the socialist wing were concerned with the general social condition of the mass of women, the poor of London's East End and the north of the country.

In the nineteenth century working-class women struggled collectively to set limits to the hours of grinding labour, to raise their wages, and to improve working conditions that left them with no time or energy for their families. At the same time genteel ladies were struggling for the right and opportunity to break out of the confines of the home, children and the kitchen (the main alternative to which, for those who fell on hard times, was employment as governesses to other people's children), and to break into the masculine world of the professions, higher education and public life

Recent sociological theory has attempted to link the two 'worlds' of women – the world of the home and the world of 'work' – into a single theoretical structure by showing that they form part of an overall social and economic system. Thus functionalist theory, as we have seen, contrasts industrial society with peasant society, where the family was both a unit of production and a consumption unit. On the production side, women as well as men were engaged in agricultural labour: harvesting, weeding, etc. They also contributed to monetary income via petty trade (the sale of eggs, handicrafts, etc.).

Today, by contrast, the family is seen as a unit of consumption only, and the woman's role as the 'non-economic' provision of emotional support for the rest of the family, and – only indirectly related to the economy – the socialization of children into attitudes compatible with the demands of school and future work-roles.

This theory does take account of significant shifts in the internal dynamics of the family and of its changed position within the wider society. But it fails to recognize that there are now over 9 million women – two out of every five people in the labour-force – at work in Britain, and that over $5\frac{1}{2}$ million of these are married women ($2\frac{1}{2}$ million more than in 1951). Nearly a half of all married women now go out to work, before and after a quite limited period of years when they are rearing small children. In the 1890s, by contrast,

the typical working-class mother . . . married in her teens or early twenties and experiencing ten pregnancies, spent about fifteen years in a state of pregnancy and in nursing a child for the first year of its life. She was tied, for this period of time, to the wheel of child-bearing. Today, for the typical mother, the time so spent would be about four years . . .

At the beginning of this century, the expectation of life of a woman aged twenty was forty-six years. Approximately one-third of this life expectancy was to be devoted to child-bearing and maternal care in infancy. Today, the expectation of life of a woman aged twenty is fifty-five years (Titmuss, 1958, p. 91).

Hence, the typical woman worker 'is no longer the single teenager, but a middle-aged married woman with teenage or grown-up children' (Land, 1976, pp. 117–18).

Secondly, women earners are not marginal, but economically indispensable in many families. Some two million women (married; lone mothers with children; single women, many with dependants) are the chief supporters of their families, one in six of all households. Others contribute importantly to the joint income of the household.

Thirdly, as Marxist theorists have emphasized (Secombe, 1974; Middleton, 1974), the functionalist model also undervalues the female contribution to the domestic economy, treating this as 'marginal', because the household does not produce commodities sold on the market. But what goes on inside the household *is* work, and usually hard work, even if no wage is paid. Where a woman works outside, she has *two* jobs. Further, through the biological reproduction of children, and by bringing those children up, in combination with the school, to the point where they are ready to enter the labour-market, the family reproduces the labour-force as a collectivity out of its own income.

Fourthly, the daily, as distinct from the inter-generational, 'reproduction' of the labour-force – the support of the actual individuals who go out to work – is supplied by the family, which provides for the physical and mental well-being of its members.

When we turn to communist societies we find, not surprisingly, a different pattern in the jobs allocated to women and those from which they are excluded. Medicine, for instance, is predominantly a female profession, whereas only a small proportion of women have, until recently, been accepted into British medical schools even when qualified for entry. On the other hand, the profession is said to carry lower prestige in the U.S.S.R., and in the senior positions men predominate. At the other end of the occupational scale, women perform labouring jobs only performed by men in Western European countries.

These differences derive in part from the existence of a dominant State ideology, Marxism, which asserts the principle not only that 'men are brothers' everywhere, but of male–female equality, too, and which sees the involvement of women in productive labour outside the home as the main way in which relations between the sexes will become equalized. In part, however, the entry of women into employment outside the home simply reflects the demands of an expanding economy for new supplies of labour. To enable women to take their places in the labour-force, a network of crèches, often attached to factories, has been established, where children of working mothers are taken care of by trained personnel.

Yet the dual demands of home and work still leave the main work of the household to women, and relatives, especially grandmothers, still play a major role in child-minding. Moreover, women are still largely employed in low-wage industries, and the higher one goes in the social scale, the lower the proportion of women. Though women make up half the labour-force, only one in ten managers in industry is a woman. But two-thirds of professionals and specialists with higher and secondary educational qualifications are women, as against one-third in the U.S.A. (Bartol and Bartol, 1975). About half the members of local soviets are women; 35 per cent of the members of the Supreme Soviets of the Union Republics; and 4 per cent of the Central Committee; while there is only one woman to one hundred men in the Council of Ministers, and no woman on the Politbureau at all (Lane, D., 1976, pp. 195–6).

The elimination of gender inequalities, then, is not achieved solely via structural changes at the societal level, whether in capitalist or communist societies, e.g., by establishing State ownership of the means of production or Equal Opportunity Commissions. Changes in the law, of course, from the right to vote or the right to choose one's marriage-partner to the right to enter into hire-purchase agreements, to compete for jobs, or to own property – do, of course, importantly remove or inhibit discrimination and make equality of opportunity more possible. But opportunities are not necessarily taken up, or realized, since gender-based inequalities are supported by a powerful set of 'unofficial' ideologies which flourish among networks of friends, neighbours, kin, workmates and colleagues, and are as powerful as they are often implicit or silent. They therefore come into play, informally, even within the framework of formally 'open' situations, as when 'gate-keepers' select people for employment according to such criteria, or in areas such as the home where social control is less effective. Thus, it is commonly accepted that the basic work of the house is the woman's responsibility, but that the husband should make the key decisions, from buying a house to whether the couple should have more children, over the children's schooling, or even over the uses of leisure time. All these decisions have consequences for the disposal of resources, their differential allocation between men and women, and for the futures of the family members. The continuing structural inferiority of women as a gender limits their individual life-chances.

Hence home and the family are often seen, not as egalitarian, 'caring' and emotionally supportive milieux, a refuge in a competitive and hierarchical world favourable to the production of stable personalities in the young, but as a cockpit of tensions, where the inequalities of the wider world penetrate, and as a social unit, too, with its own additional inequalities and hierarchies which, in turn, feeds into the stratification-system of the society as a whole.

Race, Ethnicity, Nation

Apart from the universal and historical inferior place given to women in society, the other major inequality – running like a geological fault across the world – is that between the 'White' world of Europe, North America, South Africa and Australia, and the rest. This division has often been thought of as explicable simply in terms of its most obvious feature, race.

Yet race did not become an important concept until the nineteenth century (Banton, 1970). People do not inevitably think about society, and explain what happens in it, in racial terms. Until then race had been used to mean 'line of descent', since the best argument for the legitimacy of any institution was thought to be the demonstration that it could be traced back to Adam, the Prophet, or the beginning of time. 'Race' as meaning a sub-type of humankind gained impetus with the rise of Darwinism and the popularization of the notion of the species as the unit of analysis, in a natural world characterized by competition in the struggle for survival. This immediately gives us some sociological clues, because the world of human society was increasingly characterized by intensified competition, particularly between nations and states. Multi-cultural empires, autonomous tribes, cultures of all kinds were levelled down and incorporated as colonies or semi-colonies within capitalist empires, and combined or split up to form entities which had often never existed before: Nigeria, Indo-China or Eritrea (Worsley, 1967, Chapter 1).

A note of caution was sounded by those who observed that races were nowhere pure, but always mixed (which led them to theories of 'degeneration', rather than progress), but they were largely ignored. Before long, Disraeli could write, in *Tancred*, 'All is race; there is no other truth.'

Races were now being thought of as clearly-defined populations, usually with common culture, territory and institutions. Even a century later the more statistical conceptions of race used by biologists have hardly begun to penetrate popular thinking.

Today, however, races are seen to be much more problematic categories than once assumed. In the statistical sense, a 'population' (which is not necessarily a population of human or even living things) is a collection of individuals each of which possesses a whole set of characteristics, in the case of humans, ranging from blood-group to height, which vary from individual to individual. The incidence of such characteristics, taken in aggregate, may vary from group to group, but we will get different results depending on what characteristic we select for attention, and according to the way we select the group. Thus the population of blue-eyed people will not overlap neatly with the population of curly-haired people. The groups usually chosen are inhabitants of a given country, but most such populations show a variety of mixed characteristics, some more widely present than others, and the same features are to be found in neighbouring countries. Various classifications of 'races' are therefore used for scientific purposes, but they have little in common with popular 'racial' stereotypes. (Thus, to take skin colour, the Berbers of North Africa are much 'whiter' than most Mediterranean southern Europeans.) Again, variations *within* groups are often as striking as those *between* groups. Finally, modern biologists have paid much more attention to distributions of *genetic* features and bodily *processes* (cell-types, metabolism, etc.) as against earlier generations' concern with 'morphological' features such as body-size or brain-weight (often naïvely thought to have some correlation with 'intelligence').

In the 1930s, too, reacting against Nazi racism, physical anthropologists spent a lot of time exploding the myth that physical features had any necessary connection with culture: the great variety of European social systems and cultures, for instance, could not be explained in terms of race, as the peoples in these countries were of the same basic physical stock. Conversely, populations with different physical characteristics could co-exist within the same polity.

Social scientists now began to move away from studying physical characteristics, or examining the logicality or otherwise of racist ideas, towards analysis of the conditions under which racism emerged, and the function of racism in society.

Social psychologists had begun to explore the ways in which racial prejudice was learned, rather than something innate – sometimes, however, assuming that the drawing of lines of social exclusion and inclusion is a natural propensity of the human mind (a tendency to think in terms of like and unlike, which they assumed to be a distinction fundamental to any kind of coherent thought). In terms of social institutions it led them, usually, to concentrate upon socializing agents such as the family or the local community as the source of racist ideas, or upon ideologies as systems of thought. A great deal of important research, notably the studies of 'the Authoritarian Personality' by Adorno and his colleagues, however, explored connections between attitudes towards 'race' and people's positions in society.

Sociologists developed this approach by asking not just about the processes by which people learned to think and behave in a racist fashion, but how these ideas and practices got produced in the first place, what kinds of people typically held them, how they were used, and their function in the total social system. This meant putting the emphasis upon societies as wholes, and particularly upon structures of political and social stratification. Further, the accent upon the totality was pushed to an even higher level by identifying racism as a world phenomenon, international and transnational in scope, and deriving from the experience of fascism and of earlier modern imperialisms.

Before the nineteenth century, empires, often enormous in scale – those of the Islamic world, the Turkish Empire, Imperial China, those of India and South America, for example – had been built up by incorporating whole peoples, with different languages and cultures. Equally, such populations might be split between neighbouring political units. As long as they accepted the authority of their rulers, it was not thought necessary to force them to adopt the language or culture, not even the religion, of those who ruled them. Nor, in their turn, did the ruled consider the ethnic identity of their rulers all that important. What was more important was whether they ruled them more or less benevolently. 'Minority' peoples, as in the cosmopolitan city of Cairo, might live and work, often at occupations largely monopolized by them, in their own areas of the city (Abu-Lughod, 1971), though their rights may be more limited than those of more favoured sections of the population (e.g., Muslims in the Turkish Empire). On the other hand, their 'externality' – as we saw in the case of female relatives of African kings above – made them at times highly suitable as government officials, even ministers, as soldiers, and the like. Whole corps of administrative officials were often recruited from categories marginal to the main population and its ruling class; from the ranks of eunuchs, slaves, commoners and foreigners, and from ethnic groups such as Mamelukes and Circassians in Egypt, Germans in Imperial Russia, or Janissaries in Turkey. (Sometimes they failed to stick to the expected role of 'neutral' servant, and seized power for themselves.)

The horrors which were unleashed upon the world in the 1930s and 1940s by those who used racism for political ends had led biologists and physical anthropologists to dismiss the notion of clearly distinct 'races'. Now social scientists began to express similar doubts about ethnicity. Obviously, whatever their physical characteristics – which might be quite heterogeneous – people who lived together over centuries produced a set of customary ways of living which we call 'culture', shared within groups which thought of themselves as being marked off from other groups by virtue of this cultural distinctiveness and common descent.

Yet if racial purity was largely mythical, ethnic identity was not necessarily always important, either. Indeed, assimilation has always been a major process, applauded by internationalists and feared by those striving to preserve their distinctiveness. Why, and under what circumstances, they should *want* to preserve their distinctiveness, are questions which are not always asked by those who assumed ethnicity to be a natural thing. But not all peoples do wish to remain distinct.

The occurrence of migration on a massive scale in the late nineteenth century provided a splendid laboratory for examining the durability of ethnic identity, as tens of millions of people left Europe for North America. It had been known from older studies that the 'Baba' Chinese who had emigrated into Malaya centuries ago had lost their Chinese culture and adopted that of the Malays. Now – under Western eyes – Czechs, Poles, Italians and English in the United States, together with people of very diverse African descent were changing their ethnicity, and often doing so readily – despite the pains – since, for them, this was a progressive step, whether in terms of higher income and living standards, wider opportunities, or access to 'civilization'. 'Changing one's language,' Gellner has noted, 'is not the heart-breaking or soul-destroying business which it is claimed to be in romantic nationalist literature' (Gellner, 1964, p. 165).

In the U.S.A. the theory of the 'melting-pot', for instance, and studies of the 'ghetto' by the Chicago School of sociologists in the 1920s and 1930s, saw the preservation of separate identity as a phase in an intergenerational history. The first generation banded together to protect themselves and to share their valued and familiar ways of life (they were also often simply *forced* to live under ghetto condi-tions). The second generation, however, was socialized into the American way of life particularly via the school and by contact with members of other ethnic groups at work and in general social life, though their home life was different. To them, marriage-ties or land-owning in some remote village in Sicily or Poland were of little interest. They were often ashamed of these 'old country' cultures, and wanted to be 'modern'. Their social ties were no longer confined to the ethnic community in its 'ghetto'. The third generation, however, *were* confidently American, and therefore no longer ashamed; they began to learn the ancestral language and visit the homeland. Ethnicity was reviving, albeit now largely of a 'cultural' kind only. As Gellner puts it, 'The grandson tries to remember what the son tried to forget' (*op cit.*, p. 163).

But assimilation does not occur when those who wield power use it to block off access by minorities to the good things of life and especially access to societal power itself. 'Minority', it should be noted, is used here as a sociological, not a quantitative term, referring to the collective position of inferiority ascribed and imposed upon some section(s) of society (Glass, 1962). Thus, in South Africa, the numerically preponderant Africans are a 'minority' in this sense. The attempt to keep such minorities permanently disprivileged, whether in terms of jobs, education, housing, political rights, etc., consolidates the ethnic consciousness of those subject to this process, and then produces resistance, as Black nationalism, Zionism, or the innumerable 'reactive' nationalisms generated by colonialism bear witness. Rapidly-growing societies like the nineteenth-century United States, with mushrooming industry and expansion into the West, could not easily be structured on rigid ethnic lines. Populations were too mobile, too heterogeneous for this. But if not easy, the attempt can be made, given an intransigent and determined ruling class operating under the influence of a deeply-held ideology. In the U.S.A., the South failed in its attempt. Today, a parallel resistance to those forces in industrial society which work towards open mobility and a free labour market, across ethnic lines, has been most marked in South Africa, where a modern industrial capitalism has been built precisely on a racial basis (Wolpe, 1970; van Onselen, 1976). The labour compound and the 'pass' are the mechanisms of control that enforce this rigidity.

Entrenched and powerful groups justified their exploitation of minorities by branding the newcomers as inferior. The latter soon reacted to being labelled as members of a disvalued ethnic group: as 'Wops', 'Wogs', 'Dagos', 'Pakis', etc. Some of them were very surprised to find that this was the identity they now possessed (Pakistanis, for example, had never conceived of themselves as 'coloured people' like West Indians): previously they may have thought of themselves as members of such-and-such a village, family or region. On arrival in the new land, or on reaching the city from the countryside, they had no ready-made ethnic consciousness at all relevant to city life, and, in consequence, little solidarity or organization. Some of them formed quite novel voluntary associations to defend their interests, to assist each other through the tribulations of the new life (especially sickness and unemployment), and to afford some expression of their religious, cultural and other values in their leisure time. Those who came from superior strata within their village or homeland were particularly shattered to find themselves looked down on as inferiors. But however much *they* might regard themselves as superior, and see their new inferior status as some kind of cosmic mistake, however much the people from different tribes – Yoruba, Malinke, Kongo, Akan – now enslaved in the U.S.A., might have previously been unknown to each other, or mutually hostile in their homelands, they were now transformed into inferior 'Negroes'. Over two centuries this identity was consolidated by the experience of plantation life, the Civil War, and finally the exodus into the ghettoes of the northern cities. The ethnic identity of 'Negro', then, was the product of a relationship with a dominant Other – the 'White man' – as owner and employer and authority-figure-in-general. The syndrome of deference to Whites, and passivity – even the attempt of many Negroes to 'pass' and *become* Whites – and the compensatory culture of mutual aid and religion typical of the plantation era gave way, under more autonomous conditions of life, wider educational horizons, and awareness of the possibility of change, to a new-found 'Black pride' – even 'Black rage' – that turned its back on the 'Uncle Tom' Negro of the past. The 'Negro' now became transformed into the 'Black', as the demand for 'Black Power' replaced humility and acquiescence. Similarly, under persecution, submissive Jews became transformed, firstly, into Zionists, and then into militant Israelis.

The emphasis in recent sociological studies, then, has been to question the very label 'race relations' as an adequate framework of analysis. 'A theory of race relations,' Marvin Harris has said, 'must be a sub-case of a theory of social stratification.' Alternatively, as Rex puts it, 'without the power and stratification element there would be no race relations problem' (Rex, 1970, p. 48).

A more recent minority phenomenon – the mass immigration of eleven million workers from the Mediterranean countries into the factories of Western Europe – has been analysed in very similar terms by Castles and Kosack; as a matter of 'political economy' and 'structured social inequality' rather than of racial prejudice 'in itself'. They explain antagonism to immigrant workers on the part of indigenous workers, rather, in terms of competition for jobs; the immigrants are given the hard, dirty, unskilled and low-paid work. In Switzerland, for example, where immigrants make up 40 per cent of the labour-force in factories, only one-tenth of young Swiss people in Geneva become unskilled or semi-skilled manual workers; only 22 per cent of the children of labourers become labourers themselves (Castles and Kosack, 1973; Berger, J., 1975). The indigenous workers, then, become what has been described as a 'labour aristocracy'. They do not necessarily become aggressively *racist*, however; unlike Nazi Germany, there is no mass expression of racial prejudice. Indeed, race may not be the basis of discriminating against immigrants at all. Italians in Switzerland, and blond Finns in Sweden, are subject to the same kinds of prejudiced treatment as 'coloured' immigrants in England. Nor does mass mobilization against the immigrant population as scapegoats necessarily occur, for there has been no need for a scapegoat. Indeed, the presence of immigrants has meant better jobs for indigenous workers. In conditions of over-full employment (which is why the immigrants are there), the immigrant (and his social disabilities) has been ignored rather than persecuted. Since he is too vulnerable – being liable to deportation – to organize, he is 'benignly neglected'. More explicit and active racism might well emerge given continued economic depression and/or resistance of the kind developed by Black nationalist movements in the U.S.A.

As long as immigrants keep their place, and can be absorbed into the economy, the emergence of racism, as a systematic ideology and practice, is unlikely. Racialism exists, but is not articulated into '*racism*', which seeks to justify the treatment of groups as inferior by reference to some *theory* of their (believed) inherent biological or cultural inferiority.

These processes, then, whether in the U.S.A., Europe or the colonies, are consequences of the transformation of the world brought about by modern imperialism, rather than intellectual errors; the outcome of inadequate socialization in infancy; or some natural propensity to separate and distinguish. They are increasingly seen as part of world-wide relations between entire populations, differently situated in an international and unequal division of labour and power, and not simply to be comprehended as the outcome of face-to-face relations between persons or interactions at the level of the local community.

So far, though we have spoken of race and ethnicity within the framework of this inter*national* relationship between states, we have refrained from speaking of nationalism itself. This, too, is another quite recent growth. Ethnic identity of some kind, of course, is probably as old as, or even coterminous with, human society. But the large, often ramshackle and loose-knit ancient empire, on the one hand, and the tight-knit tribe on the other, both differed crucially from the modern nation-state.

Nationalism was absent, too, from the medieval feudalism of Europe. Its growth is clearly connected to the rise of the modern capitalist State, particularly in its formative period, as in Tudor England, when a consolidated centralized State with a country-wide internal market was being established; and, later, whenever the survival or power of that State was threatened by other States (in the case of the U.K., notably during the struggles with Spain, Holland and France for commercial domination of the new colonial world, during the Napoleonic Wars, and during the First and Second World Wars). The doctrine of nationalism thus developed in the West was exported along with liberalism, socialism and communism to the rest of the world in the era of imperialism. But colonialism also refused the extension of these doctrines to subject peoples, and consolidated that refusal by the colour-bar. Hence a new kind of 'reactive' nationalism emerged, rather than acceptance of the conquerors' national superiority. Nationalism, like those other ideologies, rapidly became a weapon turned against the conquerors. These were nationalisms of the ruled rather than of the rulers.

Nineteenth-century liberalism had assumed that the nation would disappear as world society became more integrated, more rationally organized and more evenly prosperous. Marxism, too, accepted the Enlightenment belief in the transient and irrational nature of attachment to the nation, which was a product of capitalist class society. The proletariats of each country had no common interests with the bourgeoisies that exploited them. The 'national community' was a sham and delusion. The only true community was that of the international proletariat, in the singular, which would act in cooperation to overthrow international bourgeoisies of all countries, and then establish a fraternal classless society across the globe.

The first serious blow to these theories of the inevitable disappearance of nationalism was the First World War, when the proletariat of each country marched off to fight for its respective nation-state. Fascism in Italy, Germany and Japan constituted a second heightened form of nationalism in 'latecomer' countries, coupled with a virulent racist ideology. Nation and race, it seemed clear, were by no means being displaced by class as identities that moved men into action, however much they might be discounted as 'non-scientific', or seen simply as the outcome of other, deeper causes, by social scientists.

The Left had also to adapt its theories so as to recognize a benign or 'progressive' variant of nationalism, as when Chinese resistance to Japanese fascism, or British to the Nazi threat of invasion, led to a *justified* 'national unity', even between bourgeoisie and proletariat.

Yet, on Left and Right, there has been remarkably little attempt to grapple with the topic of the nation, and of nationalism, in the literature of the social sciences – a phenomenon which calls for explanation. Most research has traced the philosophical origins of the idea of the nation, and of the historical process of connecting up nation and State – usually going back to Hegel and Kant – or describing the subsequent spread of these concepts across the globe. Others have constructed taxonomies of types of nationalism (Smith, A. D., 1971).

Such explanations of the massive and swift rise and spread of nationalism have generally pointed to the obvious coincidence with the rise of (a) the capitalist State, and (b) modern imperialism. The *nature* of the connection, however, has rarely been made clear.

One attempt to fill the gap is Gellner's argument that before the era of modern imperialism, there were, conceptually, two polar types of society: the tight-knit, small tribe, which was a cultural as well as a political unit, at one end, and the large, conglomerate empire at the other. In both kinds of society, however, the individual was clearly located in a definite position in the social structure, usually by the fact of birth, and the local groups he belonged to were articulated with the structure of the society as a whole. Modern society, by contrast, though by no means devoid of strong structures (e.g., bureaucratic organizations), are 'looser', being built upon dynamic industrial economies which require geographical and status mobility. Relationships between people, therefore, tend to be more ephemeral 'encounters' between persons who interact for specific purposes, rather than a many-sided knowledge of each other gained through spending lifetimes as fellow-members of 'intimate, given structures'. In such societies, structure is strong, but culture by no means uniform or important, as a mechanism of integration.

Since we now have to communicate with people *un*familiar to us, a standardized culture, and especially the language we communicate in, becomes of central importance. What that language contains is the knowledge needed for life in modern industrial society. The village cannot provide that; it can only fit a person to be a member of village society, which is a 'part-society'. It can, that is, equip him to become a peasant *within* an industrial society. If he wants access to the wider culture, he must learn the language and culture of the centres of that society, i.e., the culture of the city. This analysis, however, requires a further explanation of the rise of the centralized State and of industrial society (Gellner, 1964).

Countries which develop first as industrial nation-states constitute a model for latecomers, Gellner argues. The 'demonstration-effect', however, gives rise to unintended imitations in the form of new independent movements of national liberation and mobilization for development, rather than the evolution of Africans into little Frenchmen, since colonial society in fact provided Africans scarcely any opportunity to become either French or prosperous. In the growth of such 'reactive' nationalism, the intelligentsia is crucial. Unlike traditional intellectual groups – clerks and priests in pre-industrial society – their role is not to ensure the functioning of the society and to defend its ideas, but to change the social order and bring in the new. Mass support is forthcoming from the new urban proletariat, itself uprooted from traditional attachment to the village. The intellectuals therefore turn to the masses.

It is not the case that every nationalism that tries to do so is successful in becoming a nation, of course: many fail, usually because they are simply suppressed by more powerful neighbours (e.g., the fate of Armenian, Kurdish or Biafran nationalism). Others come to terms with more powerful, or equally balanced, neighbouring nationalities within multi-national states (Canada, Belgium, U.S.S.R.).

The question of why it is the State to which nationalism becomes attached has received most attention from Marxists, who have shown how the unification of the market and the centralization of power under the Absolutist state proceeded hand-in-hand: two dimensions of a single explanation in terms of 'political economy', firstly, during the early emergence of capitalism, and later, on a world scale, with the expansion of these countries, now industrialized, to absorb the rest of the world. Nationalism was the cultural consolidation of the centralized State. Nairn has argued that the colonized countries, in order to throw off the control of the West and mobilize for development – 'the great compensatory drive to catch up' – has had to mobilize *people*, 'more or less all the nationalists had going for them' (Nairn, 1975, p. 12), since they lacked capital:

Through nationalism . . . societies try to propel themselves forward to certain kinds of goal (industrialization, prosperity, equality with other peoples, etc.) *by a certain kind of regression* – by looking inwards, drawing more deeply upon their indigenous resources, resurrecting past folk-heroes and myths . . . [They] have to look desperately back into the past to gather strength wherever it can be found for the ordeal of 'development' (p. 18, italics in original).

Nation triumphed over class, he argues, because the dominant bourgeoisies in each country took over an ideology of the nation, and developed it to fit their interests, at the same time as they took over the running of the State. Hence socialist *inter*nationalism could only be a premature 'utopia'. Capitalism could organize successfully on the basis of a cross-class, national appeal precisely because the class consciousness and organization of the working class were weak and embryonic. This triumphant bourgeois nationalism is now challenged by a 'new nationalism' in the Third World, because the latter is infused with socialism. Nevertheless, *all* forms of nationalism are flawed, he argues, since they fall short of the ideal of the 'social development of the *whole* world'.

Stratification, then, involves much more than simply occupation. It involves our memberships of all kinds of social groups and categories which affect our access to social 'goods'. In modern industrialized societies gender and ethnic identity still remain important bases for allocating whole categories of people to positions of lower or higher status and reward. Yet they are no longer – like castes or estates – absolute and fixed bases of discrimination. Today, they are challenged both legally and informally.

Discrimination on the basis of ethnicity, race or gender, though, as we have seen, both ancient and universal, has taken its modern forms largely in response to the demands of the economy for supplies of cheap labour. It is to the analysis of the latter, therefore, that we must now turn.

We will take each of the three major dimensions of stratification classically formulated by Max Weber: economic inequalities (usually called 'class' on its own), status inequalities and power inequalities: and discuss each in turn.

Class

Most people who live in class societies are aware that they do, though their ideas about class may not coincide with the sociologist's model of the class-system nor with his evaluation of their particular class position. A person's class position may also be differently evaluated by others besides sociologists: by neighbours, workmates, relatives, etc. People in society have their own understanding of the class-system, of the graduations of prestige, and of the way power is distributed. These 'folk-models' are not merely cognitive – making *intellectual* sense of the stratification-system – they also have a moral or normative element: people evaluate the system as good or bad. Even where individuals or groups operate with the same intellectual model, they may differ in their moral evaluation of the system according to their position in it: the poor may regard their own poverty as divinely ordained or they may regard it as unjust.

There are, however, criteria such as a person's occupation or the amount of money he earns, which *all* can agree about, irrespective of their ideas about class in general or this or that person's position in particular. It might seem possible, then, to find a way of defining class quite *objectively*. But we all know that it is very often the case that whilst X's neighbours insist that X is working-class, X obstinately considers himself to be *middle*-class. X's ideas (and his neighbours') cannot be ignored, because they affect their behaviour. He is more likely, for instance, to associate with people he regards as middle-class, follow middle-class patterns of recreation, try to use a middle-class accent, have middle-class ambitions for his children, etc. His *subjective* perception of his class position cannot, therefore, be simply written off as 'wrong' or – more sophisticatedly – as 'false consciousness', to use the Marxist term, if we are to understand why people behave as they do, for although in other people's eyes a man may be 'wrong' in his opinion of himself, his belief, as W. I. Thomas, the American sociologist put it, is '*real* in its consequences', that is, it affects the way he behaves.

Any adequate sociological account of social class in all its dimensions must include and explain the conceptions of the social actors themselves. We will see later how inadequate many well-known models of social class are, because they do not take account of people's ideas; the subjective measure of social class is as much a reality as any objective measure of a man's income, though it is harder to get at.

A further difficulty is that we are dealing with rapidly changing societies, in which social class changes rapidly also, and in which people realize that such changes are taking place. So it becomes difficult to draw hard-and-fast borderlines between classes when hundreds of thousands of people move into occupations different from those of their parents, or marry people of different class backgrounds, or feel perhaps that class is not as important or as rigid as it was in Dickens's day.

There certainly have been significant changes in the way people are distributed *within* the class system. (It is much more debatable whether the system as a whole has changed to any significant extent.) (Westergaard and Resler, 1977.) But some kinds of change are obvious, notably the expansion of the 'tertiary' sector of the economy which has meant a decrease in the number of low-paid manual jobs and an increase in the proportion of jobs in the service occupations, the clerical sector, etc. Though such jobs nowadays are not necessarily paid any better than manual occupations (especially when overtime is so generally worked), they still retain an aura of 'middle-classness' and some real differences in treatment at work and in society generally. And with so many of the new jobs going to women, even though the women are less well-paid, their income makes the *family* appreciably better off. Many other kinds of change are equally apparent. We all know that the growth of educational opportunities and expanding industrial production have both led to an increased volume of upward social mobility as well as to new avenues for achieving such mobility, and that the very worst extremes of physical poverty have been eliminated. On the other hand, not only do the poor obstinately remain with us, but their numbers are legion, and welfare provision by the State has been seriously eroded in recent years (in some respects, the provision is less effective than it was half a century ago) (Titmuss, 1958, p. 24). Nor has 'progressive' taxation made any serious impact upon the wealthy (Titmuss, 1962), or abolished poverty (Kincaid, 1973). And by and large enhanced social and political equality – notably the extension of rights formerly restricted to the upper classes to the whole population (Marshall, 1950) – had made little difference as far as the elimination of economic inequality is concerned.

These complex changes have led naturally to varying interpretations. Some argue that one result has been the adoption of middle-class styles of life by the new non-manual workers; others argue that not only has the gap between non-manual workers and the middle class diminished, but that the gap between non-manual workers and manual workers has also narrowed (whether in terms of income or in the uses to which they put their incomes). Yet others accept one or both of these propositions, but go on to argue that class differences of a new kind have emerged: that as gross inequalities diminish, more refined distinctions spring up in their place, usually in the form of visible items of consumption – cars, clothing and so on. This argument assumes that a sense of deprivation and actual discrimination does not simply arise at a given level of poverty, but depends on the comparisons people make between their own life-situations and those of others. Poverty is a relative, socially-defined matter; what is poverty in one society is comfort in another, and the same applies *within* a society. The people we compare ourselves with tend to be those we live amongst rather than those we only know about at second hand (Runciman, 1966).

These fairly common views, which we will examine in more detail below, obviously reflect real recent changes, for people also make comparisons over time: between their contemporary life-experience and the era of the Second World War, the depression which preceded it, or their 'folk-memories' of nineteenth-century conditions. For many of us, the history of massive over-crowding, endemic and industrial disease and alcoholism is a part of family, not simply school-book history. Charles Booth's *Life and Labour of the People of London* and other works showed that around 1890 a third of the families lived in poverty. Only slowly did successive Factory Acts lead to improvement of conditions in the work-place. Trade Unions also gradually recruited more and more workers into organizations which brought collective pressure to bear on employers to raise wages, limit hours and improve working conditions for those at work, and on the State to provide minimal relief for those without work.

These limited advances, however significant, by no means generated a completely new and autonomous working-class culture, opposed intransigently to the culture of capitalism. Indeed, the very concessions won, both in the field of politics and in industrial relations, made it possible for the power-wielders to generate a new kind of social support. Working-class habits and values of deference, partly derived from the pre-industrial past, were strongly ingrained: in 1868, the Birmingham branch of the Conservative Working Men's Association had nearly 3000 members. This 'great constitutional army' (as Disraeli called it) grew to 700 local associations and branches in 1875; it was the political expression of working-class deference to established society. But there was also political and industrial resistance. Indeed, the very fear of such resistance – and of increasing working-class self-expression, whether through the ballot-box or otherwise – was an important stimulus to the deliberate political organization of the masses. 'Tory Democracy' was a response to an era during which the common people had begun to create their own quite untraditional and often radical mass organizations, from Chartism through to the wave of trade unionization in the 1880s and the formation of the Labour Party in 1900.

In other industrialized countries, working-class politics and trade unionism were often much more radical, as in the anarcho-syndicalism of France at the turn of the century. Yet, in the longer run, the political parties founded upon the basis of large-scale working-class support, though sometimes Communist (as in France and Italy), were not revolutionary in practice, and mainly oriented themselves to 'reformist' political struggles. We can use the experience of England, then, as an example of this wider pattern of development in advanced capitalist countries, despite the fact that there are also other significant differences which we do not discuss here (e.g. the existence of a revolutionary tradition in countries like France).

Social class, indeed, is pre-eminently visible in England, so that this country constitutes a strategic case to study. It is literally visible in differences of dress and audible in differences of accent. It even continues, if not beyond the grave, at least into the graveyard, where the major differences in mortuary furniture are determined by wealth, not denomination. In the nineteenth century, when the lower classes could be referred to as the 'great unwashed', class was no doubt registered by the nose also. The growing prominence of social class as the major feature shaping the general structure and culture of society was reflected in changes in linguistic usage as well as in new organizations and laws. When we look back at the nineteenth century, it often seems to us a very clear and simple picture, patently a 'class society'. Yet it by no means appeared so simple and self-evident to people at the time, nor did they necessarily perceive it as a highly-visible *system*. They did not even use the term 'class' with economic connotations until well into the century. Asa Briggs has pointed out that citizens and writers alike continued to use terms like 'ranks', 'orders' and 'degrees' (Briggs, 1960, p. 43), terms reflecting their origins in rural society, for the new urban population was made up of recent immigrants from the countryside: ex-peasants (tenants, agricultural labourers, cottagers, etc.), and still used the concepts and language of a traditional rural social order, despite its disruption which reached its climax with the enclosures.

Today class divisions are plainly of crucial importance in all areas of life. They are much more than just analytical or administrative categories. As we shall see, though classes are, in one sense, certainly abstractions (since they only partially have any institutional form), classes nevertheless produce numerous organizations and other kinds of grouping which tend to behave in the same way (in 'parallel') or to act together. They think of themselves as having like interests, and share similar cultural patterns.

Many researchers are only interested in using some indicator of class for limited purposes, as we noted. They are not in fact trying to carry out a many-sided analysis of social class in general. They are not interested necessarily in explaining how it arises or what consequences it has for the social order, but simply in collecting and using information about it. So they may, for their specific purposes, use a single indicator of class, and this may be quite accurate and usable enough in order to tell you, say, where you would be best advised to put your advertisements. For more complex analyses, however, we need to use several different indicators, as indeed people commonly do in their everyday social intercourse. Thus we classify and rank people by income, by their housing (a recent study speaks of 'housing classes' (Rex and Moore, 1967)), by their educational level, by occupation or by wealth. These are the main aspects of class, and each can be used for different purposes, or they can be combined.

Many operations of classifying the population are not concerned at all with the all-round behaviour of people in different classes, or with the nature of the relationships *between* the classes. They are often concerned simply with the individual, or with a single dimension of a person's social being, not with other attributes. It may be their individual purchasing power the analyst is interested in, not their clubs or trade unions, or their conflicts or other relationships with other classes. The analyst, that is, may be interested only in class as a category or set of individuals, not in its group aspects.

If we just want to tax income, then all we need is an estimate of income; we do not even need to know a person's job. Since ability to pay a given level of rent or mortgage depends on income, housing officials or hire-purchase firms can be satisfied with income, too. But the Registrar-General in Britain, or the Bureau of the Census in the U.S.A., need better indicators of the totality of a person's social attributes than income alone, because governments need to know about the characteristics of their population for a great variety of purposes, not just to tax them or house them, but for educational purposes, for transport policy, for military purposes, for health and social welfare purposes, and a hundred and one other reasons.

Simply to classify by income will probably give us a good indicator of class, for some limited purposes. Income depends more on occupation than anything else (except, mainly, for the very wealthy). But the income-bracket between, say, £2000 per annum and £2999 will in fact contain people of quite different occupations and therefore classes: some skilled workers, some small shopkeepers (independent proprietors), some managers of small firms and so on. Since these are very different occupations, this means that people from different social classes fall within the same income-bracket, for some will be independent, others employers, others the employed.

So income is not enough for many sociological purposes, because income-brackets constitute 'logical' classes, *categories* of people sharing some property in common. Classes, on the other hand, are collectivities that exist in society and not simply in the shape of sets of figures. A 'logical' class like an income-bracket may *reflect* social class, it does not constitute it.

If we do want to economize and use as few indicators as possible, one alone is likely to be satisfactory – occupation. Hence it is widely used by researchers and administrators. It is economical, since other characteristics need not be added; many of these other characteristics, if we do record them, are usually found to be sufficiently closely dependent upon or associated with occupation that to use several of them tells us little extra, so that for most purposes occupation is enough. Given a person's occupation, we can estimate fairly well the probability of the kind of income, educational level, housing, politics, etc., he will have, for these things tend to hang together.

Occupation is, in fact, the single most commonly used indicator of social class, particularly by governments and advertising agencies. In Britain, for instance, over 30,000 officially-named different occupational titles are recognized by the Registrar-General, so the attempt is made to group sets of occupations together to form what are claimed to be 'social classes' (see Cole, 1955, p. 6). In the Registrar-General's scheme of five social classes, Class I is not very satisfactory because, being based on occupation, it neglects wealth and ownership; the extremely wealthy and powerful are therefore lost to view amongst thousands of much less important 'directors' (and even 'university teachers', who are also Class I). Class II contains over half the minor administrative, professional and managerial occupations, as well as farmers, shopkeepers and small employers. It thus mixes up groups which belong to quite *different* social classes: some belonging to what Mills describes as the 'old' middle classes, on the one hand, and others to the 'new' middle classes: the one-man shopkeeper, say, as against the departmental manager in a big firm.

Class III, critics have remarked (Carr-Saunders *et al.*, 1958, p. 117), 'is too mixed . . . to serve any useful classification', for it includes half the male population, mostly skilled manual workers but also a high proportion of 'lower-middle-class' occupations, as well as shop assistants, clerks, foremen and supervisors.

There is an equally unsatisfactory further grouping of occupations to form 'socio-economic groups', constructed sometimes by classifying occupations in the same *industry* together, sometimes by grouping occupations that *cut across* industrial divisions. Thus crane-drivers are lumped together, whether they work in the building industry or on the docks; captains of ships, fishing-vessels and planes are also grouped together.

The confusion is compounded because these classifications inevitably involve not just the listing, but the *ranking* of the differing occupations according to prestige, power, income-level, skill, or some such criterion.

Some occupations are ranked 'high' and some 'low'. The criteria used are remarkably inconsistent, nor is there any satisfactory explanation of the logic or practical procedures used. Thus, as well as simple occupation, we find that 'employment *status*' is used, that is, whether a person is an employer, or pursues an occupation in which he is *employed*, or is his own employer. Yet at other times 'employment status' means the *level* of a job, for example, whether one is an apprentice, foreman or suchlike; 'farmers' are distinguished from 'agricultural workers'; 'employers' and 'managers' are divided into different sets according to the size of the enterprise.

Thus all sorts of inconsistent criteria are used, and this is in the nature of things, for no adequate analysis of social class can be developed simply on the basis of occupation. Even apparently 'objective' indices such as income or occupation, then, prove inadequate for sociological purposes (they may be perfectly adequate for governmental purposes). The inadequacy derives from trying to reduce the three dimensions of stratification – economic role, status and position in the system of power – to one single indicator, and from trying to eliminate the subjective aspects. In the end, they are smuggled in: occupations are *evaluated* according to skill, prestige, power, etc. Since different people judge things in different ways, there can be no general agreement. In the United States three different major occupational scales devised by different sociologists place farmers in social classes I, II and III respectively, and insurance agents likewise (Caplow, 1954, ch. 2).*

Putting whole groups into different categories can thus lead to radically different pictures of the over-all class structure.

Since purely 'objective' criteria, such as income, are inadequate for many sociological purposes, and since the 'subjective' prestige attaching to different kinds of jobs is obviously a crucial element in social class, some researchers have tried to develop models of 'social class' on a purely subjective basis. They have not tried to rank occupations so as to form classes at all: instead, they asked people to say what class *they* put themselves in, or asked a panel of informants what class they thought other people belonged to.

The problem here is that people's responses are affected by the jobs, people and statuses they know about, and by the categories you offer them (and by the categories you use to group their answers if you leave them free to answer in any terms they like to use), as well as by the situation at the time of the inquiry. Thus a famous Gallup inquiry of 1939 found that 88 per cent of a sample of the U.S. population classified themselves as 'middle class'. 'America is middle class', ran the headlines. But Gallup had only allowed people to rate themselves as 'upper', 'middle' or 'lower' class. Few evidently liked to call themselves 'lower', for when the survey was repeated shortly afterwards and the term 'working' class was introduced instead of 'lower', 51 per cent now described themselves as *working* class! Obviously, no revolution had taken place in people's self-images; it was just that different questions and different possible answers had been used. A purely subjective approach to social class thus leaves us with no firm conclusions.

Indeed, the answers people give will always be relative and situational. Their attitudes will be affected by national developments – by strikes, by the degree of national prosperity, by their personal

*Caplow has shown how various attempts to classify occupations in the U.S.A. also use many different criteria: technical distinctions (such as between farming and non-farming); distinctions of level (some jobs are labelled 'professional' or 'executive'); a public/private distinction (policemen, soldiers, firemen are 'public' workers, not ranked with other workers who are classified as 'skilled', 'semiskilled' or 'unskilled') and so on. And, he asks, how do we classify 'deviant' occupations – gamblers, prostitutes and so on (should they be 'skilled workers')?

degree of success or their experience of their own or other people's mobility, etc.

Class consciousness, then, is constantly shifting and people will think about class in quite different ways in different contexts. We can never hope, then, to get an *absolute* picture of social class in its totality, for there is no such uniformity in people's thinking or behaviour. What we can do is to develop usable indicators, which will help us predict, and to work out how variables hang together (say, occupation and racial discrimination). Though we cannot reach complete agreement about class, we are by no means prevented from discovering how it works or from developing quite useful ways of measuring it for our given purposes.

A purely subjective concept of class is certainly as unsatisfactory as objective ones which omit the subjective altogether, for underlying people's varying ideas are common experiences of real things happening in the world around them. Too many people in similar occupations think in similar terms for class to be simply an arbitrary matter of self-definition. Underlying these shared views of the world – and the conflict between vital models of class – are real inequalities of wealth, power and prestige. So common patterns of behaviour emerge amongst people in common life-situations and the range of variations is not likely to be very large on many matters.

The search for a model of class which can command the agreement of all is, in the end, an illusion, for in class-divided societies consensus about the social values which underly different perceptions and evaluations of class and status does not exist. There are only different views of the class structure held by different groups in that structure, and normally the views of the most powerful classes become the official cultural pattern, even though it may be constantly challenged by many of the less privileged. We should scarcely be surprised to find, then, that there is no consensus about the shape of the class system, or how it works, for this is exactly what we should expect to find in a class-divided society: different, even radically opposed models. The existence of many differing conceptions of the class system is naturally even more likely in rapidly changing societies.

The complexity of conceptions of class, that is, reflects not only the different positions and interests of people in the system, but also the constant changes going on in society. The idea that class divisions used to be much simpler and more obvious in the nineteenth century is undoubtedly wrong. They are no more self-evident or simpler today. Few people think, for instance, of social class solely in terms of one single factor – whether it be income, educational level, residence area, job or accent. They usually think of a *cluster* of related variables (Martin, 1954a, pp. 60–62).

Some sociologists, too, attempt to 'decompose' class into lower-level groupings, arguing that it is these that people recognize and identify with: a given occupation or profession, rather than classes, or argue that the different technologies used in different industries produce quite different attitudes towards work and towards authority, and different wage- and skill-structures and opportunities for promotion. Hence, they argue, there will be marked variations in the kinds of class consciousness, in the incidence of satisfaction and dissatisfaction, and in militancy or otherwise, according to industry rather than according to occupation or class (Blauner, 1964).

Occupational identity, however, is not the same thing as class membership or class consciousness. Indeed, the two can be seen as intrinsically opposed, as Westergaard has argued:

[There] is an assumption that the kind of working-class unity which finds expression in industrial, or more especially in political, action draws its nourishment from the simpler and more intimate loyalties of neighbourhood and kin. Consequently, it is postulated, as the latter are weakened so the former declines. The assumption is highly questionable. For its implies that the solidarity of class – which is societal in its sweep, and draws no nice distinctions between men of this place and that, this name and that, this dialect and that – is rooted in the kind of parochial solidarity which is its very antithesis . . . Sectional loyalties of region and occupation have contributed in the past to the formation of wider loyalties of class; but the permanence of that contribution has depended upon a transcendence of the original narrow basis of solidarity. Thus the developing labour movement has in many cases drawn special strength from the workers of such locally cohesive, homogeneous communities as the mining valleys of Britain and the timber districts of Scandinavia . . . and the industries located in communities of this kind are still characterized by a comparatively high incidence of strike action. Yet, at the political level especially, the collective force of the labour movement grew precisely as the local isolation of these and other working-class communities declined (Westergaard, 1972, p. 147).

Differences of occupation, and differences from industry to industry – differences within the productive process – certainly reflect technical imperatives of the organization of labour required by the use of different kinds of machinery, but there is a more fundamental common pattern running through all kinds of capitalist industrial organization: a division, not of labour, but of property (which is mostly, too, inherited wealth rather than income earned as a result of playing some managerial role within industry) (Gouldner, 1970, ch. 8).

Most people, as well as most sociologists, recognize these economic facts of life (though they may not necessarily be aroused to protest at such patent inequality). Even the most capitalistic of advertising managers follows Marx in taking class as the most important social grouping. He will therefore divide the population into income-brackets when carrying out his surveys of consumer habits; the Registrar-General divides the country into social classes he has constructed mainly on the basis of occupation; and even the most conservative political parties break down electoral constituencies in terms of their class composition so that they can calculate where their main vote lies and where it is worth canvassing.

But the basic economic inequality, it is often forgotten, is not that of *occupation* at all. The social relations of economic domination and subjection at work and in the market-place which result in inequality themselves derive from inequalities in the distribution of *property*: possession of goods – capital, land, plant. These constitute sources of income that, in turn, may be used for further acquisition (Atkinson, 1974). For there are wealthy people who do not work, or whose income from various kinds of property means that 'earned income' is not vital or their largest source of income, or who work because of the social value placed on work, or because they must do something. Often they work (e.g., as directors) in an occupation which is the source of their property – managing a farm they own, an enterprise they hold a key block of shares in, and so forth. And rich people often 'work' at such activities as politics and other forms of 'public service', too, such as running voluntary associations. This explains the curious phenomenon we noticed of the disappearance of the extremely wealthy in census categories for *wealth* disappears when they are only classified by 'occupation' (much of their income, we saw, also disappears in taxation records). The great bulk of the population, conversely, owns little beyond their 'personal' property. This difference between personal property and property as a source of income means that, for most people, property consists largely of houses on mortgages and cars on hire-purchase (Westergaard and Resler, 1977, Part 2; Atkinson, 1974, p. 4).

It follows that the reduction of general inequalities, in a class system based on private property, depends primarily on making changes in the distribution of property. Despite the elimination of extreme poverty, despite the mobility we have described, and despite the greater power of labour in periods of full employment, little redistribution of property has occurred. In 1973, over a quarter of all personal wealth was owned by the richest 1 per cent of the adult population; a half by the richest 5 per cent; and two-thirds by the richest 10 per cent (Royal Commission on the Distribution of Income and Wealth, 1975, Tables 29 and 45, pp. 80, 138). So the chances that those born into different social classes will stay in those classes are still very high.

Though there is a good deal of mobility, most of it is, in fact, very short-range mobility. The myths of 'long-distance' mobility – 'from log-cabin to President' – are, overwhelmingly, myths as far as the life-chances of the mass of the population are concerned. Though something like a third of the population moves upwards, if one compares the jobs they do with the ones their fathers did, a further third also moves down, and these proportions remain remarkably constant for industrial capitalist countries such as the U.K., the U.S.A., W. Germany, France and Sweden which otherwise differ greatly in culture and in historical development. In the U.K., Westergaard remarks, 'no change of substance in the amount of movement up and down the social scale [occurred] till about the time of World War II. And there seems to have been little increase in social circulation after that either' (Westergaard and Resler, 1977, p. 315). Job-changing is a fairly common phenomenon: about two in every five people at work in the U.K. changed employers between 1953 and 1963, for example. But only one in five changed job *level*. Most such changes, too, occur when people are starting their working lives; only few of them later in life. Much mobility is caused by migration from the countryside into town, much by the availability of new jobs and the displacement of others due to technological innovation. People change their social class, too, not solely by changing their job, but by changing their status in other ways. Thus Illsley and his colleagues found that 46 per cent of Aberdeen women with professional and managerial class origins married skilled-worker husbands, and 40 per cent of the wives of professionals and managers had fathers who were skilled workers (quoted in Lipset and Bendix, 1959, p. 46).

The two countries with the highest rates of long-range mobility are the U.S.S.R., and the U.S.A., precisely the most dynamically-expanding economies.

In contrast to feudal or caste stratification, then, class membership within an individual's lifetime, in industrial society, is much more variable, due to changes of the types just mentioned, even if people do not move very far above or below their parents. Intergenerational upward and downward mobility are the consequences of these changes. Comparatively, too, the strata in a class system are more open. The sheer multiplication of occupations in modern societies, moreover, divides such vast categories as 'working class' into innumerable specialized occupations, many of which (like 'clobberer', 'plugger-up', 'poker-in', or 'roarer') we would not recognize even if we were told their (quite official) names.

Individual mobility is by no means the sole form of mobility, however, for corporate groups also use their organized strength to promote the interests of their members as a collectivity. This kind of collective mobility is the main kind for most people whose chances of improving their position are likely to depend on trade union action rather than on individual advancement. But there are other avenues for individual mobility, for example, promotion, the acquisition of qualifications, etc.

The lives of a great many people, however, are not characterized by mobility at all, rather by a continuity of life, even between their lives and those of their parents, which gives rise to stable groups, within classes, marked off from each other by 'traditional' differences of behaviour, dress, marriage-patterns, areas of residence and the like – and a strong sense of these differences as marking them off from other such groups: what Parkin has termed 'social closure' (Parkin, 1974). Nor is individual mobility, where it occurs, very impressive. For most people it is usually restricted to one move across a class line in a lifetime, and then, as we have seen, not very far and usually early in life. Most people know this, for their social aspirations do not usually aim very far. Skilled workers typically aim at higher education for their children, but not, usually, *university* education. They have more limited aspirations which are consonant with their industrial experience: they hope their children will go on to technological studies. The educational system is, of course, the single major new channel of social mobility available to the working class, and a quarter of the students at British universities today come from working-class homes. Only 4 per cent of them, however, had fathers who were manual workers, nor has the proportion at university changed significantly since before the Second World War.

The one group of working-class people which does have exceptionally high educational aspirations for its children is the new clerical strata, whose ambitions indeed exceed those of professional and executive parents (Martin, 1954b, p. 172). The education industry itself provides many jobs for intelligent and ambitious young working-class men and has done so since mass education began: in the 1930s, for example, working-class recruits typically became teachers who staffed the expanded secondary and primary school systems. One of them was D. H. Lawrence, whose biography is typical: not only the son of a miner, but also under the close influence of a mother who had married 'beneath her'.

His history of social mobility thus brings us to one of the most crucial social groups, membership of which profoundly affects one's prospects for mobility – the family. Though we do not often think of it as such, the family is, in fact, a unit of *social class*, not merely a private domestic arrangement. Thus the family may 'sponsor' a son's advancement, and families like Lawrence's, where the mother is more highly educated than the father, are likely to produce more ambitious and successful offspring than families where the father is the more educated of the two parents; since the mother's relationship to the children is usually closer than that of the father, she influences them more. The family is the critical unit in the class system at the upper end of the class hierarchy, too. The kinship connections of the British 'power élite' have been well documented (Lupton and Wilson, 1959), and family connections in business are, of course, often very important. The continuity of the privileged classes too, then, depends upon another aspect of the family – the inheritance system. And more widely, the position of children and wives in most societies has been primarily dependent upon the father's and husband's place in it; they are 'dependent variables'. The family is also a central socializing agent through which children are prepared for their future roles. The role of the family as a unit of social class demonstrates, then, that it is far too simplistic to describe modern society as predominantly 'achievement-oriented'. There are indeed important areas open to individual achievement, but ascriptive considerations – the roles one is 'born into' or has allotted to one – remain very significant.

Marx's Theory of Class

It has been said that all modern sociology is a debate with the ghost of Marx. Certainly, much of it is, and a key element in Marx's sociology is the role he gives to class. For him class is the motor of social development. True, there was a period of primitive communism, according to Marx, and there will be a classless society in the future, but most of hitherto recorded human history, as the Communist Manifesto declares in its opening lines, has been the history of class struggle. More fundamentally, class struggle itself is only one manifestation of change and conflict which are endemic in society. Society is continually undergoing development, and different groups of men have different interests at stake which they seek to promote and defend: the most important of such groups are those occupying a similar position in a system of production–classes.

Because they occupy different positions in the productive system, these classes come into conflict with each other. The class which owns the means of production is able to secure the surplus product and keep other classes in subordinate positions. The exploited class, however, does not inevitably resist, nor even question the ruling class's right to rule. In the earlier phases of development of a new productive system, too, they may even secure certain benefits by allying themselves with a dynamic new class which overthrows an older dominant class standing in the way of both of them.

Thus, despite this division of society into potentially-conflicting classes (since the surplus social product produced by the peasants or workers is appropriated by those who own the means of production – the land, machines, capital), the antagonistic classes do not necessarily always come into open and direct conflict. The exploited do not, indeed, necessarily even become aware that they are a *class*. By virtue of their situation, then, men may be 'objectively' opposed whilst, subjectively, they lack this 'consciousness of class'.

Marx, following quite orthodox classical economic theory, distinguished three major classes, each of which was characterized in its role in the productive system by the 'factor of production' it controlled – the land-owners, obviously, by their ownership of *land*; the capitalists ('bourgeoisie') by their ownership of *capital*; and the proletariat (working class) by their 'ownership' of their labour power.

For classical economics, each of these classes was a necessary and economically creative component in the productive process, each performing a functionally useful role in providing the needed 'factors' of land, capital and labour. Marx, however, regarded the relationship between the classes not as one of functional complementarity, even less harmony, but as one of social inequality, economic exploitation and political domination of the workers by the bourgeoisie. Thus the return to the capitalist on his capital – profit – and the return to the landlord on his land – rent – were of a different order from the return secured by the worker on the labour he expended. For the labourer was the only one of these three economic actors who was actually a *producer*: even the capital of the capitalist was not something the capitalist had produced. It was simply the past labour of worker-producers, 'congealed' or locked up in the form of capital. Since the worker produced *more* than he received back in the form of wages, this 'surplus value' went to the owner of the means of production. The capitalist's capital first came from this surplus extracted from the worker – hence the intrinsic conflict beween them. The exploited class was not inevitably revolutionary. Industrial workers, in defending their interests by fighting for improvements in wages or working conditions, commonly restricted their demands to such narrow economic issues, and confined their interests to their particular trade, shop, factory or industry. They did not automatically associate and collaborate with other workers to form 'working-class' organizations even for strictly economic ends. Even less did they necessarily move beyond the economic issues to a wider concern with political ones. They might thus have what Lenin was later to call a 'trade union consciousness', but not a 'political consciousness'. But the workers might not even possess a simple 'trade union consciousness' of themselves *as a class*, especially where they had only recently come from the countryside (like so many newcomers to the city in the Third World today), and were wholly preoccupied with sheer survival in a quite unfamiliar and appalling world where, when they did find work, there were always hundreds of others waiting for their jobs if they stepped out of line, and where they were working in small-scale workshops, under a master who controlled them personally and directly, whether by paternalistic or repressive methods. They might thus be a class in so far as they occupied a *common situation* in a productive system, but even though the observer could see that they were all in the same boat and similarly exploited, even though each man individually might feel or even understand that he was being exploited, they did not necessarily feel themselves to *be*, even less act *as*, a class. They were, in Marx's classic phrases, a 'class *in* themselves' but not yet a 'class *for* themselves'.

The *objective* situation of having a common position in the production system needed complementing by *subjective* class consciousness of their common interests before they could fully become a class. Marx's theory is thus not just 'economic determinism', as is often commonly assumed, nor is his theory an 'objective' theory of class, because for him, a class could never become fully a class without this interplay between their subjective consciousness and their objective life-circumstances which he called a 'dialectical' interplay. Subjective consciousness, then, was not an automatic concomitant of exploitation, for Marx: it is something that develops and emerges over time. Poor people, indeed, have been very passive throughout history. Class-consciousness develops in part because the antagonistic parties engage in struggle, and find themselves lining up with different allies on different sides. They come to know who is friend, and who enemy, in action. Yet men do think, too, and some have the training and leisure to do so more effectively: intellectual and political leadership is often given to the masses by 'intellectuals' whose role is to generate ideas, analysis and consciousness and thereby stimulate others to act. Without some idea of where they were going; without some identification of who their friends and enemies were, respectively, some theory of how power can be seized, and some understanding of the respective strengths and weaknesses of themselves and of the bourgeoisie, the working class, Marx believed, would not move into action, or, if it did, would make serious mistakes.

As we have seen, economic power, for Marx, gave the wealthy the resources and the authoritative control over men which enabled them also to exercise *political* power, for if production was a highly co-operative social activity, appropriation of the surplus was a highly anti-social act, resulting from private ownership. Each class of people, further, tended to associate socially with its own kind and have its characteristic outlook and sets of ideas about the world. Class was therefore not simply an 'economic' phenomenon, but a *social* one. It permeated all areas of social life. Power, wealth, religious and social prestige, and culturally distinctive ways of life tended to cohere and to form a different pattern – a 'culture of class' – for each social class. But the 'weight' of each of these various attributes was not equal, for it was the position of a person in a system of production that was the factor that Marx saw as underpinning all his other relationships. The 'mode of production' in a society – the way it organizes labour and capital, men and instruments to produce goods – is the foundation or basis on which are built the other major institutions of social life.

The major institutions of society reflect the interests of the dominant social class. These institutions are congruent with, or at least do not endanger the interests of, that minority which controls both economic production and society: the complex cultural life of a whole society thus reposes upon an economic foundation.

All these other spheres of life – the dominant ideas of the time, the family, religion, the law – 'reflect' or are shaped by relationships established in production – for example, in law, the importance of the *contract* reflects the basic relationship between employer and worker in capitalist society – the contract, under which the worker undertakes to work so many hours and the master to pay specified wages in return. Their relationship outside work was of no legal concern to either partner; the master had no responsibility for the worker's housing, for the health of his children, etc. The relationship was an economic one, in which each party contracted to perform certain services, and had no other social obligation towards the other. The contrast between this pattern of relationship, symbolized by the contract, which Marx thought to typify capitalist society, in which the only important relationship between man and man was a relationship established by what he called the 'cash nexus', and the pattern of relationship in, say, feudal society, is very marked, for in a feudal society a man owed his lord a whole variety of social obligations, and his lord owed him various services likewise. The relationship between the two, that is, was not simply a one-stranded economic relationship, but a much wider, even total, social relationship, albeit an exploitative one. The relationship of worker to employer under the law in capitalist society, however, appears to be one of two formally equal parties freely entering into an agreement, for specific and limited purposes only. Each pursues his own interest: both benefit in different ways.

In fact, Marx says, this equality is spurious and the workers' freedom illusory. The law formally seems to treat each party equally, but this is a deception. The law works to the advantage of the powerful, sometimes because the worker is directly deprived of legal rights (as when trade unions are proscribed), or, more obliquely, because in any case the worker can be dismissed, whilst he cannot similarly sanction his employer. Only by collective organization (trade unions, political parties) can the workers' position be strengthened; this strengthening of the workers' hand would lead eventually to revolution. Revolution would occur in the most developed capitalist countries where the social nature of production was most advanced since thousands of workers co-operated in producing a product, but where the owners still appropriated the surplus privately. Under such conditions of 'socialized' production, the private appropriator was clearly an anachronism. He would be swept away, and the surplus made available to society in general. Hence the term 'socialism'. Thenceforward, the already social production-system would proceed without the capitalist, but would be run instead by the producers in the general interests of the whole society.

The advanced capitalist industrial countries have indeed seen a great development of working-class institutions, notably trade unions and socialist and communist political parties. The working class, however, has also continued to give massive support to non-socialist parties (two in five voted Conservative in 1974, including about a third of trade unionists). And the very power of the Labour movement has led to major improvements which seem to have muted the appeal of revolution rather than led the workers to move on to a revolutionary total challenge to capitalism and to its overthrow. Instead, the revolutionary countries of the twentieth century have been backward, mainly agrarian countries such as Russia, China and Cuba.

There has thus been no serious threat either to the continued social domination of the ruling classes, or even to capitalist ownership of industry on which the whole system clearly depends. This is not to say that the working class plays no part, exercises no power, or does not have its own institutions, even culture. It is to say, simply, that the working class does not *dominate* society.

As we noted, Marx's theory is essentially a theory of development. He saw history as a succession of historical epochs each with its characteristic and dominant mode of production: the ancient, Asiatic, feudal and capitalist epochs and – to come – the communist. In each epoch, there was an early phase, when the owners of the decisive resources (in the feudal era, the owners of land; in the capitalist, the owners of capital) were real agents of expansion and progress – pushing production towards the limits possible within a given state of technology. Later, however, when the productive capacity of a given system came into contradiction with the interests of the owners, they no longer promoted the expansion of the productive powers of industry, but resisted innovation, whether technical inventions or ways of involving workers in the running of industry, which threatened their profits or their untrammelled control of decision-making. Private profit, not the social needs of the mass of the people (and especially of those who produced the wealth of society), was the driving force of the system. This growing contradiction between the system of production and the relations of production does not lead the controllers to give up their grip on power, prestige and wealth easily; they are likely to resist being replaced, and to have to be removed by revolutionary violence.

For Marx, the relationship between economic power and political power was clear: the capitalists were not simply an *owning* class; they were a *ruling* class too. Their decisive control over the key type of property (capital) was the basis for control over the society's political life, whether parliamentary democracy existed or not.

Since technological advance leads to intensified competition, those with most capital tend to come out on top. As a result, the bourgeoisie grows smaller in number, and intermediate classes – the petty bourgeoisie (e.g., owners of small factories and businesses, shop-keepers, etc.) and the independent professionals – suffer downward mobility towards the proletariat. The same spiral of competition increases the numbers, and the misery, of the working class. Differences of skill between the kinds of worker a developed industrial system needs also diminish: more and more people come to see their common interests and are drawn into the class struggle. They find, too, that they cannot make serious progress via personal, isolated actions. An understanding of what needs to be done, and appropriate machinery for doing it, are thus generated, that is, a 'scientific' socialist theory and the organizations through which the class struggle can be waged.

Marx, then, was not simply a determinist. But there are elements of determinism in Marxism. Engels responded to the failure of the revolutions of 1848, for instance, in part by insisting that inexorable economic processes would ultimately produce the collapse of capitalism, despite this temporary setback. At the same time, Marx and Engels also responded to this failure by emphasizing the need for organization and leadership: the revolution would not just 'happen', but had to be organized carefully and *made* to happen, when circumstances were right.

The conditions needed for revolution are thus two-fold: an appropriate 'revolutionary situation' and an appropriate revolutionary agency (a party). It is always possible to emphasize one or the other. 'Deterministic' Marxists insist that one must wait until the situation matures, wait for the inevitable crisis, conflict and breakdown of capitalism and meanwhile use the opportunities legally available through the ballot-box to press for social change and even to win decisive State power. The 'Euro-Communism' of the mass electoral Communist parties of Italy and France has thus come to terms with advanced capitalism as a system likely to continue for a long time, with themselves as the Opposition within a 'bourgeois' democracy, with the prospect of transforming it into a socialist society without violent revolution. The 'voluntaristic' Marxists insist that the revolution must be created, notably the recent Marxisms which hold that the situation in the 'Third World' is everywhere a revolutionary one already (Guevara, Maoism, Debray), as well as the militant activistic Marxism of the 1968 Paris student revolt. Marxism can thus accommodate very different courses of action; it does not provide an unambiguous 'scientific guide' to action. There are parallel disputes amongst Marxists about just how much emphasis can be laid on the 'economic base', and how much 'autonomy' can be allowed to the 'superstructure' of social arrangements and ideas erected on that base. One emphasizes the 'inevitability of history', the other the importance of men, ideas, creativity, innovation, activity. Neither of these schools of Marxism, however, have provided very satisfactory explanations of why the revolution has not occurred in advanced capitalist countries. Some Marxists have explained capitalism's survival in terms of imperialism or of a 'permanent arms economy'. But little attention has been given either to rises in real living standards or to increased social mobility.

Marx himself had noted that the ruling class might make its rule 'more solid and dangerous' by providing a selective avenue of individual upward mobility. He paid less attention to the possibility – which his enemies pointed out – that the working class might, by wresting concessions from the ruling class, take the edge off a potentially revolutionary militancy, so that group mobility of this kind might be a much more effective prophylactic against revolution than the mere individual mobility of a privileged few, or even larger privileged minorities: the 'labour aristocracy' of the skilled craft workers.

The effect of newer avenues of mass upward mobility, such as the education system, were not foreseen, though Marx and Engels were aware that the new working-class parties, unions and co-operatives themselves constituted sizable new channels of mobility for ambitious working-class men, who became full-time bureaucrats with an interest not only in maintaining themselves in office, but also in not disturbing the wider social system in which they now occupied (however minor) a privileged position. These concessions to a rising and ever better-organized working-class movement were of course only possible in an expanding economy, and under developed capitalism. Fanon, indeed, has argued that not just a small 'labour aristocracy', but the whole of the working class benefited from imperialist exploitation of the Third World (Fanon, 1967). The situation in underdeveloped countries today is one in which the ruling classes, even if they wished to (which is rarely the case) are unable to offer similar concessions to the demands of the mass of their populations, because the economies they dominate are stagnant. The possibility of making concessions is thus very much more limited than it was for the ruling classes of Great Britain in the nineteenth century. But as the effects of the actions of the oil-producing Powers on the economies of the capitalist world show, the future of even the advanced capitalist societies is by no means unproblematic.

But there seems little evidence that any major breakdown of the internal functioning of the highly-developed and rich societies – including the U.S.S.R. – is likely. The era of comparative freedom from 'boom and slump' trade-cycles in the capitalist countries has been upset by the instability engendered by the disturbances in the world outside the capitalist 'West' (notably through revolution in the non-communist 'Third World'), as well as by the ever-growing competitive challenge of the communist countries. Some kind of long-term 'co-existence' with the planned economies of the communist countries seems quite conceivable; the stability of the capitalist Third World less so.

Status

Let us turn now to the second dimension of social stratification – status. Apart from the word 'class', 'status' is the only other term quite so widely used in studies of social stratification, and in everyday speech too – and so is inevitably loaded with a variety of meanings. The term is often used interchangeably with 'class' in everyday usage, however, and some sociologists have compounded this confusion, but it is necessary to keep them analytically distinct. One use of the term refers to a *position* in a structure, whether determined by formal rules (laws, articles of association, constitutions, etc.) or informally, by custom. Individuals occupying such positions are treated differentially according to the position they occupy. 'Status' here is thus used where others use 'role', in the sense of an 'office' in an organization or a position in a family. Thus a man may be a sergeant, an 'in-law', a manager, or a member of a congregation. Or you may have a status ascribed to you, not because you are part of an organized structure, but by virtue of belonging to some social category with particular social characteristics which others can observe: by being 'coloured', female, young or old. But such distinctions involve much more than simply classifying people; they involve allotting people different jobs in the social division of labour and these positions have different amounts of prestige and power attached to them, and different rewards. Thus being a 'minor' or a 'pupil' means that one is treated in a special way, both within and outside the courts.

So when motor-car advertisements suggest that the car you have is a symbol of your *status*, 'status' here does not merely refer to the position a man occupies in a division of labour in which some do one job and others different ones. For the jobs are not just 'different', they are also ranked *hierarchically* in a system of inequalities of power and of material and other reward. They are further ranked as 'higher' or 'lower' in a hierarchical system of prestige: *esteem* is unequally distributed too. 'Status' in this second sense thus refers to the way in which prestige is differentially distributed, so that people on different levels of the social structure are marked off from those below them, and from their 'superiors' or 'inferiors', by a whole complex of ways of thinking, acting and feeling recognized by members and outsiders alike – what are normally called 'class distinctions', but which the sociologist usually labels 'status differences', reserving the term 'class' to refer primarily to a person's productive role with its correlates of property and power. Status, in the sense of prestige, is thus usually visible in a particular 'style of life', in a person's everyday behaviour at home as well as at work, and notably in the way he uses his income. One's ability to consume in a certain way and the models of behaviour one adopts are certainly affected by one's position in a system of production, but one can adopt models which are more usually appropriate to people whose occupations are very different. The basis of membership in a status-group is the possession of the appropriate status-characteristics. Such status-groups commonly turn themselves into classes: they monopolize opportunities and exert power over others. Thus in South Africa, Whites constitute a status-group, membership of which can never be acquired by Africans: an African cannot become a White man. No matter how wealthy or skilled he may become, he can never acquire *the* crucial status-characteristic. Hence, status-groups often operate in ways that have little to do with maximizing efficiency or economic growth or with encouraging achievement, but rather with maintaining superiority.

Extremely inflexible status-groups may go so far as to ruin themselves rather than give up the exclusive position they prize so much. In an open class system wealth, possession of capital, etc., provide the person who has it with the resources through which he can exercise both economic and political power. He usually also uses his wealth to buy his way into a superior status-group. Thus class and status come to coincide. But the phenomenon of status-'dissonance' is only too common: people may be high on one criterion, but lower on others. And to become *socially* accepted into a status-group may be difficult, since highly status-conscious groups may keep the wealthy *parvenu*, the 'social climber' or *nouveau riche* at arm's length, since he lacks the cultural characteristics and the social graces required by his (often poorer) 'superiors', and is therefore denied full status equality. If he himself may not be able to adapt his behaviour to that demanded by the status-group he aspires to join, his wealth will usually enable him to buy his children the formal education and the instruction in 'proper' ways of behaviour such as the 'correct' accent and etiquette of everyday social intercourse called for, so that *they* will be accepted, a lag of a generation. So one's ability to be accepted does not simply 'go with the job' one does, and situations in which we experience contrary demands from different status-groups, common enough wherever a person is socially mobile, induce strains of 'cross-pressure' and 'status-anxiety'. Thus, though they commonly do overlap, a person's class position and the status he aspires to may not exactly coincide: he may have 'more respectability than means' (and have to open his family estate and mansion to the public in order to maintain his mode of life). Conversely, an unskilled worker may hold high political office, as mayor or trade union leader.

A person's self-image, his conception of his status, may also differ from that which is more usually attached to his occupation; other people's definitions of your status may differ from your own, and have to be taken into account, for not to do so would be to have 'delusions of grandeur'. There are situations, of course, in which people glory in being of *low* status, as when people contrast 'honest' ordinary folks' standards with the 'artificial' pretensions of their so-called 'superiors'. Amongst unskilled workers, but especially the 'lower classes' below the 'working classes' (Klein, V., 1965, Section 1) who lack stable jobs and have unstable family lives, we find 'upside-downers', who reject the values of those who normally have the power to set the pattern for 'proper' behaviour. 'Upside-downers' rate doing a hard manual job or a socially valuable job highly. Thus they put nurses and agricultural labourers high in their scheme of things, and company directors low (Young, M. and Willmott, P., 1957b). Such ideas, of course, are not peculiar to the 'lower classes'. Socialist ideas include similar notions that people should be rewarded according to their usefulness to society, that labour is honourable, and that usurers, 'coupon-clippers', rentiers and capitalists in general are either functionally unnecessary or an actual negative force, a 'fetter on production' whose removal would liberate initiative, help rationalize and humanize economic life and permit a 'social-ized' economy because industry would no longer be run for private benefit, but in the interests of the mass of society.

Status, in the prestige sense, thus depends very much on *subjective* factors: ideas and feelings, both on the part of the social actor and those with whom he interacts, even though one's pretensions are also controlled by one's pocket. In general, because of this last consideration, people's status-aspirations are not likely to be very ambitious. Skilled or clerical workers may imitate lower-middle-class models; they are scarcely likely to aim higher. Their 'reference-group', in sociological language, will not be very remote; their hopes of social mobility are fairly realistic. Indeed, if people are asked about their *expectations* as against their *aspirations* – what they *expect* to be, as against what they would ideally *like* to be – their expectations are usually much humbler than their aspirations. One's aspirations may, of course, be focused not upon one's own career-possibilities, but, vicariously, upon those of one's children. Social mobility is thus by no means confined to *intra*-generational movements within a single person's lifetime; it can be *inter*-generational. We have seen that the family is itself a unit of social class. This is where people acquire much of their class behaviour, their ideas and feelings about classes and status-groups. Inevitably, too, their hopes of upwards mobility (or fears of downwards mobility) are projected onto others in the family besides themselves.

These quite common divergences between people's personal conception of their own status (or their aspirations to higher status) and the status ascribed to them by others makes for difficulties in classifying many people unambiguously as belonging to one social class or another, since there is great room for such differences of subjectivity, and social class is by no means just a matter of occupation, regardless of how important this may be. People's ideas are a vital part of social class, too, and affect their behaviour deeply. Status considerations therefore have to be added to strict economic position in order to produce a rounded understanding of social class.

We have seen that many people who write about class, and devise models of class, are only concerned with showing how people from different class backgrounds behave, or predicting how they will behave. They are not concerned to explain the genesis or basis of class – how it comes into being, what it is caused by, what its significance is for society – for they are not engaged in that kind of sociological explanation.

We can easily classify people according to occupation. We can even rank occupations according to such objective criteria as amount of income so to form a table of 'higher' and 'lower' occupations. For many practical purposes, such as estimating likely political behaviour, these rough-and-ready divisions may be good enough. Scales or tables of this kind are often used in business, in politics, in census work, and so on, by people whose ideologies in general and ideas about class in particular may otherwise differ widely. But, plainly, they are only very crude divisions. Even these classifications usually take into account additional elements, however, usually status-distinctions, as when 'non-manual' occupations are distinguished from 'manual' ones, for even though both categories may be wage-earners, ideas about status still often cause white-collar workers to behave in aggregate in somewhat more middle-class ways, in some areas of their lives, than their manual-worker colleagues. Similarly, clerical workers, or even 'affluent' well-paid manual workers, brought up to think of themselves as *working* class, may continue to behave in working-class ways.

There is thus no simple, neat overlap between class and status, and people may follow quite different models in different areas of their lives. Non-manual workers are now increasingly prepared to join trade unions, for so long the characteristic institutions mainly of manual workers. The new trade unions in Britain, growing in numbers, militancy and political power, recruit distributive workers, technicians, airline pilots, supervisors, local government officials, welfare workers, bank clerks, now even teachers, junior doctors and managers. This reflects the bureaucratization and 'proletarianization' of jobs formerly regarded as middle-class occupations – and even the professions – the growth of 'service' and technical occupations in the 'tertiary' sector of the economy, and the decline of older manual occupations, of which mining is perhaps the most obvious case. These changes are reflected in the general shift of power within the trade union movement from the older 'proletarian' unions to these new unions.

If the contemporary analysis of social class derives mainly from the 'debate with the ghost of Marx', modern discussions of status derive from Max Weber's original formulation in the 1920s (Gerth and Mills, 1948, p. 7). A person's *class*, Weber recognizes, is 'unambiguously' a function of his position in the economic system. The worker, for example, is a worker because he sells his labour-power on the market. But – Weber goes on to say – we accept or reject people as social equals, inferiors or superiors, not just on the basis of their economic standing, but on the basis of their social standing as a whole. One's social standing may depend upon one's economic position, but the connection is not necessarily always a direct one. In particular, people's ideas are not automatically the same just because they do the same job. A skilled engineer may be 'upwardly-mobile' and middle class in his orientation; he may be a craft-conscious militant unionist; and he may be both together. Nor are his other social characteristics directly determined by his occupation. He may be a Presbyterian, a Catholic, or religiously indifferent. These differences are of crucial importance: he will belong to, or seek membership of, quite different social circles and be accepted or rejected. Membership of these status-groups, and exclusion from others, will have important consequences for his whole life, even for his work. Conception of status and actual membership of status-groups may well vary independently of his economic position and be as important in affecting his behaviour. Yet normally, even though we cannot predict for the individual engineer what his religion or politics will be, we can be pretty sure about the likely behaviour of engineers in general on particular issues. Indeed, there is normally a good degree of association between occupation and other characteristics, including some very important ones. Even religion, for instance, is likely to be very broadly linked with class, for though many people think of religious experience as a peculiarly personal thing, religion is usually transmitted via the family, like ideas about class. Historically, Nonconformist denominations like Methodism did recruit primarily amongst the working class and provided opportunities for working-class leadership; the Anglican Church of England, or the Episcopalian in the U.S.A., reserved leadership for the gentry class. ('The Tory Party at prayer' was one sardonic description of the Church of England in the nineteenth century.)

And despite the fact that some third of the working class vote Conservative, a distinct relationship persists between class and party politics, too:

National Opinion Poll Profile of the Electorate, February 1974: Social Class and Voting (%)

	Occupations			
	Managerial Professional and Administrative	Other non-manual	Skilled manual	Unskilled and semi-skilled manual
Conservative	67·3	51·4	30·1	24·6
Labour	10·4	21·3	47·2	53·7
Liberal	19·6	24·7	19·6	16·6
Other	2·7	2·6	3·1	5.1

(Source: Adapted from Butler and Kavanagh, 1974, p. 263.)

Nearly half of the working class, then, still vote Labour. But these figures show that the 'fit' between class and political parties is by no means neat. Both 'class' parties have lost voters to the Liberals and to the Celtic nationalist parties, and there are increasing numbers of non-voters. A lack of fit between class and political party is not surprising, however, in a society with a high degree of short-range social mobility at the lower levels, since people move away from parental influence, have different jobs from those of their parents, meet different people, and experience the world differently. Thus those growing up during the Depression of the inter-war period; those maturing during the Second World War; the children of the immediate post-war 'austerity' period; those of the 'affluent' fifties; the new youth of the sixties, have, without resorting to purely rhetorical language, really experienced significantly different worlds. Hence the much-discussed phenomenon of the 'generation gap', or, in the extreme, 'the war of generations' which is held to underly much of the contemporary revolt of youth.

In less mobile societies the 'fit' between occupation and other social characteristics may be much closer. In the least mobile, such as caste societies, it is likely to be very close indeed. We have seen that in India there was thus a tight-knit 'clustering' or overlap of economic, religious, marital and other norms of behaviour, the whole forming a *system* which brought all the separate castes together in a complex, hierarchical order buttressed by religion.

Such a system exhibits unusual consistency in the extent to which status differences and class differences coincide (or are 'congruent'). It is because of this extreme congruence and because of the rigidity of the system until recent times, that a special label – caste – has been used to distinguish a system like this from more open systems of stratification. Yet even in caste societies, changes took place, as we saw, and though a person belongs to a caste whose very title may indicate a traditional occupation (such as 'Distiller') most lower-caste villagers are, in fact, peasants working the land, whatever their caste-title, and Brahmins are more likely to be wealthy landowners than full-time religious functionaries. This dissociation of caste and occupation is, of course, greatly intensified in modern urban life. Although Brahmins are predominant in the higher occupational reaches, and caste remains an important force in determining whom one marries, in the specifically religious life and to some degree in political life, one's caste and one's occupation are much more likely to vary independently these days. Moreover, new solidarities and oppositions emerge on the basis of occupation, displacing or at least rivalling traditional ties of occupation and caste. In the town, the *jatis* of the abandoned village become irrelevant and are replaced by new *class* relationships.

The traditional overlap of economic, religious and political positions resulted in one single over-all hierarchy of prestige. The weaving together and elaboration of all of these separate elements into one large cultural scheme may seem remote from the experience of those living in industrial societies. But, Weber points out, it is only carrying to its logical conclusion of patterns of stratification found nearer home, for here, too, one's politics, religious denomination, family life, tastes in entertainment, place of residence, etc., are all likely to differ for different classes, and thus form broad 'clusters' similar to those found in more exaggerated form in caste society. So we can easily distinguish the different class-areas of a city's residential districts, or, by looking at his dress, can judge a person's social status. Even such apparently quite personal and private things as the age at which toilet-training is begun are very closely associated with class (see Table 2, p. 187). So too is the kind of language we use (Bernstein, 1971). Since most people marry partners from similar backgrounds there is a degree of endogamy, too. We tend to marry those near and like ourselves, though since it is not obligatory to do so, and since only a category (a social class) is involved and it is usually one's family rather than any wider group (such as an Indian village *jati* with its own caste council) which exercises pressure on us, we usually speak of *homogamy* – like marrying like – or 'assortative' mating rather than endogamy (marriage within the group) proper.

Social distance is maintained in class society as well as in caste society by delicate, though often rigidly observed, distinctions of etiquette, just as notions of pollution or defilement keep the Indian castes apart. Classes may be split internally by status-distinctions; status-distinctions may overlap with class divisions. The division within the working class between the 'rough' and the 'respectable', or the wider gulf between the 'working classes' and the 'lower classes' are striking instances of the importance of these distinctions. Where such distinctions coincide with other divisions – say, religious or ethnic – where differences of class and status coincide, the one reinforces the other and the divisions are therefore deeper. Thus it is one thing in Britain for the stable, employed working class to resent the 'roughs' who float from job to job, lead irregular domestic lives, etc., but when this resentment is focused upon 'rough' groups that also happen to be Irish, West Indian or Pakistani immigrants, the division is reinforced: it is based on more than one element, and the conflict is the more intense.

Power

We have seen that one of the implications of Weber's analysis is that though status and caste very often overlap, status-distinctions can cut *across* class solidarity. Classes, then, need not progressively develop greater class-consciousness; in particular, the working class may not become more cohesive, or, if it does become organized and self-aware, may not be in any significant degree revolutionary. Much depends on the skill of those who seek to mobilize the working class, whether in support of capitalism or against it, and on the organizations and policies they adopt.

Control of the working class by conservative régimes and parties, for instance, does not necessarily simply rely upon the application of brute force ('coercive' sanctions, in Etzioni's terminology), but normally also involves appeals to reason, constitutionality, tradition and the like – what Etzioni calls 'normative' appeals. Further, people may be induced to conform or to accept authority if they feel that they are getting at least something out of it: if wages and living-standards are tolerable or even improving – Etzioni's 'remunerative' inducements.

The working class (or any other class) can thus be conceived of as a 'constituency', an 'arena' or 'field', where different groups compete for support, proselytize, recruit and try to impose their views. Thus Parkin has argued that there are at least three distinct ideological attitudes to be found amongst the working class (Parkin, 1972). The 'dominant' ideology is propagated by the bourgeoisie (what the Italian Marxist theoretician, Antonio Gramsci, called the 'hegemonic' political culture in capitalist society) (Gramsci, 1957). It seeks to persuade people that their lot in life is a just one, or dictated by the logic of industrial organization, or by virtue of the immanent necessity for authority, or that their ability to find work depends upon the wise conduct of industry by those who own and control it (something that the workers themselves are held to be functionally disqualified from doing, since they lack experience and expertise in management). Or there is held to be a need to reward the owners of capital for their initiative, efficiency and social responsibility in the form of profits, without which they would not continue to invest or play their part in managing industry.

Counterposed to this ideology is the 'oppositional' outlook, which rejects all or part of the 'dominant' ideology, arguing that capitalists are self-seeking, not socially responsible altruists providing for the welfare of all classes of society; exploiters, not partners; a 'fetter upon production' rather than innovators constantly expanding output; and the operators of a system that constantly seeks to drive down wages, and therefore creates periodic crises of overproduction and structural unemployment and is incapable of providing a decent life for the mass of the people.

In between these positions, Parkin argues, are those with an 'accommodational' ideology: people who may not necessarily be contented, nor very radical, but who 'get by' in life in a variety of ways: some by finding their satisfactions, not in work, money or public life, but in interpersonal relations – in the family, with their friends, in sex, etc., or who are concerned with their local community rather than with society as a whole. Others discount this life and seek 'other-wordly' satisfactions in religion, whether organized religion or highly individual mystical and transcendental experience, or withdraw from the world into communes, religious or secular. For yet others, life is inherently random and unpredictable, but the unpredictable includes the possibility that good things as well as bad may come about: they *might*, therefore, win £500,000 on the football pools.

Among the working class, Parkin suggests, we can find people who hold each of these ideological positions fairly systematically; others adopt bits of them (often inconsistently) or move from one to another at different times and in different situations. Earlier, and more generally, Max Weber had insisted that 'social class' is potential rather than always actual: that people in common situations in a social structure do not necessarily see that situation in the same way, but interpret it in a variety of ways available to them or suggested by the cultural milieux in which they live. A plurality of constructions, therefore, can be put upon the 'same' reality, and quite different conclusions arrived at as to the justice or injustice, or the inevitability of one's lot in society, and of the over-all social system or the possibilities of any alternative to it (Parkin, 1972).

In this sense, the term 'social class' is a very abstract concept, whose significance changes in different historical circumstances. It is not an absolute. Class-consciousness, that is, may change over time, indeed may not exist, especially in formative periods of any new social formation. If and when it does come into being, it may be either 'accommodational' or 'oppositional', or people may accept the 'dominant' outlook. Since there are several competing ideologies, the working class does not possess a unitary class-consciousness. Nor does it, in fact, necessarily exist in institutionalized form. The 'working class', in fact, is a *category*, not a *group*. True, there are institutions – in Britain, trade unions, the co-ops, the Labour Party – which claim to be 'working class' and undoubtedly are in the sense that they draw their membership primarily from this class and base their programme on policies designed to improve its lot (or even to make it predominant in society). It can further be argued – in a more historical (others would say 'metaphysical') way – that such organizations are 'working class' because they promote the interests of the working class, whether members of it belong to such institutions and believe in them in any numbers or not.

We saw earlier that social strata are different from natural strata. Again, class in the *socio*logical sense involves more than class simply in the logical sense. In logic, we can classify all red-headed people together; they form a logical class. But red-headed people are not a *social class*: they are a *category*, rather than a collectivity that behaves similarly, becomes conscious of its own identity and separate interests and thereby gives rise to organized groups. Red-headed people do not organize themselves, let alone engage in struggles with the blonde or the dark-haired.

Social classes, by contrast, exhibit common patterns of behaviour. People within their ranks, and outsiders, become conscious of them as a collectivity; numbers of them create organizations of a more structured kind to represent the class's interests. In the process, what is only a *category* ('the working class') becomes a group (the organized working class) or, more exactly, a whole set of groups (trade unions, parties, co-ops, etc.) which not only see themselves as 'working class' but act in accordance with that notion. Other classes oppose them. (Yet recruitment may be far from complete, so that we can have the paradoxical position of micro-sects of revolutionaries claiming that they, and no one else, authentically speak in the name of the proletariat, or the situation where a movement composed over-whelmingly of peasants, as in China or Viet Nam, claims to be 'pro-letarian'.)

Stratification, as we have seen, has three principal dimensions. Two of these we have already examined: *class* (arising out of differences in economic role), and stratification by *status* into inferior and superior groups with different styles of life and claims to prestige. We come now to the power dimension or, more exactly, the *political* power dim-ension: the stratification of society into ruling, ruled and intermediate groups. Economic power and the competitions of status-groups have already been discussed in part, but we must examine now the inter-relationship of all of these kinds of power: the combinations of class, status and other inequalities which make up the total phenomenon, social stratification.

Parties and other groups are specially organized to mobilize and exert power on behalf of interest groups. Such groups may have only limited interests in common. A much wider basis for collective action is provided normally by religion or ethnicity. These may or may not coincide with economic interests in common. In Britain, the major factor uniting the supporters of the major political parties is not religion or ethnicity, but social class.*

But not all political parties are built upon class interests, as Weber pointed out. They may be based upon status-identity. Thus mass parties of the Right have commonly appealed to workers on some other basis than that of their common economic interests as a *class*. They have been appealed to as status-groupings: Christian workers as against Jews, White men as against Blacks. Another type of appeal based on status is to those who may have humble jobs, but who prefer to think of themselves as 'middle class' or 'respectable':

* Lipset shows, contrary to what is often believed, that class is a major de-terminant of voting behaviour in the U.S.A. also, though the two major parties are not linked to the class divisions in the nation as a whole in the same way in every part of the country: the association between class and political orien-tation is local or regional rather than national (Lipset, 1960, Ch. 9).

the 'little man'. Such status-identifications cut across class definitions based on occupational identity. A further source of support by working-class people for their social superiors arises for quite opposite reasons – because, far from aspiring themselves to join the middle classes, they believe that the latter, and even more the upper classes, are so skilled and well-equipped to rule them that things are best left in their hands. This is the so-called 'deference vote'.

There are also other ties cutting across class ties based on occupation. Though class solidarities are engendered in production – particularly at what Marxists call the 'point of production' and others the 'work-situation' – other kinds of interests, even economic interests, may cut across these. Thus a worker may find his job threatened because other workers are on strike; he may find himself in conflict with fellow-workers even in the same shop, over demarcation problems: who is to do what job. The organizations of labour – here the trade unions – may be involved in conflict with each other over such issues as well as in conflict with management. As a consumer, the worker may find that wage-increases in other industries for his fellow-workers mean dearer goods in the shop for him. Collectively, too, farmers and their farm-labourers – though one group are employers and the other their employees – often combine politically in the face of city interests that threaten them: agricultural machinery corporations, banks, organized labour, grain exchanges, railways, etc.

There are thus cross-cutting interests which divide classes internally as well as ties which link segments of one class with another. In addition, status-distinctions within a class also operate, often very fine distinctions invisible to the outsider. Thus groups severely discriminated against, like urban Africans in South Africa, who are both a class (unskilled workers predominantly) and in part almost a caste (because virtually no social intercourse with Whites is allowed by law outside the work-situation), develop exquisite distinctions of status within their own ranks, as well as voluntary associations (like football teams) which have lots of officers and elaborate displays of status-symbols and thus provide a source of dignity and self-esteem to the deprived (Kuper, 1965, ch. 22). If there were not these cross-cutting ties between classes and divisions within them, all classes would evince 'instant solidarity', and overt class warfare would be a constant phenomenon. The capitalist class, Weber points out, is similarly divided between finance-capitalists and industrialists, by differences of interest between different branches of industry, or, most fundamentally, because one firm competes with others on the market.

There are thus many ties which cut across class, and which more positively unite members of different classes via personal or local-level links, or even via national institutions which cut across class divisions. Dutch sociologists have called the latter phenomenon 'pillarization' or *verzuiling* in contrast to 'stratification', the former being the division of society into *vertical* 'pillars' as against division into horizontal 'strata'. Clearly, *verzuiling* is a very important phenomenon, for ethnic and religious divisions in particular may well cut across horizontal class divisions in the modern world. We will look at this phenomenon in underdeveloped countries later, but it is equally to be found in countries like Belgium, with its Walloon–Flemish division, in larger multinational societies such as the U.S.S.R. or India, and in any country with strong 'vertical' religious or ethnic divisions.

Though, as we have seen, religion and class may coincide, churches are status-groups (groups of believers) which very often cut across class lines, too. They commonly encourage their members to focus their attention on future salvation rather than 'this-world' concerns. They have often been ideologically hostile to any emphasis on class, which might be a divisive factor within the body of the church. At other times, churches have drawn their memberships almost entirely from one social class or another. Religions have therefore been revolutionary as well as conservative. But today, in an era of secularization, and in a world where the gulf between the underdeveloped and the developed parts of the world is of such major importance, racial and ethnic vertical divisions usually loom larger than religious ones. Racial divisions, like religious ones, can be horizontal as well as vertical, for the bulk of the population in the new societies of the former colonial world as well as the immigrant population in advanced countries tend to be both poor and coloured. When racial divisions overlap with those of class, in this way, society threatens to split open. But ethnic, religious or other status-groups may also cut *across* classes and thus constitute a stratum *or* a 'pillar'. There is a third (and very common) possibility: that of the 'plural' society in which there may be a common national government, an over-all economy, etc., but where one group lives in one part of the country with its own culture and specialized economic role (say, coffee-growing), while another speaks a different language, lives in *its* own area, and engages in trade. These divisions are *vertical*, but they divide the society into separate compartments. Vertical 'pillars', on the other hand, *integrate* the society because their members are not confined to one level in the social structure in one area of the country but are to be found at every level. Pillars cut across strata; 'plural' units do not, even though they do interact (e.g. in the market place) with other communities and thus form part of a wider society. These ethnic communities are something like the segments of a worm: together, they form a whole, but each segment is distinct and only linked weakly. In a subsistence economy, the segments would be liable to break away, but in an increasing market-economy, such groups cannot survive on their own economically, no matter how segregated the rest of their social life from that of other ethnic groups.

We may thus find a variety of institutions, showing one or the other of these patterns. In Britain, there are vertical 'pillars' with members widely distributed at all horizontal levels in society. Thus there are Anglicans and Catholics at all social levels in Britain (even if the former are over-represented in the higher reaches of British society and the latter in the lower reaches of some cities in the North West). The social category, Whites, too, is distributed at all social levels. Blacks, conversely, predominate only at low levels. The former constitute a 'pillar', the latter a stratum. And where depressed 'ghettoes' of coloured people occur, we have an instance of segmented form. Yet there are few real ghettoes in Britain, unlike, say, the U.S.A. The society generally (least, it is true, for coloured people), is characterized by 'cross-cutting' ties, as Gluckman has called them (Gluckman, 1956). The horizontal divisions of class are indeed very profound, but there are also innumerable ways in which institutions are brought into contact, consultation and interconnection, even where they have opposed interests (e.g., trade union and employer representation on Government committees), because at another level they recognize a common interest: in keeping the system going so that there will be some cake to fight over. Such cross-cutting ties also operate importantly at the inter-personal level as when foreman and worker may belong to the same church, see each other in the local pub, support the same football team, etc.

Reformers, as well as reactionaries hoping to preserve existing divisions of power and wealth, have long dreamed of actually creating institutional 'pillars' which would create cross-cutting ties not between individuals but between the groups and organizations of the different classes, so as to counteract and reduce class conflict. They have usually pinned their hopes on religious institutions, or – more recently – on industrial 'corporations' which would link all those engaged in the steel industry, say, from blast-furnace operatives through foremen and managers to the top directors, in one organization, where their representatives could thrash out problems of the industry together. This idea has been canvassed from the time of Comte and Saint-Simon, in the work of Durkheim, and in the era of fascism (Mussolini actually did establish corporations of this kind and a national council linking them together into one 'corporative' state, but they remained in effect paper institutions).

The notions of co-operation, participation and the rational planning of production are important elements in socialist thinking, too – with one crucial difference; they postulate the prior removal of the capitalist and the establishment, not of class co-operation, but of social control by the working class, in forms ranging from state nationalization to 'workers' control'. Attempts to institutionalize vertical ties have remained ineffective, however, in capitalist societies, though there are constant attempts to regulate strikes and wage-claims through legislation which hinge upon similar notions of inter-class co-operation, mediated by government, in which all co-operate to achieve generally agreed goals, though each plays a different functional role in the division of labour.

The increasing intervention and the wider area of activity of the State in capitalist societies, and the role of State and Party in communist ones, raises the question of how it is that order and continuity are maintained, a problem we will discuss more fully in Chapter 9. Plainly, differences of interest and of culture as extensive as those we have seen existing in class societies have to be contained or counterbalanced somehow, if society is not to fly apart into its constituent components.

Social stability can be achieved by enforcing conformity, or as the outcome of positive support for the government in power. In the latter case, the government is said to have *legitimacy*, because people think it has the *right* to be in power. Its ability to get its policies accepted depends on more than mere coercion through monopoly of the means of violence (arms). Such a government has authority, not just power, because it has both the means of force and legitimacy as bases for its operation. In between these situations, a population may simply put up with its government, not according it positive support, but having as little to do with politics as possible. Many variations upon these situations are possible. Where the conflicts in a society between different strata run deep, there is little room for the kind of compromise that is often called 'agreement to differ'; the 'balance of power', or as Rex calls it, the 'truce situation' can no longer be operated (Rex, 1961, ch. 7). Instead, the conflict becomes sharper and is resolved by a move towards one extreme solution or its opposite – increased reliance upon force by the dominant classes and the established government, or successful resort to force on the part of those challenging their rule. The former Rex labels 'the ruling class' situation; the latter the 'revolutionary'. These extremes of class polarization seem very different from the 'consensus' politics of Britain or the U.S.A., where parties defeated in elections by only a few percentage points, commanding some half of the nation's allegiance, refrain from using this undoubted power to resist the rule of their opponents, but allow them to take over the government, whilst they go into 'loyal opposition'. Because of the existence of ideas about the legitimacy of the political system, divisions which elsewhere would result in revolutionary confrontations here only produce the ins-and-outs of parliamentary party politics.

Class conflict in developed societies has not matured as Marx believed it would. Whilst there is a powerful Labour movement, not only are most workers quite un-revolutionary but they even fail to participate in working-class organizations. Many identify themselves with other classes, or at least are not greatly or generally hostile to them. Class-consciousness and class-militancy also vary over time, and with the issue and the level at which the issues arise.

A worker may be conscious of belonging to a working-class community; a localized status-group of this kind, composed of people of common economic position, may be very 'working class' (Hoggart, 1958). It is a kind of *communal* class-consciousness, however. Then there is what Lenin called 'trade union consciousness': the militant defence of wages and working conditions. Distinct from this again is *political* working-class consciousness. Most people in Britain only think about politics when the occasion calls for decisions to be made – say, during an election – and pay little attention to such matters in more normal times. A person may thus combine high 'working-class consciousness' over economic issues with a low interest in politics. This common situation reflects itself in widespread shop-steward agitation, and unofficial disputes at shop-floor level, combined with disinterest in official trade unionism at higher levels and even less in political Labour (or great interest in neighbourhood affairs, but none in local government) (Lane and Roberts, 1971; Beynon, 1973; Hyman, 1972).

These different kinds of class consciousness, displayed at different levels in different situations, have been looked at in a slightly different way by David Lockwood who has argued, in his study of clerical workers, that the broad concept of 'class' is too crude, and that for more refined understanding we need to break it up into three component elements: work-situation, market-situation and status-situation. In the work-situation, for instance, in contrast with manual workers on the shop-floor, clerks have in the past tended to work alongside their employers in small offices. They were often drawn via personal links from middle-class families themselves, and this personal contact at work reinforced their tendency to emulate the life-style of their employers, as well as giving them a certain amount of 'reflected' status, despite their lack of real power. Though offices are now larger and more mechanized, and though clerks may now earn only as much as manual workers, most clerks still have closer contact with management than do manual workers. The result is the continuation of distinction between non-manual and manual employees. To manual workers, clerks are part of 'Them' (Lockwood, 1958).

In the past a shipping clerk could not move to a solicitor's office, so that standardized wages and a supply of interchangeable labour comparable to that for manual labour did not emerge. This situation naturally gave rise to a sense of exclusiveness on the part of clerks in different branches of industry and commerce, and was reinforced by marked wage-differentials instituted by employers, so that unionization of clerical workers was limited (also discouraged) between the two world wars. However, after the First World War, the clerical labour-force increased in size and the work itself now took place within ever-larger units, whether in industry, business or government. The enormous growth of the tertiary sector has various sources: hundreds of thousands of people are employed in handling and taking care of private property in capitalist societies: bills of sale, title-deeds, transfers of stocks, shares and other forms of wealth, insurance, wills, trusts and the like. Disputes arising from property ownership and management, and from taxation, generate further legal work. Advertising also employs another 1·3 million workers. The growth of the State, whether in the administration of taxation or welfare services, has generated large increases in the clerical labour-force. And the 'knowledge industries', from universities and colleges to information-gathering and data-processing businesses, has created further new demands both for 'proletarian' non-manual labour, and for a new type of 'intellectual proletariat' of junior management and even of non-managerial posts that now require high educational qualifications (Adelstein, 1969). The road to promotion became more formal and dependent on education, and the recruitment of managerial trainees of higher educational level above the heads of clerks set limits to promotion opportunities. The market-situation of black-coated workers has declined, especially if one compares them to manual workers. Clerical jobs used to be singularly well-paid and secure, even during the Depression. But with continuing full employment and overtime for manual workers, the superiority of non-manual jobs is by no means so clear-cut today. A growing proportion of clerks, too, are now drawn from manual workers' families.

Clerks are thus in a status predicament. Cross-cutting ties pull them in contrary directions. Changes in their work-situation have reduced the chances that their claim to middle-class status will be accepted by the middle classes, whilst changes in the over-all labour market, the effectiveness of the manual workers' trade unions, and wider access to secondary education, have narrowed the gap between them and the manual groups to whom they used to feel superior. The consequence is that the superior status the clerk lays claim to – at work or in his neighbourhood – is increasingly open to successful challenge. This changing class-situation reflects itself in the wide range of differences in the political identifications of clerical workers: for example, there is no clear-cut commitment to either major party. The more successful, who see themselves as 'middle class', reveal a marked preference for the Conservative Party. But the tendency to identify with the middle classes varies between industries in which clerical workers are employed. Thus, the Railway Clerks' Association always had close industrial and political contact with organized Labour and its members evinced a relatively high degree of working-class consciousness and loyalty.

Today, many more clerks are no longer clearly middle class either in their own eyes or in the eyes of others. Black-coated workers are split between Labour and Conservative, and move towards one or the other party with the general political swings in the country. Growing numbers, even of bank clerks, join trade unions and take strike action. Similar processes are affecting nurses, teachers, local government officials and other occupations once resistant to unionism, and yet also underlie the parallel claims of such occupations to 'professional' status. Both unionization and professionalization, however, involve collective group mobility as distinct from purely personal advancement.

These problems are examined by Goldthorpe and his colleagues in their discussion of the thesis of the 'embourgeoisement' of the British working class: the notion that, far from disappearing, as Marx predicted, the middle classes are growing in size, as more and more manual occupations disappear, as new jobs in the tertiary sector grow in number, and as now-affluent manual workers merge with the lower middle class (Goldthorpe *et al.*, 1969, 1970, 1971).

It is indeed the case that the work-force employed in traditional extractive and heavy manufacturing industries has declined, whilst the consumer-goods industries, transportation and service occupations have grown. It is also argued that the incomes of non-manual workers are no longer so superior, and that increased geographical mobility has gone hand-in-hand with upwards social mobility, too, as people move to better jobs in the Midlands and the South East, or move from slum areas in the older parts of the city to the new estates in the suburbs. Thus many workers experiencing affluence also experience the loss or weakening of the family and neighbourhood milieux within which their working-class attitudes and values were formerly created and sustained. Working-class affluence has followed a consumption pattern similar in some respects to that pioneered by the middle class: the telly, the washing-machine, home decoration and perhaps a car. But accommodation to such a 'consumption-oriented' style of life does not eliminate dissatisfaction with work. The 'effort-bargain' (boring work undergone for the sake of high wages, themselves used to purchase a more satisfying life away from work) still involves alienation (Baldamus, 1967) and those working in the Luton car-plant went on a very bitter strike shortly after the study was completed. (The very split between work and non-work, indeed, is what many writers have meant by alienation.)

This emphasis on consumer durables is held to represent a new shift towards the home for the working class, a shift towards family consumption goals and perhaps more joint family life, and away from the older pattern of life in a traditional working-class community such as a mining town.

Here coal-mining was the single major industry in the community, and a man was bound to his workmates at work, and in the pub, by strong ties of solidarity that pulled him away from his family and the home (Dennis *et al.*, 1956). But the miner's job is changing, and the importance of the industry has declined. The emergence of the affluent 'home-centred' family, and the decline in the class-conscious solidarity of the older proletarian occupations such as mining, some people have argued, spells not merely the social 'embourgeoisement' of the mass of the population, but the ultimate eclipse of socialist and other organizations based on the working class and oriented to the collective restructuring of society.

In criticizing this thesis, Goldthorpe and his colleagues examine the evidence under three headings: economic, normative and relational. Firstly, the economic evidence for 'embourgeoisement' of the workers is not impressive, for when one takes income over the whole working life, as opposed to weekly wages, the apparent levelling up as between manual and non-manual workers is not so apparent, for pensions, prospects of promotion, sustained earnings, job security, loans and 'perks' are important inequalities as between non-manual and manual occupations. Secondly, in normative terms, the extent to which the working class is in fact losing its traditional attitudes and values and acquiring those of the middle class has little serious basis in research findings. And thirdly, there is little evidence to show that relational patterns have changed: that middle-class groups have relaxed their exclusiveness and begun to admit working-class occupational groups to social equality. There is, in fact, little social intercourse.

In order to fill in the gaps themselves, these authors undertook a study of Luton car-workers, and other well-paid workers in prosperous modern industries, because these workers were exactly the people amongst whom the changes postulated should have gone furthest: among the most affluent in the working class, many of them residentially mobile and usually younger. They found, in fact, that loyalty to class organizations such as the unions and the Labour Party have not been affected by affluence. Nor have they become more satisfied with their work-situation; the boring and repetitive nature of detailed car assembly-line work whose operations are timed in seconds rather than minutes (Beynon, 1973) means a very high degree of alienation from the work-task. The dominant motive for taking up the work was strictly instrumental – high wages and opportunities for overtime. Alienation from work reflected itself in 'privatized' pre-occupations with home and family, though a bitter strike subsequent to their study indicates that alienation might take more collective and activistic forms at work also. There was still a very high degree of commitment to class organizations (80 per cent voted Labour), but in contrast with the traditional solidarity of the working class their collectivism was much more 'instrumental'; the union was just a means to an end, a way of getting better incomes through collective bargaining, industrial action and political change, rather than part of the 'communal' solidarity of the older mining town. The over-all picture was clear: there was little indication that this new working class was being assimilated into middle-class society or that they even aspired to be part of it. Simply because they purchased consumer durables did not mean that they were becoming middle class in outlook. As the authors put it, 'a washing machine is a washing machine is a washing machine'; using one was a way of washing clothes, not a way of turning oneself into a middle-class person. Their life-chances, consumption-styles, attitudes and values remained substantially different from those of the middle classes.

The 'embourgeoisement' thesis is concerned with quite low levels of the stratification system: the manual/non-manual dividing-line.

Other theories which purported to show that Marxist conceptions of class were outmoded have concentrated on higher levels in the class system. They have questioned whether ownership does any longer carry with it decisive power in the running of industry (Nichols, 1969). Writers in the 1930s and 1940s noted that joint-stock companies were becoming a mass phenomenon, since many large corporations had hundreds of thousands of shareholders. Under these conditions, they argue, 'ownership' had become a fiction; the really decisive people were no longer the share-owners but those who ran the corporation from day to day; these, the real decision-makers, were the managers or directors. The capitalist was, in fact, disappearing.

The Second World War saw the involvement of Labour in government, and the growing intervention of government in industry, including direct government ownership of many enterprises. One influential analysis of these developments was James Burnham's *The Managerial Revolution* (1941), in which he announced that not only capitalist but also communist society was in reality coming under the control of the new managers.

In the more extreme versions of these theories, the giant corporations were seen as virtually 'socialist' enterprises: the thousands of workers, shareholders and managers were said to form a partnership, and the health of the enterprise was said to come before any 'sectional' considerations such as profits and wages. The corporation was also held, in this view, to have become more conscious of its contribution, hence more 'responsible'.

An alternative view was the notion that what was emerging was neither capitalist nor socialist – a 'mixed' economy in which the State represented one corner in a three-sided triangle, the others being Business and Labour. No longer was the State to be seen as a 'committee of the whole bourgeoisie', in Marx's phrase, only concerned with reconciling the differing interests of sections of the capitalist classes, but as equally amenable to the influence of organized Labour. Sweden, a highly developed industrial country, was held out as an epitome of 'modern' industrial relations of this kind: though industry remained decisively in private hands, the Social-Democratic Party had been in power, with only minor interruptions, since 1932.

By contrast, the growing power of the State, and of the giant corporations in the U.S.A. – and their growing together – was seen by radical writers like Mills as an increase in the capacity of the dominant 'power élite' to control the masses, and, in particular, to control the State in their interests. The components of the power élite were, firstly, the corporations; the military, whose orders for advanced and expensive technology (missile, atomic weapon and aerospace programmes especially) were increasingly vital to the economy; and the controllers of the society's political machinery, including both that of the parties and of the State. In this view, the State had become integrated into what President Eisenhower called the 'military-industrial complex', in such a way as to strengthen and consolidate capitalism, and in a way, too, which promoted expansionist, 'forward' policies and military involvement abroad. The notion that the State was becoming more autonomous, or the 'supreme' institution, or some 'neutral' balancing force mediating between Business and Labour was discounted (Mills, 1956).

Since Mills wrote, the 'multi-national' corporations have greatly extended their operations over the entire world capitalist market, to

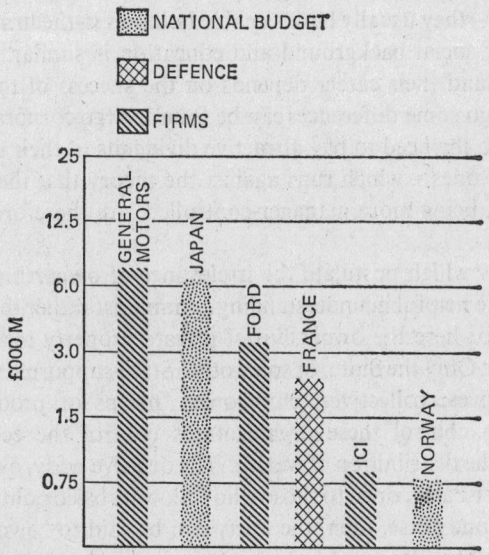

Figure 12 Today's world organizations compared
(Source: After A. Wedgwood Benn, 'Learning to Use Power', *Roscoe Review*, 1970, University of Manchester Department of Extra-Mural Studies, p. 18.)

such an extent that General Motors spends more than the Japanese Government every year (and Japan is the fourth largest industrial power in the world); Ford spends more than the French Government spends on defence; and I.C.I. spends more than the Norwegian Government spends in its entire budget.

Whatever the relative powers of manager and shareholders, then, the crucial phenomenon is the growing power of giant capitalist corporations in political as well as economic life, rather than the eclipse of capitalism. Research has demonstrated in fact that not only have enormous inequalities of wealth persisted, but that despite the wide diffusion of share-holding, the wealthy still dominate the large corporations, because they still own decisive blocks of shares. Even if they are a minority of the total, these blocks still enable a few such large shareholders (often 'institutional' rather than individual shareholders – banks and insurance companies) to outvote the hundreds of thousands of inactive small shareholders and thus control huge corporations with numerous subsidiaries. Sargant Florence has shown, too, for the U.K., that managers are not a quite separate class from capitalists – they usually have sizeable holdings in the firm, and in any case, their social background and education is similar, as are their attitudes, and their career depends on the success of the company. And though some differences can be found, large corporations are as sensitive to the need to pay attractive dividends to their shareholders as smaller ones – which runs against the theory that the bigger corporations, being more manager-controlled, are therefore less profit-conscious.

Theories which postulate the irrelevance of ownership are in fact much more helpful in understanding communist rather than capitalist society. For here the ownership of private property really has been eliminated. Only the State, or some other State-supported social group (co-operatives, collectives, etc.), owns 'means of production'. So those who control these organizations control the economy and therefore the distribution of wealth. The decisive body, over-all, is the Communist Party, open to those who follow its basic political requirements. In one sense, then, the Party can be said to 'own' the whole economy and its leaders to constitute, collectively, a class which is in effect the owning class. The model here is virtually the obverse of Marx's picture of capitalism. In that picture, political power was the outcome of economic power. The state was a 'committee of the ruling class'. In communist society, writers like Djilas (1957) have argued, it is the other way round: wealth is a function of political power. One becomes rich by becoming a politically powerful leading Party or government official. The 'New Class', which controls the Party and the State, is firstly a ruling class, but by virtue of its political power, becomes an economic class too.

Djilas's analysis drew considerably on earlier writing by Trotsky and other Marxists, of which Trotsky's remains by far the most powerful and the best-documented analysis (Trotsky, 1974). There are major differences, however, between his interpretation of the U.S.S.R. and Djilas's, and between Trotsky's interpretation and that of other Marxists who have variously seen the U.S.S.R. as 'State' capitalism, 'degenerated' communism and so forth. These differences in analysis, of course, have led to very different opinions over the conclusions to be drawn for practical political action, and have led to severe sectarian quarrels.

Djilas denounced the 'New Class', and the system it operated, as a new despotism, and a self-perpetuating one at that. Many theorists have seen the Soviet experience as a further demonstration that, even given a gigantic revolution, any complex society will always require an apparatus of social control and a division of social labour in which there will be rulers and ruled.

Functionalists, in the 1960s, had explained this concentration of power in terms of the 'logic of industrialism', which, they argued, made for uniformities between one industrial society and another, overriding other factors such as differences in national culture or differences of political systems. As with Rostow's theory of development, discussed in Chapter 3 (pp. 143–4), the idea was that as countries reached the stage of advanced industrialization, their institutional arrangements and social systems – from mobility-patterns to class-systems – would become more and more alike.

Goldthorpe tested this thesis by comparing developments in Soviet society with those in the United States. He concluded that there was, in fact, no single 'logic of industrialization', but rather several ways in which development could occur, and no single mode of relationships between the polity and the economy either. In the West, 'economic, and specifically market forces act as the crucial stratifying agency within society . . . They are the major source of social inequality.' In the U.S.S.R., on the other hand, 'stratification . . . is subjected to *political* regulation: market forces are not permitted to have the primacy or degree of autonomy that they have even in a "managed" capitalist society' (Goldthorpe, J. H., 1964, pp. 110–11). In the U.S.S.R., then, because Marxism makes a distinction between 'productive' and 'non-productive' labour, the numbers of administrative and managerial personnel are kept as low as possible. Ideological factors thus explain the marked differences in the composition of the work-force as between the U.S.S.R. and the West: clerical workers, for instance, make up less than 4·5 per cent of the Soviet labour-force, as against 10–15 per cent in Western countries. Contrary to popular stereotypes of the Eastern European communist countries as being highly bureaucratized, they are strikingly underprovided with administrative services (which may, in part, explain the familiar accounts of delays, bottle-necks, queues and the like).

Again, far from following identical stages of modernization to those which occurred in the earlier capitalist development of Europe, Soviet industrialization took place very rapidly and in a very centralized fashion, under the aegis of State and Communist party, and with unusually heavy reliance upon the rapid development of heavy industry at the expense of agriculture and light (especially consumer) industry. Hence, Soviet agriculture is labour-intensive: at least 39 per cent of the labour-force was still employed in agriculture in the U.S.S.R. as late as 1960, compared to only 4·2 per cent in the U.K. and 7·3 per cent in the U.S.A. Some thirty million people are still engaged in agriculture, a figure which has remained steady, rather than declining (Garnsey, 1975).

Rather than a single pattern of development inexorably dictated by a technical 'logic of industrialism', we find that ideology and historical circumstances make for great differences not only in growth-patterns and output, but of social structure and culture. They bear little resemblance to the Industrial Revolution in Britain a century and a half earlier.

Taking the two key factors of production, capital and labour, capital was accumulated in Britain's Industrial Revolution, abroad, through the despoliation of other countries, and at home by reinvesting profits from an already capitalized agriculture and from growing industry. A labour-force was created out of the dispossessed rural population. In the Soviet case, there was no 'primitive' accumulation of capital from abroad; rather, the agricultural sector (which meant mainly the peasantry) were the source of the capital which paid for industrialization as well as providing the labour-force needed in the new urban factories. Finally, Britain's Industrial Revolution – though it involved State intervention much more than *laissez faire* ideology recognizes – was in many ways the polar antithesis of State- and Party-directed industrialization in the U.S.S.R.

Some theorists regarded this concentration of power in the hands of a 'modernizing élite' – in this case, a communist one – as essentially a phenomenon of *transition*. The early phase of industrialization, they argued, inevitably entails the mobilization of factors of production. In the case of the British Industrial Revolution, the accumulation of capital had been decisive; in the Soviet case, the mobilization of labour.

More recently, Lane has sought to avoid any counterposing of Marxist versus functionalist arguments. The early period of development of Soviet society was a revolutionary phase, 'best explained by the theory of class struggle devised by Marx and applied by Lenin (Lane, D., 1976, p. 64). Once the Soviet State, however, had become established and consolidated under the leadership of a Party dedicated to mobilization for industrial development, the Soviet polity and society became a singularly co-ordinated one, unified, ideologically, by a single system of values (Marxism-Leninism), and institutionally, by the dominance of the Communist Party. Hence, Parsonian functionalism, which emphasizes precisely these things, becomes a more suitable intellectual framework for analysing contemporary Soviet society (see below, pp. 494–533). The adaptation of functionalist theory to Marxism, in the U.S.S.R., has also been stressed by Gouldner, who sees both theoretical systems as orthodoxies against which 'radical' sociologists are beginning to react (Gouldner, 1970, ch. 12).

The so-called 'élite' theorists, on the other hand, regard any notions of progress towards democracy, let alone towards 'classless' society, as delusions, perhaps admirable as ideals, but fundamentally non-scientific, and inherently doomed to remain *only* dreams, especially in large-scale complex modern industrial societies. They usually draw their theoretical inspiration from Vilfredo Pareto (1848–1923), who built his sociology around the simple notion that societies could always be divided into two differing populations: those who exhibited qualities of excellence in their given sphere of activity – the élite – and the rest, the non-élite (Pareto, 1966). A governing élite was constituted by those with the best-developed skills at ruling others, whether by the use of force or fraud. The masses, by contrast, were incompetent and ineffectively organized. In any case, mass and majority rule, he held, were both impossible in reality. Pareto believed that changes of régime and government merely reflected the periodic transfer of power from one type of élite to another, not from one class to another. Such a theory is psychologistic rather than sociological, for it explains social change in terms of there being reservoirs of *individuals* with fixed characteristics rather than as the outcome of conflicts in institutional arrangements. The economic and political dominance of the élites is explained as the outcome of their personal characteristics. Other élite theorists, notably Gaetano Mosca, produced more sociological versions in which they do not postulate the existence of different types in this way, but simply observe that some people perform more effectively than others in any activity; that in changing societies new people are constantly being recruited into the various élites, that the political ruling class is the most important of these élites and that modern democracy therefore represents a way of retaining 'open-ness' of the élite (Bottomore, 1964). An open system actually *increases* the effectiveness of the ruling class because it preserves allegiance to the system on the part of the most energetic and enterprising amongst the non-élite who always hope to rise in the social hierarchy, and who otherwise, if frustrated, might constitute a dissident force. Democracy thus depended on having a reservoir of talented middle-class people, some of whom could be recruited into the élite; it was also a more stable and popular political system than more reactionary and less flexible ones.

The model of a society in which key political power is firmly in the hands of a *political* class, whose power does not derive from their economic holdings, has also been used in analysing the situation in some of the newer and more backward 'neo-colonial' independent states. These are agrarian societies; the decisive power is held not by a bourgeoisie or a class of capitalist landowners but by a political class of 'new men' of no great substance who, by founding and dominating the party, and then the government, become a new ruling élite rather than a ruling class in the Marxist sense, but do not develop the country. It is significant that so many studies use the label 'new élites' for these countries rather than 'new ruling *classes*', for decisive economic power lies outside the country – with those who own the plantations and mines, control the financial institutions, regulate world-market prices and monopolize modern technology.

In communist societies, where private property has been abolished, and in backward 'neo-colonial' societies where the internal ruling class is not the decisive property-owning class, élite theory thus seems useful and helps complement theories which emphasize the economic basis of class alone.

Social classes in the full Marxist sense, characterized by a sense of solidarity amongst their members, and by class organizations which express and articulate conflict with other classes over the radically unequal division of property, are not yet clearly consolidated in many underdeveloped countries, and vertical divisions of ethnicity – tribal, regional and 'ethnic' differences – often divide classes and unite people, as 'pillars', despite economic differences of position and wealth. Classes are, of course, developing in all these countries, and in some are already well developed, since most of the world's peasants have long been drawn into the money economy as cash-crop producers, virtually all as consumers, and many into urban industry or plantations as labourers. Indigenous capitalist enterprise also emerges or continues to develop after independence. Hence, social classes are indeed coming into existence. But the ruling élites are not classic ruling classes, and ethnic divisions (usually labelled 'regionalism', 'tribalism' or 'separatism') are strong.

The bourgeoisie in such countries, we noted in Chapter 3 (pp. 151–2), has often been condemned as incapable of bringing about modernization, in particular industrialization. Though it is often large, containing myriads of petty traders, artisans working on their own account, owners of small workshops and shops, and small landowners, the bulk of these are very tiny operators indeed. In countries like India and Nigeria there are, of course, some very wealthy men: not a 'petty' bourgeoisie such as we have described, but a full-blown bourgeoisie proper.

Nevertheless, most of them are involved in importing manufactured goods from the developed world, or in exporting raw materials, or in commercial, financial and middlemen activities rather than in developing manufacturing industry. Again, in newly independent countries the State has assisted entrepreneurs, including members of the reigning parties and public officials, to invest by providing them with cheap finance, producing a new kind of 'state bourgeoisie' which identifies strongly with the political authorities, unlike the fiercely independent liberal bourgeoisie of early nineteenth-century Britain (Leys, 1975).

That bourgeoisie had come into violent conflict with the established land-owning classes, though it eventually reached a compromise with them politically once the latter had ceased to put obstacles in the way of unbridled industrial development. In any case, agriculture itself became organized on capitalist lines.

In the Third World agriculture remains backward, polarized between declining smallholder farming and large estates, *latifundia* or plantations increasingly managed on thoroughly capitalist lines, and worked by a wage-labour work-force of landless people. In the extreme, farming is being rationalized along the lines of American 'agribusinesses', which have made U.S. agriculture the most productive in the world. Elsewhere, the old *latifundia* have been split up in land reforms and distributed to peasants, in the hope that a mass prosperous peasantry, committed to capitalist farming, will grow up in the countryside.

Such land distribution often goes hand-in-hand with attempts to modernize the methods of farming, of which the use of new 'miracle seeds' in the 'Green Revolution' is the best-known instance. In general, the evidence seems to be that the poorer peasants with little or no capital soon find themselves unable to continue in business, since the new seeds require considerable investment in fertilizers, irrigation, etc., and sell out to their more prosperous neighbours. We have seen that the city offers them one way out but – as in the extreme situation represented by Calcutta – the majority of the urban population are often not absorbed there, as urban industry is quite incapable of providing enough work for the ever-growing urban population. Commonly, the *majority* of town- and city-dwellers live, somehow, outside industry. They may engage in a bit of street-trading, get a casual labouring job for a while, steal, starve, or live off their more fortunate kin who *do* have jobs, and have been described, therefore, by the pejorative word 'lumpenproletariat', or as 'sub-proletarians' or 'marginal' people.

A coherent proletariat of the type Marx had in mind thus hardly exists. Where the urban workers are organized, hitherto they have not often constituted a very dangerous challenge to the State, and have been readily controlled when they have. More often, it has been the peasantry, when given leadership and organization, who have provided the most successful revolutionary challenges in this century (Shanin, 1971; Wolf, 1966 and 1971).

But these have been exceptional situations. Peasants are no more 'naturally' revolutionary today than they have been throughout history, where they have been known, rather, for their passivity, fatalism and deference to authority. They were also usually thought to be so parochial and 'privatized', so weak and so ready to bow before powerful authorities, that they were practically incapable of working together. Yet they have been successfully organized by revolutionary 'cadres' who themselves usually come from urban backgrounds. It is these people who, by immersing themselves in peasant life, develop the ideologies and programmes which eventually meet with a response because they promise to fulfil the unsatisfied wants of the peasantry, and provide the machinery through which these ideas get translated into action. Energies which would otherwise remain only latent are thereby unleashed, whether for revolutionary struggles or for post-revolutionary development campaigns. Parties which have this mobilizatory function thus constitute an independent political variable. Poverty and frustration are more likely otherwise to result in despair, resignation or escape, or resort to illusory solutions or 'amoral' individualism.

The capture of power, the nationalization of industry or distri-bution of land, does not eliminate all forms of inequality. In com-munist societies, new kinds of classes based on access to the sources of political power, rather than on possession of private property, emerge, as we have seen, and, despite major changes, women have still to reach equality with men, whether in the home, in positions of power, or in many occupations. The 'Cultural Revolution' in China was an attempt to counteract these tendencies, and to break down not only inequalities of wealth, but all forms of inequality generated and entrenched over millennia: the differences between life in the town and life in the countryside, and the traditional inferiority of those who work with their hands producing material commodities and those who engage in 'mental labour' producing pieces of paper or ideas, or who do 'people-work' (Worsley, 1975). Though the outcome of that attempt to overcome the routinization that affects even revolutions cannot yet be known, it represents a counter-instance of great importance to those deterministic theories that assume that all revolutions will inevitably become fossilized and develop new forms of inequality.

Chapter 9
The Problem of Order

Individual and Society

In previous chapters we have discussed various aspects of sociology, showing how it is divided amongst such areas of specialization as 'sociology of work', 'sociology of the family', 'urban sociology' and so on. Whilst sociologists may be differentiated from one another by their substantive interests in such areas they are also separated from one another by their theoretical allegiances.

Sociologists by no means agree with one another on the nature of their subject. They do not see eye-to-eye on questions about the proper tasks of their discipline or the ways in which they should go about their work (some idea of the scope of these differences has been given in Chapters 1 and 2). They do not agree, either, in their general conceptions of the nature of the reality with which they deal. There are radically different views on the nature of man and the way in which society is 'put together' and 'works'. In this chapter we shall be examining *some* of the principal points of view on those matters which have been current in sociology, particularly in the period since the Second World War.

The different 'camps' of sociological thought can be defined in many different ways – for example, in Chapter 2 we distinguished between 'positivist' and 'interpretivist' views of sociology on the basis of attitudes towards the relation between natural and social science. For the purposes of this chapter we will demarcate between schools in terms of their views of the problem of social order, since we can then contrast very basic views of the nature of the elements of social organization and of the place of man in society.

To say that the problem of social order involves asking whether and how social organization is possible may seem perverse, for obviously social life does exist. But it is by no means obvious as to how and why this persistence of organized social life comes about. Nor do we get much help in our efforts to solve this problem if we try to use many commonly held beliefs about society and human nature – whether they be popular beliefs or theories developed by major thinkers. Those theories, if carried through to their logical conclusions, would lead us to believe that social life can never exist.

Theories of this kind were spelled out most systematically by Thomas Hobbes in his *Leviathan*, published some three hundred years ago, and they have been repeated in whole or in part by many other social theorists since then.

The most basic assumption is that human beings are entirely selfish, concerned only with the fulfilment of their own desires. We need not concern ourselves with the kinds of things different individuals will want, we need only assume that desires are randomly distributed amongst them with the result that they will often want the same things. The next assumption is that the resources needed to satisfy human wants are in scarce supply, that there are not sufficient of them to satisfy everybody's wants. The last assumption is that people have the power of reasoning, that they are capable of determining the most effective ways of getting the things they want.

The first implication of these assumptions is that human relations must be intensely competitive, given the condition of scarcity, for one man can have what he wants only if another is denied it. Each individual is compelled to look upon his fellows as obstacles standing between him and the things that he wants. Being quite selfish he will have no compunction against dealing with his fellows in whatever ways are most favourable to his self-interest and a principal preoccupation will be that of ensuring that others do not come between him and the things he wants. He will come to realize that force and fraud are the most effective means of dealing with his fellows, for through their use he can either destroy his competitors or reduce them to the service of his own purposes.

The only difficulty with this reasoning is that it is available to everybody. Each and every individual is capable of concluding that force and fraud are the most effective ways of realizing his self-interest, and therefore they will *all* resort to the use of those means, creating amongst themselves a dangerous and mutually destructive anarchy in which, in the words of Hobbes, there would be 'no arts; no letters; no society; and which is worst of all, a continual fear and danger of violent death; and the life of man, solitary, poor, nasty, brutish and short' (Hobbes, 1962, p. 100).

The implication of these assumptions is that anarchy is the inevitable outcome of the pursuit of self-interest in a condition of scarcity. There is, however, something of a paradox here, for it is hardly in anyone's interests to be exposed to the inevitably fatal hazards of a lethal anarchy. There is little pleasure in having unrestricted freedom to pursue one's interests by whatever means one deems best if one is unlikely to live long enough to make any use of that freedom. Survival must be assumed to be a *special* interest of the individual's, for he needs to be assured of that before seeking any of the other things he desires. Anarchy is not, then, the automatic extension of self-interest that it first seemed to be, for since it threatens the individual's very survival it goes against the most important interest of all. Each person will, therefore, want to avoid the danger of anarchy, but cannot do so alone, since anyone who unilaterally abandons the use of force and fraud merely makes himself into an easier victim for others. Anarchy can be avoided only on a collective basis, through the simultaneous sacrifice by all men of their freedom to engage in unconstrained mutual destruction.

It seems, then, that if men come together and make a 'social contract' – an agreement to surrender their freedom to make use of force and fraud – they can take care of their predominant interest in staying alive and thus liberate themselves to pursue their other desires by the best means they can devise – provided, of course, that these involve neither force nor fraud. The mere making of such an agreement does not guarantee security, for nothing ensures that the parties to it will in fact abide by the terms of the agreement, they may merely have assented to them as part of a strategy of deception. It is, therefore, necessary that as part of the agreement itself some arrangement be made to ensure that it will be honoured. An effective means of doing this is to agree to the creation of a 'sovereign power', an impartial authority which will oversee relations between individuals, constraining and punishing any who breach the agreement they have made.

By allowing the interest in physical survival to assume primary status we can now conclude that society *can* exist, even if it is only as a means by which its members defend themselves against one another. Even so, the assumptions do lead to conclusions which are not very satisfactory. The idea that society could be created through a social contract, for example, is one that has no historical foundation, for nothing even remotely resembling the making of a social contract has ever taken place. At best the idea of a social contract might have a metaphorical value, enabling us to understand society by looking upon it *as though* it were created and sustained through some form of explicit agreement amongst its members. Similarly, the view that some sovereign power is necessary to prevent society disintegrating into anarchy is incorrect, for there are societies which are orderly and peaceful enough but which have no monarchy, no State administration or other kind of differentiated authority.

In 1937, in his *The Structure of Social Action*, Talcott Parsons argued that although assumptions of a Hobbesian kind were patently inadequate, they had not been improved upon, but more effective assumptions could be found in the work of some of Parsons's predecessors, sociologists such as Emile Durkheim and Max Weber amongst others.

Durkheim's main aim was to establish that sociology could be a *bona fide* science, and one of his principal strategies was to argue that society is a perfectly natural phenomenon, just as natural as any other and, hence, just as suitable a subject for scientific study as any other. Given this emphasis, Durkheim could hardly make use of assumptions of a Hobbesian kind for they, in essence, suggest that society is unnatural, an artificial contrivance which has been imposed upon a basically anti-social human nature. Durkheim had to develop a different conception of the nature of the individual and society and of their mutual relations.

In his analysis of *The Division of Labour in Society*, Durkheim postulated two principles which serve to keep societies together and prevent their collapsing into internal disorder. He thought that two main types of society could be identified, distinguished from one another by the degree to which they were dominated by one or other of his two 'principles of solidarity'. These were societies of the 'mechanical' and of the 'organic' type.

The mechanical type is dominated by *similarity*. Its members are like one another, they undergo similar life-experiences, have similar skills and capacities and develop the same thoughts and attitudes. Societies of this type are simple and undifferentiated, and their organization insufficiently complex to allow much variety of experience and outlook. A small nomadic band of hunters with very little specialization and made up of individuals all of whom must master the same basic skills – those of hunting – if they are to keep themselves alive, exemplifies this kind of society. Such a society survives because of the similarity of its members, no one person is indispensable to it. To the society as a whole, it does not greatly matter if some of its members are lost, for they do not monopolize any special skills or expertise which might be essential to those remaining. Only skills and knowledge which are readily available to the other members of the society are lost when anyone moves away from the community or dies.

By contrast, the organic type is organized on the basis of *difference*. That type of society – in which our own would be included – is complex and differentiated, characterized by a high degree of division of labour (by which expression Durkheim means *all* forms of specialization, not just those of an economic kind), and containing many different occupations and life-styles, each with its own associated practices, skills and esoteric knowledge. Members of this type of society are confronted with a vast array of possibilities and can, therefore, develop in many different directions and can acquire skills, knowledge, experience and attitudes which will be quite unlike those of most of the other members of their society, perhaps even unique to themselves.

It might seem that a society containing such extensive variation would be most unstable, for the differences between members would surely encourage and exacerbate conflicts. Durkheim argues that the opposite is true; that the difference contributes to the cohesion of the society because it creates interdependence. The spread of specialization may mean that we can do certain things which our fellows cannot do, but it also means that they can do things which we cannot. We therefore *need* our fellows because we depend on them to use their special skills on our behalf. From the point of view of a society of this type, its members are indispensable, for should some of them break away they may take with them irreplaceable knowledge and skills which are necessary for the continuance of the life of the society.

There is, in Durkheim's view, a continuing tendency for movement to take place from mechanical and towards organic solidarity; complex and differentiated societies developing out of simpler and less differentiated ones. This tendency was, he thought, due to the pressure of growing population, since larger populations could be sustained and organized through developing specialization.

Durkheim's analysis of the different forms of social solidarity shows the fallacy of arguments of a Hobbesian kind. Hobbes, and those who hold similar views, attempt to understand society by making some initial assumptions about the nature of individuals and then attempting to extrapolate from those to conclusions about the nature of society. The arguments about the two types of solidarity shows, however, that, if anything, it is the characteristics of the individual which need to be derived from those of the society rather than the other way around. The difference between organic and mechanical solidarity is not to be understood as resulting from differences between the kinds of individuals who make up the two types of society. A society of a simple and undifferentiated kind does not develop into one which is complex and differentiated because, overnight, the nature of its members has changed. There may be a great deal more variety in the traits of those who live within a society of an organic kind, but this is not because their natures are different from those who live under mechanical solidarity. Variation and difference are *possible* in a society of the organic type but they are not possible within one of the mechanical sort simply because there is no room for them. The difference between the populations follows from the difference between the social structures of the two types of society.

In discussing the division of labour, Durkheim attacked the view that society could be based upon some kind of social contract. In a society like our own – one of the 'organic' type – contracts are extremely widely used as the basis of relationships between people; explicit and binding agreements set down the terms on which people are to deal with each other. However, whilst two parties may, in making a contract, create a new relationship between themselves, they are depending upon certain underlying rules and understandings which are not spelled out in the contract but which are assumed by those who are drawing it up. These are the rules and understandings which specify what is to count as a contract, what can and cannot be done in such an agreement. In summary, says Parsons, they

regulate in the first place what contracts are and what are not recognised as valid. A man cannot for instance, sell himself or others into slavery. They regulate the means by which the other party's assent to the contract may be obtained; an agreement secured by fraud or under duress is void. They regulate various consequences of the contract once made, both to the parties themselves and to third persons. Under certain circumstances a party may be enjoined from enforcing a contract quite legally made, as when the holder of a mortgage is sometimes prohibited from foreclosing when interest payments are not made. Similarly, one party may be forced to assume obligations which were not in his contract. They regulate, finally, the procedure by which enforcement in the courts is obtainable (Parsons, 1949, p. 312).

If we think of an 'institution' as a set of practices which are established through rules and understandings which are widely known and accepted amongst the members of society, we can see that the burden of Durkheim's argument is that contract is an institution and that it is this which makes possible the drawing up of specific contractual agreements between the members of society. Contract, therefore, cannot be seen as the basis of social organization because it can only exist within an already organized society with established rules and understandings. We need, therefore, to explain, first, how institutions are possible, how people come to establish stable and standardized practices and how they develop shared rules and understandings – contract is not something which explains social order, it is something which needs explanation as part of social order.

In arguing that sociology is a science, Durkheim insisted that society is quite as real as any physical thing, such as a chair, and that it must therefore be studied in the same way as any other real thing. Society is real, he maintained, because it exists independently of the will and wish of any single individual, because it is external to its members and constrains what they do, simply imposing itself upon them. In arguing this Durkheim sounds rather as though he was taking a Hobbesian position, for that view, too, insists that society is an imposition upon the individual. Durkheim's argument is rather more subtle, as his discussion of *Suicide* shows. As we have already seen (cf. above, pp. 80–82), Durkheim wanted to account for the remarkable stability of suicide rates over time and, by doing so, to show that what is seemingly the most individualistic of actions – that of self-destruction – is to be accounted for in terms of social factors. We need not concern ourselves here with the full scope of Durkheim's argument on suicide and the different types which he identified but can focus our attention upon one type only, that which he identified as 'anomic' suicide.

This type, the anomic, was intended to identify that kind of suicide which relates to changes in economic circumstance. Durkheim noted that suicide rates increased both in times of economic collapse *and* of economic boom. That suicides result from the *loss* of fortunes that occur in slumps or depressions is perhaps obvious enough, but it is not quite so obvious why booms, and the associated *making* of fortunes, should also result in increases in the suicide rate. Durkheim thought that variations in the suicide rate in both booms and collapses could be accommodated under one single explanation, since both are times of rapid social change in which the lives of many individuals are radically disrupted. Such times create conditions of 'anomie', situations in which the rules and standards by which an individual is accustomed to live are rendered irrelevant by changing circumstance.

In relatively stable periods, the members of different social classes live according to different standards of living which are deemed appropriate to them. Members of the different classes accept as appropriate to themselves those standards which are deemed proper for their class. Rapid economic change, however, involves the redistribution of fortune and people may find that their economic position is no longer congruent with their class position, that they are in a position in which they can – or may *have* to – live in a way different from that to which they have become accustomed.

People can, of course, learn to make adjustments and change their ways of living to match their economic position, but this takes time, and gradual change is not possible in times of rapid economic transformation. People find their lives have changed overnight and that the standards they have hitherto followed no longer apply. If someone acquires a new fortune in a short time, then, unlimited possibilities lie before them. Now, in Durkheim's view, human appetites and desires are inherently unlimited, which means that they can never be completely satisfied. If desires are unlimited then no matter how much one gets, one will always want more. This means that desires can only be satisfied if, somehow, they are limited, if some discipline is imposed upon them, and in Durkheim's account it is society which imposes that discipline. Through life in society the individual learns to accept those standards which set certain conditions of material life for people of his type, and comes to see socially approved standards of living for his class as those which he may legitimately want and expect to see fulfilled. He does not go on indefinitely wanting more, but is satisfied to have what he feels he is entitled to get.

Radical redistribution of fortune disturbs that situation and breaks down the discipline which the society has imposed upon the individual's wants. The individual's desires, no longer being subject to the standards which he has learned, are now free to become enlarged, to run out of all control, leading the individual to develop wants and expectations which are quite unrealistic and which cannot be satisfied. The result will be frustration and disappointment, and these may eventually encourage the individual to attempt suicide.

Just as the loss of wealth can precipitate suicide because it means that the individual can no longer live according to his habitual standards and, hence, leads to his frustration and disappointment, so too can the sudden acquisition of riches lead to the same result by releasing the individual's desires from society's 'control' and allowing them to expand beyond all possibility of fulfilment, again producing frustration and disappointment.

An account of the Hobbesian sort leads us to think of the individual as bringing his desires already formed into society with him, the purpose of society being to regulate the conditions under which he can pursue his wants and to provide him with some security in the process. Durkheim is suggesting something very different: that the individual comes to want that which the society deems it proper for him to want. Society regulates not just the *means* of human actions but the very *ends* themselves, and it is only when social regulation collapses – as in conditions of anomie – that the individual is enabled to develop genuinely spontaneous wants. But that, Durkheim claims, is no good thing, for the individual is by no means assured to be so good a judge as society of what he may practicably and realistically want. The result of the individual's self-determination of his wants may be his self-destruction rather than the advancement of his happiness.

Society is not, it now appears, *only* external to the individual; it is internal too, shaping our minds and feelings, shaping the things we want and expect. This is the broadest conclusion that can be drawn from Durkheim's account of anomie, for it suggests that society disciplines the individual's desires by 'injecting' itself within the individual in the form of the standards by which he learns to live. The constraint which society imposes upon the individual is a real one, Durkheim maintains, in that it sets limits to what we can do and be. This we can rapidly discover for ourselves if we attempt to go against the laws of our society. If we do so, we shall find that we are constrained from doing so, physically incarcerated or even killed. Murder, for example, is something that is forbidden by the laws of society and if we attempt or commit it we shall find ourselves restrained and punished. The constraint which society can impose upon us to prevent murder is not, however, experienced by most of us as an imposition. We are not prevented from murdering by the thought that we shall be arrested and tried. The thought of murdering someone simply does not occur to us; we do not murder because we do not want to. We would receive any suggestion that we should kill someone with revulsion: we just couldn't do that. We abide by society's rules, then, because we feel spontaneously inclined to do so.

To say that society has 'injected' itself into the individual might seem rather strange. After all, Durkheim began by saying that society is 'external' to its members and now it is being said that society is 'internal' to them. How can this be so, how can something which is external also be internal? Durkheim takes the view that society is *in essence* its moral codes, the rules which govern the relations between its members. It can be external, therefore, in the sense that the moral rules of society pre-exist for all of us and have been developed out of the association of our innumerable predecessors – those rules are not the invention of any single one of us. It can be internal also because we can, each of us, learn those rules from and through our association with our fellows, and can incorporate them into our own personalities so that they come to shape our thoughts, feelings and desires.

The argument was developed further in Durkheim's reflections upon religion. Since he did not believe in the supernatural, Durkheim was convinced that religious ideas could not be about that, for it did not exist. They must, therefore, be a symbolic expression of something else. The question was, what?

The essence of the religious experience, Durkheim thought, is a feeling of awe which arises from being confronted with something that is larger, more powerful and much greater than we human beings are, something which is much more encompassing than our individual consciousness. What we worship is not really a supernatural force but something which is greater and more awe-inspiring than our individual selves. The obvious candidate, in Durkheim's view, is society itself, since that encompasses the individual and is substantially more powerful than ourselves. However, our social relations with other individuals are relatively transitory things and are hardly likely to fill us with a sense of awe. If we are worshipping society then it must be in some other form than that in which we experience it through our direct relations with our fellows. The main element of continuity in social life, which persists despite changes in our relations and in the personnel who make it up, is the *moral* order, that set of rules governing social relations; that is so transcendentally superhuman that we can fittingly feel respect towards it. We are, in Durkheim's famous formula, when worshipping, really worshipping society itself in the form of the moral rules which are its essence. The actual rites of worship are themselves of great importance for the maintenance of the society's life, for when we engage in them we remind ourselves of the codes which order our life and to which our attachment tends to become attenuated under the strains of daily life, therefore requiring periodic revival and re-dedication. Religious ritual, then, keeps alive the morality it embodies (Durkheim, 1976).

Durkheim's arguments thus run counter to those of Hobbes. In Hobbes's terms, the relation between the individual and society is based upon fear and calculation. The member of society abides by its rules because he sees it as being in his own interest to do so, or because he fears the consequences if he does not. Durkheim asserts that the individual is a moral creature, who reacts in terms of right and wrong and who acts as he does not from expediency or fear of external sanction but because of internal conviction. The relationship between individual and society is that of a subscriber and his moral code.

Arguments complementing those of Durkheim were developed by Max Weber, who also emphasized the importance of religious institutions in society, though in a different way, since the questions he was asking were of a different kind.

Weber was primarily concerned to give some account of the origins of modern industrial capitalism in the Western world. Although capitalism had appeared in other societies and at other times, only in the contemporary West had it developed in a world-historic way. The problem was to understand the peculiarity of this development: why had it taken place *only* in the West?

Weber sought a main part of the solution in the differing religious traditions of the West and the Orient respectively. Through their influence upon attitudes towards work and economic activity, religious traditions can affect the propensity of people to undertake those activities which are necessary for the creation of modern industrial capitalism. The religions of the Western world had, Weber argued, encouraged such propensities in a way that those of the East had not, there being the most pointed connection of all between the Protestant ethic and the spirit of capitalism (Weber, 1952).

The most distinctive thing about Western capitalism was, thought Weber, its spirit. It took an attitude towards work and economic enterprise which was quite unique, which stressed that industry and the endless accumulation of riches were things which were desirable in their own right. Other societies may have encouraged industry and the accumulation of great wealth but these were, in such cases, approved of because they could eventually result in luxurious and gratifying consumption. Under Western capitalism hard work and the making of profits were approved not because they served the end of making possible consumption but because they were good things in themselves, the things which any upright individual should be engaged in. Unwillingness to work and the dissipation of wealth in consumption rather than investment were viewed as signs of moral weakness.

This attitude, Weber pointed out, is by no means one that is natural to men or one that is found everywhere. A quite different attitude, one which he labelled 'traditional', is every bit as natural and just as widespread and that outlook views work as a necessary evil, something that is undertaken only because it has to be. Work is seen as a means of sustaining an established standard of living, and it is not undertaken to any greater extent than is necessary to keep up that standard of living. Faced with the choice between working more and obtaining a higher standard of living and working less to retain a customary standard of living, the worker with a traditional orientation will prefer to work less.

A society like capitalism could not work if its labour force was imbued with a traditional attitude, for it requires that its economic enterprises be kept in continuous operation, that capital be accumulated and that plant and machinery be used as much as possible. It therefore requires a disciplined work-force which will work regular and predictable hours and will do so despite changes in the return upon their labour. It needs workers who are motivated by the desire to improve their material standard of life and who will, therefore, continue to work the same hours as before should their wage rates rise. A worker with a traditional orientation would not behave in the requisite fashion but would take the opportunity presented by a rise in wage rates to reduce the number of hours worked.

Since the disposition to work regular hours and to be motivated by a desire for a higher standard of living is not one which is universal it must, somehow, have been 'created' in the inhabitants of capitalism, must have some kind of specific historical origins.

Weber noted that there were many resemblances between the spirit of capitalism and the religious attitudes which developed amongst the members of the Protestant sects at the time of the Reformation, attitudes which he thought made up a Protestant ethic. Those resemblances, Weber thought, indicated the likely existence of a causal connection between the Protestant ethic and the spirit of capitalism.

Calvinism was seen as the purest example of the Protestant attitude, and it was therefore Calvinist beliefs which Weber used as the central instance for his argument.

The central Calvinist doctrine holds that God has predestined the world and that all the individuals in it have already been assigned to salvation or damnation. What God has decided must be the fate of each person cannot, however, be known nor can anything be done to change the decisions which God has already made. The consequence of this doctrine, for those who accept Calvinism, is to place them in a psychologically intolerable position, for the fate of their immortal soul must be a matter of the most intense concern to them and yet they cannot hope to know about it, they are condemned to ignorance and uncertainty. Such strains upon the Calvinists of the Reformation period, Weber argued, had to have some kind of resolution, and one way in which believers could achieve that was through the 'distortion' of the Calvinist doctrine in such a way as to allow that they *could* know what God had decided. They were able to persuade themselves that whilst 'good works' could not change any decision God had made they could indicate the nature of that decision:

Good works, while they could not influence salvation, could be interpreted as *signs* of grace. A good tree could not bear evil fruit. Then gradually the elect [i.e. those who were saved] came to be identified with the 'righteous', those who did the will of God, and the damned with 'sinners', those who failed to obey His will (Parsons, 1949, p. 525).

The believer could convince himself that he *did* know the fate of his immortal soul, could do so because he could tell from the evidence of his own conduct. If it was God's will that men should act in the world in such a way as to enhance His greater glory then surely he must look with favour upon those who fulfil that injunction and act in accord with his commandments. Therefore those who are most obedient to His law must be those whom he has saved.

The doctrine of predestination may appear to license the believer to act in whatever ways he pleases since his actions can have no consequences for his ultimate salvation, even the most sinful conduct being unable to change the decision which God has already made. The Calvinists, however, drew entirely opposite conclusions and came to adopt the most stringent, rigorous and ascetic control over their own conduct, eschewing anything that might be viewed as sinful. The reason for this, Weber argued, was because the believer could create within himself the *feeling* that he was saved and that the need to sustain his own conviction of salvation must place him under the most intense pressure to avoid all things which could cast doubt upon that conviction.

By acting in accord with God's laws as expressed in the Commandments, the individual is not earning salvation but creating within himself the conviction that he already has it. Such a conviction is of the most intense significance to the believer and the occurrence of any kind of conduct, no matter how trivial, which might seem to cast doubt upon his salvation could not be allowed. The believer must simply take the most enormous care in the organization of his own conduct, always ensuring that any possible taint of sinfulness be avoided, and this would require the most rigorous self-control and self-scrutiny on the part of the individual at all times. One single instance of misconduct would be enough to unseat his conviction and it was not, therefore, possible for him to relax his self-discipline for one single moment: he must *always* be alert to the danger of failing to comply with God's precepts.

This self-discipline was applied by the Calvinist in all spheres of life, including the economic. A man's occupation was something to which he had been 'called' by God and he was, therefore, obliged to pursue its responsibilities with the same scrupulousness that he must apply to all the other duties which God had placed upon him.

The main parallels between the spirit of capitalism and the ethic of Protestantism are that both require the application of systematic self-discipline in economic activities and both view the fulfilment of one's occupational responsibilities as something which is morally worthy. Capitalism requires that the worker proceed in a disciplined and systematic way about his task, whilst the Protestant ethic leads him to exercise similar self-control in order to sustain his rather fragile conviction of his own salvation. Capitalism looks upon work as something good in itself, something people *ought* to do if they are good and upright citizens. Calvinism's attitude parallels that, for it too sees work as something which people ought to do, that it is morally worthy to work because that is something which God requires of man.

The spirit of capitalism looks rather like a secularized version of the Protestant ethic. There are some grounds for thinking that the *by-product* of the Protestant ethic might be the creation of capitalist activity and the capitalist spirit. The assiduous application of the Calvinist to his work must surely mean that he would be successful in his calling, and that in turn would mean he would become increasingly prosperous. Since those things which are normally used to consume wealth – pleasures and luxuries – were generally identified in Calvinism with sin, the believer who became prosperous would be unable to dispose of the wealth he was accumulating: he could not spend it upon himself since he had to lead an ascetic daily life. There would be nothing else for him to do but to re-invest his wealth in productive work. That, of course, would make him even more prosperous, leaving him with an even greater surplus which he could not consume and must therefore invest, and so on, in a cycle which involved him in becoming more and more wealthy. In this situation we may have the roots of capitalist society itself, for the inability of the Protestant faithful to do anything with their wealth except to plough it back into industry could provide just the motivation necessary for the accumulation of capital essential for the creation of capitalism's economic structure.

The spirit of capitalism does not itself derive directly from religious attitudes and motives, but it is at least possible that the Protestant ethic made a vital contribution to its creation by providing religious sanctions to underpin motives appropriate to the early stages of capitalist growth. Once capitalist society is firmly established, of course, it can itself imbue the appropriate motivation necessary for its functioning into its members, and it no longer needs religious ideas to support it. People in capitalist society act as they do because that is how everyone else acts: they do not need to be told that they should act that way because it is God's will.

Weber's argument also runs counter to the assumptions we outlined above. There we argued that we could assume that desires were randomly distributed amongst members of society and that we need not concern ourselves with the nature of individual wants. Weber's discussion of the genesis of capitalism suggests, however, that there is some systematic relationship between the organization of social structures and the nature of individual desires. He argues that modern capitalism simply could not function if its members were motivated by randomly assorted desires and that it depends upon the successful inculcation into them of certain specific kinds of motivation – those associated with work and accumulation of wealth. Weber concurs with Durkheim that the individual acquires his motivation 'from society', in and through association with his fellows. In fully developed capitalism the individual internalizes those attitudes which make up the spirit of capitalism.

The combined effect of the arguments of Durkheim and Weber is to rebut the assumptions we began with. Together they argue that the sort of assumptions made by Hobbes are accurate enough in certain respects but grossly over-generalized: what has happened is that the experience of industrial/capitalist society has been treated as though it were a universal one. Assumptions of the Hobbesian kind make the individual out to be a competitive self-interested creature bound to his fellows only through some contractual relation and kept in order by the authority of the centralized state. These descriptions may fit those of us who live in that kind of society which does employ contract and which has a state authority, but they are not universally characteristic of all human beings, nor expressive of a basic human nature. Competition, the pursuit of self-interest and contract are *institutionalized* within societies like our own.

A more basic fault has been found with the initial assumptions. Argument of the Hobbesian sort proceeds as though the existence of society makes no basic difference to the nature of individuals. We begin by imagining what individuals are like before there is any society, then we work out what is necessary to get them into some kind of stable association and we then conclude that we understand the nature of society. Durkheim and Weber seek to show that the individual is *unthinkable* without society, does not exist outside it.

In our initial specification the individual living outside of society is conceived of as having some clear self-interest, the power of reason and, we must presume, some kind of language in which to communicate with his fellows and to make the initial social contract. The only difference between this individual and ourselves is that he has not, as yet, agreed to take part in society. To Weber and Durkheim the human individual can only exist within society, and any creatures existing outside it would not be recognizable to us as fellow human beings but would be more like animals, lacking the power of reason, interests and language.

Both Durkheim and Weber have argued that human desires are formed within society, the individual internalizing the wants that are current and appropriate within the social settings he inhabits. Exactly the same argument can be applied to language. We can speak of something as a language only if it is shared amongst and serves to communicate between the members of a community. By definition language is an instrument of sociation and can only exist within society. Since our capacity for thought, its elaboration and expression, is part and parcel of our capacity to use language, we cannot conceive of creatures without a language as really being endowed with the power of reason.

System and Function

If the conclusions arrived at in the preceding section are correct, society is not in perpetual danger of collapse because of the intrinsically anti-social inclinations of its members. It *is* possible for human beings to establish enduring mutual relations. However, whilst social relations may last for fairly considerable periods of time they do not persist for ever – they do disintegrate or change beyond all recognition. The problem, now, is to understand how societies do manage to contain such tendencies towards anarchy as do exist within them and how established forms of social organization undergo changes, i.e., we need a general theory of stability and change in social life.

One of the main attempts to create such a theory is that known as 'functionalism'. It rests upon an analogy between society and the living organism. In assuming that society is like a living creature it does not suggest that we need to identify the social equivalents of legs, eyes, ears, etc., for the analogy is not being drawn in that way. We are being asked to consider society and the organism as being alike in that both face and, somehow, resolve the problem of survival. The body can and will die but it does not promptly do so. It often survives for relatively extended periods of time. Likewise, a society can collapse, but it does not necessarily do so. It, too, often survives for a long period of time. If we think of the disintegration of a society as being equivalent to the death of a living thing, then by drawing upon the relatively extensive biological knowledge of how creatures are kept alive we may be able to acquire a deeper understanding of what it is that keeps a society together.

The living body is a *system*. It is made up of a number of distinguishable parts but those parts are inter-related with one another so that if one of them is somehow changed the other parts will be affected also and will change in response. The body is made up of such parts as eyes, brain, lungs, heart, legs and so forth, and it is apparent that those different parts are most significantly interconnected, such that the failure of the heart, for example, will result in the death of the entire body, of the whole ensemble of parts. These parts are interconnected because each one has a particular role to play within the organization of the body as a whole: the heart has the vital task of supplying blood to all the other parts for they cannot, without that supply, perform their own roles in the body. Similarly, the brain has the task of processing information from the external world which comes in through eyes and ears and touch and smell, as well as co-ordinating the operation and movement of other parts of the body. Damage to it, therefore, means that such things as the capacity to think, move, see, hear, touch, breathe may all be affected and, if the damage is substantial enough, death of the entire body may result. We may, therefore, look upon the different parts of the body to see what *functions* they have, what part they play within the entire organization and what contribution they make to the continuing survival of the body.

As we have suggested in the previous paragraph, the body is an *open* and *adaptive* system in that it takes in information, food, energy and similar things from its external environment and is capable of adapting itself to changes in that environment. Certain conditions of heat and cold, for example, cannot be tolerated by the body and if they are exceeded it will die, but short of these extremes there are quite large variations in temperature in the external world which do not prove fatal, even though the body's survival requires that its own temperature remain within narrower limits than those in the external world. The body's own temperature does not rise in simple correspondence with the external one because the body is so organized that as the external temperature rises it begins to produce perspiration and the production and evaporation of that has a cooling effect so that the body's own temperature is rising more slowly. The various parts of the body can function to keep the entire organism alive by changing in ways that adapt to and compensate for changes in the environment which might otherwise threaten its continuing survival.

In its simplest form the functionalist doctrine in sociology advises us to take over these ideas from biology and to look upon society as an open and adaptive system whose different parts may function to keep it unified and unchanging.

Stated in this way, the doctrine does not tell us much, for it does not tell us what is to count as a 'part' of society, nor how we are to *determine* the nature of the inter-relations between parts, or weigh the *value* of the contribution that any single part makes to the survival of the whole.

Sociological functionalists have usually assumed that the 'parts' which make up society are its different institutions: its economy, political system, family system, religions, educational organizations and so forth. Some functionalists have argued that there are a number of 'functional prerequisites' which those institutions must meet, some very basic conditions without which society could not hope to survive at all (cf. Aberle *et al.*, 1950). They point out that society must have some kind of economy, for unless goods and services are produced, its members will die of starvation and exposure. Likewise there must be some kind of family system to regulate sexual relations and provide for the birth and raising of children, for without new members to replace those who die or move away the society will simply die out.

Observations of this sort, however, are hardly the kind that require elaborate analogies with biological systems. It is obvious enough that without people societies cannot exist and that if any kind of relationship which procreates and socializes children is called a family then societies must have some kind of family system if they are to survive. If the functionalist analogy is to have any significant use it must draw our attention to less apparent conditions of societal survival.

Religious institutions have always been especially attractive to functional theorists, for they offer an excellent opportunity to reveal functions which are not perhaps so readily apparent as those of family and economy. Indeed, many people feel that religion is the opposite of a functional asset, that it is an irrational and unnecessary institution whose elimination would probably improve things. Functionalists, as we shall shortly see, think that religion does fulfil some very vital functions.

Functionalist analysis in sociology is often (though not always) identified with a 'consensus approach'. They are frequently associated because many functionalists are followers of Durkheim and they share his conviction that society involves *shared* moral codes, shared standards, rules and understandings. Social organizations, to them, is necessarily premised upon a consensus, a substantial measure of agreement as to what is right and good. Thus Talcott Parsons drew from his reflections upon the work of Durkheim and Weber the conclusion that, far from being randomly distributed, ends were systematically organized by and related to the social structures in which they existed, and that any relatively stable society must have some general agreement upon values amongst its members.

This does not mean that the members of society must agree upon each and every little thing – far from it. In Parsons's usage values are understood to be very general, very vague and very abstract conceptions of what is good and desirable: the same value can underlie the most disparate wants and preferences.

The members of our society want very different things: this one a car, that one a television set, that one a swimming pool, another a refrigerator and so on. We can, however, classify all these different things in more abstract terms as the same *type* of things: consumer durables. Becoming even more abstract, we can say that people wanting these different consumer durables are all expressing a preference for an improved standard of material life. What Parsons means by the values which he thinks must be shared by the members of a society refers, then, to these very general and basic conceptions of what is worth having. For him, such a conception as 'desiring an improved standard of living' may still be too specific, itself an expression of an even deeper conception of the desirable, that of expanding man's control over the world in which he lives.

Western man does not take a fatalist attitude to the world in which he lives. He does not regard whatever may befall him as being inevitable and therefore something that he must accept and learn to live with. He tends to be activistic, treating the world as something which he can control and subordinate to his will, refusing to accept that there are things which he cannot change or improve. Such seemingly diverse things as his economic acquisitiveness and his scientific curiosity can both be seen as expressions of this activistic attitude. In expanding his economic activity he takes material resources and shapes them to satisfy his wants; in pursuing his scientific inquiries he demonstrates that Nature can keep no secrets from him: he can dominate Nature and make it what he wants it to be. It is attitudes as basic and general as this which make up the values which are agreed amongst society's members.

Parsons noted, too, that both Durkheim and Weber see the most profound values of society as being intimately connected with the religious institutions in society, that both of them viewed religions as being well equipped to shape and sustain the consensus. Parsons and other functionalists have tended to follow this line of reasoning and to view religion as the institution which plays the major role in expressing elemental values and in keeping the society together.

Religions are appropriate institutional forms in which to express basic social values, the argument goes, because they are involved in dealing with the ultimate issues in human life, facing the most inclusive questions about the nature of reality and the significance of our existence.

Religious doctrines purport to tell us what the world is really like, what we are doing in it and what is truly important for us. Thus, for example, the Judaeo-Christian tradition tells us that the universe is God's creation within which we have a very special place because we have been created in His image and are subject to His endless attention and scrutiny: it is we human beings that are significant to God, not inanimate things or other animals. Indeed, we can look upon the world as having been created by God *for* man and we can therefore make of that world whatever we can – it has been placed at our disposal by God himself. Such an attitude towards reality is quite consonant with the activist attitude which we have noted is characteristic of Western man.

Religions not only tell us what reality is fundamentally like, they also indicate the significance of our own lives. Weber pointed out that we can broadly classify religions into two types – those which take a 'this-worldly' attitude and those which take an 'other-worldly' one – on the basis of their views of the meaning of human life. Those of the 'other-worldly' type completely devalue the significance of life on this earth, viewing it as being at best a period of waiting and preparation before death and the beginning of the truly important life after death. 'This-worldly' religions, by contrast, emphasize the importance of life in the here-and-now and stress that it is what happens in our earthly existence which counts and not whatever may take place in some possibly imaginary after-life.

Those sharply differing views upon the meaning of life may have strong implications for conduct. Other-worldly deprecation of life on this earth can encourage an indifference to or distaste for the secular and practical affairs of day-to-day life: it is not the individual's place to engage himself with mundane matters or to tamper with the earthly distribution of power and misery in some attempt to put things right but, rather, to concern himself with his religious situation, preparing himself to meet his ultimate fate. A this-worldly attitude can encourage involvement in secular affairs: it is what happens *now* that is important and therefore it is worth attempting to improve things on this earth and attempting to improve one's own lot, getting the maximum benefit from the things this life offers.

Weber further pointed out that religions answer that question which men seem to find one of the most crucial of all, how it is that good and bad fortune, respectively, come to be distributed. They attempt to account for the discrepancy between destiny and merit. In life the things which befall us are not necessarily the things which we think we are deserving of and so we often find ourselves in the position where we ask: Why me? What have I done to deserve this?

We find, for example, that right conduct does not result in the continuance and improvement of our well-being and that though we have seemingly done nothing to deserve it we are visited by misery and disappointment. Religions do try to explain such things: they tell their followers that the forces which govern the cosmos also shape the distribution of fortune amongst men and that though there may be no immediately apparent justice to its distribution there is a pattern and meaning to it all. Many religions, therefore, carry to the poor and the oppressed the message that their suffering will eventually be alleviated and that the trials which they have undergone in this world will – if they are borne with faith – be amply compensated for in the next life. Weber notes that it is not only the poor who require this kind of explanation from religion: those who are successful are not satisfied just to be wealthier or more powerful than their fellows. They need to feel that they *deserve* to be wealthier and more powerful than others and there are religions which tell the successful that they are deserving because they are good people, that their success is their reward.

Addressing itself to such elemental matters as the nature of reality and our place within it, religion must inevitably be associated with our most basic values, since the things we will consider right and good will obviously be much affected by our ideas about what we are and what we can be. Religions are, therefore, excellent vehicles for the expression of values. They are also potent instruments for ensuring the acceptability of these values.

Religious conceptions of what is good and proper in human life are deeply entangled with conceptions of supernatural powers and forces which, they claim, govern our world and our lives. Thus, they do not merely describe the good and proper way for us to act, they recommend them to us in the very strongest terms, warning us that to fail to adopt those ways of acting may result in the most terrible punishments. If we reject Christian teachings we do not merely reject an idea of what the good life should be, we reject *God*'s idea of how man should live and in so doing we may well reject the opportunity for the salvation of our own immortal soul. If we do accept those teachings then we are, of course, under great pressure to remain faithful to them because if we do not we take the most profound risks of damnation. Thus religions seek to sanction orientations towards the world and activity in it at the level of deep and basic concerns about supernatural punishment and approval, linking attitudes with the most powerful forces in the universe.

Although Weber and Durkheim both emphasized the importance of religious doctrines in society, they were at pains to remind us that there must always be a tension between such teachings and the life of the believer in the world. Religious teachings offer *ideals* for conduct, standards with which the faithful should comply but which they cannot always fulfil. Mundane and practical considerations have a greater immediacy for the individual in the course of his day-to-day life, and there is a tendency therefore for religious obligations to be accommodated to the give-and-take of secular life. Durkheim, as we have noted, argued that this attenuation of religious commitment could be prevented through religious practice and ritual. He maintained that collective ritual occasions excite extraordinary emotions of awe and respect in the individual and that these emotions are associated through the symbolic activities and paraphernalia of the religious occasion with the values being expressed. The values expressed by the ritual are thereby suffused in the mind of the individual with the most intense feelings and he is thus given a most potent emotional reminder of them. This kind of expressive and resuscitatory role of ritual is well illustrated in the following description of the British Coronation ceremony of 1953, as interpreted by two sociologists holding views very close to those of Durkheim. The Coronation service is said to be

a series of ritual affirmations of the moral values necessary to a well-governed society. The key to the Coronation service is the Queen's promise to abide by the moral standards of the society. The whole service reiterates their supremacy above the personality of the sovereign. In her assurance that she will observe the canons of mercy, charity, justice and protective affection, she acknowledges and submits to their power. When she does this she symbolically proclaims her unity with her subjects who, in the ritual – and in the wider audience outside the Abbey – commit themselves to obedience within the society constituted by the moral values which she has agreed to uphold (Shils and Young, 1953, p. 224).

The occasion of the Coronation involves an impressive display of the regalia and paraphernalia of the State. Many of the most powerful, prestigious and high-status members of society are involved as active participants. The more ordinary members of society are given holidays in order that they may witness the ceremony itself or take part in activities which celebrate it. The act of crowning a new monarch is therefore made memorable for the members of society, who will associate it with powerful feelings such as those of admiration or excitement. In short, the Coronation is a *dramatic* occasion and, as such, will impress itself upon the attention and memory.

Through that ceremony the bonds which bind together those who rule and those whom they rule are reaffirmed, and presented, too, as expressions of values which are blessed by God Himself. The sense of respect which citizens should have for their monarch is reinforced by the association, throughout the ceremony, of the monarch with the paraphernalia of State power, she being dressed in elaborate robes, presented in the context of displays of military strength, and surrounded by and receiving homage from the most powerful of her subjects. Seeing all this, her subjects cannot help but see that she is someone special and powerful.

The Coronation draws our attention to another crucial aspect of religious practice. Not only important moments in the life of the whole society, but also critical moments in the life cycle of the individual – particularly those of birth, marriage and death – are highly ritualized. There are points in time when the social relationships of the individual undergo radical change. Births, for example, involve the introduction of a new member into the family unit, and they realign relattions between the conjugal pair. Marriage involves the creation of new relations between the spouses and between the separate groups of kin to which they belong. Death breaks established relations and obliges those who remain alive to reconstruct their lives and to go on living without someone who was of great importance to them.

The rituals associated with such occasions of transition provide support and comfort for anyone who has been bereaved, or bestow community or supernatural approval upon the creation of new ties. It has been found that some rituals cannot be undertaken if those who must take part in them are at odds with one another, in a state of dispute or disagreement. The relevant parties must settle their dispute if the ritual is to be carried out, and the wish to have the ritual performed places pressure upon them to repair their relations. In all these ways, then, ritual is involved in the actual repair and maintenance of particular social relations. The Coronation ceremony does this too, for it is the creation of a new relation between new monarch and subjects.

The functionalist case is, then, that religion is a highly functional institution, for though it may make no obvious contribution to the material well-being of people it does play a crucial social role. Indeed, that role is almost a purely integrative one: religion's central social contribution is keeping society together, presenting, legitimizing and reinforcing values which are essential to its life.

Social stratification is another institution whose social uses are often seen as being just as obscure as those of religion and, again, the functionalists have sought to show that they do exist and are important.

They have argued that society as a whole must face the problem of distributing the members of its population amongst the various tasks that need to be done. Society must ensure that there are husbands, wives, priests, physicians, refuse-collectors, political leaders and so on, for society could not survive if everyone were a physician and no one a farmer or manufacturer of clothing. Hence the members of society cannot simply be allowed to select their task in life on some utterly random and unorganized basis, for everyone might gravitate towards the same tasks and vitally necessary things might be left undone. It is not, either, merely a matter of ensuring that all available tasks are filled, for not all such tasks are of equal significance: some are of greater importance to society than others. A society might be able to survive and operate quite satisfactorily if a few labouring jobs, say, were not filled, but might be in jeopardy if some crucial positions of political leadership were left unoccupied. Since the skills which are necessary to different tasks vary, it is not just a matter of ensuring that *someone* is available to fulfil them, it is important that people who occupy positions be capable of discharging their obligations, that they have the appropriate skills.

Functionalists argue that through the manipulation of its reward system society can ensure an appropriate distribution of its members to the various positions. It can ensure that people will be willing to take on the extra and perhaps onerous responsibilities of the more important positions in society, and that where the talents needed to fulfil the requirements of some posts are scarce, the people who have those talents will be motivated to come forward and offer their services. Further, where specialized skills are required and can be learned, people will be prepared to undergo such deprivations as may be involved in a prolonged period of training in them.

Social stratification, they conclude – the unequal distribution of wealth, power, prestige and other gratifications – is society's way of motivating people to occupy the positions in society to which they are most suited and in which they are most needed. By attaching the highest rewards to those positions which require rare talents, which are of most importance to society or which need skills that require prolonged apprenticeship, society is able to motivate people to come forward to take those positions. Were all positions rewarded at the same level, there would be nothing to motivate people to take on more difficult responsibilities that are attached to some significant positions, nothing to motivate those with uncommon skills to apply them where they are most needed. Stratification, therefore, is functional: it contributes to the survival of society by ensuring that socially necessary tasks are done.

It is towards this kind of model of the relation between institutions and society as a whole that functionalism tends. The question must now be: how do common values fit into the functionalist schema and into a social system made up of interdependent parts? Surely it is the complementary nature of different institutions' functions which produces social integration: are values therefore necessary?

The notion of the body as a system does not only involve the idea that there is an interdependence between its parts. It also means that the relation of interdependence imposes constraints upon the constitution of each separate part. Each part must have the right size, capacity and construction to perform its specialized role and must do so in just such a way as to be compatible with the other parts. The human body may need a heart but it does not need just any heart: it requires one of the right sort. A human heart is necessary, not that of some other species of animal. Similarly, if the body is that of a human child, the heart of a fully grown adult human will not do because it is too large.

This idea of compatibility has also been taken over into functionalist sociology. Though society must have an economy if it is to survive, it cannot just make use of any type of economy whatsoever. It must have one which is 'compatible' with those other institutions which make up the same society. We have seen that it has been argued (pp. 176–194) that the characteristics of the nuclear family system are compatible with the economy and other institutions of an industrial society in a way that those of the extended family system are not. The process of industrialization and the development of an industrial economy are, therefore, associated with a transition from an extended to a nuclear family system. How, then, is this compatibility between the various parts of a system brought about?

Since the concern of functional analysis is to understand how the integration of the social system is maintained, then parts of the system will be seen as incompatible if their relations are such as to cause the system to fall apart and, of course, conflict is identified as one of those things which does bring the system to a state of collapse. System parts will, therefore, be incompatible if they are in conflict. What ensures compatibility between them is the existence of a consensus about shared values.

If such a consensus is absent then conflict will develop between institutions because they are 'pulling' in different directions. Suppose, say, that the religious institutions recommend values which lead the individual to look upon life as meaningless and unimportant and to regard political action as irrelevant, but that the political institutions in the same society enjoin upon all citizens an active and deep involvement in politics and a constant concern to improve life on this earth. The religious and political institutions would, inevitably, conflict, since they are delivering their different messages to one and the same citizenry and they cannot both be satisfied: if citizens do their political duty, they will fall down on their religious commitments. If, on the other hand, they take the appropriate religious attitudes they will fail to fulfil their obligations as citizens.

Though we are talking about institutions those institutions are, in the last analysis, made up of human beings. The conflicts that will develop are not only between institutions but within individuals, since the same ones can be involved in different institutions. If those who are involved in political organizations are the same ones who are involved in the religious ones, then if those two types of organizations were making the sort of radically disjunctive demands we have sketched above, those individuals would be in a most difficult position. What are they to do: behave in one way when involved in their political activities and at other times in the entirely contrary manner which their religion demands of them? None of us is altogether consistent, but we *are* whole human beings and most of us would find it utterly impossible to behave in the schizophrenic way that such a situation of conflict would create. The implication is clear: disjunctions in the values to which different institutional sectors of the same society were committed would lead to conflicts between them and, ultimately, to intolerable conflicts within the people who staff them. Consensus upon values between such institutional sectors means that the institutions are 'moving' in broadly the same directions and that the ways in which one institution requires people to act are consistent with those which other institutions require of them.

The parts of society are not like those of the organism, for they are not made up of the mindless activities of cells but of the activities of sentient human beings. How, then, are the broad injunctions supplied by the basic societal values translated into the actual, smoothly dovetailed organization of activities as the members of the society go about their day-to-day affairs? By definition, values are *very vague* conceptions of the desirable; they carry no specific instructions as to how we are to act, but only indicate the most general directions in which we are supposed to go. We can, for example, be told to go to New York but that does not tell us how we are to get there: do we walk, take a plane, sail or what? Likewise, we can be told that we should seek an activistic mastery over the natural world but that does not tell us how we should act at home.

Talcott Parsons recognized that society faces the problem of translating its basic values into more specific directives to its members as to how they are to act. He sees the parts of society as being composed of what he terms 'status-roles'. We can see the organization of a nuclear family as being made up of a number of 'positions' which are, typically, those of 'mother', 'father' and 'child'. These positions Parsons terms 'statuses': they have certain ways of acting associated with them, these patterns of behaviour being termed 'roles'. We have seen (cf. above, pp. 199–203) that until recently at least it was thought that the father should have an occupation and should provide an income for the family, the mother should assume responsibility for the day-to-day management of the household and care of the children, whilst the children should be obedient to their parents and so on: these different patterns of behaviour appropriate to each of the different statuses in the family are their roles.

Of course, these ways of behaviour are not necessarily those which family members *do* follow, they are, rather, ways in which family members *ought* to act. The relations between the occupants of the different statuses which make up some unit are governed by rules which specify how they should behave towards one another. Their roles are, in fact, the rules which specify what they should do, those rules being what Parsons terms 'norms'. The orderly conduct of members within a social unit is assured if they abide by the norms, since they then act in ways which complement one another, as the husband and wife divide up responsibilities within the nuclear family.

Since norms now assure the organization within institutions it may seem that the notion of values must be redundant, but the point of Parsons's account is that the norms are only a detailing of the things required by the values.

One of the key values towards which, he claims, industrial societies are oriented is 'universalism', the principle that all persons should be evaluated in the same way, regardless of who they might be. An example of what is meant by this is that people should be appointed to jobs through the use of quite impersonal mechanisms such as public examinations, which allow selection of those who give evidence of possessing the greater talent for the occupation. Appointments ought not to be made on the basis of 'particularistic' considerations, e.g., because the appointee has some special relation to the person making the appointment – perhaps a kinsman or close friend of the employer. The normative requirement that the father assume the role of income earner within the family is one that 'implements' the value of universalism. It does so because its application produces a separation between the family and the household, on the one hand, and occupation and industry on the other. In the early phases of the Industrial Revolution in Britain there was no such normative requirement; all family members were expected to contribute to the earning of family income and this meant that the entire family unit would often find employment together in the same plant and would work there as a team (cf. below, pp. 526–528). The development of a norm which placed the onus upon the adult male of the family to provide it with an income meant that the rest of the family unit no longer took employment with him and that those with whom the father worked during the day were not those bound to him by the particularistic ties of kinship. The norms regulating the relations of members of the family unit served to separate work and household, and thus prevented the intrusion of particularistic relations into the sphere of work where, it is held, they would have been inimical to the needs of a developing industrial society to employ people on the basis of their competence in the job rather than because they were the kinsmen of some other employee.

Norms, in this view, represent detailed implementations of the ends indicated by societal values and thus contribute to the compatibility of the various parts of the system, encouraging activities in one area that assist the functioning of some other area. Thus, considering the organization of the school class in the American educational system, Parsons argues that the class is so organized as to encourage competitiveness and the desire to be successful, the child being evaluated relative to others on the basis of how well he performs in class, *not* on the basis of his social status or any other characteristics which he may have acquired by birth or inheritance. He learns that his ranking within the class is decided on the basis of his 'achievements', on what he does, and not on his 'ascribed' characteristics, on who he is, where he lives, and so on. The child is effectively taught that these ascribed characteristics are irrelevant to his competitive success and that his performance is all-important, and he is, therefore, taught an orientation to 'achievement' as a criterion in terms of which he himself and others may *properly* be evaluated. This, the argument goes, prepares the child for life in the occupational world of American society, where success is something which must be achieved.

The fact that the norms implement the society's values also serves to make the norms themselves more acceptable. American parents would not, presumably, continue to tolerate the organization of the school class through competition and achievement did they not think that it was *in general* a good thing for people to be competitive and to be assessed in terms of their achievements.

The next question must, of course, concern the operation of norms and the acceptance of values. Why do the members of a society accept its values and abide by its norms? Parsons, like Durkheim, argues that they do so because they 'internalize' those norms and values, make them into their own inner convictions, personal preferences and expectations of others. We do not merely notice that parents provide for the welfare of their children, we expect them to do so, thinking it right that they should and being shocked if they don't. We feel, too, when we become parents in our turn, that it is our responsibility to provide for our own children and we know that other people will be expecting us to do so and will disapprove of us if we do not.

Norms are internalized, Parsons argues, because people are highly sensitive to one another, finding that the reactions of others bring them pleasure or discomfort. Imagine two people who have had no previous contact and who have no knowledge of each other. They meet for the first time. One of them does something and the other finds that he liked what was done. He therefore hopes that the first person will act that way again and to encourage him to do so himself acts in a way he thinks the first will like. If the first party is gratified, he will then repeat the action the second has been wanting, but if he is not pleased by what the second has done he may well do something to distress the second. By experimenting with their actions in this way, our two people will develop knowledge of one another and they will each come to know what things the other likes and dislikes. By manipulating his own behaviour each will be able to control the other. If the other does not do what is wanted then something he does not like will be done to him. A stable arrangement should develop between these two because they will each come to *expect* certain kinds of response from the other in reaction to anything they may do and they will enforce their expectations upon one another through the exchange of rewarding and punishing actions.

Such an imaginary encounter is, in Parsons's view, a simple model of the processes which underlie all forms of social organization. The sensitivity of each individual to the actions of others as rewarding or punishing, and their tendency to form expectations for the future, provide the basis for internalization. The individual comes to learn the same expectations as are current in his social environment because those who have already internalized those expectations will in turn train the newcomer into them through the manipulation of rewards and punishments.

The period of childhood is seen as being a particularly critical one for the internalization of norms and values, the child's relations with its parents being managed by them in terms of rewards and punishments. The parents will react to their child's actions by giving it things it likes if they approve of what it does, withholding those things if they disapprove of what it does. What they will approve and disapprove of is, of course, decided by the norms which they, the parents, have already internalized. The child will eventually learn the pattern of its parent's responses and will come to grasp that certain things regularly bring pleasure, others result in discomfort; it will, therefore, come to expect that they will continue that way in the future, expecting its parents to continue administering gratifications when the child produces the appropriate conduct.

Of course, although childhood is a particularly critical period for internalization, it is not the only time at which that occurs. On entering any new sphere of life at any age, we must learn the appropriate norms and will do so because others will reward and punish our behaviour in the light of what they see to be appropriate. Once we have internalized the norms they become our commitments to action, things we feel we should do. Should we be tempted to do otherwise we will, of course, find that others react punishingly and so we will tend to continue complying with the norms.

The model of internalization provides a simple model of the way orderliness in social relations is preserved. It provides for a predictability in everyday activities, people tending to act in the ways in which others expect because they *want* to act in those ways, established patterns of action which are created by people fulfilling mutual expectations tending to remain stable because of the threat of punishment associated with any departure.

As should now be apparent, Parsons's idea of the organization of the total society sees it as being made up of many different 'levels', building up from the simple pattern of the face-to-face encounters between individual members of the society, through larger organizations of relations such as, for example, the family unit or school class, to the total social system which includes these 'lower' levels of organization. Each of these levels is co-ordinated with those above and below it by the central values of the society and the norms which spell them out: individual mothers and babies act in the ways required by family organization in their society because they have internalized the relevant norms. The total system is comprised of differentiated parts, which complement one another and which contribute, in some way, to the continuing operation of the social whole. Compatibility between these different parts is assured because they are directed towards the same values and, hence, there will tend to be no conflict between them. Any tendency towards change in the institutional structure which might result in misalignment between one institution and another will lead to a restructuring of relations in order to bring those deviating institutions back into line with the basic values. The values themselves will tend to continue unchanged because there are institutions in the society – such as religious ones – which sustain those values and encourage loyalty to them, and because there are other forms of organization – such as the family and educational systems – which tend to inculcate established values into new members of the society. People will continue to act in accord with the values because they are, in their personal dealings, likely to be punished by others if they 'deviate' and because, on the level of the total society, there are specialized forms of organization – such as the legal system and police force – which act as agents of 'social control', having the task of locating and punishing those who violate the society's rules.

Conflict, Change and Power

Functionalist theory has been subjected to a good deal of criticism. Much of it has to do with its adequacy *as* theory. It has, for example, been argued that functionalism is nowhere stated with the clarity, consistency or precision that any self-respecting scientific theory should have. Functionalism certainly does lack those characteristics when compared with theories in, say, physics, where those theories can often be stated in mathematical terms. The same objection could, however, be made to most – if not virtually all – sociological theories and there seems to be little point in singling out functionalism for failings which are hardly unique to it.

Other critics of functionalism point to what they consider to be the conservative political implications of functionalist doctrine, the failure of the theory to give an adequate account of such important things as the distribution of power in society, the possibility of radical social change, and the significance of social conflict. Certainly, the claim has commonly been made that functionalist theory's main weakness is its failure to understand power, change and conflict. Since Parsons has been one of the most important and systematic exponents of functionalism, he has been the target of much of the criticism.

Not all the criticism of functionalism has come from the same direction, nor has all of it involved the production of any coherent alternative doctrine to the functionalist one, but there has been sufficient coherence amongst some of the objections for it to be possible to speak of a 'conflict theory' which did attempt to provide some kind of alternative.

The conflict theory could effectively claim that Parsons – in his early work, at least – simply ignored the problems involved in explaining social change and conflict and had nothing to say about the role of power in society. This criticism has, however, been obviated since Parsons has, in his later writings, devoted much of his attention to power, change and conflict. As we shall see, the kinds of things he has had to say on those matters are not the kinds of things that will satisfy his critics from the conflict school.

It should be stressed that many of the critics of Parsons and of functionalism more generally have no objection to the idea that society can usefully be viewed as a system of interconnected parts. They take exception to what they see as the functionalist tendency to pay attention only to the 'beneficial' effects of interrelation amongst system parts.

Thus the heart of the objections that the conflict school make to Parsons's work is that he adopts an excessively benign view of society and of the *status quo*, the already established and ongoing order of society. This leads him to look upon conflict and change as essentially detrimental and leads him, too, to fail to see that the established arrangements within society do not benefit everyone equally and may be to the positive disadvantage of many. Many of these objections are inspired by the work of Karl Marx, perhaps the most significant sociological theorist whom Parsons did not number amongst his predecessors and whom he regarded as falling outside the tradition which inspired his own work.

Marx's theory is one which addresses itself directly to the problem of social change: it asks the question 'Under what conditions does the replacement of one form of society by another take place?' Marx assigns a significant role to the economy in generating social change, and sees the evolution of society in general as following from the development of its economic activities. The reason for the priority given to the economic structure is this: that before men can create other social forms such as political or religious ones they must *first* provide themselves with a livelihood, and we may therefore expect that the ways in which they ensure their subsistence will set limits to the ways in which they can organize their other affairs. The changing character of economic activities is the basis of social change, that change taking place through conflicts between social groups and, most centrally, through revolutionary transformations of the whole society. Social stratification is another critical institution, for in Marxist theory social classes are the main agents of social transformation.

A given social class acquires a vested interest in a certain way of organizing productive activities, and this means that as the organization of production evolves, that class finds that the mode of production with which it is associated is being eliminated and that, therefore, its interests are being undermined. It will, therefore, seek to protect those interests and prevent the changes which are detrimental to them. Other classes, however, will have developed interests vested in the new ways of producing which are developing and they will want to improve their own position. There is a conflict between the interests of these classes, and each must struggle to eliminate the other if their own interests are to be effectively protected, the revolutionary transformation of society taking place when an emerging class finally achieves the overthrow of an established one.

The emphasis upon the decisive role of those institutions which shape the material conditions of life is one which is behind much of the criticism of functionalism from a conflict viewpoint. As should be apparent, the placing of such a determining weight upon one institution is at odds with the functionalist view of the interdependence and complementarity of institutions: all institutions have a part to play in keeping the society going and they exercise mutual effect upon each other's natures, no single institution being so much more significant than the others.

It is this idea of the predominant importance of the material conditions of life which gives rise to the objection that Parsons is an excessively 'normative' sociologist, seeing activities as following in accord with norms and therefore failing to see the extent to which the possibilities of action are decisively limited by the material and economic resources available to people. For Parsons, the description of the organization of society is principally a description of its rules. Since, by and large, people do act in the ways they are supposed to, we can describe the rules which govern them and we thus more or less describe what they do: if, say, we want to describe how people play chess then we can, because they tend to obey its rules, describe the way chess is played by outlining its rules. The critics, however, argue that descriptions of a society in terms of its normative order is not like outlining the rules of chess: they may say how the game *should* be played but they do not accurately describe *how* and *why* it is played that way.

Take, for example, the norm which says that we are all equal before the law and that we are all free to seek redress for any wrongs in the courts. Though we may be 'free' to take other people to court the simple fact is, of course, that most of us cannot afford to settle our disputes or resolve our problems through the courts. Whether or not we actually can take people to court is going to depend upon how much money we have and that, of course, is related to our class position. The possibility of obtaining redress in court may be one which is *formally* available to all of us, but *in reality* is restricted to very few of us. If, therefore, we were to look to see who is making use of the courts, we could find that they were relatively prosperous people and we might conclude, therefore, something like 'prosperity does not bring happiness', because the prosperous are the ones who have problems as can be seen from the fact that they are in court. Such a conclusion may, of course, be utterly false: there is no reason to suppose that the wealthy are more or less troubled by problems than the poor: it is just that when the former have problems they can get legal help in settling them.

Similar arguments have been developed concerning the interrelation of institutions. We have already noted how the school class can be seen as having a normative order which stresses that people should be evaluated in terms of their achievements, without regard for any ascribed statuses such as social class membership. Research on educational achievement, of course, remorselessly reveals correlations between educational achievement and social class affiliation. It is not that working-class children are graded poorly *because* they come from the working class, but they will none the less tend to be educationally unsuccessful. The normative order does not *require* a connection between stratification and education: there is no rule which says that working-class children must do relatively poorly in education when compared with their middle- and upper-middle-class counterparts. If anything, the norms governing education are in entirely the opposite direction, and a description which was cast entirely in terms of norms would, therefore, fail to recognize the real and consequential connection between stratification and educational success which results from the fact that the working class suffer many material disadvantages and many consequences following from those which limit their children's opportunities to perform well in the classroom.

Conflict theorists, therefore, tend to reject the emphasis upon normative order because it ignores, in their view, the fact that the capacity to implement norms may be powerfully constrained by other features of the society's organization. Certainly the distribution of material resources amongst the members of society will be a major limitation upon their potential to obtain those things to which they may have a right, and it is for this reason – among others – that an emphasis upon conflict is associated with the view that stratification is a most decisive institution. The source of conflict, all too often, is the struggle over the distribution of material resources and advantages, and since stratification is the means by which those are distributed it must obviously be deeply involved in patterns of conflict.

The difference between functional and conflict approaches is one of fundamental evaluation, of the kinds of assumptions that are made about the nature of man and society and about the worth of social institutions. The criticisms of functionalism are not simply based upon questions about descriptive accuracy: they themselves are only surface reflections of more basic differences in outlook.

As we showed above, functionalism advances a view of man as an animal with an essentially social nature, one who can only become truly human through socialization and through membership in society. It stresses the essentially co-operative nature of society itself, arguing that through the organization of a great number of people into complex patterns of association we are able to accomplish tasks which we could not perform as individuals. We benefit in concrete and material ways from living in association with others. However, co-operation is not something we undertake solely out of some kind of profit motive, for we appreciate the company of other human beings and want to participate with them in common enterprises. The unity of human society arises 'naturally' from the associations amongst people, as a result of the kind of integrative processes which we have already described. That unity is built, in the end, around the common beliefs and sentiments of people, and the value system which stabilizes their relationships is the value system of the *whole* society.

The conflict view is also founded upon the assumption that man is essentially a social animal but it does not assume that every society is equally well suited to the realization of his social nature or that any society is well suited to realize the social nature of all its members equally. It may provide extraordinarily good lives for some but this is usually only possible because the great majority are oppressed and degraded, and unable to develop their capacities to their fullest extent. Nor is co-operation necessarily a good thing in itself, for some people can co-operate together to ensure the more effective exploitation of their fellows. Differences of *interest* are therefore as important to society as agreements upon rules and values, and most societies are so organized that they not only provide greater benefits for some than for others but in such a way that the accrual of benefits to a few causes positive discomfort to others.

Upon the basis of different situations within society, then, people are likely to develop different interests and this will inevitably lead to conflict over many issues. The possibility of the kind of anarchic strife which we initially considered now appears to be arising again: if groups with different interests come into conflict, why does society not simply disintegrate into internal warfare? The answer that conflict theory gives is a simple one. There is inequality amongst groups with respect to power, and some groups, simply because they are the most powerful, can impose their will upon others. They preserve the order of society by dominating subordinate groups and compelling them to comply with whatever policies the ruling groups consider best serve their own interests. Conflict theorists argue that Parsons and other functionalists underestimate the extent to which a society can be held together through the exercise of power, failing to see that profound differences in interests and values can be contained if one group has enough power to keep things going and to assert its will over others, keeping everyone within the framework of the *status quo*.

Parsons has, however, replied to such criticisms. He says that a functionalist account of power can be given and that it is a more realistic one than that which his opponents offer. They tend to think of power in 'zero-sum' terms. They think, that is, that within a society the amount of power which is available is fixed, and if any group increases its share of power then it can only do so by taking it from another group. An increase in the power of one group means a diminution in the power of some other group. The natural consequence of this is that power *must* be used in domination, since groups are involved in struggling against one another and can only keep their own position by holding others down. Indeed, power is simply 're-invested', it is primarily used *in the power struggle itself*. Any group which does manage to increase the amount of power available to itself must then use that power to hold the new position, defending its gains.

Parsons holds that such a view is a mistaken one. Whilst it may be true at a given moment in time that the amount of power available in society is fixed, it is perfectly possible that, over time, the total amount of power may be increased. In just the same way that a society may benefit from economic growth, involving the expansion in the total amount of wealth available to the entire society, so may it benefit from a growth in its power resources. This means that it is possible for *all* groups in the society to become more powerful than they previously were without having to wrest that power from one another: there is simply more for all. Power need not, then, be reinvested in protecting the advantages of the most powerful, it can usefully be employed in other ways and is often employed in executing tasks on behalf of the entire society.

Parsons sees power as something which operates not – as his critics see it – as a cement holding society together but as a lubricant which smoothes its functioning. It is used to get things done and it ensures that these are the things which further the goals and values of the system. Power is, of course, mainly concentrated in the political system: those who discharge the political tasks in society exercise power *on behalf* of the social system. The political institutions, that is, seek to do what the members of the society want, as that is specified within the broad framework of common values.

In describing power we have employed economic metaphors of growth and investment and in describing how power is exercised on behalf of the system we can employ yet another parallel with economic affairs – there is an exchange between the political system and the rest of society. If the political institutions are to achieve the society's common goals then, in order to do so, they must be able to command special use of some of society's resources – time, labour, wealth and so on – so as to organize the activities which will fulfil the relevant goals. The 'return' which people receive for the sacrifice of those resources to the needs of the political system is that they obtain more of the things which they want in so far as their shared goals are furthered. In a society with an electoral system the transaction can be seen to take place through the offering by the politician of his electoral promises and efforts to fulfil them in return for the votes and support of the electorate. The politician 'produces' the 'goods' which the electorate desire in the form of legislative and executive decisions; the people, in their turn, are willing to accept and obey the laws which politicians pass. In so far as the electorate are imbued with certain values then, of course, the politician will only be able to gain their votes and continued support if the things he offers appeal to those values: hence, once again, the value system constrains the operation of the political transaction.

Within such a scheme of thought there is *some* use of power in the oppression of some of society's own members, but only a relatively small quantity of the total amount of power available is seen as being used for such a purpose. As part of its efforts to 'mobilize' the resources of the entire society towards the fulfilment of its goals, those holding political power do have to control those recalcitrant members who will not fulfil their obligations or who seek to block the realization of the values which the majority of people want. Of course, if society does start to disintegrate, revolutionary groups begin to assume major importance, then more and more power will be invested in controlling them, but *in the vast majority of societies for most of the time* relatively little power *is* devoted to internal oppression. This is the functionalist argument.

These different interpretations of the social role of power bring us to another important difference between the two outlooks. Parsons and other functionalists are concerned with the operation of society *as a whole*, with the way in which society encounters and deals with such problems that it faces as a totality. Those who adopt a conflict perspective will not, of course, deny that there are 'functional prerequisites'. They accept, for example, that a society must have an economy and perhaps other essential institutions but do not consider this to be more than a trivial observation to make. The question, for them, is how such 'functional prerequisites' as there are can be met, and how the benefits accruing from their solution are distributed amongst people and groups. Though several different solutions can in principle be envisaged for any functional problem, different solutions will produce different effects upon the distribution of resources, and conflict theorists tend to suspect that the solutions which 'the system' selects will just 'happen' to be those which most favour the interests of those groups which are already dominant. They are, therefore, much more concerned than functionalists are to examine institutional arrangements from the point of view of different interest-groups, and predisposed to find that, in most cases, matters work to the advantage of the powerful. Conflict theory comes to see functionalism as an ideology which seeks to conceal these differences of interest behind a mask of consensus.

They see functionalism not as a *bona fide* scientific theory which says how things really are but as an attempt to present the way things are now as the best way for things to be, something which certain people or groups in society might well like us to believe. The kinds of views which functionalism takes can be seen to parallel rather closely those which are held by ruling groups. After all, those in power do often seek to defend their position by arguing that they are the only ones who can take an 'over-all view' of matters, can look upon things from the point of view of society as a whole and hence do things which, in the end, are to the benefit of each and every one of us. Those who disagree with such arguments are denounced as being guilty of sectional, partial, prejudiced and interested views and cannot therefore be considered as providing an realistic alternative to the *status quo*.

By emphasizing the role of dominant values and of dominant groups as representatives and agents of the consensus, functionalist theory can begin to look as though it is validating the claims which the powerful are making, giving those pretensions the additional aura of appearing to be supported by objective scientific findings.

Those who are at the top of hierarchies of stratification are often apt to claim that they are there because they deserve to be, that they have qualities which are highly valued in society and that they contribute much more to the general welfare than does the average person. They are apt, too, to reject the claims of those who call for equality on the grounds that their critics are envious and truly motivated by their own private interests, incapable of taking a more than sectional view of what is good for society. Above all else, the dominant are likely to insist, equality is a practical impossibility, there *must* be some kind of stratification in society, and the choice is not between domination by this or that group and the abolition of stratification altogether. It is a choice between one sort of stratification and another, between domination by this group or by some other (compare this with élite theory, discussed above, pp. 472–3). The final step in the argument is apt to be this: the *status quo* is to be preferred because alternative ways of stratifying would not work so well, would not be so adapted to the needs and interests of the society as a whole.

In their emphasis upon the inevitable and valuable nature of stratification and in their stress upon the worth of the contributions they make to society, those who defend advantage sound rather like functionalist theorists of stratification except in so far as these last are laying claim to the status of scientist. Of course, the conflict theorists are apt to note, the best way to present what is only a justification is to present it as though it were something demanded by the very laws of nature themselves, and for this reason they suspect that the functionalist theory may be only ideology masquerading as science.

The functionalists are not, however, inclined to collapse in the face of such arguments and will concede that people do justify their advantages in terms very similar to those of the functionalist theory. But, they will continue, justifications cannot be empty verbiage: they cannot be persuasive unless they touch upon some genuine beliefs and sentiments of those they are meant to persuade. Though the advantaged may be the ones who expound the case for their own privilege it is worth noting that the case is accepted by those who are less privileged. It is accepted because the dominant and their subordinates do agree and the less privileged will often accept that those who are above them have a *right* to be there.

The fact that powerful and powerless may share in common certain sentiments, beliefs and values does not, however, carry any great weight in the eyes of conflict theorists. Marx argued that those who have power in society can control the means whereby ideas, beliefs, values and attitudes are communicated, and they can therefore ensure that those ideas, etc., which become widespread in society are those which suit them best. The dominant values of a society will be those of the dominant groups *even if those values are accepted by every-*

one. It is no use looking to see which groups people belong to in order to decide whether their ideas are those of a dominant group or not. The principal institutions of society are often staffed or controlled by people who are not, themselves, members of the groups which actually and decisively control power but, if they are not actually members of such groups, they will be bound to them in many ways and will tend to accept and express the ideas of that dominant group. The channels of communication, therefore, will spread the ideas of the ruling group even though members of the ruling group take no part in the process of communication. Conflict theorists often complain that functionalism is lacking in historical grasp, and nowhere, they feel, is this more exemplified than in relation to the question of 'shared' values. The only way to see whether they are genuinely shared is not to look to see if everyone accepts them but to look *at their historical development*: where did these values originate, amongst which groups did they first arise, how did they become so widespread? The answer which they expect will regularly be found to such questions is that the ideas will have arisen in specific interest groups, will have become widespread because those groups have been able to extend their influence throughout the society, and will serve, once established, to protect the interests of those groups from which they sprang. If we are to look to the 'functions' of common values we should not see what contribution they make to the well-being of 'social systems' but should examine how they function on behalf of interest groups.

We have already remarked on functionalist views of political institutions, but some additional remarks are in order here. The two-party system of Government and Opposition of some of the industrialized democratic societies might seem to controvert the idea of shared values, because it seems to show that fundamentally different interests exist and achieve representation in the form of competing parties. But the fact is that although there are competing parties little political violence occurs. This is said to show that there is a fundamental consensus, for the two parties do disagree but they do so within the framework of common values. Values, remember, are very vague and carry no very precise indications as to how they may best be realized: it is therefore possible for people to come to different conclusions as to the best means by which the values may be furthered.

And it is over means that the conflict between elected political parties takes place: they tend to differ less about what is wanted – e.g., in our society material prosperity – than over questions about how the things that are desired may be obtained. There is, too, consensus upon the rules for political operation: elections are decisive and the party in office surrenders power upon electoral defeat without making any attempt to use force to retain its position.

The conflict school does not see the workings of democracy, the distribution of power and the role of political institutions in the same light. To them, political institutions like Parliament and the Civil Service work basically for the interests of the ruling groups, and the political parties are manned by people who are either part of those groups or dependent upon them. They stress, too, that political institutions are dependent institutions, subject to the power of others. The power which is exerted over political institutions is not, however, that of the mass of the people, expressed through elections, public action or the organized pressure of secondary associations, but the power of those who command other major institutions within society. Such institutions as religion, the economy and the political system have their own internal hierarchies of power, and it is those at the top of these hierarchies who exercise pressure upon one another, through ties of friendship, kinship, common association or even expedient self-interest. C. Wright Mills argued that the three dominant institutional spheres of American society today are the political, the military and the industrial. He also argued that they have become increasingly interdependent. The government is an increasingly significant consumer of the products of the industrial sector, a massive proportion of its expenditure being on supplying equipment for the military. The military themselves become increasingly dependent upon the industrial sector as they become increasingly dependent upon technology in their operations. The industrial sector is, therefore, so dependent upon government and military contracts that without these it would virtually collapse. The mutual dependence which is created in this way is transformed into a social dependence: the top staff in all three sectors are drawn from the same kind of social and educational backgrounds, they are often bound to one another through ties of kinship and marriage, and it becomes increasingly commonplace for their careers to carry them through all three sectors, moving from the Armed forces into business and from there into government and then, perhaps, back into business. The superficially separate spheres of military, industry and government are, then, united by all kinds of ties, and it must be expected, therefore, that they will have the same interests to a great extent and that the people who staff them will come to look upon things from a shared point of view. Mills concluded that the U.S.A. has come to be dominated by a single power élite.

The implication of his argument is that the political institutions are subject to pressure from and dominance by the military/industrial complex. Although it is government that *formally* decides what the military shall and shall not have and what industry shall provide for it, those in government may be in no position to judge such matters and to take such decisions, thus being compelled to accept the advice they are given by those in the forces or business who are expert on such matters. Since, however, these men are enormously dependent on each other for their own continuing success, they must seek to accommodate and oblige one another and to avoid conflicts of interest where they can, and they, together, are the ones who decide what 'must' be done, even though their conclusions may be publicized as a governmental decision. Their decisions are not shaped by the pressure of mass opinion or by the popular consensus, for they are taken in the light of the power élite's conception of its collective interest. The people may back whatever decisions are made in its name, but they are seen as doing so only because they have been subjected to propaganda and control by those who really are in control.

The existence of alternative political parties and of competition between them begins to look like the operation of a formality, for changes in the party in office may produce changes in the different individuals who occupy the positions but the *type* of people in command is not changed. The competition between the parties seems to serve only to mask the political realities, for it focuses attention upon points of difference and gives the electorate the feeling that they actually have some choice about the directions the society will take, but in practice the differences between the parties are only of the most marginal kind and the interests of the people in parties are broadly identical. Indeed, it is in the nature of the electoral system to lead parties to converge on much the same kinds of policy positions in elections, since they are competing for a majority of the votes and hence for the same voters to a considerable extent; they need, therefore, to make the kind of promises those whose support they seek will believe and they will end up making much the same kind of promises to the same people. The feeling of choice and the sense of political conflict which the electorate may experience are, when looked on in this way, largely illusory, being artefacts of the electoral process itself rather than expressions of real differences in ideas and outlook amongst those who compete for votes. The electorate is therefore 'fooled' into thinking that politicians are doing what the electorate want because they have been voted for, and do not realize that much the same decisions would have been taken anyway, the choices of the decision-makers being profoundly constrained by the interlocking needs of the power élite.

The parties serve to absorb the political interest of the broad mass of the population and they serve, too, to 'incorporate' some groups into the society: they do so by involving even the most dissident groups with the central institutions, and by persuading them to follow procedures which are already established within those institutions. Such procedures usually outlaw radical demands and practices with the result that, once involved with them, dissidents must, if they want anything whatsoever to be done, be prepared to modify their demands in such a way that they can be dealt with by the established procedures. The leaders of dissident groups are those most likely to be drawn into involvement with orthodox political institutions and, once involved, they are treated like orthodox political celebrities and are offered the possibility of adopting the life-styles and values current in those institutions. Finding themselves accepted amongst those who run the orthodox institutions who have formerly been their opponents, dissidents are apt to modify their conceptions of these people, to see that they are not perhaps so bad after all, and their enthusiasm for radical and rapid change begins to moderate, their hostility to the *status quo* dissipates. In order to retain the positions of leadership within the groups which give them their position in these orthodox institutions they have to attempt to keep support, persuading their followers to accept the modification of radical demands in favour of more 'reasonable' ones – the leaders of dissidents are thus given the task of controlling their own supporters and leading them in directions the established powers can accept and respond to.

For the conflict theorist, consensus is a temporary state, conflict being endemic in society because of the deep-rooted differences of interest that divide groups. If there is a consensus of values that is merely the result of the successful inculcation of the outlook of dominant groups in the minds of subordinate ones. That consensus will surely dissolve under the stresses and strains that must arise from the real conflicts which differences of interest between groups will create.

The functionalist theory views conflict as a pathology, something which menaces the stability of the social system. The functionalist does not recognize that conflicts may be means whereby people seek redress for real injustices. In a position of subordination, a group may be able to further its own interests only if it is able to 'cause trouble' for super-ordinate groups and is thus 'bought off' from creating further difficulties by having some of its demands met. Conflict can, in that way, be profitable. The revolutionary transformation of society – which from a functionalist viewpoint would be looked upon as its disintegration – may be desirable, conflict theory holds, because it may represent the attempt to create a new society, to eliminate injustices and inequalities present in the old order.

The functionalist will tend to believe that this is to make altogether too much of conflict in any society. The functionalist model, it must be recognized, *is* a *model*, not the representation of any real society. Its purpose is to represent the conditions under which society will remain stable and unchanging, and to know something about the things which keep society together is to know something about the things which will break it apart or change it. No real society could be perfectly integrated, eternally unchanging, entirely free of conflict. There will, in any real society, be conflicts between institutions, roles and people, but it is misleading to say that conflict is *endemic* in society! Indeed, many of the things which create conflicts within a society actually arise from outside that society, in changes in its ecological or technological environments. It is also erroneous to assume that change can only come through conflict or that those changes induced by conflict are never pathological.

The question of social change has been a major issue between the two sides. Conflict theory has claimed its superiority because of its capacity to deal with social change, whilst functionalism has been severely criticized for its inability to account for rapid and abrupt changes.

Parsons's own treatment of social change begins, once again, with the analogy between the living body and the social system. If we think about the living body then we immediately recognize that it does not remain unchanging throughout its life: it is constantly changing. It develops from a child into an adult and this involves great changes in its size and in many other features. Such changes as occur during processes of maturation and ageing have to be compatible with the functional requirements of the body: they do not threaten its survival. Society, too, goes through major changes but those are often within the limits set by conditions necessary for its continued survival. The society changes, but not into another *kind* of society; nor does it disintegrate. An example is the change which has affected the American economy in this century, involving the replacement of small businesses by very large organizations indeed. That process of replacement can be looked upon as a development in American society which is wholly compatible with its basic values, particularly those which stress the domination of the natural world. Indeed, an increase in the size of the economic organization is an 'upgrading' of the American's capacity to turn natural resources to his own uses. Even quite radical modifications of social life of this sort may, then, occur without being counted as changes *of* the society: they are changes *within* the society because they fall within the limits set by its values.

Parsons has developed a more long-range conception of social change, one which has been called 'progressive social differentiation'. In pre-industrial society, there is little separation of function: within such societies, kinship is commonly the institution through which religious, political, economic and other activities are organized. In industrial society, by contrast, these activities are generally separated from kinship and each of them is performed by an institution which specializes in that functional task. Thus economic activity is separated from the household and family, and is carried on in industrial organizations which are physically distant from the home; politics are conducted by organized political parties; and even the socialization of children is carried on by educational organizations. The transition from pre-industrial to industrial societies involves, then, an increasing specialization of functions and the emergence of new organizational bases for the execution of those functions. No *new* functions have been created: the society is still fulfilling the same functions that it did before but new ways of meeting the relevant functional needs have developed. This process is seen to be adaptive, since this specialization allows for the development of more complex patterns of social organization: the great bureaucracies of modern society could not work in the impersonal ways they do if economic and occupational relationships were still regulated by kinship ties. The particularistic demands of kinship would make the impersonal attitude of bureaucracy difficult to maintain.

The process of structural differentiation does produce strains and conflicts. In the course of the development of the Lancashire cotton industry in the eighteenth and nineteenth centuries, economic activities were progressively separated from home and kinship relations. In the early stages of the process the family often moved *en bloc* into the mills and worked there as a team but

the enlargement of mules [a kind of machine] and the introduction of power-looms threatened to separate the labour of children from that of adults (often parents). These technological pressures, while long in the maturing, reached a critical point in the mid-1820s. For the family economy of the factory operatives, the pressures represented a serious dissatisfaction ... The worker and his family could no longer work on the old basis which fused the family economy with other, more general family functions. If the worker refused to accept the new conditions of employment, he could no longer suppor this family satisfactorily; if he accepted labour on the new basis, certain non-economic relations in his family – particularly the rearing of children – might suffer. These pressures, magnified by an appeal to independence and personal responsibility as a family value, pressed for a thorough-going reorganisation of family relationships.

The factory operatives, especially the adult male spinner, reacted immediately and fiercely to this pressure in a number of disturbed social movements . . . a series of vigorous but unsuccessful strikes to resist the new machinery; a commitment to the ten hour agitation of the 1830s, one effect of which would have been to preserve the old work structure; a prolonged attempt to subvert the Factory Act of 1833, which threatened to separate the labour of adult and child even further; and a brief though intensive flirtation with the Utopian co-operative movements (Smelser, 1959, p. 406).

These kinds of changes resulted in the structural differentiation of family and economy, but their occurrence induced tensions in social relationships and gave rise to political disturbances, including some of a revolutionary kind. In this model, those tensions and the disturbances which follow from them are not viewed as legitimate causes and expressions of grievances on the part of those most affected by the changes, and who stood to lose the position they had previously held as a figure of authority within the family and in the work-place. Instead, they are regarded as 'threats' to the integrity of the social system, a danger to the social fabric which must be 'handled and channelled' by agencies of social control so that people are eventually brought to accept the new, and more differentiated, structure of relationships that make for a more adaptive social system.

It could be claimed, once more, that the functionalist looks at things from the point of view of the powerful, those who have an interest in separating the household from the occupational sphere, but who do not want, in doing so, to lose their own power. Political opposition to them is treated as a danger to the stability of the total system rather than as a challenge to a dominant group alone. The suppression and containment of disturbances leads to the successful 'reintegration' of society around a more functional arrangement of system parts, but these same developments could be seen as involving the subjugation of political dissidents by those who benefitted from the destruction of the dissidents' previous way of life.

Thus the functionalist does provide an account of change, particularly of the kind involved in the gradual evolution of specialized functions. Such change is thought of as occurring within the framework set by established values and, thus, as representing no basic changes in the nature of the society. Where the process of structural differentiation does give rise to social tensions and to radical or revolutionary social movements, these are not viewed as legitimate attempts at social change but as 'temporary' disturbances, symptomatic of the 'readjustments' that must necessarily take place in the relations between institutions at such times. Disturbances occur because, for a while, institutions are relatively imperfectly integrated, but these imperfections will, with time, be eliminated and the disturbances will cease.

There are, of course, cases in which the changes that occur in society do result in its complete transformation or dissolution, but the functionalist theory generally treats such radical changes as unpredictable things that cannot really be accounted for within a sociological framework. The impetus for such changes comes from 'outside' the social system, from the natural or technological environment, or from the activity of other social systems (as through invasion or conquest). Where radical changes are seen to have their source *within* society they are, again, treated as the product of rather random factors which cannot be foreseen by the theory itself.

The simple fact is, the argument goes, that random variations in the activities of members of society will mean that the socializing done by some of them will not be wholly effective or will have been misdirected, with the result that some new recruits to society will not have been adequately and properly socialized, will have failed to internalize the norms and values. Equally, other random variations will ensure that some of those who have been socialized properly will, even so, become dissociated from the norms and values they have previously accepted. On occasion the number of people who are not sufficiently affiliated to the normative order will become sufficiently great for them to constitute a threat to the integrity of the system. Since the emergence of a significantly under-socialized population is a result of randomly distributed variations from the normatively specified pattern it is not possible for theorists to say when and how such populations will develop.

Conflict theory claims great superiority in its capacity to deal with radical social change, especially those changes which involve the creation of new basic values. It asserts that the functionalists cannot deal with that kind of change because they cannot identify any sources within the social system from which new values might arise. Functionalist analysis has been wholly directed towards showing how the basic values are maintained unchanged. Dominant values, for functionalism, are those which are most widely accepted and most thoroughly institutionalized; but for the proponents of conflict theory they are dominant values only in so far as they are *politically* dominant: even where some values seem to be accepted throughout a society that is only because they have been imposed. Subordinate groups in society tend to develop different values from those who dominate them, unless they are prevented from doing so by the indoctrination of the powerful. Subordinate groups are, then, always potential sources of and constituencies for alternative values, and are always the agencies which may stage a revolutionary transformation of society, institutionalizing novel values of their own. The argument is not that oppressed groups will necessarily have different values but that they are always a possible source of such values: conflict theory can locate something which makes radical social change a theoretical possibility.

Conflict theory and functionalism tend to match one another point for point, each having views on the same things but looking at them in very different ways. The controversy between them ultimately proved an inconclusive one and it has, in recent years, tended to diminish in importance as new issues have moved to the centre of debate.

A decisive choice between these two perspectives is not readily made: they cannot be assessed in the light of certain decisive facts which would enable us to assert that the evidence supports one side of the argument rather than the other. The perspectives are often in agreement about the facts but disagree as to the significance of those facts, the interpretation that is to be placed upon them. The disagreement, that is, concerns what the facts are evidence for and of. Let us now illustrate our assertion that they disagree as to the significance of evidence, by a couple of examples.

The first is that of common values. As we have shown, both conflict and consensus perspectives will accept that in contemporary Western society there is a rather broad agreement as to certain values. People generally want an improving standard of living, and generally accept the values that Weber identified as being peculiar to modern capitalism. Neither side of the argument questions whether – as a matter of fact – there is such agreement, but they differ profoundly over the question of whether the agreement is spontaneous or spurious. The proponents of the conflict view see consensus as spurious, a mere *appearance* of agreement which is really created by – to use a term from Marxist theory which is now acquiring wider currency – the hegemony of the ruling class, a product of that class's capacity to control the thought of society as a whole through domination of the means of communication. Consensus thinkers react to such claims by pointing out that there is no reason to think the value consensus spurious *unless one first accepts the assumptions of conflict theory itself*. It is conflict theory which assumes that groups have 'interests' which may be quite different from the overt values which members of those groups hold. The conflict theorist is claiming that some things are in the interest of a given group even though its own members do not seem to think they are. So the conflict theorist tends to argue that if he can show that a set of values originated with some other group than the one that now accepts them, this is evidence that those values are really more in the interest of the group that devised them than in the interest of those who now subscribe to them. Hence conflict theorists suppose that their criticism of consensus theory for failing to explain the origins of norms is a potent one, because they suppose that such explanation will show the norms to have sectional origins.

Those who are criticized thus do not accept that one can make this kind of distinction. Why should one suppose that there are things which 'really' are in the interest of certain people if those people do not even want those things. If both ruling and subordinate classes want the same things, this can mean that they have the same interests. If this keeps the ruling class in power it demonstrates that people support those who want and are trying to get the same things as themselves.

A second instance is that of resort to force. As we have noted, conflict theory asserts that social stability rests upon power, whilst the functionalist stresses the role of agreement. Again, the facts are not really in dispute: if we examine the society we live in we can easily see that ruling groups *relatively* rarely make use of force to control life in society. There are, of course, certain critical occasions when force is used – riots, for example, are often put down by violence. However, in general, the members of our society go about their affairs in their regular ways without having to be forced to do so.

Those who take a conflict line generally accept that this is so but, they say, the point is surely that *in the last resort* there are armed troops and police who will be organized to put down the citizenry if they should constitute any real threat to the *status quo*. Though there may appear to be a consensus which props up the State, the truth is that in the last analysis the State relies for its authority on the fact that it can call out the troops.

To this, the consensus reply is that the precise and relevant point has been made: *in the last resort* naked force is available but it *is* only when all other mechanisms of maintaining order have broken down that naked force is used on a substantial scale to keep society working. One can legitimately say that order 'rests' upon force in the sense that, if all else fails, force will be used to support it, but can one not, therefore, more legitimately say that order 'rests' upon consensus since a substantially greater part of society's life is carried on without any appeal to force at all?

Some conflict theorists have argued, further, that the functionalist view is too narrow and benign. The functionalist does not acknowledge the violence that is routinely inflicted upon *most* members of society, e.g., by an education system which indoctrinates children with class-biased ideas, or a stratification system which allocates an undue share of sickness, suffering, disease, poverty and death to the lower classes, compelling them to lead lives which are considerably more nasty, brutish and short than those of their social superiors. Stokely Carmichael makes the same point by distinguishing two types of racisms:

individual racism and institutional racism. The first type consists of overt acts by individuals, with usually the immediate result of the death of victims, or the traumatic and violent destruction of property. This type can be recorded on TV cameras and can frequently be observed in the process of commission.

The second type is less overt, far more subtle, less identifiable in terms of specific individuals committing the acts, but is no less destructive of human life. The second type is more the overall operation of established and respected forces in society, and thus does not receive the condemnation that the first type receives.

Let me give you an example of the first type: When unidentified white terrorists bomb a black church, that is an act of individual racism, widely deplored by most segments of the world. But when in that same city, Birmingham, Alabama, not five but 500 black babies die each year because of lack of proper food, shelter and medical facilities ... that is a function of institutionalised racism (1968, pp. 151–2).

The reply from a consensus point of view is that the problem has not to do with such facts, for the correlation of illness with social class position is well known. The question is simply one of the use of words, for conflict theorists are using 'violence' much more widely than are those they are criticizing. The consensus theorist can recognize that death does follow from inadequate facilities and services but the problem, as he has posed it, does not involve counting that as violence, for by that term he refers to fairly direct physical encounters, the use of weapons and so on. If conflict theory wants to call other types of things 'violence' then it can do so, but it simply poses a different problem from that which functionalism is trying to answer.

The differences between these two approaches, then, derive from the assumptions they make and the ways in which they define their terms and specify their problems. A particular state of affairs only shows what the rival theories claim is shown if one accepts their assumptions and definitions.

Deviance, Rule and Interaction

To say that the case for or against a given 'approach' to sociology cannot be settled by any decisive facts, but involves assessment of definitions and assumptions, is not necessarily to imply criticism, for that same point can be made against *all* sociological frameworks. Controversy within sociology is usually over assumptions and interpretations rather than particular factual matters. The direction of controversy away from the conflict–consensus argument in recent years has resulted from the emergence of other approaches which rest upon assumptions quite different from those of both functionalism and conflict theory.

Despite the fact that they are contentiously divided, functionalism and consensus theory do have much in common. Both, for example, are attempting to account for the organization of total societies, explaining why society *as a whole* changes or fails to do so. Both, too, are inclined to look upon society as a system of interlinked parts even though they may differ on the nature of what it is that keeps those parts together.

The movement away from these two approaches has followed from objections to the treatment of society as a system and to the emphasis upon looking at matters in relation to the organization of the society as a whole. The argument, during the last decade, has shifted to a point which is centred upon what we may – conventionally, but somewhat inaccurately – call the 'interactionist critique'. The issues arise, first, in relation to the problem of deviance.

(a) Anomie theory

Functional theory could, at one time, be accused of treating all conduct which did not conform to norms – all deviance – as a product of random factors such as the failure of some parents, teachers, etc., to adequately socialize their young. Or social tensions were seen as resulting from factors which arose outside society: invasion, say, or depleted natural resources. Recognizing the force of this criticism, Robert K. Merton sought to construct a theory which, though of a functional kind, would show how deviance could be *systematically* created by society.

Taking the example of the U.S.A., he argued the standard functional case, that there are certain core-values which are widely accepted and pursued by members of society, access to those values being regulated by norms. Only in certain ways can those values be legitimately pursued. In the U.S.A. the predominant value is that of financial success, and the appropriate means for its pursuit are hard work and industry. Merton then notes a point which critics of functionalism have often claimed is ignored: that the structure of American society involves an unequal distribution of opportunity and advantage. Thus, although all Americans are supposed to seek financial success, they cannot all expect to achieve it if they use only legitimate means. The most disadvantaged members of society cannot really hope to become financially wealthy simply by working hard.

There is, Merton argues, a disjunction between ends and legitimate means in that the end – financial success – is one which has been inculcated into everyone more or less equally, but the means – the avenues to success through hard work – are not equally distributed, so that some have a far greater chance of success than do others. The result of this incongruence between ends and means – which Merton terms 'anomie' (though he means by this something rather different from Durkheim) – places pressure upon people to use other than the approved means in pursuit of success.

The majority of people in society will remain 'conformist', for they have internalized strong attachments to both ends and means: they will continue to seek financial success by working hard even though the task may be hopeless. Some others, however, will react to the strain that anomie imposes by rejecting the end, the means or both. Since the means of achieving success are differentially distributed throughout the stratification system it is likely that the reactions to the pressures imposed by anomie will also be differentially distributed throughout that system. It is the members of the lower classes, Merton argues, who are most likely to 'innovate': to seek success by resorting to illegitimate means. The pressure upon them to deviate is greatest, since the only legitimate route to success available to them is that of hard manual work, and that does not offer much prospect of high reward. Members of the lower middle classes are more likely to become 'ritualists': they will abandon the pursuit of success as fruitless yet will continue to adhere to the prescribed means. They 'go through the motions' of their occupation, meeting its demands meticulously, but without seeking their own advancement. They make this response because they have come to regard the norms as sacred. They cannot bring themselves to violate them, but they can resolve the tensions of anomie by lowering their aspirations.

Others 'retreat' from society, refusing to pursue wealth either by legitimate or illegitimate means, and refusing, also, to lead a 'conventional' life:

Sociologically, these constitute the true aliens. Not sharing the common frame of values they can be included as members of the *society* (in distinction from the population) only in a fictional sense . . . In this category fall some of the adaptive activities of psychotics, autists, pariahs, outcasts, vagrants, vagabonds, tramps, chronic drunkards and drug addicts (Merton, 1968, p. 153).

This withdrawal from society is the response of those who have been unable to succeed by either legitimate or illegitimate means. They are unable to achieve success 'honestly', but have internalized a prohibition upon resort to dishonest means which they cannot break: their solution to this dilemma is to 'drop out' of society.

One other possible deviant response remains, that of rebellion. Those who have rejected both the value and the means for their realization that society makes legitimate can struggle to substitute new ends and means for those already in existence.

(b) Labelling theory

The critique eventually developed against Merton began – as arguments against functionalists invariably do – by objecting to his assumption that there is general agreement about the nature of right conduct. The position is stated bluntly by Lemert:

it is theoretically conceivable that there are or have been societies in which values learned in childhood, taught as a pattern, and reinforced by structured controls, serve to predict the bulk of everyday behaviour of members and to account for prevailing conformity to norms. However, it is easier to describe the model than it is to discover societies which make a good fit with the model (1967, p. 7).

Most societies do not fit the functionalist model very closely, and American society is as remote from its requirements as any. It is a complex society made up of different ethnic, religious, class, regional, occupational and other groupings which will have varying conceptions of proper behaviour. If there is no agreement amongst such groups as to what is right then there will not, either, be agreement as to what is wrong and deviant.

Merton attempts to say which activities are 'deviant' for American society but his critics argue that there is no consensual American viewpoint on conduct, so that the very same activity may be looked upon by one party as deviant, by another as conduct properly in accord with the relevant rules. Becker exemplifies:

Italian immigrants who went on making wine for themselves and their friends during prohibition were acting properly by Italian immigrant standards, but were breaking the law of their new country (as, of course, were many of their Old American neighbours). Medical patients who shop around for a doctor may, from the perspective of their own group, be doing what is necessary to protect their health by making sure they get what seems to them the best possible doctor; but from the perspective of the physician, what they do is wrong because it breaks down the trust the patient ought to put in his physician. The lower-class delinquent who fights for his 'turf' is only doing what he considers necessary and right, but teachers, social workers, and police see it differently (1963, pp. 15–16).

He suggests that the functionalist theory needs replacing by an alternative view, one which has come to be known as 'labelling theory'. The functionalist account requires that the sociological analyst look upon events in society 'from the point of view of the social system' in an attempt to determine which people are and which are not acting in accord with its rules. Labelling theory, on the other hand, suggests that society is less of a system than a 'pluralist' arrangement, an ensemble of different and competing groups which may be loosely inter-related but which have a great degree of autonomy from one another. In such a situation there cannot be a viewpoint which is the equivalent of that of 'society as a whole', only the different viewpoints of the various groups which make up society. The sociological analyst cannot, therefore, rely upon any single outlook or standard to guide his judgement as to what is deviant *for that society*, unless he illegitimately 'takes sides' and – perhaps unwittingly – adopts the viewpoint of some one group as the standard by which to judge all the others, as if that were better than those of any other group.

Rather than attempting to work out, for a given society, which actions are to be counted as deviant, the labelling theorist proposes to recognize that it is in the nature of deviance for there to be disagreement about it, that there will be no general agreement as to how people should properly behave *even in the same society*. The sociologist should simply study the ways in which some activities are 'picked out' by some people as deviant and some people set apart from others by being 'labelled' as deviant. Adopting that attitude, the sociologist is encouraged to look not at norms and values but at the rule-making and rule-enforcing practices, at the ways in which rules for right conduct are set up, and at the ways in which some people come to look upon others as being 'outside' the boundaries of proper social life.

The examination of these things shows up the naïveté with which functionalism has looked upon the relation between rules and the life of society.

The functionalist view of rules is that they are an expression of the common sentiments of society. However, if one takes the case of legal rules in the U.S.A., for example, it is not true that these are automatic expressions of the common sentiments of everybody. The law-making procedures of that society are complex – the activities of zealous pressure groups and of those with expert knowledge or special interests can act in such ways as to lead to the enactment of laws which are standard for the entire society but which in no way represent the sentiments of the majority who are subject to them. Becker cites the marijuana tax act and the enactment of prohibition as instances of legislation which are quite unrepresentative of common sentiment, but enacted simply because they were sponsored by relatively small groups of what he calls 'moral entrepreneurs' and imposed upon everyone else.

Of course, Becker continues, the creation of a rule is not the same as its enforcement, and there is a complex and complicated relation between defining conduct which might be construed as action in violation of a rule, and actually identifying some actual person as a deviant who has performed that action and broken the rule.

Merton, in the course of his discussion of anomie, assumed a fairly simple and direct connection between acts of deviance and the identification of persons as deviant. The latter are seen as being readily identified as deviant because they have engaged in a proscribed action. Thus, for example, Merton argues that his claim that there are greater rates of 'innovation' in the lower strata is substantiated by the fact that official statistics show that there are higher rates of crime among the lower classes. Becker's point is, in contradiction of Merton, that one cannot easily assume that the conviction rates of lower-class people in the criminal statistics do indicate greater rates of criminal activity among those people.

One of the purposes of many studies of deviance is to understand what it is that *makes* people behave in deviant ways by examining groups of deviants to see what, if anything, differentiates them from the population at large: are there any social, personality or other characteristics which are peculiar to the deviants? If so, then it is usually assumed that these special characteristics are the things which explain the fact that the person is deviant. Thus, for example, the disproportionate representation of low-status people in prisons is assumed, by Merton, to show that it is low status which is causative of their criminality; the low availability of legitimate means forces them to innovate.

This kind of study, the argument from labelling theory goes, is not a study of people who are deviant in the sense that they have broken some specific rule, but a study of people who have been *identified* as deviant by others, who have been *judged* to have broken some rule. We require, Becker observes, a two-fold table to express the possibilities:

	Perceived as Deviant	Not Perceived as Deviant
Rule-Breaking Behaviour	Pure Deviant	Secret Deviant
Obedient Behaviour	Falsely Accused	Conformist

Some of the people who have been identified as rule-breakers may indeed be guilty of the offence with which they are charged – the pure deviant, in Becker's typology – but many people who have been identified as deviant may not have broken those rules, though their supposed offence against the rules has led to their being publicly stigmatized: these are the falsely accused. At the same time, there are people who have in reality broken the relevant rules but who have not been singled out from their fellows for having done so – secret deviants.

The populations which are treated by sociologists as populations of deviants may, then, be made up of a mix of pure deviants and of those who have been falsely accused whilst, at the same time, the population at large with which the supposed deviants are to be compared may contain a proportion of secret deviants, people who have performed the deviant acts in question but who have never been discovered. Studies of prison populations have been used as bases for studies of criminals but, of course, they are not so much studies of criminals as they are of people who have been convicted and imprisoned, some of whom might be innocent of any crime whatsoever. If we find that there are differences between the characteristics of the prison population and the rest of us outside, we have identified not those things which make people into criminals but, perhaps, those things which get people imprisoned.

It can be argued that the disproportionate representation of the lower classes in the criminal statistics and in prison is not so much evidence in support of Merton's theory of anomie as it is evidence of bias in the law enforcement system against the lower classes.

In the first place, it is probable that the vast majority of us are as guilty of criminal acts as are those who have been convicted and imprisoned. Most of us will have broken some law or other – those governing traffic, petty theft, drug use and so on – but these violations have had no consequences: our offence was not noticed or tied to us. Those who are in prison may consider themselves unlucky to the extent that someone did notice such violations of law as they have committed.

The simple fact is, of course, that when some law is set up it has to be enforced, and there is a vast organizational machinery which, in modern society, has the task of enforcing laws – it involves the police, lawyers, courts, prisons, probation officers and so on. Those who staff such organizations recognize that it is a practical condition of life within them that they have been charged with a task they cannot realistically hope to fulfil. If, say, it is their task to apprehend people who commit speeding offences, they know that they are far too few to be able to catch more than a very, very small proportion of the people who speed. Given that those who must enforce the law cannot be everywhere at once, they are apt to deploy their energies and resources in line with organizational policies. The traffic police, say, may decide to patrol the highway in those places in which they think people are most apt to speed or where they think speeding may be most dangerous. Similar considerations apply to other kinds of law enforcement: the police cannot be everywhere and must decide where to put their effort. In deciding where to patrol, then, they may be inclined to patrol lower-class neighbourhoods where 'trouble' may be expected, whilst middle-class neighbourhoods are 'quiet'. The possibility of being 'picked up' by the police may, therefore, be greater for those who frequent lower-class neighbourhoods since that is where the police will be.

The bias in the enforcement of law against the lower classes is due to the fact that those who are engaged in law enforcement have theories of their own about the nature and causes of crime and the characteristics of criminals, and see those things as being class-related. In his account of the administration of juvenile justice in some American cities, Cicourel shows that the theories of judges, police, probation officers and other officials are used in making decisions about the disposition of juvenile cases. White middle-class children who appear before the courts constitute a 'puzzle': they are 'known' to come from 'good' homes, to have the advantages associated with them, 'nice' parents and so on, and the judge therefore faces the question: How can someone in that position have 'gone wrong'? Unless, of course, there is something 'wrong' with them: perhaps they are mentally sick? Lower-class, Black juveniles pose no such problems: they come from 'poor' homes and 'bad' neighbourhoods and could not help but mix with 'wrong' people and get involved in crime and trouble with the police: they will get worse. In deciding what to do, the court is therefore likely to declare the White, middle-class adolescent a suitable case for psychiatric treatment because, as we have suggested, that juvenile will be looked upon as being 'sick': in addition, the juvenile's family will be seen by the court as one that can be relied upon to keep its promise to the court and see its child through a programme of therapy. The lower-class Black is not a candidate for such treatment because his family cannot be relied upon to support a programme of psychiatric treatment and because, in any case, that is not thought appropriate. Whether one will end up in the statistics of crime or those of mental illness may well have to do with one's class and ethnic characteristics, but not because they 'in themselves' bring about mental illness or criminality. They do so because they feature in the theories of police, judges, probation officers and others as things which affect one's predispositions to crime or mental illness (Cicourel, 1968).

Whilst the law-enforcement system has something of a bias against the lower classes, then, the processes involved in singling out some people and publicly identifying them as deviants are not entirely organized in class terms. Many of the factors which affect those passing through the processes of arrest, arraignment, conviction and incarceration are shaped by organizational considerations; others are simply 'contingencies'.

Labelling theory has inspired a number of studies of processes of plea-bargaining which go on between defence and prosecution lawyers. Suppose, for example, that someone is arrested for child-molesting. The prosecution will often offer the defence lawyer a 'deal' if his client will make a guilty plea, saving the prosecution the necessity of a trial: the prosecutor will reduce the charge and accept a guilty plea to a lesser charge than that with which the defendant is now accused. The defendant will be allowed to plead guilty to 'loitering' rather than child-molesting. What the defendant will be identified as in the criminal statistics, then, – child-molester or loiterer – will depend not so much on 'what he really did' as upon his willingness to accept a deal with the prosecutor. The process of plea-bargaining shows that law-enforcement is done by people who work in and manage organizations, and that their decision-making is governed by their organizational setting. Prosecuting attorneys are concerned not only with convicting the guilty, but with obtaining convictions quickly and efficiently. Any case they have to prosecute will be only one amongst many, and they will be concerned to keep the cases flowing through court. The making of a plea-bargain not only expedites the processing of cases, it also guarantees the prosecutor a conviction: he runs no risk of losing as he might in a contested charge (Sudnow, 1965).

Police work too is done within organization and organizations are apt to develop specialized departments assigned to specialized tasks. In the course of their work policemen organize themselves in the light of the fact that they are in a particular department. One who is attached to the narcotics squad will, for example, recruit informers whom he knows are involved in, say, handling stolen property, but he will take no action against them because it is not his business but that of some other department.

Police work is, after all, work, and policemen, like other workers, are inclined to make their job as comfortable and congenial as they can. They arrange things so that they are convenient and making an arrest can be more or less convenient, depending on the circumstances in which it is to be done. At the end of the policeman's working day it can be very inconvenient for him to make an arrest since he has to take the person he has arrested back to the police station and complete all the necessary paperwork himself. He can, thus, find himself with unwanted overtime. At other times of day the prospect of something interesting to do might make an alternative to the boredom of continuous patrolling and offer an opportunity to return to the station. Whether or not someone gets arrested or is simply given an informal caution can depend, then, upon the policeman's assessment of the relevant advantages and disadvantages *for himself* in the different courses of action.

The point of these arguments is that they show that between a citizen's initial contact with law-enforcement agencies and their eventual public identification as deviants there is a lengthy process in which organizational considerations and sheer contingencies can dictate how things develop and shape the eventual fate of the people being processed through the organizations. Labelling theory thus pays attention to rather different issues than does functionalism, suggesting that the emphasis should be upon the study of the processes whereby people are defined as deviant rather than upon attempting to identify the things which 'make' deviants act in the ways they do. It emphasizes that there is a 'political' aspect to the making of social rules. People who get labelled as deviant are often those who are caught between the demands of centralized authority and the traditions of the sub-cultures and communities to which they owe their loyalties. There is nothing 'special' about them which makes them different from the rest of us and causes them to behave like 'deviants', for, all too often, *rather than people who have been 'lawlessly' breaking the law, they are people who have been following the rules of their own community*.

Labelling theory has not, of course, itself escaped criticism. Those who take a conflict approach, for example, are apt to look on labelling theory as the liberal reaction to the conservatism of the functional-consensus line. Labelling theory is accused of a sentimentalist bias toward the underdog, and of looking at the problem in terms of a superficial view of the conflict between central bureaucracy and subcultures. In classic liberal fashion, labelling theory – it is said – fails to recognize the fact that class represents a more fundamental form of social organization than others like ethnicity and regionalism, and that the social definition of crime and the enforcement of the law are dimensions of class rule, in which, notably, the protection of private property is a central concern. In short, it fails to see that agencies of social control are extensions of the power of a dominant class and instruments of class oppression.

Although labelling theory may look upon 'making the rules' as political, the criticism continues, it does not see that 'breaking the rules' is often an act of a political kind, an act – real or symbolic – of resistance and political challenge. The rule-makers can, by making laws, and defining certain acts as criminal, try to get people in society to look upon those acts as the acts of criminals, rather than as those of political opponents. Identifying them as criminals ensures that the public will not give them sympathy or take notice of their cause or any legitimate grievances they may have. The contemporary question of terrorism exemplifies this problem, the authorities typically seeking to treat the terrorists as 'gangsters', emphasizing that they are criminals, breaking laws against murder, kidnapping, theft, hijacking, arson and so on, whilst the terrorists themselves claim that their actions are those of a political opposition, employing the only available means to make others conscious of their cause.

Another common objection to labelling theory has been that it is not internally consistent. Becker's typology, for example, has received much attention in this connection. If, it is argued, we adopt labelling theory's view of deviance as *that which is publicly identified as such*, then Becker's typology cannot be valid. It contains 'impossible' phenomena like secret deviance: that category implies that a person really is a deviant even if he has not been publicly identified as such – but that is a contradiction of the theory's definition. Likewise, the notion of 'false accusation' is also dubious, if the policy of labelling theory is strictly adhered to, for it postulates someone who is publicly identified as deviant but who is *not* deviant. In effect, in constructing his typology Becker is employing both a labelling conception of deviance – that which is publicly identified as such – *and* that of the functionalists which he has supposedly rejected – deviants are people who break rules and laws. A secret deviant is someone who has not been publicly stigmatized and hence is *not* a deviant in the labelling theory sense but who *has* broken rules and is therefore deviant in the functionalist sense.

(c) Symbolic interactionism

Underlying the approach to deviance used by the labelling theorists is a rather loosely articulated general perspective on sociology which is usually referred to as 'symbolic interactionism'.

Symbolic interactionists see the kind of systems theorizing in which both functionalist and conflict theory engage as overly determinist, treating the things that the members of the society do as though they were done *by* the system itself or by its parts, rather than by the individuals who actually perform the relevant actions. Social order is viewed as the product of an interplay between system parts and this, in the view of symbolic interactionists, underestimates the extent to which social order is created *in and from the interaction of the members of society*.

At the heart of the functionalist theory is the idea that man is a socialized participant, but that idea has been referred to as being an essentially 'over-socialized' conception, underestimating the degree to which the individual is a shaping force in his own right. Symbolic interactionists do not deny that the individual is socialized. G. H. Mead, one of the main thinkers upon whom symbolic interactionism has drawn, argued no less strongly than Durkheim that the individual is a social creation who comes into being only in social relations with others and who internalizes the society into his own personality in the form of what Mead called 'the generalized other' – meaning by that something similar to a shared moral order. However, Mead also insisted that the individual did not consist *only* of the norms of conduct which he had internalized; he may always act impulsively and inventively in ways that have not been learned from society. The socialized individual is, in the terminology of symbolic interactionism, a 'self', capable of thought, invention and self-determination (Strauss, 1964).

The inadequacy of the 'over-socialized' conception follows not only from the fact that people are not totally dominated by learned rules but also from the fact that those rules which are learned do not completely and precisely specify the details of individual conduct. The rules of society are often vague, ambiguous and quite unclear in their implications. To have internalized them is not to be in possession of some very definite set of instructions on what to do. If we were creatures who could *only* act upon socially supplied rules, we would be quite unable to carry on our social life as we do.

The point being made here is one which is practically exemplified in the world of work by the 'work to rule': if people abide strictly by the rules which have been supplied to them then the organization of work begins to fall apart because that organization relies upon the workers acting in ways which are *not* specified in the rules. Symbolic interaction simply extends this point to the entire society: that only 'works' as it does because its members do things which they are not explicitly called upon to do.

In conducting the affairs of his society, then, the individual is not simply moving through a sequence of explicitly pre-defined steps which make up a stable pattern of interaction as imagined by functionalism. The emphasis of symbolic interaction is upon the extent to which interaction is 'improvised', worked out upon the occasion on which it is done. Just as there is no reason why improvised music cannot be built around some themes and ideas which are elaborated as the music is played, so there is no reason why interaction cannot develop from the rules and understandings which are learned from society. Just as improvised music develops and changes through the emerging mutual interactions of the players, so may patterns of social interaction develop out of and beyond the initial expectations which the participants brought to them, being shaped by the emerging mutual responses of the interactants. This conception of interaction has been crystallized in a conception formulated by Anselm Strauss and his colleagues, one of 'negotiated order' (Strauss *et al.*, 1964).

Their study was specifically intended to examine psychiatric hospitals as organizations, but many of their ideas are applicable to patterns of interaction of any sort. The study shows that psychiatric hospitals are ostensibly governed by laws, rules and understandings which specify an hierarchy of authority, a division of labour and routine courses of action, but such rules, laws and understandings do not adequately describe the observable patterns of authority, division of labour and activities which will be found on the wards of the hospital. The actual day-to-day life of the organization is, they argue, constantly under negotiation, being worked out amongst those involved in its life.

The hierarchy of authority in a hospital, for example, may specify that doctors have authority over the administrative staff, nurses, orderlies and other para-medical and untrained staff, and over the patients themselves. The facts of life in a hospital are, of course, that though the doctors may *formally* have complete control, the doctors are *dependent* upon the co-operation of nurses, administrative staff and all the others to make their own working lives effective and comfortable. If others are not co-operative and are not willing to assist the doctors in various ways not specified in the rules, then the latter may well find their work becoming impossible. The division of labour itself will come to be negotiated in that doctors will come to trust and rely upon others and will allow them to do things which *should* be done by the doctor himself – thus quite untrained staff will end up applying medications which should be given by the doctor.

Having been allowed to perform certain tasks which they ought not, people can begin to use that as a basis for claiming further rights and privileges. Similarly, the fact that one can acquire some power over one's formal superiors by being co-operative with them may allow one to further enhance one's power by, say, becoming so co-operative that people become wholly dependent upon one's services. One can then begin threatening to withdraw these unless one's demands for increased autonomy and self-control are met.

The understandings which govern actual practice, then, permit situations which develop in ways that the rules cannot provide for. The very general nature of such rules involves 'understandings' of how to interpret them, and they can be interpreted differently by different people and from situation to situation. Different parties may strike quite different bargains: some doctors, for example, may insist very strictly upon their formal rights and privileges, and upon the fact that they are in control and that it is their task to apply certain medicines, whilst others may adopt a very informal approach, treating their formal subordinates very much as equals, allowing lines of demarcation in the division of labour to become very vague and permitting 'subordinates' to arrogate to themselves privileges which, in other contexts, are restricted to medically trained professionals.

The conception of negotiation is intended – in a rather metaphoric fashion – to capture the fact that the participants in an organization are 'working it out' even as they carry it on. It is not meant to suggest that the pattern of interaction is negotiated in the way that, say, a union–employer contract is negotiated through explicit offer, counter-offer, argument, bargaining, and eventual making of an agreement (though sometimes, certainly, such things may occur as they do in union–employer bargaining). The notion of negotiation is meta-phoric in the sense that it suggests that interaction is conducted *as though* the parties to it were bargaining in some implicit fashion, and it therefore points to the extent to which the interactional process is one which involves mutual adaptation between parties, arising from adjustments they make in response to one another's preferences, at-titudes, doings, etc., often in the form of tacit agreements as to what they will allow each other to do, how far they can go.

This is, of course, to some extent the view that functionalist theory takes of the process of social interactions, but that approach sees the eventual end-product of that process as being clear, stable and sanc-tioned understandings. The conception of a negotiated order, how-ever, is meant to emphasize that the 'agreements' are never stable, that they can be and constantly are being changed in response to the unfolding life of the organization, to the turnover of personnel, to modification of understandings in other parts of the organization and so on. Whereas functionalism postulates a system with built-in mechanisms which are designed to control tendencies for change and thereby to restore the *status quo*, the concept of negotiation offers a conception of order as something which is 'open-ended', which may certainly build upon existing patterns of relationship but which may very well bring about modifications and changes. Just as symbolic interactionism encourages a shift in the study of deviance away from the concentration on what it is that makes people *act* in deviant ways towards the study of the ways in which actions *come to be counted* as deviant, it also encourages a shift in the analysis of social order away from a concentration upon social systems and their properties and towards the examination of the practices and interactional patterns through which people come to build up and develop relationships and patterns of organization.

A central notion upon which interactionism has come to place great emphasis is that of 'the definition of the situation', and the way in which that is accomplished. The notion of the 'definition of the situation' means that people react to circumstances as they see them, that different people see circumstances differently, and that, therefore, it is important for sociologists to see how situations are defined to appreciate 'how things look' to those they study.

The emphasis in functionalism, as we have made plain, is in looking at things 'from the point of view of the social system': all activities are looked at in relation to the contribution they will make to the functioning of the system, and in relation to the over-all pattern of norms and of social integration. Actions are, therefore, viewed as rational or otherwise in terms of their contribution to the system as a whole. This is not a view interactionists can accept – they are inclined to see host activities as being rational enough if they are assessed in relation to circumstances *as those appear to the actors and relative to the ends the actors have in mind*.

Insanity has been to interactionism what religion has been to functionalism, the topic to which the approach has been applied to greatest and most surprising effect.

Insanity seems, by definition, to be the supreme exemplar of irrationality. The insane person is one whose mind cannot function adequately, who cannot obtain a realistic grasp on reality and who cannot, therefore, be expected to relate ends to means in effective ways. A number of interactionists, however, have tried to show that if things are seen as they are seen by people who are supposedly insane, what those people do may be much more rational than it looks to us.

Two studies in particular have argued this case most vividly. In *Asylums*, Erving Goffman attempted to show that if one looks at the behaviour of the inmates of insane asylums, relating their behaviour to the way in which such institutions are organized, that behaviour appears to be well adapted to the environments the inmates must live in. It may look bizarre in the context of daily life, but the asylum is not daily life, and in such institutions as large mental hospitals the bizarre conduct of inmates is quite appropriate. Goffman examined asylums on the assumption that its inmates were nothing less than absolutely psychologically normal and was able to argue that their behaviour was fully explicable on that basis.

He coined the expression 'total institution' to denote those organizations which encompass the total daily round of their inmates' lives. Asylums, ships, monasteries, concentration camps are all instances of total institutions, places where the inmates eat, sleep, work, play and indeed live their entire daily lives together within the same physical confines. The thrust of Goffman's commentary on the asylum is, however, to show that it is a totalitarian institution within which the inmates' entire existence is subjected to the rule of the staff: there is, for the inmate, no privacy, no freedom, even his thoughts cannot be kept to himself, and the domination of the institution over its charge is expressed through the often punitive and coercive use of what is supposed to be medical treatment.

The asylum, from the point of view of the inmate, is not so much a hospital designed to help him and care for him, but an enclosing, depriving and punishing world which attacks even his sense of self, his sense of being an autonomous, self-determining entity. In the face of such an environment, the individual struggles to assert himself and develops patterns of adjustment which enable him to overcome deprivations and avoid punishments.

Within the psychiatric frame of mind which dominates the orientation of the staff of the institution, however, these things which patients do to adapt themselves to necessities of life in the asylum are looked upon as potential symptoms of the mental illnesses which have brought the patient into hospital. In line with psychiatric doctrine, what the patient does is seen as expression of his personality, not the social circumstances of the milieu he lives in. The necessities which the hospitals, because of their coercive and depriving character, place upon their charges to adopt novel means for acquiring quite ordinary rights and satisfactions are not considered by the staff: the things inmates do in response to the conditions provided by the hospital are seen as signs of sickness.

A classic case, here, is that of hoarding behaviour. The inmates of mental hospitals often hoard all kinds of mundane things about their person, walking the wards with pockets filled with string, books, cigarettes, toilet paper and so on. The hoarding of such things can be seen as symptomatic of excessively developed anxieties and insecurities since, after all, the compulsive accumulation of quite worthless possessions is hardly normal. The burden of Goffman's argument is that though it may not be normal in life outside the asylum to accumulate worthless possessions and keep them about one's person, in the eyes of the inmate those seemingly valueless commodities may be invaluable. They are difficult to acquire within the economy of the hospital and they are also difficult to keep, for the inmate has no secure and private places of storage except those which are about his person and, therefore, in order to prevent prying into his possessions or loss of them the inmate keeps them with him all the time.

It can perhaps be argued against Goffman that even the inmates themselves do come, sooner or later, to admit that they have been or are mentally ill, but this case is one that Goffman has anticipated. The patient is in a difficult bind, for psychiatric theory typically maintains that realizing that one has been mentally ill is a sign of progress and refusal to recognize that one has been mentally sick may well mean that one still *is* mentally ill. No matter how strong an inmates' sense of wrongfulness about his incarceration, no matter how strong his sense of his own sanity, once hospitalized he is advised to say that he has been mentally ill if he wants to obtain his release. Until he does so the staff will look upon him as refusing to 'face up' to the fact of his illness: once he has agreed that he is, or has been, mentally ill, then the staff can begin to look upon him as 'making progress'.

In a study of paranoia paralleling Goffman's study of asylums, Edwin Lemert advanced the argument that the paranoid, one who is supposedly suffering delusions of persecution at the hands of an imaginary conspiracy, is actually undergoing persecution at the hands of a real and well-organized conspiracy. Viewed from the paranoid's vantage-point, other people *are* organizing themselves against him in a conspiratorial and secretive fashion and *are* trying to put him out of circulation and into the hands of psychiatrists. Both Goffman and Lemert argue that other people act towards those they fear are mentally ill in a fashion which gives to the one who is supposed to be mentally ill a feeling that he is being betrayed. Those who begin to suspect that someone is mentally ill are usually afraid to express their fears directly to him, for they see mentally sick people as being dangerous and perhaps inclined to be violent. They then try to take action to arrange for the supposedly insane person to see doctors and psychiatrists, to go to hospitals and so forth, but they usually go about that in surreptitious, dishonest and evasive ways with the end result that their 'victim' arrives in hospital with the thoroughly justified feeling that he has been persecuted and betrayed by those nearest and dearest to him – the very fact that he is in the mental hospital is evidence that other people have been lying to him, arranging things behind his back, talking about him and so on. The paranoid's 'irrational' feeling of being got at begins to seem like a realistic assessment of what is happening to him.

In general, then, the symbolic interactionist perspective sees social order as emerging from the ongoing process of interaction between the members of society as they define and react to situations. It is not, therefore, much concerned to see things 'from the point of view of the social system', since the organization of society is seen as a fluid and changing organization, liable to endless modification through the continuing negotiations which are taking place between its innumerable members.

(d) Ethnomethodology

'Ethnomethodology' is the name of an approach to sociology which, as a name, has caused many people difficulty as being 'hard to understand', 'an outstanding example of the ugliness of sociological jargon', and so on. That name does not mean anything very mysterious, meaning only 'the study of the methods which people in society use to make sense of what is going on around them'. Why this should constitute a distinctive approach to sociology is something that needs to be explained.

Ethnomethodology (to which, for brevity, we shall refer as EM) is, like symbolic interactionism, opposed to functional analysis and to the idea that conduct is organized solely through internalized rules. EM does not deny that rules are important in society or that much everyday conduct is organized by reference to them: it simply points out that *more* is involved in understanding conduct which does follow rules than simply spelling out the rules which are followed. All rules carry with them what is called an 'et cetera clause', which means that it is understood to say more than is actually put into its words. For example, a sign which says 'No Parking' is not usually understood as forbidding the emergency parking of police and fire vehicles, even though the rule says nothing about legitimate exceptions. In following rules, then, the members of society show the capacity to grasp the et cetera clauses, to see the meanings and implications of rules which are nowhere spelled out. Furthermore, the following of a rule involves a pairing of action and circumstance: a rule indicates that in certain circumstances a given way of acting is appropriate. An individual's capacity to follow a rule, then, depends upon his ability to see that it is applicable *here*, to identify his circumstances and see they are relevant to the rule. Functionalism, it can be argued, gives no account of the capacity of members of society to appraise relevant situations in this way. It does not do so, it can be argued, because it has misconceived the problem of order and hence must produce an inadequate solution.

The term 'order' is one which takes its sense from the implicit contrast it is used to make and it has been understood, this far, to be opposed to 'anarchy'. That way of looking at order involves the sociologist in seeking to understand what it is that prevents society disintegrating into anarchy, how force and fraud are restricted. The term 'order', however, may be used to draw a quite different contrast – with 'confusion'. It could be argued that the pre-social man which we imagined above would not be in real danger of involvement in a lethal and anarchic struggle against his fellows because he would be in total confusion, unable to make any sense of what was going on around him and, hence, quite unable to take *any* action of *any* kind.

The functionalist solution to the problem of order is open to the same kind of criticism as that which Durkheim made of the idea of contrast as a basis for social organization: it relies upon those things it is meant to be explaining. Thus, to talk in terms of shared values and norms requires that people must be able to learn from one another – for it is only through socialization, through learning from others, that each one of us learns norms and values. But learning can only take place if we share with one another some mutually intelligible means of communication, if we can make sense of each other's actions. But if we can do that, then we are already involved in orderly social transactions with one another – society *already* exists.

Ethnomethodology, therefore, focuses centrally upon that problem which is often spoken of as the 'problem of meaning' but which is perhaps better thought of as the 'problem of sense': how do people make sense of the things which are going on around them and of the way in which their social environment is organized?

Men experience the worlds in which they live as sensible and meaningful places; the things that happen to them, the people and objects that confront them, are recognizable and behave in more or less expected ways. Men feel with some confidence that they know about their world, that they can account for it and deal with it, that the things they have done in the past will contrive to produce the same results that they have previously done, now and in the future.

For most of the time men take it for granted that they know the world, feeling that there is nothing either problematical or curious about that fact. If they keep their eyes and ears open and their wits about them they cannot fail to understand what is going on about them, for they need do no more than recognize the obvious; anyone else in their situation would see the world in exactly the same way as they do.

They think of themselves, in many ways, as passively registering experience, seeing the world in the way they do because that is how it is; things in the world simply present themselves and are seen. But a naked eyeball, passively observing, will not serve us as a model for human perception. Although men often regard themselves as doing no more than recognizing what takes place under their eyes, they are also, on other occasions, capable of recognizing that the world is not quite so transparently self-evident. Thus, although we may assert that 'anyone' ought to be able to see certain things because they are obvious, we nevertheless exclude children and strangers from the category 'anyone', and treat them with special patience and tolerance because we classify them as people who have not yet learned how to see the world in the way we see it. We thus implicitly recognize that seeing the world this way is *not* obvious, but has to be learned.

The world is not 'given' to men, something which is simply seen through wide open eyes. What is seen is as much a function of who is looking, how he is looking, and what he is looking for, as it is of what is 'out there'. We may, after all, see the 'same' thing as several quite 'different' things, now as this, now as that:

In the course of my professional work for a fire insurance company . . . I undertook the task of analysing many hundreds of reports of the circumstances surrounding the start of fires, and in some cases, of explosions. My analysis was directed towards purely physical conditions, such as defective wiring, presence or lack of air spaces between metal flues and woodwork, etc. and the results were presented in these terms . . . Indeed it was undertaken with no thought that any other significances would or could be revealed. But in due course it became evident that not only a physical situation *qua* physics, but the meaning of that situation to people, was sometimes a factor, through the behaviour of the people in the start of the fire . . . Thus around a storage of what are called 'gasoline drums', behaviour will tend to a certain type, that is, great care will be exercised; while around a storage of what are called 'empty gasoline drums', it will tend to be different – careless, with little repression of smoking or of tossing cigarette stubs about. Yet the 'empty' drums are perhaps the more dangerous, since they contain explosive vapour (Whorf, 1964, p. 135).

Whether the same gasoline drums are to be seen as 'full' or 'empty' is not dependent upon the drums themselves, for they can be seen as *either* one or the other; how we shall see them depends upon the yardstick that we are using to evaluate them; whether we are assessing them in terms of the amount of gasoline or the amount of gas they contain. The yardstick we will choose to employ as a measure will relate to the interests, purposes and knowledge that we have. If we are *interested* in the storage, distribution and sale of gasoline then it is the amount of gasoline in the drums that will concern us, whilst it will be the vapour content in them that we will want to know about if it is our job to investigate and prevent fires. If we are storage workers we are likely to see the 'empty' drums as being 'safe', because we do not have much technical knowledge of fire hazards and thus do not see that these drums are in fact more likely to be dangerous than are the 'full' ones which we treat so circumspectly. We are unlikely to discover this danger because our work does not involve us in having access to information the insurance investigator can come by, nor does it require us to meditate upon the possible causes of explosions.

Thus the way in which something is seen depends upon the 'perspective' from which it is viewed, upon the interests that we have, and upon the knowledge, information and opportunity that are available to us. People can, then, be seen as *making* the sense that the world has for them: what the world 'looks like' to them depends upon the things that they bring to 'making it out' as the recognizable, familiar place it is. The aim of EM is to give an account of the ways in which experience of the world *as* an orderly, intelligible place, in which things happen in expected and explicable ways, is produced.

The argument from EM begins in fairly Durkheimian style: from the point of view of the members, society is experienced as a real and objective thing which is already organized and 'out there', operating independently of the wish of any one of us and providing intractable circumstances to which we must adapt. It is a world taken for granted: we relate to this world on the basis of a number of important unquestioned assumptions. In going about our daily affairs we simply assume that things will happen today as they have in the past, and that people will continue to conduct themselves today as they have on previous occasions. When we enter a room and press the light switch we assume, simply, that the light will go on as it usually does. We do not, say, imagine that today pressing the light switch will release hot water from the ceiling onto our heads, and therefore press the switch and dive from the room before that can happen. Our assumptions about how things will go have an 'until further notice' character for, of course, reality can always deal us a nasty surprise and fail to follow through as we expect it to; we simply rely upon those assumptions and take it for granted that things will work as we are accustomed for them to do – until they fail to do so. *Then* when things do not happen as we expect we begin to make inquiries: if the light switch does not put on the light, *then* we check to see if someone has taken out the bulb, if it has failed, if there has been a power cut and so on. We negotiate our way about the world without paying all of it equal attention: indeed, in order that we may focus our attention upon some matter in hand we must disregard other things, simply assuming they will go on their way as they usually do. In order, for example, to focus attention upon the reading of our newspaper on our way to work we must assume that the bus driver is doing his job as he routinely does: we *cannot* concentrate on our newspaper and on everything else as well.

In living in society we must invest an enormous amount of trust in other people. We cannot inquire into everything that might conceivably be doubted because anything and everything can be called into doubt. If we want to do anything or even inquire into something then we have to take many things at face value and simply trust that appearances are genuine. If, say, we enter a hospital and see in the corridors various people in white coats with stethoscopes and other medical implements protruding from their pockets we *could* imagine that they are all impersonators and phonies engaged in some enormous charade to deceive us for some nefarious reason and we *could* start to investigate them – interrogating them, checking credentials, etc., to establish *bona fides* – but we do not typically do these things.

We simply take it on trust, assume that those who 'look like' doctors in places where doctors usually are *will be* genuine.

As members of society we have at our fingertips a great deal of knowledge about 'how this society works', and we invoke our knowledge of the society as we know it to decide what is going on around us and what is happening before our eyes. We are able to invest the kind of trust we have just been discussing because we suppose that we are competent in the ways of our society, and knowledgeable enough to understand the social arrangements which underpin the events which go on around us. We 'know', for example, that medical staff gather in certain settings such as hospitals, and we know, too, that medical personnel may routinely be recognized by their dress and ornamentation, may be spotted by a white coat or possession of a stethoscope.

We do not normally bother to make special points about such things in this society as, say, that medical staff work in hospitals, simply because we do not think that the reader needs to have such things spelt out. We presume that the readers, because they live in society, will take it as a matter of course that they have a good grasp of an enormous number of 'facts of life' in their society and we expect, too, that they will *require* of one another a knowledge of just such things. That medical staff wear white coats, that red lights signify danger, that families are made up of spouses and their children, that shops are open between nine a.m. and six p.m., are all things that we should expect, along with countless others, should be known by people who seem otherwise competent in the ways of our society. Likewise we expect our cohabitants to know how to do a good many things such as, say, speak the language, tell the time, cross the street, make coffee, unlock a door, etc., etc. We live our lives in society on the assumption that we share with others a grasp upon an extensive corpus of 'common-sense knowledge', of things which anyone should know, which are apparent to all of us and which need not be spelt out. If, say, we see that a traffic light has turned from green to red and see a vehicle come to a halt in front of it, we need not ask the driver why he has stopped. We can 'see' from the fact that the light is red that he has stopped *because* of the red light, since we know that motorists have to stop for red lights: *everyone* knows that. The presumed grasp of our fellows of such a 'common-sense knowledge of social structures' is used by us to make sense of what they are doing: just as we use the driver's supposed grasp of the significance of red traffic lights to see that he 'stopped for the light'.

The decisions which people in society make as to 'what is happening' are often such as to cause some people to complain that they are less than rational. Compared with the ways in which, say, scientists arrive (or are *supposed* to arrive) at decisions on matters of fact, the manner in which things are routinely decided in day-to-day life often looks quite scandalous. The scientist is supposed, if he is conducting his inquiries properly, to engage in systematic policies of doubt, taking nothing on trust that has not been carefully established as a matter of fact. If he does not have sufficient information upon which to make sound decisions then the scientist should refrain from making judgements as to what the facts are until such time as more adequate information becomes available to him. It does not matter, in this context, whether scientists really do live up to these exacting standards; we mention them only because they are sometimes appealed to as yardsticks against which we assess the rationality or otherwise of conduct in day-to-day affairs; against such standards we are likely to find that every day conduct wanting in rationality. People living daily lives will take things on trust without inquiring into them, without requiring the substantiating evidence the scientist would need. However, it can be argued that it is quite inappropriate to apply the standards of science to the way life in society is conducted, for that life is a thoroughly practical affair, and those who live together require of one another that they make and accept from others judgements of evidence and proof which are adequate for 'all practical purposes'. The life of the scientist is *not* a standard against which other people's activities should be assessed, since scientists can be seen as people who are exempted – in certain exceptional circumstances – from having to obey requirements that the rest of us have to accept.

Scientists, notably, are expected to take an interest in things with no practical ends in view, purely for the sake of acquiring knowledge, and they are, too, permitted as an integral part of their working lives to follow to remote and unlikely conclusions things which are purely speculative constructions in the first place – they can follow things through just to see where they lead. They can also work systematically through alternative possibilities in any line of inquiry, thinking up many different ways of explaining the same things to see which ones are best, most comprehensive and so on. Such luxuries are not allowed to most of us. We *have* to organize things with practical ends in view, *have* to make decisions whatever difficulties we may face in arriving at them, however short may be the information or however scarce the resources necessary to pursue our inquiries. We cannot delay decision until 'all the facts are in' or until all the conceivable possibilities have been explored. Others are usually waiting upon us and demand we decide so that they can get on with the organization of their affairs. One cannot, for example, once a defendant has been charged and arraigned in court, seriously propose that since, by the standards appropriate in science, there is insufficient evidence for a decision as to his guilt, the case ought to be suspended indefinitely until such times as some more decisive evidence emerges. Once the legal proceedings are initiated then they must be carried to some conclusion, to a finding one way or another, and whatever evidence is presented as part of those proceedings *has to be* 'enough' to serve as the basis for a decision: if there is not 'enough' evidence of guilt then that is grounds for a finding of 'not guilty' and dismissal of the case, rather than for delay in taking the decision.

In deciding what *is* fact, the members of society routinely make use of what is called by Harold Garfinkel – whose work was the basis for EM – 'the documentary method'. To show what this method involves Garfinkel constructed a kind of laboratory experiment (see above, Chapter 2, p. 118). He asked some students to take part in what they were told was an experiment in psychotherapy. They were to talk about their problems to an adviser whom they could not see, since he was concealed behind a screen. They were to ask the adviser questions about their troubles and he would give his advice in the form of 'yes' or 'no' answers to their queries. In truth, the 'adviser' was merely an experimenter giving his answers in an entirely random fashion which had nothing to do with the questions that were asked at all.

Although there was no sensible relation between the questions and the experimenter's responses, the students nonetheless treated those responses as real answers to the questions asked. Although the experimenter never said anything except 'yes' or 'no' the recipients of his 'advice' interpreted it as telling them to do things which he never said in so many words. The experimental subjects tried to work out what a 'yes' or 'no' might mean by reference to the things that they, the subjects, had already said. Thus, if a subject had asked, say, 'Shall I drop out of school?' and the response from the 'adviser' was 'yes', then the 'adviser' was heard as telling the subject to drop out of school.

Since the 'answers' were given on a random basis then inevitably they would give rise to strange positions: a subject asked, say, 'You think I should drop out of school?' and received a 'yes' reply, and then asked, say, 'You really think I should drop out of school?' only to receive a 'no' response. The 'adviser' thus appeared to be contradicting himself, but the experimental subjects would devote considerable effort to attempting to make sense of what the 'adviser' was telling them, recalling things that they and the 'adviser' had previously said, attempting on the basis of that to determine what the 'adviser' must mean.

This 'experiment' serves to show that people do make sense of each other's actions and will continue to attempt to do so even when what they are being given are, in reality, senseless and random responses. In making such sense whatever materials are to hand will do if they have to – since the adviser can only say 'yes' and 'no' those flat answers *will* serve as the experimental subject's basis for working out the adviser's advice. More specifically the 'experiment' is used to bring out the features of the documentary method which

consists of treating an actual appearance as the 'document of', as 'pointing to', as 'standing on behalf of' a presupposed underlying pattern. Not only is the underlying pattern derived from its individual documentary evidences, but the individual documentary evidences, in their turn, are interpreted on the basis of 'what is known' about the underlying pattern. Each is used to elaborate the other (Garfinkel, 1967, p. 78).

In one of those exchanges between experimenter and subject, the following talk occurs:

Subject: . . . under those conditions, should I still date the girl?
Experimenter: My answer is yes.

Subject: Well I am actually surprised at the answer. I expected a no answer on that. Perhaps this is because you are not quite aware of my dad and his reactions and he seems to be the type of person that is sensitive . . .

The subject treats the experimenter's answers as expressions of an 'underlying' pattern which is the adviser's reasoning and advice about the subject's problems. Since the only knowledge that the subject has of the adviser is the answers the latter is giving to his questions then the subject has to work out, from those answers, what it is that the adviser thinks – thus from the fact that he gets a 'yes' answer he begins to work out whether or not the adviser is 'aware' of the subject's father's character, etc. *At the same time*, the subject is using what he supposes to be knowledge of the adviser's reasoning, etc., to decide what the adviser is telling him to do: the adviser is telling him to defy his father, continue to date the girl and so on. The answers the adviser gives are used by the subject to find out about, to get to know, the adviser, even as what is known about the adviser is used to make out what he is saying. This is what Garfinkel is talking about when he refers to the use of 'one to elaborate the other'.

It may be objected, now, that such a documentary method is the sort of thing that justifies the earlier comparison between scientific method and everyday decision-making to the disadvantage of the latter. Surely one cannot defend a 'method' in which some particular thing is used as evidence of a pattern, even as the pattern is used to justify the claim that that particular thing is what it is? However, Garfinkel's point is this, that the documentary method *is* used in making sense of what goes on and that though its use may cause logicians pain that is not our problem, for it is our task to study the methods people *do* use to their own satisfaction, to make sense of the things that happen.

In making sense of something through the use of the documentary method members of society do so through reference to the context in which those things occur. This draws our attention to something which Garfinkel calls 'indexicality' and which he suggests is a pervasive feature of sense-making. By this is meant only the following: that the sense of a remark or activity can only be decided by reference to the circumstances in which it is produced. We can, that is, only make sense of what someone says or does if we see such things as who says it, when they say it, where they say it, in response to what, what is being assumed and so on. Human activities are inextricably circumstanced and we can only hope to understand them if we look at them relative to their circumstances. There is a difference, in Garfinkel's view, between what is literally *said* and what is *meant* by what is said: if we attend only to the words that people utter we shall never understand what they understand one another to be talking about because they rely, in talking to each other, upon many things which they never say, which they assume their hearers can see or supply. Suppose, for example, that we have some simple exchange which goes:

A: What time is it?

B: Five.

B's remark 'five' could present an enormous puzzle to us: what does it mean, five what? We are able to grasp that it is 'five o'clock' even though B *does not say that*, because we can see that 'five' is an elliptical way of saying 'five o'clock' and because the remark is in answer to a request for the time.

Now it is often claimed that 'plain' or 'everyday' talk is 'confused', 'unclear', 'vague' and similar apparently undesirable things, and it could well be claimed that our assertion that B means 'five o'clock' is just the sort of instance about which the complaint could be made. How can we be sure that B does mean that and not something quite different? Garfinkel conducted some now notorious 'experiments' with his students to illustrate some of the points he wanted to make and one such experiment was designed to deal with just this question. He asked his students to conduct themselves like those people who complain that ordinary language is vague, fuzzy, etc. and to treat the commonplace talk of other people as requiring clarification, explanation and increasingly precise expression. All remarks which could, in any way, be found less than absolutely clear were to be questioned. Following this policy should produce dialogues of the following sort (where E is the experimenter, S his subject – or perhaps, victim):

E. What time is it?

S. Five.

E: What do you mean, five: five o'clock, five eggs, five days?

S: Five o'clock.

E. What do you mean, five o'clock – exactly five o'clock, two minutes to five, five minutes past?

S: Five o'clock exactly.

E: What do you mean: five at night, five in the morning?

and so on and on . . .

The dialogue did not however develop in this way since those subjected to this kind of experiment rapidly lost patience with it and simply refused to continue taking part in it. They would *insist* that their interlocutor did know what they meant, that their speech was perfectly plain and did not require this kind of explanation. They regarded it as incumbent upon their hearer to see how they were talking, to recognize the sense of loose, idiomatic and other remarks. Seeing that some remark such as 'five' is offered as an answer to a question about the time is integral to seeing what it means.

For EM language and speech have assumed a centrality that they have not really been given by other sociological approaches and EM has stressed the extent to which the making of sense of the social world *is* the making of sense of other people's remarks since to an enormous extent our social life is the exchange of talk between people.

Sociologists often want to make a distinction between 'talking' on the one hand and 'acting' on the other, and they puzzle a great deal about the relation between these two: do the things people say have any connection with the things they do? EM seeks to avoid such puzzles by abolishing that distinction and by pointing out that talking *is* acting. Thus, for example, when B 'says' 'five' he also 'does' something, he answers a question. This policy, it is claimed, can be extended to all speech exchanges, and any utterance in a conversation can be looked upon as some action in a process of social interaction. Hence, to understand how members make sense of each other's doings is in substantial part to be engaged in understanding how they identify the actions that each other's utterances perform, for utterances can perform such actions as blessing, cursing, promising, warning, hinting, debating, denouncing, describing and so on *ad infinitum*.

In attempting to dissolve this distinction between 'saying' and 'doing' EM has employed an additional notion, that of 'reflexivity'. This means, essentially, that all descriptions are to be treated as part of the things they describe.

As we have said, sociologists are inclined to puzzle over the relation between words and deeds and they are particularly puzzled over what to do with the descriptions people make of the societies they live in: are the descriptions people give of life in their society true and accurate or must they be biased and partial? Questions of this kind give rise to considerable difficulty and once again EM has tried to bypass them. After all, to ask if members' descriptions of society do accurately and truthfully describe society is to talk as though there was, on the one hand, society, and on the other the descriptions which its members make of it. However, there is no need to think that way, for one can equally well think of society as something which describes itself: the descriptions people give are part of the society they are describing and it is our task, as sociologists, to see what those descriptions 'do' there. This may seem paradoxical but it is really to claim nothing out of the ordinary. In the course of giving a lecture, for example, it is possible at a certain point to say, 'In this lecture I have been outlining the principles of functionalist theory . . .', where that statement is made in the very course of the lecture it is describing. It is less interesting to start asking questions like, 'Is it true he has been talking about functionalist theory, etc.', than it is to see that making such a remark can 'do' such things as summarizing the lecture content, beginning to conclude the lecture and so on.

The policy that EM recommends, then, is that *all* remarks and descriptions be looked at as themselves parts of the society. Suggesting that we do so involves us in nothing more bizarre than is involved in, say, writing an editorial on a newspaper's policy which will be published in that same paper.

EM argues, then, that the production of social order is *identical* with the assignment of sense to events, and to understand how social order is produced is to identify the procedures or methods which people who live in society use to enable themselves to 'see' 'what is happening' or 'what he is saying to me': how do people go about the commonplace work of spotting doctors in hospital corridors, figuring out what their therapeutic adviser is telling them to do, knowing how to decide guilt and innocence when acting as a member of a jury and so on and on.

As will be apparent, the kinds of things that EM proposes to do are very far removed from the kinds of things which are envisaged as the proper tasks for sociology by those who take functionalist or conflict approaches, and EM has naturally enough been attacked by them for failing to deal with what they see to be the proper, important, real and significant tasks of sociology itself. Again, of course, the acceptance of such objections does require the acceptance of assumptions that functionalism or conflict theory have identified tasks which are more properly those of sociology than are those pursued by EM – and again, if one accepts the initial assumptions of EM then these objections do not have a great deal of force. The interactionist critique simply shifts the relevant assumptions and problems away from those which underlie functionalism and conflict theory.

Conclusion

We have presented the arguments in this chapter in a sequential form and in a roughly chronological order in that functionalism came first, conflict theory being the first reaction against it, symbolic interaction being roughly simultaneous with that, ethnomethodology coming along quite late in the argument. However, whilst that process is chronological we do not wish to imply that it is one of succession, with later perspectives eliminating their predecessors. This has not happened in sociology, and functionalism, conflict theory, symbolic interactionism and ethnomethodology are still busy disagreeing with one another.

We shall not attempt to pull together the various strands of our argument in order to provide a misleadingly systematic portrait of the state of sociological thought. We have tried, more than anything else, to show that sociology is currently diversified and divided and that it faces many problems. Our discussion of deviance, for example, was intended to show that great difficulties are involved in relating very general theories about the working of complex societies to the everyday activities and situations which constitute that society, but that the failure to make this connection weakens and undermines the usefulness of the theory. Sociologists have yet to solve the problem of relating their two levels of analysis together, but this is only one of many problems which theory faces. There are interesting problems to solve; much constructive work needs to be done.

Sociology thus has a great variety of tasks ahead of it, and difficult problems to resolve. Throughout this book, we have seen that there is an extraordinary diversity of approaches to the study of society, approaches which are not only different, but see themselves in rivalry to other 'schools'. Most sociologists are fairly eclectic; even though they try to systematize their thinking, they draw their ideas from a variety of sources. Some of these are, however, attempts to construct consistent 'world-views' or theoretical systems which lay claim to be *the* way of looking at the world. Some of these visions are political ideologies, such as Marxism, and hence carry a special attractiveness to some because they are backed by institutional loyalties and express special ideals; others are more academic 'schools' of thought.

The reader will, by now, be aware of the kinds of problems and approaches to these problems these schools of thought represent. He will probably find that mastering them is quite hard work, but then, thinking about anything problematic is not easy; that is why we have to do some work in order to become better at it. As for finding one's way between the rival schools, that, in the end, is the reader's own job. We cannot pontificate about what are ultimately matters of judgement, necessarily affected by the kinds of values one holds. We have tried, in this book, to give the reader basic tools with which to make his own judgements in a more informed and better equipped way, and have tried to draw a map for him. We hope that he has enjoyed his intellectual journey so far, and that he will continue to enjoy it, as we have enjoyed ours – or, more exactly, have enjoyed ours *so far*, for there is only one thing certain about intellectual journeys; that though we do get somewhere, the journey itself never ends.

References

Aberle, D., Cohen, A., Davis, A., Levy, M., and Sutton, F. (1950), 'The Functional Prerequisites of a Society', *Ethics*, Vol. LX, pp. 100–111.

Abu-Lughod, J. (1971), *Cairo: 1001 Years of the City Victorious*, Princeton University Press.

Adams, R. N. (1960), 'The Nature of the Family', in J. Goody (ed.), *Kinship*, Penguin, pp. 19–37.

Adams, W. (1968), *The Brain Drain*, Free Press.

Adelstein, D. (1969), 'Roots of the British Crisis', in A. Cockburn and R. Blackburn (eds.), *Student Power*, Penguin, pp. 59–81.

Advisory Commission on Intergovernmental Relations (1971), 'The Pattern of Urbanization', in L. K. Loewenstein (ed.), *Urban Studies: An Introductory Reader*, Free Press, pp. 3–40. (Reprinted from *Urban and Rural America: Policies for Future Growth*, a report by the Advisory Commission on Intergovernmental Relations, Washington, D.C., April, 1968.)

Alavi, H. (1972), 'The Post-colonial State', *New Left Review*, 74, pp. 59–81.

Althusser, L. (1971), *Lenin and Philosophy and Other Essays*, New Left Books.

Amin, S. (1974), *Accumulation on a World Scale: A Critique of the Theory of Underdevelopment*, Monthly Review Press.

Anderson, P. (1974a), *Lineages of the Absolutist State*, New Left Books.

Anderson, P. (1974b), *Passages from Antiquity to Feudalism*, New Left Books.

Arensberg, C. M., and Kimball, S. T. (1940), *Family and Community in Ireland*, Harvard University Press.

Asad, T. (ed.) (1975), *Anthropology and the Colonial Encounter*, Ithaca Press.

Atkinson, A. B. (1974), *Unequal Shares: Wealth in Britain*, Penguin.

Aubert, V. (1965), 'The Sociology of Sleep', in *The Hidden Society*, Bedminster.

Babchuk, N., and Thompson, R. (1970), 'The Voluntary Associations of Negroes', in F. Baali and J. F. Vandiver (eds.), *Urban Sociology: Contemporary Readings*, Appleton-Century-Crofts. (Reprinted from *American Sociological Review*, Vol. 27, No. 5, pp. 647–55, October, 1962.)

Baldamus, W. (1967), *Efficiency and Effort*, Tavistock.

Banks, J. A. (1954), *Prosperity and Parenthood: A Study of Family Planning among the Victorian Middle Classes*, Routledge & Kegan Paul.

Banton, M. (1965), *Roles*, Tavistock.

Banton, M. (1970), 'The Concept of Racism', in S. Zubaida (ed.), *Race and Racialism*, Tavistock, pp. 17–34.

Baran, P. A. (1957), *The Political Economy of Growth*, Monthly Review Press. (Penguin, 1973.)

Barker, D. (1972), 'The Confetti Ritual', *New Society*, June 1972, pp. 614–17.

Barker, D., and Allen, S. (eds.) (1976), *Sexual Divisions in Society: Process and Change*, Tavistock.

Barthes, R. (1973), *Mythologies*, Paladin.

Bartol, K. M., and Bartol, R. A. (1975), 'Women in Managerial and Professional Positions: the United States and the Soviet Union', *Industrial and Labor Relations Review*, Vol. 28, July, No. 4, pp. 524–34.

Beauvoir, S. de (1953), *The Second Sex*, Four Square. (Penguin, 1972.)

Bechhofer, F. (1974), 'Current Approaches to Empirical Research: Some Central Ideas', in J. Rex (ed.), *Approaches to Sociology*, Routledge & Kegan Paul, pp. 70–91.

Becker, H. S. (1963), *Outsiders: Studies in the Sociology of Deviance*, Free Press.

Becker, H. S., Geer, B., Hughes, E. C., and Strauss, A. L. (1963), *Boys in White*, Chicago University Press.

Becker, H. S., Geer, B., and Hughes, E. C. (1968), *Making the Grade*, Wiley.

Bell, C. (1968), *Middle Class Families*, Routledge & Kegan Paul.

Bendix, R. (1969), *Nation-Building and Citizenship: Studies of our Changing Social Order*, Anchor Books, Doubleday.

Benedict, R. (1934), *Patterns of Culture*, Houghton Mifflin.

Berger, J. (1975), *A Seventh Man*, Penguin.

Berger, P. (1963), *Invitation to Sociology*, Penguin.

Berger, P. (ed.) (1964), *The Human Shape of Work*, Macmillan.

Bernard, J. (1976), *The Future of Marriage*, Penguin.

Bernstein, B. (1962), 'Social Class, Linguistic Codes and Grammatical Elements', *Language and Speech*, 5, pp. 221–40.

Bernstein, B. (1965), 'A Socio-linguistic Approach to Social Learning', in J. Gould (ed.), *Penguin Survey of the Social Sciences*, Penguin.

Bernstein, B. (1971), *Class, Codes and Control, Vol. I.*, Routledge & Kegan Paul.

Bernstein, B. (1975), *Class, Codes and Control, Vol. 3: Towards a Theory of Educational Transmissions*, Routledge & Kegan Paul.

Beynon, H. (1973), *Working for Ford*, Allen Lane. (Penguin, 1973.)

Bittner, E. (1973), 'The Concept of Organization', in G. Salaman and K. Thompson (eds.), *People and Organizations*, Longman, pp. 264–76. (First published in *Social Research*, Vol. 32, 1965.)

Blackburn, R. (ed.) (1972), *Ideology in Social Science: Readings in Critical Social Theory*, Fontana.

Blau, P. M. (1963), *The Dynamics of Bureaucracy*, University of Chicago Press.

Blau, P. M. and Scott, W. R. (1963), *Formal Organizations: A Comparative Approach*, Routledge & Kegan Paul.

Blauner, R. (1964), *Alienation and Freedom: the Factory Worker and his Industry*, University of Chicago.

Boal, F. W. (1969), 'Territoriality in Belfast', *Irish Geography*, Vol. VI, pp. 30–50. (Reprinted in C. Bell and H. Newby (eds.), *The Sociology of Community: A Selection of Readings*, Frank Cass, 1974.)

Bodmer, W. F. (1972), 'Race and IQ: The Genetic Background', in K. Richardson and D. Spears (eds.), *Race, Culture and Intelligence*, Penguin.

Boissevain, J., and Friedl, J. (eds.) (1975), *Beyond the Community: Social Process in Europe*, Government Printing and Publishing Office, The Hague.

Bonilla, F. (1970), 'Rio's Favelas: The Rural Slum within the City', in W. Mangin (ed.), *Peasants in Cities: Readings in the Anthropology of Urbanization*, Houghton Mifflin. (First published 1961.)

Bose, A. (1973), *Studies in India's Urbanization 1901–1971*, McGraw Hill.

Bose, N. K. (1965), 'Calcutta: A Premature Metropolis', *Scientific American*, Vol. 213, No. 3. (Reprinted in *Cities*, Penguin, 1967.)

Bott, E. (1957), *Family and Social Network*, Tavistock.

Bottomore, T. B. (1954), 'Social Stratification in Voluntary Organizations', in D. V. Glass (ed.), *Social Mobility in Britain*, Routledge & Kegan Paul, pp. 349–82.

Bottomore, T. B. (1964), *Elites and Society*, Watts. (Penguin, 1966.)

Boudon, R. (1974), *Education, Opportunity, and Social Inequality*, Wiley.

Bowles, S., and Gintis, H. (1976), *Schooling in Capitalist America*, Routledge & Kegan Paul.

Briggs, A. (1960), 'The Language of Class in Early Nineteenth-century England', in *Essays in Labour History*, Macmillan.

Brody, H. (1974), *Inishkillane: Change and Decline in the West of Ireland*, Penguin.

Brown, R. (ed.) (1973), *Knowledge, Education and Cultural Change*, Tavistock.

Bruyn, S. T. (1966), *The Human Perspective in Sociology*, Prentice-Hall.

Burnham, J. (1941), *The Managerial Revolution*, Penguin.

Burns, T. (1955), 'The Reference of Conduct in Small Groups: Cliques and Cabals in Occupational Milieux', *Human Relations*, Vol. 8, pp. 467–86, Bobbs-Merrill.

Burns, T., and Stalker, G. M. (1961), *The Management of Innovation*, Tavistock.

Burt, Sir C. (1961), *The Backward Child*, University of London Press.

Butler, D., and Kavanagh, D. (1974), *The British General Election of February 1974*, Macmillan.

Caplow, T. (1954), *The Sociology of Work*, University of Minnesota Press.

Carden, M. L. (1969), *Oneida: Utopian Community to Modern Corporation*, Johns Hopkins Press.

Carmichael, S. (1968), 'Black Power', in D. Cooper (ed.), *The Dialectics of Liberation*, Penguin.

Carr-Saunders, A. M., Caradog-Jones, D., and Moser, C. A. (1958), *A Survey of Social Conditions in England and Wales*, Clarendon Press.

Castells, M. (1968), 'Y a-t-il une sociologie urbaine?' *Sociologie du Travail*, 1, pp. 72–90. (English translation in C. G. Pickvance (ed.), *Urban Sociology: Critical Essays*, Tavistock, 1976.)

Castles, F. G., Murray, D. J., and Potter, D. C. (eds.) (1971), *Decisions, Organizations and Society*, Penguin.

Castles, S., and Kosack, G. (1973), *Immigrant Workers and Class Structure in Western Europe*, Oxford University Press for the Institute of Race Relations.

Centre for Urban Studies (1964), *London: Aspects of Change*, MacGibbon & Kee.

Chapin, F. S. (1947), *Experimental Designs in Sociological Research*, Harper.

Chapman, J. M., and Chapman, B. (1957), *The Life and Times of Baron Haussman: Paris in the Second Empire*, Weidenfeld & Nicolson.

Chesneaux, J. (1971), *Secret Societies in China in the Nineteenth and Twentieth Centuries*, Heinemann.

Chombart de Lauwe, P. H., Antoine, S., Couvreur, L., and Gauthier, J. (1952), *Paris et l'agglomération Parisienne*, Presses Universitaires de France.

Cicourel, A. (1968), *The Social Organization of Juvenile Justice*, Wiley.

Cicourel, A. (1971), in J. D. Douglas (ed.), *Understanding Everyday Life*, Routledge & Kegan Paul.

Cicourel, A., *et al.* (1974), *Language Use and School Performance*, Academic Press.

Clark, B. R. (1960), *The Open Door College*, McGraw-Hill.

Cloward, R. A. (ed.) (1960), *Theoretical Studies in the Social Organization of the Prison*, Social Science Research Council, New York.

Cockburn, A., and Blackburn, R. (eds.) (1969), *Student Power: Problems, Diagnosis, Action*, Penguin.

Codere, H. (1966), *Fighting with Property*, American Ethnological Society Monograph No. 18, Augustin.

Cohen, S. (ed.) (1971), *Images of Deviance*, Penguin.

Cohen, S. (1972), *Folk Devils and Moral Panics*, MacGibbon & Kee.

Cohn, N. (1957), *The Pursuit of the Millennium*, Secker & Warburg. (Paladin, 1970.)

Cole, G. D. H. (1955), *Studies in Class Structure*, Routledge & Kegan Paul.

Coleman, J. S. (1964), *Introduction to Mathematical Sociology*, Collier-Macmillan.

Coleman, J. S. (1967), *The Adolescent Society*, Free Press.

Comaroff, J. (1976), 'A Bitter Pill to Swallow: Placebo Therapy in General Practice', *Sociological Review*, Vol. 24, pp. 79–96.

Cook-Gumperz, J. (1973), *Social Control and Socialization*, Routledge & Kegan Paul.

Cooke Taylor, W. (1968), *Notes of a Tour of the Manufacturing Districts of Lancashire*, Frank Cass. (First published 1842.)

Cooley, C. H. (1964), 'Primary Groups', in L. A. Coser and B. Rosenberg (eds.), *Sociological Theory*, Collier-Macmillan, pp. 311–14. (Reprinted from C. H. Cooley, *Social Organizations*, Scribner's, 1909, pp. 23–8.)

Coser, R. L. (ed.) (1974), *The Family: Its Structures and Functions*, 2nd edn, Macmillan.

Damer, S. (1974), 'Wine Alley: The Sociology of a Dreadful Enclosure', *Sociological Review*, Vol. 22, pp. 221–48.

Davin, D. (1976), *Woman-Work: Women and the Party in Revolutionary China*, Oxford University Press.

Davis, K. (1965), 'The Urbanization of the Human Population', *Scientific American*, Vol. 213, No. 3. (Reprinted in *Cities*, Penguin, 1967.)

Dawe, A. (1971), 'The Two Sociologies', in K. Thompson and J. Tunstall (eds.), *Sociological Perspectives*, Penguin.

Dennis, N. (1958), 'The Popularity of the Neighbourhood Community Idea', *Sociological Review*, Vol. VI, 2, pp. 191–206. (Reprinted in R. E. Pahl (ed.), *Readings in Urban Sociology*, Pergamon Press, 1968.)

Dennis, N., Henriques, F., and **Slaughter, C.** (1956), *Coal is Our Life*, Eyre & Spottiswoode.

Djilas, M. (1957), *The New Class*, Thames & Hudson.

Dobriner, W. (ed.) (1958), *The Suburban Community*, Putnam.

Douglas, J. D. (1967), *The Social Meanings of Suicide*, Princeton University Press.

Douglas, J. W. B. (1964), *The Home and the School*, MacGibbon & Kee.

Douglas, J. W. B., Ross, J. M., and **Simpson, H. R.** (1968), *All Our Future: A Longitudinal Study of Secondary Education*, Peter Davies.

Dubin, R. J. (1956), 'Industrial Workers' Worlds: A Study of the "Central Life Interests" of Industrial Workers', *Social Problems*, Vol. 3, pp. 131–42.

Durkheim, E. (1976), *The Elementary Forms of the Religious Life*, Allen & Unwin. (First published in French in 1912.)

Durkheim, E. (1964), *The Division of Labor in Society*, Free Press. (First published in French in 1893.)

Durkheim, E. (1970), *Suicide: A Study in Sociology*, Routledge & Kegan Paul. (First published in French in 1897.)

Durkheim, E. (1973), *Moral Education: A Study in the Theory and Application of the Sociology of Education*, Free Press. (First published in French in 1925).

Elkins, S. M. (1963), *Slavery: a Problem in American Institutional and Intellectual Life*, Grosse & Dunlap.

Elvin, M. (1973), *The Pattern of the Chinese Past*, Eyre Methuen.

Emmanuel, A. (1974), 'Myths of Development versus Myths of Undervelopment', *New Left Review*, 85, pp. 61–82.

Engels, F. (1975), 'The Condition of the Working-class in England', in *Marx–Engels on Britain*, Progress Publishers, Moscow. (First published in 1845.) The page references in Chapter 7 are to the Panther edn, 1974.

Epstein, A. L. (1967), 'Urbanization and Social Change in Africa', *Current Anthropology*, Vol. 8, No. 4, pp. 275–96. (Reprinted in G. Breese (ed.), *The City in Newly Developing Countries*, Prentice-Hall, 1969, pp. 246–84.)

Esland, G. M. (1971), 'Teaching and Learning as the Organization of Knowledge', in M. F. D. Young (ed.), *Knowledge and Control*, Open University, pp. 70–115.

Etzioni, A. (1961), *A Comparative Analysis of Complex Organizations*, Free Press.

Etzioni, A. (1964), *Modern Organizations*, Prentice-Hall.

Eysenck, H. J. (1971), *Race, Intelligence and Education*, Temple Smith.

Fanon, F. (1967), *The Wretched of the Earth*, Penguin.

Feldman, K. A., and Newcomb, T. M. (1969), *The Impact of College on Students*, Jossey-Bass.

Festinger, L., Riecken, H. W., and Schachter, S. (1966), *When Prophecy Fails*, Harper & Row.

Fine, B. (1958), 'Educational Problems in the Suburbs', in W. Dobriner (ed.), *The Suburban Community*, Putnam, pp. 317–25. (Reprinted from *The New York Times*, 30 January 1957.)

Finer, S. E. (1962), *The Man on Horseback: The Role of the Military in Politics*, Pall Mall.

Finnigan, R. (1970), 'The Kinship Ascription of Primitive Societies: Actuality or Myth?', *International Journal of Comparative Sociology*, Vol. 11, pp. 171–94.

Firestone, S. (1972), *The Dialectic of Sex*, Paladin.

Firth, R., Hubert, J., and Forge, A. (1969), *Families and Their Relatives*, Routledge & Kegan Paul.

Folger, J. K., and Nam, C. B. (1967), *Education of the American Population*, Bureau of the Census.

Fortes, M., and Evans-Pritchard, E. E. (1940), *African Political Systems*, Oxford University Press.

Foster, J. (1968), 'Nineteenth Century Towns: A Class Dimension', in H. J. Dyos (ed.), *The Study of Urban History*, Edward Arnold, pp. 281–99.

Foster, J. (1974), *Class Struggle and the Industrial Revolution: Early Industrial Capitalism in Three English Towns*, Weidenfeld & Nicolson.

Foster-Carter, A. (1974), 'Neo-Marxist Approaches to Development and Underdevelopment', in E. de Kadt and G. Williams (eds.), *Sociology and Development*, Tavistock, pp. 67–105.

Frank, A. G. (1967), *Capitalism and Underdevelopment in Latin America*, Monthly Review Press. (Penguin, 1971.)

Frank, A. G. (1969), 'The Sociology of Development and the Underdevelopment of Sociology', in *Latin America: Underdevelopment or Revolution?*, Monthly Review Press.

Frankenberg, R. (1957), *Village on the Border*, Cohen & West.

Fraser, R. (ed.) (1968), *Work: Twenty Personal Accounts*, Penguin.

Freire, P. (1972), *Pedagogy of the Oppressed*, Penguin.

Gans, H. J. (1962), *The Urban Villagers*, Free Press.

Gardner, J. (1971), 'Educated Youth and Urban-Rural Inequalities 1958–66', in J. W. Lewis, *The City in Communist China*, Stanford University Press, pp. 235–86.

Garfinkel, H. (1967), *Studies in Ethnomethodology*, Prentice-Hall.

Garnsey, E. (1975), 'Occupational Structure in Industrialized Societies: Some Notes on the Convergence Thesis in the Light of Soviet Experience', *Sociology*, Vol. 9, No. 3, September, pp. 437–58.

Gellner, E. (1964), *Thought and Change*, Weidenfeld & Nicolson.

Gerth, H. H., and Mills, C. W. (eds.) (1948), *From Max Weber, Essays in Sociology*, Routledge & Kegan Paul.

Gillespie, D. L. (1972), 'Who has the Power? The Marital Struggle', in H. P. Dreitzel (ed.), *Family, Marriage and the Struggle of the Sexes*, Recent Sociology No. 4, Macmillan.

Ginsburg, H. (1972), *The Myth of the Deprived Child: Poor Children's Intellect and Education*, Prentice-Hall.

Glaser, B. G., and Strauss, A. L. (1968), *The Discovery of Grounded Theory: Strategie s for Qualitative Research*, Weindenfeld & Nicolson.

Glass, D. V. (ed.) (1954), *Social Mobility in Britain*, Routledge & Kegan Paul.

Glass, R. (1962), 'Insiders-Outsiders: The Position of Minorities', *New Left Review*, 17, pp. 36–45.

Gluckman, M. (1956), *Custom and Conflict in Africa*, Blackwell.

Gluckman, M. (1963), 'Rituals of Rebellion in South-East Africa', in *Order and Rebellion in Tribal Africa*, Cohen & West.

Godfrey, M. (1970), 'The Brain Drain from Low-income Countries', *Journal of Development Studies*, Vol. 6 (April 1970), No. 3, pp. 235–47.

Goffman, E. (1961), 'On the Characteristics of Total Institutions', in *Asylums*, Doubleday, pp. 1–24. (Penguin, 1968.)

Goffman, E. (1969), *The Presentation of Self in Everyday Life*, Penguin.

Gold, D. (1964), 'The Janitor', in P. Berger (ed.), *The Human Shape of Work*, Macmillan.

Goldthorpe, J. E. (1975), *The Sociology of the Third World: Disparity and Involvement*, Cambridge University Press.

Goldthorpe, J. H. (1964), 'Social Stratification in Industrial Societies', in *The Development of Industrial Societies, Sociological Review*, Monograph No. 4, Keele, pp. 97–122.

Goldthorpe, J. H., Lockwood, D., Bechhofer, F., and Platt, J. (1969, 1970, 1971), *The Affluent Worker* 3 vols., Cambridge University Press.

Goode, W. J. (1960), 'A Deviant Case: Illegitimacy in the Caribbean', in R. L. Coser, *The Family: Its Structures and Functions*, 2nd edn, Macmillan, 1974, pp. 64–77.

Goode, W. J. (1970), *World Revolution and Family Patterns*, Free Press.

Goodman, P. (1962), *Compulsory Miseducation*, Penguin.

Goody, J. (ed.) (1971), *Kinship*, Penguin.

Gorer, G. (1955), *Exploring English Character*, Cresset Press.

Gough, E. K. (1960), 'Is the Family Universal? – the Nayar Case', in N. W. Bell and E. F. Vogel (eds.), *A Modern Introduction to the Family*, Free Press, pp. 80–96.

Gouldner, A. W. (1954), *Wildcat Strike: A Study in Worker-Management Relationship*, Routledge & Kegan Paul.

Gouldner, A. W. (1955), *Patterns of Industrial Bureaucracy*, Routledge & Kegan Paul.

Gouldner, A. W. (1970), *The Coming Crisis of Western Sociology*, Heinemann.

Gramsci, A. (1957), *The Modern Prince, and Other Writings*, Lawrence & Wishart.

Gramsci, A. (1971), *Selections from The Prison Notebooks*, Lawrence & Wishart.

Habenstein, H. (1962), 'The American Funeral Director', in A. M. Rose (ed.), *Human Behaviour and Social Processes*, Routledge & Kegan Paul.

Hambley, J. (1972), 'Diversity: A Developmental Perspective', in K. Richardson and D. Spears (eds.), *Race, Culture and Intelligence*, Penguin.

Hammersley, M. (1974), 'The Organisation of Pupil Participation', *Sociological Review*, Vol. 22, No. 3, pp. 355–68.

Hannerz, U. (1966), *Soulside*, Columbia University Press.

Harvey, D. (1973), *Social Justice and the City*, Edward Arnold.

Havighurst, R. J., and Neugarten, B. L. (1975), *Society and Education*, Allyn & Bacon.

Heffernan, E. (1972), *Making it in Prison: The Square, the Cool and the Life*, Wiley.

Hellman, E. (1948), *Rooiyard: A Sociological Survey of an Urban Native Slum Yard*, Rhodes-Livingstone Papers No. 13, Oxford University Press.

Hillery, G. A. (1955), 'Definitions of Community: Areas of Agreement', *Rural Sociology*, Vol. 20, pp. 111–23.

Hinton, W. (1966), *Fanshen: A Documentary of a Revolution in a Chinese Village*, Monthly Review Press. (Penguin, 1972.)

Hobbes, T. (1962), *Leviathan*, Collier Books. (First published 1651.) (Penguin, 1968.)

Hobsbawm, E. J. (1964), *The Age of Revolution, 1789–1848*, Mentor.

Hobsbawm, E. J. (1968), *Industry and Empire: An Economic History of Britain since 1750*, Weidenfeld & Nicolson. (Penguin, 1969.)

Hoggart, R. (1958), *The Uses of Literacy*, Penguin.

Holly, D. (1973), *Beyond Curriculum: Changing Secondary Education*, Hart-Davis, MacGibbon.

Holt, J. (1971), *The Underachieving School*, Penguin.

Hunter, A. (1974), *Symbolic Communities: The Persistence and Change of Chicago's Local Communities,* University of Chicago Press.

Hunter, A. J., and Suttles, G. D. (1972), 'The Expanding Community of Limited Liability', in G. D. Suttles, *The Social Construction of Communities*, University of Chicago Press, pp. 44–81.

Hyman, R. (1972), *Strikes*, Fontana.

Illich, I. (1971), *Deschooling Society*, Calder & Boyars. (Penguin, 1973.)

Illich, I. (1975), *Medical Nemesis*, Calder & Boyars.

Ionescu, G., and Gellner, E. (1969), *Populism: Its Meanings and National Characteristics*, Weidenfeld & Nicolson.

Irwin, J. (1970), *The Felon*, Prentice-Hall.

Jackson, B., and Marsden, D. (1962), *Education and the Working Class*, Routledge & Kegan Paul. (Penguin, 1966.)

Janowitz, M. (ed.) (1964), *The New Military: Changing Patterns of Organization*, Russell Sage.

Jen Ku-ping (1974), 'Third World: Great Motive Force in Advancing World History', *Peking Review*, No. 44, p. 6.

Jencks, C. (1972), *Inequality: a Reassessment of the Effect of Family and Schooling in America*, Harper & Row. (Penguin, 1973.)

Jenkins, R. (1970), *Exploitation: The World Power-structure and the Inequality of Nations*, Paladin.

Kadt, E. de, and **Williams, G.** (eds.) (1974), *Sociology and Development*, Tavistock.

Kapferer, B. (1969), 'Norms and the Manipulation of Relationships in a Work Context', in J. C. Mitchell (ed.), *Social Networks in Urban Situations*, Manchester University Press, pp. 181–244.

Kay-Shuttleworth, J. P. (1970), *The Moral and Physical Condition of the Working Classes employed in the Cotton Manufacture of Manchester*, new impression of 2nd edn, Frank Cass. (First published in 1832.)

Keddie, N. (1971), 'Classroom Knowledge', in M. F. D. Young (ed.), *Knowledge and Control*, Open University.

Kerner Commission (1968), *Report of the National Advisory Commission on Civil Disorders*, Bantam.

Kerr, C., Dunlop, J. T., Harbison, F. H., and **Myers, C. A.** (1962), *Industrialism and Industrial Man*, Heinemann.

Kincaid, J. C. (1973), *Poverty and Equality in Britain*, Penguin.

Klein, J. (1965), *Samples from English Cultures*, Routledge & Kegan Paul.

Klein, V. (1965), *Britain's Married Women Workers*, Routledge & Kegan Paul.

König, R. (1968), *The Community*, Routledge & Kegan Paul. (First published in German in 1958.)

Krapf-Askari, E. (1969), *Yoruba Towns and Cities: An Enquiry into the Nature of Urban Social Phenomena*, Clarendon Press.

Kuhn, T. S. (1962), *The Structure of Scientific Revolution*, University of Chicago Press.

Kuper, L. (1965), *An African Bourgeoisie*, Yale University Press.

Labov, W. (1972), *Language in the Inner City*, University of Pennsylvania Press.

Lacey, C. (1970), *Hightown Grammar*, Manchester University Press.

Laclau, E. (1971), 'Feudalism and Capitalism in Latin America', *New Left Review*, 67, pp. 19–38.

Laing, R. D., and **Esterson, A.** (1970), *Sanity, Madness and the Family*, Penguin.

Land, H. (1976), 'Women: Supporters or Supported?', in D. Barker and S. Allen (eds.), *Sexual Divisions in Society*, Tavistock, pp. 108–32.

Lane, D. (1976), *The Socialist Industrial State: Towards a Political Sociology of State Socialism*, Allen & Unwin.

Lane, T., and **Roberts, K.** (1971), *Strike at Pilkingtons*, Fontana.

Laslett, P. (1965), *The World We Have Lost*, Methuen.

Leach, E. (1968), 'Ignoble Savages', *New York Review of Books*, Vol. 10, No. 8, pp. 24–9.

Leete, R. (1976), 'Marriage and Divorce', *Population Trends*, 3, H.M.S.O., pp. 3–8.

Lemert, E. M. (1967), *Human Deviance, Social Problems and Social Control*, Prentice-Hall.

Lenin, V. I. (1975), *Imperialism, the Highest Stage of Capitalism*, Peking, Foreign Languages Press. (First published in Russian in 1916.)

Lewis, J. W. (1971), *The City in Communist China*, Stanford University Press.

Lewis, O. (1951), *Life in a Mexican Village: Tepoztlán Restudied*, University of Illinois Press.

Leys, C. (1975), *Underdevelopment in Kenya: The Political Economy of Neo-colonialism, 1964–1971*, Heinemann.

Liebow, E. (1967), *Tally's Corner*, Little, Brown.

Linton, R. (1963), *The Study of Man*, Appleton-Century-Crofts.

Lipset, S. M. (1960), *Political Man*, Heinemann.

Lipset, S. M., and **Bendix, R.** (1959), *Social Mobility in Industrial Society*, Heinemann.

Lipset, S. M., and **Smelser, N. J.** (eds.) (1960), *Sociology: The Progress of a Decade*, Prentice-Hall.

Littlejohn, J. (1963), *Westrigg: The Sociology of a Cheviot Parish*, Routledge & Kegan Paul.

Lockwood, D. (1958), *The Blackcoated Worker*, Allen & Unwin.

Long. N. (1961), 'The Local Community as an Ecology of Games', in O. P. Williams and C. Press (eds.), *Democracy in Urban America*, University of Chicago Press. (First published in the *American Journal of Sociology*, Vol. 64, 1958.)

Lupton, T. (1963), *On the Shop Floor: Two Studies in Workshop Organization and Output*, Pergamon Press.

Lupton, T., and **Wilson, C. S.** (1959), 'The Social Background and Connexions of "Top Decision Makers"', *Manchester School of Economic and Social Studies*, Vol. 27, pp. 30–52.

McClelland, D. (1961), *The Achieving Society*, Princeton University Press.

McGregor, O. R. (1957), *Divorce in England*, Heinemann.

McHugh, P. (1968), *Defining the Situation: The Organization of Meaning in Social Interaction*, Bobbs-Merrill.

MacIver, R. M. (1937), *Society*, Macmillan. (Also in the revised edition of R. M. MacIver and C. H. Page, *Society*, Macmillan, 1961.)

McKinlay, J. B. (ed.) (1975), *Processing People: Cases in Organizational Behaviour*, Holt, Rinehart & Winston.

McMichael, P., Petras, J., and **Rhodes, R.** (1974), 'Imperialism and the Contradictions of Development', *New Left Review*, 85, pp. 83–104.

McPherson, A. (1973), 'Selections and Survivals: A Sociology of the Ancient Scottish Universities', in R. Brown (ed.), *Knowledge, Education and Cultural Change*, Tavistock.

Macpherson, B. (1970), *The Political Theory of Possessive Individualism: Hobbes to Locke*, Oxford University Press.

Malinowski, B. (1922), *Argonauts of the Western Pacific*, Routledge & Kegan Paul.

Malinowski, B. (1930), 'Parenthood, the Basis of Social Structure', in R. L. Coser (ed.), *The Family: Its Structures and Functions*, 2nd edn, Macmillan, 1974, pp. 51–63.

Mangin, W. (ed.) (1970), *Peasants in Cities: Readings in the Anthropology of Urbanization*, Houghton Mifflin.

Mannheim, K. (1948), *Ideology and Utopia*, Routledge & Kegan Paul.

Marcus, S. (1967), *The Other Victorians: A Study of Sexuality and Pornography in Mid-nineteenth Century England*, Weidenfeld & Nicolson.

Marcuse, H. (1968), *One-dimensional Man: The Ideology of Industrial Society*, Sphere.

Markley, O. W. (1967), 'A Simulation of the S I V A Model of Organisational Behaviour', *American Journal of Sociology*, Vol. 73, pp. 345–69.

Marshall, T. H. (1950), *Citizenship and Social Class*, Cambridge University Press.

Martin, F. M. (1954a), 'Some Subjective Aspects of Social Stratification', in D. V. Glass (ed.), *Social Mobility in Britain*, Routledge & Kegan Paul, pp. 57–75.

Martin, F. M. (1954b), 'An Inquiry into Parents' Preferences in Secondary Education', in D. V. Glass (ed.), *Social Mobility in Britain*, Routledge & Kegan Paul.

Marx, K. (1942), *Capital: a Critique of Political Economy*, Vol. 1, Everyman. (First published in 1867.) (Penguin, 1976.)

Marx, K., and **Engels, F.** (1975), 'The Future Results of British Rule in India', in *Marx and Engels on Britain*, Progress Publishers, Moscow, pp. 385–92.

Mayeske, G. W., and **Beaton, A. E., Jr.** (1975), *Special Studies of our Nation's Students*, U.S. Department of Health, Education and Welfare.

Mayo, E. (1949), *The Social Problems of an Industrial Civilisation*, Routledge & Kegan Paul.

Mellor, R. (1975), 'Urban Sociology in an Urbanized Society', *British Journal of Sociology*, Vol. XXVI, No. 3, pp. 276–93.

Mencher, J. P. (1965), 'The Nayars of South Malabar', in M. F. Nimkoff (ed.), *Comparative Family Systems*, Houghton Mifflin, pp. 163–91.

Merton, R. (1968), *Social Theory and Social Structure*, Free Press.

Merton, R. K., Gray, A. P., Hockey, B., and **Selvin, H. C.** (eds.) (1952), *Reader in Bureaucracy*, Free Press.

Merton, R. K., Reader, G. G., and **Kendall, P. L.** (eds.) (1957), *The Student Physician*, Harvard University Press.

Middleton, C. (1974), 'Sexual Inequality and Stratification Theory', in F. Parkin (ed.), *The Social Analysis of Class Structure*, Tavistock, pp. 179–203.

Mills, C. Wright (1956), *The Power Elite*, Oxford University Press.

Mills, C. Wright (1959), *The Sociological Imagination*, Oxford University Press. (Penguin, 1970.)

Miner, H. (1963), *St Denis – A French-Canadian Parish*, Phoenix. (First published in 1939.)
Mitchell, J. C. (1956), *The Yao Village*, Manchester University Press.
Mitchell J. C. (1966), 'Theoretical Orientations in African Urban Studies', in M. Banton (ed.), *The Social Anthropology of Complex Societies*, A.S.A. Monograph No. 4, Tavistock.
Mitchell, J. J. (1971), *Woman's Estate*, Penguin.
Mitford, M. R. (1951), *Our Village*, Dent. (First published in 1824.)
Moore, F. Barrington (1973), *The Social Origins of Dictatorship and Democracy*, Penguin.
Moser, C. A., and **Kalton, G.** (1971), *Survey Methods in Social Investigation* (2nd edn), Heinemann.
Murdock, G. P. (1949), *Social Structure*, Macmillan.
Musil, J. (1968), 'The Development of Prague's Ecological Structure', in R. E. Pahl (ed.), *Readings in Urban Sociology*, Pergamon Press.

Nairn, T. (1975), 'Marxism and the Modern Janus', *New Left Review*, 94, pp. 3–29.
Newsom, J., and **Newsom, E.** (1963), *Patterns of Infant Care in an Urban Community*, Penguin.
Nichols, T. (1969), *Ownership, Control and Ideology*, Allen & Unwin.
Nisbet, R. A. (1962), *Community and Power*, Oxford University Press. (First published in 1953 under the title *The Quest for Community*.)
Nisbet, R. A. (1970), *The Sociological Tradition*, Heinemann.

Oakley, A. (1975), *Sociology of Housework*, Martin Robertson.
Olives, J. (1972), 'La lutte contre la rénovation urbaine dans le quartier de "La Cité d'Aliarte" (Paris)', *Espaces et Sociétés*, 6–7, 9–27. (English translation in C. G. Pickvance (ed.), *Urban Sociology: Critical Essays*, Tavistock, 1976.)
Onselen, C. van (1976), *Chibaro: African mine labour in Southern Rhodesia 1900–1933*, Pluto Press.
Opie I., and **Opie, P.** (1959), *The Lore and Language of Schoolchildren*, Oxford University Press.

Pahl, R. E. (ed.) (1968), *Readings in Urban Sociology*, Pergamon Press.
Pahl, R. E. (1975), *Whose City? And Further Essays on Urban Society*, Penguin.
Pahl, J. M., and **Pahl, R. E.** (1971), *Managers and Their Wives*, Penguin.
Pareto, V. (1966), S. E. Finer (ed.), *Sociological Writings*, Pall Mall.
Park, R. E. (1916), 'The City: Suggestions for the Investigation of Human Behaviour in the Urban Environment', *American Journal of Sociology*, Vol. XX. (Reprinted in P. K. Hatt and A. J. Reiss (eds.) (1951), *Reader in Urban Sociology*, Free Press, pp. 2–32; also in R. Sennett (ed.) (1969), *Classic Essays on the Culture of Cities*, Appleton-Century-Crofts, pp. 91–130.)

578   References

Parkin, F. (1972), *Class Inequality and Political Order: Social Stratification in Capitalist and Socialist Societies*, Paladin.

Parkin, F. (1974), 'Strategies of Social Closure in Class Formation', in F. Parkin (ed.), *The Social Analysis of Class Structure*, Tavistock, pp. 1–18.

Parsons, T. (1949), *The Structure of Social Action: A Study in Social Theory with Special Reference to a Group of Recent European Writers*, Free Press. (First published in 1937.)

Parsons, T. (1962), 'The School Class as a Social System: Some of its Functions in American Society', in A. H. Halsey, J. Floud and C. A. Anderson (eds.), *Education, Economy and Society*, Free Press.

Parsons, T. (1964), *Essays in Sociological Theory,* revised edn, Free Press.

Parsons, T., and **Bales, R. F.** (1956), *Family, Socialisation and Interaction Process,* Routledge & Kegan Paul.

Pearse, A. (1973), 'Structural Problems of Education Systems in Latin America', in R. Brown (ed.), *Knowledge, Education, and Cultural Change*, Tavistock.

Perrow, C. (1970), *Organizational Analysis: A Sociological View*, Tavistock.

Pickvance, C. G. (ed.) (1976), *Urban Sociology: Critical Essays*, Tavistock.

Pizzey, E. (1974), *Scream Quietly or the Neighbours Will Hear*, Penguin.

Pons, V. (1956), 'The Changing Significance of Ethnic Affiliation and of Westernization in the African Settlement Patterns in Stanleyville (Belgian Congo)', in D. Forde (ed.), *Social Implications of Industrialization in Africa South of the Sahara*, UNESCO, pp. 638–69.

Pons, V. (1961), 'Two Small Groups in Avenue 21: Some Aspects of the System of Social Relations in a Remote Corner of Stanleyville, Belgian Congo', in A. Southall (ed.), *Social Change in Modern Africa*, Oxford University Press. (Reprinted 1969.)

Pons, V. (1969), *Stanleyville: An African Urban Community Under Belgian Administration*, Oxford University Press.

Presthus, R. (1962), *The Organizational Society*, Knofp.

Pugh, D. S., Hickson, D. J., and **Hinings, C. R.** (1964), *Writers on Organizations*, Hutchinson. (Penguin, 1971.)

Rapoport, R., and **Rapoport, R.** (1971), *Dual-career Families*, Penguin.

Redfield, R. (1930), *Tepoztlán: A Mexican Village, A Study of Folk Life*, University of Chicago Press.

Redfield, R. (1947), 'The Folk Society', *The American Journal of Sociology*, Vol. 52, No. 4.

Redfield, R. (1955), *The Little Community: Viewpoints for the Study of a Human Whole*, University of Chicago Press.

Reiss, I. L. (1967), *The Social Context of Premarital Sexual Permissiveness*, Holt, Rinehart & Winston.

Reissman, L. (1964), *The Urban Process*, Free Press.

Reitzes, D. (1960), 'The Role of Organizational Structures: Union Versus Neighborhood in a Tension Situation', in S. M. Lipset and N. J. Smelser (eds.), *Sociology: The Progress of a Decade*, Prentice-Hall, pp. 516–21.

Rex, J. (1961), *Key Problems in Sociological Theory*, Routledge & Kegan Paul.

Rex, J. (1970), 'The Concept of Race in Sociological Theory', in S. Zubaida (ed.), *Race and Racialism*, Tavistock, pp. 35–55.

Rex, J. (ed.) (1974), *Approaches to Sociology: An Introduction to Major Trends in British Sociology*, Routledge & Kegan Paul.

Rex, J., and Moore, R. (1967), *Race, Community and Conflict*, Oxford University Press for the Institute of Race Relations.

Richardson, K., and Spears, D. (eds.) (1972), *Race, Culture and Intelligence*, Penguin.

Richman, J. (1972), 'The Motor Car and the Territorial Aggression Thesis: Some Aspects of the Sociology of the Street', *Sociological Review*, Vol. 20, pp. 5–27.

Riesman, D., Glazer, N., and Denney, R. (1950), *The Lonely Crowd: A Study of the Changing American Character*, Doubleday.

Rist, R. (1970), 'Student Social Class and Teacher Expectations: the Self-fulfilling Prophecy', *Harvard Educational Review*, Vol. 40, No. 3, August 1970.

Roberts, B. R. (1973a), 'Education, Urbanization and Social Change', in R. Brown (ed.), *Knowledge, Education, and Cultural Change*, Tavistock.

Roberts, B. R. (1973b), *Organizing Strangers: Poor Families in Guatemala City*, University of Texas Press.

Roberts, R. (1971), *The Classic Slum*, Penguin.

Roethlisberger, F. J., and Dickson, W. J. (1964), *Management and the Worker*, Wiley. (First published in 1939.)

Rose, S. (1972), 'Environmental Effects on Brain and Behaviour', in K. Richardson and D. Spears (eds.), *Race, Culture and Intelligence*, Penguin.

Rosen, H. (1972), *Language and Class: A Critical Look at the Theories of Basil Bernstein*, Falling Wall Press.

Rostow, W. W. (1960), *The Stages of Economic Growth: a Non-Communist Manifesto*, Cambridge University Press.

Rudé, G. (1959), *The Crowd in the French Revolution*, Clarendon Press.

Runciman, W. G. (1966), *Relative Deprivation and Social Justice*, Routledge & Kegan Paul.

Sachs, H. (1972), 'Notes on Police Assessment of Moral Character', in David Sudnow (ed.), *Studies in Social Interaction*, Free Press.

Sahlins, M. (1972), *Stone Age Economics*, Aldine.

Salaman, G., and Thompson, K. (eds.) (1973), *People and Organizations,* Longman.

Salisbury, R. F. (1962), *Structures of Custodial Care*, University of California Press.

Schnore, L. F. (1958), 'The Growth of Metropolitan Suburbs', in W. Dobriner (ed.), *The Suburban Community*, Putnam, pp. 26–44. (Reprinted from *American Sociological Review*, Vol. 22, April 1957, pp. 165–73.)

Schnore, L. F. (1967), 'Community', in N. J. Smelser (ed.), *Sociology: An Introduction*, Wiley, pp. 79–150.

Schofield, M. (1968), *The Sexual Behaviour of Young People*, Penguin.

Schram, S. (ed.) (1974), *Mao Tse-tung Unrehearsed: Talks and Letters, 1956–71*, Penguin.

Schwartz, B. (1971), 'Pre-institutional vs. Situational Influence in a Correctional Community', in *The Journal of Criminal Law, Criminology and Police Science*, Vol. 62, pp. 532–42.

Secombe, W. (1974), 'The Housewife and Her Labour under Capitalism', *New Left Review*, 83, pp. 3–24.

Seeley, J. R., Sim, R. A., and Loosley, E. W. (1963), *Crestwood Heights: A Study of the Culture of Suburban Life*, Wiley.

Sen, S. N. (1960), *The City of Calcutta: A Socioeconomic Survey, 1954–55 to 1957–58*, Bookland, Calcutta.

Sennett, R. (ed.) (1969), *Classic Essays on the Culture of Cities*, Appleton-Century-Crofts.

Sexton, P. (1961), *Education and Income: Inequalities of Opportunity in Our Public Schools*, Viking Press.

Shanin, T. (1971), 'The Peasantry as a Political Factor', in T. Shanin (ed.), *Peasants and Peasant Societies*, Penguin.

Shils, E. (1972), *The Intellectuals and the Powers and Other Essays, Vol. I, Selected Papers*, University of Chicago Press.

Shils, E., and Young, M. (1953), 'The Meaning of the Coronation', *Sociological Review*, Vol. 1, pp. 68–81. (Reprinted in S. M. Lipset and N. J. Smelser (eds.), *Sociology: The Progress of a Decade*, Prentice-Hall, 1961.)

Simmel, G. (1950), *The Sociology of Georg Simmel*, ed. K. A. Wolff, Free Press.

Sjöberg, G. (1960), *The Preindustrial City: Past and Present*, Free Press.

Skolnick, A., and Skolnick, J. H. (eds.) (1974), *Intimacy, Family and Society*, Little, Brown.

Smelser, N. J. (1959), *Social Change in the Industrial Revolution: An Application of Theory to the Lancashire Cotton Industry 1770–1840*, Routledge & Kegan Paul.

Smith, A. (1950), *An Inquiry into the Nature and Causes of the Wealth of Nations*, Dent, Everyman's Library. (First published 1776–8.) (Penguin, 1969.)

Smith, A. D. (1971), *Theories of Nationalism*, Duckworth.

Sorokin, P. (1955), Foreword to F. Tönnies, *Community and Association*, Routledge & Kegan Paul.

Stacey, M. (1960), *Tradition and Change: A Study of Banbury*, Oxford University Press.

Stacey, M. (1969), 'Family and Household', in M. Stacey (ed.), *Comparability in Social Research*, S.S.R.C./B.S.A., pp. 32–64.

Stafford-Clark, D. (1952), *Psychiatry Today*, Penguin.

Stambouli, F., and Zghal, A. (1976), 'Urban Life in Pre-colonial North Africa', *The British Journal of Sociology*, Vol. XXVII, No. 1.

Staples, R. (1974), 'Towards a Sociology of the Black Family', in A. Skolnick and J. H. Skolnick (eds.), *Intimacy, Family and Society*, Little, Brown, pp. 536–64.

Stedman Jones, G. (1971), *Outcast London: A study in the Relationship Between Classes in Victorian Society*, Oxford University. (Penguin, 1976.)

Stein, M. R. (1960), *The Eclipse of Community*, Princeton University Press.

Storr, A. (1968), *Human Aggression*, Allen Lane The Penguin Press. (Penguin, 1970.)

Strauss, A. (1961), *Images of the American City*, Free Press.

Strauss, A. (ed.) (1964), *Geroge Herbert Mead on Social Psychology*, University of Chicago Press.

Strauss, A., *et al.* (1964), *Psychiatric Institutions and Ideologies*, Free Press.

Strauss, A. (ed.) (1968), *The American City: Sourcebook of Urban Imagery*, Allen Lane The Penguin Press.

Strauss, A., Schatzman, L., Bucher, R., Ehrlich, D., and **Sabshin, M.** (1964), *Psychiatric Ideologies and Institutions*, Free Press.

Sudnow, D. (1965), 'Normal Crimes: Sociological Features of the Penal Codes in a Public Defender's Office', *Social Problems*, 12, pp. 255–72.

Sudnow, D. (1967), *Passing On*, Prentice-Hall.

Suttles, G. D. (1968), *The Social Order of the Slum: Ethnicity and Territory in the Inner City*, University of Chicago.

Swift, D. (1965), 'Educational Psychology, Sociology and the Environment: A Controversy at Cross-purposes', *British Journal of Sociology*, Vol. 16, 1965, No. 4, pp. 336–41.

Swift, D. (1972), 'What is Environment?' in K. Richardson and D. Spears (eds.), *Race, Culture and Intelligence*, Penguin.

Sykes, G. (1958), *The Society of Captives*, Princeton University Press.

Sykes, G., and **Messinger, S.** (1960), 'The Inmate Social System', in R. Cloward (ed.), *Theoretical Studies in Social Organization of the Prison*, Social Science Research Council, New York, pp. 5–19.

Taylor, L., and **Walton, P.** (1971), 'Industrial Sabotage: Motives and Meanings', in S. Cohen (ed.), *Images of Deviance*, Penguin.

Thompson, K. (1975), 'Religious Organizations', in J. B. McKinlay (ed.), *Processing People: Cases in Organizational Behaviour*, Holt, Rinehart & Winston, pp. 1–40.

Thompson, K., and **Tunstall, J.** (1971), *Sociological Perspectives*, Penguin.

Titmuss, R. M. (1958), *Essays on the 'Welfare State'*, Allen & Unwin.

Titmuss, R. M. (1962), *Income Distribution and Social Change*, Allen & Unwin.

Tönnies, F. (1955), *Community and Association*, Routledge & Kegan Paul. (First published in German in 1887.)

Trotsky, Leon (1974), *The Revolution Betrayed: What is the Soviet Union and where is it going?*, New Park Publications. (First published in 1937.)

Tugendhat, C. (1973), *The Multinationals*, Penguin.

Turner, R. H. (1962), 'Modes of Social Ascent through Education: Sponsored and Contest Mobility', in A. H. Halsey, J. Floud and C. A. Anderson (eds.), *Education, Economy and Society*, Free Press.

Turner, V. W. (1957), *Schism and Continuity in an African Society*, Manchester University Press.

Wakeford, J. (1969), *The Cloistered Elite*, Macmillan.
Wallerstein, I. (1974), *The Modern World-System: capitalist agriculture and the origins of the European world-economy in the sixteenth century*, Academic Press.
Warner, W. L. (1959), *The Living and the Dead: A Study of the Symbolic Life of Americans,* Yale University Press.
Warner, W. L., and Lunt, P. S. (1941), *The Social Life of a Modern Community*, Yale University Press.
Warner, W. L., and Lunt, P. S. (1947), *The Status System of a Modern Community*, Yale University Press.
Warner, W. L., and Low, J. G. (1947), *The Social System of the Modern Factory*, Yale University Press.
Warner, W. L., Meeker, M., and Eells, K. (1949), *Social Class in America*, Harper & Row.
Warner, W. L., and Srole, L. (1945), *The Social System of American Ethnic Groups*, Yale University Press.
Warren, B. (1973), 'Myths of Underdevelopment', *New Left Review*, 81, pp. 3–44.
Watson, J. (1968), *The Double Helix*, Weidenfeld & Nicolson. (Penguin, 1970.)
Webber, M. M., Dyckman, J. W., Foley, D. L., Guttenberg, A. Z., Wheaton, W. L. C., and Wurster, C. B. (1964), *Explorations into Urban Structure*, University of Pennsylvania Press.
Weber, M. (1952), *The Protestant Ethic and the Spirit of Capitalism*, Allen & Unwin. (First published in German in 1904/5.)
Weber, M. (1960), *The City*, Heinemann.
Weber, M. (1963), *The Sociology of Religion*, Methuen. (First published in German in 1922.)
Weber, M. (1964), *The Theory of Social and Economic Organization*, Free Press. (First published in German in 1925.)
Weinberg, I. (1967), *The English Public Schools: The Sociology of Elite Education*, Atherton Press.
Wertheim, W. F. (1974), *Evolution and Revolution: The Rising Waves of Emancipation*, Penguin.
Westergaard, J. H. (1972), 'Sociology: the Myth of Classlessness', in R. Blackburn (ed.), *Ideology in Social Science*, Fontana, pp. 119–63.
Westergaard, J. H., and Resler, H. (1977), *Class in a Capitalist Society: a study of contemporary Britian*, Penguin.
Whorf, B. L. (1964), 'The Relation of Habitual Thought and Behaviour to Language', in J. B. Carrol (ed.), *Language, Thought and Reality: The Selected Writings of Benjamin Lee Whorf*, M.I.T. Press. (First published in 1941.)
Whyte, W. F. (1955), *Street Corner Society: The Social Structure of an Italian Slum*, University of Chicago Press. (First published in 1943.)
Whyte, W. H., Jr (1957), *The Organization Man*, Cape. (Penguin, 1960.)

Williams, R. (1968), *Culture and Society* 1780–1950, Penguin.
Williams, R. (1976), *Keywords*, Fontana.
Wirth, L. (1963), 'Urbanism as a Way of Life', in P. K. Hatt and A. J. Reiss (eds.), *Cities in Society*, Free Press, pp. 46–63. (First published in *American Journal of Sociology*, 1938, Vol. 44.)
Wolf, E. (1966), *Peasants*, Prentice-Hall.
Wolf, E. (1971), *Peasant Wars of the Twentieth Century*, Harper & Row.
Wolpe, H. (1970), 'Industrialism and Race in South Africa', in S. Zubaida (ed.), *Race and Racialism*, Tavistock, pp. 151–79.
Woodward, J. (1965), *Industrial Organization: Theory and Practice*, Oxford University Press.
Worsley, P. (1967), *The Third World*, Weidenfeld & Nicolson.
Worsley, P. (1970), *The Trumpet Shall Sound: A Study of 'Cargo' Cults in Melanesia*, Paladin. (First published in 1957.)
Worsley, P. (1975), *Inside China*, Allen Lane.
Worsley, P. (ed.) (1978), *Modern Sociology: Introductory Reading*, Penguin.

Young, M. (1961), *The Rise of the Meritocracy 1870–2033*, Penguin.
Young, M., and **Willmott, P.** (1957a), *Family and Kinship in East London*, Routledge & Kegan Paul. (Penguin, 1962.)
Young, M., and **Willmott, P.** (1957b), 'Social Grading by Manual Workers', *British Journal of Sociology*, Vol. 7, pp. 337–45.
Young, M., and **Willmott, P.** (1975), *The Symmetrical Family*, Penguin.
Young, M. F. D. (ed.) (1971), *Knowledge and Control*, Open University.

Zubaida, S. (ed.) (1970), *Race and Racialism*, Tavistock.

Further Reading

Chapter 1

Two reference books are invaluable: Raymond Williams's *Keywords* (Fontana, 1976) and J. Gould and William L. Kolb (eds.), *A Dictionary of the Social Sciences* (Tavistock, 1964). Philip Abrams's *The Origins of British Sociology, 1834–1914* (University of Chicago Press, 1972) provides a fascinating account of the emergence of sociology in one country, while Thomas Kuhn's *The Structure of Scientific Revolution* (University of Chicago Press, 1962) develops a general theory of how both gradual and radical change occur in science, social or natural.

C. Wright Mills's *The Sociological Imagination* (Penguin, 1970) remains the most stimulating general discussion of the moral implications of the social sciences and the uses made of them by practical policy-makers. But he also sees sociology as a critical discipline, as does Peter Berger, whose *Invitation to Sociology* (Penguin, 1966) is a lucid and thought-provoking discussion of the effects of sociological analysis upon our thinking.

Lewis A. Coser and Bernard Rosenberg's *Sociological Theory* (Macmillan, 1969) is the best general collection of key passages from classic writings in sociological theory. Philip E. Hammond's *Sociologists at Work* (Basic Books, 1968) shows that sociologists' theories about the methods they use do not always square with their actual practice. In *The Discovery of Grounded Theory* (Weidenfeld & Nicolson, 1968), Barney Glaser and Anselm L. Strauss suggest that theory is best developed in the process of doing research, anyway.

Chapter 2

A detailed study of the logic of inquiry would lead us eventually to fundamental problems of philosophy or to complex mathematical statistics. For the purposes of the ordinary student of sociology, however, the problems of epistemology set out by Ernest Nagel in *The Structure of Science* (Routledge, 1961), by Abraham Kaplan in *The Conduct of Inquiry* (Chandler, 1964), by Peter Winch in *The Idea of Social Science* (Routledge, 1958) or by Quentin Gibson in *The Logic of Social Enquiry* (Routledge, 1960) are probably adequate. The more advanced reader will find Cicourel's *Method and Measurement in Sociology* (Free Press, 1964) a useful examination of the epistemological foundations of common research procedures. This critique is taken a stage further in Derek L. Phillips's *Abandoning Method* (Jossey-Bass, 1973).

There are several books dealing with research methods in general. Margaret

Stacey's *Methods of Social Research* (Pergamon, 1969) is a clear and relatively simple account of the basic procedures suitable for a British public. W. Goode and P. Hatt's *Methods in Social Research* (McGraw-Hill, 1952) has been a stand-by for many years. J. Madge's *The Tools of Social Science*, (Longmans, Green, 1953) provides a British equivalent. The book by C. Selltiz, M. Jahoda, M. Deutsch and S. W. Cook, *Research Methods in Social Relations* (Methuen, 1965) is probably the most comprehensive of this sort of book. The book edited by Norman K. Denzin, *Sociological Methods: A Source Book* (Butterworth, 1970) provides a comprehensive set of more advanced readings on methods in general.

As far as statistical procedures are concerned there are many elementary textbooks for the beginners in general. The books by Hubert Blalock, *Social Statistics* (McGraw-Hill, 1960), however, and the older one by Margaret Hagood and Daniel Price, *Statistics for Sociologists* (Holt, Rinehart & Winston, 1952), address themselves specifically to the needs of sociologists. James A. Davis's *Elementary Survey Analysis* (Prentice-Hall, 1971) provides a clear readable account of methods of analysing several variables simultaneously.

A more advanced consideration of research procedures from the 'subjectivist' perspective is provided by Severyn T. Bruyn in *The Human Perspective in Sociology* (Prentice-Hall, 1966). The book edited by William J. Filstead, *Qualitative Methodology* (Markham, 1970), provides a wide-ranging set of readings relating to these procedures.

Chapter 3

For a wide-ranging historical perspective on the development of the different countries of Europe, leading up to the emergence of modern capitalism, Perry Anderson's two books, *Passages from Antiquity to Feudalism* and *Lineages of the Absolutist State* (New Left Books, 1974) offer challenging interpretations that are both scholarly and readable.

Recent development studies in sociology have been so much a 'debate with Gunder Frank' that it is worthwhile reading the key writings that sparked off that debate: 'The Sociology of Development and the Under-Development of Sociology' (in A. G. Frank, *Latin America: Underdevelopment or Revolution*, Monthly Review Press, 1969), and his series of case-studies of various Latin American countries, *Capitalism and Underdevelopment in Latin America* (Penguin, 1971).

The impact of these writings is apparent in *Sociology and Development* (eds. Gavin Williams and Emmanuel de Kadt, Tavistock, 1974), particularly A. Foster-Carter's essay on 'Neo-Marxist Approaches to Development and Underdevelopment'.

For a non-Marxist approach which contains much valuable material, see J. E. Glodthorpe, *The Sociology of the Third World* (Cambridge University Press, 1975).

Older, but still influential approaches are represented by W. W. Rostow's evolutionist *The Stages of Economic Growth* (Cambridge University Press, 1960), and Reinhard Bendix's Weberian *Nation-Building and Citizenship* (Anchor Books, 1969).

Robin Jenkins's *Exploitation* (Paladin, 1970) and Pierre Jalée's *The Third*

World in World Economy (Monthly Review Press, 1969) contain useful material on the gap – and the relationship – between the underdeveloped countries and the developed world, and Colin Leys's *Underdevelopment in Kenya* (Heinemann Educational Books, 1975) provides an exemplary case-study.

Chapter 4

There are several good readers and collections of articles. In addition to the collections edited by R. L. Coser and by Skolnick and Skolnick, the reader's attention is drawn to N. W. Bell and E. F. Vogel (eds.), *A Modern Introduction to the Family* (Free Press, 1960), a good example of functional theorizing in the Parsonian tradition, and to M. Anderson (ed.), *Sociology of the Family* (Penguin, 1971). Readers with an anthropological interest will find several detailed studies in A. R. Radcliffe-Brown and D. Forde (eds.), *African Systems of Kinship and Marriage* (Oxford University Press, 1950) and the collection edited by Nimkoff cited in the bibliography.

On the general theme of industrialization and the family there is, in addition to the international survey by Goode, a useful collection edited by J. N. Edwards on *The Family and Change* (Knopf, 1969), and a detailed historical case-study by M. Anderson, *Family Structure in Nineteenth-Century Lancashire* (Cambridge, 1971). The functional approach is already represented in the collections edited by Bell and Vogel and Coser; a straightforward introduction to the work of Parsons as a whole may be found in Guy Rocher's *Talcott Parsons and American Sociology* (Nelson, 1974). The approaches of Parsons and other theorists to the study of the family are also examined in D. H. J. Morgan's *Social Theory and the Family* (Routledge & Kegan Paul, 1975).

The contemporary feminist movement has lead to a rapid growth in collections dealing with women in society. One of the most militant is R. Morgan's collection *Sisterhood is Powerful* (Random House, 1970), while readers with a more socio-logical interest will find useful papers in N. Glazer-Malbin and H. Y. Waehrer's collection, *Women in a Man-Made World* (Rand-McNally, 1972) and, especially, D. L. Barker and S. Allen's *Sexual Divisions and Society: Process and Change* (Tavistock, 1976). Similarly, the question of the future of the family has been treated extensively in a variety of collections, including those of Coser and Skolnick and Skolnick. A good general summary is provided in J. Bernard's *Future of Marriage* (Penguin, 1976), and a more general account of American communes is to be found in R. Houriet's *Getting Back Together* (Abacus, 1971).

Chapter 5

A recent survey of the debate about the uses of language and their relationship to learning in school-situations is found in Michael Stubbs's *Language, Schools and Classrooms* (Methuen, 1976). Some of the issues are taken up in H. Ginsburg's fascinating and polemical account, *The Myth of the Deprived Child* (Prentice-Hall, 1971). Colin Lacey's *Hightown Grammar* (Manchester University Press, 1970) remains one of the clearest and most detailed studies of pupil interaction within schools and provides a comprehensive account of the effect of school organization (e.g., streaming, house organization, etc.) and of social and economic background on the performance of children. The debate over the effects of schooling in creating or reducing social inequality is most readily available in Christopher Jencks's *Inequality* (Peregrine, 1975). This book brings together much of the survey work relating educational performance to IQ, occupational attainment and to salary. A more theoretically sophisticated account of the relation of educational systems to economy and society is S. Bowles and H. Gintis, *Schooling in Capitalist America* (Routledge & Kegan Paul, 1976). This book also provides a useful review of studies of the values communicated by schooling.

Chapter 6

A useful and recent collection of British material is to be found in D. Weir (ed.), *Men and Work in Modern Britain* (Fontana, 1973). William A. Faunce has edited an excellent reader, concentrating on American material, called *Readings in Industrial Sociology* (Appleton-Century-Crofts, 1967). The theme of alienation is discussed to some extent in the work by J. H. Goldthorpe *et al.*, already cited. A more extensive treatment, referring to four specific work-situations, can be found in R. Blauner's *Alienation and Freedom* (University of Chicago Press, 1964). For a more theoretical treatment see B. Ollman, *Alienation: Marx's Conception of Man in Capitalist Society* (Cambridge University Press, 1971). The best work on strikes is R. Hyman's *Strikes* (Fontana, 1974) which puts a lot into a few pages. A detailed account of a particular strike is to be found in T. Lane and K. Roberts, *Strike at Pilkingtons* (Fontana, 1971). Huw Beynon's *Working for Ford* gives a vivid picture of work in a car factory. For role theory, reference has already been made in the text to the works by Banton and Merton. A more detailed collection of articles on this topic is found in B. J. Biddle and E. J. Thomas (eds.), *Role Theory – Concepts and Research* (Wiley, 1966).

The main comparative studies of organizations have been referred to in the text. For a critical summary of Etzioni's thesis, see 'Sociological approaches to organizations' in S. R. Parker, R. K. Brown, J. Child and M. A. Smith, *The Sociology of Industry* (Allen & Unwin, 1967, chapter 7). Weber's discussion of bureaucracy is to be found in H. H. Gerth and C. W. Mills (eds.), *From Max Weber* (Routledge & Kegan Paul, 1948), and in Merton *et al.*, *Reader in Bureaucracy* (Free Press, 1952), an excellent collection of writings on all aspects of bureaucracy in many different types of organization. Other useful collections of articles on the structure and functioning of large organizations are A. Etzioni (ed.), *Complex Organizations: A Sociological Reader* (Holt, Rinehart and Winston, 1969, second edition) and G. Salaman and K. Thompson (eds.), *People and Organizations* (Longman, 1973).

There are, of course, numerous studies analysing individual organizations. As well as those mentioned in the text, the following may be recommended: S. Cohen and L. Taylor, *Psychological Survival: the Experience of Long-Term Imprisonment* (Penguin, 1972); S. H. Stanton and M. S. Schwartz, *The Mental Hospital* (Basic Books, 1954) and W. Caudill, *The Psychiatric Hospital as a Small Society* (Harvard University Press, 1958); J. Lofland, *Doomsday Cult* (Prentice-Hall, 1966) (a religious sect); P. Selznick, *TVA and the Grass Roots* (University of California Press, 1949) (a development organization); S. M. Lipset, M. A. Trow and J. S. Coleman, *Union Democracy* (Doubleday, 1962) (a trade union); R. Michels, *Political Parties* (Free Press, 1949).

On the concept of network, J. C. Mitchell *Social Networks in Urban Situations* (Manchester University Press, 1969) is recommended.

Chapter 7

Maurice Stein's *The Eclipse of Community* (Princeton University Press, 1960) (especially parts 1 and 2) needs no further recommendation. Two British books partly inspired by Stein's work are Ronald Frankenberg's *Communities in Britain* (Penguin, 1966) and *Community Studies* by Colin Bell and Howard Newby (Allen and Unwin, 1971).

As the title of the book suggests, the essays in R. Sennett (ed.), *Classic Essays on the Culture of Cities* (Appleton-Century-Crofts, 1969) are seminal for the urban sociologist. A well-known empirical collection of readings on urban sociology in general is P. K. Hatt and A. J. Reiss (eds.), *Cities and Society: The Revised Reader in Urban Sociology* (Free Press, 1957). The essay by C. D. Harris and E. L. Ullman on 'The Nature of Cities', H. Miner's 'The Folk-urban Continuum', and R. D. Mackenzie's 'The Rise of Metropolitan Communities' are particularly succinct. Also useful is L. G. Bourne (ed.), *Internal Structure of the City* (Oxford University Press, 1971). C. G. Pickvance (ed.), *Urban Sociology: Critical Essays* (Tavistock, 1976) gives the English reader a valuable insight into recent Marxist-oriented urban research from Europe. J. Boissevain and J. Friedl (eds.), *Beyond the Community: Social Process in Europe* (Government Printing Office, The Hague, 1975) provides useful examples of recent European rural studies.

R. E. Pahl's *Readings in Urban Sociology* (Pergamon, 1968) contains more British material, including N. Dennis's interesting article on 'The Popularity of the Neighbourhood Community Idea' (first published in *Sociological Review*, vol. VI, 1958) and Ruth Glass's 'Urban Sociology in Great Britain' (first published in *Current Sociology*, vol. IV, 1955). *The Sociology of Community* edited by Colin Bell and Howard Newby (Frank Cass, 1974) is another interesting collection and contains a provocative foreword, 'Towards a Theory of Communities', by Norbert Elias.

A. L. Epstein's 'Urbanization and Social Change in Africa' (originally in *Current Anthropology*, vol. 8, No. 4, 1967) takes us out of the developed world, as do all the other contributions to G. Breese (ed.), *The City in Newly Developing Countries* (Princeton University Press, 1969). Various aspects of problems of urbanization in the developing countries are well illustrated in D. J. Dwyer (ed.), *The City in the Third World* (Macmillan, 1974), and studies of the incorporation of migrants into Third World cities are the main theme in W. Mangin (ed.), *Peasants in Cities: Readings in the Anthropology of Urbanization* (Houghton Mifflin, 1970).

The community study 'method' is discussed at length in M. R. Stein's book and also in A. J. Vidich, J. Bensman, and M. R. Stein (eds.), *Reflections on Community Studies* (Wiley, 1964).

Chapter 8

André Béteille's reader, *Social Inequality* (Penguin, 1969) contains many key passages from key writings on this subject, from varied cultural and historical settings. Celia S. Heller's introductions to the various parts of her selection of writings on *Structured Social Inequality* (Free Press, 1969) are also useful. O. C. Cox's *Caste, Class and Race* (Monthly Review Press, 1970) provides a stimulating theoretical overview of the relationship between these three phenomena. John Berger and Jean Mohr's *A Seventh Man* (Pelican, 1975) and Stephen Castles and Godula Kosack in their *Immigrant Workers and Class Structure in Western Europe* (Oxford University Press, 1973) show the relationship between contemporary racism in the West and the unequal development of the world capitalist economy. D. L. Barker and S. Allen (eds.), *Sexual Divisions and Society* (Tavistock, 1976) is an excellent collection of studies of the inequalities attached to gender. A. B. Atkinson's *Unequal Shares: Wealth In Britain* (Penguin, 1974); John Westergaard and Henrietta Resler's *Class in a Capitalist Society* (Penguin, 1976); and the four *Reports of the Royal Commission on the Distribution of Wealth and Income* (H.M.S.O., 1975 and 1976) all contain abundant factual information on the United Kingdom.

Industrial Society: Class, Cleavage and Control (ed. Richard Scase, Allen & Unwin, 1977); *Poverty, Inequality and Class Structure* (ed. Dorothy Wedderburn, Cambridge University Press, 1974); and *The Social Analysis of Class Structure* (ed. Frank Parkin, Tavistock, 1974) all contain varied sets of more theoretical essays of high standard. Parkin's *Class Inequality and Political Order* (Paladin, 1972) is a closely argued discussion of current theories about class in contemporary industrial societies, both capitalist and communist. David Lane's *The End of Inequality?* (Penguin, 1971) is an equally succinct discussion of the direction in which Soviet society is moving, as is his later *The Socialist Industrial State* (Allen & Unwin, 1976).

Franz Fanon's *The Wretched of the Earth* (Penguin, 1969) presents a forceful Third World view of the division of the world into 'haves' and 'have-nots'.

Chapter 9

A comprehensive discussion of 'the Hobbesian problem' and of the theories of Weber and Durkheim may be found in Talcot Parsons's *The Structure of Social Action* (Free Press, 1937). Parsons's own work, at least to 1960, is reviewed in Max Black (ed.), *The Social Theories of Talcott Parsons* (Prentice-Hall, 1961), the paper by E. C. Devereux Jr. being particularly useful. An extensive selection of papers on the function/conflict controversy is contained in N. J. Demerath III and R. A. Peterson (eds.), *System, Change and Conflict: A Reader in Sociological Theory and the Debate about Functionalism* (Free Press, 1968).

Jerome G. Manis and Bernard N. Meltzer (eds.), *Symbolic Interaction: A Reader in Social Psychology* (Allyn & Bacon, 1967) assembles many papers on interactionism and Howard S. Becker's *The Other Side: Perspectives on Deviance* (Free Press, 1964) contains papers of a largely interactionist character but focussed upon aspects of deviance.

Don H. Zimmerman and Melvin Pollner's 'The Everyday World as a Phenomenon', in J. Douglas (ed.), *Understanding Everyday Life* (Routledge, 1970), is a good brief statement of ethnomethodology's general position, and in Roy Turner (ed.), *Ethnomethodology* (Penguin, 1974) there is a good sample of papers.

Author Index

Chapman, B. and Chapman, J. M., 371
Chesneaux, Jean, 147
Chombart de Lauwe, P. H., 378, 379, 380
Cicourel, A., 117, 223, 254, 541
Clark, B. R., 237
Cohen, Stan, 377
Cohn, Norman, 147
Cole, G. D. H., 426
Coleman, J. S., 112, 114, 250
Comaroff, Jean, 296
Comte, Auguste, 73, 136, 137, 144
Cook-Gumperz, Jenny, 219–20
Cooke Taylor, W., 364
Cooley, C. H., 343–4

Damer, Seán, 377
Davin, Delia, 173
Davis, K., 345–6
Dawe, Alan, 63
Denney, R., 369
Dennis, Norman, 284, 301, 349–50, 369, 464
Djilas, Milovan, 157, 469
Douglas, J. W. B., 217–18, 223–4, 231
Douglas, Jack, 81
Dubin, R., 285
Durkheim, E., 80, 82, 137, 252, 303, 342, 344, 346, 480–88, 493, 497, 498, 500, 501, 508, 535, 553, 555

Elkins, S. M., 402
Elvin, Mark, 129
Emmanuel, Arghiri, 159
Engels, Friedrich, 41, 138, 361, 382, 385ff.
Epstein, A. L., 365
Esland, G. M., 262
Etzioni, Amitai, 305, 307, 315–18, 452
Eysenck, H. J., 145, 213, 215

Fanon, Frantz, 151, 152, 442
Feldman, K., 251
Festinger, L., 100
Fine, B., 366
Finer, S. F., 52, 157

Finnigan, Ruth, 191
Firestone, Shulamith, 207
Firth, Raymond, 180
Folger, J. K., 240
Fortes, Meyer, 396
Foster, John, 384
Foster-Carter, Aidan, 160
Frank, A. G., 149, 152
Frankenberg, R., 100, 339
Fraser, Ronald, 290
Freire, Paolo, 256
Friedl, J., 340

Gans, Herbert, 356ff.
Gardner, John, 270
Garfinkel, Harold, 118, 559, 560, 561, 562
Garnsey, E., 470
Geiger, H. Kent, 173
Gellner, Ernest, 412, 413
Gerth, H. H., 448
Gillespie, D., 186
Ginsburg, H., 223
Glaser, B. G., 352
Glass, Ruth, 376, 413
Glazer, Nathan, 369
Gluckman, Max, 196, 400, 458
Godfrey, Martin, 272
Goffman, Erving, 232, 295, 313–15, 330, 549, 550, 551
Gold, D., 284
Goldthorpe, J. E., 148, 156, 383–4
Goldthorpe, J. H., 27, 286, 291, 301, 317, 321, 463–5, 470
Goode, W. J., 173, 177, 196
Goodman, Paul, 253
Goody, Jack, 172
Gorer, Geoffrey, 54
Gough, Kathleen, 172
Gouldner, Alvin, 146, 283, 294, 310, 311, 431, 471
Gramsci, Antonio, 148, 452

Habenstein, H., 246
Hambley, J., 214

Swift, Donald, 215
Sykes, G., 327–8, 330

Taylor, Laurie, 292
Thompson, Kenneth, 305
Thompson, R., 365
Titmuss, Richard, 43, 52, 406, 422
Tönnies, Ferdinand, 341–3, 344, 346
Trotsky, Leon, 157, 469
Tugendhat, C., 289
Turner, R. H., 239
Turner, V. W., 120, 279

Wakefield, John, 232
Wallerstein, Immanuel, 152
Warner, Lloyd, 112, 353ff., 375, 376
Warren, Bill, 159
Watson, James, 65
Webber, M. M., 378
Weber, Max, 44, 55, 138–40, 143, 147,
    307–11, 336, 390, 448, 451–3, 488,
    489, 492, 493, 498, 499, 500

Weinberg, I., 232
Wertheim, W. F., 143, 148
Westergaard, John, 235
Westergaard, J. H. and Resler, H.,
    421, 430, 432
Whorf, Benjamin Lee, 555
Whyte, W. F., 101, 334, 361
Whyte, W. H., 312
Wolf, Eric, 475
Wolpe, Harold, 413
Williams, Raymond, 169–70, 276, 288
Willmott, Peter, 348, 366
Wirth, L., 347ff., 364
Woodward, J., 321
Worsley, Peter, 55, 122, 128, 147, 161,
    379, 409, 476

Young, M. D. F., 255
Young, Michael, 146, 246, 348, 366, 501
Young, Michael and Willmott, Peter,
    185, 206, 277, 282

Zghal, A., 390

Subject Index

Communes, 204–5
Communications, 146
Communism, 142, 154–5, 156–8
  polycentric, 155–6
Communist societies, 471
  education in, 268–70
  industrialization in, 469–71
  women in, 406–7
Community, 288
  and school, 223–9
  'communities within community',
    337
  concept of, 332–45
  ethnic communities, 381
  community identity, 374–5
  communities of interest, 367–8
  in urban studies, 345–51
  local communities, 370–71
  quest for, 350–51
  studies, 352ff.
  the eclipse of, 351ff., 371–2
  the 'little' community, 335
Comprador bourgeoisies, 151
Concepts, 49, 340
  operational and analytical, 344
Conflict
  and work, 281, 290–94
  in small groups, 339
  in the community, 350
Consciousness, 44, 61–2, 70
Consensus, 496, 505, 525
Consumption, social, 277–8
Contract, 438–9, 482–3
Convergence theory, 144, 469–71
  in education, 236–7
Correlations and causal connexions,
  107–9
Correlation coefficient, 107
Counter-cultures, 147–8, 228
Credentialism, 245
Cross-cutting ties, 458–9
Culture, 116
  accumulation of, 23
  and biology, 22–8
  and education, 216–17
  definition of, 24

  discontinuities of, 26
Cultural reproduction, 227–9

Definition, of the situation, 548–9
Dependency, 151–2
Deprivation, relative, 422
Deschooling, 248
Determinism, 27, 57–8, 69–71, 142,
  441–2
Development
  and nationalism, 419
  education and, 244, 269–73
  in China, 135, 148, 161
  in colonies, 133, 138
  in Eastern Europe, 155–6
  in Japan, 135
  in Russia, 135
  in Third World, 156
  in U.S.A., 134
  religion and, 138–9
  uneven, 418–19
Development gap, 122–8, 159
Deviance, 434ff.
  and class, 540–41, 543–4
Division of labour, 279–80, 481–2
  at work, 307, 432
Divorce, 166
Documentary method, 559–61
Domains in social science, 33–4
Double contingency, 45–6
Dysfunctions, 309

Ecology, 128–9, 351, 370–71, 377ff.,
  387
  and schooling, 225
Economics, and sociology, 29–30
Education
  and development, 244, 269–73
  and family, 217–21
  higher, 232–3, 250–51
  in communist countries, 268–70
  in middle-class suburbs, 366
  medical, 253–4
  private, 231–2
Elaborated codes, 219–23

Elites, 472–3, 522–4
  kinship links, 434–5
  ruling, 146
Embourgeoisement, 463–6
Empiricism, 41–2
Enclosures, 130
Environment, 216–17
Estates, 396
Et cetera clause, 552
Ethics, and social science, 71–2
Ethnicity, 411–13
  and education, 230–31, 240
  and social class, 473
Ethnography, 116
Ethnomethodology, 115–19, 552–65
  use of tape-recorders in, 118
  laboratory techniques in, 118
Evolution, social, 21
Experiments
  natural, 105
  controlled, 105–6
Expressive/instrumental approach to
  work, 321

Face-sheet data, 90
Family
  alternatives to, 165, 173, 204–8
  and social class, 434–5
  as universal institutions, 172–6
  definitions of, 168–72, 204
  functions, 175, 177, 180–84, 199
  future of, 165, 204–8
  in industrial society, 176–94, 527–8
  in West Indies, 172–3
  nuclear, 172, 177, 178–80, 191–2, 199
  relative autonomy of, 182–3, 191–2, 199
Fertility decline in the nineteenth
  century, 85–6
Feudalism, 134, 138, 145, 151, 152, 153–4
Force, 478–9, 531–2, 553
Formal theory, 50, 56–7
Frame of reference, 42
Framing of knowledge, 257–8
Frontier, 134

Function, 494ff.
Functional relations, 111
Functionalism
  and development, 149
  and family, 175, 180, 184, 199–203
  and schooling, 252

Gemeinschaft, 341, 344
Generalized other, 48, 545
Genes, 213–14
Genotypic phenomena, 111
Gesellschaft, 341, 344
Government and social science, 38–41, 70–72
Groups
  primary and secondary, 343, 347
  ethnic, 357ff.
Growth-models, 160–61

Hegemony, 531
Heredity, 145, 212–17
'Hidden curriculum', 211
History, and sociology, 31, 45, 53, 57
  historical documents, as sociological data, 84–6
Home, and school, 217–26
Housework, 186, 188–9, 200, 201–2, 207, 274–5, 404ff.
Hypothesis, 75–6
Hypothetico-deductive method, 74

Ideal type, 336
Ideology, 'end' of, 144
Imagery, urban, 372ff.
Immigrants, 351, 356ff.
Immigration, 412–16
  and education, 240–
Imperialism, 132–3, 141
Incorporation, 524 45, 150–52
  of working class,
Index of social st 132
      112   atus characteristics,
Indexes and scales, 104, 111–13
Indexicality, 561–3
Indicators, 78
  and underlying dispositions, 111–12

Individual, 471ff., 485–8, 493
Industrial action
  strikes, 354
Industrial society
  and family, 176–94
  and work, 282–90
Industrialism, 'logic of', 27, 143–4,
  469–71
Industrialization, 140–41, 158–9, 353ff.
  in communist countries, 469–71
Informal relations
  in organizations, 322
Instincts, 23, 25–6
Instrumental/expressive approach to
  work, 321
Intelligence, 145, 212-17
Intelligence quotient (I.Q.), 212–17,
  245, 262
Interaction, in education, 252–62
Interests, 305, 516, 531
Internalization, 493, 508–10
Interpenetrating samples, 95
Interpretive sociology, 61, 74, 88, 104
  methods of, 115–19
Interview-situation, 221–2
Interviewing, 95–8

Juvenile delinquency, 117

Kinship, 169, 178–80, 183–4, 192–3,
  197
Knowledge, classification and framing,
  257–8

Labelling theory, 377, 536ff.
Labour aristocracy, 132
Language, 25, 493–4, 563–4
  and education, 215, 219–23, 227
  and interpretive procedures, 77
Legitimacy, 459–60
Logic and practice of scientific method,
  76
Love
  and mate-selection, 195–9

Mail questionnaires, 89–90
Management systems, mechanistic and
  organic, 310–12
Managers, 466–8
Market-situation, 461
Marriage, 165–6, 168, 175, 177, 179,
  184–5, 186–9, 205–6, 208
  and love, 195–9
  and social class, 450–51
Marriage-rates, urban and rural, 347–8
Marxism, 59
  and development, 140–41, 150–55,
  160
  and education, 228–9
  and family, 199, 200–203
  and work, 275–6
Mass culture, 322
Meaning, 44, 553
Mechanical solidarity, 480–81
Medical education, 253–4
Medicine, 247–8
Mental illness, 549–52
Mental institutions, 60, 303–4
Meritocracy, 144, 246
Migration, rural-urban, 348, 383
Military organization, 302
Minorities, national, 413, 418–19
Mobility
  contest, 238
  in U.S.A., 239–40
  sponsored, 239
Mode of production, 153–4
Models, 113
  folk models, 333, 420ff.
  of rural-urban contrast, 240ff.
Modernization, 355
Multinational corporations, 158–9,
  289, 467–8
Multivariate analysis, 106
Mystification, 248–9

Nation-state, 122, 153
Nationalism, 82–4, 145–7, 416–19
  and education, 273
  and minorities, 413, 418–19
Nature, and society, 21, 128–9

Retrodiction, 69
Revolution, 423–4, 436–9, 441–3
  Cultural Revolution (China), 476
Roles, 149, 506
  and work, 294–7, 300, 301
  multiple, 296–7
  of interviewer, 97–8
  of observer, 98–102
  sex-roles, 181, 184–5, 186–9, 206–8,
    297–300, 401–3
Role-set, 296–7, 298
Rules, 536, 538, 540–43, 545–6, 552
Ruling classes, 146

Sampling, 91–3
  interpenetrating, 95
  quota, 91
  random, 91–2
Scientific law, 75
Scientific method, 73–4
Secondary analysis, 79
Self, Mead's conception of, 47–8
Sex
  and gender, 23
  roles, 181, 184–5, 186–9, 206–8,
    297–300, 401–3
Simulation studies, 113–14
Slums, 356ff., 381, 384ff.
Social change, 57–8, 340ff., 355, 512,
    526–30
Social class, *see* Class, social
Social closure, 433, 445
Social contract, 479–80, 482, 493
Social distance, 316, 398, 450–51
Social dramas, 114
Social formations, 153
Social meanings, 99, 104, 115–16
Social mobility, 397–8, 432–5, 441–2,
    445
  and professionalization, 463
Social problems, 51–4
Social reform, and sociology, 39–41,
    52–3
Social sciences, divisions of, 28–35
Social solidarity, 342–4
  in slums, 358ff.

Social surveys, 88–94
Social system, 54–5
  and sub-systems, 55
Socialism
  in colonized countries, 133
Socialization, 22–7, 180–82, 183, 185–6,
    187, 189–90, 529, 545
Societies
  age-set, 397–8
  caste, 396, 398–9, 450–55
  folk, 336, 341, 344
  urban, 336, 344
Sociological problems, 51–4
Sociology
  and philosophy, 21
  divisions of, 34–5
  growth of, 19–20, 38–41
Socio-economic groups (in U.K. census)
    426–7
Solidarity
  mechanical, 480–81
  organic, 506
Sovereignty, parcellized, 132
Spurious relationships, 107
Stages of growth, 143–4, 149
State, 493
  absolutist, 131, 153–4
  formation of, 131, 153–4, 416
  in colonies, 416
State capitalism, 466–70
Statistical sources of information,
    80–84
Statistical population, 92–3
Status, 398–9, 443–6, 506
  achieved and ascribed, 280–81,
    298–9
  and class, 452ff.
  and power, 455ff.
  and work, 276–7, 280–81, 283–6,
    295, 300–301
  anxiety, 445
  characteristics, 321–4, 326
  groups, 398–9, 443–6
  situation, 461
Stratification, social, 395–6
  folk models of, 420

definitions of, 274–7
in industrial society, 282–90, 301, 304
in pre-industrial society, 301–2
instrumental and expressive, 290
separation from home, 286–8, 289, 301
situation, 461
Working class, incorporation of, 132
World-system, 57, 122, 151–2, 155–61

MORE ABOUT PENGUINS, PELICANS, PEREGRINES AND PUFFINS

For further information about books available from Penguins please write to Dept EP, Penguin Books Ltd, Harmondsworth, Middlesex UB7 0DA.

In the U.S.A.: For a complete list of books available from Penguins in the United States write to Dept DG, Penguin Books, 299 Murray Hill Parkway, East Rutherford, New Jersey 07073.

In Canada: For a complete list of books available from Penguins in Canada write to Penguin Books Canada Ltd, 2801 John Street, Markham, Ontario L3R 1B4.

In Australia: For a complete list of books available from Penguins in Australia write to the Marketing Department, Penguin Books Australia Ltd, P.O. Box 257, Ringwood, Victoria 3134.

In New Zealand: For a complete list of books available from Penguins in New Zealand write to the Marketing Department, Penguin Books (N.Z.) Ltd, Private Bag, Takapuna, Auckland 9.

In India: For a complete list of books available from Penguins in India write to Penguin Overseas Ltd, 706 Eros Apartments, 56 Nehru Place, New Delhi 110019.